Perspectives

Global Perspectives

In a time of ever-increasing global phenomena, the series *Global Perspectives* offers regionally focused volumes that attempt to move beyond the standard regional studies model. Each volume includes a selection of previously published articles and an extensive introduction by the volume editor, providing an overview of the history and cultures of the region under discussion. The articles are chosen to illustrate the dynamic processes by and through which scholars have described and understood regional history and culture, and to show how profoundly the ethnography of each region has influenced the direction and development of anthropological and social theory. The *Global Perspectives* series thus furnishes readers with both an introduction to the cultures of a vast array of world regions, and a history of how those cultures have been perceived and interpreted. The contributors include anthropologists, historians, philosophers, and critics. Collectively they show the multiplicities of voice in regional studies, and reveal the interpenetration of ideas and concepts within and across disciplines, regions, and historical periods.

Published

1. *Perspectives on Africa: A Reader in Culture, History, and Representation,*
   edited and introduced by Roy Richard Grinker and Christopher B. Steiner

2. *Perspectives on Las Américas: A Reader in Culture, History, and Representation,*
   edited and introduced by Matthew C. Gutmann, Félix V. Matos Rodríguez,
   Lynn Stephen, and Patricia Zavella

3. *Perspectives on the Caribbean: A Reader in Culture, History, and Representation,*
   edited and introduced by Philip W. Scher

EDITED AND INTRODUCED BY PHILIP W. SCHER

perspectives on
The Caribbean

A Reader in Culture, History,
and Representation

WILEY-BLACKWELL

A John Wiley & Sons, Ltd., Publication

Library of Congress Cataloging-in-Publication Data

Perspectives on the Caribbean : a reader in culture, history, and representation / edited by Philip W. Scher
       p. cm. – (Global perspectives; 3)
   Includes bibliographical references and index.
   ISBN 978-1-4051-0565-1 (hardcover: alk. paper) – ISBN 978-1-4051-0566-8 (pbk.: alk. paper)
1. Ethnology–Caribbean Area. 2. Ethinicity–Caribbean Area. 3. Folklore–Caribbean Area. 4. Culture and globalization–Caribbean Area. 5. Cultural fusion–Caribbean Area. 6. Caribbean Area–Social life and customs.
I. Scher, Philip W., 1965-
   GN654.C37P47 2010
   306.09729–dc22

                                                  2009008317

A catalogue record for this book is available from the British Library.

Set in 9.5/11.5pt by SPi Publisher Services, Pondicherry, India
Printed and bound in Singapore by Ho Printing Singapore Pte Ltd

1   2009

Contents

Acknowledgments

This project began a long time ago when I was teaching a course on African cultures at George Washington University. Part of the way through compiling a massive reading list for my students I spoke with my colleague Richard Grinker who handed me a copy of *Perspectives on Africa* that he had edited with Christopher B. Steiner. It turned out to be such a useful resource that later I proposed the idea of compiling something like it to Professor Kevin Yelvington at the University of South Florida. His enthusiasm, suggestions and hard work are felt everywhere in this volume and it was really only his very busy professional life that prevented him from being listed on the cover of this book as a co-editor. If this book is a successful tool for students and scholars it is due to the initial model set by Grinker and Steiner and the enviable erudition of Kevin Yelvington. Our early efforts were eagerly supported by Jane Huber at Wiley-Blackwell, and I have been subsequently fortunate to have worked with a number of wonderful people at the press including Deirdre Ilkson, Helen Gray, Julia Kirk and Rosalie Robertson. I would also like to thank Garth Green for his suggestions, along with Lynn Stephen, my colleague at the University of Oregon, whose experience editing *Perspectives on Las Americas* also proved valuable. A deep debt of gratitude goes to my many students at George Washington University and the University of Oregon who, over the years, have made it quite clear which readings were most helpful to them in learning about the Caribbean. As I am completing this volume I am very fortunate to be a visiting scholar at the University of the West Indies, Cave Hill, Barbados. My wonderful colleagues and students there have continued my enthusiasm for a collection of this nature and it is to them and to my family, Constance, Julia and Marston, that I dedicate this volume.

Philip W. Scher
Enterprise
Barbados April, 2009

Acknowledgments
of Sources

Roger Abrahams, "Joking: The Training of the Man-of-Words in *Talking Broad*," from *The Man-of-Words in the West Indies: Performance and the Emergence of Creole Culture*, pp. 55–76. Baltimore: Johns Hopkins University Press, 1983.

Barry Chevannes, selections from Barry Chevannes (ed.), *Rastafari and Other African-Caribbean Worldviews*, pp. 1–42. New Brunswick, NJ: Rutgers University Press, 1995.

Leslie G. Desmangles, "The Faces of the Cosmic Gods," from *The Faces of the Gods: Vodou and Roman Catholicism in Haiti*, pp. 92–130. Chapel Hill: University of North Carolina Press, 1992.

Carla Freeman, "Designing Women: Corporate Discipline and Barbados's Off-shore Pink-collar Sector," *Cultural Anthropology* 8(2), 1993, pp. 169–86.

Jorge Duany, "Reconstructing Racial Identity: Ethnicity, Color and Class among Dominicans in the United States and Puerto Rico," *Latin American Perspectives* 25(3), 1998, pp. 147–72.

Faye V. Harrison, "Women in Jamaica's Urban Informal Economy," *New West Indian Guide* 62(3–4), 1988, pp. 103–28.

Aisha Khan, "What is 'a Spanish'? Ambiguity and 'Mixed' Ethnicity in Trinidad," from Kevin A. Yelvington (ed.), *Trinidad Ethnicity*, pp. 180–207. London: Macmillan Press, 1993.

Frank E. Manning, "Celebrating Cricket: The Symbolic Construction of Caribbean Politics," *American Ethnologist* 8(3), Symbolism and Cognition, 1981, pp. 616–32.

Elizabeth McAlister, "Rara as Popular Army: Hierarchy, Militarism, and Warfare," from *Rara! Vodou, Power, and Performance in Haiti and Its Diaspora*, pp. 135–57. Berkeley: University of California Press, 2002.

Sidney Mintz, "Houses and Yards among Caribbean Peasantries," from *Caribbean Transformations*, pp. 225–50. New York: Columbia University Press, 1989.

David Murray, "Homosexuality, Society, and the State: An Ethnography of Sublime Resistance in Martinique," *Identities* 2(3), 1996, pp. 249–72.

Mona Rosendahl, "To Give and Take: Redistribution and Reciprocity in the Household Economy," from *Inside the Revolution: Everyday Life in Socialist Cuba*, pp. 28–50. Ithaca, NY: Cornell University Press, 1997.

Philip W. Scher, "Copyright Heritage: Preservation, Carnival and the State in Trinidad," *Anthropological Quarterly* 75(3), 2002, pp. 453–84.

Nina Glick Schiller and Georges Eugene Fouron, " 'The Blood Remains Haitian': Race, Nation and Belonging in the Transmigrant Experience," from *Georges Woke Up Laughing: Long-Distance Nationalism and the Search for Home*, pp. 92–129. Durham, NC: Duke University Press, 2001.

Elizabeth Thomas-Hope, "Globalization and the Development of a Caribbean Migration Culture," from Mary Chamberlain (ed.), *Caribbean Migration: Globalised Identities*, pp. 188–99. London: Routledge, 1998.

Steven Vertovec, " 'Official' and 'Popular' Hinduism in the Caribbean: Historical and Contemporary Trends in Surinam, Trinidad and Guyana," from David Dabydeen and Brinsley Samaroo (eds.), *Across the Dark Waters: Ethnicity and Indian Identity in the Caribbean*, pp. 108–30. London: Macmillan Caribbean, 1996.

Introduction

The Caribbean in Perspective

Philip W. Scher

A volume entitled *Perspectives on the Caribbean* implies that there will be more than one viewpoint. Indeed this must be so, as there can be no complete understanding of a region as vast, complex and vibrant as the Caribbean. But we can, through multiple viewpoints, begin to layer our understanding a bit better. The aim of this collection is to provide many perspectives, but it is also organized around a basic theme. That is, that any perspective on the contemporary Caribbean is improved by illuminating connections between cultural forms, political economy and history. Toward that end, I have provided brief part introductions with short lists of suggested readings to help further guide student interest.

One perspective on the Caribbean might be that of recognizing the archipelago and its related cousins on the mainland of North, Central and South America as a forgotten or perhaps, better, an elusive space. In many compendia of the "world's peoples" the Caribbean is absent, generally subsumed under the Latin America heading, a strategy only partially accurate. And perhaps this is because of the elusive nature of the region. Sidney Mintz has encouraged looking at the Caribbean as a socio–cultural continuum, one that might include those New World slave and plantation societies from Brazil to Louisiana. Indeed this seems a very good place to start. The cultural, political, economic and historical continuity is undeniable. Mintz was responding to the generally baffled attempts, especially by outsiders, to categorize the Antillean experience. Pointing out that the Caribbean was only reluctantly accepted as a legitimate area of study by early anthropologists, Mintz reminds us that this was in part because Caribbean anthropologists and social scientists themselves were eager to take their region seriously as an object of study. And although stereotypes of the region abound in popular discourse, the intellectual's neglect seems to have resulted in the fact that no single overriding descriptor has plagued the Caribbean. The metaphors, tropes and other literary devices that have been dissected by contemporary scholarship with regard to those places outside of the West have generally focused on such things as Africa: the Dark Continent, or the Orient as Asia. But what of the Caribbean? In contrast to the Dark Continent, nothing comparable ever emerged. The unique history of this region, with the early near decimation of the Amerindian population by Europeans and the subsequent repopulation of the islands by African slaves, Asian indentured servants and other immigrants, the Caribbean was never simply "savage" or "civilized." From the intellectual perspective of the West it could have been called the Twilight Archipelago, that is, neither the "darkness" of Africa nor the fully bright light of European "civilization."

And perhaps they could be then, with a wink to the long history of tourism, the Sunset Islands. In that respect, in the contemporary world, it is really a different idea of a brightness that attracts, a light without enlightenment, a space dedicated to one side of the human condition: play, lightness and indulgence. As Derek Walcott has written:

> Sadly, to sell itself, the Caribbean encourages the delights of mindlessness, of brilliant vacuity, as a place to flee not only winter but the seriousness that comes only out of culture with four seasons. So how can there be a people there, in the true sense of the word? (1993:13)

And as for the rest of Caribbean life that not dedicated to tourism, there has simply been the charge of imitation. The contemptuous dismissal of a whole world as a faded approximation of something much better, more fully realized, complete. Then we might call them, after Naipaul, the Mimic Islands. Or possibly the Magic Islands, inasmuch as they have inspired, especially in North America and Europe, a rather two-dimensional stereotype as a place of sorcery, black magic, midnight rites and sacrifice or a land of perpetual sensuality: the sorcery of seduction. And all of this conceals history. Whatever focus we choose to describe the culture of the Caribbean, none of it makes much sense without contextualizing the emergence of these societies within the historical conditions that brought these people, in a certain way, to this place.

And yet it does seem to make sense to continue to conceive of the Caribbean as an area with commonalities. Area studies in Anthropology have often turned out to be crucibles in which certain theories are advanced, tested and then dwelled upon sometimes for much longer than their usefulness would seem to warrant. This process may or may not be in direct relation to any specific data the area itself can yield, but may even be a sort of accident of history. If Africa, for British Anthropology, came to be the area of the world in which early theories of structural functionalism were most heartily tried and then later came to be the site of their refusal, does that say anything about Africa itself? It may, of course, say much about the British colonial relationship to Africa, but that is not entirely the same thing. The Caribbean, too, has had its share of "local" theories. Yet many of these ideas do indeed derive from the specific nature of Caribbean society and are connected to issues within the region, not to the general interests of discipline building. The concepts of syncretism and acculturation as developed by Melville Herskovits, for instance, began life in the Caribbean and in the African diaspora in general. In keeping with the American anthropological focus at the time, begun largely by Franz Boas and his students, Herskovits was interested not in building grand theories about human social institutions, but in using anthropological insights to combat social injustice, especially racism. And these theories have certainly enjoyed increasing attention in the social sciences as notions of "creolization" and "hybridity" have come into vogue. Furthermore, the unique historical circumstances that shaped the Caribbean after Columbus have also garnered newfound interest. Indeed, the very forces that created the kind of creolized societies initially shunned by anthropology and sociology in the West are now the processes studied with redoubled energy as the earliest examples of globalization. And yet, for the most part, this volume does not sample from the "classic" theoretical frameworks: that is, the

Caribbean as matriarchal in kinship studies, or the idea of representation vs. respectability as advanced by Peter Wilson. Nor does it include specifically the writings of Herskovits in which he develops his idea of "acculturation." I have avoided these "greatest hits" of Caribbean theory, mainly because I found that their legacy was well represented in the articles chosen and that the ideas themselves were often embedded in larger ethnographic or historical works.

The essays in this volume are culled from an enormous body of literature. The aim is to give a broad sense, in a small space, of the diversity of approaches, voices and subject matter that have come from the region. Always there is the difficult task of balance in terms of the representation of authors and their language groups, nationalities, ethnicities and genders. This poses a great problem as the region has for so long been written about by a wide range of people both local and foreign. Because of the necessary limits on such a volume, I have tried to provide some measure of redress in the Suggested Readings lists at the end of each short introductory section. I have also shied away, somewhat, from including works that seemed purely rooted in a particular academic discipline. That is, I have tried to find articles that are interdisciplinary and combine history and sociology, or anthropology and political economy, etc. This was a way of both providing depth for students and highlighting the interdisciplinarity of the volume as a whole. I feel that this approach carries the general theme of the volume well. That is, that "perspectives" on the Caribbean are informative and more three-dimensional if readers are continually reminded of the keen relationships between such areas as folklore, history, sociology, political economy and anthropology, and that these disciplinary boundaries maintain strong connections to art, literature, music, dance and architecture. With this view we can contribute to an evolving idea of the Caribbean that finds something like knowledge in recurring patterns, and challenges in diversity and unpredictability. The articles reproduced here should be seen, I think, as part of a long conversation. Some of the older voices still resonate while the newer ones offer new concepts that are responding to, perhaps challenging, but always building on what came before. My hope is that the book will give a sense of the range of Caribbean studies and will suggest where these studies may be going in the future.

Reference

Walcott, Derek, 1993. *The Antilles: Fragments of Epic Memory*. New York: Farrar Strauss Giroux.

Part I

Living and Livelihood

Introduction

Caribbean life was defined early in the colonial period by issues surrounding labor and these issues helped shape settlement and work patterns into the contemporary period. The radical and mostly forced reorganization of the traditional labor and living practices of the indigenous population in order to satisfy the needs of the colonists quickly decimated the native inhabitants. The changing fortunes of the Spanish and the arrival of new European powers in the region led to changing economic priorities as many of the islands were turned into enormous sugar production "camps." As a result, possibly the largest forced transplantation of human beings in history was embarked upon via the slave trade from Africa and continued with the importation of indentured labor from Asia and South Asia. The emergence of a Caribbean peasantry both during and after slavery can be attributed to a variety of sources included small-scale yeomen farmers, runaways and maroons, squatters, outlaws and most significantly the former slaves themselves. The Caribbean was shaped, ultimately, by agriculture, but in the modern era economies have diversified to include manufacturing, off-shore banking, tourism, data processing and other industries. This section of the volume gives readers a sample of studies devoted to how many Caribbean people earn their living and how domestic life and traditional work patterns have changed and adapted in the contemporary political and economic climate.

Suggested Readings

Cross, Malcolm and Gad Heuman, 1988 Labour in the Caribbean. London: Macmillan Caribbean.

Kale, Madhavi, 1998 Fragments of Empire: Capital, Slavery, and Indian Indentured Labor Migration in the British Caribbean. Philadelphia: University of Pennsylvania Press.

Look Lai, Walton, 2004 Indentured Labor, Caribbean Sugar: Chinese and Indian Migrants to the British West Indies, 1838–1918. Johns Hopkins Studies in Atlantic History and Culture. Baltimore: Johns Hopkins University Press.

Mintz, Sidney, 1974 Worker in the Cane: A Puerto Rican Life History. New York: W. W. Norton.
Potter, Robert B. et al., 2004 The Contemporary Caribbean. New York: Pearson/Prentice Hall.
Safa, Helen, 1995 The Myth of the Male Breadwinner: Women and Industrialization in the Caribbean.
    Boulder, CO: Westview Press.
Yelvington, Kevin, 1995. Producing Power: Ethnicity, Gender, and Class in a Caribbean Workplace.
    Philadelphia: Temple University Press.

1

Houses and Yards among
Caribbean Peasantries

Sidney W. Mintz

Today's rural Caribbean folk may be divided roughly into rural proletarians, who work on and for plantations; peasants, who have access to land and produce their own food and market commodities; and people who fall somewhere between the rural proletariat and the peasantry, and generally both work their own (rented or shared) land and engage in wage labor (Cumper n.d.; Comitas 1964; Frucht 1967; Handler 1965, 1966).

Many of the social characteristics of rural Caribbean populations are shared by persons in all of these categories. Others are largely limited to persons in one or another category, for reasons having to do with their particular style of life. Thus, to take one obvious example, control over the labor of one's family members is much more typical of peasants than of rural proletarians, while the purchase of a large proportion of the family's food is obviously more typical of rural proletarians than of peasants. Hence any discussion of similarities and differences among rural Caribbean peoples must take account of major differences in the activities associated with making a living.

But there are of course other reasons why Caribbean rural peoples are culturally homogeneous or heterogeneous. We have seen that the origins of these peoples are very diverse, and that the populations of different Caribbean societies have been subject to many different cultural influences. We do not seek to "explain" the presence of African religious elements in Haiti and Trinidad, for instance, in terms of the economic history of these two societies, but in terms of the strength of the particular cultural traditions or heritages borne by those who settled them. Again, that the Jamaican people speak one language, the Haitian people another, and the Puerto Ricans a third is plainly due to the respective metropolitan cultures to which their peoples were subject, rather than to any general feature of economic history, or to any contemporary difference in rural life-style.

Any comparative study of the rural subculture of the Caribbean region plainly requires some plotting of similarities and differences. The historically oriented scholar will want to know how a particular cultural feature became part of contemporary life, and to examine its distribution in the region as a whole. He will recognize that both similarities and differences may be attributable to traditions that have persisted or that have been differentially discarded since newcomers from other parts of the world came to inhabit the islands; or to influences that shaped the life of local peoples during or after the slavery epoch; or to particular local conditions – economic, demographic, ecological – that affected the creation of living patterns over the centuries.

Scholars interested in the Caribbean region in the past have often been preoccupied with the survival of one or another particular cultural tradition. Herskovits, for instance, a pioneering anthropological student of the African tradition in the New World, was especially concerned with the tracing of African elements in Caribbean life (cf., for instance, 1930, 1937, 1945, 1947), while other scholars have been more interested in documenting the importance of various European traditions (cf., for instance, Greenfield 1966). Amerindian elements have attracted the attention of still other observers (cf., for instance, Taylor 1951; Sturtevant 1969). All of these research workers have been aware that there was no single, unified European or African or Amerindian tradition, and each has made contributions to our understanding of the processes by which one or another cultural element or complex has been modified, synthesized, and reworked, in terms both of its particular form and content and of its symbolic meanings, values, and associations for those who perpetuated it. Haitian religion, for instance, is rich in features that can be traced, more or less precisely, to the African past, but these features have rarely survived in any unmodified, or "pure," form. The processes of change are in some ways even more interesting than the particular origins of one or another trait, since these processes exemplify a general characteristic of human cultures: their complex capacity simultaneously to change and to remain the same.

But for reasons unconnected with the intellectual quest itself, retentions are sometimes perceived as more interesting than losses or replacements in culture, and some cross-cultural similarities are thought to be more interesting than others. This may be illustrated with a few Caribbean examples. Almost everywhere in the Caribbean, rice and beans (or "peas," as they are sometimes called) are a key item in local cuisine. Puerto Rican rural proletarians call the combination *"el matrimonio"* (the married couple), and clearly prefer the dish to cornmeal, another common food, which is somewhat disdained. Haitian

peasants eat rice and beans every day, if they can afford it, and prefer the combination to millet which, like cornmeal in Puerto Rico, is a less acceptable common food. Just as Puerto Rican folk are reluctant to serve *funche* (boiled cornmeal) to a foreign visitor or an honored guest, so Haitians dislike to serve their guests *piti-mi* (millet). Much the same is true in Jamaica, where rice and peas are a preferred item, not replaceable by "food" (which here means root crops such as yams and taro, or green bananas, or breadfruit). These taste preferences are probably all traceable to the period of slavery, when rice and beans constituted a luxury dish, as compared to the other foods mentioned. People do not describe their preferences this way, of course; but rice and beans were not a traditional dish in the original homelands of any Caribbean population, and the taste was probably acquired in the islands.

But the interest of scholars in this cross-cultural uniformity seems slight. They seem to display far more interest in an item such as akee (*Blighia sapida* Koen.), a tree crop of particular importance in Jamaica, the origin and name of which is clearly African (Cassidy and Le Page 1967). Akee is usually eaten with what the Jamaicans call "salt fish," which is dried cod, and which, probably like rice and beans, became standardized in Caribbean cuisine under slavery. Yet akee is unknown in the Eastern Caribbean (where a wholly different fruit, the guinep or *quinepa* or *kénèp*, *Melicocca bijuga*, is called "akee"), and it is hardly known in Haiti or the other Greater Antilles. We can specify easily the date the akee arrived in Jamaica; apparently it reached Haiti considerably later. In Jamaica, the akee remains a comfortably specific African retention; in Haiti, it is not eaten.

Both the Jamaican and the Haitian rural subcultures exhibit numerous features of African provenience; the differential distribution of akee is one way in which these societies are unlike; but the "retention" of akee in Jamaica is somehow regarded as "more interesting" than its absence in Haiti. In contrast, the "retention" of *akansan*, a cornmeal mush of African provenience (though corn itself is American in origin) in Haiti seems to be considered more interesting than its absence in

Jamaica. And the presence of such foods as *akra* and *doukounou* in both islands, both African foods, both with African names, is even more "interesting," it seems, because here we have two parallel "retentions," surviving the holocaust of slavery in both societies.

Why some of these facts should seem more exciting than others is, indeed, not difficult to determine. Features of Caribbean life that can be traced to the preslavery African past appear as testaments to the toughness and pride of the human spirit – which, indeed, they are. But survivals from slavery seem to be viewed merely as testimony to cultural defeats and losses. The use of words from African languages, the cooking of foods originating in Africa, the worship of gods of African provenience all appear to document the will to endure, to resist; but the significance of survivals from the slavery epoch is apparently diminished by the circumstances of their origin.

However such a view risks belittling the accomplishments of Caribbean peoples during their period of sorest trial. The slavery experience tested to the limit the strength and resourcefulness of millions of newcomers from other lands. The significance of that experience is expressed in the contemporary cultures of Caribbean peoples, just as are both the preslavery and post-slavery pasts. The task of historians of these cultures is to disentangle the origins and growth of the life-styles of the Caribbean region, and to seek to analyze the very complex processes by which cultural forms changed and were consolidated. This is not a different task from documenting the capacity and will of people to resist oppression. To survive at all under slavery was a mode of resistance; the cultures of contemporary Caribbean peoples are in their entirety a testament to such resistance.

Cultures lack pedigrees, and it is not surprising that the Caribbean peasantries of today expend little effort in disentangling the varied sources of their beliefs and practices. Haitian peasants apparently see no contradiction in a religion that contains elements drawn from the African, European, and Amerindian pasts; Jamaican peasants draw no distinctions among words of African origin and words of English origin. Puerto Rican peasant singers worry little that their *agui-*

naldos are of substantially European derivation, while their *plenas* are much more "African." This is by no means to say that consciousness of such differences is entirely lacking. But rural folk in these societies are much more likely to perceive differences of these kinds in terms of differences between rural and urban life-styles, or between one class and another, than in terms of particular historical origins.

Implicit in the above argument is the need to bear in mind certain general points about the nature of similarities and differences in the rural subcultures of the Caribbean region. First, economic, ecological, or demographic similarities and differences unite or divide different rural populations in the same society. Second, there are similarities, either within one society or between comparable peasant sectors in two or more societies, that are traceable to a common cultural heritage predating slavery, as in the case of important features of African origin, including lexicon, cuisine, religion, language, folklore, and music. Third, there are commonalities that may be traced to the experience of slavery itself, as well as to the parallel impact of European domination – as in the case of the common use of Spanish in both Cuba and Puerto Rico, or the parallel proto-peasant adaptation in both Jamaica and Haiti. Finally, there are similarities and differences arising from the conditions of life following the slavery epoch and intermingled with the influences cited in the first point. Thus, for instance, Puerto Rican peasants and rural proletarians share many features of life, but also differ in significant ways. Their similarities are traceable in large measure to common historical experiences; their differences are due in good part to differences in their economic style of life, stabilized during their earlier development, and still operative.

From a systematic or analytic point of view, similarities traceable to the colonial period are as significant as those that hark back to an earlier past. Both similarities and differences are useful and important means for reconstructing the past, be it the recent past, the period of slavery, or the ancient pasts of the homelands – including, in the case of Amerindian cultures, the pre-Columbian pasts of the islands as well.

Though the volume of historical research on the Caribbean region is vast, relatively few books and papers have dealt with the origins and history of peasant subcultures and the similarities and differences among them. Even rarer are historical studies which deal in a detailed fashion with one or another aspect of rural life in the region as a whole. Marshall's research on the origins of (British) West Indian peasantries (1968) is promising. Wolf's study of the peasant subculture of Puerto Rico (1956) provides a useful introduction to the structural attributes of one Caribbean peasant society. Several precisely focused and detailed papers, such as Sturtevant's (1969) on the processing of root starches, and Handler's on arrowroot (1971), indicate both what is possible and what remains to be done in documenting fully the development of peasant technology in the region. Not only must such research provide a full picture of this development for any one island or peasant subculture, but the studies of comparable phenomena among different island populations must be combined to pinpoint similarities and differences in the processes of development.

Here we need to remember that the peasant subcultures evolved in most cases in the face of metropolitan or insular government opposition, and that observers, both contemporary and in the past, have paid very little attention to the life-styles of rural Caribbean peoples. Only a few historically minded scholars have sought to get behind the so-called imperial tradition of historiography sufficiently to document what peasant life-styles are really like. Price's (1966) paper, on Caribbean fishing and the history of Caribbean fishermen and fishing techniques, stresses the growth of a fishing subculture in the margins of Caribbean societies and documents its importance as a way in which local people could escape the tyranny of plantation life. Much the same sort of treatment should be given the peasantries, and the work is only now beginning.

Characteristics of the House-and-Yard Pattern

In the present chapter, a tentative first attempt is made to organize a little of what is known about one aspect of Caribbean peasant life, the house

and yard, and the meaning of these for rural people. The importance of the house and yard as a setting for daily activity is obvious: here decisions are made, food is prepared and eaten, the household group – whatever its composition – sleeps and socializes, children are conceived and born, death is ceremonialized. To speak in terms of some common house-and-yard pattern, without taking account of the many factors that produce variation and difference within the pattern, would be entirely unjustified. Yet there are certain very general similarities, even cross-cultural – that is, occurring across the boundaries of different Caribbean societies – that require description and explanation, and it is principally around such similarities that the chapter is built.

But it is also intended to relate the concrete, material character of the house and the yard to the activities which go on in and around them, to suggest the ways that things and ideas are fitted together, made into (and learned as) patterns, as systems and subsystems of culture, and passed on to the next generation. Too often "material culture," the term by which anthropologists refer to the concrete expression of culture in tangible objects, is seen as divorced from the world of values, ideas, beliefs, and behavior. But it is through such material representations of culture that people relate to each other, express themselves and their values, interact, and carry out their activities. Hence the house is far more than a fabrication of wood and thatch, the yard far more than a locale for the house. Together, house and yard form a nucleus within which the culture expresses itself, is perpetuated, changed, and reintegrated.

A number of writers, some geographers, some ethnologists or historians, have examined the houses of Caribbean rural folk from the vantage point of their history as architectural forms. Doran, a geographer, has interested himself in what is technically known as the "hip-roofed" cottage, a distinctive house-type widely distributed through the British and Dutch Antilles; found less commonly in Haiti, the French Antilles, and Trinidad; rare in the Dominican Republic; and almost entirely absent from Cuba and Puerto Rico (1962). Doran weighs four possible historical sources for the hip-roofed cottage:

aboriginal America, Spain, Africa, and Western Europe. He concludes that aboriginal America and Spain may be discounted as possible places of origin, holds in abeyance the possibility of African influences, and opts for a "circum-English-Channel" hearth of origin. His analysis is based both on the contemporary distribution of the form, and on what can be learned about its historical spread during the seventeenth and later centuries. Métraux, an ethnologist, has concentrated narrowly upon Haitian house-types (1949–51), but has dealt more exactly with details of construction and type variants; though he stresses the importance of European architectural influences, he leaves open the question of African traditions. Métraux expressed the hope that Africanist colleagues would evaluate his Haitian materials in the light of what was known about West African house-types, past and present, but such comparative treatment remains unrealized. Moral, a geographer, has also concentrated on Haitian house-types (1957), but discounts African influences; Revert, also a geographer, reaches similar conclusions for the rural homesteads of the French Antilles (1955). Pérez de la Riva imputes African origins to the rural houses in Cuba (1952), but his argument is poorly developed, particularly since he seems to accept the notion of a single African architectural prototype. All of these authors deal, on one level or another, with the question of origins; all admit that the information is insufficient for any firm conclusions.

The question of architectural origins is, in one sense, fairly straightforward; if we had enough information about African and Caribbean house-types, past and present, we would at least be able to chart similarities and differences, and perhaps to indicate the evidence that argues clearly for one or another place of origin, even if firm and definite answers were not forthcoming. Houses are a useful unit of comparison, precisely because they consist of a limited number of different materials (wood, stone, thatch, mortar, mud, cement, metal, etc.) and elements (roofs, doors, lintels, frames, window openings, floors, stoops, etc.), which may or may not be diffused as interrelated assemblages. Studies of such forms are consonant with North American ethnology's traditional concern with the origins and diffusion of elements

and complexes of culture, and with the way such forms change in space and in time, as they are adapted to new uses or new environments.

In seeking African origins for Caribbean house-types, however, the historical ethnologist or geographer faces certain clear-cut difficulties. For instance, we have no certain evidence that newly arrived Africans were ever able to build their houses according to their own traditions. If African elements are present, we must assume that the migrants were able to retain their architectural knowledge until they became free and could build their own houses, or that some variants of the original types were constructed and the techniques preserved by runaway slaves, by early generations of freedmen, or in some other way. Patterson, who has amassed considerable evidence on the daily life of Jamaican slaves (1967), is silent on this point; Brathwaite (1971) tells us what he can. Research workers on other islands have done little more. The comparable task is probably no easier when we deal with such features of culture as folklore, religion, musicianship, ethnobotany, crop uses, and the like, though the attribution of features, particularly lexical features, can sometimes be more certain.

But the cultural forms of a people are not only historically derived – products or consequences of the past, so to speak – but must also fit in with the needs and beliefs of those who employ and preserve them today. Such needs and beliefs are reflected in use, in behavior, and in the values people maintain. The houses of Caribbean peasantries are more than historical aggregates of past tradition; as the settings for many of the most important contemporary rural activities, they must be studied as behavioral contexts and not merely as historical products. The questions this pursuit raises are concerned more with similarities and differences arising from the differential adaptations of newcomer populations to the pressures imposed upon them by the Caribbean experience, and less with the specific historical origins of particular traits or complexes.

Such an exercise requires that some attention be given to the background conditions of peasant life in the region, the customary or usual distribution of population, and the forms of settlement and land use that peasant populations employ.

Though peasant settlement and land-use patterns vary not only from one Caribbean country to another, but also from one region to another within the same island society, certain general characteristics provide a context within which to examine house uses and the attached values and attitudes of the peasantries. Seven such features are enumerated here, each of which will be dealt with in turn: (1) the peasant adaptation is primarily to the highlands and to sloping terrain, rather than to coastal floodplains and alluvial fans or to intermontane valley floors; (2) main cultivation grounds do not usually adjoin the houses of their owners; (3) house plots are often dispersed rather than clustered and are sometimes scattered along a slope or strung out upon a mountain spur; (4) usually, only one sexually cohabitant couple occupies a house, though several houses (and several couples) may share a yard; (5) each homestead, whether consisting of one house or more, is usually surrounded by at least a small quantity of land, and set off from the outside by a fence, clumps of vegetation, or a hedge or living fence; (6) the yard may be associated intimately with the house, and its land may have important ritual or kinship significance; (7) house and yard often have particular symbolic meaning for local people, though this may be implicit and little noticed by outsiders.

The Highland Adaptation

These seven features may now be discussed at greater length, in order to clarify the place of house and yard in the daily life of Caribbean peasantries, and to indicate something of the history of the features. We have seen that peasant agriculture is predominantly a highland adaptation on the major islands because the coastal plains and interior valleys were frequently taken over for plantation cultivation at an early stage. In general, this division between coastal estates and highland small-scale farming on the larger islands has not varied significantly, except in the case of Haiti. There, the plantation system was largely destroyed by the Revolution, reappeared briefly thereafter, withered away once more, and was then reinstituted in certain narrow coastal regions of the north and around Port-au-Prince in the twentieth century. By and large, the countryside

remains a peasant domain. In Jamaica, the plantation adaptation is ancient and has, if anything, expanded since the nineteenth century; coastal areas, except in the south, are largely monopolized by plantations. Much the same is true of Puerto Rico, where the expansion has been very intensive since 1900.

In all three countries, however, the peasant adaptation is paramount in the highlands of the interior. Peasant holdings are prevailingly small – one to ten acres, and more commonly one than ten – and owners often cultivate several plots, which may be held by various arrangements, including leaseholding, sharecropping of various kinds, and renting. In some regions, both within these three countries and elsewhere in the Caribbean, the peasant adaptation may rest heavily upon a tradition of rented land; but access to land to permit small-scale cultivation with family labor is very common, even when land is not owned. The agriculture itself is typically very diversified. Such diversification is a means of distributing risk, as we have seen in the case of Jamaican peasant farming; it also provides a perennial trickle of food crops, both for subsistence and for sale; maximizes the utility of the land, relative to the availability of labor; and may even serve to maintain fertility, as by intercropping, the use of catch crops, and the like. Sauer (1954) has suggested that the reputation of Caribbean peasant agriculture as a "land-killer" may be undeserved, arising from the need to cultivate on hilly slopes with sharp runoffs and shallow topsoils, rather than from the agricultural techniques themselves. However, it is true that the failure to use fallowing, fertilizer, rotation, terracing, and other land-protective practices typifies such agriculture; it is also true that the farming of widely scattered plots greatly increases the necessary investment of time and energy – though this difficulty is hardly the fault of the peasants, unless one wishes to hold them responsible for traditional systems of inheritance that often lead to the progressive fragmentation of holdings.

Kitchen-Gardens vs. Provision-Grounds

Normally, agricultural holdings are separate from the houses of their owners, and may even be located some distance away – as much as ten miles, in many cases. Both in Haiti and in Jamaica there is a clear historical precedent for this separation which does not, however, completely explain it today. We have already seen that estate slaves commonly grew their own subsistence on plantation uplands, using lands judged unsuitable for the major plantation crops. It was on such lands that the slaves acquired or perfected their horticultural skills, developed their own standardized agricultural practices, learned the characteristics of Caribbean soils, mastered the cultivation of new crops, and otherwise prepared themselves for their reconstitution as peasantries. A wholly distinctive crop repertory, adapted to the new settings, was created by combining familiar African crops, such as "guinea yams" (*Dioscorea sativa*) and okra, with native American crops, including corn, sweet potatoes, potatoes, tomatoes, and species of *Xanthosoma*; European vegetables, such as cabbage and carrots; and Southeast Asian cultigens, including the breadfruit. Such agricultural tools as the short-handled hoe, the mattock, and the bush knife were adjusted to new conditions – though we are still uncertain about the provenience of these items. Citrus, avocado, mango, coconut palm, papaya, soursop and akee trees were cultivated, to provide cover, fruit, and wood – together they illustrate well the intersection of different agricultural and orchard traditions. Techniques of land-clearing – by burning, tree-girdling, and the removal of stones for walls and shelters – were developed, again probably by combining different traditions of land use. Moreover, techniques associated with food processing, storage, preservation, and seed selection were perfected, though the origins of these techniques have never been wholly disentangled.

But these myriad skills and usages took shape during slavery for the most part, either on the plantation uplands where slaves grew their own food, as in Jamaica and Haiti, or in the maroon communities of the interior. We have seen how frontiersmen developed a pattern of casual cultivation in the interior of Puerto Rico – again, outside the normal routine of plantation cultivation, or even in open opposition to it. Pérez de la Riva has developed the theme of the Cuban

maroon community, or *palenque*, as a by-product of the concealed cultivation plots of runaway slaves (1952) – though the role of such communities in Cuba has been overshadowed by the better-known exploits of the maroons of Jamaica, Dutch Guiana, and Brazil. According to Pérez de la Riva, so developed was the palenque adaptation in Cuba that one famous community – Bumba – was able to carry on agricultural trade not only with neighboring haciendas in Cuba itself, but also with Santo Domingo and Jamaica, by means of small craft!

All this, however, is a far remove from the more common pattern of "proto-peasant" adaptation, developed within the confines of the plantation. There, the separation between house plot and provision ground was a clear function of the control wielded by the plantation system over the slaves. The "garden," or provision ground, was always located in portions of the plantation that were not used for the major crop, and in which it was not normally intended to plant that crop – as we have seen, plantation owners tried to avoid taking up for sugarcane any of the land they habitually provided the slaves for growing their own provisions.

But the huts of the slaves, unlike the provision grounds, were regularly located near the center of the plantation itself, on or near the "plaza" and below the "great house," where the slaves could be guarded and watched. "Adjoining to the [slave's] house is usually a small spot of ground," wrote one Jamaican observer in 1823, "laid out into a sort of garden, and shaded by various fruit-trees. Here the family deposit their dead, to whose memory they invariably, if they can afford it, erect a rude tomb. Each slave has, besides this spot, a piece of ground (about half an acre) allotted to him as a provision ground" (Stewart 1823: 267).

This separation of subsistence plot from house plot, and the use of the house plot for fruit trees (as well as spices, etc.) and as a family cemetery, is typical of Jamaica and Haiti to this day, though probably not at all of Puerto Rico. There is little evidence that the division into house plot and provision ground, so ubiquitous in Jamaica and Haiti, was ever pronounced in Puerto Rico, nor is there evidence in Puerto Rico of familial house-plot burial grounds.

Dispersal of Houses

In many parts of these three island societies, it is difficult to define community boundaries in terms of settlement, particularly in the highland interiors. Admittedly, the coastal plantation areas exhibit nucleated settlement patterns, with rows or clusters of houses formed into company towns, *colonias*, or line villages. Such aggregates are also common along principal roadways, near major towns and cities, and around special enterprises, such as the bauxite mines of Jamaica and Haiti. But the highland countrysides show little comparable nucleation, even though national populations may be quite dense, as in Puerto Rico and Haiti. In Jamaica, the missionary-founded free villages still show coherent patterning and form, as we have seen in the case of Sturge Town; but in general, all three of these societies display scattered highland settlement. This dispersion is revealed in the actual distribution of households: in a straggling row along a ridge; scattered around a central water supply in the form of a spring, well, or standpipe; set unevenly into the side of a hill; or, often, substantially isolated from one another. This is by no means to say either that such settlement is incoherent and random or that people entirely lack a sense of community – but all three societies contain substantial numbers of rural folk who have chosen to remain dispersed in terms of household occupancy.

Household Composition

As yet, we have said nothing about the composition of groups within households. This is obviously a question of very considerable importance in any study of marriage, family, and kinship in Caribbean rural society, and it has received much attention in the literature (cf. particularly Solien 1960, Greenfield 1961). To begin with, one of the most striking characteristics of Caribbean peasant subcultures in these regards is the fact that the domestic unit or kin group housed under one roof only rarely includes more than one sexually cohabiting couple (Mintz 1956, 1960; Davenport 1961). In fact, the rule of independent residence for cohabiting couples appears to hold for almost all rural Caribbean folk, proletarians as well as

peasants – as in the case of Cañamelar, the Puerto Rican plantation community discussed earlier (Mintz 1951, 1953, 1956). In effect, this signifies that the establishment of new conjugal associations depends on access to an unoccupied house plot and, commonly, to possession of the means to build a house.

Though the point may sometimes be given exaggerated importance (cf., for instance, Otterbein 1965, and Price's 1970 critique), the linkage between most forms of domestic union and the availability of a house plot or house is nonetheless very significant in Caribbean rural life. In Haiti, Métraux (1951: 116) writes, "the peasant builds his hut when he intends getting married or taking up employment. It represents a young man's first effort and action to free himself. An offer of marriage is out of the question unless the man proves he is in earnest by laying the foundations of the future family home." Davenport (1961: 446), writing of Jamaica, describes the invariable rule by which young men set up a separate household when they take wives: "As long as their father remains fully active, they will move out and establish their own households with their spouses, even though this might only be across the yard. ... The rule of household formation, then, is that no single household will contain more than one active conjugal pair." Cumper (1961: 398–99) points out that in Barbados, where the definition of a peasantry is open to some question, the establishment of an independent household – usually on rented land, at first – is a customary precondition for the establishment of a family by those who approximate a peasant status. While it is indeed true that some kinds of conjugal union and the fathering of families can and do occur in these societies *without* the prior establishment of an independent household for the cohabiting pair, the relationship between independent domicile and cohabitation is the basis of certain important types of conjugal union.

But a significant exception should be noted. In fieldwork carried out among Puerto Rican peasants in 1948–9, Wolf found that newly married couples sometimes moved in with the wife's family: "This ideal form of residence removes the young husband from the circle of his own father's family and avoids conflicts between the young wife and her mother-in-law" (1956: 206). Apparently, under certain circumstances neolocal residence near the home of the wife's parents is also a possible choice; but Wolf gives no figures on the percentages of different modes of residence in the community he studied.

The importance of this exception is twofold. On the one hand, it runs counter to what is otherwise usual in domestic settlement, both peasant and proletarian, in the Caribbean. On the other, it suggests the possibility of the presence of an extended kinship group under one roof: a phenomenon as common in West Africa as it is rare in the peasant subcultures of the West Indies. In fact, the insistence on separate residence for cohabiting couples in Caribbean peasant life stands in stark contrast to what is known of the African past. It is all the more interesting, then, that this exceptional form is reported for highland Puerto Rico, which, in terms of its culture history, is probably the least "African" rural sector of the three societies.

The point, of course, is that a mode of residence, a pattern of settlement, a form of marriage shared by peoples in differing cultures may be traced either to a common origin on the one hand or to parallel or convergent experiences or present-day needs on the other. If Puerto Rican highland peasants do, indeed, display characteristics reminiscent of an African past, such features may be attributable either to that past or – as is in this case much more likely – to local historical (economic, ecological, demographic) factors producing an analogous form.

Contrariwise, the general absence of more than one cohabiting couple within a single household cannot be regarded as an aping of "European" residence patterns. If anything, it more closely resembles the domestic life-style of European urban proletarians than that of the European middle classes; and this resemblance is not likely to be wholly fortuitous, given the historical experience of Caribbean peoples in past centuries.

The value placed on separate residence is expressed neatly in the Puerto Rican pun-proverb, "Que se casa pa' su casa" – "Let those who marry go to their own house." But separate residence does not necessarily mean a separate yard, as we have already seen. Often, more than one house

occupies a yard, though the occupants of two or more such houses are usually related consanguineally. For instance, the traditional Haitian house-and-yard unit, the *lakou*, often included several households (Bastien 1951: 29–36; 1961: 481; Métraux 1951: 10). The unit was headed by a senior male, usually with his wife and unmarried children in one house, his married sons and their families, and perhaps other relatives, in other houses. Though this kind of multihouse homestead has declined swiftly in Haiti, losing its organizing influence as an economic, social, and religious unit, Bastien describes a lakou as follows:

> In 1948 one was found which still included ten households with a total of twenty-seven members, all related, and belonging to three generations. A father and his four sons held about two-thirds of the whole estate, while the rest was divided between the father's sister, two nephews, half-brother, and the concubine of one of the sons and her infant. (Bastien 1961: 481)

There may appear to be certain superficial similarities between such a group and the residence group living on indefinitely indivisible family land in Jamaica (Clarke 1957), but analogies of this kind are risky, not only because the actual compositions of such groups are different, but also because their social functions differ as well. The Jamaican residence group normally consists of both the male and female children of the deceased progenitor, who are supposed to share equally in the land, though the land is to be held undivided. But the group cannot be viewed as a corporate group – engaged in common activities as a group – and it is rarely co-residential (in the sense that several homesteads occupy the same plot, as is true of the traditional Haitian lakou). "Family land, in the process of transmission and use has in the main long ceased to have agricultural value," Clarke (1957: 44–5) tells us, "apart from the economic trees with which it is usually well stocked. It represents security in the sense that any member 'in need' can erect a hut on it and live rent free. ... On the other hand it runs counter to the ambition to own land [individually] and the dislike of usufructuary communal rights only." In Haiti, a somewhat comparable situation is described by Comhaire-Sylvain (1952). Though Haitian law holds that no inheriting individual need accept a share in undivided property, actually such property may be held unchanged by a group of inheritors for one generation or more (Métraux 1951). Such holdings can come into being on the death of a landowner, since it is customary in Haiti not to divide up such land for some time.

In Jamaica, a man can create family land simply by leaving his property to his children undivided (Clarke 1957). Unless they are willing to undergo litigation for division, the property will continue to be held by several persons, or some inheritors will sell their shares to others. Indeed, there may have been a time when the landowning, land-use, and inheritance practices of the Jamaican peasantry very closely resembled those of their Haitian counterparts. In both Jamaica and Haiti – and far more swiftly in Jamaica than in Haiti – the trend has been toward individualization of land-holdings, more scattered residence, emigration of at least some of the inheritors-to-be (though often retaining continuing rights in undivided land), and the sale of some shared land to other co-inheritors.

The problems of land tenure and the transmission of land rights among Caribbean peasantries remain largely unsolved, in spite of interesting and careful work by such scholars as Clarke (1953, 1957), Comhaire-Sylvain (1952), and M. G. Smith (1956). The distinction between house plots and agricultural land has become more and more widely recognized, but cross-cultural variations among Caribbean peasantries have still been only very incompletely analyzed. Nor is it possible at present to evaluate either general patterns or local distinctions with regard to possible African influences. We can perceive certain systematic contrasts between official legal systems affecting land and its inheritance, and the locally accepted and traditional practices of the peasantries (Clarke 1957; M. G. Smith 1956), but much more work is needed before such differences can be traced convincingly to one or another tradition.

Hence, the relationship of local forms of kinship organization and family structure to the physical expression of the local group's character, as embodied in house form, homestead, and yard, in these three societies, requires further study. Scholars such as Clarke (1957), M. G. Smith (1962), Davenport (1956) and R. Smith (1956) have demonstrated that the forms of family organization extant in much of the Caribbean are stable in character, and adaptive to the contemporary social and economic circumstances of the societies in which they are found. The analyses of these family forms suggest that domestic organizations go through cycles of development, and that the "family types" to be found in the Caribbean area are probably developmental stages in one or more sequences of domestic organization. Such sequences are intimately associated with particular forms of household. Studies by R. Smith and others have illuminated the earlier period in the study of Caribbean kinship, when it was assumed that family "types" were to be explained in general historical terms, either as the products of North European and African traditions of social organization, or as the results of centuries of slavery. In fact, the importance of specific historical circumstances for particular forms of domestic organization has not yet been properly assessed for Caribbean societies. But the functionalist studies of recent years have put the weight of analysis on the relationships between domestic organization and characteristics of the wider contemporary society.

The House and the Yard

The homestead is a place, a setting: yard and house together define the sphere within which much daily life is lived. They also define (or express) the ways that the personnel of the household are divided up – by age, sex, role, and otherwise. Of Jamaica's lower-class people in general, Davenport writes:

> In physical layout the lower-class household consists of a house, a detached kitchen or cookhouse, and a yard area. Each of these areas is the location of important activities which make up the domestic routine. The house is usually used mainly for sleeping and for storing clothing and other articles of personal value. The poorer the

household, the more the use of the house is restricted to just these activities, while the houses of the more well-to-do will have space and furnishings for additional activities such as relaxing, entertaining, and eating. Houses vary from simple one-room structures made of wattle and thatch and with earth floors to multi-room buildings of frame or concrete construction, metal or shingle roofs, and plank or cement floors. ... The cook house is usually a temporary structure and has less care lavished upon it than on the living house. It is used for preparing and storing food, and in most poor households, the family eats here in bad weather. It can also serve as a general utility shed and working space when other special structures have not been erected in the yard for these purposes. The yard is the scene of great miscellany of activities. On this swept ground between house and kitchen, the children play, the washing is done, the family relaxes, and friends are entertained. In it and surrounding it a few food-producing trees are grown, the small animals are tethered, and space is given over to a small vegetable garden. The yard is frequently fenced to keep animals in, and neighbors pay respect to this boundary by never entering without being asked. Far more respect, however, is paid to the house, for this cramped space affords the only real sanctum of privacy for the household against the rest of the neighborhood.

The house, yard, and kitchen are dominated by the adult women of the household, for most of the perennial work which goes on in them is in their charge. Women prepare the food, do the washing and mending, tend the kitchen garden, look after small animals, and most important, look after the children. ...

The adult men and older boys of the household assist in heavier tasks, such as looking after the larger and more valuable animals (if there are any), repairing the house and cook-house, chopping logs, spading a new kitchen garden, and even assisting with the processing of food products which are to be sold. But men's work is not nearly so confined to the round of domestic duties as is the women's. To them falls the major responsibility of the cultivation plot, or 'ground,' as it is called. In many instances this is removed some distance from the house site, and the men go to and from it daily, leaving the

women in charge of the household activities and children. Men, of course, do most of the wage work which takes them away from the domestic scene. They alone congregate in one another's yards or at the local shops to socialize. ...

Although the division of adult labour is not rigidly fixed by sex, it is the context of the household group which makes it clear. The rule, as in many European societies, is that women dominate the services of the domestic scene, while the men are concerned with productive working outside. Each sex may assist the other in some of his or her work, but this assistance is supplementary to the major responsibilities in each sphere. ... It is this general but flexible plan which enables the household group to adjust and maintain itself in a variety of situations and with a variety of different compositions. (Davenport 1961: 435–37)

This careful description, quoted only in part, reveals well how the house and yard express the division of labor within the household, the flexible character of the household group in dealing with the round of daily and yearly activities, and the different activities for which house and yard are a common setting.

The Yard: Material Uses

The integrity of house and yard as a unit, and its degree of intactness and separation from the outside varies greatly, and cannot be judged solely in terms of its physical form. But usually the peasant homestead is set off from the outside by some physical barrier. Often in highland areas, a visitor is not even aware of the presence of a house until he reaches the barrier which shields it. This barrier may consist of scattered clumps of vegetation, walls, living fences, ditches, picket fences, trees and groves of bamboo, or even the slopes of gullies (Métraux 1951; Mintz 1962; Street 1960). When living fences are used to separate the yard from the outside, they may serve several purposes at once. In Haiti, for example (Mintz 1962), living bamboo is sometimes used for fencing; it can be used to make an important musical instrument (*vaksin*), for rain gutters, to make carrying baskets for chickens, etc. Sisal (*Agave rigida*, var. *sisalana*), commonly grown alongside a living fence, can be cut for sale as fiber, and can be used to make rope, bridle headstalls, and croupiers, and as a reinforcement for baskets. Other plants used as living fences or to supplement such fences have comparable uses; a few are grown largely for their decorative effect, including varieties of croton.

Some plants are commonly grown within the yard, on the house plot. Such plants are to be distinguished in several ways from those grown on provision grounds. Thus, in Haiti, in terms of their eventual use, at least three sorts of plants are grown on house plots: (1) minor vegetables, which may also be decorative, such as egg-plants, hot peppers, and tomatoes; (2) items which may enter into commerce but which also have domestic uses, such as cotton (for lamp wicks), sisal (for rope), and vetiver (for thatch, and to keep out insects); and (3) trees which provide fruit, shade, or craft materials, such as avocados, guavas, coconut palms, and lataniers. Plantains and bananas, which can be stolen easily, are also sometimes planted inside the yard. In Haiti, the minor foods, especially spices, grown near the house are called *"diab diab"* and often serve as small presents to visitors. The distinction between these kinds of cultivation and the cultivation of provision grounds, principally by men, is quite clear.

The Yard: Symbolic Meaning

But the yard is far more than a site for occasional cultivation. We have seen that the land on which the house stands often links groups of kinsmen. The significance of such links is far greater when the plot has been used as a family cemetery, as is commonly the case in Haiti and as was once the case in Jamaica. The organization of affective and ceremonial life around the yard as a repository of tradition, and as expressing the continuity of a kin group, is one of the most promising subjects of research for those interested in the role of the African past. This is perhaps particularly the case in Haiti, where the yard often served both as a burying ground and as the locus of the *oûmfo*, or *vodoun* temple, which expressed the religious continuity of the family group with its ancestors (Métraux 1959: 59–60). Métraux (1954) also

points out that the burying group is considered indivisible and inalienable by Haitian peasants, and that even when the house plot is sold, its burying ground remains accessible to the original owners, even to the right of burying kinsmen there. Some of the same reverence for the yard, especially as a repository of ancestors, is observable in Jamaica as well.

What is more, the yard may express continuity at the beginning of life, as well as at its end. In Jamaica, if a fruit-bearing tree is "given" to a newborn child by burying his umbilicus at its foot, the tree is usually within the yard. The placenta is often buried beneath the door stoop, as are other effluvia of birth, and the protective intent of these procedures is clear in what people say when describing them. The yard thus protects the continuity of the kin group, as well as the individual; the links between dead ancestors and newborn children are represented in the yard, expressed and maintained by the generation which stands between them.

But the wider symbolic meaning of house and yard goes even beyond these quite specific details. What might be called the ritual significance of the yard and house is revealed in behavior. One approaches the yard circumspectly in all three societies, indicating one's presence in some way before entering the yard, and usually awaiting acknowledgment. In Haiti, the guest shouts "hònò!" (honor) before entering, and does not cross the threshold until he hears the reply "réspè!" (respect). In Puerto Rico, the peasant's words for house and yard, *bohío* and *batey*, are Arawakan (Taino) terms having a certain emotional significance. The batey, or yard, is where men normally congregate to talk, and the overtones of the word are revealed in various ways. The name of the Popular Party newspaper was *El Batey*; and Governor Muñoz Marín greeted his party cohorts at the insular convention of 1948 with the words: "How large is our batey." In Jamaica, the word *yard* is sometimes used to define one's total span of activities. When one is told by another person to keep out of his yard, this means essentially to stay out of his way, out of his life. Cassidy and Le Page (1967) point out that yard often means both house and yard in Jamaican speech and thought: /nómbari nó da a yáad nou/ means "no one is at home now"; /wi kyan go a mis mieri yáad/ means "we can go to Miss Mary's place."

Conclusions

We have argued that the seven features of the house-and-yard complex stem from the histories of Caribbean rural peoples, particularly the experience of slavery and the plantation system, and the usefulness of the peasant adaptation as a response to regimentation and oppression. It remains to consider some of these features in the light of this general assertion. The earliest post-Columbian settlement of the highland interiors of these societies by independent cultivators was uncontrolled, irregular, and often secretive. The Puerto Rican highlander, the *jíbaro* – a word which, to this day, means "shy" – has remained a symbol of the half-wild, the cimarron or feral, the withdrawn peasantry. Though such a peasantry has now almost disappeared in Puerto Rico, and was in any case much overdrawn in the political propaganda of recent decades, this image of the peasantry and the stereotypes attributed to it still persist (Steward 1956). In Jamaica, the reconstruction of the peasantry began in 1838, but we have seen that many of the basic skills of the freedmen were learned before Emancipation, within the confines of the plantation. Much the same was true in Haiti, though slavery was ended there by revolution. In all three cases, there is substantial evidence of the role of runaway slaves in creating the beginnings of a peasant adaptation while slavery was still in its hey-day; and in all such cases, there are good grounds for supposing that many continuities with the African (and, particularly in Puerto Rico, the Amerindian) past might be best preserved. These are histories, then, of disengagement and of resistance; and the characteristic features of the peasant adaptation are bound up with an escape from various modes of regimentation. We have seen that the reconstituted peasantry of Jamaica received strong support from the missionary churches, and such communities still manifest, in some instances, the institutional sponsorship they enjoyed. But peasant settlement otherwise has always been, for the most part, unorganized, unofficial, and sporadic.

This is the basis, then, for supposing that such characteristics as scattered settlement, the intactness of yard and house as a unit, the insistence on separate households for each cohabiting couple, and the circumspection with which the yard of another is approached, are all derivable to some degree from the historic conditions under which the peasantry was formed. The thought that a man's freedom begins inside his own fence has other origins besides the Caribbean experience; but it may have taken on additional significance in terms of that experience. Given the very special circumstances by which the ancestors of today's Caribbean peoples were "modernized," and the extremely early development of capitalist modes of production in the islands, it may be more apposite than it seems to recall Luther's insistence that "good fences make good neighbors."

For much of rural Caribbean life, as we have seen, the house-and-yard complex is much more the domain of women than of men. Cooking, garden care, washing, and especially the care of children are largely in the hands of women; the "lap-baby," "knee-baby" and "yard-baby"[1] stages of childhood typical of the United States South find their ready parallel in the Caribbean rural setting. But the activities of males may also be centered in the yard, even if men frequently gather elsewhere. If the yard contains fighting cocks, beehives, a burying ground, a ceremonial temple; if it is what the Jamaicans call a "balm-yard" (where healing is done; cf. Hogg 1964); if food or liquor is sold as part of the household's activities; if fishing boats are beached or stored there – in all such cases the yard's uses are divided and complementary, sometimes overlapping but more commonly separate. The relationship between yard and house may thus be viewed partly in terms of the conjoined activities of males and females, partly in terms of the different uses to which each, yard and house, is put by members of one or both sexes. The house, particularly among poorer peasants, is not important in itself as a material representation of the domestic group or family; houses are often moved from one site to another. But the yard is an extension of the house, and land remains immensely important for Caribbean peasants.

The yard is an extension of the house, just as the house is the living core of the yard; the outer limits of the yard come to represent the outer "walls" of the house itself, as it were.

None of the similarities among Caribbean peasantries with regard to the house-and-yard pattern should be allowed to conceal important exceptions, however, or the very considerable variation within a common pattern. Both the exceptions and variations cannot be written off as deviant or idiosyncratic, but require equal attention as variants. Thus, for instance, the use of the yard for minor subsistence items is clearly correlated with some particular tradition; but the practice does not – indeed, cannot – persist under circumstances of intense crowding of houses, aridity, saline soil, etc. The movement of highland migrants to the sugarcane region of the south coast of Puerto Rico was marked by the transfer of the kitchen-garden habit to the new setting, a setting wholly unsuited for it. Over time the pattern was eroded, and it has largely disappeared. But highland migrants to the coast – most of them of peasant origin – share the coastal pattern of separate (neolocal) residence on marriage, a pattern that seems to typify the proletarian population as well as substantial portions of the peasantry. And whereas fences do not typify all coastal proletarian dwellings in Puerto Rico,

migrants from the highlands are accustomed to put them up when they can, and to retain them, even if old-time coastal proletarians do not. Thus the picture is in fact complex, and requires more study.

Under the circumstances, is it possible or useful to attribute a common characteristic of the life-styles of three Caribbean peasant peoples to some general aspect of the past, in view of the many differences among them? The answer must be as tentative as the propositions advanced here. There is need for much more careful study of the intimate life-patterns of Caribbean peasantries; the expressed values and attitudes of the people themselves must be recorded: Until that time, such propositions simply enable us to ask more and, it is hoped, better questions. Because the three peasant subcultures discussed here may differ dramatically from those with which other observers are familiar, and because they often appear to differ in some common direction, there is a strong temptation to generalize about them, and about the Caribbean region as a whole. Only careful functional and historical studies, carried out on a comparative basis, afford the means of assessing the forces that have given these peasantries their form, and of weighing the effects of particular forces over time.

Note

1   In Jamaica, however, the term *yard-child* has a special meaning. A yard-child is the illegitimate child who lives at the house of its father, rather than with its unmarried mother. Those who live with the mother may be called "illegitimate" (Cassidy and Le Page 1967). This curious usage – which may be extremely rare – strikes a different note, for

it calls our attention to those children born of cohabiting couples that do not coreside, an extremely important aspect of familial and domestic organization in rural Jamaica, though far less so in Haiti and Puerto Rico. This subject is relevant to present considerations, but cannot be dealt with in this chapter.

References

Bastien, Rémy. *La Familia Rural Haitiana*. Mexico: Libra, 1951.

Bastien, Rémy. "Haitian Rural Family Organization," *Social and Economic Studies* 10 (1961): 478–510.

Brathwaite, Edward. *The Development of Creole Society in Jamaica 1770–1820*. Oxford: Clarendon Press, 1971.

Cassidy, F. G., and Le Page, R. B. *Dictionary of Jamaican English*. Cambridge: Cambridge University Press, 1967.

Clarke, Edith. "Land Tenure and the Family in Four Communities in Jamaica." *Social and Economic Studies* 1 (1953): 81–118.

Clarke, Edith. *My Mother Who Fathered Me*. London: George Allen and Unwin, 1957.

Comhaire-Sylvain, Suzanne. "Land Tenure in the Marbial Region of Haiti." In *Acculturation in the Americas*, edited by Sol Tax. *Proceedings of the 29th*

International Congress of Americanists, vol. 2. Chicago: University of Chicago Press (1952): 180–84.

Comitas, Lambros. "Occupational Multiplicity in Rural Jamaica." In *Proceedings of the American Ethnological Society, 1963*, edited by V. Garfield and E. Friedl. Seattle: University of Washington Press (1964): 41–50.

Cumper, George E. "Household and Occupation in Barbados," *Social and Economic Studies* 10 (1961): 386–419.

Cumper, George. *The Social Structure of Jamaica.* Caribbean Affairs. Jamaica: University College of The West Indies, n.d.

Davenport, William H. "A Comparative Study of Two Jamaican Fishing Communities." PhD dissertation, Yale University, 1956.

Davenport, William H. The Family System in Jamaica," *Social and Economic Studies* 10 (1961): 420–54.

Doran, Edwin, Jr. "The West Indian Hip-Roofed Cottage," *The California Geographer* 3 (1962): 97–104.

Frucht, Richard. "Caribbean Social Type: Neither 'Peasant' nor 'Proletarian,'" *Social and Economic Studies* 16 (1967): 295–300.

Greenfield, Sidney M. "Socio-Economic Factors and Family Form," *Social and Economic Studies* 10 (1961): 72–85.

Greenfield, Sidney M. *English Rustics in Black Skin.* New Haven: College and University Press, 1966.

Handler, Jerome. "Some Aspects of Work Organization on Sugar Plantations in Barbados," *Ethnology* 4 (1965): 16–38.

Handler, Jerome. "Small-Scale Sugar Cane in Barbados," *Ethnology* 5 (1966): 264–83.

Handler, Jerome S. "The History of Arrowroot and the Origin of Peasantries in the British West Indies," *The Journal of Caribbean History* 2 (1971): 46–93.

Herskovits, Melville J. "The Negro in the New World: the Statement of a Problem," *American Anthropologist* 32 (1930): 145–55.

Herskovits, Melville J. *Life in a Haitian Valley.* New York: Alfred A. Knopf, 1937.

Herskovits, Melville J. "Problem, Method and Theory in Afroamerican Studies," *Afroamèrica* 1 (1945): 5–24.

Herskovits, Melville J., and Herskovits, Frances S. *Trinidad Village.* New York: Alfred A. Knopf, 1947.

Hogg, Donald W. "Jamaican Religions. A Study in Variations." Ph.D. dissertation, Yale University, 1964.

Marshall, Woodville K. "Peasant Development in the West Indies since 1838," *Social and Economic Studies* 17 (1968): 252–63.

Métraux, Alfred. "L'Habitation Paysanne en Haïti," *Bulletin de la Société Neuchâteloise de Géographie* 55 (1949–51): 3–14.

Métraux, Alfred. *Making a Living in the Marbial Valley (Haiti). Occasional Papers in Education 10.* Paris: UNESCO, 1951.

Métraux, Alfred. "Rites Funéraires des Paysans Haïtiens," *Arts et Traditions Populaires* 4 (1954): 289–306.

Métraux, Alfred. *Voodoo.* Trans. by Hugo Charteris. London: André Deutsch, 1959.

Mintz, Sidney W. "Cañamelar: The Culture of a Rural Puerto Rican Proletariat." PhD dissertation, Columbia University, 1951.

Mintz, Sidney W. "The Folk-Urban Continuum and the Rural Proletarian Community," *American Journal of Sociology* 59 (1953): 136–43.

Mintz, Sidney W. "Cañamelar: The Sub-Culture of a Rural Sugar Plantation Proletariat." In *The People of Puerto Rico*, edited by J. H. Steward *et al.* Urbana: University of Illinois Press, 1956.

Mintz, Sidney W. *Worker in the Cane.* New Haven: Yale University Press, 1960.

Mintz, Sidney W. "Living Fences in the Fond-des-Nègres Region, Haiti," *Economic Botany* 16 (1962): 101–5.

Moral, Paul. "La Maison Rurale en Haïti," *Les Cahiers d'Outre-Mer* 10 (1957): 117–30.

Otterbein, Keith F. "Caribbean Family Organization: A Comparative Analysis," *American Anthropologist* 67 (1965): 66–79.

Patterson, Orlando. *The Sociology of Slavery.* London: MacGibbon and Kee, 1967.

Pérez de la Riva, Francisco. *La Habitación Rural en Cuba.* La Habana: Contribución del Grupo Guamá, Antropología No. 26, 1952.

Price, Richard. "Caribbean Fishing and Fishermen: A Historical Sketch," *American Anthropologist* 68 (1966): 1368–83.

Price, Richard. "Studies of Caribbean Family Organization: Problems and Prospects," *Dédalo. Revista do Museu de Arte e Archeologia da Universidade de São Paulo* 3 (1970).

Revert, Emile. *La France d'Amérique.* Paris: Editions Maritimes et Coloniales, 1955.

Sauer, Carl O. "Economic Prospects of the Caribbean." In *The Caribbean: Its Economy*, edited by A. C. Wilgus, pp. 15–27. Gainesville, Florida: University of Florida Press, 1954.

Smith, Michael G. "The Transformation of Land Rights by Transmission in Carriacou," *Social and Economic Studies* 5 (1956): 103–38.

Smith, Michael G. *West Indian Family Structure.* Seattle: University of Washington Press, 1962.

Smith, Raymond T. *The Negro Family in British Guiana*. London: Routledge & Kegan Paul Ltd., 1956.

Solien, Nancie L. "Household and Family in the Caribbean," *Social and Economic Studies* 9 (1960): 101–6.

Steward, Julian, Manners, Robert A., Wolf, Eric R., Padilla Seda, Elena, Mintz, Sidney W., and Scheele, Raymond L. *The People of Puerto Rico*. Urbana: University of Illinois Press, 1956.

Stewart, John. *A View of the Past and Present State of the Island of Jamaica*. Edinburgh: Oliver & Boyd, 1823.

Street, John M. "Historical and Economic Geography of the South-west Peninsula of Haiti." PhD dissertation, University of California, 1960.

Sturtevant, William C. "History and Ethnology of Some West Indian Starches." In *The Domestication and Exploitation of Plants and Animals*, edited by Peter J. Ucko and G. W. Dimbleby. London: Gerald Duckworth & Co., Ltd., 1969.

Taylor, Douglas MacRae. *The Black Carib of British Honduras*. Viking Fund Publications in Anthropology no. 17. New York: Wenner-Gren Foundation for Anthropological Research, Inc., 1951.

Wolf, Eric R. "San José: Subcultures of a 'Traditional' Coffee Municipality." In *The People of Puerto Rico*, edited by J. H. Steward et al. Urbana: University of Illinois Press, 1956.

2

Women in Jamaica's Urban Informal Economy

Insights from a Kingston Slum

Faye V. Harrison

Introduction

The West Indian legacy of colonialism and imperialism is the world's oldest and possibly the world's harshest.[1] The work, adaptations, and struggles of Caribbean women, particularly poor Afro-Creole[2] women, warrant scholarly attention, for these experiences can reveal much about the part that gender inequality, especially in its intersection with race and class oppression, plays in colonial and post-colonial domination and in dependent forms of national development.

Much of the material that exists on gender and on women in Caribbean societies can be found embedded in the many studies of lower-class family structure and in the works on internal marketing among peasants.[3] However, over the past decade or so, increasing attention has been more directly focused on the socio-cultural, political, and economic underpinnings of women's lives.[4] The purpose of this chapter is not to provide a general framework for analyzing the varying statuses of women across class boundaries in West Indian societies, but to offer a perspective on the positions occupied and roles played by women within what is sometimes called the "informal economy" of urban Jamaica, specifically the Kingston Metropolitan Area.[5] Drawing upon ethnographic data from "Oceanview," a slum in downtown Kingston, the ensuing discussion attempts to elucidate and provide a context for understanding important facets of the everyday lives and struggles of those women who occupy the lowest strata of the Jamaican class structure: women who represent some of the most marginal segments of the working class and the petty bourgeoisie; and who, together with their young and aged dependents, constitute the largest proportion of their nation's poor.

A basic premise of this essay is that the problem of sexual inequality as it obtains in Jamaica today is integrally related to the broader processes of uneven development within the Caribbean periphery of the world capitalist system. That is, sexual oppression must be viewed in the national and international contexts of class and regional disparities which condition the specificity of women's everyday lives (Nash and Safa 1980:x–xi). The world capitalist system embodies a structure of labor market segmentation wherein workers in peripheral countries receive no more than one-sixth of the wages received by their counterparts in the advanced industrial center (Amin 1980). Since female workers receive considerably less than their male counterparts, Third World women represent a *cheaper than cheap* segment of the international workforce (Lim 1983:80; Nash 1983:3). Capital accumulation and transfer on a world scale is based upon relations of superexploitation, the brunt of which Third World women bear. The interplay of class and gender is, therefore, integral to capitalist development at both national and international levels.

Patterns of Uneven Development in Jamaica

Jamaica, formally independent since 1962, has historically been one of the most important countries, politically and economically, in the Commonwealth Caribbean. Its current population is approximately 2.2 million, one-half of which is urban and one-third of which is situated in the primary city, Kingston (Department of Statistics 1978b:3). The Jamaican economy is marked by uneven development or "underdevelopment," i.e., historically constituted processes that distort and subordinate domestic production and exchange to the accumulation interests of metropolitan capital (Mamdani 1976:6). Based largely on the production of sugar and bananas, the mining and partial refining of bauxite, tourism, and manufacturing, Jamaica's economic structure is extroverted in that its dominant enterprises and sectors are largely foreign owned or controlled and oriented toward an export market. The economy is internally disjointed, for there are few organic links between domestic sectors (Beckford and Witter 1980:66,81). Instead, the major linkages are vertical; that is, agriculture, bauxite, tourism, and branch-plant manufacturing are integrated into North American (and largely American) corporations. Accordingly, all inputs – raw materials, services, technology, and skilled personnel – are imported, and virtually all outputs from these industries are exported.

However, all of the economy is not directly controlled by corporate capital. Jamaica's peripheral capitalism encompasses variant forms of production and exchange which are subordinate to the dominant capitalist pattern. Some of these subordinate economic forms, e.g., subsistence agriculture, have their origins in earlier non-

capitalist modes of production/exchange that have been absorbed into the domestic capitalist system due to the consolidation and widespread penetration of large-scale and primarily foreign capital (cf. Post 1978). Other patterns, such as many of those found within the small-scale, unlicensed sphere of the urban economy, have developed out of contradictions and complexities endemic to peripheral capitalism itself (cf. Kowarick 1979:83).

Crisis of the 70s and 80s

During the 50s and 60s, foreign investment, principally American, propelled a rapid and sustained growth in the economy (Jefferson 1972). This capital-intensive growth benefitted the national bourgeoisie and middle class while it engendered a rise in unemployment and a decline in the poor's share in national income (Girvan and Bernal 1982:37). In sharp contrast to the boom period, the 1970s brought two world recessions, quadrupled oil prices, sharp price increases for manufactured imports, and acute price and demand instability for Third World exports (National Planning Agency 1978:6). The People's National Party (PNP), the ruling party of the 1972–80 period, instituted various reforms to redistribute national income and to secure greater "Jamaicanization" or sovereignty over the economy. One of the most dramatic actions the government took in response to international conditions and pressures from segments of the national bourgeoisie was the imposition of a production levy on the bauxite companies in 1974. Following the levy and Jamaica's part in the formation of the International Bauxite Association, the PNP announced its commitment to democratic socialism and to liberating itself from imperialism.

Fearing that Jamaica would move further leftward and expropriate investments, foreign and domestic capitalists, largely through the agency of the Jamaica Labour Party (JLP) opposition, mobilized a destabilization campaign to undermine the legitimacy of the PNP administration and oust it from office (Keith and Girling 1978:29). Bauxite companies cut back production and filed a litigation suit; the American press discouraged tourism, Jamaica's second largest foreign exchange earner; local capitalists cut back production and, in many cases, closed down business and fled the island with their capital; and international commercial banks ceased making loans to Jamaica.

Facing an economic collapse, in 1977 the country was compelled to seek foreign exchange from the International Monetary Fund (IMF), whose restrictive policies exacerbated the island's economic slump as well as its volatile political climate (Girvan and Bernal 1982:39, 40). In order to gain eligibility for IMF loans, the government had to undertake a number of drastic readjustments, among them cuts in real wages and retrenchment in the public sector. Initially the administration resisted the IMF strategy, but a severe credit squeeze forced it to re-open negotiations. Adhering to the terms of a standby loan, in April, 1977 the government was forced to devalue its currency by almost fifty percent, impose indirect taxes, lift price controls, and limit wages increases. These measures resulted in a 35 percent decline in real wages and a 50 percent rise in the price level (Girvan and Bernal 1982:43). After failing fiscal performance tests for two consecutive years, in early 1980 the government called for general elections in order to determine the nation's economic path. A month later the negotiations with the IMF were discontinued. The continuous shortages of basic commodities (even food staples), the rising unemployment (35 percent in 1980) especially affecting young adults and women, the constant currency devaluations and sharp price increases, and the unprecedented wave of political violence accompanying the campaign demoralized the population and eroded its confidence in the PNP government. Within several months the opposition party had electorally ousted the PNP as the country's ruling party and returned the economy to the orbit of Western banks, transnationals, and the IMF.

In spite of massive support from the United States government and international institutions, principally the IMF, the Jamaican economy has deteriorated since the JLP's rise to power. Following stringent IMF directions, the administration de-nationalized public-owned businesses, drastically cut back in public employment, abolished price regulations and food subsidies,

imposed restraints on wages, and devalued the national currency several times. The IMF strategy for economic recovery has increased the balance of payments deficit and imposed a degree of austerity on living conditions more severe than the hardships that prevailed during the PNP administration (Headley 1985).

The Urban Informal Economic Sector

Since the consolidation of the capitalist mode at the turn of the century, Jamaica, like many Third World countries, has been unable to offer secure and stable employment opportunities for most of its working-age population. The chronic problem of "surplus" population, severely aggravated by the balance of payments crisis, is manifest in high rates of unemployment, immeasurably rampant underemployment, and successive waves of emigration; and is the consequence of the displacement of labor from both subsistence and modern sectors of the national economy. Much of the surplus working population – the dislocated peasants, displaced and landless wage-workers, and the marginally self-employed – is absorbed into the urban informal economic sector, which encompasses income-producing activities outside formal sector wages, pensions, and gratuities (Portes 1981:87).[6]

Within the urban informal economic sphere are myriad productive, marketing, and service activities and enterprises, most of which are unlicensed, untaxed, and able to circumvent the expenses imposed by State safety and sanitary regulations. This petty-scale sector of the economy is dependent upon large-scale and capital-intensive industry and complements it by taking on tasks that the latter generally neglects because of unprofitability (Roberts 1978) or illegality. Because of the export orientation of capitalist production in most of the Third World, the dominant economic spheres are not organized to satisfy all market demands. Whereas the formal, corporate sector meets the demands of the export market, the informal sector caters to many of the requirements of the domestic market. For example, due to the gravity of economic conditions during the latter years of the PNP administration (when I collected most of my field data), the

formal = export market
informal = domestic market

importation of a wide range of consumer and capital goods virtually ceased. A premium was, therefore, placed on items that had become scarce or unobtainable in the formal domestic market. The informal economy, particularly its illegal segments, became a major source of many goods and services, including such staple foodstuffs as rice, milk, flour, and cheese.

An integral and fairly stable component of Jamaica's illegitimate economic sphere is the production of and trade in ganja or marijuana. While the local and national trade is important, the international distribution of "herb" is even more economically significant (Lacey 1977). In fact, at the height of the balance of payments crisis of the 70s, ganja production and trade was "the only healthy [sector] of the Jamaican economy. The 1.1 billion dollar business [was] the economic lifeline of Jamaica ... after traditional segments of the economy failed" (*Newsweek* 1980). This starkly illustrates how integral informal sector activities often are in peripheral capitalist economies.

While it may be clear that informal economic processes are subordinate to and dependent upon formally recognized economic sectors, it is also important to realize that capitalist accumulation itself is dependent upon the subsistence-oriented and other petty-scale activities of the informal sphere. The largely unlicensed and unregulated small-scale domain plays a critical role in subsidizing part of the costs of transnational corporations operating in Third World nations, enabling these firms to enforce comparatively low wages on their labor (Portes 1978:37). Moreover, by lowering the costs of reproduction, informal economic activities indirectly subsidize workers in core nations, e.g., the United States, and, thereby, help maintain the rate and transfer of profit (Portes 1981:106). The urban informal sector helps reduce labor costs for corporations in two major ways: first, by providing relatively cheap and/or accessible goods and services and, hence, reducing some of the costs of subsistence for the urban population, particularly wage-workers; and, second, by decreasing the relative size of the formal labor force with its abundant labor available for casual and disguised forms of wage-work.

"Self-employment" or "own-account" work represents a pattern of concealed wage-work which permits capital to extract surplus labor from petty producers and traders. Several scholars, e.g. Portes (1981), Birkbeck (1979), and Scott (1979), have shown that much informal sector activity is actually work done for the benefit of formal sector firms. For example, the informal marketing of formal sector goods constitutes a well-organized business ultimately controlled by capitalist firms. Rather than invest in retail chains, distributing firms utilize "independent" traders. In this case, informal trading represents an efficient and profitable means of circulating both national and imported goods in the domestic market. The character of this inter-sectoral linkage is concealed, because capital does not intervene directly in the informal labor process, which is generally organized around personalized, often familial relationships. The informal labor process, therefore, should be distinguished from the underlying social relations of production and appropriation which permit capital to superexploit informal labor (cf. Amin 1980:25).[7]

Informal economic relations, which are typically embedded in kinship and peer networks, permit the use of free or nominally paid labor and, consequently, "an output of goods and services at prices lower than those which could be offered under formal productive arrangements" (Portes 1981:86). While these conditions reduce the costs of reproduction for the petty-scale sphere and, therefore, permit its viability, ultimately, these very conditions maximize surplus extraction by reducing the costs that the dominant sector must pay to reproduce labor power.

The "feminization" of the informal economy
The part the informal sector plays in lowering the general costs of reproducing labor power for formal sector capital is also the role attributed to a reserve army of labor.[8] Saffioti (1978) bases her theoretical discourse on women in class societies upon the premise that intrinsic to capitalism is the existence of a reserve resulting from the exclusion of considerable segments of the working populations from a secure position in the labor market. Under capitalist social conditions, a large proportion of women, particularly housewives

who have been displaced from what are socially defined as productive economic roles, constitute a reserve labor force, whose surplus labor power is absorbed into the domestic domain of the social economy.

While women as housewives, working to reproduce their mates' labor power without the benefit of wages, may indeed represent an important and, in analytic terms, neglected component of the labor reserve, the quintessential reserve in peripheral societies such as Jamaica, where women constitute a sizeable component (47%) of the workforce as well as of the displaced workforce (i.e., informal workers),[9] includes those women who, as breadwinners and quite often as heads of households, must operate within the context of an insecure and informal opportunity structure to eke out a livelihood for themselves and for their young and aged dependents. From these segments of the reserve, middle- and upper-class housewives recruit and hire their domestic helpers, who for pitiably low wages perform most of the functions necessary for maintaining privileged households. From this informal labor force also come many of the female street vendors, called "higglers," who are responsible for distributing staple foodstuffs throughout the urban population, particularly to the poor.

The rate of formal unemployment for Jamaican women (39%) is more than twice as high as that for men (16%), resulting in more than twice as many women (167,900) being unemployed as compared to men (79,200) (Department of Statistics 1978b:26). The relative feminization of unemployment and poverty is manifested in the informal economy wherein females participate in survival and subsistence activities in comparatively larger numbers and proportions. Moreover, in view of the pivotal position women occupy within familial and domestic configurations,[10] they tend to play principal mobilizational roles in "scuffling" ventures, i.e., small-scale income-generating processes.

The Sexual Division of Labor in the Informal Sphere

The urban informal economy consists of an expansive, competitive tertiary sector, a small sphere of secondary production or petty manufacture, and, in light of the physical constraints of the urban economy, a restricted sector of primary production, e.g., gardening and animal husbandry. The principal focus of informal sector activity in the Kingston Metropolitan Area, therefore, tends to be that of commodity circulation and services rather than that of production. The latter process is concentrated largely within the formal sphere of the urban economy. That is to say that petty producers have been substantially displaced by large-scale capital, and this displacement has affected women more drastically than men.

According to government data for the late 1970s and early 1980s, approximately 70% of all female workers in Jamaica were employed in the tertiary sector (i.e., commerce and services), while only about 32–33% of all male workers were active in this sector (Department of Statistics 1978b:27; 1984:308; Statistical Institute of Jamaica 1984:10). Only 7–8% of the female work was in manufacture, whereas on average 14% of the male workforce was concentrated there.

The respective distributions of female and male workers in the informal sector of one neighborhood's economic structure (that of Oceanview) indicate that both women and men shared exceedingly large concentrations in the tertiary sector of the locality and metropolitan economy. Still, the percentage of women workers in this sector exceeded that of men by about 11%.[11] Moreover, while a substantial percentage of men worked as producers (35%), a much lesser percentage of women (20%) was engaged in productive labor. It seems, therefore, that although most informal sector participants were involved in commercial and service activities, the concentration of women's work in this particular domain was especially high (88%). This evidence suggests that compared with women, men tended to have access to income opportunities across a wider range of occupations, activities, and sectors. Furthermore, the income opportunities accessible to men, e.g., those in construction, provided higher levels of remuneration than female-specific jobs. Many of the higher paying jobs available to males, however,

tertiary sector - commerce & services

tended to be insecure, or available only on a temporary, casual basis.

Nelson (1979) shows that within the informal economic sector of Nairobi, Kenya, women by and large are restricted to marketing skills (e.g., preparing beverages, cooking, caring for children, and washing clothes) practiced in the home, whereas men market a much wider range of skills and services.[12] Evidence from Oceanview confirms this kind of sexual division of labor. For instance, close to 33% of the working women in my sample were engaged in some sort of domestic service, while about 26% were employed in general services (e.g., casual street-cleaning, hairstyling, and spiritual healing). In contrast, 40% of the men in the sample were engaged in general services (e.g., taxi-driving, vehicle repair, and photography).

Approximately 46% of all of the women sampled were involved in either or both the marketing of domestic services (33%) and the marketing of domestic or household consumer goods (24%), e.g., foodstuffs, cooking utensils, and clothing. Few (i.e., 3%) of the men were engaged in services (e.g., baking and cooking) that could be classified as domestic; nonetheless, approximately 18% were involved in marketing domestic commodities – food, durable domestic goods, and clothing. It is important to realize that the majority (78%) of these female marketers were "higglers," i.e., street vendors selling fresh, and, therefore, perishable vegetables and fruits, and only about 22% of the female retailers were shopkeepers.[13] Conversely, 64% of the male retailers were proprietors of small grocery shops, stores, or restaurants while only about 36% were street vendors. Male retailers were more likely to manage larger-scale enterprises. Furthermore, whereas these male proprietors generally benefitted from the labor of their spouses and/or kinswomen, their female counterparts were less inclined to have adult males as regular sources of labor.

Although perhaps the large higgler category may evince salient management and organizational skills among women as instrumental actors, these abilities and achievements were not widely channelled into other important areas. Men were more likely to hold supervisory positions and to market leadership skills and services, for example, as foremen of construction and public works crews and as informal labor recruiters and political party brokers. Further, a larger proportion of men than women was engaged in productive and service activities (e.g., vehicle repair, electrical work, plumbing, carpentry, masonry, welding, etc.) which demanded some readily recognized degree of technical expertise.

It is also noteworthy that male and female informants had different patterns of participation in the small urban primary sector. Women, for instance, tended to raise fowl and tree fruits for household and domestic subsistence, while men were more inclined to produce for commodity exchange. Half of the men involved in primary production were engaged in raising pigs or goats for the market. Women's involvement in secondary production, viz., petty manufacture, was largely restricted to the production of children's and women's clothing, while men produced men's clothing, shoes, furniture, woodcarvings, and were involved in building construction. Women's work across all sectors was linked largely to domestic needs and functions.

Another discernible category of informal economic activity is that related to entertainment or recreation.[14] Approximately 22% of the males in my sample admittedly participated in this sphere as barkeepers (5%), ganja traders (14%), and gambling vendors/brokers (3%). Approximately 31% of the women were involved in often multiple and interrelated occupations within this sphere as barkeepers (13%), ganja traders (7%), gambling vendors and housemistresses (11%), and "sportin gals" or prostitutes (5%). Of course, these percentages, which represent only what informants were willing to divulge, grossly underestimate the extent of involvement in illegal activities, particularly in the ganja trade and prostitution. These two illegal spheres seem to reflect a division of labor by gender, in that although women are indeed active in the production and exchange of ganja, the trade is a domain in which males predominate. On the other hand, prostitution at the local level is largely organized by women, who tend not to have pimps or male superiors. This relative autonomy, however, is absent in the major tourist zones, where

evince = reveal

commoditized sexual exchanges are typically mediated by male brokers.

Nelson (1979) treats prostitution as well as those serial mating practices in which an economic motive or dimension is apparent as instances of the marketing of services that women practice and perform within the domestic domain.[15] Although she places prostitution and those mating practices which, for all intents and purposes, represent an economic survival strategy into the same category, the two behaviors should not be equated. The sexual services embodied in mating behavior are not commodities, as are the services prostitutes market, but use-values.

In view of this conceptual distinction between commodities and use-values, it is necessary to underscore the fact that the informal economy is not limited to the production and exchange of petty commodities. Of great significance is the production and non-market exchange – what Lomnitz (1977) calls "reciprocal exchange" – of such resources as information and any good and service which contribute in some way to subsistence and economic viability. Non-market exchange is especially crucial for the subsistence of a considerable proportion of ghetto (i.e., slum and shantytown) populations that cannot regularly engage in monetary transactions.

The Social Organization and Construction of Gender

Social networks – or very fluid and diffusely structured social relationships organized primarily around kinship, co-residential, and/or peer ties – constitute the basis for much of the socioeconomic activity within the informal economy. Kinship groupings extend beyond individual residential units, and the embeddedness of these households in broader domestic configurations is critical given the absence of State aid or welfare benefits for the formally unemployed or the non-wage working poor.

The primacy of extended consanguineal ties characterizes the situations of both women and men; however, ghetto women tend to be comparatively more reliant on or committed to kin and domestic groupings for salient and sustained social relationships. Women informants (particularly those in the 18–30 year range) tended to express distrust for friendship and marriage,[16] suggesting that investments in such non-kin relationships would lead to additional demands on limited resource, "trouble" and "war" over gossip and men, and, in the case of legal marriage, constraints on female independence and autonomy. "Me naa keep friends" was the claim of several women who restricted most of their intimate, reciprocal interactions to relatives. Women who were higglers with relatively stable retail enterprises, officers in local-level political party associations or mutual aid societies, or "bankers" in rotating credit networks called "partners" tended to have more intense relationships outside the domestic sphere. For these women peer relationships were often significant; nonetheless, kin ties were viewed as much more reliable and valuable.

While the idiom and organization of kinship are key in the everyday lives of poor urban women, among ghetto men peer bonds are highly valued and play a central role on the street corners where male networks are based (cf. Brana-Shute 1976; Lieber 1976; Wilson 1971). The peer networks of men between the ages of 15 and 35 often assume the form of gangs which may combine to form gang hierarchies extending over the territory of an entire neighborhood or an even more inclusive district or zone. Street corners and their associated gangs provide the context within which subsistence-related information is exchanged, material resources are redistributed, casual labor is recruited for government-sector employment, and legitimate and illegitimate hustling strategies are devised and carried out.

Interestingly, in the way that both women and men talked about their lives and survival struggles, women seemed to place greater emphasis on independence and autonomy than did men. Despite their actual dependence on the "baby-fathers" (i.e., consensual mates), mothers, sisters, and special neighbors of their active networks, women underscored the importance and necessity of independent action in surviving Kingston's slums and shantytowns. They viewed their participation in familial networks, which extend and contract according to need and circumstance, as the outcome of their individual strategies and negotiations rather than as the result of group obligations and duties. "Networking," even among kinspeople, was described as voluntary and instrumental, and it involved no fixed, long-term commitments to a clearly defined social unit.

The assertion of female independence is not at all controverted by kin alignments. In fact, the extended organization of kinship and domesticity, with its internal division of labor and forms of cooperation, frees some women for work and other activities outside the home. Those women remaining at home and in the immediate neighborhood supervise and care for the children, while also carrying out other household-based tasks, some of which generate income. Independence does not, therefore, imply "a shedding of social attachments . . [but] is linked to a strong sense of interpersonal connectedness ..." (Sutton and Makiesky-Barrow 1981:496).

Manifestations of female autonomy, particularly in the economic domain as evinced by the high rate of female participation in the labor force, have sometimes been taken by the public and by scholars to mean that women enjoy sexual equality (cf. Mintz 1981; Sutton and Makiesky-Barrow 1981). However, evidence indicating that women indeed suffer from underemployment, unemployment, low-paying jobs, and de facto disenfranchisement more disproportionately than their male counterparts serves to dispel this conception. Sexual inequality is also reflected in the incidence of wife-battering and sexual violence as well as in ideological representations in, for instance, mass media advertisements and popular music (Antrobus and Gordon 1984: 120; Henry and Wilson 1975:193–4). Male resentment against female competence and assertiveness is expressed in song lyrics which often encourage men to control or dominate women lest the latter's alleged cleverness, deviousness, and promiscuity endanger men's standing in the home and community (cf. Henry and Wilson 1975:193).

Despite the ambivalence men may feel toward women's presence outside the home, women's work is expected and tolerated. The tolerance for female independence and for individual independence regardless of gender originated during

the slavery era when both sexes were equally involved and exploited in the "public" domain of plantation work (Sutton and Makiesky-Barrow 1981). Mintz (1981) hypothesizes that since enslaved men could not assert "paterfamilial" domination over female slaves, and since slave masters relegated both male and female Africans to the status of chattel property, respect for individual rights and prerogatives for both men and women was strong among Afro-Jamaicans.

Historically, the masses of Jamaican women have been conspicuous as workers not (wholly) dependent on their kinsmen and mates for their sustenance and security. During the post-emancipation period, peasant women complemented the work of male producers through a system of internal marketing controlled largely by the market women themselves. However, with the expansion and consolidation of capitalist social relations at the turn of the century, the autonomy of Afro–Jamaican women – and that of peasants, artisans, and traders as a whole – diminished. Owing to the entrenchment of colonial state power over the hitherto independent peasantry,[17] male dominance gained further legitimacy and was imposed on the society by established churches, schools, laws, and a system of job segregation and wage differentials.[18]

Gender and Politics

In the mid-1970s, a government redevelopment agency charged with upgrading housing, utilities, and social services in the Oceanview vicinity conducted a survey in order to identify the neighborhood's leadership on the basis of reputation. These "area leaders" were then to comprise an advisory committee that would aid in implementing the government program's objectives. Out of the 23 persons identified, only one was a woman. In a locality where women are quite visible in the economic arena and where their membership and work keep alive and active local-level political party groups and branches, why were women underrepresented as area leaders?

The term "leader" tends to connote authority and official status and is typically applied to middle-class political party functionaries. In this sense, Oceanview respondents would claim that there are no leaders among the locality's residents. With a qualified, expanded definition of leader as one with the respectability, personal influence, mobilizational skills, and resources to determine and implement local or factional goals (Swartz 1968:1), respondents would generate a list of persons strategically situated in grassroots sociopolitical fields. The redevelopment program sought to identify the latter persons; yet the survey results yielded a predominantly male pool.

Contrary to the impression the neighborhood survey may have given, and although females may be denied legitimate recognition, it is not at all unusual for women to be principal political agents, i.e., de facto protagonists, catalysts, directors, and sustainers of sociopolitical action at the local level. Beckford and Witter (1980:99) confirm this observation by pointing out that women are the main party workers in groups and branches. They maintain the party machinery during terms of government office, and they are the most committed campaigners during electoral contests. Their activism is manifested not only in association membership, but also in the leadership of neighborhood party organs, for they often appear as secretaries, vice-presidents, and presidents. Nonetheless, by and large, despite various exceptions, women's power is largely confined to the lowest levels of political party structure and the inclusive State apparatus; they are not highly visible in the decision-making echelons. Even at the local level, the power and leadership of party women may be preempted by gang brokers who are often more strategically placed in the party machine.

In view of the constraints on their political role and participation, women are inclined and, in some respects, encouraged to assert their unevenly formed power by manipulating and influencing those men who are authorized or empowered actors in parties, government, street gangs, and mainstream churches.[19] For example, a former female group president recounted how she was pressured to become "friendly" with higher level party brokers in order to gain access to important information and job opportunities for her local area. Another woman, one who never joined a party association, used her acquaintance and intimacy with a party broker and a police

officer to acquire favors which were crucial in securing and expanding her ganja trade business. In another case, a former group leader resigned from party activism because of the sexual harassment she encountered. She claimed that sexual services were often expected of women in exchange for party patronage. While women may sometimes gain power, influence, and control over resources through their relationships with male brokers, this dependent access to political capital leaves women vulnerable to manipulation and abuse.

The greatest proportions of women are found in informal fields of power, e.g., revival churches, school associations, and markets, wherein there arise opportunities for women as individuals and as groups to define and implement strategic local goals – Swartz's definition of politics (1968:1). Generally, this sphere of activity is not perceived or designated as political, despite its intrinsic political dimensions and its articulation or interpenetration with formal political domains. Henry and Wilson suggest that because of the subservient role women play in society, they predominate in lower-class religious cults or sects (1975:190). They claim that

> religion is one of the few areas ... where women find some measure of equality with significant others. It is also an area where women have free access and the fact that they can hold positions of office gives them a measure of status outside the religious group which they might not otherwise be able to achieve. (1975:190)

In localities like Oceanview, where inter-party rivalry often attains volatile and life-threatening proportions, a large percentage of residents tends to retreat from "politricks" and are distrustful of partisan activities and activists. Parent Teacher Associations, mutual aid societies, and churches are more likely to be perceived as non-partisan and therefore potentially more reflective of the interests and needs of a broader cross-section of the neighborhood. It is in such extra-domestic situations that many women are able to mobilize their limited resources for the survival of their families and neighborhoods as well as for a sense of collective defense and autonomy.

Through their involvement in these often predominantly female spheres of action, women produce an emergent praxis of sisterhood marked by ambiguity and contradiction. The sisterhood engendered in certain informal fields can be seen as a constructive reaction to the constraints women confront as single parents, formal and informal workers, and political constituents. For example, many of the members of Oceanview's PTA consider that organization an alternative to the local party associations that have been unable to promote community development, peace, and unity. The PTA (whose agenda encompasses much more than educational objectives) represents a non-partisan vehicle for actively resisting the various forms of victimization and oppression its members experience in their everyday lives.

Nonetheless, sisterhood may also comprise elements of collusion (cf. Westwood 1985) and escapism. Some Oceanview women believe that politics is intrinsically "wicked" and not a righteous means of meaningful change. The recurring statement "Me naa deal in politics; only God can save Jamaica" reflects this view. For these women any politician or political activist, leftist or rightist, sincere or opportunist, is suspect and unworthy of support; and churches, friendly societies, or other associations provide a refuge. Whereas the informal sphere may provide women with alternative outlets for constructive political expression, it can also offer a means of retreat, suppressing effective opposition and resistance.

An informally organized sector of Oceanview's social organization not readily open to women's mobilization and empowerment is that of the Rastafari. Local followers of Rastafari, particularly the more senior and devoted "true Rastas," organize their religious worship, economic activities, and domestic life along clear lines of male dominance.[20] Rastafari represents one of the most significant mass movements, culturally and politically, in contemporary Jamaica.[21] Its ideology and idiom of protest and rebellion have permeated the slums and shantytowns, where displaced wage-workers and the marginally self-employed dwell. In Rastafarian views and practices, women are essentially spiritual and political dependents (Kitzinger 1969:260, 1971:583; Rowe 1980). Men must guide women in order for the latter to achieve spiritual wholeness and "sight," the "I/eye."[22] I broach this issue of patriarchy among Rastafari simply to highlight the sexist character of important elements in Jamaican culture and to suggest some of the contradictions within sociocultural forces that exert considerable influence on the uneven and often contradictory patterns of opposition, protest, and accommodation within some of the most alienated segments of Jamaican society.

The sexism that shapes and inhibits the political behavior of women active in the informal economy impedes the political development of the entire informal and casual workforce. While this relationship between the social construction of gender and political underdevelopment holds also for the organized working class as well as for any class, it is especially critical for informal workers, because women are disproportionately represented among them.

I raise this question of the political character of informal labor, because anthropologists and other social scientists have questioned whether the urban informal sector functions as a safety valve reinforcing the status quo or whether it represents a potential source of pre-revolutionary rebellion (McGee 1971; Worsley 1972). Roberts (1978:135) claims that the fragmented organization of small-scale socioeconomic enterprises, combined with the present-day survival orientation of the actors themselves, gives rise to sporadic and inhibited patterns of political action. Elsewhere I have argued that supralocal or State-level political processes also contribute to the containment of rebellion. Patronage–clientelism undermines solidarity among grassroots constituents; police and army repression thwarts efforts to disrupt or challenge the social order; and by labelling many forms of protest and rebellion as crime, the State delegitimates certain political behaviors and isolates rebels from potential allies in, for instance, the formal working class (Harrison 1982:326–35).

An additional factor that contributes to the underdeveloped political character of the informal labor force, and one that has not been pinpointed, let alone accentuated, is the suppression of women's participation in politics, particularly in those fields most strategically aligned to or embedded in national- (and international-) level political structures. These most strategic fields, arenas, and institutions are male dominated and conditioned largely by middle- and upper-class interests.

Conclusions

Sexual or gender inequality represents an essential and integral feature of social relations and cultural construction in Jamaica, where for the past four hundred years colonial and imperialist exploitation has governed the development of economic, political, and sociocultural patterns and structures. Although the focus of this chapter has been on women and, more generally, on gender differentials within the urban petty-scale sphere of the Jamaican economy, it is extremely important to further contextualize the subordination and oppression characterizing these women's position by taking into account the pervasive impact of racism. During the course of Jamaica's history, the exploitation of the masses has been legitimated and rationalized by a system of ideas and symbols which has elaborated the allegedly inherent and functional inferiority of Africans as a distinct racial grouping and as bearers of a peculiar, "cultureless" culture. Racist ideology and institutional arrangements have historically supported and permitted the superexploitation of Afro-Jamaicans as a labor force, the violation of black and brown women as objects of sexual indulgence, and the political alienation and repression of the island's majority.

The many segments of the working-age population which, to varying extents, are absorbed into the urban informal economy may represent a surplus labor force from the point of view of their surface relationship to corporate capitalist spheres; however, the casual workers, scufflers, hustlers, and the petty producers and traders who fill the streets, lanes, and yards (i.e., communal residences) with their daily survival struggles are vertically integrated into peripheral capitalist structures that depend upon the articulation and interpenetration of variant socioeconomic patterns, the asymmetrical conjuncture of which constitutes a socioeconomic formation specific to the complexities and contradictions of Jamaica's historical development within a world system.

In a central way, the feminization of the informal sphere contributes to the reproduction of a cheap, casual, and concealed workforce accessible to capital for performing its temporary and largely unskilled tasks. Although responsible for supporting appreciable proportions of the nation's dependents and for organizing their non-wage-compensated work into minimally lucrative household-based ventures, women have the most limited access to income and capitalization opportunities. Despite the undisputable existence of substantial numbers of higglers, visible with the results of their mobilization of petty capital, the informal sector is not ruled by matriarchs. The economic status higglers have rests upon the marketing of domestic and household use goods and, therefore, on a sexually segregated system of economic opportunities which confines women to spheres related to domestic consumption. Moreover, whatever status and power individual higglers and other female retailers may in fact have within their communities, associations, and their primary networks of kinspeople, friends, and clients, this power and status cannot be generalized to depict the situation of the majority of women in the slums and shantytowns of urban Jamaica. These latter women scuffle under fluctuating and unpredictable circumstances to eke out minimal subsistence for themselves and their "pickney" (children), either with or without sustained support from their "babyfathers," and under diffuse and ambiguous contracts of support and alliance with kin and fictive kin.

The mass of Jamaican women, who in some form or another operate as informally organized workers, have a legacy to inform their lives and struggles. On one hand, that legacy is long with the pain and blood of "sufferation" and "downpression," but, on the other hand, that legacy is also marked by the integrity of a people at some levels conscious of its potential power as resisters, rebels, and rulers of its own destiny. Despite obstacles and constraints, Afro-Jamaican women have historically made their footprints in paths of struggle on both economic and political planes. In light of the critical current state of affairs in Jamaica, it is becoming increasingly obvious that for "deliverance"[23] and change to come, Jamaica has to mobilize all of its people, men and women. How exactly this proposisition will be translated into political discourse and applied to organization and praxis is a question for which only the unfolding of social history can provide answers.

Notes

1   Williams (1944) and Knight (1978) have written on political and economic aspects of Caribbean history. For studies of underdevelopment and dependency, see Beckford (1972; 1975), Beckford and Witter (1980), Girvan (1973; 1976), Mintz (1977), and Thomas (1974).

2   The term *Creole* refers to the Caribbean-born descendants of the Africans and Europeans who peopled the West Indies during the colonization and slavery era. The category is not applied to post-emancipation immigrants such as the Chinese and East Indians.

3   For examples of classic family studies, see Blake (1961), Clarke (1957), and Gonzalez (1969). See Bolles (1983) for a more current analysis of urban working-class households in crisis-torn Jamaica. For work on internal marketing, see Mintz (1955; 1964; 1981).

4   Henry and Wilson (1975) have addressed the general status of Caribbean women; Moses (1981) treats women's status in Montserrat, and Sutton and Makiesky-Barrow (1981) focus on Barbadian women. Bolles (1983) deals with women's family and work responsibilities in the context of the economic austerity exacerbated by the International Monetary Fund.

5   My perspective is based largely on fieldwork done on political and economic processes in a locality in the Kingston Metropolitan Area in 1978–9.

6   It is impossible to directly measure the actual extent of participation in the informal sphere of an economy, because informal activities and enterprises tend, for the most part, not to be recorded or registered. We can assume, however, that this sector absorbs the unemployed (defined as those actually seeking wage-work or those willing to do wage-work) and those segments of the population which have never sought formal wage-employment. It is also important to note that, to varying extents, formal workers – even members of the established middle-class – are involved in informal economic activities as a means of supplementing their income. While the informal economy acts as a buffer against unemployment, it also provides capitalization opportunities for petty entrepreneurs and petty capitalists. In fact, Stone (1977) claims that an indeterminant number of businesspeople from the most precarious segments of Jamaica's petty bourgeoisie commonly engage in informal and sometimes in illegal means of capitalization and appropriation (e.g., gambling and ganja ventures) in order to maintain and expand their legitimate enterprises.

7   This distinction between labor process and social relations of production is pertinent in light of the argument that the informal sector represents a distinct mode of production (cf. Davies 1979).

8   The reserve, surviving under tenuous and insecure social and economic circumstances, consists of unemployed workers, casual workers moving from job to job, displaced peasants and agroproletarians forced into cities, and long-term "scufflers" and the marginally self-employed. See Braverman (1974:388) for a discussion of Marx's formulation of surplus population.

9   In 1978 women represented approximately 47% of Jamaica's total recorded labor force (Department of Statistics 1978b:26). Over 65% of all women above the age of 14 were part of this force. In light of the factor that in 1978 38% of the female labor force was formally unemployed, and an even larger percentage underemployed, it appears that women are dislocated and excluded from normal labor market opportunities at a higher rate than men, who suffered a 16% rate of unemployment in 1978.

There is a history of relatively high rates of both formal and informal employment among women in former plantation slave societies such as Jamaica. During the slavery era, both men and women were fully employed as slave labor. Scholars (e.g., Patterson 1967; Mintz and Price 1976) have suggested that at this juncture the sexual division of labor was slight; however, women experienced a double drudgery in that they were responsible for both field and household tasks (Davis 1981). Women also played pivotal roles in the "proto-peasant" sphere of the slave economy, and were partly responsible for marketing their agricultural surplus. The peasant economy of the post-emancipation period was organized around a clear sexual division of labor in which men were primarily responsible for cultivation while women were largely responsible for marketing.

10   One-third of all households in Jamaica are headed by women (Department of Statistics 1978a:10).

11   The data for this discussion were collected from a small sample of 45 women and 56 men. These data were gathered as part of a broader investigation of the organization of socioeconomic and political life in Oceanview. Although the sample is limited, the data it yielded are consistent with the results of government surveys (e.g., those done by the Urban Development Corporation) conducted in the 1970s.

12   This pattern of sexual segregation in work (domestic vs. non-domestic) has been noted by anthropologists such as Rosaldo (1974) who underscore the relevance of the domestic vs. public dichotomy in a wide variety of sociocultural cases.

13   Of all the women sampled, 16% were higglers and 5% shopkeepers (e.g., grocers). Among the men, 7% were street vendors and 12% grocers and restaurateurs. Interestingly, outside of this domestic goods realm, female proprietors outnumbered their male counterparts. For instance, whereas 13% of the women in the sample were barkeepers, only 5% of the men were proprietors of bars. Most of the regular clientele of neighborhood bars are men and their guests. I am suggesting that women play an important role in entertaining men, for whom public drinking and, perhaps, less open gambling, are regular features of peer-related socializing and recreation.

14   This category which Nelson uses in her Kenya study is misleading in the sense that ganja traders may also be seen as providing a product necessary for religious rituals and healing, and gamblers may consider their activity hard work rather than mere recreation.

15   Nelson's conception of prostitution as domestic activity is consistent with the generally held definition of domesticity or domestic functions: all those activities involved in the production or preparation of food, in childrearing, in consumption, and in sexual reproduction or mating (Yanagisako 1979).

16   Most women in the sample as well as in the population at large were not legally married but involved in common-law unions and visiting relationships.

17   In the aftermath of emancipation, a reconstituted peasantry arose in opposition to the declining plantation system. This peasantry emerged before the formation of a capitalist mode of production and the consolidation of a class of agrarian capitalists. At this juncture peasants were in a strong position relative to large landholders. The former usually owned their own plots and paid little or nothing in taxes to the State. Furthermore, they were able to circumvent the expropriation of some part of the product of their labor by controlling exchange relations through networks of higglers – the mothers, wives, sisters, and daughters of peasant households (Post 1978).

18   See Henry (1983:100–7) for a discussion of the post-emancipation cultural colonization of Afro-Jamaicans, and Post (1978:34–5) for a treatment of the role of colonial State policies in thwarting the development of a free peasantry and enhancing the power of an emergent capitalist class. I have extended this line of argument to the realm of gender.

19   Henry and Wilson (1975) bring out that in the popular view women are often depicted as devious, manipulative, and conniving. It is also noteworthy that these stereotypes also apply to perceptions of lumpenproletarians who also commonly activate strategies of manipulation when dealing with politicians.

20   Whereas a large number of "youths" (i.e., male adolescents and adult males under 35) wear their hair in dreadlocks and claim to be Rastafarian, I am concerned with that minority of males who are committed to Rastafari religious beliefs and lifestyle, and who are designated as "true Rastas" within the locality. This segment exerts considerable influence over the secular "dreads."

21   See Smith, Augier, and Nettleford (1960), Nettleford (1970), Barrett (1977), Chevannes (1981), and Campbell (1987) for analyses of the Rastafari in Jamaica. See Austin (1983:236) for comments on the routinization of the movement during the past two decades.

22   Within the past decade, however, women have become more visible and vocal within the Rastafari movement. For instance, in 1980 three women's organizations were established. While "daughters" claim not to challenge the patriarchal tenets and structure of the movement, their very mobilization and "reasonings" (i.e., consciousness-raising rituals) seem to be generating new perspectives on women and on Rastafari itself.

      The concept of "sight" refers to spiritual vision and knowledge of truth. That of the "I" also refers to vision, but "I" also signifies the collective Rastafari, the "I and I," whose shared "reasonings" and sacramental rituals (ganja smoking and Nyabingi) lead to heightened transcendence.

23   "Deliverance" is a religious concept applied to popular political discourse in Jamaica. During

the 1980 electoral campaign against Michael Manley and the PNP, Edward Seaga, the present Prime Minister, promised deliverance to Jamaica. Politicians commonly manipulate popular religious symbols when mobilizing the electorate. The PNP made use of Rastafarian and revivalist (i.e., syncretist Christian) symbols in earlier campaigns.

References

Amin, Samir, 1980. The class structure of the contemporary imperialist system. *Monthly Review* 31 (8): 9–26.

Antrobus, Peggy and Lorna Gordon, 1984. The English-Speaking Caribbean: A journey in the making. In Robin Morgan (ed.), Sisterhood is global: The international women's movement anthology. Garden City, Anchor Books/Doubleday, 118–26.

Austin, Diane J., 1983. Culture and ideology in the English-speaking Caribbean: A view from Jamaica. *American Ethnologist* 10: 223–40.

Barrett, Leonard, 1977. The Rastafarians: Sounds of cultural dissonance. Boston: Beacon Press.

Beckford, George L., 1972. Persistent poverty: Underdevelopment in plantation economies of the third world. New York, Oxford University Press.

Beckford, George L., (ed.), 1975. Caribbean economy: Dependence and backwardness. Mona, Institute of Social and Economic Research, University of the West Indies.

Beckford, George and Michael Witter, 1980. Small garden ... bitter weed: The political economy of struggle and change in Jamaica. London, Zed Press.

Birkbeck, Chris, 1979. Garbage, industry, and the "vultures" of Cali, Colombia. In Ray Bromley and Chris Gerry (eds.), Casual work and poverty in third world cities. Chichester, John Wiley and Sons, 161–84.

Blake, Judith, 1961. Family structure in Jamaica: The social context of reproduction. Glencoe, Free Press.

Bolles, A. Lynn, 1983. Kitchens hit by priorities: Employed working-class Jamaican women confront the IMF. In June Nash and Maria Fernandez-Kelly (eds.), Women, men, and the international division of labor. Albany, State University of New York Press, 138–60.

Brana Shute, Gary, 1976. Drinking shops and social structure: Some ideas on lower-class male behavior. *Urban Anthropology* 5: 53–68.

Braverman, Henry, 1974. Labor and monopoly capital: The denigration of work in the twentieth century. New York, Monthly Review Press.

Campbell, Horace, 1987. Rasta and resistance: From Marcus Garvey to Walter Rodney. Trenton, Africa World Press, Inc.

Chevannes, Barry, 1981. The Rastafari and urban youth. In Carl Stone and Aggrey Brown (eds.), Perspectives on Jamaica in the seventies. Kingston, Jamaica Publishing House, 392–422.

Clarke, Edith, 1957. My mother who fathered me. London, George Allen and Unwin, Ltd.

Davies, Rob, 1979. Informal sector or subordinate mode of production? In Ray Bromly and Chris Gerry (eds.), Casual work and poverty in third world cities. Chichester, John Wiley and Sons, 87–104.

Davis, Angela, 1981. Women, race, and class. New York, Random House.

Department of Statistics, Jamaica, 1978a. The labour force. Kingston.

Department of Statistics, Jamaica, 1978b. Statistical abstract. Kingston.

Department of Statistics, Jamaica, 1984. Statistical Yearbook of Jamaica, 1982. Kingston.

Girvan, Norman, 1973. The development of dependency economics in the Caribbean and Latin America: Review and comparison. *Social and Economic Studies* 22: 1–33.

Girvan, Norman, 1976. Corporate imperialism: Conflict and expropriation. Transnational corporations and economic nationalism in the third world. New York, Monthly Review Press.

Girvan, Norman and Richard Bernal, 1982. The IMF and the foreclosure of development options: The case of Jamaica. *Monthly Review* 33 (9): 34–48.

Gonzalez, Nancie L. Solien, 1969. Black Carib household structure. A study of migration and modernization. Seattle, University of Washington Press.

Harrison, Faye V., 1982. Semiproletarianization and the structure of socioeconomic and political relations in a Jamaican slum. Unpublished doctoral dissertation. Stanford University.

Headley, Bernard D., 1985. Mr. Seaga's Jamaica: An inside look. Monthly Review 37 (4): 35–42.

Henry, Frances and Pamela Wilson, 1975. The status of women in Caribbean societies: An overview of their social, economic and sexual roles. *Social and Economic Studies* 24: 165–98.

Henry, Paget, 1983. Decolonization and cultural underdevelopment in the Common-wealth Caribbean. In Paget Henry and Carl Stone (eds.), The newer Caribbean: Decolonization, democracy, and development. Philadelphia, Institute for the Study of Human Issues, 95–120.

Jefferson, Owen, 1972. The post-war economic development of Jamaica. Mona, Institute of Social and Economic Research, University of the West Indies.

Keith, Sherry and Robert Girling, 1978. Caribbean conflict: Jamaica and the United States. NACLA *Report on the Americas* 12 (3): 3–36.

Kitzinger, Sheila, 1969. Protest and mysticism: The Rastafari cult of Jamaica. *Journal for the Scientific Study of Religion* 8: 240–62.

Kitzinger, Sheila, 1971. The Rastafarian brethern of Jamaica. In Michael Horowitz (ed.), Peoples and cultures of the Caribbean. New York Natural History Press, 580–8.

Knight, Franklin W., 1978. The Caribbean: The genesis of a fragmented nationalism. New York, Oxford University Press.

Kowarick, Lucio, 1979. Capitalism and urban marginality in Brazil. In Ray Bromley and Chris Gerry (eds.). Casual work and poverty in third world cities. Chichester, John Wiley and Sons, 69–85.

Lacey, Terry, 1977. Violence and politics in Jamaica, 1960–1970. Manchester, Manchester University Press.

Lieber, Michael, 1976. "Liming" and other concerns: The style of street embedments in Port-of-Spain, Trinidad. *Urban Anthropology* 5: 319–34.

Lim, Linda Y. C., 1983. Capitalism, imperialism, and patriarchy: The dilemma of Third World women workers in multinational factories. In June Nash and Maria Fernandez-Kelly (eds.), Women, men and the international division of labor. Albany, State University of New York Press, 70–91.

Lomnitz, Larissa Adler, 1977. Networks and marginality: Life in a Mexican shantytown. New York, Academic Press.

Mamdani, Mahmood, 1976. Politics and class formation in Uganda. New York, Monthly Review Press.

McGee, T. G., 1971. Revolutionary change and the third world city. In McGee, The urbanization process in the third world. London, G. Bell and Sons, Ltd., 64–93.

Mintz, Sidney W., 1955. The Jamaican internal marketing pattern. *Social and Economic Studies* 4: 95–103.

Mintz, Sidney W., 1964. The employment of capital by market women in Haiti. In Firth and Yarney (eds.), Capital, savings and credit in peasant societies. Chicago, Aldine Publishing Company, 256–86.

Mintz, Sidney W., 1977. The so-called world system: Local initiative and local response. *Dialectical Anthropology* 2: 253–70.

Mintz, Sidney W., 1981. Economic role and cultural tradition. In Filomina Chioma Steady (ed.), The black woman cross-culturally. Cambridge, Schenkman Publishing Company, 515–34.

Mintz, Sidney W. and Richard Price, 1976. An anthropological approach to the Afro-American past: A Caribbean perspective. Philadelphia: ISHI.

Moses, Yolanda T., 1981. Female status, the family, and male dominance in a West Indian community. In Filomina Chioma Steady (ed.), The block woman cross-culturally: Cambridge, Schenkman Publishing Company, 499–514.

Nash, June, 1983. The impact of the changing international division of labor on different sectors of the labor force. In June Nash and Maria Fernandez-Kelly (eds.), Women, men, and the international division of labor. Albany, State University of New York Press, 3–38.

Nash, June and Helen I. Safa., 1980. Sex and class in Latin America: Women's perspectives on politics, economics and the family in the third world. South Hadley, Bergin & Garvey Publishers.

National Planning Agency, 1978. Five year development plan, 1978–82. Kingston, Ministry of Finance and Planning, Jamaica.

Nelson, Nici, 1979. How women and men get by: The sexual division of labor in the informal sector of a Nairobi squatter settlement. In Ray Bromley and Chris Gerry (eds.), Casual work and poverty in third world cities. Chichester, John Wiley and Sons, 283–302.

Nettleford, Rex, 1970. Mirror, mirror: Identity, race and protest in Jamaica. Kingston, William Collins and Sangster (Jamaica) Ltd.

Newsweek, 1980. Jamaica: Back in business. December 15, 86.

Patterson, Orlando, 1967. The sociology of slavery, an analysis of the origins, development and structure of Negro slave society in Jamaica. Rutherford, Fairleigh Dickinson University Press.

Portes, Alejandro, 1978. The informal sector and the world economy: Notes on the structure of subsidized labor. *Institute of Development Studies Bulletin* 9: 35–40.

Portes, Alejandro, 1981. Unequal exchange and the urban informal sector. In Portes and John Walton.

Labor, class, and the international system. New York, Academic Press, 67–106.

Post, Ken, 1978. Arise ye starvelings: The Jamaican labour rebellion of 1938 and its aftermath. The Hague, Martinus Nijhoff.

Roberts, Bryan, 1978. Cities of peasants: The political economy of urbanization in the third world. Beverly Hills, Sage Publications.

Rosaldo, Michelle, 1974. A theoretical overview. In Michele Rosaldo and Louise Lamphere (eds.), Women, culture, and society. Stanford, Stanford University Press, 17–42.

Rowe, Maureen, 1980. The woman in Rastafari. *Caribbean Quarterly* 26 (4): 13–21.

Saffioti, Heleieth I. B., 1978. Women in class society. New York Monthly Review Press.

Scott, Alison MacEwen, 1979. Who are the self-employed? In Ray Bromley and Chris Gerry (eds.), Casual work and poverty in third world cities. Chichester, John Wiley and Sons, 105–29.

Smith, M. G., F. R. Augier, and Rex Nettleford, 1960. The Ras Tafari movement in Kingston, Jamaica. Mona, Institute of Social and Economic Research, University College of the West Indies.

Statistical Institute of Jamaica, 1984. The labour force, 1983 preliminary report. Kingston.

Stone, Carl, 1977. The political economy of gambling in a neo-colonial economy. In Stone and Aggrey Brown (eds.), Essays on power and change in Jamaica. Kingston, Jamaica Publishing House, 58–64.

Sutton, Constance and Susan Makiesky-Barrow, 1981. Social inequality and sexual status in Barbados. In Filomina Chioma Steady (ed.), The black woman cross-culturally. Cambridge, Schenkman Publishing Company, 469–99.

Swartz, Marc J., 1968. Introduction. In Swartz (ed.), Local-level politics: Social and cultural perspectives. Chicago, Aldine Publishing Company, 1–52.

Thomas, Clive Y., 1974. Dependence and transformation: The economics of the transition to socialism. New York, Monthly Review Press.

Westwood, Sallie, 1985. All day, every day: Factory and family in the making of women's lives. Urbana, University of Illinois Press.

Williams, Eric, 1944. Capitalism and slavery. Chapel Hill, University of North Carolina Press.

Wilson, Peter, 1971. Caribbean crews: Peer groups and male society. *Caribbean Studies* 10 (4): 18–34.

Worsley, Peter, 1972. Frantz Fanon and the lumpen-proletariat. In Ralph Miliband and John Saville (eds.), The Socialist Register. London, The Merlin Press, 193–230.

Yanagisako, Sylvia J., 1979. Family and household: The analysis of domestic groups. *Annual Review of Anthropology* 8: 161–205.

3

To Give and Take

Redistribution and Reciprocity in the Household Economy

Mona Rosendahl

The national economy of Cuba is characterized by its redistribution and planning. Since 1961, when the socialist system was introduced, the Cuban economy has functioned as a tightly controlled field guided principally by the Party and monitored by local organizations. The data in this chapter deal with the period before 1990, when the Soviet Union discontinued its special trade arrangement with Cuba and the economic crisis began. An update on the economic situation since then is given in the epilogue.

Other than a very small group of *particulares* (own-account farmers, artisans, hairdressers, manicurists, and so on), everyone is employed by the state or state organizations, and farmers sell only to the state.[1] Profits from all products sold go to the state exchequer and are then redistributed in different ways – through free medical care, inexpensive drugs, free education, and subventions on food and other goods.[2] People do not pay income taxes but do pay fees to the mass organizations; to the Party, if they are members; and to the militia. These fees go to support these organizations, but also in part to the state. The economy of the state is planned both long and short term, and the provinces and municipalities have overall budgets drawn up by higher political levels. Within the guidelines assigned, local governments can use the resources as they see fit, for education, sports, or construction, for example.

Although the Cuban economy provides most citizens with a comfortable standard of living, there is also a considerable bureaucracy. The lack of goods is something Cubans struggle with every day. Although rationed basic foodstuffs and other necessities can almost always be obtained, everything else is either lacking because of deficiencies in distribution or is in scarce supply. The scarcity results from the lack of foreign currency, which in turn stems from the difficulties in trading with Western countries because of the US trade embargo on Cuba. Foreign currency must thus be used for the most important items, such as raw materials for industry, so that there is not enough money to import goods people would like in more abundant supplies.

In everyday life, the planned economy is evident principally in the rationing system and the *emulación socialista* (the socialist competition). But an informal economy, with "gray" and black markets, also exists, as well as a system of reciprocity and barter, which brings people together through the constant giving and receiving of articles and services (see Hart 1973; Smith 1989; Gudeman and Rivera 1990; Humphrey and Hugh-Jones 1992).

The Rationing System

The core of the Cuban household economy is the rationing system, which guarantees every citizen basic goods in equal amounts and at very low cost. Every person has two *libretas* (booklets) – one for food and one for clothes and other household items – in which rationed items are listed and checked off when purchased. Foodstuffs that can be bought on the libreta are those that are the most often consumed, such as rice, beans, lard, sugar, detergent, and soap.[3] Each person also is allowed one-third of a loaf of bread each day, which costs 12 centavos (15 cents).[4] Rationed items can be bought for approximately 9 pesos per month per person (US $12), not counting cigars and some special articles for children. Every second week each person also gets one-half pound of beef, which costs 30 to 40 centavos (40 to 50 cents).

Many people buy all the items in the libreta and sell or exchange those they do not use. Libreta household products can be bought once a year. This list includes such items as sheets (one set for 2.20 to 3.00 pesos), work shoes (one pair for 6 to 10), dress shoes (one pair for 15 to 30), cloth (4 meters for 1.20 to 17.50), towels (one for 2.50), and underpants (four for 1.20 to 2.20). Many people feel that the clothes offered on the libreta are so unattractive that they do not want them. Other items, such as underpants and socks, are perennially in short supply. When people speak about the scarcity of goods, they say that goods do "not come" in sufficient quantities, which emphasizes the perceived and real distance between consumers and the system of central distribution. Insofar as this system is nationwide and state controlled, entities at the local level have very little control over distribution. The shops receive goods from higher levels and cannot order more themselves if something is sold out. This leads to constant vigilance awaiting the "coming" of goods and a complicated informal queuing system. The use of the libretas for household products is organized in a complicated way, so that there are specific buying days for each person, thus giving people access to goods at varying times. Finally, there is also the Plan Jaba, which gives precedence in the ever-existing queues to women who work outside the home.

In addition to rationed goods, some foodstuffs (vegetables and tubers), canned goods, clothes, and household items are sold *por la libre* (on the free market) at the parallel state market.[5] These articles are subject to some market principles of demand and supply, so that vegetables, for example, are cheaper when there are a lot available. Other items are always much more expensive on the free market. Rice, for example, costs 1.50 a pound (compared to 24 centavos when it is rationed) and peas cost 2.15 a kilo (compared to 37 centavos a kilo when rationed).

Four Households and Their Economies

Data on the economies of four households were obtained through interviews with the women of these families.[6] These women usually buy the goods and are responsible for the household economy. Since none of the women made budgets, it was impossible to get exact figures, but almost all the women could estimate rather closely how much they spent each month on different items. The two father-and-mother households have joint household economies, but in some other families the men keep most of their salaries and contribute only a portion to the women for household expenses. Three of the women said that "there is always enough money for our needs," and the fourth claimed that "there is never enough money for our needs." None, however, felt any need for more control over her domestic economy. Three of the families lived in apartments, and one lived in a small house. All had the installment payments for housing deducted from their salaries, together with a sum for other items bought on installment.

Single-person household

Juana is rather unusual in Limones in that she has lived alone since she was divorced. She has a good job and earns 265 pesos a month (US $331). Her former husband left her his libreta when he moved out, and she buys some of the items on this libreta as well as her own. Juana estimates that she uses about 10 pesos for rationed food and household items and 1.20 for meat but says that she does not always buy all the allotted alcohol and kerosene for the stove. She also buys about

20 pesos of food on the free market, mostly fruit, vegetables, and tubers. She eats many of her lunches in the canteen at work, which costs her about 40 to 50 centavos (50 to 60 cents) for each meal. Previously, she saved 45 to 50 pesos a month, and when she has paid for her furniture and refrigerator, she will start saving the same amount again. Because of her job, Juana has a telephone, which is a real luxury and costs her quite a lot each month. She is a prominent person in Limones and receives many gifts of food from friends and neighbors, as well as from her big family, which has animals and fruit trees. Juana's monthly budget would look approximately like this:

Food	42.00 pesos
Housing	45.00 pesos
Electricity	8.00 pesos
Fees	5.50 pesos
Telephone	11.00 pesos
Furniture	17.00 pesos
Refrigerator	25.00 pesos
or	
Savings	45.00 pesos
Total	153.50 (173.50) pesos

This means that Juana has about 100 pesos left from her salary when she has paid for her monthly expenses. She spends much of this 100 pesos on clothes. She likes to dress well and buys cloth, which her sister sews for her, or clothes in the free-market shops.

Household of mother, father, and two children
Papito, the father, in this household, is an administrator and earns 190 pesos (US $241) a month. Anita, the mother, is a teacher and earns 283 pesos (US $353) a month. The children, nine and fourteen years old, are both in school. The family has four libretas, since all children get a libreta the day they are born. The family buys all the rationed items it is allowed and spends about 25 to 30 pesos on these items. They also buy food on the free market – canned items, vegetables, fish, ice cream, and so on – for about 30 pesos. Anita saves some money each month, and both parents occasionally save a sum for the children. They bought their television set for cash but have paid for a refrigerator and their apartment on

installment. They have many relatives and friends in the neighborhood and receive food as gifts or buy it inexpensively from them. Anita also raises chickens and sometimes a pig at the finca of a relative. Their approximate monthly budget is as follows:

Food	60.00 pesos
Housing	50.00 pesos
Electricity	10.00 pesos
Fees	6.75 pesos
Refrigerator	14.00 pesos
Savings	40.00 pesos
Total	180.75 pesos

This family lives rather inexpensively. After they have spent their monthly fixed amounts, they still have about 290 pesos left for clothes, recreation, and other items.

Household of mother, father, and one child
In this family, the father, Jesús, earns 230 pesos (US $287) a month as a cook, while the mother, Gloria, earns 118 pesos (US $147) doing manual labor. Their nine-year-old child is in school. They buy everything they can each month on their three libretas and estimate that they use 20 pesos for that, which is probably a low estimate. They also buy about 30 pesos of food from the free market. Jesús can also buy leftover food inexpensively at work. He eats every second day at work, paying the full canteen fee. Gloria also eats at her workplace, for 25 to 35 centavos a meal (35 to 45 cents). They save occasionally, but Gloria says that they are wasteful with their money. They spend a lot every month on cigarettes and smoke two packs each day. Gloria is often sick and has to stay home from work. On these days she is paid only 40 to 60 percent of her salary. They sometimes receive gifts from relatives and friends, but not often. The biggest aid to their domestic economy is that Jesús can buy food cheaply at work and sometimes can take leftovers home. Their budget would look approximately like this:

Food	50.00 pesos
Housing	47.00 pesos
Electricity	10.00 pesos

Fees	7.75 pesos
Furniture	22.00 pesos
Transport	12.00 pesos
Cigarettes (free market)	77.00 pesos
Total	225.75 pesos

After this family has paid for all its expenses, it has about 120 pesos left.

Household of mother and two children
Graciela has one thirteen-year-old child who is in school, while her eighteen-year-old son is now working. She has a manual job earning 100 pesos (US $125) a month. Her son pays 40 to 50 pesos to his mother each month. He keeps the rest of his salary of 114 pesos (US $132) for himself. They have three food libretas, and Graciela says that she buys the food for the three of them but does not use the full ration. Graciela estimates that she uses 15 pesos for libreta items but that she spends about 30 to 40 pesos a month for food, cigarettes, and other things on the free market. She very seldom buys any clothes or other items and is always pinched for money. The children's father sometimes pays when they need something special. Graciela seldom receives food from others and only occasionally raises chickens or pigs. Her budget would look like this:

Food	50.00 pesos
Housing	8.50 pesos
Fees	1.50 pesos
Refrigerator	30.00 pesos
Total	90.00 pesos

Graciela makes a very low estimate of her monthly expenses. She most certainly uses more money for food and other necessities. In this budget she has 60 pesos left for non-essentials, but Graciela often borrows money from friends and claims that she cannot pay required fees to her union and the mass organizations. The only way she can moderate her domestic economy, she says, is to reduce her food costs, which she does when possible.

From these examples, we can see that many people have more money than they spend. This is in part why dissatisfaction with the lack of available goods is probably the most common complaint that people in Palmera express about their life situations.

Good Food and Nice Clothes

The cost for food on the libreta is very low, but most families buy food on the free market and therefore use about 15 percent of their salary for food. In addition, they purchase beer and rum for parties.

Most people in Palmera like to eat well and a lot. They eat hot meals twice a day (rice, tubers, meat, fish, or anything else available). Rice and often beans are served in abundance with a little meat or fish to go with it.

Food also has a symbolic value which is related to society and gender. Having enough to eat is associated with a good life and a good society. Eating heartily, especially meat, connotes masculinity, whereas cooking and serving plenty of good food is connected to female gender ideals. The female tradition of serving platefuls of food still persists in many families. The mother first serves the father a large plateful of food, then the sons, and then the daughters, who get less. Finally she takes what is left.

The favorite foods among most men (and many women) in Palmera are the traditional foods of the Cuban countryside, *macho asado* (roast pork), which is served mostly at parties, and yucca or yams.

The gendered importance of meat was illustrated by a bitter saying a female friend quoted to me: "El día de la carne es el día de los padres, porque los otros días son de madre." This is difficult to translate with all its connotations, but the closest is "The day of the meat [when the ration is distributed] is father's day, because all the other days are *de madre*" [which literally means "mother's day" but also means "terrible," "hellish," or "disappointing"].

Muñoz, an older man, once said to me in talking about the scarcity in the Cuban economy: "What we Cubans want is to eat good and dress well. Therefore it is difficult when we cannot get hold of clothes and good food." He explained that he, a manual worker, had his niece buy *guayaberas* (traditional dress shirts) for him *por la libre* in the city where she lives. They cost 60 pesos each, about half his monthly salary, and he paid her in installments. His wish to be well dressed made it worth the economic sacrifice.

As we have seen, food and clothes are indeed what people in Palmera generally spend most of their money on, the women buying cloth to sew for themselves, their children, and sometimes their husbands. People buy clothes on the free market or in *tiendas de amistad* (shops where imported goods are sold very expensively), or they buy them in the street from black marketeers. Some people also buy household appliances *por la libre*, but that is so expensive that few can do so. An electric fan, for example, costs 90 to 120 pesos depending on the size, a refrigerator 700 to 1,000 pesos, and a TV set 500 to 600 pesos. Instead, most people wait to win these articles in the emulación socialista, the socialist competition, which is open to people at all workplaces except those who have political appointments.

Emulación Socialista

Cuba's planned economy is closely connected to its socialist ideology. This is evident in the discussions about the need for economic versus moral incentives, which have been going on in Cuba for the more than thirty years under socialism. In the early 1960s, Che Guevara advanced the idea that good revolutionaries should not need economic incentives to work productively for their society (Deutschmann 1987:159–68); the mere satisfaction of doing a good job for the revolution should be enough. It was evident, however, that this did not work very well, and economic rewards, so-called *estímulos* (stimuli), were introduced.

Under this arrangement, the state distributes desirable articles to the central union, which in turn distributes them to the municipality branch unions those in the central union feel have done good jobs. The branch union leader then awards the articles to different local unions, from which a group is elected to choose the persons who have earned the most merits and therefore will be awarded the article. The article is not awarded free of charge but may be bought at a much lower price than in a shop or on installment. A small

electric fan, for example, costs 40 pesos compared to 90 pesos on the free market.

This arrangement, of course, leads to conflicts among workmates when someone feels unfairly treated. While I was in Palmera, the biggest conflicts arose when housing was at stake, since shortages are severe. The conflicts usually arise over the way merit points are counted. Every worker collects merit points by doing voluntary work, by being a conscientious worker, and by being a good workmate. Some workers think they have not received all the points they should and that they therefore lose in the competition.

Sometimes foreign travel is also distributed as estimulos. One of my neighbors who had been a vanguard worker for many years was awarded a two-week trip to the Soviet Union. Everything for her and her husband was paid for, and they even got some money to buy winter clothes since the trip was in October. For most Cubans, this is the only way of ever traveling abroad.

Queuing

One of the most salient features of Cuban society today is its queues. Everywhere and almost constantly one sees people gathering, not in straight lines but in clusters. After a while, one learns to do like the Cubans and join a queue before even asking what is being sold. Some people do not like the queuing system and say that it is not necessary, but almost everyone who can uses it, not daring to wait, since desirable articles might then be sold out. Some people, such as teachers, however, cannot leave their jobs to stand in lines for hours.

The queuing is, of course, a result of the scarcity of almost everything in Cuban society, but it has become a great pastime as well as a habit. The rules of queuing are very well defined. Everyone arriving at a queue will ask for *el ultimo* (the last person) in a loud voice. This person waves a finger in the air. This "last person" then announces who is in front of him or her and maybe also the second-to-the-last person, so as to guarantee that if he or she leaves for a while or drops out, the new person will know who precedes him or her in the queue. If the "last person" is not there when the new person arrives, someone else provides the information.

A queue is a place for conversation, jokes, and gossip, and those who have time to spare can enjoy themselves thoroughly. The queues are not always orderly, however. In Limones, the three days every second week when meat is distributed are a busy time for the sales-persons in La Pescadería. The queues are enormous, and the police are often called in, to put men and women in different queues and to break up fights, which occur when discussions get too heated. The same ruckus occurs when perfume, underpants, or shoes come to the shop on the main street. When cloth arrives at the one time during the year when Palmerans may buy the four meters they are allowed, there is not always enough for everyone and the queues are at their most intense.

One Tuesday night, a couple of days before Marta "had her letter" – that is, before it was her turn to buy her ration of cloth for the year – she heard that there was a queue forming outside the shop. She changed to her street clothes, put on some lipstick, and walked over there. A few people were waiting, and a man had started to organize the queue, giving out little pieces of paper with numbers on them. Since Marta was early, she got a very low number, twelve, and was thus guaranteed that there would be cloth for her. The man told her to come back at one o'clock that morning to confirm her place in the queue. She went home and watched a popular telenovela, content that she had a good spot in the queue. At a little before one o'clock, she walked tiredly to the queue and confirmed her place once again. There were loud discussions between Marta and some other women who felt she had cheated them of their places, but she went home to sleep. For the next confirmation call, at six o'clock that morning Marta sent her daughter, who again confirmed their place. By now some people had dropped out, and Marta received an even lower number. During the day, she checked several times with the queue, and after lunch she went to the shop to stand in line herself. After a few hours she came out with her four meters of cloth, one piece for a friend of hers and two pieces for herself and her daughter.

In addition to queues, there are other ways to get scarce goods. Someone can bring along a friend's or a relative's libreta and buy for her. If the article is sold por la libre, some people buy as many items as possible and resell them to friends and relatives for the same price as they are sold on the free market. Many working women complain, however, that they never have the opportunity to buy popular items since they are always sold out when they have time to shop.

The "Gray" and the Black Markets

The queues are sometimes instruments of the gray market, which recirculates legal commodities. There are people, for example, who buy items in the official stores and then resell them privately to others at higher prices. Goods bought on the libreta that a family does not consume may also be sold or exchanged. There are even people called *coleros* (queue sitters), who are said to stand in every line there is and to make good livings on the articles they then resell. There are also legitimate libretas floating in the community that do not belong to the people who hold them. These persons can thus buy more than they use and resell the surplus to others, at a profit. These transactions are usually not made with friends or relatives since they would sever the reciprocal relationships that ideally should exist between them. More often these articles are offered to casual acquaintances.

The black market in clothes is especially widespread. Most people in Palmera want to be nicely dressed and like the modern, foreign clothes they can obtain from the *bisneros* (a slang expression for black marketeers). The bisneros operate in the bigger cities, changing money with foreigners to get hold of dollars, which until 1993 Cubans were forbidden from owning. The bisneros then get foreigners to buy clothes and sometimes other items at the Cubalse (the foreigners' shop), where Cubans usually cannot buy. They then resell these articles in the street at exorbitant prices.[7] A T-shirt that costs US $2 to $3 in the Cubalse is sold for 50 to 60 pesos (US $65 to $75) in the street. Jeans that cost US $10 in the Cubalse cost 150 pesos (US $200) or more in the street. Since most Cubans have more money than they can spend on the few items available in the shops, they can afford to buy these black market items every now and then.

Another illegal activity that is widespread is taking articles home from work. This can range from the rather innocent activity of pilfering light bulbs or paper to the much more serious crime of organized theft of construction materials or other high-value goods.

Reciprocity

Marcel Mauss (1969) introduced the idea that the exchange of goods includes both an economic and a social component, which builds and reinforces social relations. Many others (Scheper-Hughes 1992; Smith 1989; Stack 1974) later discovered that the relations involved in giving, receiving, and repaying gifts is not only the basis of many traditional societies but also operates widely in contemporary, large-scale economic systems. Within many socialist planned economies, there exists an informal economic sector that depends in part on loans, gift giving, and the cultivation of reciprocal relationships (Evans 1993; Yang 1988). Reciprocity has always been important in Cuban society, but since the revolution and the introduction of socialism, new forms of reciprocity have developed.

In Palmera reciprocity is a vital part of the informal economy.[8] There is one form of reciprocity that is almost totally social and in which the monetary value of the articles, goods, and services subsumes a subordinate role to the creation and maintenance of social relations. At times there are no gifts involved in the transactions, just "symbolic capital" (Bourdieu 1977), via *cultura* (cultured behavior) that strengthens one's reputation as a "good person" within the context of an established relationship.

With other forms of reciprocity, the goods and services exchanged become a very important part of the household economy although the transactions also serve to cement and create social relations. Scarce goods can thus be exchanged and both parties profit. A friend of mine who maintained several hobbies, including photography and fishing, complained that these hobbies involved much work and even stress. But, he said, "through my hobbies I get many friends and they help me and I can easily *conseguir* [get hold of] almost everything." To him, his hobbies were also an investment in the future.

The acts of giving, receiving, and repaying gifts are clearly present in reciprocal relations in Palmera, but the way transactions are accomplished varies. When the economic aspect is more important, the repayment is swift and the gift is expected to be equivalent in value to the gift that is given. When the social aspect is the vital component, the gifts can be less equivalent in value, and the interval before repaying can vary greatly. The closeness of the relationship also makes a difference. Friends who have established relationships can allow themselves to exchange less symmetrical gifts, while looser acquaintances must follow more timely and symmetrical patterns in the gifts exchanged. Under certain circumstances, however, friends may have a reciprocal relationship that is mainly economic, and acquaintances may build a friendship through their mainly economic reciprocity. Repayment is extremely important. The person who does not repay is excluded from the relationship, or the nonrepayment is taken as a sign that he or she wants out.

Evidence of reciprocity can be found in all corners of what we might call the informal sector, the entire array of economic transactions that exist side by side with the formal state economy. These transactions involve the exchange of money, goods, and information in differing combinations.

Economic aspect of reciprocity

For most people in Palmera, having acquaintances with access to scarce items is crucial for success in procuring goods and is a constant preoccupation. The exchange that transpires very much resembles balanced reciprocity in Marshall Sahlins's (1972:194–5) terms, or what Caroline Humphrey and Stephen Hugh-Jones (1992) call barter, which they define more broadly than do most scholars.

I was once approached by a woman who wanted me to buy some clothes for her child at the Cubalse. We did not know each other well but had met and chatted in the street at times. She wanted to pay me in pesos for what I bought for dollars. Since this is a felony for both parties, I always refused such requests. I told the woman that I would buy her the clothes, which cost me a very small sum, but I gave them to her as a gift. She then said that she had a chicken at her mother's house and she would go there to get it and give it to me. I replied that she should keep the chicken, that I did not want anything for the clothes. Nonetheless, two days later she came with the chicken and presented it to me. In my eyes her repayment for my gift was much too much, but if she had bought the clothes on the street from a bisnero, she would have had to pay much more than the value of the chicken.

Every conversation in Palmera starts with a discussion of where one can buy something. The most common form of reciprocity, in which everyone takes part, is the giving, receiving, and repaying of information about the availability of various articles.[9] The scarcity of goods, the erratic distribution system, and the disorganization of the market make it extremely time-consuming to procure things. *Conseguir*, which literally means "obtain" or "procure," has become an activity of great importance in maintaining reciprocal relationships. Since there is almost always a scarcity of goods, people cannot just go out and buy what they want, even if they have the money. They have no choice but to enter into the process of *consiguiendo*. Thus, everyone is always on the lookout for articles to buy or advising others about where they can find what they are looking for.

Maria called Margarita from her office to talk about a problem at work. After having greeted one another, Maria started by telling Margarita that she had seen some nice suede shoes at a shop in a mountain village. "They cost 30 pesos and they come in your size four," she said. "Miguel is going there tomorrow. I can ask him to buy some for you." Margarita jumped at the opportunity and would look up Miguel and give him the 30 pesos. When she in turn gets news of something that she thinks Maria needs, she will tell her, and so the reciprocal flow benefits them both. This means, of course, that a person can also withhold information from others and give it only to preferred friends, thereby strengthening the relationship with them.

Another aspect of reciprocity is begging; it is not unusual and is considered acceptable among friends. The item asked for is often given since it is something the person who is asking knows that the giver can and might well give him. Some items are also asked for as a compliment, or to express interest, but are not meant seriously. Eva wore a pair of white tennis shoes when visiting her friend Maribel. Maribel admired the shoes and said: "Give them to me! I've always wanted a pair of white sneakers." Eva just laughed, saying that Maribel would have to cut her toes off to get her feet to fit in the shoes since her feet were so much bigger than Eva's. "Come on," said Maribel, "I'm sure they will fit." Both laughed knowing that Eva would not give away her shoes. Eva said, however, that she would ask her sister in town who had bought the shoes to look for a pair in Maribel's size.

When the begging is no longer considered acceptable – when someone asks too much or of the wrong person – it causes embarrassment or shame to the beggar and also to the person who has to say no. José was approached by a person who wanted to be given or possibly lent one hundred pesos. Quite upset, José afterward told me that he hardly knew the person, had not seen him for two years, and that, of course, he refused the demand. He felt embarrassed, mostly because the person was so forward and did not have the cultura to understand that one does not do such a thing. First of all, the sum was too large. One might lend or give a very good friend or a relative such a sum but definitely not an acquaintance. Second, they did not know each other well enough to support such a reciprocal relationship, and José did not want to develop such a relationship with the other person.

A short while after I moved into the barrio, I started to get visits from people who begged for different things, from plastic bags to pants or other clothes. Those who had already become my friends were embarrassed about this behavior and told me never to give anything to these people. They might themselves very well ask me for things, although always small items, but this was in the process of ongoing reciprocity, since they also gave me things, invited me to dinner, and helped me in many ways.

In all of these examples, an element of economic gain guides the relationship, but the transaction also has social implications. The context, the status of the people involved, and their relationship determine whether or not the exchange is successful (cf. Hugh-Jones 1992).

Social aspect of reciprocity

The more symbolic aspect of reciprocity in Palmera also involves gifts, but in this case their significance is more social than economic. Small gifts and loans constantly move back and forth between people, tying them more and more closely together.

When I moved into the little, spartan apartment where I lived during my fieldwork, a neighbor immediately came to visit with a glass of strong, sweet Cuban coffee. She welcomed me and said that if I ever had any problems or needed help with anything, I was to feel free to ask her and her family, who would try to help. After some days, she came knocking on my door asking if I could possibly spare a *cubalse* (a plastic carrier bag). Bags are scarce in Cuba, and cubalses, which are used for all purposes, are extremely popular and washed until they disintegrate. I gave her two cubalses, and she departed happily. This was the beginning of the kind of reciprocal relationship most people keep up with their neighbors.

Being generous and hospitable is a very important part of being a good person in Palmera (cf. Gilmore 1990:88; Herzfeld 1987). There is a saying Palmerans like to quote with pride, that the people of this region are especially warm and hospitable. Children are taught from their first months to be sociable, to kiss and talk, and to relate easily to others. By the time they are older, they have learned the socially correct way of entertaining a visitor and always bid a visitor to sit and offer him or her something to eat or drink.

This is part of the concept of having cultura, which can be translated as "being cultured" but which really means much more than that (cf. Gilmore 1980:59). The concept includes the notion of knowing how to behave toward other people, not being coarse or vulgar, and knowing the rules of social reciprocity.

Part of having cultura and being a good Cuban is being "happy," or at least acting as if you are. Many people said to me that they did not show their unhappiness to their friends and acquaintances, because "they are not the cause of it and should not be made to suffer for it." Showing too much suffering to the outside world causes embarrassment, which should be avoided at all costs, and demonstrates a lack of cultura. Showing suffering

to a friend in private, is totally acceptable, however, and women at least do much serious talking about their problems and give advice to each other.

Having cultura also means being generous, especially with one's house and one's time. Very few people in Palmera would ever say that they have no time to talk to or see someone. They stop what they are doing when visitors come, or if the visitor is a close friend or relative they continue with what they are doing and invite the visitor to stay anyhow. This is partly because it would be very rude not to welcome visitors, but also because people do not enjoy being alone. Most Cubans live close to many people during their lives, with siblings and parents while they are unmarried and then with others, sharing a place of their own. Many people say that they cannot imagine living alone and that they do not like, almost fear, being alone.

When I arrived to visit the Martínez family, the door was half open to let in some cool air. Papito, the man in the house, was lying bare-chested on one of the beds. Excusing himself for not wearing a shirt, he got up and greeted me with a wave of the hand, exiting to put one on. Anita, his wife, shouted her hello from the kitchen. Nena, their eleven-year-old daughter, was washing the floor in the sitting room. She greeted me with a kiss in the air toward my right cheek, and using the respectful *usted* address, asked me how I was. Anita came out to the sitting room, kissed me on the cheek, and beckoned me to come into the kitchen. She was cutting yucca for lunch. Rice was simmering in a big pot. "Nena," she shouted, "fetch the stool from the bedroom for Mona." Nena brought it to the small, dark kitchen and invited me to sit. While Anita prepared the food, she gave me cold coffee, which she had left from breakfast. Papito came into the kitchen and, asking Anita if she had given me coffee, greeted me with a handshake. We talked a little about the carnival, which was to be held in the community the following weekend. Anita invited me to have lunch with them. I could not stay, and I said that I felt embarrassed because I ate there so much. "Don't talk rubbish," said Anita, "estás en tu casa [you are in your own house]" (cf. Herzfeld 1987). As I left, Anita gave me yucca and plantain to take home.

This scene includes many aspects of cultura that one encounters when visiting Cubans. Greetings are made either by kissing on the cheek or shaking hands. Although people may meet several times in a day, they always greet each other formally. Palmerans say that the custom of kissing on the cheek is fairly new there and that it was not done before. When people meet in the street they usually stop and shake hands or kiss, ask "How are you?" and exchange a few words, mostly about the welfare of the family or other friends. ¿Y Pepe?, for example, is the ritual phrase for inquiring about someone. The equally ritualized answer is Bien (cf. Gilmore 1980:96). A throw-back to the times when people used to shout to each other in the mountains is the greeting used to someone across the street – "¡Ayeeeeeeeee, compay (mate)!" – compay being the familiar word for compadre, the ritual godparent-parent relationship seldom referred to today. What is important, however, is not how a person greets but that he or she does so.

The offer of a seat and something to drink or eat is equally important when someone comes to visit. It is said that it does not matter what one offers as long as one offers something. A glass of water can be sufficient. If the host does not have anything in the house, which is not unusual since scarcity is the rule in Cuba, he or she makes excuses and says, "I don't even have coffee to offer you." Very often, though, a visitor is offered coffee, homemade juice, ice cream, and sometimes soft drinks or sweets.

As important as the offer of something to eat or drink, the guest must be invited to sit down. In every sitting room, however small, there are as many chairs as could possibly fit into the room, and the invitation to sit down is made immediately and at times quite demandingly if the guest, as in the case of a Swedish newcomer, does not understand that she should accept the invitation.

Conversation is also an important part of having cultura and validating oneself as a true Cuban. In a group of people, the conversations are often about daily events and mutual acquaintances, activities such as weddings, or, of course, what there is to buy where. Being able to tell jokes and being amusing are also important parts of being a fully social person (cf. Gilmore 1980:114). Being quiet is seen as somewhat threatening, and people who say little are urged to talk and asked what is wrong and why they do not say anything. A television is almost always on in all houses, and if it is off

when a visitor comes, it is put on and acts as a sound wall to the conversation. If there is something very interesting on the screen or the conversation falters, the events on the screen become welcome topics for continued conversation.

Cultura is built on giving and receiving. Guests receive total attention but are also expected to be entertaining and, above all, to open their homes just as generously.

One organized way to show generosity and hospitality is to throw a party. There are some events that should be celebrated, such as the first birthday of a child, los quinze (the fifteenth birthday of a girl), and weddings. Such parties almost always have a fixed form, although they might seem completely chaotic to an outsider. Their most important features are the photography and the food and drink.

Weeks before Suleyda's one-year birthday party, Popi, the father of the little girl, invited me. He reminded me of the party every time I met him after that. It was going to be on the afternoon of her birthday, which fell on a work-free Saturday, at the home of the young family who lives with the father of the wife. I went with a neighbor and her little son. We were told to arrive at 2:00, and at 2:30 we set off.

When we arrived, some other guests were already present and the place was chaotic. The women, who were preparing the rice and beans and tubers and making the decorations, were still in hair rollers and work clothes, while the men, shirtless, were roasting a pig over an open fire and making a goat fricassee. Every now and then they cooled themselves with beers taken from a plastic container filled with ice. Children were running and playing all over the place. Popi and his wife, Tania, came to greet me and my friend and gave us each a beer. The son of my neighbor gave a little present to Suleyda, and I gave a bottle of rum to Popi. We sat down and talked on chairs that the hosts had carried out onto the patio, while the host family was running around making last-minute preparations. At 4:00, more guests arrived. The family emerged newly showered and in their party clothes. The photographer and some of Popi's relatives, who were coming from another place in Palmera, had not arrived yet. Everyone was drinking, talking, and joking, and the atmosphere was very relaxed. When Popi's relatives arrived, his brother brought a huge casette recorder and tapes, and soon music blared all over the neighborhood.

Now it was really a party. People had to shout to make themselves heard, but they didn't mind. Some danced, and the rum was brought out. Then the photographer, who was also a friend of the family, came, and all activities stopped as Popi urged everyone to go to a neighbor's house, where the cake was being kept, to be photographed. The cake, which was pink since the party was for a girl, was enormous and mounted on a table decorated with little boxes of candy and bottles of soft drinks. The birthday girl was put behind the table, while her small friends gathered around. First the girls, then the boys, and then different sets of adult friends and relatives all had to be photographed.

When the photo session was finished, everyone trotted up to the house again as Popi and his father carried the cake. Now it was dark and the patio was lit with one single light bulb hung in a tree. The women of the family went into the house, where the men had brought the pig and the goat fricassee, and for each person, they filled two little brown paper boxes of a type that is always used at parties, one with the hearty food, the other with a piece of cake, some *ensalada fría* (a macaroni salad with mayonnaise), and sweets. Meanwhile, Tania gave out presents – books, paper masks, paper hats, and some small toys – to all the children. A piñata, filled with sweets and small toys, was suspended above the children and then broken so that all the items fell out. The children threw themselves on the ground and fought for the bits and pieces. The bigger children could hoard more things, and the little ones cried. A big girl gave some candy to one of the little boys, who walked away happy.

The boxes containing the food and cake were passed around first to the children, who also got soft drinks, and then to the grown-ups. People ate with their hands or with a piece torn from the box. During all this time Popi and Tania passed around beer and rum, urging people to drink and asking if they were having a good time. People were becoming a little tipsy. They danced and talked, and everyone was given boxes of food to take home for those who could not come to the party. The night was cool and all of us were enjoying ourselves. When my neighbor and I left at 11:30, people were still dancing and drinking.

This was a lavish party with lots of gifts for the children and lots of food and drink. Weddings and fifteenth-year parties are similar, except that there are no children's gifts or piñata. Many parties are much simpler than Popi's, for although he does not earn much money, he has many relatives and a job that takes him around the municipality so that he can obtain a lot of things. Hosting a grand party might also be more important to him because he does not have a prestigious position in society. Parties can be a way of repaying gifts or help received or seen as investments for assistance needed later.

People also like to throw parties spontaneously when they have the means. Especially in the summertime, many a pig, a cherished party food, is roasted out of doors, at a beach, or on a riverbank. Then people eat, drink beer and rum, and immerse themselves in the cool water, making conversation, joking, and laughing. Since food is scarce and it is difficult to get hold of what is needed beyond rationed foodstuffs, one has to have access to a farmer who can sell a pig or raise one oneself in a back yard.

People do not go to parties uninvited because it is so difficult to get food and drinks, and, as a friend explained, it would be a terrible embarrassment for the host if there was not enough for everyone to eat, or, preferably, more than enough. Having more than people can drink is virtually impossible, so that the number of crates of beer available at a party is a valid measurement of its success.

Following the rules of social reciprocity is a way of showing one is a good Cuban, a socially competent and acceptable person. It is also a way of creating and maintaining social relations. A person who cannot or does not want to act according to these rules is excluded from enjoying many social relations. With relatives, reciprocity is important in maintaining the relationship. With friends, reciprocity is necessary to have a relationship at all.

Social relations not only are extremely important as emotional outlets in Cuba but are imperative for the survival of the Cuban people, since the social dimension of reciprocity is intimately linked to and necessary for the economic dimension of reciprocity to continue.

Notes

1 Today many more occupations have been introduced as *particulares*, and "private" farmers' markets are allowed.
2 For a discussion of Cuba's national economy, see
   Brundenius 1984 and Zimbalist 1989.
3 *Libreta items and their prices in 1990*

Product	Amount/person/month	Price (pesos)
Rice	5 pounds	1.20
Beans, peas, lentils	40 ounces	0.41–0.54
Lard	1 pound	0.30
Cooking oil	1 pound	0.40
Sugar, brown	5¾ pounds	0.46
Sugar, white	¼ pound	0.11
Coffee	4 ounces	0.20
Condensed milk		
7–13 years	10 tins	3.00
65– years	4 tins	1.20
Fruit purée		
0–13 years	15 tins/jars	2.25–3.75
Tomato purée	2 tins	0.60
Noodles	1 pound	0.20
Canned meat	1 tin/3 months	0.36
Cigarettes	4 boxes	1.20
Cigars	4 cigars	0.60–0.80
Toothpaste	1 tube	0.65
Detergent	3 ounces	0.06
Soap		
for washing	1 bar	0.25
for bathing	1 bar	0.20–0.25
Cleaning rags	2/family	0.40
Kerosene (1 person)	3.5 gallons	1.12
Kerosene (5 persons)	9 gallons	2.88
Alcohol	5 litres	0.50

*Information from the local shopkeeper in Limones. Cf.
Pérez Lopez 1989.*

4 When transforming pesos to US dollars, I have
   used the rate 1 peso = US $1.25 (approximately).
   This is not really a valid measurement, however,
   since the peso is nonconvertible. The best way to
   assess the value of the peso is to compare salaries
   and costs.
5 After fall 1990, all items became rationed and
   household items have not been sold at all for several
   years.
6 For a comparison of a household economy in an
   urban working-class Argentinian setting, see Jelin
   1991b.
7 During my fieldwork these prices *were* exorbitant,
   but compared with the prices on the black market in
   1993 they are rather low.
8 Reciprocity in the form of work exchange and ritual
   gift giving are common in many Latin American
   societies (see Hugh-Jones 1992; Isbell 1978; Gudeman and Rivera 1990), but in my opinion the contemporary Cuban type of reciprocity more
   resembles the kind Carol Stack (1974) describes
   since it is not organized on the community level
   but more informally, although it still has rules and a
   structure.
9 Elisabeth Jelin (1991a:30) calls this "information
   capital," paraphrasing Pierre Bourdieu (1977).

References

Bourdieu, Pierre (1977) *Outline of a Theory of Practice.*
   Cambridge: Cambridge University Press.
Brundenius, Claes (1984) *Revolutionary Cuba: The
   Challenge of Economic Growth with Equity.* London:
   Heinemann.

Deutschmann, David, ed. (1987) *Che Guevara and the
   Cuban Revolution: Writings and Speeches of Ernesto
   Che Guevara.* Sydney: Pathfinder/Pacific and Asia.
Evans, Grant (1993) Buddhism and Economic Action
   in Socialist Laos. In Chris M. Hann, ed., *Socialism.*

Ideals, Ideologies, and Local Practice, pp. 132–47. London: Routledge.

Gilmore, David (1980) *The People of the Plain*. New York: Columbia University Press.

Gilmore, David (1990) *Manhood in the Making: Cultural Concepts of Masculinity*. New Haven: Yale University Press.

Gudeman, Stephen, and Alberto Rivera (1990) *Conversations in Colombia: The Domestic Economy in Life and Text*. Cambridge: Cambridge University Press.

Hart, Keith (1973) Informal Income Opportunities and Urban Employment in Ghana. *Journal of Modern African Studies* 11:61–89.

Herzfeld, Michael (1987) "As in Your Own House": Hospitality, Ethnography, and the Stereotype of Mediterranean Society. In David Gilmore, ed., *Honor and Shame and the Unity of the Mediterranean*, pp. 75–89. Washington, DC: American Anthropological Association.

Hugh-Jones, Stephen (1992) Yesterday's Luxuries, Tomorrow's Necessities: Business and Barter in Northwest Amazonia. In Caroline Humphrey and Stephen Hugh-Jones, eds., *Barter, Exchange and Value: An Anthropological Approach*, pp. 42–74. Cambridge: Cambridge University Press.

Humphrey, Caroline, and Stephen Hugh-Jones (1992) Introduction: Barter, Exchange and Value. In Caroline Humphrey and Stephen Hugh-Jones, eds., *Barter, Exchange and Value: An Anthropological Approach*, pp. 1–20. Cambridge: Cambridge University Press.

Isbell, Billie Jean (1978) *To Defend Ourselves: Ecology and Ritual in an Andean Village*. Austin: University of Texas Press.

Jelin, Elizabeth (1991a) Family and Household: Outside World and Private Life. In Elizabeth Jelin, ed., *Family, Household and Gender Relations in Latin America*, pp. 165–96. London: Kegan Paul International.

Jelin, Elizabeth 1991b. Social Relations of Consumption: The Urban Popular Household. In Elizabeth Jelin, ed., *Family, Household and Gender Relations in Latin America*, pp. 12–39. London: Kegan Paul International.

Mauss, Marcel (1969) *The Gift. Forms and Functions of Exchange in Archaic Societies*. London: Routledge.

Pérez-López, Jorge F. (1989) Wages, Earnings, Hours of Work, and Retail Prices in Cuba. *Cuban Studies* 19: 199–224.

Sahlins, Marshall. 1972. *Stone Age Economics*. London: Tavistock.

Scheper-Hughes, Nancy (1992) *Death without Weeping: The Violence of Everyday Life in Brazil*. Berkeley: University of California Press.

Smith, M. Estellie (1989) The Informal Economy. In Stuart Plattner, ed., *Economic Anthropology*, pp. 292–463. Stanford: Stanford University Press.

Stack, Carol (1974) *All Our Kin: Stategies for Survival in a Black Community*. New York: Harper.

Yang Mei-hui, Mayfair (1988) The Modernity of Power in the Chinese Socialist Order. *Cultural Anthropology* 3:408–29.

Zimbalist, Andrew (1989) Incentives and Planning in Cuba. *Latin American Research Review* 24:65–93.

Part II

Questions of Identity: "Race," Ethnicity, Class, and Gender

Introduction

The essays in this section begin to address the enormous diversity in class, color, ethnic and gender identity that marks the Caribbean region. Because of the dramatic and pervasive immigrant character of the majority of the population, this region has historically presented difficulties to the social sciences in Europe and North America. Scholars operating within disciplinary paradigms that sought a kind of pure indigeneity, such as anthropology, or complexity, such as sociology, found in the Caribbean societies that defied categorization. Formed by European colonial forces in a climate of imperial and capitalist expansion that coerced native populations into labor, and that brought many thousands of Africans and Asians into the plantation economy, the Caribbean became, very quickly, a place of "mixed" populations working in a kind of indeterminate economic space. Neither industrial nor fully agricultural, the Antillean experience resisted analysis by social sciences formed in a European context. That is, by the time the social sciences were being developed in the nineteenth century, the Caribbean was already several hundred years occupied by foreign powers and peopled by representatives of many ethnic and language groups. Furthermore, these groups had long intermixed and produced class and color divisions of their own. Thus, with regard to the question of "identity," color, "race" and class are intimately connected as a result of the historical conditions that allowed or prevented access to wealth and standing on the basis of these identities. To further add to the complexity, gender identities in the Caribbean have also been critical to the division of labor and to ideas of the family and of sexuality.

Suggested Readings

Dabydeen, David, and Brinsley Samaroo, eds., 1996 Across the Dark Waters: Ethnicity and Identity in the Caribbean. London: Macmillan Caribbean.

Forte, Maximilian C., 2006 Indigenous Resurgence in the Contemporary Caribbean: Amerindian Survival and Revival. New York: Peter Lang Publishing.

Whitten, Norman E., Jr., and Arlene Torres, 1998 Blackness in Latin America and the Caribbean: Social Dynamics and Cultural Transformations, 2 vols. Blacks in the Diaspora. Bloomington: Indiana University Press.

Williams, Brackette, 1991 Stain on My Name, War in My Veins: Guyana and the Politics of Cultural Struggle. Durham, NC: Duke University Press.

Yelvington, Kevin A., ed., 1993 Trinidad Ethnicity. London: Macmillan Caribbean.

4

✷ What is 'a Spanish'?
Ambiguity and 'Mixed' Ethnicity in Trinidad

Aisha Khan

> Man No. 1: "My father is mix with white and Portagee. Trinidad is such a mix country, Spanish, French, white, Indian. My mother is from Arima, a Spanish. If you see she hair! *Straight* and jet black".
> Man No. 2: "Women in Arima are all mix".
>
> (Conversation overheard in taxi, Trinidad, 1987)

The Problem of 'Mixed' in Perspective

Recent anthropological work on ethnicity, nationalism, and transnationalism has emphasised that social identities are constructed – that is, are composite and multivocal, and that multiple identities can be activated in different combinations depending on the contingencies in question. Furthermore, these combined constructions, particularly categories of ethnic identity, are not necessarily isomorphic or without ambiguities. This is not to say they are ambiguous in the sense that persons have trouble comprehending or applying particular ethnic categories in any given social situation. They are ambiguous in that they are 'capable of being understood in two or more possible senses' (*Webster's New Collegiate Dictionary*, 1975), in that these categories are frequently equivocal: contingent upon individual perception (though obviously not entirely) and upon varying and not always predictable emphases of combinations of attributes. Categorisations of ethnic identity that marshall a variety of historical, social, and cultural dimensions in their construction may also encompass apparently contradictory images, since traits, qualities, stereotypes, and the like are not self-contained or mutually exclusive. Indeed, the very fact of combination and ambiguity foregrounds the fluidity of ethnic identity.

In Caribbean research the fluid and protean nature of ethnic and racial identities has been evident for some time. In these studies the units of analysis tend to be distinct *racial* categories (such as 'African' or 'East Indian' or 'Chinese') and *colour* terms (such as 'black', 'brown', 'white', 'red', etc.) involving pliable meanings, designations, and significance. An important issue to emerge from this literature was that so-called intermediate categories – that is, combinations lying between the extremes of 'black' and 'white' – signal important questions about the nature of ambiguity and the significance of the relationship between appearance (phenotype) and background[1] in social relations, and more broadly, between social identity and social stratification, and ultimately between ideology and power. Sidney Mintz observed early on that perceptions of colour (and I would add appearance in general) are not merely 'a matter of observed phenotype but of observed phenotype taken together with many other factors' (1957); that perception of appearance is variable not only with context but within a dialectic between *self-consciousness* and perception of an Other (1957); and that the social meaning of an intermediate category 'may depend upon the indefiniteness with which its boundaries are drawn, and the difficulties people experience in trying to draw such boundaries, . . .' (1971:443). Also recognised in the literature is that in mediating appearance, background does not simply connote position in the social hierarchy but descent as well, in the form of alleged cultural history and traditions and in the notion of family pedigree. Moreover, although appearance can attest to background, it can belie background as well, because it is negotiable, situational, and to a degree observer-specific. In other words, looks can be deceiving.

The phenomenon of 'mixing' – often referred to as 'miscegenation' – has always been a key issue for colonial and post-colonial societies (e.g., Stoler, 1989), and in the Caribbean ever since European master and African slave produced socially problematic offspring – that is, slave or free; and if free, with an uncertain place in the social structure. When intermediate categories (that is, 'mixes') are taken up in studies of the Anglophone Caribbean, discussion is by and large couched in terms of the rubric 'coloured' or 'brown', mixtures of 'black' and 'white' that either subsume or overshadow other categorisations of 'mixed' possibilities. In the literature, 'mixed' and 'coloured' often stand for each other, implicitly calling forth variations on a 'black'-plus-'white' theme. Hence, Trinidad has been characterised historically as a social class-colour pyramid consisting of three strata: upper/'white', middle/'coloured' or 'brown', and lower/'black', a social pyramid more or less

incorporating subsequent influxes of foreign (e.g., East Indian, Chinese, Portuguese) immigrant labourers (cf. Braithwaite, 1975 [1953]; Brereton, 1979). Discussions of racial or ethnic 'mixing' tend to be placed within a larger agenda of race relations research.

In this chapter I want to explore the notion of 'mixed' in Trinidad on its own terms, as an overarching rubric for glossing ethnic or racial combinations, and to analyse the importance of ambiguity for defining, sustaining or resisting hierarchy in systems of social stratification – a subject not of primary interest to researchers until relatively recently (viz. Cancian, 1976).[2] I do this by focusing on one of its specific manifestations, that of 'Spanish'. I also want to raise a related issue of critical importance not yet thoroughly studied in Caribbean literature. Since all ethnicities are somehow 'mixed' (i.e., 'pure' and 'impure' are social constructs, not biological facts), how and when is 'mixed' ('combined', 'impure') socially emphasised as the primary identity marker and how and when is an ethnic identity principally perceived as a socio–cultural 'whole'? My premise is that in polyethnic New World societies such as Trinidad, 'mixed' is more than 'coloured', beyond 'black'-plus-'white', and should not be confined within implicit assumptions – scholarly or popular – of distinctly bounded categories of 'race'.

In exploring the concept of 'mixed' ethnicities, it is instructive to consider Ardener's (1982) notion of the simultaneous process of classifying an event and the 'event' itself (1982:11). Applying this idea of simultaneity to analyses of 'mixed' ethnicities broadens our appreciation of these categories as windows into understanding ethnic identity as being both structural and processual (Chapman et al., 1989:9). Ambiguity can be seen as a nexus, if you will, between classification/definition and action. More than a continuum of categories (viz. Chapman et al., 1989), 'mixed' ethnicities are fluid in the sense of consisting of a *dialectic* between boundary and content rather than as shifting boundaries that encompass interchangeable attributes. In other words, once the attributes are exchanged, the boundary itself that separates 'who are' from 'who are not' is transformed. Barth's (1969) landmark turn away

processual - involving study of processes rather than discrete events

nexus - connection or series of connections linking 2 or more things

from the content ('cultural diacritica') of ethnic groups toward a focus on ethnicity in action through boundary shifts was critical for understanding ethnicity as process. Problematic, however, was that content tended to be construed in rather static or secondary terms (viz. Fox, 1990:6). In order to better understand situations where, simultaneously, boundaries are negotiable and their content is plastic, and where ethnic categories may function as mediators that modify other ethnic categories, we must analyse the operation of ambiguity and its functions and role in 'mixed' ethnicity, as it is central to the manipulation, contingency, and idiosyncrasy of ethnic identity. Ambiguity both reveals and negotiates the extant system of social stratification and the power relations upon which it rests. That is, ethnic category constructs possess diverse qualities, meanings and uses in social action and at the same time form, maintain, and challenge hierarchical structures.

The notion of 'mixed', accepted as both empirical reality and metaphor, is multivalent in local Trinidadian ideology. For instance, one of my informants could recite without hesitation (and with dubious sincerity) what he conceived as appropriate nationalist rhetoric: 'Over time, a few generations, with mixing the future wouldn't have race consciousness.' And in grappling with the issue of defining a Trinidadian, Merle Hodge (1975:31) suggests that 'perhaps the epitome of a Trinidadian is the child... with a dark skin and crinkly plaits ... decidedly Chinese eyes ... [named] Maharaj'. Although the child, symbol of a heterogeneous identity, is a 'mixed', every attribute in this composite is disaggregated and identified. Yet 'mixed' is not *necessarily* one concrete end result of a prior act of mixing, precisely measurable, an always exact set of specified attributes that are 'situationally' activated. While 'mixing' does not necessarily mean haphazard, since most attributes are accounted for – recollected, traced, and thus defined – in some way, 'Spanish' indicates a 'mix' whose attributes may or may not be unanimously acknowledged or verified.

It is not merely that one may choose to be or not be 'a Spanish'; 'Spanish' itself as a ('mixed') designation fluctuates. By this I do not mean that 'Spanish' is not a clearly understood ethnic des-

ignation in a particular/individual's reckoning; rather, many of its constituent attributes are ambiguous and variable, as are the ways it is meaningful in Trinidadian society. For example, the definition and function of what 'a Spanish' *is* depends on a number of variously selected criteria such as colouring, hair texture, area of origin (e.g., Venezuela or locales in Trinidad with historical Spanish and/or Amerindian populations such as Arima, Santa Cruz, or parts of southern Trinidad), lineage (i.e., individual forebears), class position, and what is generally associated with class as one of its markers: presentation of self – behaviour, comportment, and speech.[3] Also critical are the specific reasons for their attribution to particular individuals, the moment in which the designation is made, and by whom. Therefore, 'Spanish' is both a malleable category and a negotiable identity for individuals who may differentially promote a variety of criteria. It can conjure up different associations to different people. Thus while 'mixed' is also a generalised rubric, the attributes of specific kinds of 'mixed' come together in various numbers and combinations and, as in the case of 'Spanish', can be again sub-categorised. 'Mixed' constitutes both a fluid ethnic category and an individual's negotiable membership. In fact, as will be discussed, certain kinds of 'mixed', such as 'Spanish', are terms describing individuals (rather loosely designating an aggregate) and emphasise cultural and phenotypic characteristics rather than social – i.e., jural, political – dimensions. As a 'mixed' category, 'Spanish' lets us get at these various processes as it: 1) identifies or emphasises particular qualities and their combinations; 2) reveals how various kinds of 'ethnic'/'racial'/'cultural' combinations are valorised; and 3) throws into relief actual or putative historical events and relationships. While some of these issues arise in connection with more clear-cut race and colour categories in Trinidad (all of which are, of course, social constructs and hence to some extent malleable), more multivalent and thus potentially ambiguous 'mixed' classifications such as 'Spanish' permit even less to be assumed or taken for granted.

'Spanish' is certainly a label that is used by some Trinidadians to describe themselves. In this chapter I will not refer to self-referential

extant -surviving
idiosyncratic peculiar or individual.
valorized - validated or enhance value or status
putative: supposed

[handwritten margin notes: idiomatic-using containing expressions that are natural to a native speaker; elucidate — explain]

statements of 'Spanish' persons.[4] Rather, my intention is to underscore the significance and sharpen the concept of ambiguity in 'mixed' ethnicities through the example of Trinidad's 'Spanish'. I am dealing with the idiomatic usage of ethnic categories, conceptualisations of 'mixed' persons, and the ideological construction of kinds of groups. I do this by considering two distinct yet connected domains: 1) historical evidence taken from secondary sources, and 2) contemporary ethnographic data gathered during fieldwork undertaken in Trinidad (1984, 1987–9). While my interpretation of the historical material is somewhat speculative, I think it can stand as a provisional attempt to elucidate some of the antecedent dimensions underlying the current significance of a 'Spanish' ethnicity among the general population in Trinidad. The ethnographic data offered here, however, emphasises Indo-Trinidadian perception and use of the construct 'Spanish', rather than those gleaned from a cross-section of the society. The focus of my field research in Trinidad did not specifically address 'Spanish' ethnicity but ethnicity among Indo-Trinidadians. Moreover, my research was conducted in a relatively small, semi-rural area, traditionally perceived – with some degree of accuracy – as a particularly conservative (both politically and culturally) region of the country. For these reasons my observations in this chapter should be seen as exploratory and provisional. Due to the nature of ethnic group relations in post-colonial Trinidad, however, especially between the two demographically most significant ethnic groups – Afro-Trinidadians and Indo-Trinidadians – Indo-Trinidadians' conceptualisations can provide a useful window through which to view the meanings and social significance of both 'Spanish' and, by extension, 'mixed' as ethnic categories.

A number of my informants referred to 'Spanish' in three senses: 1) as a distinct ethnic category, 2) as occupying a particular symbolic space in Indo- and Afro-Trinidadian relations, and 3) as a form of 'African' or 'black' identity – a diluted or 'softer' variation that in a sense upgrades the person designated 'Spanish' in an ethnic hierarchy where elements of colonial ideology have relegated Afro-Trinidadians and

Indo-Trinidadians to the bottom, where both struggle against being last. To a significant extent my informants' perceptions of 'Spanish' discussed in this chapter act as what I will call an ethnic modifier (cf. Alexander, 1977:421). By this I mean a category of ethnicity that modifies other ethnic categories, indicating a positive condition which improves another ethnic referent into something more highly valued, at least by certain sectors of society. While the constructions of 'Spanish' discussed here are *by no means* Indo-Trinidadians' *exclusive* conceptualisation of this category, as ethnic modifier, 'Spanish' functions *in part* to affirm an ethnic hierarchy where 'softened' or ambiguous 'African' or 'black' convey and confer a higher status that modifies the perceived stronger or more clear-cut expression of 'African' or 'black' attributes.

Yet it is also significant that because of the particular history and social use of the colour 'black'/concept 'African' in Trinidad, the category 'Spanish', in this capacity as ethnic modifier, has not been a focal point in local discursive traditions avowing a positive image of 'blackness' or 'Africanness'. Examples of the latter include philosophical treatises from the turn of the nineteenth century such as J.J. Thomas' *Froudacity* or social movements like the Pan-African Association; Trinidad's Black Power movement of the 1970s; contemporary political bodies such as the National Joint Action Committee; or that evinced in aesthetic expression, particularly in some calypsoes and cultural competitions such as Best Village.[5] Labour unions and political parties (such as the Oilfield Workers' Trade Union, the former Workers and Farmers Party and United Labour Front) that embrace notions of class unity in rejection of ethnic (and other) factionalism fostered by colonial ideology have also subscribed to cultural equality and pride. While 'blackness' or 'Africanness' is not today a principal theme in everyday discourse among the majority of people, these examples are all clear illustrations of the positive associations and imagery of 'Africanness' and 'blackness' in Trinidadian society. Moreover, in individuals' personal estimations, 'Africanness' or 'blackness' can certainly be emphasised. For example, an acquaintance remarked to me that although his Trinidadian wife 'is a Spanish', she refers to herself as 'Afro-Trinidadian', emphasising her African heritage and identity.

From both a national Trinidadian perspective and that of my informants, the category 'Spanish' illustrates that categories of ethnicity are ways of talking about power that reveal the tensions around the nature and construction of ethnic boundaries and the cultural contents they enclose, within structures of group conflict and competition. The category 'Spanish' also allows us a means to explore how people use multiple and contrastive *ideas about* ethnicity, history, and culture to understand their place and/or create places for themselves in society.

Before discussing the foundations and contemporary significance of the category 'Spanish', I will briefly sketch the historical context of Trinidadian social structure and then locate the concept of 'mixed' within it.

Ethnicity and Politics in Trinidad

The development over time of particular world views and definitions of social identity is part of a broader question of how material conditions are experienced and expressed as particular ideologies. The nature of colonial society is, in most cases, that economic and social boundaries are made to correspond with racial, ethnic, religious and other communal groups, which are differently incorporated into the stratification system of the society (Hintzen, 1989:6). Through this unequal incorporation, which fosters conflictual political and economic interests, adversarial relations can develop between the communal groups (ibid.). In Trinidad's origins as a colonial society, a system of stratification based on a class-race-colour hierarchy – beginning with slavery and continuing through emancipation and indenture – laid the foundations for a post-colonial society whose hallmark has been ethnic group competition fostered by class inequalities and state control of certain resources. While an analysis of the genesis of all salient Trinidadian categories of ethnicity is beyond the purview of this chapter, noting the historical context in which ethnic identities evolve, are evaluated and contested clarifies how ethnic hierarchies become salient in social life. Labour deployment and its associated standards of value and prestige helps shape the way people classify their world – and each other – as well as the rationalisations marshalled that ratify these classifications.

After the abolition of West Indian slavery in 1838 a cheap and ready labour supply was still needed to continue the colonial production of sugar. Under an indentured labour project between 1845 and 1917, the British brought East Indians to Trinidad from India to work on sugar estates. Mid-nineteenth century Trinidadian society was permeated by '... the whole intricate experience of the Afro-European encounter since the Renaissance, the stereotypes formed by slavery, the legacy of the master and servant relationship, and, equally important, the growing dogma of the superiority of European culture and technology' (Wood, 1968:248). To this we can add another critical influence, noted by Brereton (1979:193ff.), the development of British and European concepts of racial types and the 'natural' inequalities between them. These ideologies and their institutionalisation formed the context within which the various sectors of the Trinidadian population interacted and into which the East Indians entered.

As a 'segmented society' divided by occupational hierarchies, status groups of colour and race, and class levels partly determined by race/colour and differential access to key resources (such as land or employment possibilities), nineteenth century Trinidad had clear lines of demarcation among a population 'conscious of belonging to definite and separate groups' (Brereton, 1979:205). Constituting these groups were, according to Ryan (1972:19–20): a) whites, subdivided between 'principal whites' (wealthy European and creole planters and merchants, and British officials), 'secondary whites' (wage-earning employees of 'principal whites'), and Syrian, Lebanese, Portuguese, and Jewish small business people; b) coloured persons, of whom the middle class was mostly comprised; and c) at the lowest point, blacks and the indentured labourers.

Such a complex social structure as this assuredly produces diverse, cross-cutting, ambivalent and ambiguous ideologies of social place and privilege. While elite whites asserted racial (and class) superiority, there were other (lesser) whites

Salient: important.
genesis: formation
purview. limit purpose or scope

who could not make the same claims. Moreover, as Brereton (1979:208) points out, an emergent 'Creole identity' participated in by both whites and middle-class coloureds and blacks was evident, creating a unity that contrasted with the feelings toward British representatives and indentured immigrants. Within the coloured and black middle class itself, many scholars of the Caribbean note that to an extent the analogy between 'whiteness' and 'superiority' had been accepted (e.g., Ryan, 1972; Patterson, 1975; cf. Brereton, 1979). It is a familiar characterisation in the literature that many of this group 'accepted and internalised' notions of black inferiority (Ryan, 1972:20) and '... compensated to some extent for the negative racial self-image ... by turning it against those lower in the shade hierarchy ...' (Patterson, 1975:317).

For the mid-nineteenth century Wood (1968) and Brereton (1979) assert that there was little conflict between the indentured East Indians and blacks, separated to a great extent by regional distance and occupational concentration. After the early 1880s, however, when increased recruitment of indentureds within a depressed economy exacerbated the competition between lowest rung East Indians and blacks, the latter increased their perception of East Indians as an 'economic threat' (Brereton, 1979:189–90). In this vein the coloured and black middle class articulated a 'systematic critique' of immigration and these immigrants, and 'a whole collection of unfavourable stereotypes was built up' against them throughout the nineteenth century (ibid: 186) from various sectors of the society. According to Wood (1968:136–7), even by the 1850s Negro Creoles '... who had been at the bottom of the social scale now had an easily recognizable class beneath them'. Feeling similar pressures, the East Indians in turn imbibed local Trinidadian stratification and elaborated upon traditional forms of bias, particularly regarding their nearest competitors.

Beginning from a largely separate existence, as constraints in the economy tightened, Indo- and Afro-Trinidadians increasingly – though not exclusively – began to voice their interests in communal terms, reflecting their interests as ethnically segregated workers. This process was encouraged and made more complex after World War II by the needs of the state and the efforts of political leadership that mobilised support through platforms of race/ethnicity.

The strength of communal politics derives from the implementation of voting in Trinidad, where 'the most important, visible, and salient dimension of political cleavage is race ...' (Hintzen, 1989:20). As Hintzen (1989:3, 39) succinctly explains, by the 1950s the appeal to race was a principal aspect of mass political mobilisation. The notion of majority rule required aspiring leaders to amass the support of the largest voting blocs. With little overt class mobilisation, this pointed to the black and East Indian populations (1989:39). However, through the significance of the black and mixed populations, 'majoritarianism' gave rise to a black political party (the People's National Movement) 'which relied on communal mobilisation to gain control of the state' (Hintzen, 1989:3). Reliant on communal politics, the state became synonymous with 'black' and opposition parties largely with 'Indian'. While the ruling National Alliance for Reconstruction from 1986 up to December 1991 rested on a self-conscious (if not entirely successful) platform of multi-ethnic representation, the previous PNM regime's strategies of racial politics fomented ideologies of interests based on ethno-cultural identification rather than that of class (Phillips, 1990; Hintzen, 1989). Although today there is also a local discourse of ethnic group harmony regarding Afro- and Indo-Trinidadians, in many social and political contexts it is largely rhetorical.

We have seen so far that a curious combination of forces is at work in Trinidadian society: a ready acknowledgement of its multiple cultural influences and the 'mixed' quality of its history and population, along with an apparently clear ethno-political division into Afro- and Indo-. This local characterisation of Trinidad as having experienced its entire history as a 'callaloo' (literally, a kind of multiple ingredient stew, and designated a national dish) or 'mixed' society, the presence of large numbers of variously 'mixed' persons in Trinidad,[6] and the existence of a formal as well as informal ethnic category 'mixed' (evident, for example, in the official census listings[7] and in everyday parlance) pose an interesting, if submerged, conundrum for Trinidadians. On the one hand, an image of cultural, religious, and ethnic heterogeneity and amalgamation is evoked – a 'cosmopolitan' nation with Amerindian, African, Spanish, French, Portuguese and English influences (from centuries of colonial endeavours), flavoured with subsequent 'foreign' ethnic cultures, such as East Indian or Chinese. On the other hand, in the competition for scarce, state-dispensed resources, ethnic groups' cultural legitimacy, distinctive historical roots and separate-but-equal representation form the discourse through which political claims are made. In other words, the degree of cultural presence is deemed commensurate with the degree of political efficacy, since the social and political voices of competing ethnic groups are framed in an essentially cultural idiom (cf. Williams, 1989, 1990). As Williams (1989:420) points out, '... when cultural distinctiveness becomes a criterion of group identity formation in a single political unit it is certainly a product of the power relations existing among citizens of that unit'.

The popular local credo 'unity in diversity' exists simultaneously with a socio-cultural 'callaloo'; both serve as key metaphors for national unity and ethnic group harmony. In other postcolonial societies, nationalist ideology has taken 'miscegenation' – putatively resulting in a particular kind of person – as a symbol of national identity (cf. Morner, 1967; Stutzman, 1981; Wright, 1990). Williams' (1989:433) comment on works dealing with these issues applies here: '[i]n short, creating a new race through such mixed union would [ostensibly] eliminate the inevitable conflicts assumed to be the consequence of racially distinct groups' struggle to maintain their purity and a "homeland" for their culture'. Trinidad, though a self-proclaimed 'callaloo' society, cannot *unequivocally* or *uniformly* embrace an ideology of a 'mixed' national identity, given the concern over potential cultural oblivion that competing ethnic groups allegedly risk. In Trinidad it is the concern over the assumed intrinsic relationship between racial/ethnic assimilation (mixing) and acculturation (cultural change or demise) that makes for a 'callaloo' society that remains unamalgamated (cf. Morner, 1967:5); it

is synchronously 'mixed' and distinctive (cf. Alexander, 1977). It is this, in part, that allows 'mixed' to be both a formal and informal ethnic category.

This dual quality figures in the question of how a particular 'mixed' designation is socially meaningful. As Alexander (1977:429) points out for Jamaica, '... the notion of union between persons of different races has an air of illegitimacy around it'. In Trinidadian society these unions have many possible social interpretations. By embracing a 'callaloo' identity, Trinidadians modify and broaden any implicit suggestion of 'illegitimacy' within the category 'mixed'. Although not necessarily overtly denigrated, all types of 'mixed' are not deemed, *vis-à-vis* each other, equally desirable or distasteful. What makes any given 'mixed' category positive, negative, or somewhere in between depends on how and by whom the constituent attributes are valorised individually, assessed in composite, and seen in relation to the wider ethnic arena. Two brief examples illustrate this.

First, the modification (mixing) of socially devalued racial traits is ironically and disapprovingly commented upon by a character in Merle Hodge's *Crick Crack, Monkey:* '... Mrs Harper muttered about the 'lil 'Panol prostitute down in the Place-Sainte who had a chile o' every breed God make and couldn' tell yu which Yankee sailorman she make that pissin'-tail runt for – what these people wouldn' scrape-up outa the rubbish-truck to sharpen they gran-chirren nose, eh!' (1970:139). Second, the category *'dougla'* (East Indian and African mix) is, at least among some Indo-Trinidadians, an at times tacitly avoided and to a certain extent disapproved identification, in large part because ultimately it symbolises the potential engulfment of a minority[8] or subordinate ethnic group. In a letter to the editor in the *Sunday Guardian* newspaper (24 June 1990, p. 11), there is a call for 'conservation' of pure Indian and African races, lest the proliferation of *douglas* result in a 'homological' [*sic*] Trinidad that ultimately loses the 'beauty' of distinct 'races, cultures, and religions', who need to 'develop their language, religion, culture, economic and political power *now*'. Given the nature of Trinidad's ethnic politics, this letter reflects

efficacy - effectiveness
commensurate - equal. corresponding

the concern over establishing the possibility of Indo-Trinidadians', and other 'distinct' ethnic groups', political and thus cultural demise.[9]

The meaning and significance of *'Spanish'* are as complex as the examples of other 'mixed' categories. In this chapter we will see that, for differing yet related reasons, on both a national and community (i.e., Indo-Trinidadian) level one important connotation and use of 'Spanish' is that which is socially acceptable, a positive condition.

What is 'a Spanish'?: Historical Context

In determining *what is* 'a Spanish', we must first consider *who were* the Spanish, for this historical population of colonisers provides a heritage symbol that functions as a key image in the ideological construction of the *category* 'Spanish'. Claimed by Columbus for Spain at the turn of the sixteenth century, Trinidad offered no significant caches of precious minerals or vast numbers of indigenous inhabitants to be harnessed in large-scale labour schemes. Trinidad's most important role for Spanish colonialism was as a military base to launch expeditions to El Dorado (Newson, 1976:235). Consequently, Spanish colonisation and settlement was very limited. As Laurence (1980:214) puts it, the Spanish colonial era was one in which Trinidad lay in a '... state of neglect ... for almost the entire period it remained a Spanish colony'. This situation had significant consequences for the path of Trinidad's development as an increasingly populated, revenue-producing colony. But more significant for our purposes, the peculiar nature of the Spanish occupation likely had repercussions for retrospective assessments of Trinidad's history. I suggest that the Spanish colonial experience holds a qualitatively different kind of place in contemporary estimation than that of the British, rendering the Spanish a more or less neutral, if not benign, coloniser.

This hypothesis is based on four possibly contributing factors: first, the Spanish are sufficiently far back in Trinidad's history not to be seen as leaving detrimental legacies felt in contemporary times, contrary to British colonialism. Perhaps contributing to this view is that, as

Hintzen (1989:21) points out, unlike the British, 'who considered themselves colonial expatriates, the [nineteenth century] French and Spanish creoles developed a special pride in their Trinidadian identity'. Second, Trinidadian perceptions of European identity are not uniform. There is a difference between 'white' (most notably the English) and 'Trinidad white' – those Europeans alleged to be variously if minutely 'mixed' with non-Europeans (notably Africans) or Europeans assumed to be 'darker' than northern Europeans. These can include French Creoles, Portuguese, and Spaniards. Moreover, from their arrival, the Spanish were interacting with the indigenous Amerindians on sexual as well as other terms.[10] This resulted in the Hispanicisation of Amerindian culture and society (Laurence, 1980:220–1) and undoubtedly to some extent the Amerindianisation of Spanish life in Trinidad. Hence, the Spanish identity carries with it vestiges of Trinidad's original, 'authentic', and somewhat romanticised past, in the form of aboriginal Amerindian 'blood' and cultural survivals.[11]

Third, the eighteenth century saw an influx of wealthy colonists into Trinidad who 'tended to displace the original Spanish inhabitants down the social scale' (Newson, 1976:193). Furthermore, Spain was defeated by England (who annexed Trinidad in 1802). History records that in 1802 Governor Picton observed that there were 'only six or seven Spaniards of "any respectability" in Trinidad' (Newson, 1976:194). These factors potentially enable Spain to be rendered, with hindsight, an underdog of sorts, or at least potentially more sympathetic.

Finally, it can be provisionally suggested that the debated and largely dismissed but influential claim in histories of the colonies that the supposedly paternalistic and benevolent nature of slavery among the Spanish and Portuguese, compared to the harsher attitude of northern European countries, has influenced perceptions of Spanish colonisation *vis-à-vis* that of the British. Thus, Ottley's (1955:86) comment:

> The free people of colour and the Negroes found in Trinidad [after the Cedula of 1783] a Spanish government which gave them liberty to indulge in, to the fullest extent, and to expound on, and

Hypothesis

glorify the new Republican doctrine of liberty, equality, and fraternity. ... These exponents of the new order ... were in no way different from the other free society of nobles and semi-nobles, although the two groups lived in complete isolation. Both were rich, in money and in quality.[12]

Although Brereton notes that Spanish slave *laws*, if not *practice*, 'were generally more humane and paid more attention to the slaves as individuals with human and religious rights' (1981:26), she provides a more realistic assessment than Ottley's eulogistic reconstruction. However, she also acknowledges that many historians subscribe to this unfavourable comparison between Spanish/Portuguese and northern European colonisers. While it is not possible to speculate to what extent popular sentiment or scholarly information is imbibed by the mass population over time, we can assume that some of these issues found their way into local wisdom through such avenues as oral tradition, the educational system, and the media.

Over the eighteenth and nineteenth centuries more waves of Spanish emigrated to Trinidad. A small number of wealthy Venezuelan *émigrés* assimilated into Trinidad's white elite (Brereton, 1979). From 1802 on, political refugees arrived from the Venezuelan mainland. Furthermore, large numbers of *peon* labourers were brought to Trinidad from Venezuela during the nineteenth century as immigrant workers for 'specific tasks for which they were considered particularly well suited – wood-cutting, stock-rearing, and labour on cocoa estates' (Laurence, 1980:219; Wood, 1968:33–4). Known as *payoles* or *cocoa-pañoles*, the *peon* labourers were identified with these rural pursuits and some (likely Amerindian-derived) craft production, e.g., basketry (Laurence, 1980:223). Significantly, they arrived in Trinidad as 'mixed' people – African-Amerindian-Spanish.[13] Along with the larger black and coloured labouring population, they 'were rigorously excluded from political or civic life, their most characteristic cultural forms tended to be despised by the upper and middle classes, and they were in a low economic position ...,' (Brereton, 1979:110). Rather than assimilating into the then predominantly French population, they were inclined toward the extant

Spanish population (Laurence, 1980:219). The latter were predominantly relegated, along with the fast-disappearing Amerindians, to the interior, far from existing centres of population and social amenities (Brereton, 1981:80). It would seem that now 'Spanish' necessarily takes on an association with marginality, labouring classes, and lack of social privilege, possibly particularly exacerbated by their relationship with the defeated Amerindians.

However, a contradiction becomes evident in the ethnic category 'Spanish', since nineteenth century observers also deemed the *peons* important contributors to the island's cultivation and settlement, as well as being 'the most industrious class' in the Montserrat district (Brereton, 1979:131–2ff.). According to accounts of the day, cited by Brereton, they were depicted as 'honest, active, God-fearing, law-abiding, and hard-working', 'a peaceful people', 'the original clearers of the forest', 'doing [much] for the future development of the Colony ...' and being 'the most valuable of all pioneers' (Brereton, 1979:131–2). Moreover, the small-scale cocoa farming undertaken by *peon* labourers rose dramatically throughout the century, and, by 1900, cocoa was Trinidad's primary agricultural export (Wood, 1968:34). As Wood (1968:34) notes, 'the *peons* prized their freedom and were scornful of field labour on sugar estates during the time of slavery'. The imagery of this population as skilled, proud, and worthy contributors to the nation and its ascendance (cf. Williams, 1990), albeit within the confines of contemporary class restrictions and ethnic prejudices, added to the complexity of the panoply of dimensions of 'Spanish' identity, in such a way as to preserve significant positive associations with this population.

Thus, by the turn of the century a figurative and literal transformation of the Spanish population must have occurred, in terms of the construction of 'Spanish' as a category of identity. First, as an ambivalently assessed (rather than uniformly decried) coloniser, the category gradually comes to refer to a very different, and largely dependent, population, called in general terms 'Spanish' and encompassing through historical metaphor[14] a number of ethnic groups, characteristic attributes, and class associations.

panoply - range/collection

While we must be careful in considering historical evidence in retrospective interpretation, I think it can be posited that the conceptualisation of 'Spanish' has gone from denoting foreign and essentially homogeneous nationality – Spain/Spaniard – to connoting localised 'mixed' ethnicity – 'a Spanish', one among other 'mixed' kinds of persons. But it is best to view this gradual transformation in identity as an accretive mosaic that gives rise to multivalence and ambiguity rather than as a linear falling away of a prior identity to a subsequent one. The question, then, is what is the nature and role of this mosaic: why has 'Spanish', as a contemporary 'mixed', maintained in current times a critical function as socially acceptable ethnic modifier?

What is 'a Spanish'?: Contemporary Context

As Hodge (1975:33), among others, asserts, in Trinidad 'Spanish influences are abundant' – in the form of the language which can be heard in certain parts of the island, through its proximity to South America, and, importantly, in the Christmas folk music called *parang*.[15]

We can consider *parang* at some length here, as it figures as one of the principal symbols of Trinidadian national identity, evidence of the 'callaloo' composition of the society. Although it is performed by persons from a variety of ethnic backgrounds in addition to those who are 'Spanish', *parang* implicitly and explicitly draws a focus on the Spanish presence in Trinidad, evoking notions of local *history*, 'Spanish' *culture* as part of the 'cosmopolitan' nature and 'plural' heritage of Trinidad, and the image of the ambiguous 'Spanish' *phenotype* that can blur the boundaries of (and among) such socio-politically distinct ethnic categories as 'African', 'Chinese', and 'East Indian'. *Parang* begs the question of the distinction between cultural traditions that are considered embodied in and exclusive to certain groups or collectivities, and cultural traditions that are not so contained.

'Culture' or cultural identity is harnessed in different ways and toward different ends. Creating or reinforcing an ethnic *category* is a distinct process from determining the boundaries and function of an ethnic *group*. Ethnic categories are not always isomorphic with ethnic groups. Indeed, this distinction is illustrated in one university professor's rhetorical question to me: 'Why is *parang*, which is sung in Spanish, a national symbol, yet [East] *Indians* must give up his [*sic*] language to be "national"? The language of the coloniser was, after all, also Spanish.' The underlying issue here is that *parang*, and other 'Spanish' cultural traditions, are not necessarily 'owned' by or located within one, specifically demarcated ethnic group, in the same way as, for example, the Hindi language or *bhajans* (Hindu hymns) would be for East Indians. *Parang* serves as part of the symbolic imagery of what makes Trinidad 'cosmopolitan'. *Bhajans* or Hindi are to many non-Indo-Trinidadians[16] a symbol of what makes Trinidad society parochial.

Moreover, conceding a prominent place in the national arena for Indian culture is a problematic act, since cultural representation and political competition are often synonymous. Conceptualised as a different kind of ethnic category, 'Spanish' and its constituent cultural traditions pose no such politico-cultural threat. Furthermore, while *parang* was a dying art form until it began to be promoted in the 1960s, it was revived as something that had been previously integrated into Trinidadian society and already known (Gordon Rohlehr, personal communication, 1988) – i.e., as an authentic part of Trinidad's original cultural repertoire.[17] *Parang*, as a definitive representation of 'Spanish', can serve as a legitimate, unproblematic national symbol because: 1) it is a different *kind* of ethnic identity from those that are politically salient and whose boundaries are more exclusively defined; and 2) it has a priority of claim, a putatively extensive history of integration as part of the 'original' fabric of Trinidadian society. No other ethnic group (except the partially 'reinvented' Amerindians) can make this kind of claim about their traditions for the *local* context.[18]

Given the plethora of scholarly attention to Trinidadian ethnic and race relations and national identity, and given Laurence's (1980:228, fn. 63) observation that despite a degree of creolisation,

within the Creole structure the *payoles* have always maintained, and continue to maintain their own traditions e.g. music, dancing, songs, food, *oraciones* [prayers], superstitions, and, above all, language,

one would think that there would be more investigation of the contemporary 'Spanish' as one of the ethnic segments in Trinidad's 'plural society'. Laurence (ibid.) goes on to suggest that 'this subculture has doubtless helped to create a sense of group identity which has contributed to the persistence of this minority group and its traditions'. However, this 'minority group' is being defined by its 'subcultural' traditions and only secondarily – if at all – by power relations. Critically important is that this 'minority group' of 'Spanish' subculture is not as clearly bounded (defined) as Laurence's comment might imply, given that the *political* dimensions of their corporate identity are unclear and that both phenotypical and genealogical claims to being 'a Spanish' are made by and levied at a significant variety of people.

Ethnographic Data

In answer to my queries about their designations of a particular individual as 'a Spanish', my informants were not suggesting a strict genealogical line of descent from the original Spaniards. To do so would contradict the idea of 'Spanish' as a 'mixed' category that recognises various streams of influence: Spaniards from Spain, Amerindians from Trinidad, 'mixed' Spanish from Venezuela, and African, Indian, Chinese, and European aspects.[19] Offering a Jamaican example, Alexander (1977:420) states that 'Spanish persons are generally regarded as being of darker complexion than north west Europeans. Nevertheless Spanish persons are classified as white'. In the Trinidadian context, 'Spanish' is not a colour term *per se* but a term signalling putative 'background' and 'appearance'; contemporary 'Spanish' persons are decidedly not classed as 'white'; and 'Spanish' entails a significant ambiguity in the establishment of another's ethnic identity.

My informants, and contemporaries such as Vidia Naipaul (below), use the category 'Spanish' as a descriptive device for different kinds of messages. In what follows I present some examples,

grouped to illustrate the ambiguity and hence symbolic depth of the category 'Spanish'. I will discuss each section in order to shed light on the significance of 'Spanish' in current ethnic relations.

I   This section shows various perceptions of possible criteria for 'Spanish' identity.

(a)   '"Spanish" is white Negro mixed with Indian. It also have red Negro and black Negro. White Negro is fair, clear, with straight or straightish hair' (Indo-Trinidadian woman).

(b)   'My daughter-in-law is "a Spanish". She have a [East] Indian mother and a Spanish father, [he is] a red [very light-skinned Afro-Euro mix], with kinda curly hair' (Indo-Trinidadian woman).

(c)   'We went through purely mulatto villages where the people were a baked copper colour, much disfigured by disease. They had big light eyes and kinky red hair. My father described them as Spaniards' (V.S. Naipaul, *The Mimic Men*, 1985 [1967]:121).

(d)   'If I see the hair is straightish I will say Spanish, and if it is more curly I will say red. ... I look for skin colour, hair, and what not. I say mixed if they seem more whiteish, and Spanish or Spanishy if they seem more Negro' (Indo-Trinidadian woman).

In these statements each person offers an idiosyncratic perspective on what particular attributes constitute a 'Spanish' identity. What recurs in all, however, is the notion of 'Spanish' as a kind of 'mixed'. The two principal constituent qualities of 'Spanishness' refer to appearance: hair texture and skin colouring, which derive from African, East Indian, and/or European background. Interestingly, cultural characteristics are not what is salient about 'Spanishness' to these respondents. In this sense the delineation of 'Spanish' as an ethnic group is ambiguous, and renders 'Spanish' an applicable term to whatever an observer is describing, of course within general parameters, for a particular person or situation.

Jamaican - white
Trinidadian - not white.

Colour terms, hair texture, and other appearance diacritica transcend the *cultural* boundaries of ethnic identity and are not dependent upon commonly claimed ethnic group ideologies such as a sense of community, a shared history or traditions, a feeling of kinship, and so on. Naipaul's comment comes closest to indicating a community, but primarily in the literal sense of co-residence and secondarily in physical resemblance.

The diversity of qualities or attributes in these four statements aid us in perceiving 'Spanish' ethnicity as not only a social construction like (all) other ethnic categories, but as having greater capacity as an ideologically charged symbol. Its ambiguity and more or less generalisable applicability find relevance where other, more precise ethnic categories do/can not. However, although ethnic categories may be couched in the language of phenotype, the driving force of their significance is not phenotype itself. The meanings derived from perception do not reflect 'objective' phenomena, particular attributes *per se*. Rather, meaning is derived from social relations – including those of class, politics, and history.

II   The quotes in this section illustrate historical and class dimensions of 'Spanish' in inter-ethnic relations and its consequent use as an ethnic modifier.

(a) 'Spanish people [have been] with the Hindu people since long time [the far past]. Spanish have a peaceful history with Indians' (Indo-Trinidadian man).
(b) 'Only the old midwives with Spanish [descent] does with the babies like we do, probably because they intermingled with the Indian people long time, the Hindu people. Long time we had no differentiation, there was no racialism then. Neighbours lived close together, not like now, where you become more aware of South Africa and all them kinda things …' (Indo-Trinidadian woman).
(c) 'When [an Afro-Trinidadian person] not mix with anything, you must know both they mother and father is *nigger*, they not mix with anything. When I say 'a *Negro*'

I mean a mixture, Spanish, Chinee, Indian. They just act different, you see it right away in them. You see the kind of *softness* into it, the softness in their personality. The Spanish or the Indian is coming out in the personality … They mighn't be clear, clear [very light-skinned] … Basically, the colour have nothing much to do with it. But their *personality* is different, a mix of qualities gives a complete different way [manner]' (Indo-Trinidadian woman).

(d) Indo-Trinidadian woman: 'My boyfriend is a Spanish – Indian and Negro'.

AK: 'Isn't that a *dougla?*'
WOMAN: 'Well, I doesn't use that word, I calls it Spanish. He have grey eyes, like, and soft hair. I doesn't say *dougla*.'
AK: 'How about if he had dark eyes and hard hair?'
WOMAN: 'Oh! Then he'd be *dougla*, not Spanish.'

These comments demonstrate that 'Spanish' can be used when the African/'black' element is being made ambiguous or diluted. When Indo-Trinidadians employ it, this can suggest a smoothing out of otherwise omnipresent racial antagonisms. The 'Spanish' are portrayed here as having a pacific and co-operative history with Indo-Trinidadians, learning (thus implicitly valorising and legitimising) aspects of Indian culture and not symbolising group conflict, such as is deemed an intrinsic part of the ethnic politics of Afro-Trinidadians and Indo-Trinidadians. 'Spanishy' Negroes can be less of a threat, elicit easier camaraderie, and seem more sympathetic than *'real'* ('pure'?) Negroes, who have had in Indo-Trinidadian perception a putative, culturally homogeneous, precisely defined identity as the allegedly materially envious, politically competitive, sexually covetous, sometimes threatening Other. 'Spanish' seems to efface antagonisms rather than represent them. In the ability to do this, its capacity as ethnic modifier does not render 'Spanish' as a *category* less ambiguous, because the very condition of ambiguity makes possible its appropriation in one direction or another.

Furthermore, the function of ethnic modifier is just one of its aspects.

The reference to South Africa (IIb) – the epitome of Black oppression and struggle – 'and all them kinda things' implicitly points to what this speaker sees as a relatively recent schism between local ethnic groups, where the present politically derived ethno-racial 'differentiation', and hence acrimony takes the place of a past harmony of cultural exchange. Politics divides, and divides along ethnic lines, or boundaries, but these boundaries apply to specific ethnicities with particular histories and qualities – i.e., African, Indian, but not 'Spanish'. She seems to imply that political boundaries that create ethnic identity are artificial, and that the genuine differences between groups are cultural and therefore not problematic.

In the use of the term 'Spanish' we can see the association of class and culture personified, insofar as behaviour and comportment (sometimes glossed as 'personality' or 'ways') modifies so-called 'ordinary' *black* (Hodge, 1970) into a higher social category of *'Spanish'*. The speaker of these remarks (IIc) clearly communicates her ideas about the relationship between (physical) appearance and (cultural) background, and the consequences for social position. In her statement, a 'mixed' identity is far superior to a 'pure' or clear-cut African ethnicity, which she labels with an epithet; mixing, in her estimation, improves the personality (or formation and presentation of self) by blurring stark boundaries. (In contrast, this reasoning would likely not, however, be the case with regard to Indian ethnicity – ideally to remain 'pure'.) Action or behaviour is more important than colour *per se*, and 'personality' is expressed in behaviour, which in turn is often assumed to be indicative of status in the social hierarchy. Proper comportment (respectability, manners, 'living good' with people) and the equation of being 'civilised' with being 'cultured' are implied, and seen as the province of the middle (or upper) class. A 'nigger' is low(er) class; a 'Negro' and, even better, a 'Spanish', are high(er) class. As an ethnic modifier, within a rubric of 'mixed', 'Spanish' can alter the meaning (if not the designation) of an original constituent attribute. While this is potentially applicable to any ethnic group,

since the very nature of ambiguity in the notion of 'mixed' renders it protean, given the nature of ethnic politics in Trinidad it is here notably Afro-Trinidadian-associated when used by this Indo-Trinidadian.

The sub-text of (IId), in what was at the time self-conscious distinction between *dougla* and 'Spanish', reveals the complex nature of 'Spanish' ethnicity. The 'grey eyes' and 'soft hair' of her 'Spanish' boyfriend allows this speaker to tag *dougla* as a less preferable identity, whose greater association with ostensibly non-white qualities, 'dark eyes' and 'hard [kinky] hair', would mean downward status mobility for her. Her obvious embarrassment during our conversation reveals a reluctance to assign what she considers an adverse label to a 'mixed' individual: he becomes 'a Spanish' by virtue of his ambiguous 'ethnic' qualities – *grey* eyes as opposed to light or dark, and *soft* hair as opposed to hard (but, significantly, not 'straight').

As the well-known turn of the century West Indian politician, journalist, and author A.R.F. Webber wrote in his novel, *Those That Be In Bondage*, 'His features were *soft* tinted as may be so frequently met with in those creoles of Trinidad who can trace their ancestry back to the Spanish occupation' (Webber, 1988 [1917]:140, emphasis added). Also compare Alexander's (1977:419) Jamaican informant's racial category 'Spanish-dark'. The informant explains: 'that means *soft* darkness with pretty black hair ... Spanish-dark and Indian-dark imply straight hair, and not Negroid features. I mean it could be straight nose and not very thick lips, sort of thing' (emphasis added).

In reference to comments about 'Spanish', the various associations made between the word 'soft' or 'softness' and 'Spanish' leads me to suggest that this word may be understood as conveying what social scientists sometimes refer to as the 'blurring' of ethnic boundaries. The opposite of 'soft' is 'hard', which has many meanings in local Trinidadian usage. One implication is, I think, *definitiveness* of *quality*: for example, 'hard' hair is kinky hair; 'hardened' disposition is wilful (that is, overtly expressed as opposed to the blurring or 'softness' of acquiescence or co-operation). Hence, with reference to 'Spanish', 'softness' can be read as a positive (enhancing) ambiguity.

III The following statement exemplifies the place of 'Spanish' in the contemporary politics of the 'plural society':

> 'Spanish is people from Venezuela mix[ed] with Negro, with straight hair until they mix with Negro. Most Spanish like [desire] Creole [Negro] people. Is a natural thing for them. In Venezuela Creole and Spanish get along just like natural. Venezuela people aren't racial like we [Indo-Trinidadians] are. The Spanish and Creole even here live good, because the Creole have the jobs. Spanish girls looking for security. Our ancestors made us racial in the beginning, and [former Prime Minister] Eric Williams gave the Creoles all the jobs'. (Indo-Trinidadian man)

In this text the speaker communicates two ideas of particular interest. He straightforwardly avers Indo-Trinidadian 'racialism', which he construes as inherent or at least ancient ('in the beginning'). Juxtaposed are the 'Spanish', who have proclivities for amicable relations with Negroes, either through natural sexual compatibility and the smooth interrelations that derive from this, or through the pragmatic affinity caused by economic dependence. Regarding the latter, 'Spanish' are equated in this comment with Indo-Trinidadians, who often say they have been less successful than Afro-Trinidadians in securing the benefits, rewards, and patronage of party politics. Yet the 'Spanish' simultaneously have natural fraternity with Africans and are in a sense forced into it through social inequality, i.e., the unequal dispensing of resources. The ambiguity of 'Spanish' is thrown into relief here: they are 'mix[ed] with Negro' yet akin to Indo-Trinidadians in their material condition; they are sexually associated with Negroes, but in a way that is both 'natural' and pragmatic ('looking for security'); they are, by contrast with Indo-Trinidadians, not 'racial'; yet circumstances and history rather than intrinsic essence dictate this to a degree. In Trinidad ethnic groups do not 'live good' naturally, since social inequality is paramount; it is in Venezuela that 'people aren't racial' and so can interact more naturally.

Conclusion

The category 'Spanish' is multivalent, and simultaneously refers to both one ethnic rubric, and many, diverse individual members who qualify, as it were, through various means. Thus there is more than one way to get to be called 'a Spanish': for example, through various combinations of appearance (phenotype); background (ancestral lineage, name, locales of origin, cultural traditions); social class; personal comportment or behaviour; self-identification; assessment and attribution by others; and so on. The category 'Spanish' also underscores the extent to which ethnic identity is socially constructed and based on perceptions of history. History simultaneously lends authenticity and confers legitimacy, yet threatens cohesiveness of descent through transformations in traditions and practices. Since there is not a uniform ideal model that encompasses the precise qualities that constitute its distinctiveness, attributes defining 'Spanish' as an ethnicity are perhaps even more fluid and contingent than in other, more delimited ethnic 'group' examples in Trinidadian society, such as 'African'/'Negro', 'East Indian', or 'Chinese'. I am certainly not suggesting that any of these categories are uniform or static, only that 'mixed' may offer a greater possibility for the creative use of ambiguity in social relations.

'Mixed' may also act as an ethnic modifier in the suggestive place it holds in local discourse about racial hierarchies. Alexander (1977:427) comments on the ambivalence with which racial hierarchy is conceived in Jamaica: 'This ambivalence is expressed in the touchiness with which the subject is discussed ... race is a subject people do not discuss freely and openly; it remains understood'. This 'touchiness' is similar in Trinidad, even though 'the making of ethnic [and racial] distinctions is an enthusiastic concern of most Trinidadians' (Lieber, 1981:100). What becomes evident is that a two-dimensional discourse is operative, reflecting notions of hierarchy and egalitarianism. That is, showing too much cognisance of, and hence interest in, matters of *race* veers too closely to being *'racial'* – attributing validity and legitimacy to the intrinsic inequality of racial hierarchies (and, by implication, other social hierarchies), thereby going against the egalitarianism of both the credo, 'unity in diversity' and the local wisdom of 'living good' with people by not 'showing them a bad face'. As one of my informants (a 'mixed' but not 'Spanish' woman in her mid-40s) stated it:

> In my generation no one looked for ethnicity, no one felt it was important, but if you *had* to put a category on someone, you'd go by surname, what they look like, and culture, like wearing a *sari* on special occasions or the girl who'd bring *won ton* to all our school parties. But even now ethnicity isn't important in Trinidad, because of all this callaloo [mixing] we have ...

There exists a fine line between accepting the apparently self-evident and commonsensical structure of ranked social and cultural attributes (the colour-class-ethnicity hierarchy) while not appearing to contradict (fundamentally preferable) democratic, universalistic ideals. Perhaps one of the means of negotiating this fine line is through the employment of various 'mixed' categories of ethnic identity, such as 'Spanish', where historical authenticity, contemporary ambiguity, and yet categorical distinctiveness permit both the construction and rationalisation of social place. However, it must be noted that the use of 'Spanish' certainly *does not necessarily* suggest the user is deliberately being racially hierarchical. Yet in its function as ethnic modifier discussed here, this implication in a sense serves to buttress the

system of stratification. It does this partly through redefining the perceived competitor/oppressor in terms of creating distinctions and imbuing these with different statuses, and stipulating ostensive allies in an antagonistic environment.

But evaluating the ethnic 'background' of competing ethnic groups and their presence in the national mainstream is a different process from evaluating the ethnic 'background' of 'Spanish'. As a body, 'Spanish' are not competitors in the usual sense for state-defined and state-dispensed resources meted out in post-colonial societies. At the same time it is a buttressing phenomenon, 'Spanish' is a buffer as much as (if not more so than) a clearly bounded, single-descent, same-traditions, collective voice kind of ethnic construction. It is a buffer in that it exemplifies (though not solely and not deliberately) a solution to a major issue in post-colonial nation-states: it simultaneously affirms and negates ethnic heterogeneity; a symbol of a kind of ethnic compromise in antagonisms between distinct, and competing, ethnic groups. As one kind of 'mixed', 'Spanish' allows recognition of Trinidad's empirically undeniable population diversity deriving from centuries of colonial labour schemes; it establishes Trinidad's historically deep and culturally authentic past; it symbolises a homogenised and 'typical' Trinidadian ethno-cultural group, and in its latitude remains outside the contested terrain of ethnic group competition and conflict.

Notes

1   I conceive 'background' as encompassing related dimensions of social identity such as class position, locale of origin, marriage and sexual relations, cultural heritage, and the like – criteria that can readily be translated into socially meaningful ranked classifications.

2   A well-known exception is Martinez-Alier's (1974) analysis of social stratification that recognises the importance of ambiguity in definitions of rank and their manipulation.

3   By 'speech' I mean manner or style of speaking English. While research shows that Spanish as a spoken language survives to a degree in Trinidad today (Lipski, 1990; Laurence, 1980; Moodie,

1973), I did not find it a significant criterion in people's designations of 'Spanish' identity.

4   My continuing research on this topic will include narratives to be gathered from self-identified 'Spanish' persons, and from Afro- and other non-Indo-Trinidadians. Preliminary data suggest that the term 'Spanish' as used by non-Indo-Trinidadians does not necessarily carry the same symbolic resonance as it does for my Indo-Trinidadian informants quoted here.

5   Best Village is an annual competition for local communities, involving folk music, dance, and drama. It began in the mid-1960s under the auspices of former Prime Minister Eric Williams of the

People's National Movement (PNM) ruling party, as a vehicle for fostering national identity and community pride. An implicit objective was to strengthen PNM support within the communities. Historically Best Village has been dominated by Afro-Trinidadians (see, for example, Stuempfle, 1990).

6   According to the 1980 census, Trinidad and Tobago registered 172,285 'mixed' persons, out of a population total of 1,079,791. Further breakdown within this 'mixed' category is not provided.

7   The other census categories are 'Negro', 'White', 'East Indian', 'Chinese', 'Syrian Lebanese', and 'Other'. 'Spanish' is an informal if commonly accepted ethnic designation; it is not to my knowledge an official (i.e. statistical or census) category. Another example of occasional differences in officially and informally devised categories of ethnicity is taken from an announcement in the *Trinidad Express* newspaper (10 October 1988, p. 11): a San Fernando City Queen Pageant beauty contest was held, featuring nine women representing the nine electoral districts of the borough. They paraded 'the traditional wear' of nine ethnic groups in Trinidad: 'Syrian Lebanese'; 'African'; 'Arawak-Maltese'; 'Chinese'; 'Carib'; 'French'; 'Spanish'; 'Caucasian'; and 'East Indian'.

8   I mean 'minority' in the political, not demographic sense. An interesting example of the ambivalence toward the label *'dougla'* is evident in the following statement. In June 1991 I had the following conversation with a (male) bank teller:

TELLER: My father is a Indian, Hindu, and my mother is Negro. I call myself Indian.

AK: You can be a 'mix' and an Indian at the same time?

TELLER: Yes. You see, it is the [sur] name that tells you exactly the nationality you come from. The seed is from the father, what *he* is.

AK: But isn't a Negro and Indian mix a *dougla*?

TELLER: Well, I don't receive it, I don't accept *dougla*.

AK: Why not?

TELLER: It's a kind of negative, like. I am a *Indian*. It is the seed, you see.

9   On the other hand, some categories that include 'mixed' persons have other factors that take precedence in their social evaluation, such as considerations of class. For example, the category 'French Creole' contains both 'whites' and those seen as the historical result of combined African and European colonial, particularly French, relations (at times classified as 'Trinidad white'). It is associated in contemporary usage with the nation's economic power brokers, the capitalist class of elites whose own interests are seen by others as not always corresponding with those of the rest, the nation. As such, 'French Creoles' are admired as enviable for their privilege and success, yet they are also often identified by working and middle-class Trinidadians of various ethnic identities as unjustly having more than a fair share of society's resources and rewards.

10   Such as, for example, the convents and schools organised by Spanish religious orders, particularly the Capuchins (Lipski, 1990).

11   As recently as 1988, a national newspaper (*Trinidad Guardian*, 14 August 1988, p. 7) had the following to say about the complex construction of 'Carib' ethnicity in Trinidad:

... the [post-eighteenth century] ethnic and cultural fusion among Spaniards, Africans and Carib descendants was the basis for the initiation of a slow and steady disappearance act among Trinidad's 'aborigines'. In the emerging gens d'Arime [people of Arima] of those days, the genetic endowments and cultural retentions by a people with a distinctive personality, are said to be unmistakably evident among present day Arimians ... [Arima is] still distinguished as the living quarters of an ethnically distinct group, shy and reticent, yet no [sic] fully a part of Arima's mileu [sic], in spite of apparently strong Hispanic characteristics ... With hardly more than 300 descendants of the past two centuries, the Carib heritage fails to attract the focus and interest of its young 'liberated tribesmen and women'. The integration with the Arima population appears almost complete ... [a] self-styled leader and 'President', is himself a living example of the total emasculation that insidiously undermines his efforts 'to survive as recognised ethnic entity', stubbornly refusing to be labelled [sic] and treated as 'a relic of the past'. [He] remains committed to the utmost, to revive Carib traditions still known, and to rejuvenate the glorious cultural trappings that distinguished the early Amerindian inhabitants.

12   Thanks to Sabiyha Prince for reminding me about this debate as a possible contributing factor.

13   See Wright (1990). Wood (1968:34) provides a partial illustration of the heterogeneity of *peon*

heritage: 'From the Spaniards they had inherited their language and their religion; from the Amerindians they had derived the art of weaving baskets and cassava-strainers ... and slept in bark hammocks like the Indians of the Orinoco.'

14 That is, history serves as a *symbol* as well as the *means* of the emergence of 'Spanish' as 'mixed'.

15 *Parang* (from *parranda* [Lipski, 1990]) was brought to Trinidad by Venezuelan immigrants, but has absorbed influences from Trinidad's other musical styles, such as calypso and forms of Indo-Trinidadian popular music (see Khan, n.d.).

16 And, indeed, to some Indo-Trinidadians as well.

17 Interestingly, 'Spanish' enables being 'authentic' without needing to be 'pure'.

18 Stephen Stuempfle (personal communication, 1991) points out that many Trinidadians perceive calypso as having deep roots in Trinidadian society, and it is thus also an 'authentic' national symbol. However, the time depth is still more recent than that of the Carib/Spanish presence.

19 Bridget Brereton (personal communication, 1991) points out that families deemed to be of 'pure' Spanish descent are classified as 'French Creole' and are not included in the 'mixed' 'Spanish' referred to here.

References

Alexander, J., 1977, 'The Culture of Race in Middle-Class Kingston, Jamaica', *American Ethnologist*, Vol. 4, No. 3, pp. 413–35.

Ardener, E., 1982, 'Social Anthropology, Language and Reality', in Parkin, D. (ed.), *Semantic Anthropology*, London: Academic Press.

Barth, F. (ed.), 1969, *Ethnic Groups and Boundaries*, London: Allen and Unwin.

Braithwaite, L., 1975 [1953], *Social Stratification in Trinidad*, Mona: Institute of Social and Economic Research, University of the West Indies.

Brereton, B., 1979, *Race Relations in Colonial Trinidad 1870–1900*, Cambridge: Cambridge University Press.

Brereton, B., 1981, *A History of Modern Trinidad 1783–1962*, London: Heinemann.

Cancian, F., 1976, 'Social Stratification', *Annual Review of Anthropology*, Vol. 5, pp. 227–48.

Chapman, M., McDonald, M., and Tonkin, E., 1989, 'Introduction', in Chapman, M. et al. (eds), *History and Ethnicity*, ASA Vol. 27, London: Routledge.

Fox, R., 1990, 'Introduction', in Fox, R. (ed.), *Nationalist Ideologies and the Production of National Cultures*, Washington, DC: American Anthropological Association.

Hintzen, P., 1989, *The Costs of Regime Survival: Racial Mobilization, Elite Domination and Control of the State in Guyana and Trinidad*, Cambridge: Cambridge University Press.

Hodge, M., 1970, *Crick Crack, Monkey*, London: Andre Deutsch.

Hodge, M., 1975, 'The Peoples of Trinidad and Tobago', in Anthony, M. and Carr, A. (eds), *David Frost Introduces Trinidad and Tobago*, London: Andre Deutsch.

Khan, A., n.d., 'Survey of Indo-Trinidadian Musical Forms', report for Smithsonian Institution Folklife Programs, Smithsonian Archives, Washington, DC.

Laurence, K.M., 1980, 'The Survival of the Spanish Language in Trinidad', *Nieuwe West-Indische Gids*, Vol. 54, pp. 213–28.

Lieber, M., 1981, *Street Scenes: Afro-American Culture in Urban Trinidad*, Cambridge, MA: Schenkman.

Lipski, J., 1990, 'Trinidad Spanish: Implications for Afro-Hispanic Language', *Nieuwe West-Indische Gids*, Vol. 64, Nos. 1 and 2, pp. 7–47.

Martinez-Alier, V., 1974, *Marriage, Class and Colour in Nineteenth Century Cuba*, Cambridge: Cambridge University Press.

Mintz, S., 1957, 'Review of *A Framework for Caribbean Studies* by M.G. Smith', *Boletin Bibliografico de Antropologia Americana*, Vol. 8, No. 1, pp. 189–94.

Mintz, S., 1971, 'Groups, Group Boundaries, and the Perception of "Race"', *Comparative Studies in Society and History*, Vol. 13, No. 4, pp. 437–50.

Moodie, S., 1973, 'The Spanish Language as Spoken in Trinidad', *Caribbean Studies*, Vol. 13, No. 1, pp. 88–94.

Morner, M., 1967, *Race Mixture in the History of Latin America*, Boston: Little, Brown.

Naipaul, V.S., 1985 [1967], *The Mimic Men*, New York: Vintage.

Newson, L., 1976, *Aboriginal and Spanish Colonial Trinidad*, London: Academic Press.

Ottley, C.R., 1955, *An Account of Life in Spanish Trinidad*, Port of Spain: College Press.

Patterson, O., 1975, 'Context and Choice in Ethnic Allegiance: A Theoretical Framework and Caribbean Case Study', in Glazer, N. and Moynihan, D.P. (eds), *Ethnicity: Theory and Experience*, Cambridge, MA: Harvard University Press, pp. 305–49.

Phillips, D., 1990, 'Race and the Role it Plays in National Life', *Caribbean Affairs*, Vol. 3, No. 1, pp. 186–98.

Ryan, S., 1972, *Race and Nationalism in Trinidad and Tobago*, Toronto: University of Toronto Press.

Stoler, A., 1989, 'Making Empire Respectable: The Politics of Race and Sexual Morality in Twentieth Century Colonial Cultures', *American Ethnologist*, Vol. 16, No. 4, pp. 634–60.

Stuempfle, S., 1990, 'The Steelband Movement in Trinidad and Tobago: Music, Politics and National Identity in a New World Society', unpublished PhD dissertation, University of Pennsylvania.

Stutzman, R., 1981, 'El Mestizaje: An All-Inclusive Ideology of Exclusion', in Whitten, N.H. Jr (ed.), *Cultural Transformations and Ethnicity in Modern Ecuador*, New York: Harper and Row, pp. 45–93.

Webber, A.R.F., 1988 [1917], *Those That Be in Bondage*, MA: Calaloux Publications.

Williams, B., 1989, 'A Class Act: Anthropology and the Race to Nation Across Ethnic Terrain', *Annual Review of Anthropology*, Vol. 18, pp. 401–44.

Williams, B., 1990, 'Nationalism, Traditionalism, and the Problem of Cultural Inauthenticity', in Fox, R. (ed.), *Nationalist Ideologies and the Production of National Cultures*, Washington, DC: American Anthropological Association, pp. 112–30.

Wood, D., 1968, *Trinidad in Transition: The Years After Slavery*, London: Oxford University Press.

Wright, W., 1990, *Cafe Con Leche: Race, Class, and National Image in Venezuela*, Austin: University of Texas Press.

5

Homosexuality, Society, and the State

An Ethnography of Sublime
Resistance in Martinique

David A. B. Murray

During the final weeks of rehearsals for the play "Gouverneurs de la Rosée" (based on the novel by the Haitian writer Jacques Roumain) which was to open the Cultural Festival of Fort-de-France, Martinique, the director became increasingly critical of the lead actor's portrayal of Manuel, the Haitian peasant hero. "You don't have enough presence," the director told him, "Manuel is a man of the earth." The scenes with his lover, the good-hearted Annaise, were especially problematic: Manuel was not convincing in his seduction of Annaise. One evening, the director sent the rest of the actors outside in order to work with Annaise and Manuel privately. While we were standing outside the rehearsal building, Claude, one of the supporting actors, mentioned that he was sure that the actor playing Manuel was homosexual. Several others agreed and said that they had been wondering for a while, but his problems on stage with the lead female proved it. These statements baffled me. I had been with this theater troupe for eight months and had never heard any comments about Manuel's sexual orientation before – a couple of other members had been tagged much earlier in the year, and most conversations about sexual orientation had ceased until this moment. When I asked Claude

how he knew this to be true, he replied, "Because you can see it in his body when he's with Annaise." I protested, saying that you can't make an assumption about the actor's personality from his stage actions, but Claude and the others replied that no 'normal' (meaning heterosexual) male would have these difficulties. Seduction, in other words, should not require any acting skills for any 'normal' Martiniquais male.

In the development of this play for a Cultural Festival considered by some Martiniquais politicians and bureaucrats to be the premier showcase of Martiniquais Culture[1], a rigid definition of gender and sexuality appeared in representations of Martiniquais identity. Those who failed to display the appropriate criteria for the ideal Martiniquais male risked being denigrated as homosexual, the antithesis of the normative heterosexual male and, analogically, of normative Martiniquais Cultural identity. In order to understand why only a single, specific kind of masculinity is tolerated in Martiniquais Cultural politics we must explore both Martinique's historical position as a colony of France and its contemporary socio-political position as a Département D'Outre Mer of France (Overseas Department).

I had joined this theatrical company because of my desire to understand the complexity of *creating* a regional cultural identity, which requires observing *all* stages of production. If we are to take an anthropological definition of culture as a continuous and contested process of making meaning, then the study of any social group that explicitly utilizes "Culture" as a component of its identity requires interrogation of the means of production of "the production." There is as much information about Cultural identity contained in what is edited, shifted, added, or transformed in rehearsal as there is in the polished opening night performance. Simply to watch a performance would be an incomplete ethnographic exercise: "Performance is the visible tip; rehearsal/repetition the submerged body ... the tip is not a token of the submerged body. It is a part, a moment of the process" (Fabian 1990:12).

In the 11 months that I spent with this group as a fellow actor, I learned that conversations held among the actors outside of official rehearsal time and space were equally important in understanding what "Martiniquais" consisted of. However, as I came to see the centrality of specific gender and sexual characteristics in both official and unofficial conceptualizations, I became increasingly curious about those who are invisible or slandered in public discourse; what if Manuel is a homosexual "in real life?" What is the position of a homosexual in a neocolonial society that promotes aggressive masculine heterosexuality in both its official Cultural productions and in unofficial popular discourse? How does a Martiniquais male who identifies himself as a homosexual articulate his identity in a society that provides no political or public support?

 My first objective in this chapter is to demonstrate that homosexual identity today in Martinique intersects in some ways with its French or American counterparts because of historical and contemporary political connections, but it does not replicate them. Although officially part of France and increasingly penetrated by the US, Martinique has developed gendered, sexualized, and racialized regional identities that reflect its history of multiple cultural origins embedded in exploitative political and economic relationships.

My second objective is to explore how homosexual Martiniquais (men who recognize and identify themselves as homosexual, as opposed to men who participate in homosexual acts yet identify themselves as heterosexual) define, describe, and defend themselves in a hostile public and political climate. By focusing on these men's narratives I am addressing Robert Norton's critique of studies of cultural discourses on identity that criticize the representation of "tradition" but do not adequately address the issue of how such manipulations of culture are related to sociological conditions (Norton 1993:755).

My conversations with these men reveal that despite varying racial and class differences, there are common strategies of resistance to public condemnation that reject certain qualities revolving around the "effeminate" nature of the homosexual (embodied in the Creole pejorative *macoumé*) yet incorporate aspects of a popular aggressive masculine identity and the French state's claim to the value of individualism. Such a relationship supports Foucault's argument that resistance is never in a position of exteriority in relation to power (1978:75). Sexuality and gender, like economics, religion, or kinship, cannot be understood apart from their position in relation to local and global political processes. This relationship would also seem to support another Foucauldian assertion, that the knowledge of self must exist in order for institutions of power to have any control over sexuality. That is, in order to administer a distinction based upon an aspect of sexuality there must first exist an understanding of the self as a unit with its own sexuality separable from the social and sexual whole (Hunt 1992:85).

Foucault does not, however, recognize that "relations of power" and "individualism" must be culturally situated: Martiniquais homosexuals' relationship to official and popular discourse is not simply one of repression and self-censorship in comparison to gay activism in America, but rather a compromise between the normative values, expectations, and responsibilities espoused by the state and the community and aspects of one's own personality. It is a sublime rather than fugitive position and demonstrates how a history of colonization has structured modes of resistance that cross gender, sexual, racial, and class lines at certain moments. In these situations, the normative ideals of gender and sexuality as codified by the French and Martiniquais states as well as popular discourse dissolve. Yet in other contexts these lines occupy a central structural position and reveal schisms within the homosexual community. Contextuality must be recognized if we are to continue analysis of any 'community' in contemporary societies.

Despite official rhetoric, which emphasizes an idealized Martiniquais Cultured individual (modelled out of and against French nationalist imagery) applicable to all Martiniquais citizens, Martiniquais state-sponsored productions contain highly gendered imagery reinforcing a stereotypical "hypermasculine" male. This is a popular public figure whose characteristics emphasize heterosexual promiscuity, bravery, and charm. It is supported by men and women across racial, class, and educational lines and acts as a central symbol in combating the historical, racialized imagery of the weak and powerless colonized male subject. No positive symbolic space appears on stage, screen, or page for any man that is not "properly" heterosexual. Furthermore, positive representations of homosexuality are not only absent in theater and other Cultural productions, but are also condemned in popular discourse.

Yet I maintain that homosexuality is crucial both for the maintenance of state Cultural authority and the popular ethic of hypermasculinity. Nationalism, a product of middle class interests and values, attempts to control sexuality through a prism of "respectable or normal" behaviors (Mosse 1985). George Mosse has already identified in a European context nationalism's concern with respectability that is built upon bourgeois notions of sexuality and race. Both homosexuality and "other" races are used by political leaders and intellectuals engaged in nation building as forces outside of and destructive to the nation due to their uncontrollable and passionate natures which counteract the white, serene, and almost sexless character of both the male and female national stereotype (1985:10,14). Although there is very little in the way of

Martiniquais official statements linking the interests of the nation/region to proper gendered behavior (unlike other societies. See Cohen and Mascia-Lees 1993; Mankekar 1993), recent research reveals that philosophical and intellectual ideologies in contemporary Martiniquais debates over Culture contain highly gendered assumptions and imagery (Arnold 1994; Schnepel 1993). This should not surprise us given the historic connection between nationalist ideology and its concerns with respectability and sexuality.

However, as Parker, Russo, Sommer, and Yaeger point out, gender, nationality, and sexuality are relational terms whose identities derive from their inherence in a system of differences (1992:5). A neo-colony such as Martinique striving for recognition as a distinct Cultural entity faces different obstacles from the French (or white European) nation in trying to establish a national Cultural identity as it must overcome the racialized and sexualized predispositions of national models of identity that were built out of and against colonized populations. Thus the content of "Martiniquais" is linked in an inverse, refracted relationship to French nationalist imagery. Reacting to a racialized history of effemiization and hypersexualization in French nationalist rhetoric, Martiniquais Cultural bureaucrats are unlikely to support homosexuality as a viable choice in their quest to achieve a respectable regional/national identity.

The (Heterosexual Masculine) Individual in State Cultural Programming

reason to be

The Martiniquais people have been exposed to more than 300 years of colonial rule; it is only within the last 50 years that Martinique has been "officially" included as an equal department in the French Republic, and it is less than 150 years since slavery was abolished. Prior to this, one of the state's primary *raisons d'être* was to ensure the maintenance of a plantation economy system and control of its labor force, the slave population, through legislation endorsing inequality (see Mintz 1989:64–75). This history must not be overlooked when analyzing cultural ideas and behaviors in contemporary Martinique.

No cultural reference to homosexuality in + way

As a department of France, Martinique is granted equal participation in the federal government and its citizens have full French citizenship.[2] In legislative terms, then, Martinique is no different from the departments located in mainland France. In 1983, the Socialist government of François Mitterrand enacted a policy of decentralization in order to "democratize" the government. This meant that "regions" of France would have greater autonomy – Cultural, economic, and social. At the same time, regional Cultural differences were highlighted through the activities of the French Ministry of Culture, whose budget was doubled in one year (Wangermee 1988:68), and through the establishment of Regional Cultural Affairs Offices (Directions Régionales des Affaires Culturelles). As a result, Martinique today enjoys one of the most active Cultural movements in the Caribbean. The French federal government and the two regional governing bodies of Martinique, the Conseil Régionale and Conseil Générale, each have Cultural Commissions located in Fort-de-France that fund and promote Cultural activities on the island. Furthermore, most sizeable towns like Fort-de-France, Lamentin, and Trinité have their own municipal Cultural departments.

The definitions of Culture said by Martiniquais intellectuals and politicians to be distinctive of Martinique are linked in their form and content to French national identity. Central to this imagery is the individual who stands as an independent being apart from society. The fact that both French and Martiniquais Cultural rhetoric value the individual should not be surprising – 'the individual' is a Western social category with its origins in the development of capitalism, wage labor and a philosophical revolution throughout Europe dating from the seventeenth century (D'Emilio 1993; Dumont 1986). Yet I would argue that the conceptualization of the "individual" in contemporary French and Martiniquais constructions is not the same. This differentiation must be recognized, as it plays a crucial role in many Martiniquais homosexuals' discussions about their position in relation to their society. The construction of individual identity in Martinique therefore reflects both its history of differentiation from and subordination to the contemporary French policy of recognizing and promoting regional distinctions.

In French nationalist discourse "individualism" helps to differentiate France from its colonized others. French social scientists, for example, continue to perpetuate this idea by distinguishing between French people who are able to think about themselves in relation to others (hence the ability to consciously recognize one's "individuality") and "other" cultures who, "... do not have culture so much as they are had by it, rendering them incapable of thinking critically about their own ways of being" (Beriss 1993). In a nation that claims to be founded upon a revolutionary democratic ideology, the individual is deemed the primary unit whom the nation and its supporting structure, the state, are dedicated to serve and protect. Society is envisioned as an association or partnership between individuals (Rousseau's social contract), and each individual is conceived of as an independent, autonomous, and essentially non-social moral being (Dumont 1986:61–3). Yet the logic of French individualism runs into potential conflict with another highly respected "original" construct of French national identity – that of "égalité" (equality). In a nation-state where individualism is valued and all individuals are declared to be equal, hierarchy officially disappears and with it the immediate attribution of authority to a ruling agent. Left with a collection of individuals, the problem of justifying a power above them can be solved only by *supposing* the common consent of the fellowship (Dumont 1986:77).[3] It is in the interest of those in power to project a collective identity, that is, an ideal individual who represents all that is French. The nation itself becomes a "collective individual" whose identity is described in terms of an individual's life cycle, and sets a standard or type for all citizens: "If the nation is a species, the individuals who compose it are all characterized by the same specific qualities" (Handler 1988:45). Thus, despite the emphasis that French nationness places on the individual to become uniquely oneself, being "oneself" means to be uniquely French, and "French" is conceived in counter-distinction to a racial and colonized other that is not French. Thus the individual as a feature of nationalist rhetoric simultaneously conceals and exacerbates social difference.

In Martinique, a different kind of individual emerges in the Cultural rhetoric of politicians and bureaucrats. In order to understand this difference we must first review the development of Martiniquais Culture as an official government responsibility. This story begins with Aimé Césaire, a man whose life embodies the intertwining of the Cultural and the political. Césaire, a poet and writer, is well known as one of the founders of Negritude, a philosophy that combined resistance to French imperialism and a recognition of African heritage in contemporary diasporic cultures. As James Arnold has noted in *Modernism and Negritude: The Poetry and Poetics of Aimé Césaire* (1981), the sources of Césaire's Negritude were, to a certain degree, shaped by his experiences in mainland France, from his education in the higher tiers of the French university system to his contact with influential African thinkers like Léopold Senghor. Arnold comments that Césaire was also influenced by the middle-class values of his own family and the primacy of French over Creole as the language of the educated – which remained unquestioned by Césaire, despite his recognition of Creole's symbolic differentiating value (Arnold 1981:31). In maintaining French as the official language of Negritude (albeit often applied in an experimental style) Césaire perpetuated the colonial linguistic hierarchy, which placed high value on the pure written language of the colonizers rather than the "derivative" oral language of the colonized. This situation continues relatively unchanged in contemporary Martinique, where French is the sole language of the educational system and Creole continues to be spoken in informal or private contexts.

The media through which this philosophy of blackness was to be communicated were identical to those honored in the French 'Cultural' tradition – literature, poetry, theater, painting. According to Césaire, the development and proliferation of Cultural forms such as these would not only prove the competence of *l'homme noir*, "but also contribute to the recognition of a distinct and rich cultural heritage. The development of this heritage would counteract the profound alienation suffered by the Antillais people in their subservience to France. This, in turn, would lead to political emancipation, because, "Only a culturally conscious people can lead themselves in political economic and social development" (Conseil Régional 1988).

By 1958, Césaire had formed the Parti Progressiste Martiniquais (PPM), which was dedicated to an independent Martinique. By the early 1980s the PPM controlled the Conseil Régional and was the most popular party of the left and the official opposition to the right-wing integrationist (pro-French) coalition in power in the Conseil Général (General Council) of Martinique. The center of PPM power was in the urban south of Martinique – Césaire was elected mayor of Fort-de-France in 1945 and held the position until 1993.

Following the victory of Francois Mitterand's Socialist Party in 1981, in which 48% of eligible Martiniquais voters cast their votes for Valéry Giscard d'Estaing, the presidential candidate of the right (Burton 1990:1), Césaire declared a "moratorium on the question of autonomy," thus changing his party's position from one of separation to one of cooperation with the federal French government.

Césaire is primarily responsible for the establishment, promotion and funding of Cultural activities in Martinique since the late 1950s due to his longstanding political influence as mayor, respect for his international recognition as a brilliant writer, poet, and philosopher, and his party's eventual control of the Conseil Régional's budget (Blérald 1988:127). His emphasis on "Culture's" primary role as a means to political, economic, and social development is shared by most politicians on both the left and the right. This is not unique, for as Gable, Handler and Lawson assert, "Culture" carries significant weight for groups traditionally excluded from participation in national politics. In order to gain recognition and representation in a larger political system that has actively oppressed a minority group, that group must 'solidify' an identity from which they can challenge the state on its own terms. *A* Culture becomes key to proving and legitimizing that identity (Gable, Handler, and Lawson 1992:802). Once legitimized, the

diasporic - spread of something originally confined to a local, homogeneous group as a language or cultural institution

autonomy - right of self govt [handwritten annotation at top of page]

identity can be recognized, which in turn allows representation and a means to confront the state on its own terms (i.e. as a nation).

What *is* more unusual is Césaire's abrupt declaration of a "moratorium" on the question of autonomy and his ensuing acquiescence to and support of the Socialist Government's decentralization policies. However, upon closer scrutiny, Césaire's philosophy of Negritude may be less "autonomist" than it first appears – it shares an essentialist, universalistic principle of identity with French nationalist discourse (articulated in terms of "blackness" rather than "Frenchness"), it has always presumed French over Creole as its representative language, and it has continually promoted French Cultural forms as the means of its articulation. Given the close relationship between the PPM and the French Socialist party and the latter's pledge to recognize regional differences within France, Negritude in the 1980s could no longer be declared an oppositional discourse but instead became quasi-hegemonic. Thus it is not so surprising to see why Césaire embraced the Socialist promise of decentralization – his belief in the Cultural particularities of French West Indians and his universalist assumptions embedded in French nationalist Culture could be reconciled through this policy. This recognition of Cultural legitimacy could thus be interpreted by Césaire and his party members as the recognition of Martinique as an autonomous geo-political entity. At the same time, it allowed for political and economic ties with France to be maintained, providing infrastructural support so necessary for Martinique's relatively high standard of living (compared to neighboring Caribbean islands).[4]

The majority of Martiniquais Cultural bureaucrats that I interviewed were, like Césaire, of middle-class background and had obtained their higher educational experience in France. The current generation of Martiniquais officials can be called "the children of Negritude," having been raised in a society that was increasingly influenced by Césaire and his supporters. Although many did not agree with certain aspects of this philosophy, they were unanimous in their desire to create a model of personhood that does not replicate the French individual. They saw the

Martiniquais individual as differentiated from his or her French counterpart in terms of Culture. This subtle distinction from the French Cultured citizen has been constructed out of and against it: The Martiniquais individual is conceived of as a free-thinking, independent, and self-sufficient person yet a person who must first be fully conscious of his Martiniquais identity to be "healthy." The status of "citizen" (the base unit of the state) is thus achieved through self-recognition as an individual (the base unit of the nation) which in turn is premised upon self-conscious pride in one's Culture. However, we must not forget that this Culture is one created from the experiences of a primarily middle-class, well-educated bureaucratic corps who link the cultural development of individuals with the collective development of Martinique.

In a brochure entitled "Consolidate to Better Develop", published by the Regional Council, the following statement appears: "The man who fully lives his culture, without refusal or constraint, is a man confident in the future, not afraid to face the inevitable difficulties in the building of his country" (Conseil Régional 1988). Martinique's DRAC also published a similar statement about their "mission": "Culture is a means of conscience of the self ... Culture is a productive force because a man who lives his culture is evidently more free and therefore more creative" (DRAC n.d.:4,13). A few Martiniquais social scientists present a diametrically opposed model juxtaposing a culture of individualism against a collective culture, claiming the latter indicative of true Martiniquais identity. One social scientist argued that individualism is anathema to the development of a regional, healthy culture: Individualism is the cause of the disappearance of the "vibrant and convivial exchange that characterizes Martiniquais society" (Capgras 1989:101). Although this point of view is not fully adopted by most bureaucrats, it provides a clear contrast between two models from which the official Cultured individual is drawn.

Culture is also defined for the individual in Martinique through the production of various state-sponsored Cultural programs such as theater, dance, painting, and literature. This Cultural programming also communicates a

[handwritten margin note, rotated: *abhorrent to offensive*]

number of other values to its audience, one of which – gendered identities – I will focus on here. Productions funded by the Cultural bureaucracy appear on stages, screens, and pages in Martinique. Both the Conseil Général and Conseil Régional provide complete or partial funding for both individual and institutional Cultural projects, ranging from historical research to art exhibitions to musical and theatrical groups. These productions communicate strong and rigid depictions of Martiniquais male and female identities. However, unlike the "passive, serene and almost sexless" male and female sexuality Mosse identifies as characteristic of European nationalisms, these representations portray the Martiniquais man as aggressively heterosexual. In Martiniquais productions the male is often portrayed in a strained, if not violent relationship with women, communicating what I would call a "hypermasculinity" that reflects more the characteristics deemed 'normative' in popular conceptualizations of the Martiniquais male[5] (see below).

An example of this "normative" behavior can be found in the following scene from a theatrical production. I have chosen this genre because of Martiniquais Cultural bureaucrats' view of theatrical productions as a highly desirable form of Cultural activity.[6] There is widespread support across political party lines of Césaire's view of theater as a means to building a popular resistance based on a collective consciousness of a distinctive African past (see Arnold 1981). Since the 1950s, the theatrical community has grown substantially. Currently, Martinique enjoys a number of theatrical troupes, and at any one time during my stay there were at least three plays performed nightly in Fort-de-France alone.

One of the most popular plays during my stay in Fort-de-France was *Dis Maman, Où est Papa?* It was extended for weeks beyond its original run at the Centre Dramatique Régional (The Regional Drama Center). The play is a classic farce, centered on a Martiniquais couple who had been living together, had a child, and then decided to get married. The comedy begins when the mailman, known to be a Casanova at the local bar, is challenged by the bartender to seduce this happily married mother. The mailman scoffs as he downs his *ti punch*, saying that this wasn't worth

the challenge – "married women are too easy." However, the bartender ups the ante by betting the mailman a large sum of money that he couldn't succeed within a week. The mailman looks around at the (imaginary) customers, smiles confidently, and accepts the bet.

This depiction concurs with everyday remarks made by Martiniquais concerning the behavior of males. These features have been identified by R.T. Smith as typical of West Indian males:

> Men are thought to be stronger and more dominating and are expected to be more active. They should be 'providers' while women need someone to be responsible for them. The nature of man is such that he needs sexual intercourse (Smith 1988:134)

> Men are perceived to be strong, virile, active and domineering as well as 'responsible.' They are thought to be so by nature, not by education or effort ... Masculinity does not depend on work performance; it is demonstrated by 'manly' activities with other men, by sexual conquest of many 'girl friends,' and by 'having children all about'. (ibid:147)

Both male and female conversants of varying class backgrounds reiterated these features as indicative of "normal" male behavior.[7] My Creole tutor, George Menil, age 72 and former mayor of a town in Southeast Martinique, one day waxed nostalgic about how "Women used to accept their husbands' affairs; they understood that the man had to sow his oats (*planter ses graines*)." In women's commentaries on men, these features usually emerged as part of a critique. Catherine, a basket-weaving instructor at a Cultural Action Center in Fort-de-France, told me she was convinced that all men of her generation (she was 29) are irresponsible: "Once they are married, the man abandons the woman to play sports with his friends, go to the cinema, and/or find other girlfriends. Furthermore, they are still too authoritative and won't give women enough freedom." An older woman who works in a Fort-de-France fruit and vegetable market told me that her husband is faithful now, but that he caused her much suffering when they were younger due to his philandering.

The similar theme in these commentaries – recognizing the male's "natural" desire to have sexual intercourse resulting in his "naturally" promiscuous behavior – was articulated by individuals of different ages, economic positions, and educational backgrounds, indicating a central conceptual scheme of masculinity. If we replace what is "natural" with what is "cultural," then these commentaries reveal the privileged position of masculinity in the public realm.

The prevalence of such opinions about men reveal a strongly gendered division of the world that sets the terms for relations between individuals. The primacy of the hypermasculine ethic in Martiniquais public discourse is similar to that of "machismo" found in Latin American societies:

> Machismo is not exclusively or even primarily a means of structuring power relations between men and women. It is a means of structuring power between and among men ... one must constantly be proving one's masculinity as there is little capital investment; to lose in the ongoing exchange system means a loss of status, with the ultimate threat of descending to the lowest level, 'cochon' (Lancaster 1992:236–77).[8]

In public, with his male friends, the Martiniquais male must constantly buttress his reputation as a man, and the opposite gender serves as the most straightforward means by which to do this.[9]

Why are these classic features of Martiniquais hypermasculinity replayed and reiterated repeatedly? The answer, I would argue, derives in part from Martinique's symbolic relation to France, a relationship construed in terms of female to male or child to parent. Richard Burton, in an historical review of colonial literature, observes that the relationship between Martinique and France is often sexualized. France, until 1945, was commonly referred to as *la mère-patrie*, a curiously and/rogynous term that encapsulated both its maternal power in nurturing its colonies, and its paternal role as a figure of authority and administration. Martinique and Guadeloupe were commonly referred to as *les filles* – the daughters – yet they were also labelled *la petite patrie*, the paternal in miniature. Burton maintains that despite being granted Department status since 1945,

Martinique and Guadeloupe continue to be perceived, spoken of, and acted upon as though involved in a subordinate filial relationship with the Metropole (Burton 1990:2). Whether mother or father, son or daughter, the colonizer/colonized relationship has been constructed in terms of a Western conceptualization of the parent and child, the latter being unformed and impotent. The aggressive heterosexual male combats this infantilization, yet in doing so perpetuates colonial nationalism's racial construction of the passionate, uncontrollable "other."

Macoumé!

The absence of any constructive reference to alternative sexual identities on stage speaks loudly to the Martiniquais bureaucrats' quandary in constructing a Cultural identity in relation to the political and symbolic influence of France. Martiniquais Cultural bureaucrats are dedicated to articulating an identity different from that of their former colonial oppressors, yet in order to be recognized in a world of nations it must be articulated in a specific way. As we have seen, these geo-political identities are often represented through ideal gendered and (non-) sexualized bodies. Considering the historical depictions and descriptions of the colonized as an infantilized or effeminate figure, and the concomitant tradition of the colonizing nation as a robust, virile, and respectable masculine figure, it is doubtful that homosexuality would be touted as a healthy image.

A more pragmatic explanation of the absence of alternative sexualities or gendered behavior can be found by examining popular conceptualizations of proper gendered behavior. Proper public displays of behavior are embedded in a hypermasculine ethic that clearly codifies male and female through an unequal heterosexual relationship. The theatrical community, dedicated to increasing the popularity of theater in Martiniquais society (and at least partially reliant on financial support from state Cultural offices), tends to shy away from themes that would challenge these popular norms, especially at a moment when so much effort has been made to legitimize these norms as representative of a distinct Martiniquais identity. Sexual relationships between men have not been and still are not an acceptable category of social behavior in public discourse, hence their absence in most "Cultural" domains.

As noted above, the popular Martiniquais male, a public figure, must constantly buttress his reputation as a man. Standing outside the theater workshop with a group of male actors, there are perpetual references to *les copines* (the girlfriends), comments on female passersby, or joking challenges to a friend's masculinity. In more acrimonious exchanges, the sure sign of an escalation in hostility is when one man insults the other as a *macoumé*. *Macoumé* is a creole word, roughly translating to "ma commere" in French; in English, it combines the invectives "sissy boy," "mama's boy," and "faggot." I discovered the potency of this epithet early on in my fieldwork.

Michel (a dancer at the Cultural Action Center), a friend of his, and I were leaving his home in a suburb of Fort-de-France and about to get into my car when a group of five young men, who had been hanging out on the street since our arrival an hour before, yelled something to Michel. I did not hear what was said, but before I knew it, Michel was running at them screaming that they were jealous good-for-nothing layabouts. They laughed, and one of them told Michel to *"Soti épi macou mé'ou"* (leave with your faggot friends). Michel yelled that he knew they were all *macoumés* as all they did was hang out on the street together. Suddenly, a rock whizzed by my head and hit the side door of the car. Michel picked up the rock and threw it back at the group, narrowly missing them. He yelled at the group that they were too scared to fight hand-to-hand, and that throwing the rock was evidence of their *macoumé* nature. Finally, the other group walked off laughing, and Michel got into the car trembling with rage.

At the time, I assumed that Michel's explosion was connected to a combination of class and sexuality – Michel claimed to be heterosexual and he was from a very poor neighborhood of Fort-de-France with a reputation for being "tough." However, when I later recounted this incident to a group of homosexual men from predominantly middle-class families and neighborhoods, they reacted by recounting similar personal experiences, some of which involved physical violence and all of which included hurling verbal abuse back at the offenders.

The *macoumé* insult not only questions, but actively accuses the other of a combination of feminine traits, all revolving around a passive identity. The sissy boy connotation conveys imagery of a powerless, sexually impotent child who is under the protection of a female and thus incapable of defending himself on his own; the faggot connotation refers to the act of male-to-male sexual activity, specifically anal passivity and the acceptance of penetration, but also more generally in reference to any sexual act that takes place between men. The anal-passive position resembles the female role in sex, and is thus indicative of a feminized identity. This is an insult that threatens one's equality amongst other men, as well as threatening one's public reputation as a man (see Wilson 1974:113–42). It shakes the very foundation of the man's place in his public world. Violence is a socially sanctioned means (according to hypermasculine ethics) through which a man may redress his threatened status. Even stone throwing was not "masculine" enough according to Michel, who told his adversaries that they were *macoumé* for not engaging in physical, hand-to-hand combat. The *macoumé* is a product of this macho ethic – it serves to ground the ethos of macho behavior and hold it in its place, just as the macho male grounds the *macoumé* and holds him in his place. Thus the *macoumé* faces double stigmatization – he represents a disreputable and disrespectful male in public discourse and he is the feminine, weak figure that threatens the nationalist image of heterosexual virility. A neo-colonial society such as Martinique, trying to legitimate itself as a political entity utilizing racial and sexual characteristics as prime indicators of its national identity, has no place for a "black faggot" in its Cultural portfolio. Yet his existence serves a useful purpose in delineating the difference between normal and deviant (Mosse 1985:25).

Martiniquais Society from a Homosexual Perspective

Hypermasculinity in Martinique is a predominant ideology, producing forms of consciousness that structure relations between men, women, and children. Although knowledge of alternative forms of masculinity exist[10] there is little evidence of them in public spaces.[11] In a society where male sexual status and honor are premised on the male's sexual conquests of female bodies (and reinforced and structured through its antithesis, the *macoumé*), what happens to men who desire men? How do these political and popular beliefs affect the homosexual's perception of himself? Are these negative stigmatizations internalized? If not, then what are the strategies and tactics of resistance? And finally, how does the homosexual view himself in relation to his society?

But first we must ask the question whether it is appropriate to apply the Western definition of homosexual (with its exclusivist tendency to identify two male gender individuals engaging in sexual activity as indicative of a homosexual "identity" [Dynes 1992:xi]) to Martinique. After a couple of months in Martinique, I began to wonder if there were men who identified themselves as homosexual and male (as opposed to the *macoumé* stereotype). There was certainly no kind of organization or activism representing this kind of identity equivalent to what I had seen in urban American contexts. It was not until a few months into my second trip to Martinique that one of my contacts, Xavier, spoke to me about his "homosexual" identity and this was only after I had talked about my involvement with gay support counselling in America. Through Xavier, I was introduced to other homosexual men and learned of the few public spaces in which homosexuals may congregate. There was very little in the way of class, racial, educational, or political similarities amongst the individuals that I met. However, over time, I observed similarities in how these men positioned themselves in relation to a society that condemns an aspect of their identity. These "strategies," as I call them, reflect and refract specific political and cultural features of Martinique as well as influences from France and North America. The practice of masking/inversion, the use of the *branché* label, and the individual vs. society provide partial answers to the above questions. These strategies demonstrate

that most homosexual men do not identify or internalize any of the *macoumé* characteristics. In fact, most perceive themselves to be men, and through inversion of dominant discourses, manage to redefine masculinity through same-sex desire.

The mask of heterosexuality
During my fieldwork, I met only one individual who "publicly" acted out the stereotypical *macoumé* characteristics; that is, he used a noticeable amount of make-up, wore women's style clothing, spoke in a high, lilting voice and worked as a make-up artist (a predominantly 'female' occupation) at a Fort-de-France beauty salon. As I came to know other homosexual men, I noticed a distinct difference between their public and private personas.[12] In public, men are not physically intimate and maintain a significant physical space between each other. This is basic role behavior for the hypermasculine male, and I quickly learned that homosexual men ascribe to it as well.

When I met Xavier on the street his kinesics communicated a controlled set of appropriate masculine gestures – a handshake, no touching of other body parts, maintenance of adequate distance between the two male bodies, limited gesticulations. Our conversations would rarely refer to anything about homosexuality. This was noticeably different from interactions with Xavier at his apartment. Here, Xavier would repeatedly touch his lover (placing a hand on his shoulder, holding his hand) or just sit very close to him on the couch. He would also be more physical with me, touching my thigh to make a point, or my arm to ask if I wanted something to drink.

Physicality is even more intimate at social events such as the Trinité Boite, a discothèque located on a quiet street in a suburb of Fort-de-France, where exclusively "gay" socials are held about once every three weeks (it is primarily a restaurant/nightclub that caters to a mostly heterosexual clientele). This was a new venture, and it had only come into operation a few months before my arrival. Prior to this, I was told that another occasional gay disco existed, but its popularity was apparently in decline due to Trinité's preferred location and appearance.

The Trinité is ideal for a gay social gathering. There are no windows, and to enter one must pass through a heavy, solid iron and wood door, along a dimly lit hallway, and then through a second solid wood door. There is also a security guard at the front door. Its design provides a safe transformative space from the public street to the private domain.

Once inside, homosexual intimacy can be publicly acknowledged. Although not all men present are equally affectionate, most are noticeably more animated in their gestures and speech than "public" rules of masculinity allow.

It was at the Trinité Boite that I mentioned to Leo Beausoleil my surprise at how significantly different men behaved compared to the street. Leo then explained to me *le jeu de l'homme Martiniquais* (the game of the Martiniquais man): "One wears the heterosexual mask," he said. "Each day when he leaves his apartment he must wear this mask on the streets: he walks, talks, dresses and generally behaves as a man should." Leo said he doesn't carry masking to an extreme like other men who take on a girlfriend, get married, or have children. I replied that these actions sounded hypocritical, and that in North America one of the objectives of the gay activist movement is to eradicate this self-enforced censorship amongst gay men. Leo replied that he was well aware of this, and that he had seen much the same when he lived in Paris. "But the situation is different in Martinique," he continued, "It's a small island." It was not until a few months later in a reply to a different question that Xavier highlighted what Leo was implying. I had just been listening to him complain how frustrated he was having to visit his mother every day since her cataract operation and how this was curtailing his time with his lover. I asked if his mother knew about his sexual orientation, and when he replied no, I asked why. "It's not necessary," he said. "It would only bring grief and shame to everyone." This comment helped me to realize that masking is an obligatory activity for most Martiniquais homosexuals not only to maintain and protect one's public reputation but also to protect one's family name as well. To be publicly labelled *macoumé* not only threatens the accused's public

status as a man but also his family's reputation, implying deviant behavior and sub-standard parenting skills.

Like other Caribbean societies, the "family name" represents an important component of a person's identity in urban Martinique (Williams 1990:117; Wilson 1974:114–15). Attributes of this label include knowledge of the family's geographic origins (urban dwellers are well aware of their family's rural roots), an extremely detailed mental map of kin relations, and an ability to list family members achievements in terms of socioeconomic success (the list is of course selective). Thus a Martiniquais individual not only walks the streets thinking of him/herself as a man or woman, but also as a member of a family with their reputation to uphold. Wearing the mask of heterosexuality is a compromise most homosexual Martiniquais men (who recognize their homosexual identity and socialize with other gay men) are willing to make. Nor is this considered by many to be a humiliating compromise – the importance of maintaining family and personal respect outweighs any advantages to publicly admitting one's homosexuality.

Men like Leo and Xavier accept the necessity of masking behavior but they are not necessarily supportive of it. This is partially why they search out enclaves where the duplicity of the mask may be exposed and ridiculed. In these gay "oases," the heterosexual world is inverted and the straight male is exposed as nothing more than another masquerading homosexual. Stories and rumors emerge about so-called straight men, often with wives and families, who have made seductive overtures to the story teller at a party, or who have been caught "looking" at a beach, or the ultimate, in *flagrante delicto* with another male. In these gatherings Martiniquais society is reinvented through the transformation of hypermasculinity into nothing more than a metaphor of latent homosexual desire. The exposure of the masquerading heterosexual allows for numerous reinterpretations of "normative" behavior and temporarily empowers the narrators. These actions and opinions transcend class divisions within the homosexual community. Leo is a dressmaker living with his mother in a government-subsidized apartment building. Xavier is a teacher whose parents own a prosperous business in Fort-de-France. Yet both articulated the necessity and duplicity of masking. Trinité Boite also attracted men of a variety of ages and professions. What united them was their willingness to expose themselves to each other as homosexuals due to the event's being organized specifically for this group. However, it is only at Trinité Boite or perhaps at a small social gathering that the mask of heterosexuality can be removed. But even then, Leo reminded me, we wear more than one mask at a time.

Although I am positing that masking behavior does not demonstrate a submission to and internalization of a stigmatized identity, one cannot deny at least some acquiescence to public norms. However, the following two strategies demonstrate how homosexual Martiniquais men resist, reinterpret, and to a certain extent refract these political and cultural norms through language and self-perception.

Branché dandy

Branché is the term most often used by homosexuals in Martinique to refer to other homosexuals. It is much "softer" and more discrete than *macoumé* and roughly approximates the English term "dandy." In the public domain, *branchér* is utilized in its dictionary definition as – "to switch on, to plug in an appliance." I was told that in France it has also come to mean "groovy" or "cool." As far as I could discern, *branché* as a reference to homosexual orientation was utilized only by homosexual Martiniquais. I first heard this term when I visited Tata beach, located along Martinique's southeastern shoreline.

Tata beach is another gathering place where homosexuals socialize. Unlike Trinité Boite, where privacy is ensured, the beach is public property. However, despite its location adjacent to one of the most popular tourist beaches in Martinique, it remains relatively deserted, as the beach is less aesthetically appealing than that of the main tourist section due to the lack of requisite "idyllic Caribbean beach" items such as palm trees and a wide sandy beach.

My friend Dominic warned me that we had to act discretely here, as this was not an exclusively homosexual space. With one's friend or in a group sitting under one of the *mangier* trees (a squat tree with thorny branches and waxy green leaves that provides some shelter from the sun), homosexual topics could be discussed quietly. Here, the heterosexual world cannot be shut out so safely, yet there is an ongoing struggle to maintain the freedom of a homosexual space by questioning the sexual orientation of passersby. Lying on his towel, facing the path, Dominic would watch people as they walked by, especially scrutinizing men who walked alone. Once they had passed, he would lean over and declare them *branché* or not. Dominic would often claim that a man walking hand in hand with a woman was *branché*. When I asked how he knew, he would raise his eyebrows and reply, "I *know* it."

It seems particularly appropriate in the Martiniquais context that a word imparting a subtle coded reference should be the most popular means of identifying those who share a similar behavioral trait. I never heard a homosexual referring to another homosexual as a *macoumé* – the pejorative and degrading potential contained in its meaning are such that even in the most pernicious gossip no homosexual would use the word. Unlike North America, where some homosexuals have appropriated and transformed insults into badges of pride (words such as "fag" and "dyke"), *macoumé* continues to be too taboo to risk appropriation. Furthermore, *branché* simultaneously allows for a homosexual to recognize himself as both homosexual and a man – there is no feminizing imagery imparted through the word, and in fact it may even enhance one's masculine identity with its mainland French connotation of coolness.

"I" versus a sick society

At both Tata beach and Trinité Boite the conversation would often turn to comparisons between Martinique and other countries in terms of the quality of life for homosexuals. Many Martiniquais are well travelled (even those from lower socio-economic backgrounds have at least been to France, and other Caribbean islands and European countries. France, Central and South American cities are also popular destinations for Martiniquais travellers), so there was much to compare. Despite much disagreement over which place was most appealing, Martinique was uniformly unfavorable in comparison. Martinique was critiqued in many ways, from its lack of a gay life *qui bouge* (that moves, swings), as one man put it, to its homophobic male codes of conduct. One of the most sweeping statements came from Claude Savy, who one day told me how tired he was of all the traditions that "bind and blind" people. I found criticism a salient feature in conversations with homosexual Martiniquais; many articulated insightful criticisms of *les Martiniquais*.

In these situations the speaker excluded himself from his condemnation by using the third person plural, they, and by following the critique with a caveat emphasizing his personal awareness and frustration over this weakness or problem. Individualizing and separating oneself from one's own society was thus a common feature in conversations and merits closer examination.

There is nothing particularly Martiniquais about condemning one's society. However, we must question what exactly is being critiqued and who is making the criticisms. Furthermore, the "I" that most commonly appears as the contrastive identity to "society" must be situated in specific contexts; it may not consist of the same features across different cultures. Indeed, it may not even consist of the same features within one culture.

When it comes to politics, criticism of Martinique's governing bodies traverses the divisive lines of gender, sexuality, class, and age. Time and time again, I heard people condemn local politicians, the government of Martinique, and/or the French national government. My homosexual acquaintances were no different when it came to this – they did not criticize the government for its complete disinterest in and willful silence towards their discriminated status – rather they shared with heterosexual Martiniquais a very pragmatic, cynical attitude toward the State (both regional and federal), placing very little faith in its ability to change and improve their lives. This cynicism is borne out in statistics: Voter turnout at both regional and federal elections is often below 50% (Burton 1989:1, France Antilles 1992). Politicians are often called opportunists, criminals, egomaniacs, or all three. It is

not a surprising attitude considering the fact that until recently, the state existed primarily to ensure the maintenance of a plantation economy system and control its labor force, the slave population, through legislation endorsing inequality (see Mintz 1989:64–75). For the majority of Martiniquais, whether heterosexual or homosexual, the ideology of individualism has been embraced and used as a means to claim an identity apart from, if not directly opposed to the state.

Throughout the Caribbean it seems that a similar form of individualism exists: Joseph Owens notes that the pronoun "I" has special importance in Jamaican Rastafarian language. It is expressed in opposition to "me," the latter interpreted to be an expression of subservience, and a term of self-degradation that makes persons into objects, not subjects (Owens 1976:65). The similarity between the Rasta and Martiniquais usage of "I" lies in the opposition it expresses to a state they feel wants to make a culture of a subservient "we". In both groups, "I" acts as a conceptual vehicle through which a profound distrust in the state is articulated. However, the Rasta "I" also forges a unifying link between the individual and his god Jah (Owens 1976:66). The "I" expressed in individual Martiniquais critiques of the government and society is, on the other hand, closer in terms of self-perception to that of the Western individual as described by French social scientists and embodied in the rhetoric of French national identity: The individual sees him/herself as an independent, autonomous, and essentially nonsocial moral being (Dumont 1986:61–2). Unlike the Rasta, who claims unity and brotherhood with his fellow Rastas and Jah, the Martiniquais dissident simultaneously extricates and isolates himself as one who knows the weaknesses of the other, but is alone in that knowledge. S/He is a modern dissident, however, in that s/he is using in part the rhetoric of the French nation as a "modern democratic state" decreeing individualism as a right. It is one of the supreme sleights of hand in the rhetoric of the French nation-state to its citizens embodied in its credo, *Liberté, Egalité, Fraternité*. You are free to be an individual and pursue your own interests, and speak your own mind. You have the right to declare your liberty. Yet we individuals are all equal (we are French), and equality implies sameness, and the state is the arbiter of sameness, hence the State's attempts to define the "proper" individual. The Martiniquais claim to know what is wrong with his/her society reveals the individual to be simultaneously a dissident (in the recognition of an historically subordinated position) and a member of the modern French nation/state.

Yet Martiniquais society and government were not the only targets of criticism by homosexuals. Some of the most passionate condemnations were expressed against the homosexual community. Jean Claude, I was told numerous times, had a reputation for "sleeping around," that is, having sexual encounters with numerous men. Many of my homosexual acquaintances did not think highly of this, since he was involved in a long-term relationship with a Metropole (white French) man.[13] I met Jean Claude one day at Tata beach and offered him a ride home. On the way, he asked me about the previous Trinité Boite gathering that he had not been able to attend. I mentioned jokingly that his absence was noticed by many, and when he asked why, I replied that he was "well known," raising my eyebrows indicating my knowledge of his reputation. Jean Claude became very silent and asked me what exactly I was saying. When I told him what I had heard about his reputation, he reacted angrily: "They don't know anything," he said, "The Martiniquais are all ignorant and jealous. I live surrounded by jealousy." He went on to tell me that he didn't have many homosexual friends because so few could handle the fact that he has a wonderful life – most try to *me faire tomber* (make me fall), but he was well aware of these rumors and didn't care.[14]

Jean Claude's defensive "I" opposed to a "jealous" society is not identical to the "I" used by people in their opposition to the government. Both "I"s are voiced by peripheralized people, yet the degrees of peripheralization must be recognized. The "I" that critiques the politicians finds solace in a chorus of agreeing "I"s. Criticism of corrupt politicians and an uncaring government is a socially sanctioned means of articulating one's independence of and freedom from a subordinating relationship. The homosexual "I," on the other hand, is more peripheralized. He may find a clandestine chorus of agreement amongst fellow homosexuals at a social gathering, yet he remains aware of the circumscribed circumstances in which he may voice his dissent. The homosexual knows that he harbors a secret that, if revealed, would destroy his position "as a man" in public society. The wistful conversations about far-off homosexual utopias are one of the ways to combat this feeling of isolation.

At the same time, however, I would argue that this isolation is temporary and contextually constructed. At other moments, in other situations, the Martiniquais homosexual is not feeling isolated. I do not think that Jean Claude or Xavier, dancing with a desirable man on the floor of the Trinité Boite, are at that moment thinking of themselves as they would in talking to me about their relationship to their society. Individualism, like racial and nationalist identities, is one point on a continuum of categorical references through which identities are negotiated. It does not play as central a role as the individual in American culture, rather it must be placed alongside "Martiniquais," "branché," "family name," and "male" as another means to articulating one's identity in the Martiniquais milieu. A homosexual identity, however, is not one of the publicly acceptable choices. No matter what class, color, profession, or age, most homosexual Martiniquais men do not see any reason to risk their own and their family's name in terms of public respectability and reputation.

Conclusion

Frank Browning, in exploring homosexuality in America, observes that,

> Just as the image of the black man in America is constructed of the relation between black and white people in America and is profoundly different from images of black men in Nigeria or Brazil, so Queer as a disdained minority of forbidden desire exists only in its relation to the straight majority. (1993:227)

Such is the case for Martinique as well, where the existence of "normative" male and female identities   influences   homosexual   identity.

However, unlike American gay activists who endeavor to create a distinctly "gay" identity and culture through opposition to a "straight" heterosexual world on the one hand but an identity that belongs to the American nation-state on the other, most Martiniquais homosexuals differentiate themselves through their reinterpretation of and relationship to a different set of hegemonic public values in a neo-colonial society. In an environment where the hypermasculine ethic reinforces "proper" codes of conduct, masking is a necessary strategy to prevent ostracization and humiliation, and to protect oneself and one's family. The homosexual men I refer to in this article do not perceive themselves as *macoumè* nor do they view themselves as feminine or female. Their rejection of publicly ascribed negative attributes of homosexuality is partially articulated through the defensive rhetoric of a politicized, pan-sexual "I," a subjectivity that is promoted and legitimated in French national rhetoric. Yet at other times there exists sexual solidarity – in their conversations with each other, the homosexual community transforms the hypermasculine male into a masquerading homosexual. Masculinity, one of the most popular tenets of "proper" Martiniquais Cultural identity, is temporarily inverted so that one can be a man through the conquest of other men. The taken-for-granted pillars of sexuality and gender as codified by the state and in popular discourse start to crumble when closely scrutinized through the eyes of the peripheralized, yet the peripheralized partially participate in the perpetuation of the modern state's authority. We have seen how geo-political identity building (we cannot call it "national" in the case of Martinique's official endeavors) reflects the interests and experiences of a group of educated elite and is framed in relation to nationalist features of a colonizing power. In this chapter, I have tried to show that the diversity of homosexual practices and identities is structured by variations in the positioning of countries or (neo)colonies within an international political system of "nations." The processes that elites and dominant classes use to attempt to create unity within their governed domain shape and are shaped by gendered, sexualized identities. The "governed," or citizens of the geo-political space, simultaneously reject, transform, *and* reaffirm these dominant values. It is a quirky and subversive relationship on both sides, but illustrates well the brief and powerful words of Edward Glissant (Martiniquais intellectual and playwright) – "We demand the right to obscurity."

Notes

1 In this paper "Culture" is capitalized in reference to nationalist or bureacucratic definitions in order to differentiate it from my (anthropological) usage.

2 France's Overseas Departments are integrated more or less completely in the French legal and political systems. Martinique's Conseil Général's administrative powers are equal to those of any mainland French department.

3 See also Tocqueville (1945:311) for a discussion of the tension between the individual and the nation in an American context.

4 The visible differences in terms of living standards, dress, and overall infrastructure are not lost on Martiniquais who visit neighboring islands such as Dominica or St Lucia. I was told numerous times that with neighboring islands like this, no independence movement would ever succeed in Martinique.

5 One should not assume that these "staged" interpretations are passively consumed by the viewer – a more complex relationship exists between the stage and viewers' perceptions of themselves as Martiniquais men and women (Mankekar 1993:544).

6 In France, theater has been viewed since the Revolution as a means of communicating to and educating the masses about their responsibilities as members of the great nation of France. For an excellent analysis of the relationship between theater and the nation see Lorren Kruger (1992).

7 Most of these opinions emerged in homosocial gatherings – the majority of socializing in Martinique is homosocial. Also, these remarks were generally unsolicited by me in that I did not initiate or switch the conversation to male and female characteristics. Comments on the nature of men and women would often be made in passing or

in relation to another topic such as romantic relationships.

8   The hypermasculine Martiniquais and macho Latin American male are not identical. A primary feature of the Latin American *machista* is that his masculinity may be enhanced through his sexual conquests of other men, as long as he remains in the active or inserter position in anal intercourse and fellatio (Lancaster 1992:238). In Martinique, any admission or accusation of sexual relations between men threatens male status and reputation.

9   Masculinity is managed through other all-male activities as well, such as drinking, playing dominos, and sports.

10 One such alternative is the "civilized" man, a reference alluding to French/white identity, combining features of good education, dress style, passion and respect for women, and monogamy. One can find evidence of this male identity, in personal columns of a weekly publication in Fort-de-France, where women often describe their desired mate as "*un homme civilisé*." Unfortunately, personal columns don't provide enough information to determine the class and/or color of the advertiser, so it is difficult to surmise who this kind of male identity appeals to.

11 This is not to imply that a singular form of masculinity renders all "men" identical in public environments. Class and education may be manifested through clothing and conversation. Race creates different masculinities as well, although the primary distinction is between black and white or French and Martiniquais men

(see previous note). Nevertheless, I would still maintain that these variations operate within a restricted spectrum of masculinity with heterosexuality operating as a common core feature.

12 I do not wish to set up a Jungian opposition of persona/anima, where the former represents the "facade" or public presentation of an individual and the latter represents the "true" or inner soul of the individual. I am hesitant as to whether the "anima" can ever be truly accessed by the anthropologist – there are too many subjective factors involved in the relationship between anthropologist and informant to guarantee that the written analysis represents the "actual" truth. Hence I utilize public and private "personas."

13 Although never stated directly, I believe that Jean Claude's preference for white men was, for some, as much the source for their critique as was his "loose" sexual behavior. The role of race in the Martiniquais homosexual community merits closer scrutiny as it occupies a central role in the construction of desire, yet at the same time it is less definitive as a marker of social status than it is in the heterosexual world, due to the already peripheralized position of the homosexual community. Condemnation or approval of a homosexual relationship by other homosexuals carries little in the way of social consequences when any homosexual behavior is condemned by society at large.

14 I believe that Jean Claude was also angry at the fact that I had committed a social faux pas in transmitting gossip about someone to that someone.

References

Anderson, B.
   1991   Imagined Communities. London: Verso.
André, J.
   1982   Tuer sa fernme ou de l'ultime façon de devenit père. L'homme 22(2):69–86.
Arnold, James
   1981   Modernism and Negritude: The Poetry and Poetics of Aimé Césaire. Cambridge: Harvard University Press.
Arnold, James
   1994   The Erotics of Colonialism in Recent French West Indian Literature. New West Indian Guide 68:5–22.
Beriss, David
   1993   High Folkiore: Chalienges to the French Cultural World Order. Social Analysis 33:105–29.
Blerald. A.
   1988   La Question Nationale en Guadeloupe et en Martinique. Paris: Editions L. Harmattan.

Browell, S.
   1993   The Political and the Sexual Body: Chinese Nationalism and the Western Female. Paper prescured at the 92nd Annual meeting of the American Anthropological Association, November, Washington, D.C.
Browning, F.
   1993   The Culture of Desire. New York: Crown Publishers Inc.
Burton, R.
   1989   Sexual Stereotypes and National Representations in Martinique and Guadeloupe. Sussex. Unpublished Manuscript.
Burton, R.
   1990   "Debrouya pa Peché" or "Il y a Toujours Moyen de Moyenner": Assimilation and Opposition in Contemporary Martinique. Sussex: Unpublished Manuscript.

Capgras, V.
1989 La Politique Culturelle des Municipalités Martiniquaises. La Culture: Un Enjeu pour les Communes Martiniquaises. Mémoire de DEA. Fort-de-France: Université des Antilles Guyane.

Cohen, C. and E.F. Mascia-Lees
1993 The British Virgin Islands as Nation and Destination in Representing and Siting Identity in a Post-Colonial Caribbean Social Analysis 33:130–51.

Conseil Régional de la Martinique
1988 Consolider pour mieux Développer. Fort-de-France: Conseil Regional.

D'Emilio, John
1993 Capitalism and Gay Identity. In The Gay and Lesbian Studies Reader. H. Abelove M. Barale, and D. Halperin, eds. pp. 467–76. New York: Routledge.

Directions Régionales des Affaires Culturelles
n.d. Paris: La Documentation Française.

Drummond, L.
1980 The Cultural Continuum: A Theory of Intersystems. Man 15:352–74.

Dumont, Louis
1986 Essays on Individualism. Chicago: University of Chicago Press.

Dynes, Wayne
1992 Forward. In Oceanic Homosexualities. S. O. Murray, ed. pp. ix–xii. New York: Garland Publishing Inc.

Fabian, I.
1990 Power and Performance. Madison: University of Wisconsin Press

Foucault, Michel
1978 The History of Sexuality, Volume 1. New York: Random House.

France Antilles
1992 Special Elections, France-Antilles 23 March. pp. 1–4.

Gable, E., R. Handler, and A. Lawson
1992 On the uses of relativism: Fact, conjecture, and black and while histories at Colonial Williamsburg. American Ethnologist 19(4):791–805.

Handler, R.
1988 Nationalism and the Politics of Culture in Quebec. Madison: University of Wisconsin Press.

Hunt, Lynn
1992 Foucault's Subject in the History of Sexuality. In Discourses of Sexuality: From Aristotle to Aids. Domna Stanton, ed. Ann Arbor: University of Michigan Press.

Kruger, Lorren
1992 The National Stage: Theater, and Cultural Legitimation in England, France and America. Chicago: University of Chicago Press.

Lancaster, R.
1992 Life is Hard: Machismo, Danger and the Intimacy of Power in Nicaragua. Berkeley: University of California Press.

Lebovics, H.
1992 True France: The Wars over Cultural Identity 1900–1945. Ithaca: Cornell University Press.

Mankekar, P.
1993 National Texts and Gendered Livers: an Ethnography of Television Viewers in a North Indian City. American Ethnologist 20(3):543–63.

Mintz, Sidney
1989 Caribbean Transformations. New York: Columbia University Press.

Mosse, George
1985 Nationalism and Sexuality. New York: Howard Fertig.

Norton, Robert
1993 Culture and Identity in the South Pacific: A Comparative Analysis. Man 28:741–59.

Owens, J.
1976 Dread: The Rastafarians of Jamaica. London: Heinemann.

Parker, A., M. Russo, D. Sommer, and P. Yaeger
1992 Nationalisms and Sexualities. New York: Routledge.

Schnepel, Ellen
1993 The Other Tongue. The Other Voice: Language and Gender in the French Caribbean. Ethnic Groups 10:243–68.

Smith, R.T.
1988 Kinship and Class in the West Indies. Cambridge: University of Cambridge Press.

Tocqueville, Alexis de
1945 Democracy in America, Volume II. New York: Vintage Books.

Wangermee, Robert
1988 Rapport de Groupe D'Experts Europens. In La Politique Culturelle de la France. Conseil de l'Europe, ed. pp. 9–273. Paris: La Documentation Francaise.

Williams, B.
1990 Nationalism, Transnationalism, and the Problem of Cultural Inauthenticity. In Nationalist Ideologies and the Production of National Cultures. Richard G. Fox, ed. pp. 112–29. American Ethnological Society Monograph Series #2. Washington: American Anthropological Association.

Wilson, P.J.
1974 Oscar: An Enquiry into the Nature of Sanity. London: Routledge and Kegan Paul.

6

Reconstructing Racial Identity

Ethnicity, Color, and Class among Dominicans in the United States and Puerto Rico

Jorge Duany

When people move across state borders, they enter not only a different labor market and political structure but also a new system of social stratification by class, race, ethnicity, and gender. Migrants bring their own cultural conceptions of their identity, which often do not coincide with the ideological constructions of the receiving societies. As a mulatto Dominican colleague told me recently, she "discovered" that she was black only when she first came to the United States; until then she had thought of herself as an *india clara* (literally, a light Indian) in a country whose aboriginal population was practically exterminated in the sixteenth century.

For most Caribbean immigrants in the United States, race and color have played a crucial role in the formation of their cultural identities. Two different models of racial hegemony are juxtaposed in the process of moving from the Caribbean to the United States. On one hand, Caribbean migrants – especially those coming from the Spanish-speaking countries of Cuba, the Dominican Republic, and Puerto Rico – tend to use three main racial categories – black, white, and mixed – based primarily on skin color and other physical characteristics such as facial features and hair texture (Seda Bonilla, 1980). On the other hand, the dominant system of racial classification in the United States emphasizes a two-tiered division between whites and non-whites deriving from the rule of hypodescent – the assignment of the offspring of mixed races to the subordinate group (Harris, 1964; Winant, 1994). This clear-cut opposition between two cultural conceptions of racial identity is ripe for social and psychological conflict among Caribbean migrants, many of whom are of African or mixed background and are therefore defined as black or colored in the United States (Kasinitz, 1992; Safa, 1983).

I will argue that the massive exodus from the Dominican Republic has culturally redefined the migrants' racial identity. Whereas North Americans classify most Caribbean immigrants as black, Dominicans tend to perceive themselves as white, Hispanic, or other (including the folk term *indio*, to be discussed later). This contradiction between the public perception and the self-concept of Dominican migrants is one of their key problems in adapting to North American society. In Puerto Rico, although the traditional system of racial classification is similar to that of the Dominican

Republic, most Dominican immigrants are viewed as blacks or colored (in local lore, *prietos, morenos*, and *trigueños*). Thus, in both receiving countries, Dominicans face the intense stigmatization, stereotyping, prejudice, and discrimination to which all people of African origin are subjected.

The argument is organized in four main parts. First, I will briefly review the extensive literature on race relations in the Caribbean and the United States, with special attention to the Dominican Republic and Puerto Rico. This background will help to clarify the different ideological constructions of racial identity in the sending and receiving countries. Second, I will summarize two field studies I directed among Dominican immigrants in the United States and in Puerto Rico. These studies will provide empirical support for the claim that migration has restructured the cultural conceptions of racial identity among Dominicans living abroad. Third, I will compare the Dominican communities of Washington Heights in New York City and Santurce, Puerto Rico. The data will reveal different patterns of racial and ethnic segregation, prejudice and discrimination, cultural adaptation, and identity, despite the similarity of many of the migrants' socioeconomic characteristics. Finally, I will assess the incorporation of Dominicans into North American and Puerto Rican societies and its potential impact on the Dominican Republic. My main thesis is that the racialization of Dominican immigrants in the United States and Puerto Rico has reinforced the persistence of an ethnic identity against the prevailing racial order and has largely confined them to the secondary segment of the labor and housing markets.

The theoretical framework for my argument owes much to the discussion of the racial formation of the United States by Michael Omi and Howard Winant (1994). According to these writers, race is not a fixed essence, a concrete and objective entity, but rather a set of socially constructed meanings subject to change and contestation through power relations and social movements. Hence, racial identity is historically flexible and culturally variable, embedded in a particular social context (see Winant, 1994, for an attempt to reconceptualize the study of race

relations from a Gramscian and poststructuralist perspective). I would argue that the dominant racial ideologies in the United States, the Dominican Republic, and Puerto Rico categorize and interpret race in different ways. Consequently, Dominican immigrants in the United States and Puerto Rico tend to be treated as blacks, although most of them do not define themselves as such.

My comparative analysis of the Dominican diaspora is also informed by recent thinking on transnationalism (Basch, Schiller, and Szanton Blanc, 1994; Schiller, Basch, and Blanc-Szanton, 1992; Rouse, 1991). For present purposes, Schiller, Basch, and Blanc-Szanton (1992) provide the most useful definition of transnationalism as the process whereby migrants establish and maintain sociocultural connections across geopolitical borders. The migrants' social relations, cultural values, economic resources, and political activities span at least two nation-states. Such transnational links are often sustained by a constant back-and-forth movement of people facilitated by rapid transportation and communications systems. As a result, migrants have multiple identities that link them simultaneously to more than one nation. Transnationalism interacts with ethnicity, race, class, gender, and other variables, complicating the process of identity formation. Among other consequences, transnational migration often transforms the cultural definition of racial identity.

In this context, the wider significance of the Dominican experience in the United States and Puerto Rico is twofold. On one hand, the reconstruction of racial identity among Dominican immigrants confirms that all systems of racial classification are arbitrary and contingent on varying forms of cultural representation. As a terrain of ideological contestation, the perceived racial identity of individuals and groups does not necessarily coincide with their self-perception (Omi and Winant, 1994). On the other hand, the racialization of Dominicans in the United States and Puerto Rico is part of a larger phenomenon affecting Caribbean communities in the diaspora. The prevailing definition of these migrants as black and colored tends to exclude them as biologically different from and culturally alien to the receiving societies (Basch, Schiller, and Szanton Blanc, 1994). To the extent that Caribbean migrants are racialized, their efforts to become integrated into the host countries face more obstacles than those of other ethnic groups that are not so labeled.

Caribbean Versus US Racial Discourses

Much of the academic literature on Caribbean race relations is now several decades old (but see Oostindie, 1996, and Carrión, 1997, for recent collections revisiting the topic). The pioneering essays of the 1950s (Wagley, 1958), 1960s (Harris, 1964; Hoetink, 1967), and 1970s (Lowenthal, 1972; Mintz, 1974) contrasted the social construction of race in the Caribbean, the United States, and other countries of the Americas. The clearest picture emerging from these classic studies is that Caribbean societies tend to be stratified in terms of both class status and color gradations ranging from white to brown to black. Color distinctions in the Caribbean involve a complex inventory of physical traits such as skin pigmentation, hair form, and facial structure (Lowenthal, 1972; see also Smith, 1984). Phenotype and social status rather than biological descent define a person's racial identity, especially in the Spanish-speaking countries.

The Dominican Republic

Historians have shown that the present-day population of the Dominican Republic is the result of the intense mixture of peoples of European, African, and, to a lesser extent, Amerindian origin. By the end of the eighteenth century, the majority of Dominicans were classified as colored – that is, mulattos and blacks or, in contemporary parlance, *pardos* and *morenos*. Free blacks and mulattos displaced creole whites, African slaves, and Taíno as the leading sector of the colony of Hispaniola (Moya Pons, 1986; Franco, 1989). Today, informed sources agree that approximately 75 percent of the Dominican population consists of mulattos, with about 10 percent black and 15 percent white (compare Encyclopaedia Britannica, 1994; Ferguson, 1992; Black, 1986; Wiarda and Kryzanek, 1982). Like all racial statistics,

these estimates reveal more about the official views of race than about the actual extent of racial mixture or the presence of blacks in the country.

Regardless of the exact demographic composition of the Dominican Republic, the dominant discourse on national identity defines it as white, Hispanic, and Catholic. Scholars have traced the origins and development of a racist and xenophobic ideology in the Dominican Republic since the mid-nineteenth century. This ideology has produced an idealized view of the indigenous elements in Dominican culture, a systematic neglect of the contribution of African slaves and their descendants, increasing animosity toward Haitians and other black immigrants (such as the so-called *cocolos* from the eastern Caribbean), and a marked preference for Hispanic customs and traditions (Hoetink, 1994; Sagás, 1993; 1997; Alcántara Almánzar, 1987). As in other Hispanic Caribbean countries, racial prejudice and discrimination have been central features of the conventional wisdom on Dominican identity.

Under Rafael Trujillo's dictatorship (1930–61), the pro-Hispanic and anti-Haitian discourse became the official ideology of the Dominican state. The Cibao region – with its traditional peasantry, popular music, Hispanic folklore, and "white" physical appearance – became the romantic symbol of an "authentic" Dominican culture (Hoetink, 1994). Thus, the Dominican merengue, particularly in its Cibao variant, became a powerful icon of national identity (Duany, 1994a). Meanwhile, Dominican politicians and intellectuals associated with the Trujillo regime defined Haiti as the antithesis of the Dominican Republic. If Dominicans were supposed to be white, Haitians were black; if Dominicans were Hispanic, Haitians were African; if Dominicans spoke Spanish, Haitians spoke Créole; and if Dominicans were Catholic, Haitians were voodoo practitioners. This binary opposition represented Haitians as the other – as inferior, foreign, and savage. The category "black" disappeared altogether from the official and popular discourses on race in the Dominican Republic, except in reference to foreigners (Baud, 1996; Charles, 1992; del Castillo, 1984).

Nowadays, even the darkest-skinned Dominican is considered not black but *indio oscuro* (dark

Indian) or trigueño. As a result of this cultural conception, most Dominicans are declared to be white (*blanco*), Indian (indio), or a mixture of the two races (*mestizo*); only Haitians are considered "pure" blacks. A recent essay by Peter Roberts (1997) has analyzed the importance of the concept of indio for the construction of national identity in the Dominican Republic, as well as in Cuba and Puerto Rico. Stressing the indigenous roots of the Dominican nation helped to distinguish it from the Spanish metropolis as well as from neighboring Haiti. According to Ernesto Sagás (1993), the Dominican government now classifies the majority of Dominican citizens as indios. Thus, the term has become an official racial category in the Dominican Republic. The equivalent term *mulato*, referring to a mixture of white and black, is rarely used.

The academic literature contains numerous studies on the hostile relations between the Dominican Republic and Haiti (see the extensive bibliography in Lozano, 1992). The key historiographic issue has been the impact of the Haitian occupation of Santo Domingo (1822–44) on the formation of the Dominican nation-state (Moya Pons, 1992; Franco, 1989). Whereas most historians traditionally considered this period a traumatic collective experience, Harry Hoetink (1971) emphasized the positive impact of the Haitian occupation on Dominican race relations and cultural identity. One of the recurring themes of the sociological literature is the massive migration of Haitians to the Dominican Republic and their slavelike working conditions on the sugar and coffee plantations (see Báez Evertsz, 1986; Lozano and Báez Evertsz, 1992). An invidious system of occupational segregation has isolated Haitians in the worst-paid and least desirable jobs, such as cane cutting and construction work. In both instances, directing racial and ethnic prejudice at a foreign enemy – Haitians – helped to define and consolidate a Dominican nationalist project conceived by the dominant elite and filtered down to the popular sectors.

Although many Dominican intellectuals in the post-Trujillo era have rejected the myth of Haitian inferiority, the popular sectors continue to repudiate Haitian immigrants and Haiti in general. Lower-class Dominicans attribute all kinds of social problems and negative situations to the Haitian "invasion," including racial "degeneration." According to a young Dominican cook living in Puerto Rico, "All Dominicans were blonde and blue eyed before they got dark and mixed with the Haitians." The Haitian has acquired a mysterious and legendary status in Dominican folklore as a practitioner of obscure rites such as black magic and cannibalism. It will take time to eradicate firmly held beliefs and practices that exclude Haitians (and, by extension, blacks) from the accepted definition of national identity in the Dominican Republic (see Torres-Saillant, 1992–3; 1997; Sagás, 1993; 1997). Anti-Haitianism pervades the dominant discourse on Dominican identity, from popular religion, music, and literature to economic affairs, public policies, and party politics. One of the main problems faced by the presidential candidate of the Dominican Revolutionary Party, José Francisco Peña Gómez, has been his Haitian origin and black appearance. Although racism was not the only reason for Peña Gómez's defeat in 1996, it played a key role in the electoral campaign.

In sum, the Dominican system of racial classification has two peculiar features in a comparative Caribbean context. First, it does not identify local blacks as a separate category within the color spectrum but instead reserves that category for Haitians. Second, it blurs the distinctions among creole whites, light coloreds, and mulattos, thereby creating the impression of a predominantly white and Indian population. Through these discursive strategies, the system fosters the racial and cultural homogenization of the Dominican Republic vis-à-vis Haiti. Thus, the social construction of race and ethnicity is characterized by a strong reactive or oppositional identity. It is this sense of national pride and rejection of their own negritude that many Dominican migrants bring with them and must reevaluate when they confront the US model of racial stratification.

Puerto Rico

The best empirical study of Puerto Rican race relations remains Eduardo Seda Bonilla's pioneering fieldwork, conducted in the late 1950s and 1960s, although several essays have dealt with the racial question on the island and the

US mainland since then (see Sagrera, 1973; Zenón Cruz, 1974; Ginorio, 1979; Picó de Hernández et al., 1985; Díaz Quiñones, 1985; Rodríguez-Morazzani, 1996; V. Rodríguez, 1997). Seda Bonilla (1973) argued convincingly that most Puerto Ricans use phenotype rather than hypodescent as the main criterion for racial identity. Puerto Ricans tend to think of three main physical types – white, black, and mulatto – defined primarily by skin color, facial features, and hair texture (see also C. Rodríguez, 1989). Furthermore, whereas North Americans pay close attention to national origin in defining a person's ethnic identity, Puerto Ricans give a higher priority to birthplace and cultural orientation.

Thus, when Puerto Ricans move to the US mainland, they confront a different construction of their racial identity (Seda Bonilla, 1980). In the United States, Puerto Ricans are often grouped together with black and colored people. Those with mixed racial backgrounds lose their intermediate status in a white-nonwhite dichotomy. Light-skinned immigrants are some-times called "white Puerto Ricans," whereas dark-skinned immigrants are often treated like African Americans. Most are simply classified as "Pororicans" as if this were a distinct racial category. Like other ethnic minorities, Puerto Ricans in the United States have been thoroughly racialized (see V. Rodríguez, 1997; Rodríguez-Morazzani, 1996).

Statistically, the majority of the Puerto Rican population is white by local standards. Estimates of the white group on the island range from 73 percent (Seda Bonilla, 1980) to 80 percent of the population (Encyclopaedia Britannica, 1994), with an additional 8 percent black and 19 percent mulatto in Seda Bonilla's count. These statistics are open to debate because of the fluid definition of racial groups as well as the lack of recent official data on the island's racial composition. (In 1970, the Census Bureau dropped the racial identification question for Puerto Rico.) However, the available figures confirm that most Puerto Ricans perceive themselves as white rather than as black or mulatto.

In any case, study after study has shown that blacks are a stigmatized minority on the island, that they suffer from persistent prejudice and discrimination; that they tend to occupy the lower rungs of the class structure, and that they are subject to an ideology of progressive whitening (blanqueamiento) through intermarriage with lighter-skinned groups and a denial of their cultural heritage and physical characteristics (Seda Bonilla, 1973; Zenón Cruz, 1974; Picó de Hernández et al., 1985). Thus, the main difference between the Puerto Rican and North American models of racial stratification is not the treatment of blacks – who are accorded a subordinate status in both societies – but rather the mixed group. In Puerto Rico, light mulattos often pass for whites, whereas in the United States, this intermediate racial category does not even exist officially. The symbolic boundaries among whites, mulattos, and blacks seem more porous in Puerto Rico than in the United States.

New York-based Puerto Rican sociologist Clara Rodríguez reports that many members of the so-called Neo-Rican community resist being classified as either black or white and prefer to identify themselves as "other." In the 1980 Census, 48 percent of New York's Puerto Rican population chose this category, including alternative ethnic labels such as Hispanic, Spanish, and Boricua (C. Rodríguez, 1989, 1992; Rodríguez and Cordero-Guzmán, 1992). Hence, many Puerto Rican migrants and their descendants continue to employ a tripartite rather than a bipolar system of racial classification. Contrary to Seda Bonilla's (1980) prediction that the Neo-Rican community would split along color lines, most migrants reject their indiscriminate labeling as members of a single race (see also Ginorio, 1979). Rather than dividing themselves into white or black, most Puerto Ricans recognize that they are a multiracial or – to use Rodríguez's (1989) apt image – a "rainbow" people.

In sum, the Puerto Rican model of race relations has several distinguishing features. In contrast to North Americans, most Puerto Ricans consider racial identity not primarily a question of biological descent but rather one of physical appearance. As a result, a person of mixed racial background is not automatically assigned to the black group in Puerto Rico. Rather, racial classification depends largely on skin color and other visible characteristics such as the shape of the mouth, nose, and hair. Puerto Ricans have developed an elaborate racist vocabulary for referring to these characteristics. Socioeconomic variables such as occupation and education can also affect a person's racial identity. Furthermore, Puerto Ricans usually distinguish between blacks and mulattos, whereas North Americans tend to view both groups as colored or nonwhite. Finally, because of the proliferation of multiple and fluid physical types, Puerto Rico has not established a two-tiered institutionalized system of racial discrimination such as that of the United States. For example, neither the occupational nor the residential structures of Puerto Rican society segregates its members exclusively by color. As we shall see, the island's system of racial classification has distinct implications for the racial identity of Dominican migrants.

The United States

The preceding discussion has already alluded to the key features of the dominant model of racial formation in the United States. Scholars have debated whether this model resembles a caste system, especially as it operated in the Old South prior to the abolition of the Jim Crow laws in the 1950s. In any case, the North American system is unusual (comparable to South Africa's apartheid) in its terminological simplicity and intense separation between subordinate "racial" minorities and dominant ethnic groups. Historically, the black/white division has been rigidly defined in the United States through the rule of hypodescent (Omi and Winant, 1994). North American race relations have been characterized by institutionalized discrimination against so-called racial minorities such as African Americans, Native Americans, Latinos, and Asians, defined partly by their skin color and partly by their geographic origin.

The dominant racial discourse in the United States assigns an upper status to white groups of European origin and a lower status to black and brown groups from other regions, including the Caribbean and Latin America. Racial minorities such as Haitians and Chinese are stereotyped and marginalized more acutely than other ethnic groups in North American society. As a result, the social distance between such groups is much greater than that between, say, the Irish or Italians and English or Germans, who are all defined as "white ethnics." The racialization of Caribbean immigrants has slowed their structural and cultural assimilation into North American society. Recent studies have coined the terms "segmented assimilation" and "oppositional identity" to refer to the fate of racially defined minorities in the contemporary United States (see Portes, 1994, for a conceptual discussion and empirical data focusing on second-generation immigrants).

Residential segregation is a fundamental aspect of racial and ethnic relations in the United States (Massey and Denton, 1993). Black Americans have been subjected to the highest degree of racial segregation in major urban centers over the past five decades, and so have most Caribbean immigrants, who tend to be considered black or colored (Kasinitz, 1992). Recent studies have shown that Latinos, especially Puerto Ricans and dark-skinned immigrants, suffer from a similar disadvantage in the housing market of metropolitan areas such as New York, Philadelphia, Chicago, and Hartford (Santiago and Wilder, 1991; Santiago, 1992). Some scholars have even predicted that Latinos will become a "middle race" between whites and blacks in the United States (Domínguez, 1973).

Until now, no empirical study has systematically examined the impact of the North American system of racial stratification on the Dominican diaspora. The major publications have neglected the cultural redefinition of the migrants' racial identity in the United States (see Guarnizo, 1994; Grasmuck and Pessar, 1991; Portes and Guarnizo, 1991; Georges, 1990; Georges et al., 1989; del Castillo and Mitchell, 1987). An exception to this trend is Virginia Domínguez's (1973; 1978) comparative assessment of Cubans, Dominicans, and Puerto Ricans in Washington Heights during the 1960s. One reason for this oversight may be that researchers have usually focused on Dominican migrants as lower-class workers rather than as members of a "racial" minority. Most studies have underestimated a key variable in the incorporation of Dominican immigrants into the secondary segment of the US labor and housing markets: their public perception as blacks, colored, or nonwhite.

Studying Dominican Immigrants in the United States and Puerto Rico

The fieldwork reported in this article was conducted in three census blocks, two in Barrio Gandul in Santurce, a central city subdivision of the metropolitan area of San Juan, Puerto Rico, studied in 1990, and one in Washington Heights in upper Manhattan, the main borough of New York City, studied in 1993. (The research summarized here followed the guidelines for an alternative enumeration developed by the Center for Survey Methods Research at the US Census Bureau; see Brownrigg, 1990; Brownrigg and Fansler, 1990; for more methodological details, see Duany, Hernández Angueira, and Rey, 1995.) These blocks were selected because of their high concentration of Dominican residents, primarily residential use, and safety. The samples included all housing units and persons residing within the three blocks at the time of the fieldwork. The two blocks in Puerto Rico contained 325 persons, whereas the New York block contained 352 persons. Both sites were ethnically and racially mixed urban neighborhoods with a predominantly Hispanic population, primarily of Puerto Rican and Dominican origin.

Race, a matter of considerable unease among Dominicans and Puerto Ricans, was observed rather than asked of each respondent. Many informants would consider it offensive for someone to even question their racial identity. We therefore decided to rely on our own impressions of the residents' phenotypes. In San Juan, we classified each person's physical appearance as white, black, or mulatto (a mixture of black and white). In New York, we added a fourth category, mestizo (a mixture of Indian and white). Following our informants' practice, this classification was primarily based on the person's skin color. Although this method is not scientifically valid as a measure of biological descent, it offers an approximate assessment of the residents' racial identity.

At the beginning of our fieldwork in Santurce, we sought to elicit our informants' own constructions of their racial identity by asking them what race they considered themselves to belong to. Responses to this seemingly innocuous question ranged from embarrassment and amazement to

ambivalence and silence: many informants simply shrugged their shoulders and pointed to their arms, as if their skin color were obvious. When people referred to others' race, they often used ambiguous euphemisms ("He's a little darker than I") without making a definite commitment to a specific racial label. In North American racial terminology, most of our subjects would probably classify themselves as "other," that is, as neither white nor black. For the purposes of this fieldwork, it seemed culturally appropriate to collect data on racial identity based on consensually validated impressions of people's phenotypes as coded in Hispanic Caribbean societies such as Puerto Rico and the Dominican Republic.

Following this procedure, the Santurce sample had a larger proportion of white and black people, whereas the New York sample was predominantly mulatto (Table 6.1). This trend reflects the higher incidence of racial segregation in New York than in San Juan. With regard to ethnicity, two-thirds of the Santurce sample were of Puerto Rican origin, whereas four-fifths of the Manhattan sample were of Dominican origin. One-third of the residents in San Juan were born in the Dominican Republic compared with more than half of the residents in the New York site. Again, foreign immigrants were more highly concentrated in New York than in Santurce.

Comparing the Two Communities

Socioeconomic characteristics

The two samples were similar in their lower status occupational composition, with an overrepresentation of service and blue-collar workers (Table 6.2). In both cases, most of the residents held low-paying unskilled jobs, working, for example, as domestics, porters, waiters, and parking attendants. A small minority were better-paid skilled workers – professionals, technicians, managers, and administrators. A larger proportion of Santurce's residents (nearly 22 percent) was engaged in craft and repair work as, for example, carpenters, mechanics, and seamstresses, than in Washington Heights (13 percent). On the other hand, the Washington Heights sample had proportionately more (17 percent) operators and laborers than the Santurce sample (7 percent).

Table 6.1 Characteristics of the Samples (in percentages)

Characteristic	Santurce (N = 325)[a]	Washington Heights (N = 352)[b]
Gender		
Male	51.0	48.0
Female	49.0	52.0
Age		
0–10	14.1	28.6
11–20	12.5	19.6
21–30	13.5	19.6
31–40	16.8	12.2
41–50	11.1	10.7
51–60	10.1	6.5
61–70	12.1	5.4
71 and older	9.7	4.2
Color		
White	44.8	26.2
Black	33.3	7.2
Mulatto	21.8	63.4
Mestizo	–	
Ethnicity[c]		
Puerto Rican	63.0	2.9
Dominican	33.2	78.2
Other	3.7	17.9
Country of Birth		
Puerto Rico	62.9	2.9
Dominican Republic	32.0	57.2
United States	1.6	29.5
Other countries	3.5	10.4

Note: Some columns do not add up to 100 percent due to rounding.
[a] The total number of cases varies between 296 and 307, due to missing information.
[b] The total number of cases varies between 286 and 336, due to missing information.
[c] Refers to national origin, regardless of place of birth.

Overall, the Santurce residents – especially Puerto Ricans – are slightly better represented than the Washington Heights residents in the upper levels of the occupational structure.

The main socioeconomic contrast between the two communities is that a much larger proportion (18 percent) of Washington Heights residents worked in manufacturing than in Santurce

Table 6.2 Occupational Distribution of Employed Residents (in percentages)

Occupation	Santurce (N = 107)	Washington Heights (N = 105)
Professionals and technicians	8.4	7.6
Managers and administrators	4.7	1.0
Office workers	6.5	5.7
Salespersons	8.4	6.7
Craft and repair workers	21.5	13.3
Operators and laborers	6.5	17.1
Service workers	43.9	48.6
Total	99.9	100.0

Note: The first column does not add up to 100 percent due to rounding.

(1 percent). Compared with those in New York, Dominicans in Puerto Rico were more likely to work in commerce, repair services, construction, and transportation. These findings coincide with those of previous studies showing the importance of light manufacturing, especially the garment industry, for New York's Dominican community (Grasmuck and Pessar, 1991; Hernández, Rivera-Batiz, and Agodini, 1995). The data also confirm the predominance of the service sector, including public administration and retail trade, in Santurce (Duany, 1990).

In short, the socioeconomic characteristics of the two samples for this study were predominantly those of a lower-class population. The results suggest that most of the residents of Barrio Gandul and Washington Heights were employed in the secondary segment of the labor market, segregated by class, race, ethnicity, gender, and age. This segment is characterized by low wages, little prestige, poor working conditions, lack of occupational mobility, few fringe benefits, high turnover, and little employment security. The concentration of Dominican immigrants in the secondary segment of the labor market was even more pronounced than for other residents.

Racial and ethnic segregation

Both the New York and San Juan sites represented multiracial and multi-ethnic samples.

According to our estimate, Barrio Gandul was about evenly divided between white (45 percent) and "colored" residents (55 percent), including blacks and mulattos in the latter category. Most of the white residents of Barrio Gandul (87 percent) were Puerto Rican, whereas more than half of the blacks and mulattos were Dominican (52 percent). Thus, the color line reinforced ethnic divisions within Barrio Gandul. Although more than one-third of the Puerto Rican population of Barrio Gandul was not white in physical appearance, the influx of Dominican and other foreign immigrants had increased the proportion of dark-skinned residents. However, the Santurce community did not separate blacks, whites, and mulattos or Dominicans and Puerto Ricans as strictly as in New York. This trend toward racial and ethnic integration was due partly to the neighborhood's historical background and partly to the way in which racial identity is constructed in Puerto Rico as opposed to the United States.

Barrio Gandul was established as a working-class community of Santurce between 1900 and 1930. The area's original inhabitants were former black slaves who leased the land of a wealthy landowner, Vicente Balbás Peña, whose heirs still own much of the property. Many of the older residents of Barrio Gandul were racially diverse immigrants from other parts of Puerto Rico. People of different color lived within the same streets, buildings, and even homes. Interracial relations tended to be cordial, friendly, and sometimes intimate. Married couples and some parents and children often had different phenotypes. Within the neighborhood, skin color was loosely correlated with socioeconomic status – for instance, whites tended to be home-owners, while blacks were usually tenants – but the two variables were not completely coterminous. Residents were sufficiently diverse in color and class to counter any one-to-one connection in the local stratification system. Since its inception, Barrio Gandul had been a multiracial lower class neighborhood.

With regard to ethnic composition, Barrio Gandul had one of the highest proportions of foreign immigrants in Santurce and probably in Puerto Rico. As a result, it had earned the sobriquet of "Little Quisqueya" (Quisqueya being the indigenous name of the island of Hispaniola, shared by Haiti and the Dominican Republic). The 1990 Census found that almost 27 percent of the residents of Barrio Gandul had been born outside of Puerto Rico (US Department of Commerce, 1994: Table 3). Our 1987 survey found that about 25 percent of the population of Barrio Gandul had been born in the Dominican Republic (Duany, 1990). Our most recent enumeration of the two census blocks found that a third of the residents were Dominican in origin. Apart from the Dominican Republic, foreign immigrants came from St Kitts, Anguilla, Dominica, Cuba, and Colombia. Of the Puerto Rican residents, only a few had been born in the United States. Thus, Barrio Gandul was not a predominantly Dominican neighborhood like some parts of Washington Heights.

Santurce's Dominican community was concentrated in run-down apartment buildings and poorly maintained areas of the neighborhood. In Barrio Gandul, Dominicans clustered in the worst streets and quarters and Puerto Ricans in the better maintained areas. However, we did not find a single street or building in Barrio Gandul exclusively occupied by Dominican immigrants. Whether or not they liked it, Puerto Ricans lived side by side with Dominicans in most residential areas of Santurce. Despite their growing presence in some lower class neighborhoods, Dominican immigrants did not dominate any area of San Juan as completely as in Washington Heights. Again, this pattern of residential integration suggests that racial identity is constructed differently in the two places.

In Washington Heights, we classified three-fourths of the residents as black, mulatto, or mestizo. The vast majority of the mulattos were Dominican immigrants and their descendants (96 percent). Four out of five residents of Washington Heights were of Dominican origin, compared with one out of three in Barrio Gandul. The degree of separation between New York Dominicans and other ethnic and racial groups was striking. Washington Heights was fast becoming a Dominican enclave, increasingly segregated from native whites, African Americans, and other Hispanics such as Puerto Ricans. This trend is related to a long history of institutionalized housing discrimination against black immigrants in North American urban centers (Massey and Denton, 1993; Kasinitz, 1992). In less than 50 years, the ethnic and racial composition of the neighborhood had shifted dramatically, with white ethnic groups such as Irish Catholics and German Jews being replaced by nonwhite minorities such as African Americans and Latinos.

Since the 1950s, Washington Heights had deteriorated physically and socially. Real estate values had plummeted as many buildings, especially in the southeastern part of the neighborhood, had become dilapidated. The rapid increase in the number of Hispanic and black residents had accelerated the flight of white residents to the suburbs. After 1965, Dominicans arrived en masse, attracted by the neighborhood's low rents, spacious apartments, and transportation facilities. Hispanics, especially Dominicans and to a lesser extent Puerto Ricans, Cubans, Ecuadorans, Salvadorans, and Mexicans, had replaced non-Hispanic whites as the leading sector of the population in Washington Heights.

Prejudice and discrimination
The United States, the Dominican Republic, and Puerto Rico have all been dominated by an ideology of white supremacy and black inferiority since early colonial times, but this ideology is expressed in different ways, especially in popular attitudes and practices concerning racial mixture and intermarriage. In the Hispanic Caribbean, prejudice and discrimination are primarily targeted at blacks, not mulattos. In the United States, the two racial categories are usually lumped together. As a result, light-skinned Dominican mulattos have better prospects for social acceptance in Puerto Rico than in the United States. For dark-skinned migrants, however, it is equally difficult to integrate into Puerto Rican society.

My fieldnotes for Barrio Gandul are full of references to the intermediate physical types of many residents, including mulato claro, mulato oscuro, moreno, trigueño, and prieto. For statistical purposes, all of these terms are usually grouped under the generic label "mulatto," but Puerto Ricans and Dominicans make finer social distinctions in their daily lives. For instance,

residents used the terms *grifo, jabao,* and *colorao* to refer to various combinations of hair types and skin tones. This fluid gradation of phenotypes makes it difficult to discriminate against intermediate groups exclusively on the basis of color and other physical attributes. In contrast, the dominant racial dichotomy in the United States between whites and nonwhites does not do justice to the vast majority of Dominicans, who have African as well as European backgrounds and range phenotypically across the entire color spectrum from black to brown to white. From a North American perspective, Washington Heights appears as an undifferentiated black neighborhood, albeit with a Hispanic cultural atmosphere. From a Dominican standpoint, the neighborhood is as racially diverse as the Dominican Republic.

Racial prejudice and discrimination have forced many Dominicans in New York to settle in areas adjacent to African American concentrations such as Hamilton Heights and Harlem. Despite physical proximity, most Dominicans strive to distance themselves culturally from African Americans by speaking Spanish, dancing the merengue, rejecting black hairstyles and speech patterns, and associating primarily with other Latinos. In the 1990 Census, only about 26 percent of New York's Dominicans classified themselves as black (*New York Newsday*, 1993). However, younger members of the second generation often adopt the black dialect, hip-hop fashion, and rap music popular among African American teenagers. Some dark-skinned Dominicans are following the path of a segmented assimilation in which the main frame of reference is an adversarial African American culture rather than a mainstream white identity (see Portes, 1994). Slowly but surely, Dominican immigrants are developing an awareness of their black roots and reaching out to other Caribbean and Latino peoples – including the traditionally despised Haitians (see Torres-Saillant, 1992–3).

In Puerto Rico, Dominicans encounter a system of racial classification and stratification similar to that of their home country. Thus, Barrio Gandul is not a black ghetto in the sense that it is not characterized exclusively by a black or even colored population; it is segregated primarily along class lines rather than in terms of skin color or national origin. However, to the extent that "money whitens," residents' lower-class status strengthens their public perception as black and mulatto. Ethnicity, color, and class reinforce each other in Barrio Gandul.

Despite the undeniable presence of racial prejudice and discrimination in Puerto Rico, anti-Dominican sentiment has proven a more formidable barrier to interethnic relations. Many Puerto Rican residents harbor strong resentment against foreign newcomers to the island, especially Dominicans. Some Puerto Ricans openly call Dominicans dirty, loud, greasy, pigs, and other insulting epithets. An ever-expanding repertoire of ethnic jokes and folk stories perpetuates the myth of the dumb, ignorant country bumpkin from the Cibao (see Iturrondo, 1994; Mejía Pardo, 1993). Local complaints of Dominican immigrants range from their playing music loud at night and throwing garbage in the streets to dominating the drug trafficking and prostitution businesses. According to one Puerto Rican resident of Santurce, "Dominicans have damaged the neighborhood." Ironically, many Puerto Rican stereotypes of Dominican immigrants have earlier been applied to Haitians in the Dominican Republic and Puerto Ricans in the United States.

Cultural adaptation and identity

In both New York and Santurce, Dominican immigrants strongly resist assimilation into the dominant culture. This tendency is partly a response to racial and ethnic exclusion. Washington Heights has reproduced many aspects of the migrants' traditional lifestyle and institutions, from their political parties and trade unions to their hometown clubs and religious practices. In the early 1980s, Eugenia Georges (1984) counted 125 voluntary associations, reaching about 8 percent of New York's Dominican community, especially in Washington Heights. Some current observers even call the neighborhood "Quisqueya Heights" to emphasize its predominant cultural orientation toward the Dominican Republic.

Quisqueya Heights is an eminently appropriate term for this transnational space, characterized by the constant crossover of Dominican and North American identities, the selective re-creation of key elements of Dominican society, and the incorporation of new cultural traits from the United States. The combination of Spanish and English signs in many business establishments and the musical interpenetration of merengue and rap exemplify the transformation of the cultural landscape by Dominican immigrants. Most of my Dominican informants in Washington Heights ate mostly Dominican food, spoke mostly Spanish at home, shopped mostly at Dominican grocery stores, belonged to the Catholic church, listened mostly to Spanish radio, and watched mostly Spanish TV (Duany, 1994b). Many Dominican homes and businesses had small shrines with images of their favorite Catholic saints and the Virgin Mary in a corner of the main hall or a private room. Moreover, most respondents (84 percent) identified themselves as Dominican, not American or even Dominican-American. None used the derogatory term "Dominican-York" popular in the Dominican Republic to refer to return migrants (Guarnizo, 1994). Most remained more firmly attached to Dominican rather than North American culture, although they increasingly mixed the two. The vast majority of the immigrants had not yet become US citizens. Only 18 percent of the Dominicans legally admitted to the United States in 1977 were naturalized by 1989 (*New York Times*, 1993). Two out of three respondents said they would like to go back to live in the Dominican Republic. Many traveled back and forth between New York and Santo Domingo to visit relatives living in both places.

In Barrio Gandul, Dominicans had also re-created a large share of their cultural repertoires, although not as extensively as in Washington Heights. The smaller size of Santurce's Dominican community, its greater geographic dispersion, and its stronger affinities with Puerto Rican culture help to explain this difference. For instance, about 40 Dominican associations of various sizes have been recorded in Puerto Rico (José Germán Gómez, personal communication, March 16, 1995) compared with the 125 counted by Georges in New York in 1984.

Dominicans in Barrio Gandul ate their traditional *mangú*, read their national newspapers, danced the merengue, and supported their Dominican political parties. They were not well integrated into Puerto Rican community institutions such as schools, churches, and voluntary associations. The area's two main formal organizations, the Residents' and Business Associations, excluded Dominicans, and most Dominicans in Barrio Gandul had married compatriots. The relations between the two groups were tinged with mutual suspicion and tension.

Despite their physical proximity, Dominican immigrants tend to be culturally isolated and socially distant from Puerto Rican residents. This insulation contributes to the popular stereotype of Dominicans as strange, alien, dangerous, and incomprehensible (Mejía Pardo, 1993). Like Haitians in the Dominican Republic, Dominicans in Puerto Rico are becoming scapegoats for underlying racial tensions. As a defensive strategy, many immigrants are reasserting their own cultural background. This move may be taken as an example of what has been called an oppositional or reactive identity (Portes, 1994; Waters, 1994). Cultural differences between Dominicans and Puerto Ricans are expressed both visually and musically. Symbolic icons such as the national flag and folk art of the Dominican Republic, as well as the merengue, are conspicuously displayed by Dominican homes and businesses. Dominican cafeterias and bars are places not only to eat and drink but also to meet with one's compatriots to talk about Dominican politics, share important information about jobs and housing, and reaffirm one's cultural identity.

As in New York, few Dominican immigrants in Puerto Rico have become US citizens. About 8 percent of the Dominicans legally admitted to Puerto Rico between 1966 and 1986 were naturalized (Duany, 1990: 30). Furthermore, a large proportion of the Dominican community in Santurce (about a third, in our conservative estimate) consists of undocumented immigrants who are not well integrated into the host society. Geographic proximity, cultural similarities, and circular migration between the Dominican Republic and Puerto Rico have given rise to a transnational circuit between the two islands.

Conclusion

Transnational migration often calls into question immigrants' conceptions of ethnic, racial, and national identities. In the Dominican Republic, most people perceive themselves as dark-skinned whites or light mulattos; only Haitians are considered black. The Dominican system of racial classification, labeling people along a wide color continuum ranging from black to white, clashes with the racial dualism prevalent in the United States. For most Dominican migrants, who have some degree of racial mixture, the rule of hypodescent means that they are considered black, nonwhite, or colored. Through a profound ideological transformation, the so-called indios suddenly become black, Hispanic, or "other." The data presented here suggest that most of the Dominicans who identify themselves as blacks in New York would probably call themselves indios in their home country. This process of self-redefinition is, in Frank Moya Pons's (1986: 247) graphic expression, a "traumatic racial experience."

Dominicans in Puerto Rico encounter less cognitive dissonance regarding their racial identity than in the United States. Immigrant Dominicans, like native Puerto Ricans, are classified in terms of a complex system that takes into account skin pigmentation, hair texture, facial features, and social class. This cultural conception does not automatically assume that all Dominicans are black or that they can be divided neatly along color lines. Rather, Puerto Ricans traditionally adopt a flexible definition that recognizes multiple and heterogeneous racial groups, especially among intermediate types. Still, the dark skin color and other "African" features of most Dominican immigrants, together with their low occupational status, place them at the bottom of the Puerto Rican stratification system.

The racialization of Dominican immigrants has been a prime obstacle to their successful incorporation into the labor and housing markets of the United States and Puerto Rico. Although many Dominicans oppose their classification as colored, some have become increasingly aware of themselves as an Afro-Caribbean people. Migrants' general response to external labels has been to emphasize racial diversity within their community as well as the cultural bonds of solidarity among Dominicans of different skin colors. The persistence of a Dominican identity in the United

States may be interpreted in part as resistance to the prevailing racial order.

The incorporation of Dominican immigrants into Puerto Rican society has been hampered by their class composition as well as their racial identity. Xenophobia and racism have increased with Dominican immigration over the past three decades. The age-old stereotypes of black Puerto Ricans are now extended to Dominican immigrants, who in turn attribute them to Haitians – for example, stupidity, uncleanliness, and ugliness (see Zenón Cruz, 1974, for a complete catalogue of racial infamies in Puerto Rico). The social construction of race and ethnicity in contemporary Puerto Rico increasingly conflates black with Dominican. Still, Puerto Rican society segregates Dominicans not primarily by skin color or national origin but by social class. Barrio Gandul is neither a black ghetto like Harlem nor an ethnic neighborhood like Washington Heights.

The theoretical implications of this comparative case study are numerous, but I can only underline three of them here. First, transnational migrants face different, often conflicting, definitions of their racial identity in the sending and receiving societies. This ideological discrepancy confirms the absence of any essential characteristics or fixed meanings in racial discourses and focuses attention on the socially constructed and invented nature of racial classification systems. Second, regardless of their imaginary and arbitrary character, cultural conceptions of racial identity have a practical and material impact when they are applied to concrete groups and individuals in social interaction. The racialization of Caribbean immigrants in the United States and elsewhere places them in a disadvantageous position in the labor and housing markets and excludes them from the hegemonic cultural practices of the receiving nation-states. Finally, the immigrants' lower-class standing reinforces their public perception as ethnic and racial outsiders. This intersection of ethnicity, color, and class makes it harder for Caribbean diaspora communities to shed their multiple stigmas.

At this point, it is difficult to assess the impact of the cultural redefinition of the migrants' racial identity on the Dominican Republic. More than two decades ago, the distinguished Dominican historian Frank Moya Pons (1986) claimed that massive migration had not eroded the island's sense of identity. Later, the New York-based Dominican literary critic Silvio Torres-Saillant (1992–3) went beyond this to propose that Dominican identity is reasserted in the diaspora against a backdrop of ethnic and racial oppression. In my view, increasing numbers of Dominicans in the United States and Puerto Rico are being forced to confront racially exclusive conceptions and practices, framed in the language either of biological descent or of physical appearance.

By and large, the Dominican diaspora has actively resisted its subordination as a racialized other and attempted to redefine the terms of its incorporation into the host societies. Whether this effort results in asserting that Dominicans are part of a middle race such as Latinos or Hispanics (Domínguez, 1973), making common cause with African Americans on the basis of their colored status, or embracing a wider pan-Caribbean identity that includes Haitians has yet to be determined. For the moment, transnational migration has transformed the cultural conceptions of racial identity among Dominicans in the United States and Puerto Rico. For many racially mixed immigrants, coming to America has meant coming to terms with their own, partially suppressed, sometimes painful, but always liberating sense of negritude.

References

Alcántara Almánzar, José
    1987 "Black images in Dominican literature." *New West Indian Guide* 61(3–4): 161–73.
Báez Evertsz, Franc
    1986 *Braceros haitianos en la República Dominicana*. 2nd ed. Santo Domingo: Instituto Dominicano de Investigaciones Sociales.

Báez Evertsz, Franc and Frank D'Oleo Ramírez
    1986 *La emigración de dominicanos a Estados Unidos: determinantes socio-económicos y consecuencias*. Santo Domingo: Fundación Friedrich Ebert.
Basch, Linda, Nina Glick Schiller, and Cristina Szanton Blanc
    1994 *Nations Unbound: Transnational Projects,*

Postcolonial Predicaments, and Deterritorialized States. Basel: Gordon and Breach.

Baud, Michiel
1996 "'Constitutionally white': the forging of a national identity in the Dominican Republic," pp. 121–51 in Gert Oostindie (ed.), *Ethnicity in the Caribbean: Essays in Honor of Harry Hoetink*. London: Macmillan Caribbean.

Black, Jan Knippers
1986 *The Dominican Republic: Politics and Development in an Unsovereign State*. Boston: Allen and Unwin.

Brownrigg, Leslie A.
1990 "1990 guidelines for the alternative enumeration. Part I. Geography and physical space." Washington, DC: Center for Survey Methods Research, Bureau of the Census.

Brownrigg, Leslie A. and Elaine Fansler
1990 "1990 guidelines for the alternative enumeration. Part 3. Behavioral observations." Washington, DC: Center for Survey Methods Research, Bureau of the Census.

Carrión, Juan Manuel (ed.)
1997 *Ethnicity, Race, and Nationality in the Caribbean*. San Juan: Institute of Caribbean Studies, University of Puerto Rico.

Charles, Carolle
1992 "La raza: una categoría significativa en el proceso de inserción de los trabajadores haitianos en República Dominicana," pp. 145–68 in Wilfredo Lozano (ed.), *La cuestión haitiana en Santo Domingo: migración internacional, desarrollo y relaciones inter-estatales entre Haití y República Dominicana*. Santo Domingo: Facultad Latinoamericana de Ciencias Sociales.

del Castillo, José
1984 *Ensayos de sociología dominicana*. Santo Domingo: Taller.

del Castillo, José, and Christopher Mitchell (eds.)
1987 *La inmigración dominicana en los Estados Unidos*. Santo Domingo: CENAPEC.

Díaz Quiñones, Arcadio
1985 "Tomás Blanco: Racismo, historia, esclavitud," pp. 13–91 in *El prejuicio racial en Puerto Rico*. Río Piedras: Huracán.

Domínguez, Virginia
1973 "Spanish-speaking Caribbeans in New York: 'The middle race.'" *Revista/Review Interamericana* 3(2): 135–42.

Domínguez, Virginia
1978 "Show your colors: Ethnic divisiveness among Hispanic Caribbean migrants." *Migration Today* 6(1): 5–9.

Duany, Jorge (ed.)
1990 *Los dominicanos en Puerto Rico: migración en la semi-periferia*. Río Piedras: Huracán.

Duany, Jorge
1994a "Ethnicity, identity, and music: An anthropological analysis of the Dominican merengue," pp. 65–98 in Gerard Béhague (ed.), *Music and Black Ethnicity: The Caribbean and South America*. Miami: North-South Center, University of Miami.

Duany, Jorge
1994b *Quisqueya on the Hudson: The Transnational Identity of Dominicans in Washington Heights*. New York: Dominican Studies Institute, City University of New York.

Duany, Jorge, Luisa Hernández Angueira, and César A. Rey
1995 *El Barrio Gandul: economía subterránea y migración indocumentada en Puerto Rico*, Caracas: Nueva Sociedad.

Encyclopaedia Britannica
1994 "1994 Britannica World Data," in *1994 Book of the Year*. Chicago: Encyclopaedia Britannica.

Ferguson, James
1992 *Dominican Republic: Beyond the Lighthouse*. London: Latin America Bureau.

Franco, Franklin J.
1989 *Los negros, los mulatos y la nación dominicana*. 8th ed. Santo Domingo: Editora Nacional.

Georges, Eugenia
1984 *New Immigrants and the Political Process: Dominicans in New York*. Center for Latin American and Caribbean Studies, New York University, Occasional Paper 45.

Georges, Eugenia
1990 *The Making of a Transnational Community: Migration, Development, and Cultural Change in the Dominican Republic*. New York: Columbia University Press.

Georges, Eugenia, Eric M. Larson, Sara J. Mahler, Christopher Mitchell, Patricia R. Pessar, Teresa A. Sullivan, and Robert Warren
1989 *Dominicanos ausentes: Cifras, políticas, condiciones sociales*. Santo Domingo: Fundación Friedrich Ebert.

Ginorio, Angela Beatriz
1979 "A comparison of Puerto Ricans in New York with native Puerto Ricans and Native Americans on two measures of acculturation: Gender role and racial identification." PhD diss., Fordham University.

Grasmuck, Sherri and Patricia R. Pessar
1991 *Between Two Islands: Dominican International Migration*. Berkeley: University of California Press.

Guarnizo, Luis E.
1994 "*Los dominicanyorks*: The making of a binational society." *Annals of the American Academy of Political and Social Science* 533: 70–86.

Harris, Marvin
1964 *Patterns of Race in the Americas*. New York: Norton.

Hernández, Ramona, Francisco Rivera-Batiz, and Roberto Agodini
1995 *Dominican New Yorkers: A Socioeconomic Profile*. New York: Dominican Studies Institute, City University of New York.

Hoetink, Harry
1967 *Caribbean Race Relations: A Study of Two Variants*. London: Oxford University Press.

Hoetink, Harry
1971 "The Dominican Republic in the 19th century: some notes on stratification, immigration, and race," pp. 96–121 in Magnus Mörner (ed.), *Race and Class in Latin America*. New York: Columbia University Press.

Hoetink, Harry
1994 *Santo Domingo y el Caribe: Ensayos sobre cultura y sociedad*. Santo Domingo: Fundación Cultural Dominicana.

Iturrondo, Milagros
1994 " 'San Ignacio de la Yola' . . . y los dominicanos (en Puerto Rico)." *Homines* 17(1–2): 234–40.

Kasinitz, Philip
1992 *Caribbean New York: Black Immigrants and the Politics of Race*. Ithaca: Cornell University Press.

Lowenthal, David
1972 *West Indian Societies*. New York: Oxford University Press.

Lozano, Wilfredo (ed.)
1992 *La cuestión haitiana en Santo Domingo: migración internacional, desarrollo y relaciones inter-estatales entre Haití y República Dominicana*. Santo Domingo: Facultad Latinoamericana de Ciencias Sociales.

Lozano, Wilfredo and Franc Báez Evertsz
1992 *Migración internacional y economía cafetalera: estudio sobre la migración estacional de trabajadores haitianos a la cosecha cafetalera en la República Dominicana*. 2nd ed. Santo Domingo: Centro de Planificación y Acción Ecuménica.

Massey, Douglas S. and Nancy A. Denton
1993 *American Apartheid: Segregation and the Making of the Underclass*. Cambridge: Harvard University Press.

Mejía Pardo, Diana María
1993 "Macroestructuras, superestructuras y proposiciones de opiniones en 17 relatos puertorriqueños acerca de dominicanos." Master's thesis, University of Puerto Rico, Río Piedras.

Mintz, Sidney W.
1974 *Caribbean Transformations*. Chicago: Aldine.

Moya Pons, Frank
1986 *El pasado dominicano*. Santo Domingo: Fundación J. A. Caro Alvarez.

Moya Pons, Frank
1992 "Las tres fronteras: Introducción a la frontera domínico-haitiana," pp. 17–32 in Wilfredo Lozano (ed.), *La cuestión haitiana: Migración internacional, desarrollo y relaciones interestatales entre Haití y República Dominicana*. Santo Domingo: Facultad Latinoamericana de Ciencias Sociales.

New York Newsday
1993 "Trying to make sense of census." June 24.

New York Times
1993 "Immigrants forgoing citizenship while pursuing American dream." July 25.

Omi, Michael and Howard Winant
1994 *Racial Formation in the United States: From the 1960s to the 1990s*. 2nd ed. New York: Routledge.

Oostindie, Gert (ed.)
1996 *Ethnicity in the Caribbean: Essays in Honor of Harry Hoetink*. London: Macmillan Caribbean.

Picó de Hernández, Isabel, Marcia Rivera, Carmen Parrilla, Jeannette Ramos de Sánchez Villela, and Isabelo Zenón
1985 *Discrimen por color, sexo y origen nacional en Puerto Rico*. Río Piedras: Centro de Investigaciones Sociales, Universidad de Puerto Rico.

Portes, Alejandro (ed.)
1994 *The New Second Generation. International Migration Review* 28(4).

Portes, Alejandro and Luis E. Guarnizo
1991 *Capitalistas del trópico: La inmigración en los Estados Unidos y el desarrollo de la pequeña empresa en la Repúlica Dominicana*. Santo Domingo: Facultad Latinoamericana de Ciencias Sociales.

Roberts, Peter
1997 "The (re)construction of the concept of 'indio' in the national identities of Cuba, the Dominican Republic, and Puerto Rico," pp. 99–120 in Lowell Fiet and Janette Becerra (eds.), *Caribe 2000: Definiciones, identidades y culturas regionales y/o nacionales*. Río Piedras: Facultad de Humanidades, Universidad de Puerto Rico.

Rodríguez, Clara E.
1989 *Puerto Ricans: Born in the U.S.A.* Boston: Unwin Hyman.

Rodríguez, Clara E.
1992 "Race, culture, and Latino 'otherness' in the 1980 census." *Social Science Quarterly* 73(4): 930–7.

Rodríguez, Clara E. and Héctor Cordero-Guzmán
1992 "Placing race in context." *Ethnic and Racial Studies* 15(4): 523–42.

Rodríguez, Víctor M.
1997 "The racialization of Puerto Rican ethnicity in the United States," pp. 233–73 in Juan Manuel Carrión (ed.), *Ethnicity, Race, and Nationality in the Caribbean*. San Juan: Institute of Caribbean Studies, University of Puerto Rico.

Rodríguez-Morazzani, Roberto P.
1996 "Beyond the rainbow: mapping the discourse on Puerto Ricans and 'race.'" *Centro* 8(1–2): 151–69.

Rouse, Roger
1991 "Mexican migration and the social space of postmodernism." *Diaspora* 1(1): 8–23.

Safa, Helen I.
1983 "Caribbean migration to the United States: Cultural identity and the process of assimilation," pp. 47–73 in Edgar Gumbert (ed.), *Different People: Studies in Ethnicity and Education.* Atlanta: Center for Cross-Cultural Education, Georgia State University.

Sagás, Ernesto
1993 "A case of mistaken identity: *antihaitianismo* in the Dominican Republic." *Latinamericanist* 29(1): 1–5.

Sagás, Ernesto
1997 "The development of *antihaitianismo* into a dominant ideology during the Trujillo era," pp. 96–121 in Juan Manuel Carrión (ed.), *Ethnicity, Race, and Nationality in the Caribbean.* San Juan: Institute of Caribbean Studies, University of Puerto Rico.

Sagrera, Martín
1973 *Racismo y política en Puerto Rico: la desintegración interna y externa de un pueblo.* Río Piedras: Edil.

Santiago, Anne M.
1992 "Patterns of Puerto Rican segregation and mobility." *Hispanic Journal of Behavioral Sciences* 14(1): 107–33.

Santiago, Anne and Margaret G. Wilder
1991 "Residential segregation and links to minority poverty: The case of Latinos in the United States." *Social Problems* 38(4): 492–515.

Schiller, Nina Glick, Linda Basch, and Cristina Blanc-Szanton (eds.)
1992 *Towards a Transnational Perspective on Migration: Race, Ethnicity, and Nationalism Reconsidered.* New York: New York Academy of Sciences.

Seda Bonilla, Eduardo
1973 *Los derechos civiles en la cultura puertorriqueña.* 2nd ed. Río Piedras: Bayoán.

Seda Bonilla, Eduardo
1980 *Réquiem para una cultura.* 4th ed. Río Piedras: Bayoán.

Smith, M. G.
1984 *Culture, Race, and Class in the Commonwealth Caribbean.* Mona, Jamaica: Department of Extra-Mural Studies, University of the West Indies.

Torres-Saillant, Silvio
1992–3 "Cuestión haitiana y supervivencia moral dominicana." *Punto y Coma* 4(2): 195–206.

Torres-Saillant, Silvio
1997 "Hacia una identidad racial alternativa en la sociedad dominicana." *Op. Cit.: Revista del Centro de Investigaciones Históricas* (University of Puerto Rico, Río Piedras) 9: 235–52.

US Department of Commerce, Bureau of the Census
1994 *1990 Census of Population and Housing: Population and Housing Characteristics of Census Tracts and Block Numbering Areas, San Juan-Caguas, PR CMSA.* Washington, DC: Government Printing Office.

Wagley, Charles
1958 *Minorities in the New World.* New York: Columbia University Press.

Waters, Mary C.
1994 "Ethnic and racial identities of second-generation black immigrants in New York City," pp. 795–820 in Alejandro Portes (ed.), *The New Second Generation.*

Wiarda, Howard H. and Michael Kryzanek
1982 *The Dominican Republic: A Caribbean Crucible,* Boulder: Westview.

Winant, Howard
1994 *Racial Conditions: Politics, Theory, Comparisons.* Minneapolis: University of Minnesota Press.

Zenón Cruz, Isabelo
1974 *Narciso descubre su trasero: El negro en la cultura puertorriqueña.* 2 vols. Humacao: Furidi.

Part III

Culture and Performance

Introduction

"The Language of the Caribbean artist does not originate in the obsession with celebrating his inner self; this inner self is inseparable from the future evolution of his community." Edouard Glissant, *Caribbean Discourse*, p. 236

This part addresses the idea of culture and performance in the Caribbean. There exists a vast literature on Caribbean art, culture and performance, but the focus here is on the relationship between a given expressive form or tradition and the historical, political or social circumstances that gave rise to it. In what ways does Caribbean culture and performance grow out of unique aspects of the histories of the islands such as plantation life and the slave's need to practice art, music and religion in secrecy? How are community ideals and values perpetuated through performance, such as the building of social reputations through public displays of wit? How are forms of resistance embodied in Caribbean performance such as disguising martial arts as dance? How has the Caribbean appropriated and reconfigured sport so that it acts as both a celebration of West Indian identity and a repudiation of the colonial power that introduced sports such as cricket or football (soccer)? These are the concerns of this section, with an analytical focus on Caribbean performance as having a life in the community and being shaped by the global forces that penetrate and shape it.

Suggested Readings

Abrahams, Roger D., 1983 The Man-of-Words in the West Indies: Performance and the Emergence of Creole Culture. Baltimore: Johns Hopkins University Press.

Averill, Gage, 1997 A Day for the Hunter, a Day for the Prey: Popular Music and Power in Haiti. Chicago: University of Chicago Press.

Behague, Gerard H., ed., 1994 Music and Black Ethnicity: The Caribbean and South America. New Brunswick, NJ: Transaction Publishers.

Burton, Richard D. E., 1997 Afro-Creole: Power, Opposition, and Play in the Caribbean. Ithaca, NY: Cornell University Press.

James, C. L. R., 1993 Beyond a Boundary. Durham, NC: Duke University Press.

Korom, Frank J., 2002 Hosay Trinidad: Muharram Performances in an Indo-Caribbean Diaspora. Philadelphia: University of Pennsylvania Press.

Malec, Michael A., 1995 Social Roles of Sport in Caribbean Societies. London: Routledge.

Manuel, Peter, with Kenneth Bilby and Michael Largey, 1995 Caribbean Currents: Caribbean Music from Rumba to Reggae. Philadelphia: Temple University Press.

Nunley, John and Judith Bettelheim, 1988 Caribbean Festival Arts: Each and Every Bit of Difference. St Louis: Saint Louis Art Museum in association with University of Washington Press.

Price, Richard and Sally Price, 1991 Two Evenings in Saramaka. Chicago: University of Chicago Press.

Ramnarine, Tina K., 2001 Creating Their Own Space: The Development of an Indo-Caribbean Musical Tradition. Mona, Jamaica: University of West Indies Press.

7

Joking

The Training of the Man-of-Words in *Talking Broad*

Roger D. Abrahams

One of the dominant features of life in most Afro-American communities is their continuing reliance on oral expression. This means that, among other characteristics, there is still a good deal of social value placed on oral abilities, and these can often be best exhibited in a contest fashion, contests that are waged in creole or street language rather than Standard English. Discussing the role of such verbal abilities in one Washington, DC, ghetto neighborhood, Ulf Hannerz noted that

> the skill of talking well and easily is widely appreciated among ghetto men; although it is hardly itself a sign of masculinity, it can be very helpful in realizing one's wishes. "Rapping," persuasive speech can be used to manipulate others to one's own advantage. Besides, talking well is useful in cutting losses as well as in making gains. By "jiving" and "shucking," ghetto concepts with the partial denotation of warding off punishment or retribution through tall stories, feigned innocence, demeaning talk about oneself, or other misleading statements, a man may avoid the undesirable consequences of his own misdemeanors. ... However, all prestige accrued from being a good talker does not have to do with the strictly utilitarian aspect. A man with good stories well told and with a quick repartee in arguments is certain to be appreciated for his entertainment value, and those men who can talk about the high and mighty, people and places, and the state of the world may stake claims to a reputation of being "heavy upstairs." (Hannerz, 1969, pp. 84–5)

The ability to contend effectively with words is, then, a social skill and highly valued as such. Furthermore, it seems significant that these contests bring black talk (or, as most West Indians refer to it, *patois*, or *bad, broken* or *broad talk*) to a high art. One might hypothesize that the ongoing importance and usefulness of such practices may contribute to the retention of creole speech patterns as the major code for in-group black interactions and entertainments. This argument seems even more plausible as one investigates the crucial place that certain of these verbal contests, like *playing the dozens*, take in the socialization process of young men in widely scattered black communities.

The importance of these skills in actively contending is amply testified to by many who have grown up in the ghetto environment in the United States, including Malcolm X, Dick Gregory, Claude Brown, Jr, and H. Rap Brown. Brown says of the whole language "problem":

I learned how to talk in the street, not from reading about Dick and Jane going to the zoo. ... The teacher would test our vocabulary each week, but we knew the vocabulary we needed. They'd give us arithmetic to exercise our minds. Hell, we exercised our minds by playing the Dozens. ... We played the Dozens for recreation like white folks play Scrabble. ... Though, the Dozens is a mean game because what you try to do is totally destroy somebody else with words. ... Signifying is more humane. Instead of coming down on somebody's mother, you come down on them. But, before you can signify you got to be able to rap. (Brown, 1969, pp. 25–7)

Playing the dozens is, as Brown explains here, just one of a number of oral contest traditions that ghetto boys learn and use as the basis of their entertainments. However, this kind of joking activity is not unique to ghetto blacks. The practice of mother-rhyming has also been observed in various other Afro-American communities, as well as in a number of groups in Africa, including the Yoruba, Efik (Simmons, 1962), Dogon (Calame-Griaule, 1965), and several Bantu tribes. Peter Rigby, for instance, notes among the Bantu Wagogo that "the abuse between age-mates is of the strongest kind. ... Grandparents ... may be freely included in the verbal banter, as well as references to each other's 'parents,' particularly 'mothers'. ... Completely free conversation, which therefore includes references to sexual matters, is characteristic of relations between age-mates" (Rigby, 1968, p. 150; see also Zahan, 1963, pp. 73–7). Philip Mayer similarly reports among the Gusii that "the true measure of the unique unrestraint of pals and the climax of their intimacy is to exchange pornographic references to the other's mother and particularly to impute that he would be prepared for incestuous relations with her" (Mayer, 1951, pp. 31–2).

These reports are all but unique because they make a reference to content features as a part of the process of joking. There has been a good deal of discussion concerning the social form and functions of the "joking relationships" in various African groups. But these discussions (other than those noted) focus primarily on who can joke with whom, not how jokes are generated or learned

and for what reasons they are employed. Thus, it is difficult to tell how widespread such mother-rhyming is, and what alternatives there are, in joking situations in Africa. We do know that such specially licensed behavior is very widespread on that continent and that it plays an important part in its various speech economies and expressive repertoires.

In the New World, such play is one aspect of a special kind of aggressive joking calling for oral quickness and wit. This highly aggressive joking domain is known by a number of names in the United States, such as *rapping* or *signifying*, whereas in the West Indians it is called *giving rag, making mock*, and *giving fatigue*. These joking domains, whether in Africa or the New World, are always described in terms of the giving of license because of special relationships or festive occasions. Joking is in this way related to the entire tradition of scandal performances and the various practices of clowning or playing the fool. These scandalizing practices are equally widespread and important in African and Afro-American communities. And we can infer from the range of practices and their importance in community life that when mother-rhyming is practiced by adolescents it is part of the training procedure for adult performances.

Joking at the Crossroads

Peasant and lower-class communities in the West Indies and the United States share this attitude toward effective use of words. The range of this verbal repertory includes the ability to joke aggressively (in some groups this includes riddling), to "make war" with words by insult and scandal pieces, to tell Anansi stories (any kind of folk tale), and to make speeches and toasts appropriate to ceremonial occasions. Community status is designated in the West Indies by making the man-of-words the chairman at wakes, tea meetings, or service of song, and the toastmaster at weddings and other fetes. Few, of course, achieve such distinction.

There tends to be something of a separation made between two kinds of artful word use: one emphasizes joking and license, the other, decorum and formality. The former emphasizes bringing the vernacular creole into stylized use, in the form of wit, repartee, and directed slander. The latter is a demonstration of the speaker's abilities in Standard English, but strictly on the elaborate oratorical level. From this distinction two types of man-of-words have been posited: the *broad talker*, who, using license, brings creole into stylized form; and the *sweet talker*, who emphasizes eloquence and manners through the use of formal Standard English.

Artful broad talk may occur at any time, most commonly in public places; it is not considered appropriate in the yard or the house. This is almost certainly because it involves *foolishness* or *nonsense* behavior, which is regarded as a frontal assault on family values. Therefore it occurs on the streets and at places where the men congregate apart from the women. As a rule, only on special occasions like Carnivals or tea meetings is this type of performance carried on in front of women, and, on such occasions, women may involve themselves in the by-play, especially if they are masked in any way. Further, on such occasions there may be a confrontation between such broad-talking performances and ones that call for *sweet* speechmaking. In such a case, the community dramatically presents the widest range of their performance styles.

Both types of speaking are not only useful for individuals seeking special performance status within the community; they also fit into the system of social control. Speechmaking is an overt articulation of the ideals of the community. The sweet talker achieves his position of moral authority not only by invoking these ideals but also by embodying them in a formal rhetoric. In contrast, the broad talker achieves license to joke because he commonly focuses on behavior of others that is in gross violation of these ideals. His scandalizing therefore acts as something of a moral check on community activities.

The broad talker does a good deal more than this, however, especially on ceremonial occasions. He is licensed to play the fool or the clown and, as such, may enact behaviors that would be regarded as improper on any other occasion. By playing the fool or by describing the antics of the trickster Anansi, the broad talker therefore enacts something of an antiritual for the community; he

produces a needed sense of classless liminality and serves as a creative channel for antisocial community motives. Furthermore, by giving him this power, the community provides itself with a set of people who bring a sense of liminality upon the entire participating group, permitting them to forget themselves under special circumstances (like Carnival or Christmas revels) and to enter into the licentious occasion. The importance of this lapsing of the social order for its eventual reorganization is crucial to an understanding not only of the festival but also such licentious ceremonies as wakes.

For both kinds of verbal performer there are, of course, training procedures that have been developed by the community. These differ in their particulars from one Afro-American enclave to another, but some general comments can be made about them. Throughout the West Indies (and, to a certain extent, in the United States), there is an identification of talking sweet with family occasions, especially ceremonial rites of passage. Certainly talking sweet embodies values that focus on the family as the modal institution in which proper, responsible behavior is learned and carried out. But there is also a feeling that parents or grandparents should be responsible for a child learning how to talk sweet. Therefore, if parents or grandparents do not know speeches that they can teach their children for those occasions in which such talking is necessary, they send the child to someone in the community who is an expert in such matters. This person either trains the child orally or, more commonly, writes out a *lesson*, which the child memorizes. When it is learned, the child returns, recites it, and receives help on his or her delivery.

Learning to talk broad artfully, however, is not developed within the family. Rather, there is an identification of dramatic and stylized broad talk with values that run counter to those of the family and that are associated with public life, the crossroads, ram shops, and markets. Artfully talking broad is therefore a technique developed apart from the yard and the family environment, as a function of the friendship system on which masculine identity relies. As such, a certain degree of antagonism develops between the values implicit in talking broad and those of the family, because friendships take men (especially young ones) away from the yard. This antagonism is complex and often ambivalent because friendship values in their most important expressions develop from those of the family, especially in the positive valuation and practices of sharing and trust. In a sense, the sharing dimension of friendship actually creates an area of potential conflict because there is just so much to be shared and families and friends therefore vie for what they regard as their due. But the deepest distrust that family people have of friendships arises because drinking is carried on among friends and this often means a breakdown of decorum and the possibility of any number of assaults on family values.

Nevertheless, even the strongest of family people acknowledge, openly or by implication, that both friendships and license are important for the continuing vitality of the group. This is why such value is placed on *keeping company* and why social pressure is often brought on the *selfish* (shy) person or the *garden man* (loner), who are distrusted because of their lack of sociability. Often being selfish is equated with *getting on ignorant* and means an inability to take a joke and reply in kind. A joking capacity is therefore one of the key behavioral manifestations of group membership extending beyond the family and the yard. The young, especially males, are expected to get out of the yard and the garden and to develop friends, both as a means of broadening the network of people upon whom they can rely in times of need, and as a technique for creating some kind of interlock within the community by which the problems that arise within the family may be taken care of.

The most important of these problems are related to the antagonisms arising from the distribution of power and responsibility within the family. Whether the family is headed by a male or a female, West Indian peasant groups find themselves confronted with the need to maintain an age-based hierarchy forcing the young into observing continuing respect for their elders. This naturally creates problems with those seeking autonomy, problems that are greatly increased when opportunities that may provide employment for the young exist outside the family. Whether or not these wage-earning positions

exist, there is a strong feeling of shared needs and experiences among male peers in these peasant communities, a sharing that results in a mutual and supportive friendship network in the face of common problems. Because the focus of these problems is on the social institution that most constrains them – the family – they tend to channel their performance energies into anti-familistic forms. As a licensed role (or roles) that provides a model of performance for these motives already exists, a number of broad-talking traditions may be observed, mostly joking forms. Appropriate to the peer relationship, these serve both as a training ground for future nonsense performances and as a device by which friendship can be put into action. Thus, as in many groups, joking is an index to the type and intensity of a relationship.

In such situations, learning to be verbally adept is part of the process of maturation. For the adult performer, the man-of-words provides a model of on-going masculine abilities, especially in a contentious and economically marginal world. Consequently, in the practice of the rhyming insult found through this culture area there is an element of masculine role-playing that is one facet of an informal initiation practice. It is, at the same time, a technique by which young men may voice their peer identification and, in so doing, achieve license within that segment of the community to try out their talents. Just such an orientation toward this peer-group joking practice has been exhibited by a number of those commenting on similar practices in Africa. But such verbal practices do much more, for they permit a trying-on of mature roles in the safety of the peer-group confines while arming the young men with weapons useful in adult life.

The relationship between adolescent practices and adult ones is clear in most cases because of the different subjects and formulas used to embody joking aggressiveness. Thus, in the West Indian community in Panama, the most common subject of adolescent rhyming is the same as that of adult joking – the attribution of homosexuality to the other (a focus probably borrowed from Latin American neighbors), while references to the other's mother – except to start a fight – is prohibited for the most part.

Rhyming on Tobago

Rhyming in Plymouth, Tobago, however, permits this focus on the maternal figure, a focus that is shared with the numerous songs and *ring play* (singing games played by adults and children) and verbal routines in Tobagonian bongo (*wake*), as performed by adults in the community. Some of the wake dance songs address this theme, illustrating its intensity and licentious playfulness:

An' de bull take 'e pizzle an' he make his mama whistle,
De bull, de bull, de bull jump 'e mama.

An' de bull, de bull, de bull jumped 'e mother.
De bull, de bull, de bull jump 'e mama.

An' de bull take a whistle and everybody whistle,
De bull, de bull, de bull jump 'e mama.

An' de bull down Carrera with some peas and cassava.
De bull, de bull, de bull in de savannah.

An' de bull jumped 'e mama and he bring forth a heifer.
De bull, de bull, de bull jump 'e mama.

An' de bull jump 'e sister in a open savannah,
De bull, de bull, de bull jump 'e sister.

An' de bull in de savannah, he make your sister partner,
De bull, de bull, de bull in de savannah.

An' de bull take de pizzle an' 'e make your sister whistle,
De bull, de bull, de bull jump 'e mama.
[*Repeat ad lib*]

Rover dover, roll body over,
Pam palam, knock 'em palam.
T'row way me breakfast an' gi' me de moon-a
Pam palam, knock 'em palam.

A little, little woman carry a big, big moon-a
Pam palam, knock 'em palam.
A big fat woman carry a small, small moon-a
Pam palam, knock 'em palam.

Them small, small woman, bottle neck moon-a,
Pam palam, knock 'em palam.
Them big, big, woman got a small, small moon-a
Pam palam, knock 'em palam.

Dem bottle neck moon got lard at de corner,
Pam palam, knock 'em palam.
Big fat woman serve like a sugar.
Pam palam, knock 'em palam.

This fascination with incest and female genitalia is exhibited in any number of other ways during the bongo. One example that stands out in my memory is a fifteen-minute exercise in metaphor in which a woman's genitalia were compared to a water well, the major point being the pleasures attendant upon digging and finding water.

The practice of adolescent rhyming is more easily understood in the light of these adult performance pieces. For purposes of comparison of content, I shall report one ritual argument, which I heard in November 1965, in a group of six male peers, all of whom were ages fourteen and fifteen. They punctuated each rhyme with punching motions and foot-shiftings. Each rhyme was followed by hilarity and a fight to see who would give the next, so that the underlying impersonality of the invective was even more pronounced than if only two had been trading insults. (This may have occurred because of my presence and because I was recording their contest with a promise of playing it back. They indicated that this often happened when the first assailants ran out of ready rhymes.)

1. Ten pound iron, ten pound steel.
   Your mother' vagina* is like a steering wheel.
2. I put your mother to back o' train.
   When she come back she porky strain.
3. Christmas comes but once a year.
   I fuck your mother in a rocking chair.
4. Ten crapaud† was in a pan;
   The bigger one was your mother' man.
5. If aeroplane was not flying in the air.
   Your mother' cyat wouldn't get no hair.
6. If snake was not crawlin' on the ground‡
   Your mother' cyat would not get no tongue.

---

* Pronounced "vá-ji-na."
† Inedible frogs.
‡ Pronounced "grung."

7. Beep bop, what is that?
   A tractor falling a tree in your mother' cyat.
8. Beep bop, what is that?
   Thunder roll in your mother' cyat.
9. Tee-lee-lee, tee-lee-lee, what is that?
   A tractor stick in your mother' cyat.
10. Voo, voo, what is that?
    A blue fly worrying your mother' cyat.
11. Your mother fucking a old pan,
    and bring fort' Dan.
12. A for apple, B for bat.
    Your mother' cyat like alphabet.
13. Me and your mother in a pork barrel,
    And every word a give she porky quarrel.§
14. Me and your mother was digging potato.
    Spy under she and saw Little Tobago.
15. Sixty second, one minute,
    Sixty minute, one hour.
    Twenty-four hour, one day,
    I fucked your mother on Courland Bay.‖
16. A little boy with a cocky suit
    Fuck your mother for a bowl of soup.
17. Me and your mother was rolling roti:*
    I drop the roti and take she porky.
18. I put your mother on a electric wire,
    And every wood I give she, porky send fire.
19. I put your mother on a bay leaf,
    And every word I give she was a baby free.
20. I eat the meat and I t'row away the bone.
    Your mother' eat like a saxophone.
21. Forty degrees, the greasy the pole.
    That was the depth of your mother' porky hole.
22. Three hundred and sixty-six days, one leap
    year.
    I fucked your mother in a rocking chair.
23. Me and your mother was two friend.
    I fucked your mother and bring forth Glen.†
24. I fucked your mother on a telephone wire,
    And every jerk was a blaze of fire.
25. Me and your mother was cooking rice,
    And she kill she eat and frighten Chris',‡
26. Up into a cherry tree,
    Who should come but little me.
    I held the trunk in both my hand
    And I fuck your mother in a frying pan.

27. Ding-dong bell,
    Pussy in the well.
    Your mother' pussy like a conk shell.

These rhymes cannot, however, be fully understood only in terms of content features. Rhyming is just one of many contest performances that until recently were very common in Tobagonian festivities, especially Carnival.

In the past two types of performance have been fostered by the community (in line with practices throughout Trinidad and Tobago): performances by the group as a whole or by individuals within it; and performances by individuals addressed to the group, generally while engaged in competition with other individuals. The primary occasions for these are bongo, Carnival, and St Peter's Day (29 June), which is a special event for Plymouth. Other occasions are christenings, Emancipation Day, and Christmas. All of these occasions present opportunities for both types of performance. For instance, Carnival commonly calls for the town to get together for some *Costume mas'*, a group enterprise in which a theme of decoration is agreed upon and many dress in line with the theme. Then, on Carnival Tuesday, the entire mas', along with the local steel band, goes to Scarborough to *jump up* together, to show off, in a sense, their community solidarity and strength. A great deal of time and money is expended on this enterprise (so much so that in a bad fishing season such as 1965–6 Tobagonians did not have the resources or spirit to put together a mas').

In the past, Carnival has also offered an opportunity for the individual performer to have his day. There were a number of traditional ways in which he could dress and compete with other such performers. One of these was the *Caiso Mas'*, groups led by a *chantwell*. Another such competition was *Speech Mas'*, which involved composing boasting and deprecatory speeches of inflated rhetoric and pungent invective. A further activity of this sort was the well-known *kalinda* stick-fight dance (E. T. Hill, 1972).

Lately, in Plymouth, these competitive exercises are being rejected by the younger members of the community and are dying. The young men still admire the good competitors, but not enough

---

§   Made noise.
‖   Plymouth's main beach.
*   A curry dish introduced by the East Indians.
†   The name of one of the boys.
‡   She burned her vagina and hollered.

to emulate them. The one remaining chantwell in Plymouth no longer performs at Carnival and the one Speech Mas' performer comes from another community and must go to yet another village to find others to form a troupe. It is difficult to understand why this is happening, but one possible explanation is that such competitive expression is no longer as highly valued as the more cooperative performance, or the fully solo activity that takes the calypsonian off the street and places him on the stage.

This retreat from competitive expression is seen in the need for excuses and explanations that is felt by the competitive performers. They self-consciously insist that they are involved in a harmless game of words, though the contest of the speeches, songs, and stick fights is totally aggressive and destructive.

The same rationale has been used by adolescents in their rhyming sessions. Those who play today insist that a nonviolence pact must be made before beginning:

We made an agreement that we can rhyme on your mother. Then we start. I say, "Go and rhyme." He might say, "Okay" or something like that. Then he first will start. The person who first to ask to rhyme, he won't give a rhyme first in case they break the arrangement. (Daniel Dumas, age fifteen, Plymouth, Tobago, March 1966; he aided me in gathering the rhyme texts)

Yet the idea is clearly not to play but to hurt as much as possible, to "come back with a hurtful one to make more vex; something like when two persons cursing." The rationale of play arises because the value of this invective contest has been challenged and is to an extent undermined. This defensiveness seems a recent phenomenon, judging by the reminiscences of men in Plymouth.

Whether this development is an indication that rhyming will go the same, say, as *Speech Mas'* and *Caiso Mas'* is unclear; it is more important to understand that this self-conscious reaction does not mean a rejection of all of the licentious and joking traditions that surround these practices. Rhyming is just one technique of exhibiting verbal wit and directing it toward persons outside

one's own peer group. There are numerous other such traditions, some of which provide the primary entertainment forms and themes for adolescents. Most important in this regard is a series of short legendary jokes and songs about local happenings, especially those involving ogre-fool figures. These compositions are very much in the scandal-piece tradition, for they focus on activity regarded as foolish and inappropriate. Any kind of action that elicits laughter because it is a disruption of the expectations of the group may become the subject of such scandal pieces among the boys. For instance, when a local boy, Egbert, found a ring in the road, he wore it on his penis and made an exhibition of himself. His father then compounded the indiscretion by giving him a public beating for it, and so the boys sang this song:

Egbert, he busting [he was so happy]
An' he t'ought he get a ring,
But Uncle Darnell
Pitch 'e big wood on him.

Another such song sung by the young is not only a scandal piece but also involves many of the same motives as rhyming. It is a formulaic composition into which can be fit the names of any couple who have recently been caught at illicit lovemaking. Then, however, the song sometimes is performed as a rhyming boast in which the singer becomes the fornicator. Here is an example of such a song:

People, if I hear de fix
Charlie eat up Miss Vaughnie' chicks.
People, if I hear de fix
Charlie eat up Miss Vaughnie' chicks.
Den I [or 'e] gi' she one
She started to run.
When I gi' she two
She buckle she shoe.
When I gi' she three
She cut down tree.
When I gi' she four
She break down door.
When I gi' she five
Now I started to drive.
When I gi' she six
She break up sticks.
When I gi' she seven

She t'ink she was in heaven.
When I gi' she eight
She lay down 'traight.
And I gi' she nine
She started to whine.
When I gi' she ten
Den my cock ben'.

As with rhyming, these songs are similar in content and focus to some of the song games performed at bongo by adults. In the case of the bongo pieces, however, it is assumed that everyone knows the story and therefore many little details, rather than the narrative, are given. Here for instance is the saga of Jean-Louis, a man from the town of Lescoteau [le-ki-to] who made a determined pass at a young girl, who promptly ran away and was said to have bawled out this song:

You know Mr Jean Louis
Tim bam.
Come out a Lescoteau
Tim bam.
You know wha' he hold me for?
Tim bam.
You know Mr Jean-Louis
Tim bam.
He hold me for pom-pom soir,
Tim bam.
He hold me for pom-pom soir,
Tim bam.
He know me a very long
Tim bam.
You never hear a trus' before,
Tim bam.
Well you know Mr Jean-Louis
Tim bam.
He come up from Lescoteau,
Tim bam.
He born in Tobago,
Tim bam.
He ain' never call me yet.

Rhyming on Tobago is, then, one of a number of traditional devices by which adolescents group themselves on a peer-group basis and learn how to perform while joking about their shared problems and perspectives. Although one of these problems certainly is in displaying their

masculine identities – which is attempted in part by the combination of boast and taunt in rhyming – this focus on female symbols is not the only means they have of asserting this generational unity and independence from the constrictions of the extended family. License is given them to focus on the generational split as well as the sexual one.

Rhyming on Nevis

On Nevis, rhyming is also practiced and for many of the same reasons, but here the boys rely almost entirely upon the scandal-piece tradition, or they use the closely related techniques of the taunt. As on Tobago, the focus of their joking is on females and on older people, but the rhymes never use the strategy of indirection and impersonality to make their point. Rather, in keeping with the sense of strong interpersonal antagonism, the rhymes are directed at individuals and usually refer to the names of those present. These are primarily formulaic rhymes in which names may be substituted. Others simply make fun of a class of outsiders – for example, young girls, older men – or make specific reference to an item of gossip. Here is a series of rhymes as performed by a group of fourteen- and fifteen-year-old Nevisian males during the summer of 1962. As explained to me, the idea was to attack some close relative or friend or one boy, to which he might or might not make a bantering reply. Once the rhyming begins, there is apparent license for any rhyme to be performed, whether it happens to be directed at someone's familiars or not, and thus later in the series there are a few rhymes that are scandal pieces about people who live outside the social world of the boys.

1. Just for the sake of a box of matches,
   Rose can't put in common patches.*
2. Just for the sake of a banana,
   Jim knocked Sam from corner to corner.

---

* Rose, the sister of one of the boys, does not even know how to sew, something that all girls are expected to learn.

3. Twenty boobies on a rock,
Sonny catch them by the flock.
Bobs put them in the pot
And Mirie eat them piping hot.[†]

4. The sweetest pumpkin ever born
Mirie turn some[‡] in the corn:
The pumpkin was so sweet
It knocked out three of Audrey's front teeth.

5. I went to Dolly' house last night
To tell you the truth I didn't sleep all right.
I got up in the night to make my pee,
I found bug all over biting me.
Bug is a t'ing don't have any respect
It walks from my chin to the back of my neck.
I bawl, I bawl,
For the dogs, fleas and all.

6. I went down to Booby Island [§]
I never went to stay.
I rest my hand on Dinah
And Dinah went away.

7. Just for the sake of a root of cassava,
That's why some of those young girls don't
know their pickny' father.

8. Young bee meck honey,
Old bee meck comb.
Those young girls get their bellies
Because they won't stay home.

9. I went up the lane.
I met the parson kissing Jane.
He gave me a shilling not to tell,
An' that's why me suit fit me so well.

10. When I was young and in my prime,
I used to jump around those young girls no
less and a time
Now I am old and feeble,
They call me "Dry Sugar Weeble."

11. Just for the sake of Mr Kelly's bell[*]
That's why Halstead and Berdicere[†] kisses
so well.

12. Racoon[‡] was a curious man.
He never walked till dark.

The only thing could disturb his heart
Is when he hear old bringle dog bark.

13. Penny, ha'-penny woman
Sit down on a pistol.
Pistol leggo boom boom
Knock off Miss Wallace hairy poom poom.

14. Miss Pemberton has a landing.[§]
The landing work with spring.
The wind blow her petticoat
And then you see her magazine.[||]

15. Miss Budgeon[#] has a pepper tree,
Jennifer hang she panty dey;
When the pepper tree begin to bear
It burn off all of Jennifer' pussy hair.

16. The longer I live, the more I hear.
Bullwiss bite of Rose Pig ear.[**]

17. When Mr Clark falls asleep
George Baker run with the sheep.[††]

As on Tobago, on Nevis there is a great similarity between these adolescent rhymes and adult entertainments both in content and form. In fact, a number of the same rhymes are used both by adolescents and adults; the latter only use them as part of the licentious clowning performances found in certain Christmas sports and tea meetings. In their adult uses, the rhymes are commonly associated with songs in some way, either as an introduction or within the text spoken between stanzas.

A number of Christmas troupes perform ribald and scandalous inventions, each of which portrays a powerful figure in broad comic terms. Politicians, kings and queens, preachers and schoolteachers, landlords and overseers – none are spared. One of these groups, performing a set of plays called *Nigger Business*, takes a piece of scandal that has come to its notice, and reenacts it while also performing a song with veiled references to the socially disapproved doings. This group first plays in the yard of the miscreants to

[†] The idea of eating boobies, black pelicans, is ridiculous; the rhyme also makes fun, on occasion, of a boy and girl who are courting.
[‡] Mix and fry.
[§] A small rocky island between Nevis and St Kitts.
[*] Mr Kelly was a teacher at a local school.
[†] These two were "friending."
[‡] Racoon was a "selfish" man who lived alone, had never had a wife, and constantly chased dogs.

[§] Porch, balcony.
[||] Genitalia.
[#] The name of any mother and daughter may be inserted here, but especially those who have recently been observed fighting.
[**] They are brother and sister; biting another's ear is a common practice in fights.
[††] A court case the previous year.

see if its members can exact a bribe, but even if
they are able to, there is no guarantee that the show
will not be given in other yards as well.

Groups such as the Saguas or the Buzzards or
the Schoolchildren do not have such a unity to
their performance, but rather a series of comic
routines that comment on human nature or on
recent noteworthy events heard through gossip. It
is this type of group that most performs rhymes
and songs that are closely related to those of the
adolescent boys.

The idea of the Saguas group is, for instance, for
a group to dress up in broadly rendered cutaways
and other formal wear and to go from yard to yard
at night alternating songs and dances with rhymed
speeches. These rhymes are often similar to those
of adolescents, although they are performed with a
great deal more liberty and are more often centered around an item of scandal. Here are some of
the songs and speeches performed by a group of
Saguas from the community of Brown Hill.

(*Sung*)
Monday morning, break a day,
When the old folks got me goin'.
Saturday night when the sun goes down
All those young girls are mine.
[*Repeat ad lib*]

(*Spoken*)
Here we are, the higher classes,
Of all the pie asses,
Straight from Missy Wallace, Limited and Com-
    pany.*

(*Spoken*)
I've got me business organized and planned.
Dis year when de next boat land.†
Luther got 'e paddle ready.
Charles Ward got he saw.
Shorty** got 'e pickaxe,
And me, Steel, got me clawhammer.

(*Spoken*)
One Monday morning, I went up the lane.
I met the parson fixing a Jane.

---

*   A clothing store on St Kitts.
†   Gets wrecked, as happened recently.
** Members of the community.

He shove me six pence, told me not to tell.
That's why me sagua coat fit me so well.

(*Sung*)
Dollars again, dollars again,
I put me hands on dollars again.
[*Repeat ad lib*]

(*Spoken*)
Out of the hollow tree I came,
Calabash is my name.
So long me get me long hungry gut full,
Calabash still remain.

(*Spoken*)
Hark, hark, the dogs do bark,
Beggars are coming to town.
Some give them white bread,
Some give them brown.
But I just give them a big cut-ass
And send them out of town.

(*Spoken*)
By golly, you that man Mr Clifton from
    Churchground?
He motor bike gi' in' him one fall, land him 'pon
    ground.
So when get up he say, "That won't be all.
I goin' to collect sufficient money and buy
    Mr Abbott' Vauxhall."

Similar alternations of speeches, including
rhymes and songs, occur in a number of other
licentious Christmas sports, such as the following
routines from the Schoolchildren. Here the antisocial content is more pointed.

The setting is a Sunday School, and most of
the jokes are directed at specific local Sunday
School teachers, who are scored for their pom-
posity and mock erudition. The characters are
dressed up as scholars in black robe and mortar-
board, and they invariably carry a very large
book, which they can barely handle but constantly refer to with great mock solemnity. The
other characters are dressed as little children or,
in the case of Robin (the one who scares all of the
bystanders as the group goes from yard to yard –
and thus stands in the same position as the Devil
does in many other groups) in motley, or Father
Christmas in the Mummies (St. George) Play

(Abrahams, 1968, pp. 176–201). These scenes can go in any sequence, and are more or less adlibbed. Between each scene, the fife and drum group plays and everyone dances, including members of the audience. Robin tries to scare some of the children.

ROBIN: Now here we are, Robin speaking. Yeah! Christmas come but once a year, yeah heh!
When 'e come, it bring good cheer (I'm glad, you know),
All what I see happ'nin' this year
Is the minister dem a breed off all de young girls dat come in here.
[*Music and dancing*]

WARD: I'm Godfrey Ward speaking, but I would not like do do anything before the captain reaching, which is Samuel Daniel.
[*Music and dancing*]

WARD: Hello!

DANIEL: Hello, man.

WARD: A book here.

DANIEL: I ready to meet you.[*]

WARD: To your exclusion.

DANIEL: Damned confusion.
[*Music and dancing*]

WARD: Madam, come inside here.

BRADSHAW [*man dressed as woman*]. Inside?

WARD: Inside. All you all time out to make confusion.[†]

BRADSHAW: Fix me good. [*Acting seductive*]

WARD: Is all right?

BRADSHAW: Sure.

WARD: Dat right? [*Goes up next to her*]

BRADSHAW: Is me, Miss Bradshaw.[‡]
[*Music and dancing*]

DANIEL: Well, den, I want fifty thousand men take up a me book of a dictionary. Well yes, fifty thousand men to lif' de book of a dictionary. Tha's right. So now I look [*leafing through the book*] from the fif' to de six of June, never too late and never too soon,

from six o'clock in the afternoon. Blessed assurance after three. One, two, three. ...
(*Song*, to the tune of hymn "This Is My Story, This Is My Song")
Send them a pasha[§] dey wouldn't go.
Take up my cat whip and leggo one blow.
Well dem dey reverse back, dey wouldn't go.
Dem dey reverse back, well-a chooka pooh-pooh.
   [Let them have it with whip, acted out, scaring children in audience.]
Going on a mountain, no walk with no bread.
I going use potato, dasheen and tania head[*]
Worser me boy we, de dasheen dems sprout.
I wouldn't buy no tania head to scratch out me mout.[†]

DANIEL: Now look in the back of the hymn-book for them, boy. Four-nine-nine.

ALL: Four-nine-nine.

DANIEL: Last verse, "We going on mountain" after three, One, two, three.
[*Repeat "Going on the mountain. ..."*]

WARD: Boys, open your hymn book. Four-nine-two.

ALL: Four-nine-two.

WARD: Las' time I speakin' to you; not again. I hope everyt'ing will come true. You heard me? De las' time we sang a proper program:
My sister had a penny pork.[‡]
She bind them wid a twine.
She po'k 'em in a doving[§] pot.
An' make my water shine.[‖]

[§]   Pasture.
[*]   Types of taro root.
[†]   Tanias scratch unless cooked properly.
[‡]   A penny's worth of pork, but also slang for female genitalia.
[§]   Cook.
[‖]   The pun here is on pot water, which shines with fat when pork is put into it, and semen, which is referred to as water.

---

[*]   To contest who knows the Bible better.
[†]   A mispronunciation of confession.
[‡]   The late Prime Minister Bradshaw, former labor leader.

The joking humor presents nonsense as if it were sense, putting together dialogue and song in a continuous fashion but without the usual logic that determines continuities. Thus, the laughter is directed at the nonsensical aspects of these characters. But this is just one dimension of the occasion's license, for, in addition, the high are made low and the virtuous revealed as lecherous and dishonest charlatans. The conventions of this kind of humor turn on dramatizing discontinuities and inverting the ascribed characteristics of everyday roles. Laughter arises with the introduction of the unexpected, though in this setting, such introductions are really expected (though their content is not known in advance). The mock-hymn and the rhymes all rely upon the disruption of expectations derived from the usual uses of these specific items (the hymn, the "Christmas comes but once a year" rhyme) to elicit laughter and to add to the irreverent tone. In such a setting, however, as soon as a device is introduced into the performance, an expectation of disruption arises on the part of the audience. This is also true of the adolescent rhymes, which trade both on such humorous conventions and their expectations, and the discontinuities associated with openly attacking others in the protected and licensed confines of peer groupings.

Significantly, the focus of the nonsense is on the symbols of the "sensible" world: school and church. The use of broad talk to confound talking sweet is thus all the more pointed, for nothing represents family-based ideals more fully than teacher and preacher, their books, and their usual manner of formal speech. In these mock speeches then, especially in those of the School-children, we witness a direct (but licensed) confrontation between family ideals and friendship values in which the latter, for the moment, win the day.

Why Rhyme?

The importance of license is that it permits a playful restructuring of the world. The recognized community order of things, actions, and especially interactions has a deeply felt sense of logic to it, simply because it *is* ordered and provides comfort and control to those who share this perspective. But everyone at some time feels contradictions or tensions arising from within or without the system. One way of handling this shared problem is for the community to get together ceremonially and reenact or recite in its most basic terms the condition and the genesis of the world's order. Another way is to provide license to community members to impose a new sense of order upon the social and natural environment, an order that is so different from that of the everyday that it produces laughter through manipulating discontinuities and contrasts. Masking is, of course, one of the most extreme examples of this effect, because it permits an overturning of the usual social order and the imposition of new status and power arrangements based upon assumed roles.

Joking is in many ways like masking because of its reorganization of the social order on the basis of different logics. But joking often establishes continuities on only a verbal level, through the use of puns and other *non sequitur* juxtapositions. This is essentially what produces the response to rhymes of children and adolescents on both Nevis and Tobago. Further, in both traditions, the potentially disruptive implications of the *non sequitur* and antitaboo arguments are rendered harmless not only by insisting that what transpires is only play (and verbal play at that), that there has been a joking about the most discontinuous things by virtue of the most elementary restricted verbal formulas.

This perspective is an extension of Freud's thesis that wit exists as an arbitrary order that permits a freeing of otherwise restrained motives. Or as Mary Douglas expressed it:

A joke is a play upon form. It brings into relation disparate elements in such a way that one accepted pattern is challenged by the appearance of another which in some way was hidden in the first. ... any recognizable joke falls into this joke pattern which needs two elements, the juxtaposition of a control against that which is being controlled, this juxtaposition of being such that the latter triumphs ... a successful subversion of one form by another completes or ends the joke for it changes the balance of power. ... The joke merely affords opportunity for realizing that an accepted pattern has no necessity. Its excitement lies in the suggestion that any particular ordering of experience may be arbitrary and subjective. It is frivolous in that it produces no real alternative, only an exhilarating sense of freedom from form in general. (Douglas, 1968, p. 365)

There is no joking, then, unless there is an order that can be overturned or at least challenged by the establishment of new continuities and relationships. But simply because a joke relies upon this previous social order indicates that it acts in response to certain pressures already existing within that order, tensions that are shared by the group who participates in the joking.

Joking thus helps to give the community the feeling that such situations are under control. But when we look at joking from a performance-centered perspective, we see that the joke seizes on such subjects because they already have tremendous potential to attract attention, for they deal with restricted matters. From this point of view, joking induces everyone's participation, because a potentially embarrassing situation is commonly depicted and drawn upon, but in such a context of social and verbal control that relief rather than embarrassment occurs. Laughter arises in response to the failure of expectations in a patterned situation, but joking occurs only when there has been an assent already given to articulating this failure, this abrogation. Joking uses embarrassment and other social dislocations, but puts the disruptions under a social control by framing them, by conventionalizing the behavior as play.

Social anthropologists argue that joking is essentially akin to antiritual because ritual underlines and reenacts social order and cosmology, while joking and clowning challenge this for the purpose of channeling off antisocial tendencies. However, E. R. Leach has suggestively argued that there is an intimate structural relation between rite and antirite masking and that, simply speaking in regard to their occurrence, "they are in practice closely associated. A rite which starts with a formality (e.g. a wedding) is likely to end in masquerade; a rite which starts with masquerade (e.g. New Year's Eve, Carnival) is likely to end in formality" (Leach, 1961, pp. 135–6).

Furthermore, as Victor Turner has effectively argued, it is necessary to achieve a "liminal" state for the formal ritual to be effective (Turner, 1969). This seems equally true of antirituals, Liminality is the acceptance, by the group and especially the participants, of a sense of *communitas* in which social distinctions are rejected in favor of a classless state commonly symbolized by the assumption of garb and mien of the lowest social creatures. The costumes of festivals of this sort often "joke" in the same way, combining unusual materials and colors – that is the original meaning of "motley." Joking is similar in almost every sense, given its antisocial thrust and its totally participative strategy in which the joking group coheres on an egalitarian basis.

Joking arises, at least among adolescents, as a ritualistic behavior in which hierarchical order is challenged, and something like liminality occurs in which it becomes possible – in fact necessary – to assert a new order on a peer-group basis. Thus the conventions of joking are crucial not only because they provide a sense of artificial ordering (of words) in the face of disorder (of concepts or themes), but also because the conventions are regarded as the insignia of the peer group. The adolescents' performance is therefore a statement of group solidarity in the face of those who must be considered the common enemy, the actors of hierarchically established roles and relationships within the community. This means that such jokes can be looked to as indications of where adolescents see constraint asserting itself socially. But it does not mean that these jokes focus on *all*, or even on the most important, of these problems. As I have tried to show, adolescents on Tobago and Nevis are given the cues to what subjects may be discussed licentiously in the content of the songs and rhymes and stories that arise during adult ceremonies of license. The sense of liberation is short-lived, for no real social transformation occurs in such playful occasions. Rather, a ratification of common feeling occurs in performances, which also enters into the performance preparation for adult nonsense-making.

The success of this system depends on the peers casting off these ways after a certain period and using their talents for the entertainment of the entire community. On many West Indian islands, however, there are indications that to do so would be an act of incorporation into an extended family system, which the young are not willing to go through. Because of the occasional availability of employment on the island, or the possibility of emigration to places where employment is to be found, the hold that the family exerts on the young has weakened. Consequently, this kind of grouping on a peer-group basis tends to continue, leading the older members of the community to sense that the system is falling apart, a disruption that they attribute to the rudeness of the young. Essentially, this indictment must be read not as a rejection of youthful license but as a charge that the young do not understand the proper occasions on which license is permitted. It would seem that joking has spilled over from the joking relationship into other performances and communications, and this is read by those who have lived with the system as a social disruption.

The elaboration of this kind of rude joking behavior is furthermore paralleled with some loss of respect for other parts of the speaking repertoire – specifically the ceremonial "sweet" speechmaking. Significantly, this kind of ceremony generally discusses overtly the most important features of household values in which the aged (and the ancestors) are given great respect. Thus, in a sense, this gravitation is away from an acceptance of Standard English as well as from a hierarchical, extended-family ideal. Surely this is not the only explanation of why broad-talk creole has persisted in spite of the obvious opportunities for employment and mobility accruing to those who learn Standard English. It is simply to urge that we must more fully understand the relationship between speech acts and events, the varieties used by different segments of the community and the social order that is given articulation through the interactions between and among these segments. For then we can discover why these stigmatized ways of talking have been maintained and used as the basis of linguistic and social experimentation.

References

Abrahams Roger D. (1968) Public Drama and Common Values in Two Caribbean Islands. *Trans-Action*, 5, 62–71. Reprinted as Patterns of Performance, in the British West Indies in *Afro-American Anthropology: Contemporary Perspectives*. New York: The Free Press, 1970, 163–80.

Brown, H. Rap (1969) *Die Nigger Die*. New York: Dial Press.

Douglas, Mary (1966) *Purity and Danger*. New York: Praeger.

Hannerz, Ulf (1969) *Soulside*. New York: Columbia University Press.

Mayer, Philip (1951) The Joking of Pals in Gusii Age-sets. *African Studies*, 10: 31–2.

Rigby, Peter (1968) Joking Relationships, Kin Categories, and Clanship among the Gogo. *Africa*, 38: 150–65.

Zahan, Dominique (1963) *La dialectique du verbe chez les Bambara*. The Hague: Mouton.

8

Rara as Popular Army
Hierarchy, Militarism, and Warfare

Elizabeth McAlister

I am arriving with my regiment,
  Ossagne Oh [Repeat]
Don't you hear [about the] the
  National Palace
Let it flow
I am arriving with my regiment,
  Ossagne Oh

M'ap antre ak tout kò divizyon mwen,
  Osanj O [Repeat]
Ou pa tande Palè Nasiyonal
Lese koule
M'ap antre ak tout kò divizyon mwen,
  Osanj O

Rara La Belle Fraîcheur de l'Anglade,
Fermathe, Easter Sunday 1992

The oldest Rara leader I met was well into his hundreds, a retired farmer named Papa Dieubon who lived high in the mountains off the road to Jacmel. Friends presented me to him one hot afternoon so he could bay odyans *(literally, "give me an audience"). We sat leaning back in small chairs under his porch roof, sipping* kleren *laced with sweet spices. Papa Dieubon's skin had the wizened look of a life lived under the hot sun, his face topped with snowy white hair. For a long time he did not understand what I had come to ask. "I want to talk about the Rara you led," I kept shouting. I began to have the absurd feeling that I was talking to the wrong old man. "Ah," he said at last, drawing himself up in his chair. "You mean the Army."*

An overarching ethos of militarism pervades the Rara festival because bands construct themselves as small regiments and go out into the streets in the spirit of battle. Rara bands often conceive of themselves as small statelike entities involved in diplomacy or warfare. Embedded in the social organization of Rara bands and underlying the festival conceptually is the notion of an imaginary state. Furthermore, vestiges of a royal idiom are interwoven with the military and state symbols in Rara. The social organization of Rara, then, is an articulation of power and rank based in military, state, and royal metaphors.

This chapter examines the social organization of Rara bands in historical context, viewing them as a type of militarized traditional peasant organization that has frequently marched across the pages of Haitian history. These groups were (and are) traditional forms of popular organizing that political activists, especially liberation theology advocates, tapped in the recent efforts to gain political enfranchisement.[1] As self-organized peasant groups, they can be viewed as the prepolitical forerunners of the contemporary grassroots popular organizations that make up the democratic peasant movement.

Rara hierarchy and organization reveal how the cultural practices of the Haitian popular classes display and draw attention to the local social order. In Rara, individual agents act out an implicitly political theory, asserting their right to participate in a communal endeavor, always ranked in strict hierarchical relationships with compatriots and *gwo nèg* and often united in battle against other local groups. Embedded in the bands' social relationships and performed in the roles individuals assume during their parades is the system of patronage that has fueled Haitian politics at all levels through the present day.

In the Rara bands, royal imagery has over time been replaced by military idiom. This change may be contextualized historically. Early colonial accounts of Vodou described the existence of a king and queen as the two leaders.[2] After independence in 1804, the north was headed from 1807 to 1820 by King Henri Christophe of the Kingdom of Haiti, and it was probably during or after this time that

republican titles replaced royal ranks in ritual. Dolores Yonker remarks that "Royal titles formerly used such as king, queen, princess and prince, dukes, etc., are gradually being displaced by more republican ones: president, various cabinet ministers, and the military."[3] We can compare this process to the history of other Afro-Caribbean societies like the Cuban *cabildos*, where the social structure was modeled on republican government but earlier had been borrowed from monarchy.[4]

Raras are organized into elaborate hierarchies, and their members hold specific titles known by everyone in the community. At the head of the band is the president. After the president come kings, queens, colonels, majors, rear guards, prime ministers, and secretaries of state. What follows is a list of possible titles for band members. These bestow upon their bearers the prestige and honor of publicly recognized rank. Linguistically, the titles are derived from French. They invoke multiple imageries borrowed from monarchy, from republican government, and from the French army:

prezidan	president
vis prezidan	vice-president
premye minis	prime minister
dezyèm minis	second minister
pòt drapo	flag bearer
avan gad	front guard
minis lagè	minister of war
minis dinfomasyon	minister of information
jeneral	general
kolonèl	colonel
dezyèm kolonèl	second colonel
kapitèn	captain
majò	major
majò jon	baton major
wa	king
premye renn	first queen
dezyèm renn	second queen
renn lagè	queen of war
renn kòbèy	queen of the basket
sekretè	secretary
trezorye	treasurer
minis finans	minister of finance
minis enteryè	minister of the interior
laryè gad	rear guard

The order of procession is a performance of military ethos. The *pòt drapo* walks a considerable distance in front of the band to scout for friends and foes. After him is the *kolonèl*, who directs the band with his whistle and whip. Usually he has several officers flanking him, making up the *avan gad*. *Majò jon*, dancers, and musicians follow, with the queens and women's chorus toward the rear of the band, protected from attack.

Sometimes within the orchestra itself there is a hierarchy, with a president who leads the band with the *manman* drum, and various vice-presidents who play behind him. Likewise, the women's chorus may include queens of various ranks, or officers of the band. After the musicians and the chorus come the rank-and-file Rara fans, who walk and sing with the band. Last but not least, individual *machann* (market women) affiliate themselves with specific Raras and walk with the band, selling liquor, cigarettes, and small foodstuffs. As vendors, these women too hold a recognized rank in the band. They provide service and maintain their loyalty to the group, and in return they are given "security" and protected by the rear guard.

In spite of the religious and magical practices of Rara, and even the participation of entire religious houses, the *grad* (ranks) in Rara are military and official in nature and do not indicate religious authority. Raras are modeled not on an imagined theocracy, but rather on an imagined military government. In some cases there is more at stake in Rara leadership than merely the band. I came across one Rara that owns land. Members of the family cultivate it and give a portion of the harvest to the Rara president.[5] These kinds of Raras exist as an imagined state with a territory and a population, and thus possess the means to produce and reproduce.

In order to analyze the royal, military, and state titles in Rara, we must understand the Raras as historically and structurally related to other popular societies also ranked into military hierarchies. These groups include Chanpwèl, Carnival bands, and various kinds of *sosyete travay* (work cooperatives): *konbit, èskwad, kòdon, konvre* (in the south), *mazinga* (in the northwest), *ranpono* (in the north), and *kounabe* (in the Petit-Goâve region). These various work cooperatives

often organize themselves into guards, squads, battalions, and so on.[6]

In some cases, the Rara is conceived as the army for a higher governing body such as a Chanpwèl society. According to Michel Laguerre, "The societies, comprised of mountain dwellers, retain a governmental structure with a military parallel with the structure of the army and the civil government of the country."[7] Rara band names are created to inspire fear, with groups like Ti Rayè (from *tirailleurs*, the artillery in the French army) and Chien Mechant (Angry Dog).

Rara ranks may correspond with, or may be distinct from, a sponsoring Vodou, Chanpwèl, or work society. In 1961 Paul Moral observed that work societies sometimes turn into Rara bands or engage in mass demonstrations to create political agitation.[8] In 1987 Rachel Beauvoir and Didier Dominique noted a similar line of transformation: "[B]etween January and April, many work societies transform into Rara bands; these groups dress in colored costumes and dance during the day, and punish people at night. The Society's money pays for the costumes, drinks and all the other necessary expenses."[9] Thus the president of a Chanpwèl may also be the president of a Rara band, or an *oungan* might be a *kolonèl* who leads the Rara. Often the Rara queens are women who have attained the rank of queen in a Chanpwèl society. However, Rara is its own enterprise, and those involved jockey for positions using their roles in other areas to obtain positions of power or prestige in the band, and vice versa. A Rara member who attains the rank of general is addressed as such, and as a decision-maker for several hundred people, he is in a true position of leadership.[10]

Rara's symbols and social organization reveal it to be one of the most militarized arenas of popular religious culture. At the absolute top of its hierarchies one finds the *lwa*, along with any *zonbi* that may have been captured and *mete sou bann nan* (put on the band). Together these form an invisible military force that helps the band vanquish its competitors. The true owner of the Rara called Mande Gran Moun, I was told, was the *lwa* Kouzen Azaka. Azaka "walked with" the band under the title of prime minister, and it was he who was ultimately in charge.[11] Laguerre writes about the militarizing of the *lwa* in Afro-Haitian Vodou:

> Since the colonial era, Voodooists have developed their own theological view of the supernatural world, which they see in terms of a complex politico-military structure that operates on a spiritual as well as a human level. The major spirits are known to have a specific function in this government, and each one has a military or political title. General Clermeil is believed to be in charge of springs and rivers, General Brisé is supposed to protect the trees of Chardette, Baron Samedi is a senator and a diplomat. *Zaka* is minister of agriculture and *Loko* is minister of public health while *Danbala* is minister of finance.[12]

The militarization of Haitian culture in general and of these local societies in particular is the result of a long-standing historical process: colonial Haiti was controlled and maintained by the French army, and the nation won its independence only after the bloody armed resistance that Haitians launched in the late eighteenth century. Haitian political history since that time has been a long series of military coups d'état; the last one at this writing was the ousting of President Aristide in 1991. In their study on militarism in Haitian music, Gage Averill and David Yih argue that the Haitian war of independence was the pivotal moment that crystallized Haitian identity and that Haitians responded by "embracing a deep cultural metaphor of the people as an army." When the indigenous army won its independence from the French, the idea of the army came to have a positive value and an association with victory.[13] Throughout the nineteenth century, the country was regionalized into diverse centers of power, and each region created its own army, capable of defending its own territory. Militarism thus became a generative scheme of social organization in the peasantry, each social group always reserving the potential to become an actual fighting force.[14] Michel-Rolph Trouillot writes that in the nineteenth century, "Retired or ousted officers, political leaders and local landlords ... put together small armed bands that were effective in their limited regional spheres and that sometimes

gave critical support to rebelling regular troops."[15]

There is historical evidence that peasant armies incorporated music into the work of fighting. Haiti's former rulers, the colonists of Saint-Domingue, had maintained regimental music corps called *corps de musique*, which were attached to various divisions such as the *chasseurs* (light infantrymen), *grenadiers* (grenade-throwers), *tirailleurs* (artillery), and *garde du palais* (palace guard). At one point there were sixteen *corps de musique* in Port-au-Prince and more in the provinces.[16] The colonial army also established various drum corps called *batteries sonores*, which the Independent Haitian armies maintained. Averill and Yih argue convincingly that the musical style of Rara *ochan* musical salutes derives from French military drumming. The word *ochan* probably derives from the French *aux champs* (to forward march; literally, "to the fields"). It is likely that postcolonial popular armies also made use of drums and other instruments as communication tools in symbolic displays, maneuvers, and possibly battle.[17]

It is probable that processional activity like Rara even had its origins in the colonial era. Thomas Madiou writes of maroon armies throughout the colony. He notes that a man named Halaou was a leader in the Port-au-Prince region who walked with drums, trumpets, and sorcerers: "The Cul-de-Sac insurgents (an army of two thousand maroons) had at their head an African priest of great height and Herculean strength. He ... always [carried] under his arm a large white cock which, he pretended, transmitted to him orders from heaven. He *marched preceded by the music of drums, lambis [conch shells], trumpets and sorcerers*" (emphasis added).[18]

But militarism in Haiti was consolidated and bolstered throughout the country's history, as peasants organized themselves into armed groups to defend their interests. In the south these were known as Piquets du Sud and in the north as Cacos du Nord. Throughout the nineteenth century, generals would march with these "armies" to overthrow the Port-au-Prince state, promising peasants they would effect their demands. A few years later, another peasant army would overthrow the state. The first *piquets* mobilized under a peasant leader known as Goman, claiming their right to cultivate land. Another southern peasant rebel, Jean-Jacques Accaau, led the same *piquets* against President Jean-Pierre Boyer (1822–44) because of his abandonment of peasant interests. In the late 1860s, the *cacos* helped Sylvain Salnave overthrow Nicolas Geffrard. When he did not move to change their conditions, they overthrew Salnave himself.

In January 1915, General Vilbrun Guillaume Sam led a *cacos* army to Port-au-Prince and named himself president. Six months later that same army killed Sam after he ordered the execution of political prisoners allied to the *cacos*.[19] This incident was the catalyst for the US invasion of that year. The killing of Sam, who was "ripped apart" by a "mob," has stayed in the middle-class and foreign imagination as the shadow side of popular gatherings, including Rara.

The United States Marines, during their 1915–34 occupation of the country, centralized, trained, equipped, and funded the Haitian military. According to one source, the title of *kolonèl* became the highest rank in Rara during the American occupation: "The title *le kolonèl* refers to the chief of the rural police. In the past, he was called 'general' because that was the highest grade in the army. Since the time of the American occupation of Haiti (1915–34), he has been known as *kolonèl*, since this was the highest rank in the American Army represented in Haiti."[20] It was during the marine occupation that one of the best-known Rara bands in Haiti was formed, making it eighty years old at the present writing. Peasant communities during the US occupation transformed themselves into armed fighting *cacos* units and launched a guerrilla resistance against the marines.[21] In 1957 Duvalier rose, and there was increased US support to the Haitian army during the Cold War. (Until the Duvalier era, Rara bands were not allowed into Port-au-Prince; they were held at bay in the outskirts of the city.)[22]

After the fall of Jean-Claude Duvalier in 1986, six military juntas forced successive coups d'état, increasing the power of the army to an extreme. In 1995, for the first time in Haitian history, President Jean-Bertrand Aristide dissolved the army and replaced it with a police force. This move was engineered, however, under the greater supervision of the occupying United Nations troops after a 1995 US military "intervasion."

Haitian militarism on the national and the local level has thus been the idiom through which hierarchies channel power to the absolute leadership of one man. Trouillot has outlined the historical pattern through which the executive branch effects the total usurping of state power. The logical culmination of this process was the totalitarianism of François Duvalier's presidency. In this politics of "big man-ism," all citizens were forced to identify their position in relation to the president, either proclaiming themselves pro-Duvalier or anti-Duvalier. Polarized and terrorized, each person learned to construct relationships of patronage and subservience with pro-Duvalierists in order to dodge the brutal repression that was sure to follow resistance or even ambivalence. "In the course of daily life anyone could claim a relationship, even fictitious, to the sole center and source of power in order to ensure a place on the side of the survivors."[23] With the construction of this shape of power relations, political patronage became the only way to survive and succeed.[24]

Local "big man-ism" is a mirror image of the national model in Haitian politics and is possibly derived in part from African roots. As Karin Barber reports of the Yoruba, "[T]he dynamic impulse in political life is the rise of self-made men. Individuals compete to make a position for themselves by recruiting supporters willing to acknowledge their greatness."[25] In Haiti, the powerful man who carries political weight is called a *gwo nèg*. The status of a "big man" derives to some extent from his performance abilities as a man-of-words. More than that, it is his everyday style and charisma, his personal power, that attracts followers. Writing on the Kono in Africa, Kris Hardin ties leadership to style, raising interesting questions about the relationship of aesthetics to power. "These aspects of social life also rely on questions of charisma, personal style, and the ability to demonstrate power, authority, and knowledge in credible ways."[26]

The ethos of *gwo nèg* leadership in Haiti is permeated with the imagery of ownership, evidenced in the phrase *moun pa'm* (my person).

The Rara presidents are local *gwo nèg* who actively attract *moun pa'l* (literally, "their people") into relationships of reciprocity wherein they offer protection from other powerful people, potential access to resources, and relationships with other *moun pa'l*. The follower in return offers up his or her loyalty and services. In extreme cases, to resist alliance with the *gwo nèg* threatens one's very survival. Thus the power of the *gwo nèg* in Haiti operates through his many dependents. Again, this is parallel to the situation among the Yoruba, where "in a fairly flexible social structure where individuals could make their own position for themselves, attendant people were the index of how much support and acknowledgement the man commanded, and thus how important he was."[27]

Heading up a Rara in the Haitian political context confers on the president the multidirectional power of the *gwo nèg*. By bankrolling and organizing the band, he signals his power in the community. The *fanatik* that he attracts enhance his power as they perform their allegiance through their bodily presence and their singing. The Rara in turn performs for even "bigger men" through *ochan* and augments its collective association with these other powerful figures. Heading a Rara increases the sphere of one's local political reputation, and by the same token, receiving a Rara is a mark of power and wealth.

The president may not be involved with the weekly *sòti* of the group, but his identity is known in the community, and often the Rara will gather in his *lakou* for a weekly *balanse Rara* (playing without walking). It is the president who is held accountable for the security of the group. In the case of accidents or deaths in the Rara, the president can be brought before a tribunal (in the Chanpwèl system) or to district court.

A band may also be financed and governed by committee, as is the case often in Léogâne, where the Raras are particularly lavish and costly. More often, the president pays the costs of the band, which can include the purchase of instruments, costumes, food, and musicians' salaries. The religious costs of Rara can also be high, and the *lwa* can demand all-night religious services, protective baths, animal sacrifices, or *wanga* made for the occasion. Also there are payments made to the police in the form of parade fees or bribes.

In more elaborate bands, each committee member has a title describing exactly what his position is to his comrades. Rara Mande Gran Moun (Ask the Elders) in Léogâne had a president, prime minister, second minister, and minister of information. In true bureaucratic style, none overstepped the bounds of another, and when I interviewed them, each carefully sent me to the next to answer questions which he deemed "out of his jurisdiction." The leadership committees in Léogâne often include absentee members of the Haitian diaspora living in Miami or New York, who send money to the group and join them during Holy Week. Financial patrons like these are sometimes given the honorary titles *parenn* (godfather) or *marenn* (godmother) in return for their support.

Rara members broadcast the reputation of the Rara leader *gwo nèg* and restate their political allegiances to him by performing praise songs in his honor. Many Rara songs are drawn from the vast repertoire of Afro-Haitian religious prayer songs, but each Rara usually has a few original songs created by its own *sanba* and *simidò*, and often these are advertisements for the leader. In 1992 La Belle Fraîcheur de l'Anglade sang that their president, Dieuvè, had all the money he needed and did not need to borrow from anybody.

> Dieuvè isn't asking to borrow
> This year, Oh, They will need him
> Dieuvè isn't asking to borrow
> This year, Oh, They will need him, Papa
> He possesses all that he wants
>
> *Dieuvè p'ap mande prete*
> *Ane icit O, y'ap bezwen li*
> *Dieuvè p'ap mande prete*
> *Ane icit O, y'ap bezwen'l Papa*
> *Li posede sa'l vle*[28]

Delen, in contrast, was a Chanpwèl leader nearby with a notorious reputation for meanness, an ability and inclination to do sorcery against people, and ties with the *tonton makoutes*. La Belle Fraîcheur de l'Anglade made the decision to turn down a mountain path and avoid this Rara altogether. Staying behind to see them, I recorded their praise song to Delen.

> Let me go, Delen, Let me go, Let me go
> Delen has a Chanpwèl band
> I won't do that work anymore
> Let me go

> *Voye'm ale, voye'm ale Delen, Voye'm ale*
> *Delen gen on bann chanpwèl*
> *M' pa sa travay ankò*
> *Voye'm ale*

A very clear example of Rara patronage was evidenced in the Rara called Ya Sezi. They named their band "They'll Be Surprised" as a *pwen* (point), a message against all of their detractors who spread malicious gossip that they were too poor to form a Rara. When a local *gwo nèg* named Papa Dieupè heard them, he adopted them as his personal band. A Chanpwèl leader holding the highest rank of emperor, Papa Dieupè is rumored to be a multimillionaire with hundreds of acres under cultivation. He calls the Rara whenever he wants to augment celebrations at his compound for birthdays, weddings, and religious ceremonies. They made a special trip on Easter of 1993 to sing at his compound for him and his five wives:

> We're arriving in Our Father's *lakou*, Oh
>   [Repeat]
> Ring the sacred rattle for me

> *Nan lakou lepè-a nou rive Wo [Repeat]*
> *Sonnen ason an pou mwen*[29]

In addition to promoting individual *gwo nèg*, Rara songs often boast about the Rara band itself. We encountered Bann Bourgeois de la Lwa outside of Saint Marc in 1993. They were a *charyiopye*, a band without instruments that uses their stomping feet as percussion. Their trademark song was about singing itself. It was a rhythmic masterpiece, a fast call and response between the *sanba* and the chorus.

S: Oh, Look at a song	C: Ya!
S: Children, I'm going to sing	C: Ya!
S: Children, I'm going to talk	C: Ya!
S: Oh, *sanba*, I'm going to roll out a song	C: Ya!
S: Children, I'm going to sing	C: Ya!
S: Children, I'm going to talk	C: Ya!
S: Oh, *sanba*, I'm going to roll out a song	C: Ya!
S: Children, I'm going to talk	C: Ya
S: O gade on konpa	C: Ya!
S: Ti moun yo m'pral chante	C: Ya!
S: Ti moun yo m'pral pale	C: Ya!
S: O sanba m pral roule	C: Ya!
S: O sanba m pral chante	C: Ya!
S: Ti moun yo m'pral pale	C: Ya!
S: O sanba m pral roule	C: Ya!
S: Ti moun yo m'pral pale	C: Ya![30]

This following boasting song by Rara Mande Gran Moun in Lèogâne brags that the *sanba* are so good people want to kill them.

> Gonaïves, I'm not going to stop in Gonaïves
> People want to kill us for our song [Repeat]
> That's the maestro standing in front; he's the leader
> He's the leader [Sing four times]

> Let them talk
> Mande Gran Moun is Number One
> It cannot be stopped
> That's why people want to kill me
> People want to eat me for my song
> That's the maestro standing in front; he's the leader

> *Gonaïves, mwen pa'p sa rete Gonaïves*
> *Se pou Konpa sa moun yo vle touye nou [Repeat]*
> *Se maestwo sa ki kanpe devan, se li ka'p kòmande*
> *Se Li k'ap kòmande [Sing four times]*

> *Kite yo pale*
> *Mande Gran Moun ki Numbè One*
> *Li p'ap ka rete*
> *Se pou Konpa sa moun yo vle touye mwen*
> *Pou Konpa sa moun yo vle manje mwen*
> *Se maestwo sa ki kanpe devan, se li ka'p kòmande*[31]

Rara bands usually pay annual visits to selected patrons that they know will receive them, in addition to spontaneously performing for new people. In these relationships between local *gwo nèg*, diplomacy is an important activity. Yonker reports a ritualized invitation process: "In a custom known as 'bois drapeau' poles are distributed to potential patrons. If they agree to be patrons, they return the poles with a patterned cloth banner, such as those preceding this band in the Artibonite Valley. The number of such banners proclaims the popularity of the group."[32]

In Port-au-Prince, a word-of-mouth system lets *oungan* in the area know that a visit is planned to their *ounfò* so they can be prepared with a contribution. If they intend to be generous with their support, perhaps offering a meal to the musicians, or even a place to spend the night, they will arrange this ahead of time with the Rara leaders. For an *oungan* who serves a *lwa* who likes Rara, this is one way to please the *lwa*. Receiving an entire Rara band is also a way to broadcast one's wealth and enhance one's reputation. Gerard reported, "We mostly dance at *oungan* and *manbo's* places. We don't dance for poor people."[33] In Port-au-Prince's cemetery neighborhood, one Rara band sent a series of typewritten letters of invitation, asking local *oungan* and *manbo* to receive the band. For a festival in which the majority of participants are non-literate, this display of literacy and formal diplomacy was a dramatic event.

Contrary to upper-class and American assumptions that Rara bands are unruly, undisciplined mobs, all bands have rules and regulations that members are penalized for breaking. One such set of rules and regulations for the Bizoton band Vapeur Vin Pou Wè was collected by Gerson Alexis in 1958. Among the stipulations are these:

> Article 1: The members of the Association must assemble on the proper days for processions before 8:00 at night, except Good Friday, Holy Saturday and Easter Sunday, when the meetings will be in the mornings: The first day before 8:00, the second day before 9:00, and the last days before 10:00. After these times, late members will pay a fine of 2 gourdes, except in case of illness or by previous arrangement.
>
> Article 6: All members of the band must wear a high hat with blue pants and a yellow shirt, or must pay a fine of 3 gourdes.[34]

Rara bands are organized local groups with formal ranks, costumes, and rituals, and they conceive of themselves as armies connected to imaginary states that move through territory, carry out armed maneuvers, and conduct diplomatic relations with other groups in the process of their musical celebrations. As local groups under the leadership of "big men," Rara bands mirror the politics of patronage that have characterized Haiti's national government. In their performances of maneuvers, diplomacy, and tribute to local notables, Rara bands distribute and redistribute prestige, reputation, and local resources.

The Army Fights: Musical Competition, Mystical Weapons, and Armed Warfare

Haiti is a populous country, so no Rara band is ever the sole performer in its locality. The wider an arc that a *kolonèl* decides to make with his Rara, the more likely it is that it will cross paths with other bands. Rara bands are always aware of each other and constantly compete to have a reputation for the "hottest" music, the best dancers, and the most *fanatik*. Each Rara band tries in different ways to destroy the others – to *kraze Rara* (literally, "crash the Rara"). *Kraze Rara* is signaled when a band's musicians stop playing and cannot get started again, or by a group disbanding altogether. The ultimate victory of one band over another is when the aggressors are able to capture the flag of the band they have "crashed."

Competition promotes virtuosity and inventiveness, though it is also potentially vicious. The public face of this competitive antagonism takes the form of performed polemics and rivalries. The most famous rivalry in the entire country is perhaps that between Ti-Malis and La Fleur de Rose in Léogâne, where to walk with one means you cannot safely walk in the other, and even Haitians living abroad form opinions about which band is best.[35] There are hidden competitions between bands as well, and these entail setting magical traps for one another in an elaborate series of war-game maneuvers. Occasionally the competition takes the form of sabotage such as kidnapping, stealing instruments, and jailing opponents. At the extreme, Rara bands enter into all-out physical battle, in which the strongest of the men fight one another with fists, rocks, clubs, and machetes. The Hôpital St. Croix in Léogâne assigns extra staff to treat the Rara wounded each year on Easter Week.[36]

Rara leaders may conduct spiritual or physical warfare for several reasons. They may be settling long-standing feuds, competing for followers, or be involved in complex local political dramas. The downward spiraling of the Haitian economy has pushed increasing numbers of people from the countryside into the capital city's slums. Many Rara bands come out of these slum neighborhoods and compete for resources, fans, and sheer reputation. Some of the most famous Raras come from Bel Air, a notorious slum that was historically the site of a maroon colony. Known for its fierce practice of the Kongo-based Petwo rites, these Raras are said to keep the slum-dwellers who are not members inside their homes at night.[37]

The goal of the Rara president, besides fulfilling his obligations to the *lwa*, is to attract the most followers. To be known as a Rara president is one way to perform one's status as a *gwo nèg* and garner its material benefits – more power and therefore more money – as well the religious benefit of being ritually remembered after one's death.

A very common Rara theme (and indeed a common theme in many Vodou songs) has to do with plots, conspiracies, and enemies waiting to entrap the singer. Rara Modèl in Léogâne sang about this plot against them:

Plot, they're mounting a plot [Repeat]
Danbala Wedo, they're mounting a plot
They're mounting a plot, What will I say to them
We can't see the people who crash a party
Get away, Get away from them

Konplo, Yo monte konplo [Repeat]
Danbala Wèdo, yo monte konplo-a
Yo monte konplo sa m'a di avè yo
Nou pa wè daso
Dekole, Dekole sou yo

David Yih perceptively relates these themes of mistrust to the history of Haitian slavery and exploitation:

In the themes, attitudes, and emotional content of the songtexts we can read the response of

Vodou to the circumstances under which it came forth. References to bondage, conflict, mistrust, betrayal, persecution, oppression, and war are frequent. These themes are often reflected in recurrent formulas – phrases encountered in several songs in the same or almost the same form.[38]

In the following Rara song, the threat of kidnapping and bondage is offset by the "talking bad" and bravado of the *sanba* who would lend his own rope to the kidnappers only to later escape:

They say they'll tie me up [Sing three times]
Here's the cord to tie me [Repeat]
When you hear midday ring, I'll throw down the cord and go

Yo di y'ap mare mwen [Sing three times]
Men kòd pou mare'm [Repeat]
Kan ou wè midi sonnen, m'ap lage kòd-la pou'm ale

In his work on the cultural patterns that inform the expressive talent and public performances of African-American men throughout the Caribbean, Roger D. Abrahams has found that verbal dexterity is a much cultivated and prized value and that men-of-words trade on oratory talent as a form of cultural capital as they compete to build reputations. Abrahams describes a multiplicity of West Indian performance troupes, often organized around a captain, who is usually the best performer. They put their talents in full view of the community during events such as Christmas serenading, Christmas mumming plays, Carnival, and Jonkonnu. "In those troupes that involve dancing, acrobatics, or fighting, [the man-of-words] has his equivalent, one we might call the man-of-action, the physically adept one who brings focus to the proceedings by his leadership and performance abilities."[39] Consider this description of the Trinidad Carnival Devil Band in 1956:

There was a reigning beast, a man so dexterous and inventive in his dancing and portrayal of the beast as to be proclaimed best. Each year aspirants for his crown would "challenge him to combat." The challenge to combat occurred automatically when the two bands met for the first time. The combat took the form of the execution by the reigning beast of various dance steps which the challenger had to imitate. If he succeeded in imitating them he then executed steps of his own for the reigning beast to imitate. The beast who first failed to imitate the other's steps lost the contest.[40]

Similar competitions can be seen in African-American traditions in the United States today. The "Black Indians" of New Orleans Mardi Gras confront one another publicly each year and enter into intense symbolic battles, each man or woman ritually showing parts of their elaborately beaded costume, thereby challenging the opposing "Indian" to "go them one better." The winner is immediately apparent, judged on the spot by the reactions of onlookers and the demeanor of the two "Indians" themselves. It is not unheard of for the "Black Indian" gangs to fight one another with fists, knives, and guns, and more than one man has lost his life in these intensely competitive processions.[41] Break-dancing, capoeira, drag balls, and jazz improvisation are performed challenges within US Black masculine cultures, just as graffiti writing is a visually performed challenge for urban "crews" or gangs.

Rara shares with all these practices a competitive spirit of artistic decoration and performance, but it is perhaps extreme in the way it spiritualizes landscape and uses mystical weapons (including poisons) and in the frequency with which bands fight one another, escalating the competition into violent and dangerous battles. Although it is a form of Black West Indian all-night reputation-enhancing performance associated with "play" values of "foolishness" and "nonsense," Rara bands are also committed to a level of battle over reputation and territory that marks it as a deadly serious event.

Poisons, powders, and magical weapons

While the musicians and *fanatik* in Rara are singing their boasting and bragging songs, playing catchy melodies on the *banbou*, and drumming as hard as they can to create a carnivalesque atmosphere, the leaders are often competing

against other bands in an inside world of secret politics. They hold nocturnal meetings and stage elaborate schemes involving espionage and magical warfare against other bands. The fears of Rara leaders about conspiracies against them are well-founded, because the magicians associated with Rara – *bòkò* and secret society leaders – perform rituals meant to weaken and *kraze* other Raras. In the first meeting of the Rara band of the season, the leaders of Rara La Belle Fraîcheur de l'Anglade got together and magically "tied up" an enemy Rara general and put him under a rock, weighing him down by magic to drain his power. General Kanep showed me a rock and a whip, explaining:

> K: You call the names of all the Rara presidents that you are going up against, and you tie them up so they can't assault you. You put them underneath you. I named another general, I put him under this rock.
>
> Q: How do you do that ceremony?
>
> K: You name him, and you place him there, and he's now underneath you. You say, "All those who live, get beneath my feet."[42]

A similar practice was reported in the colonial period. In 1758 M. Courtain, judge at the Royal Seat in Cap Français, wrote that "They place the *makandal*, loaded with curses, under a large stone, and it is indubitable that this brings misfortune to whomever they wish it."[43] "Makandal" was also the name of a slave resistance leader who carried out mass poisonings and magical warfare against slaveowners in the late eighteenth century. His name became the designation for a sort of magic object.

During Rara season, band leaders send scouts to learn the plans of other *kolonèl* and may decide to avoid or encounter neighboring bands in their weekly *ekzèsis*. There are always possibilities for spontaneous encounters as well, because each band will stop and perform at such unplanned opportunities as approaching cars, in addition to performing for patrons scheduled in advance. Even in an unplanned encounter, the music has heralded a band's approach, and flag bearers who are vigilant have spotted the oncoming flag of the competitor.

The moment when two bands encounter and pass one another is called *mariaj Rara* (literally, "Rara marriage") and is an extremely dangerous and crucial point. Each band faces the challenge of continuing its musical beat and hopes to attract the fans of the other band. When relations are very good between groups, each will stop and perform an *ochan*, the musical salute reserved for patrons and contributors. If they are enemies, the bands use the moment as an opportunity to try to *kraze* one another and force the other band to stop playing and stop their walk.

Many Rara *kolonèl* are also *oungan* and *bòkò*, knowledgeable in *zam kongo* (Kongo weapons) that include *wanga*, botanical curatives, and toxins. They commonly manufacture *pwazon* (poisons) and *poud* (powders) and leave them in crossroads for other Raras to step on. These packages are meant to create "bad air" and confuse the other band, or else lead to sickness. In a skirmish, they administer the *poud* face-to-face, with a *kou'd poud* (literally, "hit of powder") when two bands meet. The aggressor will lift the powder to his lips and blow it into the faces of the men in the opposing Rara. *Poud* are made of diverse toxins: a variety of poison ivy called *pwa grate* (itching bean), *piman* (hot pepper), and other poisonous plants and herbs. It is to the advantage of the Rara leader to boast of having *poud*, to create a sense of awe in the community about his powers and his willingness to use them. General Gerard enjoyed talking "bad" about his ability to *kraze* other Raras and attract their *fanatik*:

> Wherever it comes from, wherever it is, if there's a Rara in Bel Air I'll "crash" it. I'll make them carry their drums on their backs and go home. Any Rara I face. My Rara is the biggest Rara here.
>
> As soon as I give them a *kou'd poud*, they'll go home. Everybody will run. I'll turn that band around and everybody in it will follow me. My Rara will become the biggest Rara.[44]

Poud can reportedly cause burning and rashes on the skin, shortness of breath, blindness, paralysis, and even death. It is considered a serious weapon, and using it has historically been judged

a crime.[45] The following account, reported to me by a schoolteacher in Beaufort in the Artibonite Valley, ascribes the death of a young man to powder, but a powder that was marked magically only for him:

> A: A young man fell in the Rara, and his parents said he had gotten hit with powder. He died. This was in 1981 in Beaufort, in section Jean Denis. The guy who got the *kou'd poud* was named Lucien. He went to an *oungan*, and the *oungan* analyzed it. He said it was powder that killed him.
>
> Q: How long did it take?
>
> A: It was very quick. The same day the guy got sick, he died. After about three hours.
>
> Q: How come only one person got hit?
>
> A: Well, it was a specific guy. He blew the powder in the name of that guy. You know powder is a magical thing. When you blow it in one person's name, other people aren't affected.[46]

To be known as a someone who can manufacture *poud* and use it in the Rara is to augment one's reputation as a magician and as a feared member of the community. Karin Barber notes that among the Yoruba, "The Big Man was pictured as rising above the malicious attacks of jealous rivals and at the same time getting away with any attacks he made on *them*."[47] Surviving these attacks requires each Rara leader to carry antidotes to the powders of others. The members of Rara Brilliant Soleil in Léogâne explained:

> It's the *kolonèl* who knows what to do to go forward or to set traps. There are some Rara that go through a crossroads, and they put some "funny stuff" in the crossroads, to "crash" other Raras who come behind them. The colonel has to have a series of things with him, and he has to be smart enough to smash anything they leave for him, so he can get through.[48]

Rara leaders boasted about their ability to repair damage done by other Raras' powders. Gerard says, "If you encounter another Rara, they might blow [powder] on you. In order that your Rara doesn't 'crash,' you have to walk with your own equipment. Before you even face that Rara, if they know where you're going to pass, you can lift off anything [traps] they put down for you with your whip. So your Rara doesn't 'crash.' "[49]

In 1993 I was able to spend a few nights walking with La Belle Fraîcheur de l'Anglade, with whom I had spent two weeks in 1992. On the route from Tomasin to Kenskoff, high in the mountains above Port-au-Prince, the generals drew up elaborate battle plans, strategizing maneuvers with both friends and foes. Camping for a while with an allied band called Rara La Reine (The Queen's Rara) I heard them discussing an event that had taken place the night before. It seems that a spy sent from another Rara had walked with us and thrown powder on General Silvera's horse, trying to kill it. The horse had become sick with fever, but it had recovered, because, they said, the horse was actually mystically dedicated to a *lwa*.

Physical fighting

In both Carnival and Rara, there is always the potential for violence that exists in large public crowds where young men are drinking. In Carnival a fairly serious physical competition called *gagann* finds two men hurling themselves at each other like roosters, bashing their upper chests together in an effort to knock each other down. *Gagann* can lead to *wozèt* (strangling; literally, "bow-tie") and end in outright fights. Other small-scale warfare goes on during Carnival; Mirville reports the use of slingshots as a weapon, and rocks are thrown from time to time.[50] Rara bands sometimes perform at the site of formal physical fighting. In the south of Haiti there are wrestling matches, and onlookers bet on the young men who fight while the Raras play. This goes on presently in Port-au-Prince in the neighborhood of Delmas 31, now called "Citè Jérémie" because five hundred migrants from Jérémie have settled there in the years since 1981.[51]

Violence in Rara can be devastating, especially if two groups plan to fight. Wade Davis describes meeting Andres Celestin, a *tonton makout* and Bizango president near Saint Marc. "Now he seemed a broken man, lying prostrate on a cot with much of his face swollen and distorted by a sharp blow received, as we would learn later, when two Rara bands had met and clashed several nights previously."[52] To avoid such violence, Raras' ministers of war will engage in diplomacy, as Beauvoir and Dominique note: "Often, for example, the groups enter a state of war when they encounter one another. They throw rocks, draw their machetes and fight. To avoid this, they must send a blue flag in front and the 'Minister of War' must go ahead and make peace."[53]

I never witnessed a violent encounter between two Rara bands, but rumors of aggressive incidents were common. On 25 January 1993, the newspaper *Le Nouvelliste* ran this headline: "Confrontation between 2 Foot Bands; Shots Fired in the Air." Apparently one Carnival band held hostage a musician from another band called Konbit Lakay. The incident was reported in the newspaper only because the military arrived and fired into the air to diffuse the situation. Later that season, two Raras in Pont Sonde came to blows and a man was decapitated by a machete.[54] Someone had died in Rara Saint Rose in a fight in the mountains between Léogâne and Jacmel the year before I arrived.[55] Over the months of my research, I was told many stories of legendary battles between bands involving death, jailings, and ongoing feuds. In 1986, for example, it seems that Rara Rosalie and Rara Rosignol planned a fight; as a result of the battle, two men died, one son of each president. They crossed the two bodies over one another in the street. Five years later the two bands reconciled and invited one another to feasts.[56] Myths spring up about people dying in Rara; more than one man swore to me that he had seen a man decapitated, then saw the body continue to dance as the head, fallen to the ground, kept blowing its trumpet.

This chapter has explored the overarching ethos of militarism that pervades the Rara festival, as bands construct themselves as popular armies and move into public space like battalions prepared for war. Rara bands imagine themselves to be self-organized popular armies, which may be ritualized performances of the peasant armies that played a central role in Haitian political history.

Rara hierarchy and organization reveal how the cultural practices of the Haitian popular classes display and draw attention to the local social order. Like many other popular groups, Raras are ranked in strict hierarchical relationships, displaying and performing the system of patronage that has fueled Haitian politics at all levels through the present day. As traditional peasant groups, Raras can be viewed as the prepolitical forerunners of the contemporary grassroots popular organizations that make up the democratic peasant movement.

Notes

1 Contemporary grassroots peasant organizations include Tèt Kole (Heads Together) founded in 1986, MPP (Peasant Movement of Papay) founded in the 1970s, and Soley Leve (The Sun Is Rising) founded in 1990. These organizations represent powerful blocs on the national stage and regularly make headlines in the Haitian Press.

2 Moreau de Saint Mery, *Description topographique, physique, civile, politique et historique de la partie française de l'île S. Dominque.*

3 Dolores Yonker, "Rara: A Lenten Festival," *Bulletin du Bureau National D'Ethnologie* 2 (1985).

4 D. Brown, "Garden in the Machine," p. 58.

5 Roman, "Recherche Sur Un Rara Appele La Meprise a L'arcahaie (Merlotte)."

6 Rénald Clerismé, "Organization: For Us, It Is Our Lives," *Crossroads: Contemporary Political Analysis and Left Dialogue* 47 (1995). See also Emmanuel Paul, "Folklore Du Militarism," *Optique* 6 (1954): 24–7. Cited in Y.-M. David Yih, "Music and Dance of Haitian Vodou: Diversity and Unity in Regional Repertoires" (PhD dissertation, Wesleyan University, 1995), p. 121.

7 Michel S. Laguerre, *Les Associations traditionelles de travail dans la paysannerie haitienne* (Port-au-Prince: N.P., 1975), p. 4. Cited in Beauvoir and Dominique, "Savalou E," p. 105; my translation. Ranks in these hierarchies can include Prezidan Konsey, Vis Prezidan, Gouvene Pep, Gouvene Laplas, Dirije Laplas, Jeneral Laplas, Adjwen Laplas, Jeneral Dekouvet, Dirije, Ren Bayonet, Ren Drapo, Ren Dirije, Ren Kobey, and then Sekrete, Trezorye, Minis Lage, Minis de Finans, and Prezidan ak Ren Chita. Beauvoir and Dominique, "Savalou E," p. 106.

8 Paul Moral, *Le Paysan haitien* (Paris, 1961), p. 190. Cited in Beauvoir and Dominique, "Savalou E," p. 100. Emphasis added.

9 Beauvoir and Dominique, "Savalou E," p. 110.

10 In contrast, as in the *sosyete travay*, a member may possess an honorific title without participating in the band at all; in this case the member may be a financial supporter or a landowner who wishes to have a rank but no duties. This sometimes meets the resentment of other band members, who may have lowlier titles and perform more of the work of the band.

11 President of Mande Gran Moun, interview, March 1993.

12 Michel S. Laguerre, *Voodoo and Politics in Haiti* (New York: St Martin's Press, 1989), p. 122. Many *lwa* are contemporarily depicted as military figures, including the entire "line" of Ogou, the "god of war." Not violent per se, these spirits impart military knowledge in general, including self-control, discipline, and fearlessness. For a feminist perspective on Ogou, see Karen McCarthy Brown, "Why Women Need the War God," in *Women's Spirit Bonding*, ed. Janet Kalven and Mary I. Buckley (New York: Pilgrim Press, 1984), and Karen McCarthy Brown, "Systematic Remembering, Systematic Forgetting: Ogou in Haiti," in *Africa's Ogun*, ed. Sandra T. Barnes (Bloomington: Indiana University Press, 1989).

13 Gage Averill and Yuen Ming David Yih, "Militarism in Haitian Music," in *The African Diaspora: A Musical Perspective*, ed. Ingrid Monson (New York: Garland, 2000).

14 Beauvoir and Dominique, "Savalou E," p. 95.

15 M. Trouillot, *Haiti, State against Nation*, p. 95.

16 Constantin Dumerve, "Musique et danse vaudouesques," *Les Griots 3(3)*. Cited in Averill and Yih, "Militarism in Haitian Music."

17 Yih, "Music and Dance of Haitian Vodou," p. 132.

18 Cited in Jean Fouchard, *The Haitian Maroons* (New York: Blyden Press, 1981), p. 346.

19 For this brief outline I owe thanks to my colleague at Yale, Rénald Clerismé, who shared with me his knowledge of traditional culture history and his experience with peasant organizations. This synopsis is borrowed from his article, Clerismé, "Organization," p. 8.

20 Verna Gillis, "Rara in Haiti, Gaga in the Dominican Republic," liner notes to the album of the same name, Folkways Records Album No. FE 4531, 1978, p. 4.

21 At the present writing, the public living-room area in the headquarters of the US Embassy marine guard displays a series of photographs of Americans leading captive Cacos out of the bush, thus visually reinscribing for newly arrived marines their roles as dominators of the Haitian popular classes. I saw the photos at one of their Friday "open-house" gatherings for expatriate Americans in 1993, before the 1995 US inter-vasion.

22 Georges Corvington, personal communication, Port-au-Prince, 1993. Also see Tselos, "Threads of Reflection," note 4.

23 M. Trouillot, *Haiti, State against Nation*, p. 179. For theories on maximizing prestige, see Edmund Leach, *Political Systems in Highland Burma* (Cambridge: Harvard University Press, 1954).

24 Michel-Rolph Trouillot, personal communication, 1991.

25 Karin Barber, "How Man Makes God in West Africa: Yoruba Attitudes toward the Orisha," *Africa* 51(3) (1981): 724.

26 Kris L. Hardin, *The Aesthetics of Action: Continuity and Change in a West African Town* (Washington, DC: Smithsonian Institution Press, 1993), p. 213.

27 Barber, "How Man Makes God in West Africa," p. 728.

28 La Belle Fraîcheur de l'Anglade, Easter 1992.

29 Recorded 11 April 1993, Verettes. Another song by Ya Seizi is on a recording compiled by this author; see Artists, *Rhythms of Rapture*.

30 Bann Bourgeois de la Lwa. Recorded 27 March 1993, Route Gonaives north of Saint Marc near Beaufort.

31 Mande Gran Moun, Léogâne, 1993. *Kolonèl* of Mande Gran Moun, interview, Léogâne, March 1993.

32 Yonker, "Haiti after the Fall."

33 President Gerard of Rara Etoile Salomon, interview, Port-au-Prince, 7 April 1992.

34 Alexis, "Les Danses Rara," p. 60.

35 Videotapes of Rara in Léogâne circulate throughout New York City and Miami, giving Haitians in those two US cities the annual opportunity to hear the songs. Léogâne is the town best known for Rara in Haiti; each band sponsors a feast, called *cav*, during Lent and invites others. Then on Easter weekend bands all over the south converge between Carrefour du Fort and Léogâne for competition. Many Port-au-Prince youth and returning diaspora members go to Léogâne specially for Rara; it has become one of the cyclical tourist spots for the mobile Port-au-Prince dweller. The Rara scene in Léogâne is complex and populous and deserves a monograph on its own in the future.

36 Dr. McCleary, personal communication, Hôpital St. Croix, Léogâne, 27 March 1991.

37 M. Alphonse, drummer, personal communication, Bel Air, Port-au-Prince, 18 March 1991.

38 Yih, "Music and Dance of Haitian Vodou," p. 473.

39 Abrahams, *The Man-of-Words in the West Indies*, p. xvi.

40 Cited in ibid. See also Nunley and Bettelheim, *Caribbean Festival Arts*.

41 Larry Bannock, chief of the Goldenstar Hunters, interview, New Orleans, Mardi Gras 1990.

42 General Kanep of Rara La Belle Fraîcheur de l'Anglade, interview, March 1992.

43 Courtain, "Mémoire sommaire sur les préteudues pratiques magiques et empoisonnements prouvés au proces instruit et jugé au Cap contre plusieurs negres et negresses dont le chef, F. Macandal, a été condamné au feu et executé le 20 janvier 1758." Presented by Franklin Midy, *Chemins critiques* I, (I) (1989): 135–42. Cited in Yih, "Music and Dance of Haitian Vodou," p. 86.

44 President of Rara Etoile Salomon, interview, Port-au-Prince, 7 April 1992.

45 Moreau de Saint Mery, *Description topographique, physique, civile, politique et historique de la partie française de l'île S. Dominque*.

46 Beaufort schoolteacher, interview, 27 March 1993.

47 Barber, "How Man Makes God in West Africa," p. 729.

48 Similyen family, interview, Léogâne, 26 March 1991.

49 President of Rara Etoile Salomon, interview, Port-au-Prince, 7 April 1992.

50 Ernst Mirville, *Considerations ethno-psychoanalytiques sur le carnival haitien* (Port-au-Prince: Collection Coucouille, 1978), p. 80.

51 Wilfred, interview, Rue Xaragua, April 1993.

52 Wade Davis, *The Serpent and the Rainbow* (New York: Simon and Schuster, 1985), p. 258.

53 Beauvoir and Dominique, "Savalou E," p. 110.

54 Father Jean-Yves Urfie, editor of Newspaper *Libètè*, personal communication, Pont-Sonde, April 1993.

55 President of Rara Saint Rose, interview, February 1993.

56 Master Drummer for Mande Gran Moun, interview, Léogâne, 25 March 1993.

References

Abrahams, Roger D. (1983). *The Man-of-Words in the West Indies: Performance and the Emergence of Creole Culture*. Baltimore: Johns Hopkins University Press.

Alexis, Gerson (1959). "Les Danses Rara." *Bulletin du Bureau d'Ethnologie* 3(17, 18, 19): 41–62.

Averill, Gage, and Verna Gillis (1991). "Rara in Haiti – Gaga in the Dominican Republic." Liner notes to *Rara in Haiti – Gaga in the Dominican Republic*. Smithsonian Folkways.

Averill, Gage, and Yuen Ming David Yih (2000). "Militarism in Haitian Music." In *The African Diaspora: A Musical Perspective*, ed. Ingrid Monson, pp. 267–93. New York: Garland Publishing.

Barber, Karin (1981). "How Man Makes God in West Africa: Yoruba Attitudes toward the Orisha." *Africa* 51 (3): 724–45.

Beauvoir, Rachel, and Didier Dominique (1987). "Savalou E." Port-au-Prince: Np.

Brown, David H. (1989). "Garden in the Machine: Afro-Cuban Sacred Art and Performance in Urban New Jersey and New York." PhD dissertation, Yale University.

Brown, Karen McCarthy (1984). "Why Women Need the War God." In *Women's Spirit Bonding*, ed. Janet Kalven and Mary I. Buckley, pp. 190–201. New York: Pilgrim Press.

Clerismé, Rénald (1995). "Organization: For Us, It Is Our Lives." *Crossroads: Contemporary Political Analysis and Left Dialogue* 47: 8–10.

Davis, Wade (1985). *The Serpent and the Rainbow*. New York: Simon and Schuster.

Dumerve, Constantin (1939). "Musique et danse vaudouesques." *Les Griots* 3(3): 411–14.

Hardin, Kris L. (1993). *The Aesthetics of Action: Continuity and Change in a West African Town*. Washington, DC: Smithsonian Institution Press.

Laguerre, Michel S. (1975). *Les Associations traditionnelles de travail dans la paysannerie haitienne*. Port-au-Prince: Np.

Laguerre, Michel S. (1989). *Voodoo and Politics in Haiti*. New York: St Martin's Press.

Midy, Franklin (1989). "Mémoire" [by Courtain]. *Chemins Critiques* 1(1): 135–42.

Mirville, Ernst (1978). *Considerations Ethnò-Psychoanalytiques Dur Le Carnival Haitian*. Port-au-Prince: Collection Coucouille.

Moral, Paul (1961). *Le Paysan Haitien*. Paris.

Moreau de Saint Mery, Médéric-Louis-Elie (1958). *Description topographique, physique, civile, politique et historique de la partie française de l'île S. Dominque*. Nouvelle ed. Ed. Blanche Maurel and Etienne Taillemitte. Paris: Société de l'histoire de la Colonie Français.

Nunley, John W., and Judith Bettelheim, eds. (1988). *Caribbean Festival Arts: Each and Every Bit of Difference*. Seattle: University of Washington.

Roman, Pierre Isnard (1993). "Recherche Sur Un Rara Appele La Meprise a L'arcahaie (Merlotte)." In *Faculty of Ethnology*. Port-au-Prince: Np.

Trouillot, Michel-Rolph (1990). *Haiti, State against Nation: The Origins and Legacy of Duvalierism*. New York: Monthly Review Press.

Tselos, Susan Elizabeth (1996). "Threads of Reflection: Costumes of Haitian Rara." *African Arts* 29(2): 58–65.

Yih, Y.-M. David (1995). "Music and Dance of Haitian Vodou: Diversity and Unity in Regional Repertoires." PhD dissertation, Wesleyan University.

Yonker, Dolores (1989). "Haiti after the Fall: The Politics of Rara." Np.

Yonker, Dolores (1985). "Rara: A Lenten Festival." *Bulletin du Bureau National d'Ethnologie* 2: 63–71.

9

Celebrating Cricket

The Symbolic Construction of Caribbean Politics

Frank E. Manning

Cricket has suffered, but not only cricket. The aestheticians have scorned to take notice of popular sports and games – to their own detriment. The aridity and confusion of which they so mournfully complain will continue until they include organized games *and the people who watch them* as an integral part of their data. (C. L. R. James 1963: 191–2; emphasis in original)

The failure of art critics to appreciate the aesthetics of popular sport has been no less myopic than the failure of anthropologists to grasp its social importance. Although folklorists and protoethnologists of the previous century showed an interest in games – much of it inspired by E. B. Tylor's evolutionary and diffusionist speculations – the anthropology of play did not advance appreciably until the late 1950s (Schwartzman 1978:5). A great deal of the recent attention, however, has been directed at either children's play or at relatively small-scale games – a corpus pioneered by the early collaborative studies of Roberts and Sutton-Smith (1962, 1966). A significant literature on mass ludic spectacles such as popular sports events and public celebrations is only now emerging, much of it inspired by the interest of Gluckman and Turner in "secular ritual" (Moore and Myerhoff 1977) and by Geertz's (1972) paper on the Balinese cockfight.

The seminal work of these latter figures converges on a conceptual approach to the relationship between symbolic and social phenomena. For Turner (1977), "liminoid" performative genres such as festivals and carnivals are "proto-" or "metastructural," generating cultural comprehension by abstracting and recombining – often in novel, metaphorical ways – a social structure's basic principles. For Gluckman (see Gluckman and Gluckman 1977), whose views were articulated in the last article published before his death, symbolic events such as sports attractions and theatrical productions differ from traditional religious rites in being an imaginative "presentation" of society rather than a "re-presentation" or copy of it. For Geertz (1972), the cockfight is a fictive story about its social context, a "metasocial commentary" on it that is analogous to a literary text in using the devices of aesthetic license to disarrange conventional semantic contexts and rearrange them in unconventional ways. Geertz also under-scores a point that is less forcefully made by Gluckman and Turner: that symbolic forms are not only a reflexive interpretation of social life, but also a means through which people discover and learn their culture. The lesson for anthropology is that symbolic inquiry, besides laying bare a social system, can also tell us a great deal about the epistemological processes whereby that system is revealed to those whose lives it shapes.

Drawing from these positions, as well as other perspectives that have thrown light on public play and mass performance, this paper examines Bermudian cricket festivals. I focus on the social history of these festivals, on the manner in which they are celebrated, and on a highly significant side activity, gambling. My contention is that the total genre dramatizes a fundamental, racially oriented conflict between cultural identity and economic interest – a conflict that is generalizable to the Caribbean (and perhaps other decolonizing areas) and that underlies the region's political situation. Consistent with Cohen's (1979:87) observation that anthropology's chief contribution to the study of politics has been the analysis of nonpolitical symbols that have political implications and functions, I propose that celebration can provide a unique understanding of the conceptual parameters in which political awareness is developed and expressed.

Blacks in Whites

In the West Indies the game of cricket is played with elegant skill, studied with scholarly intensity, argued with passionate conviction, and revered with patriotic pride. Young boys with makeshift bats and balls play spiritedly in yards, fields, and beaches, learning the skills that in the past century have made West Indians among the world's outstanding cricketers. Organized competition begins in school and continues – often through middle age – in amateur sports clubs. Island-wide teams drawn from the clubs provide the Caribbean's premier sports attraction when they play annually in a touring series known as the Shell Shield. There is also a pan-West Indian team that represents the region in "test" (international) matches and that has been the outstanding exception to a catalog of failed attempts at West Indian unification.

One gleans the historical significance of the game in *Beyond a Boundary*, C. L. R. James's (1963) autobiography cum cricket analysis. A Trinidadian journalist, teacher, historian, political critic, and, above all, cricket devotee, James contends that in the West Indies cricket was traditionally seen as embodying the qualities of the classic British character ideal: fair play, restraint, perseverance, responsibility, and the moral inflections of Victorian Puritanism. Paradoxically, Afro-West Indians were taught to esteem those standards but were denied the means of achieving and demonstrating them. Cricket organizations – clubs, leagues, selection committees, governing bodies – conformed to the wider system of color-class stratification, and when the races occasionally played together, it was customary for whites to bat and blacks to bowl (St. Pierre 1973:7–12).

The phrase "put on your whites" is instructive. Literally, it means to don the several items – white or cream-colored – that make up a cricket uniform: shoes, pants, shirt, sweater, protective gloves, knee pads. Figuratively, it is a metonym of the black struggle in cricket, itself a metonym as well as an instrument of the more general black struggle under British colonialism. In cricket there were a succession of black goals: to get to bat, to gain places on island-wide teams and regional tours, and, as recently as the 1960s, to be named vice-captains and captains of test teams, positions reserved for whites even after racial criteria had been virtually eliminated from selection procedures. Cricket successes brought recognition to Afro-West Indians both internationally and, more begrudgingly, in the upper strata of local society, gradually transforming the sport into a powerful symbol of black ability, achievement, and aspiration.

Bermudian cricket is a variation on these themes, but one that, like Bermuda itself, caricatures and often strikingly illuminates the Caribbean pattern. Lying a thousand miles and a climatic zone north of the West Indies, Bermuda has a five-month summer cricket season and therefore does not participate in most major West Indian tournaments, which are held during the winter. Nor do Bermudians take the game as seriously or as professionally as West Indians do. In the Caribbean, for example, festival games – occasions when a cricket match takes place in a setting of festive sociability – are relatively informal, localized, and of little general interest (James 1963:20–1).[1] In Bermuda, however, festival games are both the highlights of the cricket season and, aside from Christmas, the calendar's most significant holidays. Bermudian festival cricket is the counterpart of Caribbean carnivals, but it enriches the spirit of celebration with the drama of a popular sporting classic.

The racial division of Bermudian cricket was shaped by an apartheidlike form of segregation, rather than by the West Indian system of color-class stratification. Introduced by British military personnel in the nineteenth century, the game was originally played in white sporting clubs. Blacks responded by forming neighborhood cricket clubs that have since evolved into the country's major centers of sport, entertainment, and sociability (Manning 1973). Through the clubs, blacks gained unquestioned superiority in cricket; when racial integration was nominally introduced in the 1960s, whites virtually withdrew from the game.

Two of the oldest black clubs, Somerset and St George's, were begun primarily to promote an informal cricket contest held each August 1st in commemoration of the 1834 emancipation of slaves in British territories – an occasion marked by varied festivities throughout the Commonwealth Caribbean. Under club sponsorship the event developed into Cup Match, the oldest and most prominent cricket festival. Now held on the Thursday and Friday closest to August 1st, the game's historical identification with blacks is maintained by the white practice of observing the first day of Cup Match as Somers's Day, named after the British Admiral Sir George Somers who discovered Bermuda in 1609.

Besides Cup Match there are the Eastern, Western, and Central County Games, each involving four clubs in a series of three matches staggered between June and September. As these series progress there is a buildup of festivity and sporting interest, so that the final games – in effect, sequels to Cup Match – are like Cup Match as occasions of mass celebration. In white

society the County Games are paralleled by summer yachting competitions, notably the renowned Newport–Bermuda race. Nowhere in the Caribbean is there a more striking example of the pluralistic segmentation that Smith (1965) attributed to British West Indian societies.

While Cup Match commemorates emancipation from slavery, the County Games celebrate diffuse aspects of the black tradition and lifestyle. The Eastern and Western series, the two most popular, reflect variants in the black situation that figure in the deeper-level meaning of festival cricket. Begun in 1904, the Eastern Games involve clubs that draw from old, demographically stable neighborhoods. In each neighborhood there is a core of black extended families, typically small property owners deriving modest incomes from family stores, trades, service jobs, and, in earlier generations more than now, part-time farming and fishing. The principle of family-neighborhood integrity is the basis of Eastern County selection rules. Eligibility is based on having been born in the club's neighborhood – the usual and preferred criterion – or having been a resident of it for at least two years. Although in a number of cases current players have moved away from their ancestral neighborhoods and play for other clubs in league games, their return for the County Games makes each club roster a roll call of familiar surnames, re-creating the networks and reviving the sentiments of traditional social organization.

The Western County Games, begun in 1962, are a product of newer social influences. The Western parishes have grown appreciably since the time when the series started, as new luxury hotels have created employment and as the demand for housing among blacks short of middle age has been met by the conversion of large estates into fashionable residential subdivisions (Newman 1972:3). Reflecting these trends, the Western Games are touted not as neighborhood rivalries, but as slick, highly competitive all-star games. Clubs vie intensely for Bermuda's best cricketers, offering lucrative incentives that lure players from outside the Western parishes and that encourage opportunistic switching between clubs from one year to the next. The clubs have even extended recruitment into the Caribbean, scouting the region for prospects and arranging their immigration. In the mid-1970s, the final game of the Western series was extended from one day to two, a move aimed at raising the caliber of play, generating wider public interest, and boosting gate receipts. The emphasis on aggressive commercialism is also seen in other areas of club activity, notably entertainment. Two of the clubs involved in the series (as well as other clubs in the Western parishes) have built elegant lounges which remain open as late as 5 a.m., offering formidable competition to the area's hotels.

Underlying the varying inflections of the Eastern and Western County Games are changes in the terms of clientage, the basis of the black Bermudian socioeconomic condition. Traditionally, Bermuda was run by a white aristocracy whose relations to blacks were paternal in both a biological and social sense. Descendants of the original seventeenth-century British settlers, the aristocracy were seafarers until the 1870s, agricultural exporters from then until the 1920s, and more recently an interlocking establishment of merchants, bankers, and corporate lawyers. Functioning as a ruling class in an almost feudal sense (Lewis 1968:323), they used the instruments of patronage – jobs, loans, credit, mortgages, charity – to maintain the allegiance and even the endearment of blacks, who make up three-fifths of the population, as well as a white underclass consisting of old "poor cousin" families, newer immigrants from Commonwealth countries, and Azorean Portuguese imported as indentured agricultural laborers. Patron–client relations were typically transacted within neighborhoods and parishes and between extended families, reinforcing residential identity and producing alliances between black and white kin groups that crosscut the system of institutionalized racial segregation. The common Caribbean metaphor of island society as a single large family (Wilson 1973:47) was powerfully resonant in Bermuda, yielding a meaningful context in which patronage took the social form of a relationship between benevolent, although demanding, white patriarchs and filial black dependents.

Since the early 1960s, however, the power and prestige of the aristocracy have been substantially eroded. The tourist boom has made foreign-owned hotels the major employers and, along with the development of an offshore corporate business sector, brought to Bermuda a class of expatriate managers who wield an appreciable influence in local affairs. In addition, the buoyancy and expansion of the economy has allowed the aggressive rise of underclass whites, notably Bermuda-born Portuguese, and a handful of black professionals and entrepreneurs. Tellingly, many of the aristocracy's merchant houses on Front Street, the commercial frontispiece of Hamilton, are now dominated by whites whose rise to economic prominence has come about within the past two decades.

What these changes have done to the patronage system is alter its character and style while maintaining, and perhaps strengthening, its grip on the overwhelming majority of blacks. The benevolent paternalism of the aristocracy has been replaced by the bureaucratic orientation of the new elite, and largess has been escalated to include company directorships, investment opportunities, business partnerships, and well-paid managerial positions. Blacks enjoy the life-style provided by an affluent economy, but at the cost of remaining in a position of clientage and subordination.

"We black Bermudians," an old man cautioned, "can easily fool you. We're laughing on the outside, but crying on the inside." This commonplace statement derives its impact from oxymoron, the figure of speech that combines conceptual and emotional antitheses. Viewed as a collectively enacted "text," festival cricket is also built on oxymoron. Overtly and purposefully, these games articulate the meaning of freedom, family, community, club, and, above all, cricket itself – symbols that manifest to blacks their identity, their solidarity, their survival. But the games also reflect, implicitly but no less significantly, the field of socioeconomic relations in which blacks are dependent on a white power structure that has lost its traditional character but preserved its oppressive force. In this juxtaposition – this dramatic oxymoron – lies the basis of both the political system and the political imagination.

Food, Liquor, Clothing, and Money

Soliciting a description of festival cricket early in my first Bermudian fieldwork, I was told it was the time "when we eat everything in Bermuda, drink everything in Bermuda, wear everything in Bermuda, and spend everything in Bermuda." Although popular interest in the game runs unusually high, festival cricket is an occasion of participation, not spectatorship. The festival ethos is one of hedonistic indulgence, gregarious sociability, histrionic exhibitionism, lavish hospitality, conspicuous consumption – behaviors that epitomize and celebrate the black Bermudian self-image. In Singer's (1955) terms, festival cricket is a cultural performance, a dramatic spectacle in which a people proclaim and demonstrate their sense of who they are.

Like Carnival, festival cricket involves a period of preparation that is considered nearly as much fun as the event itself. For weeks before Cup Match there is intense speculation about the selection of teams. Pundits offer their personal choices in letters to the editor, and the subject is heatedly discussed in bars, in buses, and on street corners. The principal centers of activity are the black clubs, where people go, in the words of one informant, "just to hear the arguments." The arguments peak a week before the game, when the club selection committees announce their picks to the membership at a meeting in which dramatic suspense, flamboyant and often fiery oratory, and uproarious entertainment combine ritualistically to induct chosen players into the club tradition. In the final days before the game there is a general buildup of festive sociability, a flurry of shopping activity for food, liquor, and clothing, and extended expressions of team loyalty through the display of club colors on cars and items of apparel. For County Games the scenario is similar, but on a smaller scale.

Game days begin early, as fans laden with coolers, umbrellas, collapsible chairs, and briefcase-sized portable radios arrive at the grounds several hours before the first ball is bowled at 10 a.m. Locations around the periphery of the field are carefully staked out, mostly by groups of friends who have made arrangements to contribute to a common supply of food and liquor. A more enviable location is in makeshift pavilions erected at the edge of the field or on surrounding hillsides. Wooden frames covered with canvas or thatch, the pavilions bear colorful names such as

"Honey Bee Lounge" and often fly flags made of liquor banners or team insignia. Organized by club-based peer groups, the pavilions accommodate 10–20 couples who pay a set fee – as much as $100[2] for the two days of Cup Match – for food, liquor, and other amenities. Most pavilions are wired to the clubhouse, enabling the use of lights, appliances, and stereos that typically have auditorium-sized electronic speakers.

In all groups there is emphasis on extravagance, sophistication, ostentation. Bottles of brand-name liquor ranging from the 40-ounce to the 1-gallon size are set out on coolers and tables, flanked by cherries, lemons, limes, angostura bitters, and more specialized garnishes and liqueurs for concoctions that gain popularity during a particular festival season (Scotch, milk, and grenadine was the favorite one year). Food is plentiful and of two kinds: the cherished "soul" dishes built around chicken, fish, and "hoppin' john" (black-eyed peas and rice); and festive specialties, notably cassava pie and a chicken- and-pork filling baked pastry made from shredded cassava. At the Eastern County Games one is also likely to see a number of festive seafood dishes, including mussel pie, conch stew, and hash shark. For those without enough food or liquor, there are at least two bars in the clubhouse and two or more bar concessions, along with 20 or more food concessions, on the grounds.

Liquor is a basis of hospitality patterns that link individuals and groups with the larger audience. People generously offer drinks to passing friends, whose visit is enlivened by joking, teasing, insult swapping, and other forms of verbal performance characteristic of Afro-Caribbean and Afro-American culture (Abrahams 1970; Kochman 1970). The visitor invariably extends an offer of reciprocal hospitality, creating an opportunity, and something of a social obligation, for the hosts to return the visit later in the day. In the pavilions persons are allowed to entertain two guests at a time, an informal rule that balances the importance of hospitality with a check against overcrowding.

The continuous traffic around the field is known as the "fashion show." Celebrants sport outfits acquired for the festival cricket season, occasionally handmade but more often purchased during the advertising campaigns that retail merchants mount in the weeks before Cup Match. Drawn from black American and West Indian trends, styles are valued for combining smartness with sexuality. [In the 1970s], for example, the style known in Bermuda as "black mod" was dominant. Women paraded in arousing "hot pants" outfits, suggestive two-piece ensembles, bell-bottom and two-tone slacks, close-fitting pants suits, wool knit skirts and jerseys, low-slung chain belts, bubble blouses, leather collars, suede-fringed handbags, large round earrings, ostentatious bracelets and necklaces, pink and yellow tinted sunglasses, and "natural" coiffures. In the same period, men wore jump suits, silk shirts slit open to expose the chest, two-tone and wide-cuffed flair pants, bolero and ruffled shirts with dog-ear collars, and suede vests over the bare skin. [Later] styles have been varied, ranging from "black disco" to "unisex chic." Women have adopted pleated balloon pants, terry cloth outfits, and "cornrow" coiffures elaborated with beads and braids – a style that can cost upwards of $100 in Bermudian hairdressing salons. Men have taken to West Indian styles, notably shirt-jacs, kareba suits, and among youth, Rastafarian dreadlocks. The jewelry portfolios of both sexes center on a half-dozen necklaces of various sizes and designs. Designer jean outfits are in vogue, as are athletic shorts that are worn by women with halter tops, by men with athletic shirts, and by both sexes with inscribed T-shirts.

The popularity of T-shirts warrants special comment. The leading black dealer in the field estimates selling 1,000 to 1,500 shirts for Cup Match alone, many of them at the cricket grounds in a concession stand that he equips with his printing and dyeing machines. His most popular line is what he calls his "black" shirts – motifs about festival cricket, pan-African identity, racial solidarity, and black entertainment genres. Next in popularity, and sometimes combined with racial motifs, are sexual themes, most of them using slang double entendres for genitalia and copulation in conjunction with humorous inscriptions of invitation, challenge, and braggadocio. The manufacture of T-shirts at the game epitomizes the rapid popularization of new styles and the ready satisfaction of customer demand for

them, central values in black Bermudian fashion culture.

Performative and provocative, the fashion show is closely observed by radio commentators, who mix accounts of the cricket game with animated descriptions of fashion plates. Indeed, one of the major reasons fans bring radios to the game is to hear these accounts of themselves and their fellow celebrants. Like liquor, fashion is a medium of exchange that integrates an aggregate audience into a cultural community. It is also, again like liquor, what Sapir (1934) termed a symbol of condensation: it exemplifies what it signifies, namely an ethos of affluence, hedonism, sophistication, and display. An observable result of this symbolism is that fashion evokes the black conversational mode known as "rapping," a lewd and lively exchange between men and women aimed both at entertainment and at the initiation or enhancement of sexual partnerships. Like Carnival, festival cricket has a rich lore as a period of license and sexual hyperactivity.

Other modes of performance compete with fashion for public attention. Steel, brass, and rock bands play on the sidelines, stimulating impromptu dancing. Also present are Gombey Dancers, masked mummers who render a Bermudian version of the John Canoe dance to the rhythm of drums, fifes, snares, and whistles. High on surrounding hillsides are groups of Rastafarians, who smoke *ganja*, translate the festival ambience into poetry, and orate philosophically about a black millennium. A profane version of that millennium is enacted on adjacent waterways, where "boojee" (black bourgeois) yachtsmen display their boats and hold swank deck parties.

The cricket match concludes at 6:30 p.m., but festivities continue well into the night. The clubhouse is jammed with revelers who fraternize with the cricketers, replay and comically argue every detail of the game, and get very drunk as the evening wears on. Other fans extend their merriment onto the field and may remain there all night. Several clubs run evening events ranging from dances and parties to outdoor concerts featuring black American and Caribbean performers.

A final ancillary activity warrants separate discussion for both ethnographic and analytic purposes. That activity is gambling, which takes place during the cricket game on the periphery of the field in a large tent known as the "stock market." As festival cricket amplifies a mode of behavior that is manifest in less spectacular ways on a day-to-day basis, stock market gambling caricatures a general style of acquisition premised on calculated opportunism (Manning 1973:87–114), as well as a particular fondness for gambling that has put soccer pool agencies and off-track betting parlors among Bermuda's lucrative businesses and has, within the club milieu, given rise to regular bingo nights, organized card games, raffles, lotteries, and so on. The significance of gambling here is twofold: first, it explicitly symbolizes a relationship between culture and money that is represented more implicitly in other phases and spheres of festival cricket; second, at a deeper level, it dramatizes the culture-money relationship in a manner that qualifies and questions the meaningful thrust of the total festival. Juxtaposed to its own context, gambling illustrates the tension that pervades black political life.

The Stock Market

Framed with wood or tubular steel and covered with canvas or sheet plastic, the stock market is a makeshift casino for a dice game known as "crown and anchor." Played on boards set atop wooden horses, the game involves betting on one or more of six choices: the four suits of cards, a red crown, or a black anchor. Three dice are rolled, their sides corresponding to the choices on the board. Winners are paid the amount of their bet times the number of dice on which it is shown, while losers have their money taken by the board. If a croupier rolls a crown and two spades, for example, he collects the money on the four losing choices, pays those who bet on the crown, and pays double those who bet on the spade.

Like cricket, crown and anchor is a game of British origin that has gained immense popularity in the Caribbean, particularly at festivals. I have personally watched it being played by Antiguans at Carnival and by Jamaican Maroons at the celebration of Captain Cudjoe's birthday in the remote moutain village of Accompong.[3] In Bermuda the game is distinguished by the amount of money that is displayed and bet. Croupiers hold thousands of dollars in their hands, and players are likely to hold several hundred. The minimum bet is one dollar, but only novices and casual players, mostly women, bet that little. Regular players tend to bet between $10 and $50 each time, although much higher bets are common. Some boards place a ceiling of $100 on bets, but the larger boards – i.e., those with bigger cash floats – generally have no ceiling. An informant lighted on the ostentatious display of cash as the chief difference between festival cricket and Christmas, the calendar's two major holidays. At Christmas, he observed, money is spent; at festival cricket, it is both spent and shown.

Crown and anchor is marked by a peculiar paradox. Although the odds marginally favor the board, regular players say that an effective strategy is to bet on choices that have not come up for two or three rolls of the dice and are therefore "due" simply by the laws of probability. A more defensive tactic, and one that is easily combined with the above, is simply to double bets on the same item until it eventually comes up and all losses, as well as the initial bet, are recouped. The only limitation is lack of ready cash, but this is minimized by the substantial sums that players carry and by the ready willingness of the boards to accept personal checks and even to loan money.

In practice, however, players tend to bet erratically and lose, often substantially. In the parlance of the stock market, they succumb to "greed" and "lose their heads" in a futile attempt to "break the board." What is potentially a game of strategy – the type associated with mastering the environment – is in effect a game of chance – the type associated with divining an uncontrollable environment (Roberts, Arth, and Bush 1959). The following example from my field notes is representative of a pattern evidenced by the stock market's "high rollers":

> Placing $10 and $20 bets unsystematically, a man lost his own money – about $60 – as well as $50 that he borrowed from the board. He then borrowed another $50 and increased it to about $85 by winning a few small bets. He next bet $70

on the club, which came up on three dice to add $210 to his money. But although he owed the board $100, he kept playing rather than pay back the debt and quit with a net winning. Within a half hour he had lost all his money, as well as a third loan of $50. As he left the board he quietly told the croupier: "I owe you $150. I'll see you Monday morning."

The familiar experience of losing is offset by the claim that gambling money is expendable. As one man put it after losing $100, "If I have money to spend, I spend it. If I lose it, I don't give a fuck. I'll go back to work next week and get some more."

Although the overwhelming majority of bettors are black, the running of boards – the profitable side of the stock market – has been dominated by the Portuguese. In the 1930s, Manuel de Souza (a pseudonym), the teenage son of an Azorean-born farm laborer, watched crown and anchor being played in the segregated white section of the racetrack. Surmising the game's appeal to blacks, he started going to festival cricket matches with a dice cup, a small table, and a tarpaulin that he stretched between some trees to make a crude tent. De Souza's winnings put him on the road to acquiring a modest complex of businesses: a fleet of taxi cabs, several small farms, and a restaurant. "You can say that I owe what I have to crown and anchor," he acknowledged. "It gave me my start in life."

As de Souza's business and gambling profits grew, he began running more boards in partnership with other Portuguese. In the 1960s he was challenged by the clubs, which successfully pressed the claim that the stock market should be under their control. De Souza countered with patronage, supporting club building projects and occasionally contributing a share of his winnings. In return he was given first option on buying the entire gambling concession, an arrangement that gave the clubs a substantial cash flow to stock their bars for festivals and that made de Souza something of a "czar" or, better perhaps, "godfather," of the stock market. With his partners he ran a half-dozen tables and reports that his share of their net profits averaged $30,000 per season. He made a further profit by selling the remainder of the space in the stock market, chiefly to a growing group of Portuguese who had acquired gambling reputations in private house parties.

Although de Souza and other Portuguese board operators were generally astute enough to hire black assistants, black gamblers gradually pushed the clubs for a bigger stake in the stock market, and ultimately for control of it. Their efforts have been partially successful; for several years the concession of Cup Match and the Western County Games has been sold to a syndicate of black businessmen, while in the Eastern County series one club continues to favor de Souza and the others run the stock market themselves. The change has resulted in more blacks and fewer Portuguese, although the new concession holders sell choice space (near the outside and sheltered from the afternoon sun) to the remaining Portuguese, including de Souza, who are respected in gambling circles and known to attract heavy bettors.

Yet the racial change in the stock market is less radical than it may appear. Many of the black-run boards, and a clear majority of those which have no ceiling on bets, are backed financially by whites, including Portuguese, or by racially mixed investment syndicates. The backers provide the cash float – as much as $15,000 at some boards – in return for a 40 to 60 percent share of the winnings. The parallel between the stock market and the wider economic system is frequently observed: blacks are in visible positions and appear to be making money, but whites are behind them and in control. Reflecting on the situation, one black gambler observed: "You know, come to think of it, I don't know a single black person in this country who has made money without having a white sponsor."

Another parallel between the stock market and the broader Bermudian situation is observed in connection with mid-1970s legislation requiring the host club to pay $500 for a one-day gambling permit and preventing the boards from taking bets later than one hour after the scheduled end of the cricket game. The cost of the permit has been passed on to the concession holders and, in turn, to individual board operators, while the time regulation has stopped boards from staying open to increase winnings, recoup earlier losses, or simply capitalize on late betting action – a restriction that has hurt mainly the smaller, black-run boards, which are on the inside and therefore wait longer for bettors. For blacks, these new statutes typify a pattern of reaction against black economic gain. As one black board operator put it, "When the stock market was run by the Portuguese, it was wide open. As soon as we boys started to get a little piece of the action, Government stepped in. That's the general trend in Bermuda."

Whatever the economic position of blacks in the stock market, their cultural presence there is highly visible and clearly dominant over whites – another correspondence, of course, to the larger society. The Portuguese play quietly and dress plainly, almost dourly. Their boards are about six feet long and staffed by two, or at most three, croupiers. They keep a supply of cold beer but do not offer it until a player has begun betting. They rarely socialize with bettors or other operators, viewing the gambling relationship as an exclusively economic transaction. As de Souza explained, "People don't play at my board because they like me. They play because they want to break me." The Portuguese leave unobtrusively after the game and abstain from the evening festivities. I once went looking for de Souza after an Eastern County Game and found him working soberly in his restaurant. He said that he cleared $1,800 from his three tables – "a day's pay" – but volunteered that his lack of emotion made it impossible for most people to tell whether he had won or lost.

The image of black gamblers, by contrast, is an ideal type of the highly performative, black-oriented expressive style that Wilson (1973:227–8) terms "reputation" – the ethos that pervades the entire festival. Croupiers dress and behave flamboyantly, standing on platforms to increase their visibility, spreading their bills like a fan, throwing their dice cups high in the air, handing out one-dollar bills to passersby to engage them in the game, and barking stock invitations to bet: "Get some money for your honey. ...Come in here on a bike, go home in a Rolls Royce. ...Take your hands out of your pocket and put your money on the table. ...Wall Street slumps, but this stock market pays double. ..." The black tables average eight to ten feet, with sets of betting squares on

each end and often with added decorations such as the signs of the zodiac. At the larger tables there may be a staff of six, typically a "house man" who shakes the dice and holds the $50 bills, two or three assistants who collect and pay the bets, and one or two others who serve as bartenders and greeters. Both liquor and beer are freely offered to onlookers as well as bettors, and when a person's drink is half empty it will be wantonly thrown on the ground and replaced with a fresh drink.

Black gamblers extend and exploit the festival's sexual license. At least two black operators have reportedly imported prostitutes, a commodity virtually absent from Bermuda, from the United States. The more common practice is to give gambling money to well-endowed women in return for their appearing at the board in plunging necklines, loosely crocheted blouses, diaphanous T-shirts, tight shorts, and similar fashions aimed at attracting – and distracting – male gamblers. As a sequel to this gimmick, a few black operators have begun hiring female croupiers and even forming gambling partnerships with women. Conversely, women have increasingly become regular and sometimes heavy bettors, a trend that is particularly noticeable in the western parishes where a good number of well-paid hotel positions are held by women. The effort to attract – and hold – women bettors enlivens the barking calls with colorful exchanges.

A middle-aged woman was about to bet on heart, but withdrew the money. The operator countered: "Don't blame me if three hearts come up, lady. 'Cause you and I – I've been looking at you for a long time – I figure our hearts could get together. We don't need no crown and anchor, honey. Our hearts could really do something."

A woman was betting, and winning, on the black choices (spades, clubs, the anchor), which are all on the bottom of the board. The operator tried to persuade her to diversify her betting: "You gotta go topside No woman in the world is satisfied on the bottom side."

A woman in her early thirties had been breaking even on small bets and drinking heavily. Towards the end of the day she put a double entendre to the operator: "All I want is a piece of you." He took up the challenge and carried on a series of lewd but playful insults that drew raucous laughter from those at the table. But she got the last word: "Knobby, you wouldn't know what to do if you tripped and fell on top of me."

Black operators indicate that their gambling success depends on establishing their reputations within a broader context of public sociability. One prominent operator spends several hours per day outside the bar that he owns in partnership with another black and two whites, engaging passersby in brief conversation, waving at pedestrians on the other side of the street, and shouting at passing cars. This strategy, he explains, provides the exposure that is needed to attract people to his crown and anchor board (as well as to his bar and to a nightclub that he owns with his partners).

A modern Bermudian proverb is at this point appropriate. "Black is black and white is white, but money is green." Culturally different and socially divided, the races nonetheless come together for a common goal: the acquisition of money. There is no better illustration of this proverb than stock market gambling, which magnifies the unique black cultural identity that is celebrated in festival cricket at the same time that it brings the races together in a staged encounter aimed at fast and easy wealth. That scenario is a dramatic rendition of what Bermudian politics, at bottom, is all about.

Festival and Politics

Racial inversion underlies the dramatic form of festival cricket. Blacks dress up in "whites" to play a white game that they have transformed into a celebration of black culture. Blacks take a white gambling game and make it the setting for a hyperbolic performance of their social personality. Whites enter a black milieu and baldly demonstrate their superordinate position. Such inversion exemplifies the carnivalesque, a genre in which the characteristic multiplexity of symbolic expression is extended by the tendency for symbols to be used playfully and for primarily aesthetic effect. This tendency creates what Babcock (1973) calls a "surplus of signifiers," a Rabelaisian profusion of images and condensed metaphors framed in a mode of liminality.

While the range of significance is vast, fragmented, and often highly individualized, the exegete can take clues from recurrent and centrally placed symbols. A major, meaningful thrust of festival cricket, manifest in the tradition and style of celebration, is the relation of a reflexive version of black identity to hedonism, high style, and money. Turner's (1964:29–31) contention, that dominant clusters of symbols interchange social and sensory-material themes, is appropriate. Like similar symbolic formulations in the club milieu, festival cricket contributes to the multifaceted process whereby black Bermudians are rejecting a stance of social inferiority in favor of a positive and assertive sense of self-awareness (Manning 1973:149–83).

There is also an antithetical thrust of meaning, reminding blacks of their economic subordination and dependency on whites. The reminder is implicit in the overall emphasis on fashion and indulgence, for Bermudian blacks are acutely aware, even in festival, that consumerism keeps them in clientage. In the stock market, however, the message is explicit: big money and effective power are still in white hands. Blacks can commemorate their traditions and exhibit their ethos, but they must also deal with whites, who have the odds – mathematical and psychological – in their favor. If festival cricket is viewed as a dramatic form, the black gamblers are both heroes and clowns. In the former role they glamorize a social vision of black culture, while in the latter they enact an economic relationship in which the vision is transparently irrelevant. Like the ludic inversion of racial categories, this sense of juxtaposition and self-parody is characteristic of the carnivalesque.

As a formative feature of the black Bermudian experience, the culture–economics interplay has a variety of demonstrable references. The most clear and currently paramount, however, is the system of party politics. An arena of intense interest and extraordinarily high participation, Bermudian politics bears both a striking conceptual similarity and an uncanny ethnographic correspondence to festival cricket. Let us briefly consider this double relationship.

Party politics came to Bermuda in 1963 with the formation of the Progressive Labour Party (PLP) by black groups who had previously been active in the successful universal suffrage movement.[4] In the election of that year, the party contested 9 of 36 parliamentary seats, winning 6 of them and clearly demonstrating the practical benefits of party organization. The aristocracy responded to the challenge a year later by forming the United Bermuda Party (UBP), which was initially joined by 24 of the 30 independents in the House of Assembly, all but one of them white. For the remainder of the decade the UBP sought to co-opt the issues pressed by the PLP, espousing, at least nominally, constitutional reform and the bread-and-butter issues of universal free education, health and welfare benefits, and the Bermudianization of the labor force. The UBP's trump card, however, was the promise of a thoroughgoing "partnership" – the term used in campaign slogans – between blacks and whites in the running of Bermuda. The partnership was demonstrated politically by strenuous efforts to recruit black candidates in the 1968 and subsequent elections, a general tactic of putting blacks in highly visible positions in both the party organization and the Cabinet; the naming of a black premier between 1971 and 1975; the appeasement of a black-dominated parliamentary "reform" group which forced the resignation of that premier's white successor in 1977; and, from the late 1970s onward, the gradual implementation of demands put forth by an internal black caucus seeking greater leverage in both the party and the national economy.

Rhetorically, the UBP presents the partnership as a guarantee of security as well as an opportunity for gain. Only through the visible demonstration of racial integration, it is claimed, can Bermuda continue to attract tourists and international companies, the sources of prosperity. The UBP couples this appeal with an emphasis on its traditional role as manager of the economy. In the 1980 election campaign, for example, Premier David Gibbons, a white who also [held] the finance portfolio and whose family controlled Bermuda's largest conglomerate, told an audience:

This election is not about personalities. It is about the conditions of people's lives. Day in and day out. People's jobs, income, housing. And, above all, the strength and stability of our economy, upon which all else depends.

Look to the United Bermuda Party's management of our economy. At a time when so many nations in the West are struggling and losing ground, Bermuda maintains one of the highest rates of per capita income in the world. ... Stability, security. These are facts. And they've come to pass because of experience and prudent, efficient management.

The UBP gave its economic theme a dimension of grave urgency in a full-page newspaper advertisement published on polling day:

Today is the day when you vote ... either to maintain Bermuda's economic growth and your own financial security and stability or ... take a chance on the PLP. Think carefully and vote UBP.

The UBP's accommodations to black interests and its emphasis on economic security have given it an unbroken winning record at the polls, albeit by successively reduced majorities. The PLP's reaction, moderated in tone as its political position has improved, has been to emphasize its "true" blackness and therefore its legitimate and logical claim to black voter support. For the first decade of its existence, the PLP projected a posture of militant racial chauvinism, articulated through American and Caribbean "Black Power" rhetoric. In the middle 1970s, the PLP embraced the idiom of revivalist religion, a move aimed at making inroads among black church groups and, more generally, at appealing to racial consciousness implicitly rather than explicitly by stirring the powerful and pregnant association between revivalism and black culture. In the 1980 campaign, the PLP balanced the emphasis on religion with a more secular appeal to racial identity. The campaign slogan was "Xpress yourself," a black Bermudian colloquialism borrowed jointly from American soul music and Jamaican reggae lyrics and combining an allusion to the marking of a ballot paper with a slang encouragement for self-assertion. One television commercial showed a group of blacks, dancing funky style, while a singer chanted "express yourself" and an announcer extolled the merits of the PLP.

Whatever their stated differences on issues – and these have converged considerably in recent years as both parties have sought a center ground – the essential partisan distinction is racial. Recent surveys indicate that whites vote almost unanimously for the UBP, and that four-fifths of the black votes go to the PLP – a division that cross-cuts and overrides class, age, sex, ideological disposition, and other pertinent social factors (Manning 1978a: 199–209). The choice for blacks remains what it has always been: cultural attachment or economic security, loyalty and commitment to blacks, or strategic alignment with whites.

The distinction between the parties is manifest ethnographically in the festival setting. Hodgson (1967:311), a black Bermudian historian and PLP polemicist, describes Cup Match as "the one and only true symbol and celebration of the black man's emancipation." Her enthusiasm, however, is offset by a skepticism that blacks will forsake such symbols in order to participate in white festivities that have now dropped the color barrier. This concern, while lacking empirical foundation, has prompted PLP politicians to present a high profile at cricket festivals, making the general environment one in which PLP supporters are familiar and welcome and UBP supporters are somewhat isolated and uncomfortable. The festival's partisan association is extended by the PLP's considerable efforts to court the club constituency (Manning 1973:210–49), a tactic exemplified by party leader Lois Browne-Evans's speech at a club dinner in 1978.

> Your long and illustrious history . . . needs to be told. Essays ought to be held for your children to write what they think Daddy's club is all about. . . .
>
> Let not economic strangulation be the cause of your enslavement. For I am convinced that you have a part to play in the Bermuda of the future, just as your forbears played a vital role in the Bermuda of the past.
>
> You must continue working until your country is free from paternalism and patronage, free from all the shackles that we know. Do not remove one form of chains for another. You must avoid the tendency to be dependent. . . .

The stock market, however, presents a striking contrast to the overall festival milieu. The black table operators, like their Portuguese counter-parts and white backers, are primarily UBP supporters. The coterie is informally led by a black UBP member of the House of Assembly, who is also renowned, on a few occasions scandalously, for the organization of invitational crown and anchor parties in private homes. At least two prominent backers also hold UBP seats in Parliament, and it is widely known that several black board operators are being groomed as future UBP candidates. Talking to me on the street, one of the blacks who operates a table on which there is no betting limit explained his support for the UBP as follows: "There is not one black person in Bermuda with any money who is PLP. Not one. . . . If the [white] man looks after you, then you've got to protect him. . . . " When a PLP member within earshot began to challenge him, the gambler yelled: "Shut the fuck up. It's niggers like you that are holding back motherfuckers like me."

PLP activists, on the other hand, tend to eschew the stock market, or at most to congregate outside or walk through without betting. Observing the action at a crown and anchor board, one PLP politician told me with a wink: "I only watch the stock market. I never invest." This avoidance is encouraged by the PLP's oft-stated position that gambling is functionally supportive of the status quo and by its general desire to adhere, publicly at least, to the strong moral condemnation of gambling made by the black churches.

Festival cricket, then, is a metapolitical commentary. It is a carnivalesque rendition of the semantic context in which Bermudian politics is conceived, institutionalized, and transacted. Through celebration, black Bermudians dramatize – and, indeed, define and discover – a fundamental aspect of their social position and its relationship, conceptual and ethnographic, to their political options. (Logically, of course, the argument is reversible; politics could be construed as a concordance for festival cricket. From a Bermudian standpoint, however, it is politics, not festival, that requires comprehension, choice, and commitment. Festival is merely for enjoyment, and perhaps profit.)

It is here that the relationship of symbolic to social phenomena, of festival to politics, is crucial, and that the convergent positions of Turner (1977), Gluckman and Gluckman (1977), and

Geertz (1972), attributing creative autonomy to ludic symbolic forms, are useful. Although festival cricket evidences myriad correspondences to the political system, it is no more a mere reflection of politics than it is a functional appendage of it. The festival version of black culture is not the ideological and instrumental type of racial awareness propounded by the PLP, but a comical caricature of the black life-style and a joyous fantasy that links racial identity to the material wealth and glamor promised by a white-dominated, consumer-oriented economy. Likewise, the festival version of biracial partnership is not the liberal and pragmatic plea for partnership advanced by the UBP, but a naked dramatization of white control that lays bare both the crass acquisitiveness of blacks and their continuing subordination to whites, and that further plays on these meanings in a burlesque of the whole patronage system that transforms money from an object of need to one of show.

In Durkheimian terms – which are the ancestry of much symbolic theory – festival cricket is a "transfiguration" of Bermudian political society (cf. Nisbet 1965:74). The semantic essence of festival cricket is that it throws the realm of politics into relief by disassembling its parts and reordering them in patterns consistent with the aesthetics of celebration, fun, and performance. Festival cricket *reveals* politics in the way that only an extended metaphor can – by creatively connecting disparate realms of experience in a manner that highlights the definitive features (in this case, the interplay of cultural identity and economic interest) on which the connection is predicated. To borrow Bateson's (1972:177–93) classic model of cognition, festival cricket is a map for the territory of politics – not a literal, drawn-to-scale map that merely replicates its referent, but a metaphorical map, an interpretive guide, that figuratively situates its referent and conveys social knowledge about it. It is this knowledge that makes Bermudian politics a comprehensible phenomenon.

Conclusion

Like any venture into the analysis of symbolic forms as texts, the interpretation offered here

rests ultimately on the anthropologist, who "strains to read over the shoulders of those to whom they [the texts] properly belong" (Geertz 1972:29). In part, the validity and value of such an interpretation depends on whether it can be generalized, as a theoretical construct and heuristic device, to other cultures. Limitations of space and scope make it impractical to address that consideration here, but a few condensed examples from the West Indies may suggest the basis of a comparative approach.

The major festival genre of the eastern Caribbean is Carnival, which evolved in Trinidad but has diffused throughout the Windward and Leeward islands with minor changes in format.[5] Like Bermuda's Cup Match, the historical referent of Carnival, for blacks, is emancipation from slavery. The festival's major performative symbols – from the canboulay parade, ritualized stickfighting, and gang warfare in earlier times, to calypso and steel bands in recent generations – make it unequivocally black. Naipaul (1973:364), one of the Caribbean's leading literary figures, describes Carnival as "a version of the lunacy that kept the slave alive...the original dream of black power, style, and prettiness...a vision of the black millennium." Calypsonians put it more simply, toasting Carnival as the "Creole bacchanal."

But the blackness of the Carnival ethos is confronted by a strong nonblack influence in the festival's economic organization. East Indian, Chinese, and Lebanese bandleaders predominate, as do white and mulatto choreographers, and, of course, the government-controlled Carnival Development Committee – all of these groups striving, rather successfully in recent years, to make the event an international tourist attraction. Celebrants are exposed to the poignant contrast between the revelry of "jump-up" on the streets and the ribaldry of the calypso tent, on the one hand, and a variety of scenarios that demonstrate the racially based socioeconomic class system, on the other hand: the judges' stand, the paid grandstand, the commercial nightclub scene, the maze of bureaucratic rules imposed by organizers and censors, and the presence of local elites, and even metropolitan tourists, in the privileged sections of masquerade bands.

Jamaica lacks a Carnival tradition but has the entertainment idiom of reggae music, a symbol system replete with religious and political significance (Barrett 1977; de Albuquerque 1979). One of the best indigenous artistic commentaries on the reggae milieu is Perry Henzell's (1973) film *The Harder They Come*. Its protagonist is a country boy who comes to Kingston to learn the fast side of Jamaican life. The voyage of discovery is twofold. He becomes a reggae star and a "rudie" (rude boy), mastering expressive styles that are quintessentially black, often in a militant, even revolutionary sense. But he also learns that the music industry is controlled by Chinese, mulattoes, and other groups deemed white from the black cultural viewpoint, and that the authorities – police, government, and international economic interests – are geared to crushing the challenge that he represents. Ultimately, he is shot down by their guns.

Are such symbolic forms a metacommentary on West Indian politics? Correspondences are harder to draw than in the Bermudian case, partly because, in the Caribbean, race is a figurative more than a phenotypical category. Virtually all local political actors are generically black, and whiteness is associated less with a visible local elite than with the abstractions of foreign ownership and imperial influence. In short, a racial analysis is a more complex and problematic task in the West Indies than it is in Bermuda.

Still, it is notable that, ever since the "Black Power" wave of the early 1970s, the most dynamic and ideologically intense political conflict in most of the West Indies has come from the challenge made to established political parties by radical movements, most of them extraparliamentary. These radical movements revive indigenous linguistic terms (Morris 1973), stress cultural affinity and social solidarity with Africa, and associate themselves with Afro-Caribbean religions, notably Rastafarianism, which has spread from Jamaica throughout the Caribbean and has become a cultural rallying ground and pervasive symbol for revolutionary politics (de Albuquerque 1980). Contrastingly, established politicians are villified as "Afro-Saxons" (Lowenthal 1972:278), imitators of white values who court foreign investment, sell out to multinational corporations, embrace the image promoted by mass tourism, and compact unholy alliances with metropolitan countries.

A litany of citations from academic, popular, and polemical literature could be introduced here, most of them familiar (and indeed, redundant), to scholars of the Caribbean. For present purposes, however, it is better to make two broad and general assertions. First, economic interest and cultural identity are often perceived in the West Indies as conflicting concerns. Second, the conflict is focused in racial symbolism, dramatized in festivity and other artistic productions, and current to political discourse. If these assertions are granted, they suggest an agenda aimed at integrating symbolic and political analyses of Caribbean societies, and perhaps of other areas that have undergone comparable historical experiences. The discussion of Bermudian cricket festivals offered here shows one direction in which such an agenda can proceed.

Notes

1 I know of no other written sources on West Indian festival cricket, but am informed by a Jamaican student that "bush cricket" in Jamaica has the same general characteristics as James's example from Trinidad.

2 [When] the Bermuda dollar [was] at parity with the US dollar.

3 I am told by Jeanne Cannizzo (1979: personal communication) that a version of crown and anchor is played at festivals in Sierra Leone. I have also seen it played at a number of fairs and amusement exhibitions in Canada, usually in booths where a wheel is spun, rather than dice thrown, to determine winning bets.

4 For a fuller discussion of Bermuda's recent political history, see Hodgson (1967), Manning (1973, 1978a), and Ryan (1973).

5 The most accessible general overviews of the Trinidad Carnival are those of Hill (1972) and Pearse (1956). Literature on other Caribbean Carnivals includes Abrahams (1970) on Tobago, Abrahams and Bauman (1978) on St Vincent, Crowley (1956) on St Lucia, and Manning (1978b) on Antigua.

References

Abrahams, Roger
1970   Patterns of Performance in the British West Indies. *In* Afro-American Anthropology: Contemporary Perspectives. Norman E. Whitten, Jr. and John Szwed, eds. pp. 163–79. New York: Free Press.

Abrahams, Roger, and Richard Bauman
1978   Ranges of Festival Behavior *In* The Reversible World: Symbolic Inversion in Art and Society. Barbara Babcock, ed. pp. 193–208. Ithaca: Cornell University Press.

Babcock, Barbara
1973   The Carnivalization of the Novel and the High Spirituality of Dressing Up. Paper presented at Burg Wartenstein Symposium No. 59, Ritual: Reconciliation in Change. Gloggnitz, Austria.

Barrett, Leonard
1977   The Rastafarians: Sounds of Cultural Dissonance. Boston: Beacon Press.

Bateson, Gregory
1972   Steps to an Ecology of Mind. New York: Ballantine.

Cohen, Abner
1979   Political Symbolism. Annual Review of Anthropology 8:87–113.

Crowley, Daniel
1956   Festivals of the Calendar in St Lucia. Caribbean Quarterly 4:99–121.

de Albuquerque, Klaus
1979   The Future of the Rastafarian Movement. Caribbean Review 8(4):22–5, 44–6.

de Albuquerque, Klaus
1980   Rastafarianism and Cultural Identity in the Caribbean. Paper presented at the Caribbean Studies Association meeting, Willemstad, Curacao.

Geertz, Clifford
1972   Deep Play: Notes on the Balinese Cockfight. Daedalus 101(1):1–38.

Gluckman, Max, and Mary Gluckman
1977   On Drama, and Games, and Athletic Contests. *In* Secular Ritual. Sally F. Moore and Barbara Myerhoff, eds. pp. 227–43. Assen/Amsterdam: Van Gorcum.

Henzell, Perry
1973   The Harder They Come. Kingston, Jamaica: New World Films.

Hill, Errol
1972   The Trinidad Carnival: Mandate for a National Theatre. Austin: University of Texas Press.

Hodgson, Eva
1967   Second-Class Citizens. First-Class Men. Hamilton, Bermuda: Published by the author.

James, C. L. R.
1963   Beyond a Boundary. London: Hutchinson.

Kochman, Thomas
1970   Toward an Ethnography of Black American Speech Behavior. *In* Afro-American Anthropology: Contemporary Perspectives. Norman E. Whitten, Jr and John Szwed, eds. pp. 145–62. New York: Free Press.

Lewis, Gordon
1968   The Growth of the Modern West Indies. New York: Monthly Review Press.

Lowenthal, David
1972   West Indian Societies. New York: Oxford University Press.

Manning, Frank
1973   Black Clubs in Bermuda: Ethnography of a Play World. Ithaca: Cornell University Press.

Manning, Frank
1978a   Bermudian Politics in Transition: Race, Voting, and Public Opinion. Hamilton, Bermuda: Island Press.

Manning, Frank
1978b   Carnival in Antigua: An Indigenous Festival in a Tourist Economy. Anthropos 73:191–204.

Moore, Sally F., and Barbara Myerhoff
1977   Secular Ritual. Assen/Amsterdam: Van Gorcum.

Morris, Desmond
1973   On Afro-West Indian Thinking. *In* The Aftermath of Sovereignty: West Indian Perspectives. David Lowenthal and Lambros Comitas, eds. pp. 277–82. Garden City, NY: Doubleday Anchor.

Naipaul, V. S.
1973   Power to the Caribbean People. *In* The Aftermath of Sovereignty: West Indian Perspectives. David Lowenthal and Lambros Comitas, eds. pp. 363–71. Garden City, NY: Doubleday Anchor.

Newman, Dorothy
1972   The Population Dynamics of Bermuda. Hamilton, Bermuda: Bermuda Government, Department of Statistics.

Nisbet, Robert
1965   Emile Durkheim. Englewood Cliffs, NJ: Prentice-Hall.

Pearse, Andrew
1956   Carnival in Nineteenth Century Trinidad. Caribbean Quarterly 4: 176–93.

Roberts, John, Malcolm Arth, and Robert Bush
1959   Games in Culture. American Anthropologist 61:597–605.

Roberts, John, and Brian Sutton-Smith
1962   Child Training and Game Involvement. Ethnology 2:166–85.

Roberts, John, and Brian Sutton-Smith
  1966 Cross-Cultural Correlates of Games of Chance. Behavior Science Notes 1:131–44.

Ryan, Selwyn
  1973 Politics in an Artificial Society: The Case of Bermuda. *In* Ethnicity in the Americas. Frances Henry, ed. pp. 159–92. The Hague: Mouton.

St Pierre, Maurice
  1973 West Indian Cricket: A Sociohistorical Appraisal. Caribbean Quarterly 19:7–27.

Sapir, Edward
  1934 Symbolism. Encyclopaedia of the Social Sciences 14:492–5.

Schwartzman, Helen
  1978 Transformations: The Anthropology of Children's Play. New York: Plenum Press.

Singer, Milton
  1955 The Cultural Pattern of Indian Civilization. Far Eastern Quarterly 15:23–36.

Smith, Michael G
  1965 The Plural Society in the British West Indies. Berkeley: University of California Press.

Turner, Victor
  1964 Symbols in Ndembu Ritual. *In* Closed Systems and Open Minds: The Limits of Naivety in Social Anthropology. Max Gluckman, ed. pp. 20–51. Chicago: Aldine.

Turner, Victor
  1977 Variations on a Theme of Liminality. *In* Secular Ritual. Sally F. Moore and Barbara Myerhoff, eds. pp. 36–52 Assen/Amsterdam: Van Gorcum.

Wilson, Peter
  1973 Crab Antics. The Social Anthropology of English-Speaking Negro Societies of the Caribbean. New Haven: Yale University Press.

10

Copyright Heritage

Preservation, Carnival and the State in Trinidad

Philip W. Scher

NCC - National Carnival Commission

You hardly ever see a Bear in Port-of-Spain anymore. The Blue Devils have mostly left the streets. And the Guarahoons (Native American warriors) are in short supply too. You have to really search for Bats and Clowns and Midnight Robbers.[1] In Trinidad, at Carnival time, the old masquerade characters are played less and less often "on the road," and almost never by the young people who swell the ranks of what are known as pretty masquerade bands, dressed in ornamented bathing suits, parading the streets to the throb of bass-heavy Soca music. The National Carnival Commission (NCC), the state-sanctioned governing body that oversees Carnival in Trinidad, laments the disappearance of traditional mas' and over the years has made attempts at correction. Some of these attempts include an annual parade of old time masquerade characters on the Saturday before Carnival, a competition called Viey La Cou (The Old Yard, in patois) that features performances of old masquerade forms, old time Steelband competitions, expositions of old style calypso singing, special museum exhibits or temporary displays of historical Carnival materials, photographs, costumes or documents. Recently, the NCC formed a Carnival Institute, part of whose mandate is to record and preserve knowledge and materials related to the traditional Carni-

val arts. In 1998, in conjunction with Trinity College in Hartford, Connecticut a World Conference on Carnival was held to bring together scholars, NCC administrators, government officials, artists, and performers. Since then, the conference has been held annually. The first conference resulted in the publication of a special issue of *The Drama Review* dedicated wholly to Carnival in Trinidad (Riggio 1998). Every article in the journal was dedicated to some form of old time Carnival masquerade form, steelband or calypso.[2] There was no sustained treatment of Soca, the music that now dominates Carnival, nor of any of the contemporary forms of masquerade, especially the "pretty mas'" bands that attract, by far, the greatest number of participants.[3] The conference, the publication of the special issue of *The Drama Review* and the various strategies undertaken by the NCC are all part of "helping to preserve and transmit invaluable Carnival traditions which have been in danger of extinction" (Foreword: Riggio 1998), according to Carlos John, former chairman of the NCC. For the scholars involved in these activities, the aim has been to redefine the scholarly understanding of "Carnival" itself, by broadening the notions of Carnival advanced by Mikhail Bakhtin (Bakhtin 1984) and Victor Turner (Turner 1983), among others.

Thus, for Riggio, the purpose of the conference and the journal issue was to "redefine theories of Carnival in light of actual contemporary practices" (Riggio 1998: Editor's Note). Yet, the "actual practices" discussed represent a very small minority of events and activities that go on during Carnival in Trinidad. Of the thousands of participants who play mas', from the opening of Jouvay morning to the exhausted partying of Las' Lap Tuesday night, the majority is registered with one of the fancy masquerade bands whose camps and headquarters dot the city. However, there is almost no official or scholarly mention of these events or masqueraders except by those who decry their excesses. To be sure, the popular press offers extensive coverage of mainstream Carnival, its costumes and colors and music, and the NCC's brochures and public relations documents are also replete with photographs of revelers playing in such bands. Despite this, what counts as Carnival, from both the perspective of the state and the scholars involved with this project, is "old time Carnival." Theoretical statements regarding the nature of Carnival based on contemporary, lived experience (as opposed to supposedly archaic forms lost in the European or African past) take into account only that which has been categorized as traditional, a myopic approach that, ironically, undermines the very goal of presenting a scholarly assessment of the experience of Carnival that is most relevant to the majority of contemporary masqueraders.

This chapter explores the impulse behind the promotion, protection, and preservation of a particular image of the Carnival in Trinidad, the erasure of competing images of Carnival and the role that certain kinds of scholarship might play in those endeavors. In pursuing this line of thought, I focus on the larger issue of preservation and protection of Heritage and nationalist ideology through recourse to international organizations such as UNESCO and the World Intellectual Property Organization. I argue here that nationalist protection of heritage must posit an interested historical narrative of both the creation and development of certain expressive cultural forms and that, by doing so, the narrative necessarily excludes both an understanding of the historical participation of certain groups within the

nation, and their contemporary participation in the ongoing evolution of such cultural forms.

The current debate over the preservation and/or protection of Traditional Knowledge, Folklore and Heritage has involved many disciplines and many state and international arenas. Generally, the provinces of Traditional Knowledge and Expressions of Folklore have been separated out on heuristic grounds with Traditional Knowledge (known as TK in the intellectual property literature) standing for native science, healing, the use of plants and animals, indigenous forms of agricultural practice, and the like. Expressions of Folklore include dancing, music, story telling, songs and other performance forms, artwork, and crafts. National governments, seen as the natural arbiters of the cultural forms of their bounded territories and the peoples that reside within them (some of whom are minority groups, others of whom are not) have increasingly tried to patent, copyright, or otherwise protect and preserve Expressions of Folklore.[4]

In some cases, organizations representing indigenous peoples, such as Australia's Aboriginal and Torres Strait Islander Commission (ATSIC), are responsible for initiating attempts to preserve and protect Folklore, among other tasks.[5] In most cases, the goal has been to solve the problem of whether or not Folklore and Traditional Knowledge can be protected from exploitation by parties outside of the community or, barring that, preserved from loss or disappearance because of either neglect or unwanted hybridization with foreign or alien cultural forms.

Although these issues have been pursued with vigor, most of the scholarly literature on the subject has largely skirted the problem of representation at the "local level." Cultural preservation and protection is not simply the province of activist groups, historical societies, altruistic cultural organizations, or even of Tribal councils, national Ministries of Culture or state-sponsored cultural organizations. Preservation and its adversary, *cultural appropriation*, are fundamentally about representation and control and these concepts imply a hierarchical relationship between the state and local organizations, on the one hand, and a larger international political and legal world, on the other. For the most part, the literature of preservation has dealt with the upper tier of this hierarchy, that is, the struggle between some local group and some outside group. This might be a First Nations struggle with the Canadian government over artifacts in a museum, an Aboriginal group's battle with corporations, organizations or individuals who use artistic designs from sacred pictures, or ethnic groups concerned about the theft of indigenous knowledge by multinational pharmaceutical companies etc. (Coombe 1998, Ziff and Rao 1997, Messenger 1999, Brown 1998, Brush 1993, Brush and Stabinsky 1996). Yet very little has been done to interrogate the next part of this equation: the relationship between the locally organized body and the people whom they claim to represent (cf. Balliger 2002). In this article, I argue that local concerns about the preservation of Carnival in Trinidad are tied to local interests of power and serve to exclude women from authorized narratives of national culture. Furthermore, the fact that scholars themselves exclude alternative narratives of Carnival, or that state organizations make use of existing scholarship and scholarly research to legitimize specific political agendas, implicates researchers in nation building. Anthropological scholarship, through its traditional form of ethnographic writing, creates both descriptions and verifications of the practices of other cultures, and a legitimizing discursive style that may selectively serve to authenticate local, cultural practices.

Questions of national or ethnic culture, long the province of anthropologists and folklorists, have gradually been configured as important political issues with concrete legal implications. The anthropological concept of culture is, in one version or another, becoming institutionalized through state and legal action as conflicts over group intellectual property rights increase. And even as the discipline of anthropology struggles to promote anti-essentialist theories of culture, much of the politics of culture outside of anthropology is concerned with the institutionalization and protection of the kinds of essentialized cultures anthropology has long helped to create.

Although the narrower problem of how to legally protect culture has been in place since at least the late 1960s with the Stockholm revisions of the Berne Convention, the problem of cultural appropriation – that is, "Who owns culture?"– has taken a decidedly new turn. This new turn concerns the extension of officially recognized and legally sanctioned definitions of heritage and culture and the increased efforts not only by minority and indigenous peoples, but whole nations, to secure binding legal rights to cultural forms. Yet while nations and even ethnic groups are often radically heterogeneous (by which I mean that other identities, such as gender and class, intersect ethnic ones) they often represent themselves as monolithic bodies, assumed to be in agreement, working to restore native property.

The presence of state agencies in the mix does require the question I stated earlier. That is, who is speaking for the group in question? Control over the national or ethnic patrimony works to sustain power in the sense that those controlling the production and dissemination of culture are in a position to mediate between the local constituency and the global agents of change, economic hegemony, or cultural imperial might. Part of the strategy of claiming the right to act for the culture[6] (as its protector and guardian) means erasing the illusion of internal differnces within the culture itself and projecting outward a generic image of a culture, shared equally by all, in danger from the outside: them. Perhaps more significantly, in the act of protecting heritage, local power structures do not merely secure the rights to some pre-existing body of collective lore or some cache of material goods. They act to define the group both inwardly and to outsiders. In many situations protection is part of the act of defining culture and thus it evokes a sense of permanence outside the vagaries of time and change. Efforts to protect expressions of folklore and heritage are generally seen by marginalized groups as not merely benign, but important steps in the emancipation of oppressed peoples or less powerful nations. Indeed the imperative to protect or restore culture (even as the concept of culture remains acknowledged as "ill defined") has proceeded to the point of being officially recognized by such international organizations as UNESCO and The World Intellectual Property Organization (WIPO).

By turning our attention to the question of who stands to gain from the preservation of heritage we shed light on the politics of representation at the local level. 1) What are the implications of preserving and documenting aspects of the Trinidad Carnival for participants not involved with or seen as being in opposition to those elements? 2) What are the implications for scholars, who either position themselves as spokespeople for a particular group or whose work is so positioned?

What is Cultural Appropriation?

Answering the question of what constitutes cultural appropriation is complex since different notions of culture as well as different ideas about "appropriation" are used across a variety of different disciplines. Cultural forms or products as diverse as archaeological artifacts or public festivals may be treated in distinct ways. For instance, we might find the concept of cultural appropriation used in relation to a number of activities: the repatriation of archaeological artifacts collected and removed from a particular site to a museum or collection overseas; the repatriation of human remains; the use of traditional stories, motif or storytelling styles by persons outside a particular community, the use of music, musical styles or musical instruments; the use of art forms, designs or patterns; the use of traditional knowledge in the healing arts, cooking, botany, agriculture or any of a number of indigenous sciences including shamanism, curing rites or other practices, either ritual or physically medicinal. These are only a sampling of possible definitions for what constitutes the cultural heritage of a group. We must also include various kinds of appropriation (Ziff and Rao 1997:6). That is, alongside notions of outright "theft" we find cultural degradation, transformation, and alteration. In each of these examples, the concept of cultural appropriation suggests that culture belongs to a corporate, definable group bounded in space and across time, and that a group's identity is, tautologically speaking, defined by its cultural forms and practices. Those cultural forms or objects that are being protected presumably *belong to* everyone in the group equally and constitute their public domain and their intellectual legacy to their children.

Contemporary progressive politics takes it as axiomatic that the degradation of the cultural forms of others is a bad thing. It is bad because, like the denial of individual rights of self-expression, cultural poaching, repression or suppression, in short cultural appropriation, denies a group of both its heritage and its ability to express an authentic, separate identity. Ziff and Rao note the following negative effects of cultural appropriation:

1 **Cultural degradation:** Cultural appropriation harms the appropriated community at the level of the integrity and identity of the local group.
2 **Cultural goods as valuable:** Appropriation can damage, distort or change a given cultural good or practice itself.
3 **Exploitation:** Appropriation allows some to wrongly benefit from the material detriment of others.
4 **Sovereign claims:** Current laws fail to reflect alternative conceptions of what should be treated as property or ownership in cultural goods (Ziff and Rao 1997).

There is still, embedded in this outlook, a vision of cultural practices as objects or at least, to some degree, as independent from the people who perform them (Handler and Linnekin 1984).

The rhetoric of contemporary organizations that represent the rights of indigenous peoples and ethnic minorities is often remarkably similar to the rhetoric of the tourist brochure and both have inherited their language from anthropological discourse. These various discourses share a conception of culture that posits a unified collection of expressive forms as *the definition* of culture. For example, consider the following statements regarding the definition of cultural appropriation:

The taking – from a culture that is not one's own – of intellectual property, cultural expressions or artifacts, history and ways of knowledge and profiting at the expense of the *people of that culture*. (The Writers Union of Canada, June 1992, emphasis mine)

…any utilization made with both gainful intent and outside the traditional or customary context

tautology - saying the same thing twice in different words

of folklore, without authorization by a competent authority or *the community concerned*. (WIPO/ UNESCO Model Provisions for National Laws on sui generis Protection of Expressions of Folklore against Illicit exploitation and other prejudicial actions, 1982, emphasis mine)

The Writers Union of Canada assumes in its statement that cultural appropriation will diminish the group, especially if the appropriator profits in some way. In the latter statement, WIPO-UNESCO implies that the control of outside usage of one or another forms must be made by consent through a representative of "the group." In both cases, culture is seen as both defining and defined by a group. It is separable and independent from, and integral and vital to, a group's identity. The thing is the culture and the culture is the thing. What is most striking about the second statement, however, is the belief that approval or consent by a group representative will lessen the destructiveness of cultural appropriation. I will return to this issue below.

Anthropology has, in large measure, moved beyond objectifications of culture and has actively promoted an anti-essentialist stance, yet the legacy of the essentializing scholarship of the past remains. And it endures most prominently in what one recent writer has called the "structures of common difference" (Wilk 1995:117), that is, the organization of diversity through mutually recognizable classification, or hegemony as taxonomy. This theory maintains that the hegemony of the contemporary global system is to be found not in the proliferation of homogeneous goods or cultural forms flowing from the west outward but in the *organization* of difference, in the standardization of *criteria* by which difference can be measured. In this view, cultures are collections of "products" whose form is consistent even as the content changes. What counts as properly cultural, what qualifies as an appropriate cultural category then constitutes an area of inquiry in which different content must be found. Examples of these categories include cuisine, costume, music, dance, the plastic arts, folklore, traditional knowledge, mythology etc. Together they form "heritage." Copyright protection of heritage reifies this notion of bounded culture groups recognizable by their expressive and material output

and, in effect, defines exactly what the nature of that cultural content will be.

The notion of culture as a set of visible forms proliferates as a supposed antidote to the ill effects of globalization, homogenization and cultural imperialism and such authenticity is said to predate the "ruptures" of modernity (Miller 1995, Garcia Canclini 1995). Policies meant to resist or counteract the epidemic of Western culture and the disappearance of "local cultures" make active use of this definition of culture. One of the central arguments of this paper is that scholarly documentation, especially that produced in the service of cultural preservation, often implicitly draws upon the "culture-as-thing" concept. Scholarship on cultural preservation contributes not only to the reproduction of these objectifications, but serves up digestible culture forms for a variety of audiences; it creates a space into which local "authorities" must step to regulate and control the definition and flow of culture, thereby gaining the power to create and maintain legitimate and authorized cultural forms. Cultural preservation authorities define the contours of "real" versus "fake" culture, marginalize certain expressive practices, and purge existing practices or elements considered foreign, undesirable or inauthentic.

The examples provided in this essay focus on the idea that those expressive aspects of Carnival considered properly "traditional" by the state are at odds with what many carnival participants imagine carnival to be. The tension here in this specific example exists primarily, although not exclusively, between what are known as Old Time Carnival and its characters and what is sometimes called, derogatorily, the "wine and jam" Carnival of young, mostly middle-class women. The official discourse of Carnival promoted by the state-run National Carnival Commission in Trinidad works to exclude a significant portion of the population in part through acts of preservation while the acts of preservation are themselves founded on "academic research."

What is Carnival?

In this section, I provide a basic description of the event in order to demonstrate the centrality of the festival to Trinidadian cultural and economic life. However, in light of the perspective outlined above, answering the question "what is Carnival?" becomes increasingly troublesome. There is almost no statement about the event that cannot be contested in some way. The ancient cultural origins of the event, who started it in Trinidad, the role that Afro-Trinidadians have played in its development versus the role that Indo-Trinidadians have played,[7] the exact contribution the festival makes to the economy, and, of course, the right way to masquerade versus the wrong way are debates that are almost as enduring as the event itself.

The Trinidad Carnival takes place each year at the start of the Catholic season of Lent. Technically, the festival lasts two days from J'Ouvay morning, the opening explosion of Carnival early on Monday morning during which the keys to the capital city of Port-of-Spain are given to the Merry Monarch, King of Carnival, to Las' Lap, the exhausted final revel on Tuesday night. At the stroke of midnight, Ash Wednesday arrives and the disheveled minions of the Monarch shuffle home, leaving the streets to the sweepers and garbage collectors. In fact, the Carnival begins long before the actual days of parading through the streets. In the late Fall, the Carnival bands (not musical groups but masquerade organizations) present their thematic portrayals for the year. At various masquerade camps throughout the city (and in other cities and towns) the year's crop of costumes are displayed in drawings on the walls of the camp. Potential patrons scan the walls of as many camps as they'd like, looking to see whose band they want to "play" with. Once the decision is made the new customers place a deposit on a costume for the section within the band that they prefer. Some of the larger bands may have twelve or more costume options. After the Christmas holidays and the passing of the New Year the latest crop of calypsos and Soca tunes are released to the eager public while the steelbands begin practicing for the various national competitions that are held just prior to Carnival Monday and Tuesday.

The Carnival season, along with Christmas, is also the busiest tourist season in Trinidad and marks the height of incoming tourism related revenue. Although the total income is difficult to calculate, it is in the many millions of dollars and includes revenue from hotel stays, restaurants, flights on the national airline, purchases of music recordings, costumes, souvenirs, and all the other collateral industries that gain from the presence of foreigners or returning natives. Carnival has been estimated by some analysts to generate well over US $30 million annually (Nurse 1999:673). These revenues are, increasingly, a vital component of the GNP (Gross National Product) in Trinidad, especially as traditional sources of income, such as oil, dwindle due to declining prices and decreasing production. As the focus on tourism has increased, so too has the focus on Carnival as *the* national festival. The state sees an increasingly professionalized Carnival as a strategy towards catering to a demanding and competitive tourist consumer. In that sense the state and the NCC are in a difficult situation: they need to balance the promotion of the "wine and jam" portion of the festival, by far the most popular aspect, and the preservation of the old time Carnival which they feel lends the event its uniqueness and therefore its marketability to tourists.

Compare and Contrast

The old time carnival consists of characters and portrayals associated with the carnival of "long ago." These characters each have a unique history and were popular at different times during the history of the festival. Most are associated with carnival before independence (1962) and some from the World War II period. In 1956, Daniel Crowley, an American anthropologist and folklorist, wrote a document for the *Caribbean Quarterly* identifying the various types of Carnival characters either in existence at the time or "extinct." That article has subsequently served as a blueprint for what constitutes legitimate carnival characters, often cited or used implicitly by the National Carnival Commission (NCC) and other organizations, as well as by Carnival scholars. Created in the late 1980s, the NCC expanded the mandate of the old Carnival Development Committee, heralding a new era of increasing the power of the state over the

1956 - Article is blueprint for legitimate
Carnival characters
1980 - NCC created.

celebration itself. Two parts of the Act of Parliament that created the NCC are noteworthy here:

1   (Paragraph c) the identification, evaluation and promotion of all Carnival related industries with a view to the enhancing and marketing of their cultural products and services
2   (Subsection ii) the possibility of marketing carnival products and activities in domestic and export markets

According to the NCC, by the summer of 2000 no real progress had been made in developing an effective marketing strategy nor had any significant steps been taken in the "preservation of... carnival traditions." Thus, the various organizations came together to produce a Strategic Plan (2001–3). The main point of the plan was to position the NCC, and consequently Trinidad, in such a way as to benefit from the explosion of overseas carnivals started, often, but not always, by émigré Trinidadians in the United States, Canada, the Caribbean and Europe. By reining in what were sometimes seen to be competing carnivals, the NCC hoped to promote a year-round Carnival industry, keeping Carnival costume makers, musicians, and others employed. One pressing issue for the NCC was to establish rights over Carnival and Carnival-related products so that Trinidad might benefit financially and symbolically from the use of "its" culture. The strategic plan included both the formation of a National Carnival Institute and the creation of legislation to protect carnival art forms.

The CITT (Carnival Institute of Trinidad and Tobago) was established in 1999. Its responsibilities include primarily the institutionalization of Carnival scholarship and craftsmanship. The institute now offers training courses not only in Carnival arts but also in judging Carnival. It also serves as a repository of scholarly works on Carnival as well as itself carrying out structured research on Carnival. As such there is at least one official anthropologist on the staff. The key word in much of the Institute's literature is *accreditation*. The Institute hopes to be able to act as the central legitimizing body of Trinidad-style carnivals in the world. A major step towards this end was the visit to Trinidad by a WIPO-UNESCO

(World Intellectual Property Organization-United Nations Educational, Scientific and Cultural Organization) mission. Although their declarations are not necessarily binding in any way, the ensuing report tied Trinidad Carnival into the larger framework of Folklore and Heritage that WIPO-UNESCO hopes will be protected through international copyright law. The visit was a symbolic boost for Trinidad and for the Institute.[8] Along with these developments the NCC has been staging shows and encouraging the portrayal of Old Time Carnival characters for some time. These characters become prime examples of what should be protected under any legislation. But beyond this they are held up as examples of true Carnival, authentic Trinidadian culture over and against the contemporary Carnival and its "unsavory" features.

What Needs Protecting?

Currently in Trinidad, performances of folklore, including the portrayal of traditional Carnival characters are just beginning to fall under the central jurisdiction of the state. Anyone can play these characters if they so choose and are encouraged to do so, but the state has begun to establish channels through which the accurate portrayal of such characters may be controlled and the unlicensed portrayal may be sanctioned. In addition, the National Carnival Commission makes use of anthropological research in order to instruct the public on and provide authentication for tourist shows containing such characters. The current proposed legislation would make the presence of legitimized and legitimating scholars central to the formation of a cultural corpus intimately bound up with the nation-state's construction of "self-expression" and "self-identity," viz. the nation. In order to explore this more fully it is necessary first to explore the sorts of cultural expressions that require protection and what sorts of strategies are being pursued.

Generally the Expressions of Folklore that the Trinidadian state would like to see protected in relation to the Carnival have to do with three areas of Carnival performance. These are *mas'* (i.e. masquerade, or costume making and the arts that accompany it with specific reference to traditional Carnival characters), *calypso* (the traditional music of Carnival) and *pan* (i.e. steelband, the acoustic percussion instruments originally created from discarded oil drums in Trinidad and proudly referred to as the only significant acoustic instrument invented in the twentieth century). These three vital areas of Carnival are intimately bound up with each other and each has its own history and body of scholarship (Crowley 1956, Hill 1993, Rohlehr 1990, Stuempfle 1995). Furthermore, each area has its own overseeing body operating with more or less autonomy under the general umbrella of the NCC.[9] The steadily increasing organization of Carnival since the early 1960s has been motivated in part by growing concern over both the exploitation of Carnival and Carnival forms for profit by outsiders and by the perception that the traditional arts of Carnival are rapidly disappearing. In an essay appearing in the *Caribbean Quarterly* in 1985, noted Carnival historian Errol Hill articulates the latter imperative quite directly, marrying the need for preservation with the art of nation-building:

> Now that most of these Caribbean territories have become independent nations, it is as if the last obstacle to achieving true Caribbean identity is the cultural one. ... [A] conscious and determined effort must be made by Caribbean peoples to discard the remnants of alien beliefs and institutions that keep us in thrall and boldly assert our freedom. ... [The] masquerades have been used to portray the struggle that still must be waged for economic and cultural freedom now that political independence has been won. (E. Hill, 1985:28–9)

The former concern, that Carnival characters will be exploited by outsiders, and that both critical revenue and the recognition of the characters place of origin will be lost, has been expressed by University of the West Indies scholar Keith Nurse (Nurse 1999). In his study Nurse notes that through processes of globalization, Caribbean migrants and their cultural forms have influenced and been embraced by the world (see also Nurse 1999). North America and Europe in particular offer an enormous market for Caribbean cultural forms, especially music. Nurse notes that the Caribbean region needs to rethink its strategies with regard to this potentially lucrative market in order to realize a greater return on its regional talent and artistic output. Toward this end he recommends pursuing options in and strengthening the regions Intellectual Property controls.

Thus the state and the NCC have a two-pronged approach to the preservation and promotion of Carnival and the Carnival arts. First, there is a desire to *preserve* the Carnival arts. The prime motivating factor here is the maintenance of the uniqueness of Trinidadian culture as an important part of creating a distinctive and independent national identity. Second, there is a desire to *protect* the Carnival arts. This project derives from the need to secure a source of recognition and revenue for the country of Trinidad. A sort of symbiosis between heritage preservation or cultural protection and the promotion of a tourism industry merges in the institution of the state. This is so because the state can offer itself as the body best equipped to pursue either international protections or sanctions or sui generis legislation in the spirit of international models of protection of folklore, and can justify these actions both economically and patriotically.

In all of this one crucial point has not been addressed: the state, in positioning itself to protect folklore, has in fact positioned itself to define folklore. This sleight of hand on the part of the state (as well as state-endorsed organizations such as the NCC and the other organizing bodies) goes largely unnoticed both in the public and academic spheres of Trinidad.

So what steps has the government taken to try to protect these Carnival forms? Until now, efforts to protect Carnival characters have not been successful. However, measures to crack down on intellectual property violations with regard to popular music have increased dramatically. The outstanding difficulty in protecting Carnival characters is that they are generally classed as Expressions of Folklore and there is no fundamental agreement, legally speaking, about what constitutes Expression of Folklore, or about how it can be protected under international copyright or intellectual property law. Nevertheless the issue is one taken seriously by both UNESCO and the WIPO (World Intellectual Property

Organization). From May 30 to June 9, 1999 the WIPO sent out a fact-finding mission (FFM) to Trinidad, Jamaica and Guyana to explore the concerns of local governments regarding Intellectual Property and Traditional Knowledge (WIPO Draft Report, 2000). The FFM met with officials from the Ministry of Legal Affairs, attorneys from the private sector, community leaders, traditional healers, artists, and representatives of the NCC. The aim of the Mission was to assess local concerns and seek out possible solutions and strategies to protect Expressions of Folklore and Traditional Knowledge.

Yet what WIPO and UNESCO actually did on these missions was to respond to invitations by centralized authorities regarding cultural depredation to *their* forms of folklore or traditional knowledge. The proprietary attitude taken by national governments toward this end was recognized by WIPO:

All government ministers encountered showed a keen interest in developing a progressive approach to these issues in the interest of their people. In some of the countries IP is recognized at the governmental level as a tool for development, the regulation of which can attract investment.

Yet groups outside of the government were not quite as enthusiastic about government management and control over issues of Expressions of Folklore and Traditional Knowledge:

The view was that there was a tendency for a nationalist approach to move towards closing access to TK or controlling it. The reality, it was suggested, was that many small island economies like exist in the Caribbean could not afford to do so. (WIPO FFM to the Caribbean Region Report 2000:16)

The issue of control, as we have seen, extends beyond the economic and into the ideological. From the perspective of the WIPO, "cultural heritage" and a "sense of community" underpin the TK system of the country (WIPO FFM Report 2000:3).

Finally, the FFM stressed the importance of documentation when identifying and recognizing candidates of Folklore and Traditional

Knowledge for protection. The FFM argued that, in efforts to protect and preserve, it is vital to communities or even individuals to regulate access by scholars to communities of people or single informants.[10] Ultimately the WIPO concluded that Intellectual Property, Copyright and Patent laws were currently inadequate to protect Expressions of Folklore. Sui generis protection, that is, laws formulated uniquely within the country in question, but possibly modeled on WIPO-UNESCO documents, such as the Model Provisions for National Laws on the Protection of Expressions of Folklore Against Illicit Exploitation and Other Prejudicial Actions, 1982, was seen as a viable strategy.[11] Toward this end, Sharon Le Gall produced, in Trinidad, perhaps the most comprehensive and sophisticated document on the issue (Le Gall 1994). Le Gall, a trained attorney, investigates all the possibilities of protecting expressions of folklore from a legal point of view and concludes that a preservationist strategy is perhaps the best course of action. Anticipating some of the same kinds of concerns voiced here she notes:

On the issue of cultural preservation, some critiques have stated that there is no "essential culture" fixed in the past that can be preserved. This view does warrant some consideration. Nevertheless, in cultures where there is a "living tradition," efforts of preserving aspects of the past *which are now visible in the present* and on the verge of extinction, are important initiatives. (Le Gall 1994:254, emphasis mine)

Le Gall mirrors the attitudes of cultural preservationists in Trinidad. This view of Carnival is that within the "living tradition" there exist remnants of the past that are being forgotten. Thus, behind certain masquerade forms such as the fancy sailors or the midnight robbers there lies a rich cultural history that should be remembered, taught, celebrated. The question is not, I suggest, whether history should be remembered or forgotten, but how the celebration of some forms and not others erases certain aspects of cultural history. That particular older forms persist even to this day is not merely a testimony to the hardiness of folk forms in Trinidad. The history of survivals and extinctions of masquerade characters is also the history of colonial, state and class-based reforms and prohibitions. It is also the history of women in mas', of other ethnic groups in mas' and of the methodical if not entirely conscious manipulation of Carnival history in the service of state agendas.

The remainder of this essay focuses on two competing narratives of Trinidadian cultural history, with specific reference to the women who participate in mas'. But before I turn to a further explication of the women's Carnival, it is important to establish what the NCC believes to be legitimate Carnival, paying special attention to the rhetoric produced by the organization about tradition and protection.

Old Time Carnival

It is not within the scope of this chapter to give a detailed history of the Carnival from its arrival with French planters in the eighteenth century to the independence of the country from the British in 1962. Some brief notes however are needed to demonstrate the rise, in the late nineteenth and early twentieth century, of what is now known as the old time Carnival.

In 1838, after the full emancipation of the slaves, the nature of the Carnival began to change dramatically as the white, elite planter class retreated from Carnival and more and more freed Afro-Trinidadians began to participate. Visiting European spectators of the festival as well as nervous Colonial officials and the local white and mixed (or Coloured) elite were scandalized by the moral license the revelers took. Pried loose from the nineteenth century social and political corset of slavery and European Victorian values, the hoi polloi claimed the avenues of the colonial city with abandon. Here is an example of the typically understated nature of elite rhetoric against this new Carnival: "In our towns ... commencing with the orgies on Sunday night, we have a fearful howling of a parcel of semi-savages emerging God knows where from, exhibiting hellish scenes and the most demoniacal representations of the days of slavery ... then using the mask the two following days as a mere cloak for every species of barbarism and crime."

The "demoniacal representations" this writer speaks of were probably antecedents of the wide variety of Carnival characters and masqueraders that evolved during the nineteenth and twentieth centuries. These characters developed slowly, often beginning as satirical reflections on people or issues in society, creatures from folklore or history or creative elaborations of French and other European Carnival figures. Other characters, like the "Neg Jadin" or "garden slave" were originally played by aristocrats pretending to be their own servants during Carnival. These portrayals were later taken on by emancipated Africans themselves in one of those role reversal performance traditions, like minstrelsy, so common in slave societies of the new world where the oppressed imitates the oppressor's impression of him/herself. Along with the Neg Jadin there were the Dames Lorraine, the Burrokeets, the Clowns, Bats, Bears, Red and Blue Devils, Jab Jabs, Jabs Molassi, the Wild Indian bands, the Moko Jumbies (stilt walkers), the Midnight Robbers and later the multitudes of sailors and soldiers commandeering the streets and sidewalks from would-be onlookers. Each character had a unique costume and attendant performance style. Often certain characters came out at different times of the Carnival. Some emerged during the early morning hours of J'Ouvert (jouvay), the explosive and ecstatic opening of Carnival, while others were better suited to the daylight hours. Many costume traditions had ritualized speeches associated with them, like the Midnight Robbers who held you up at mock gun or sword point and regaled you with terrible tales of their terrible deeds:

"For the day my mother give birth to me, the sun refuse to shine, and the wind ceased blowing. Many mothers gave birth that day, but to deformed children. Plagues and pestilence pestered the cities ... At the age of two I drowned my grandmother in a spoonful of water. For at the age of five, I this dreaded monarch, was sent to school but anything too mathematic was a puzzle to my brains, but when it come to snatching children's faces, ringing their ears, biting off a piece of their nose, I was always on top! Now be quick and deliver the hidden treasure. For I am prepared to follow you to the end of the world, as the tiger follows his prey, and pierce my dagger into your heart. Your hair will make my garments. Your eyes I will take to shine as light in my lavatory, your nostrils I will make my trumpet, your brain I will make my supper ..." (Excerpts taken from Crowley 1956)

After this tirade spectators were meant to hand over a penny or two. One of the masquerading traditions that horrified the upper classes the most was called the *pissenlit*. Literally the "bedwetter," this piece of performance entailed a grown man sporting bed sheets or linens stained red in imitation of bloody menstrual rags. The Baby Doll masquerade involved the cooperation of two performers: one, the man in drag holding the "bastard baby" (a doll) of some poor bystander and making a big scene and the other the "policeman," called in to force the poor victim to pay child support. Starting in the mid 1840s white planters began importing Indian indentured labor to work the sugar cane fields. Gradually Indians became a significant population in Trinidad and currently make up about 40% of the population. As the Indian population grew, so did increasing animosity between these dominant ethnic groups. Political competition, in particular became fierce, but rarely catastrophically violent. In 1995, for the first time, an Indian-led government gained control of Parliament and elected a Prime Minister.

In the late 1930s and right through the 1950s and early 1960s the sailor bands emerged as the most popular form of masquerade for the average (male) Trinidadian. Trinidadians had been imitating sailors since the nineteenth century (if not earlier) when the British sailors began making regular calls at Port-of-Spain. But in the 1940s and 1950s, when Americans were stationed on Trinidad during the Second World War, the sailor costume achieved the height of its popularity. Thousands of people wearing the basic white sailor outfit, some carrying talcum powder to spray on cringing spectators, would parade behind their favorite steelbands as they moved across the city. Steelbands were deeply rooted in their neighborhoods and their followers were fiercely loyal to the music, the costume and the home turf. When two steelbands coming from

rival neighborhoods met, pitched street battles, known as steelband clashes, were not uncommon. Some of them have permanently entered into the lore of the Carnival, memorialized in song and, at least in the case of one local folk artist, in sculpture. The steelbands, with glorious names like Desperados, Renegades, Red Army, and Invaders taken from American movies, advanced on the downtown in snaking columns of warriors holding banners that read "To Hell and Back" or "D-Day."

Many of these costume traditions, especially the more violent or morally questionable, were roundly decried during the colonial period by the middle and upper classes of mostly white and "coloured" or mixed elites. Campaigns to either shut down the Carnival completely (white strategy) or reform and modify it (coloured strategy) were pursued throughout the end of the nineteenth and into the twentieth century. In fact, in one form or another, there are still efforts to modify, curtail, clean up or otherwise circumscribe the license shown at Carnival time, although now the reformers are the NCC and the objects of reform, ironically, middle class women. Some of these strategies in the past included the outright banning of masks and drumming in the 1880s, elimination of certain portrayals or practices such as the *pissenlit* or the habit of sailors carrying inflated pig's bladders with which to strike unsuspecting bystanders, or the more moderate tactic of organizing competitions and contests through which to control costume portrayals and offer prizes and other incentives. The competition has been by far the most successful in corralling potentially disruptive or violent behavior and directing it both towards money-making activities (one can charge admission to a competition) and towards the contribution to a national culture. Ironically, even though it began as the white elites who were concerned with reforming or banning certain elements of the Carnival, that project was largely taken over by the black elites who lead public life after independence. Yet the main difference between the reforming strategies of the whites and those of the coloured or black middle and upper classes was the latter's concern for creating a national culture from the "folk" forms of the working class. Because the creation

old time characters are men

of a national identity was a priority for these new reformers they looked back at the oppositional forms of the working classes and embraced them as universal expressions not of a specific class and racial independence from Colonial oppressors, but as an expression of independence and resistance that all Trinidadians might share.

In 1985, the Trinidadian scholar Errol Hill wrote a significant follow up to Dan Crowley's 1956 article on old time carnival characters. Hill's article was entitled "Traditional Figures in Carnival: Their Preservation, Development and Interpretation" (Hill 1985). In this article Hill lays out a plan for how he feels the old time characters should be treated by the state. It is essentially a call to action to save these portrayals before they disappear. What is at stake, Hill argues, is no less than the cultural history of the nation. Two years later the Carnival Development Committee created a showcase called Viey La Cou, a creole term meaning "The Old Yard." This was conceived of as the first step in preserving and maintaining the old traditions. The event happens in the parking lot of the Queen's Hall auditorium, next to the city zoo. The decision to hold the event here seems strangely fitting, with endangered cultural forms sharing a public space with endangered animals in cages just beyond a chain link fence, as if the there were a conceptual continuum between them.

Largely designed for tourists, the show features performances by old time characters, presented out of their historical and sociological context as living monuments to carnivals past. The characters are predominantly those that were catalogued by Crowley and/or Errol Hill and go by the names those scholars gave them. Other scholars have suggested that these were not, in fact, the names people themselves gave to the characters during the period in which they were performed originally (van Koningsbruggen 1997:79). By the 1990s the NCC had begun actively promoting and expanding the Viey La Cou show and trying to foster the portrayal of old Carnival characters in schools along with the artistic skills to make the costumes in workshops. In 1994, John Cupid, the official anthropologist of the NCC, said of the traditional carnival characters: "[they] add to the uniqueness of the National

Festival which ... create(s) a differentiation of the product as Trinidad and Tobago Carnival claims a niche in the world economic market" (Cupid 1994:16). Similar sentiments have also been expressed by other authors, for instance, Compton Bourne and S.M. Allgrove note that a differentiated cultural product is expected and in fact demanded by the consuming public:

> This perception of cultural authenticity on the part of the consumer confers an inherent and inalienable market advantage to the musical products of the country or region in question. In effect it gives it a quality niche in the marketplace. There are substitutes of varying degrees of competitiveness but the substitutability is never total. (Bourne and Allgrove, n.d.)

Pamela Franco (n.d.) points out that almost all the traditional Carnival characters are male and that the validation of these figures by the NCC also validates the working class, male carnival of the 1930s, 1940s and 1950s as the only "real" Carnival. It is from this general period that many Trinidadians draw their conceptions of Carnival tradition while at the same time removing these traditions from their place in history. Furthermore, many of the less savory characters described by Crowley have been conveniently left out of the preservation project. Notably, the character called *pissenlit* who was known to wander the streets during carnival time dressed in bloody menstrual rags, has not been actively preserved. In summary, the NCC, while appealing to the preservation of "Trinidadian" culture, is essentially interested in advancing a historically specific and limited, working class male (mostly Afro-Trinidadian) and sanitized version of "traditional carnival." I would like, now, to return to our discussion of the women's carnival by way of contrast.

Wine and Jam

Although space does not allow for a thorough history of the Wine and Jam Carnival, the basic description is as follows. A new music began to emerge in the late 1960s/early 1970s called *soca*, a blend of calypso and American soul music that made use of amplified instruments and required

Viey La Cou The Old Yard

the use of massive sound systems. New technology made it possible for masquerade bands to bring such amplified music on the road with them. This led to the virtual disappearance of the steelband music that had formerly accompanied the majority of masqueraders on their march through the city. In addition, playing carnival gradually became more acceptable for women who slowly but steadily supplanted men as the majority of revelers on the streets, changing the demographic from about 80% men in the late 1950s to about 80% women by 1981 (van Koningsbruggen 1997).

The class composition of carnival has also changed, as more and more middle class people began to play mas'. Ironically, it was, in part, the reforming attitude of the middle class-controlled CDC (the NCC predecessor) that made Carnival more inviting to middle class women overall, by making the streets safer during the carnival season. Furthermore, the increased economic independence of Trinidadian women allowed them greater freedom in playing mas' in part because they were able to purchase their own costumes and pay registration fees, and also because the presence of women in professional positions contributed to a more relaxed attitude regarding women in public (van Koningsbruggen, 1997:80–1). By the 1980s and 1990s costumes were getting skimpier, the music was getting louder and raunchier and the carnival of "long ago" had been pushed into the background.

In trying to bring back old time characters the NCC also decried the current state of the festival, saying that it was no longer authentic carnival. True Trinidadian culture was being diluted and influences from other cultures were rendering local culture unrecognizable. Not only was there a loss of identity but Trinidad was also losing the ability to distinguish itself in the world market of cultures. It no longer had "brand name" recognition among the ocean of other, easily recognizable cultures that were out there for people to "consume." Identity, whether consciously or not, was being linked with commerce. Thus any acts of heritage preservation that were to be undertaken by the state were also acts of protecting a financial resource.

The wine and jam carnival, represented by young middle class women, was seen as not only unpatriotic, culturally destructive and morally suspect; it was potentially hurting the economy. Of course the state also recognized that many tourists were pouring into Trinidad to see the scantily clad women, but this contradiction was left relatively unexamined. The fear of culture loss lay more in the idea that soon no one would be able to tell Trinidad Carnival from any other Caribbean festival and Trinidadian authority/authorship would be lost.

At this point we can return briefly to the significant omission in the current literature on copyright and heritage protection, which is fundamentally the issue of representation. The preservation of heritage, of course, always has an agenda, but it is not always everyone's agenda. The drive to preserve heritage often becomes the province of a locally empowered group that determines what counts as legitimate culture. In our example here women become the subject of derision by a male dominated NCC that sees the middle class Carnival of women as illegitimate. By excluding contemporary developments in the Carnival from the "canon" of Carnival traditions, a significant element of Trinidadian society is silenced.

ridicule

The Poison Strike

On Carnival Tuesday 1999 the largest masquerade band[12] in Trinidad, Poison, began crossing the main judging venue at the Queen's Park Savannah in Port-of-Spain. This stage is generally considered the culminating point in anyone's Carnival journey through the city. Bands cross between two grandstands in front of several thousand spectators and in front of television cameras beaming the display to homes throughout Trinidad, the Caribbean and the world (the magic of pay-per-view). Normally the massive music trucks pass alongside the stage, providing the band with its tunes until they cross.

On this Tuesday, however, the band was so large (nearly 7,000 people according to one account[13]) and the dancers so enthusiastic that they refused to cross completely over the stage. More and more band members crowded onto the massive platform and danced, holding up all the bands behind them. As the stage grew more crowded some of the masqueraders stopped dancing (even with the music playing) and began merely mingling with each other, talking and "liming" (see below). The first of the enormous trucks that accompany the bands and are generally positioned at strategic intervals between the band's sections to provide music (some taped, some live) began to move off, leaving the crowd without music. The Poison masqueraders then began to wait for a new truck to arrive on the scene. After some exasperated minutes the NCC decided to issue a warning to the revelers to move on and let the next band on stage. In response, the mass of mostly women revelers simply sat down in an impromptu strike. After some pleading by Carnival authorities and much confusion three mounted policemen herded the reluctant band members off the stage. The act caused an immediate sensation in the press and was on the lips of most Trinidadians for the next few days. In the words of one reporter, Francis Joseph:

> Comprising mostly women, many members took a long time to move on as they played to the television and press cameras. At one point during the playing of Machel Montano's "Toro Toro" and Superblue's "Ato Party" (popular Soca hits of that year), the revellers [sic] just stopped dancing and stood on stage, leaving the audience to wonder where was the Carnival spirit. (Joseph 1998)

Letters were written to the editors of the major newspapers and people commented on the television news. Many were outraged at what they considered immature and "bratty" behavior. The National Carnival Commission maintained that the strike was selfish and echoed the comments of Francis Joseph's article that the strike was not in keeping with the Carnival spirit of allowing everyone to enjoy themselves.

Not surprisingly very few commentators bothered to delve behind the "wine and jam" phenomenon to try to cast a sympathetic or at least explanatory eye on what has become the significant component of today's Carnival. I would like to offer here some suggestions about the role Carnival plays for middle class women and

contrast this with official understandings of Carnival. My aim here is to emphasize that, in today's Carnival, the activities of the young women who play mas' can be seen as creative and performative negotiations with the society that produces them, and these activities are therefore just as "legitimate" as the romanticized carnival of the male working class.

Poison Lime

On one occasion in 1994 I had the opportunity to interview a number of women in Trinidad who routinely play in the band Poison. Poison's costumes are usually very minimal, with a bikini as the basic garment, along with a collar-piece of sequins and braid, a "head-piece," something for the shins or ankles and bands for the wrists. Masqueraders are also given a "standard," a long wooden or fiberglass rod with some emblem attached to signify the section of the band. Poison attracts one of the largest followings, with bands in recent years swelling to over four thousand people. The average masquerader in Poison is now most likely to be a young, middle class, perhaps suburban woman.

As with almost all the large "pretty" bands these days, no masqueraders actually construct their own costumes. The work is performed at the masquerade camp. The profile for the typical female Poison player articulates a whole series of social positions within Trinidad. These women are often well educated, having gone to one of the prestigious convent schools, but may not be university bound. If they are not at the University of the West Indies or at school abroad, then they are typically working in white collar professions such as a bank or other financial institution, an insurance company, advertising agency or marketing firm. There is also the chance that they are BWIA (British West Indies Airlines) flight attendants, a post commonly believed to have the most beautiful women. My interviews with these women centered on why they chose Poison. Their opinions about which Carnival bands are the best to play in give us some idea as to what they value about the festival and is quite different from what many community leaders, culture brokers and to a lesser degree, Trinidadian administrators value.

For Poison girls Carnival is all about the "lime" or group of friends involved. In one respect or another none of the five women I interviewed from this band fit the typical Poison configuration. They all seemed to agree on the above criteria for Poison players, but did not include themselves entirely within that description. Some did not go to the prestigious convent schools, did not have the right connections or the right job. All of the women mentioned that special sections were reserved within the band for the women who looked the most "with it" and that they refused registering some people in Poison, the implication being that they were too overweight or did not have the right look.

Some special sections of the band have separate costumes and people in this section are often featured on top of the music trucks or at the head of the parade. I asked how women were selected for this group and was told "if a woman comes into the mas' camp and she looks like a Coca-Cola bottle, then [she was selected]." None of the five women were in this select group and even seemed to disparage the practice. I asked them why they had joined this band in particular. In addition to the lime (their friends were playing in Poison), they all mentioned the music. Giselle noted that she had switched from another band called Hart's because the music was not as appealing, even though the costume was pretty. The music was considered better because it "got the crowd involved, they would carry on and they would get you involved." The band's role, if it is to be successful, is to provide a context in which a good lime can continue unabated for long periods of time. A sense of the solidarity and exclusiveness of Poison can be found in the fact that the group has its own theme song. Monica noted that the theme song "really sets the crowd mad, I mean you could be chipping and after you hear 'if you think that you're sexy' [lyrics to the song] and people are like 'Oh God!' and they start jumping up .... that's their song." Poison is successful because it combines a successful party atmosphere with an image of elitism and exclusivity that appeals to some women who aspire to that status within the society.

Poison attracts these women, even as they are critical of some of the band's practices and members, because it provides them with an opportunity to see themselves as members of the most privileged group. They are allowed to celebrate their position and, it is hoped, maintain or even improve that position. Further, the band provides an outlet for a community of women who, while enjoying some access to the corridors of power within their society, are still subject to discrimination and severe career limitations based on their sex. In the words of one Poison player I interviewed: "This is the one day we women rule the streets and can free up."

There is a subtle combination of "playing yourself" and playing the role you want to be or want to continue to be. It was agreed by all of the women that Poison had ugly costumes that year, but it was not enough to deter them from playing in the band because that was where the lime was. In addition my interviews revealed that these girls had a certain dissatisfaction with their prospects in Trinidad. Although, at some level, part of the elite, they still struggled against a decidedly patriarchal society in which opportunities for employment and advancement were limited. These younger, female masqueraders are much more the norm than the older, male or female ones in today's carnival. They are the ones who give Carnival its real life and the ones to whom most Carnival bandleaders must cater in order to realize a profit. Although some guardians of culture in Trinidad decry their Carnival, their actions have transformed the event. Sometimes disparagingly referred to as suburban, brown-skinned girls playing themselves, they nonetheless are the heart of the mas'. Their contribution to the "destruction" of Carnival challenges the commodification of nostalgic Carnival as national culture, even as it commercializes the event as spectacle and tourist attraction.

Yet, where those agents of official, preservationist discourse see the middle class Carnival as destructive, I suggest that, much like the role attributed to the working class Carnival, the middle class version has productive qualities related to its relevance to that specific population. Specifically, younger middle class women engage in acts of self-expression during Carnival that both reflect and are reflective of their position within Trinidadian society. Not all of these acts are obviously "resistant" or emancipatory. In fact, it may be argued that many behaviors contribute to the reproduction of an inferior status for women. But the activities of middle class women do shape the look and direction of Carnival and produce new forms of cultural expression relevant to themselves. One could argue here that the state denies the validity of a "women's" carnival, vis-à-vis the national cultural agenda merely by denying that women's (and the middle class's) self-expression is not worth as much as the male working class. Again, we need to see this in the context of a tacit state-sponsored project that has also historically denied Indians and Chinese credit in the building of Carnival. In all of these cases the minority position does not constitute an authentic or legitimate contribution to what the state sees as the central values of Trinidadian culture. And in each case the minority group's contributions vary. But in the case of the middle class woman's carnival of today whatever issues women are facing are seen as completely anathema to the official vision of Carnival.

So far my argument has explicitly maintained that the form and content of Carnival changes and that there is resistance to such change on the part of the state-sponsored agencies. But implicit in my argument is the idea that the Carnival framework itself serves the same basic agenda for every constituency that dominates it. In other words, whoever "controls" carnival controls a medium of self-expression that works the same in every case. From the 1930s through the 1950s it was Afro-Trinidadian, male, working class participants whose grievances, values and dreams were expressed. In the 1980s and 1990s middle class female desires were given voice on the streets. Along this line of reasoning Carnival itself does not change as a medium for the airing of public dissatisfaction by certain segments of the population, some of whose opinions or status is marginalized. Yet I do not wholly subscribe to this conclusion. The Carnival is not a static framework with a "job" to do. The role of the Carnival shifts with the historical context. And in none of the cases I have presented thus far has Carnival been employed as self-consciously political. Furthermore, carnival is not purely "resistant" in any easy sense. If, for example, Carnival

provides an outlet for middle class women to express frustration with a patriarchal and limiting society, it also reifies women as objects of the male public gaze. If women's "wining" on each other has been vilified for its lesbian overtones, those same overtones have excited typical male fantasies of lesbian sex as an occasion for voyeurism.

In any case the indeterminacy of public rituals such as Carnival provide more a forum for a debate than neat conclusions.[14] The key here is to recognize that the debates themselves will continue to shape the form and function of Carnival. Not only is the Poison Strike a reflection of issues relevant to the majority of masqueraders in the contemporary Carnival, it is also a product of those concerns. The bands in today's Carnival are much larger than the working class bands of the past, the routes masqueraders take through the city have changed, the judging has changed and now, with many "middle class" bands, being judged has ceased even to be a priority with many groups avoiding the chief judging venue at the Queen's Park Savannah altogether. In light of these rapid and substantial changes, the state's concern over control of the festival becomes clearer and copyright emerges as a key strategy.

Conclusion

One final issue must be mentioned. In the discussion of copyright in Trinidad, traditional characters are not the only elements under consideration. Recently, bands such as Poison have issued statements with their costumes containing warnings about pirating and many claim copyright privileges over certain designs. These copyright warnings, futile as they may be, are of a different nature than the attempts to copyright characters. In the former case the copyright applies to the designs of the band, not to a whole class of personages or a body of knowledge. In other words, these copyrights apply to original design and not to group heritage. The contemporary large-scale mas' band may be a commercial venture and may or may not make a profit but the danger of these bands to the nationalist project lies not in their commercialism, nor even their appeal to tourists, but in both their relatively undifferentiated appearance and the

presence of women "behaving badly." By elim-
inating the distinctiveness of the Old Time Carnival characters such bands are seen as diluting
the distinctiveness of Carnival. But distinctiveness is a feature that appeals to the ideology
informing the structures of common difference
and therefore heritage preservation discussed
above; it has little bearing on the performance of
actions that are directly relevant to masqueraders,
especially those masqueraders that dominate the
contemporary Carnival. As documenters, scholars
have often been guilty of ignoring these masses of
revelers, perhaps out of an implicit sense that
such groups were inauthentic.

As I have mentioned, one element in the debate
over cultural appropriation that seems routinely
ignored or downplayed is appropriation or re-
appropriation from within. Who acts to represent
the "culture" in question? What do they have to
gain? We cannot assume the monolithic nature of
another "culture" or group especially when discussing the political and legal protection of heritage. Interests are at work. Preservation, broadly
construed, has powerful resonance in that it creates a situation of "stakes" that were not there
before. We must be careful to explore all the
ramifications of preservation and appropriation
at the local level. Appropriation is not about one
group taking from another group by "reaching
into" some static, primordial corpus of cultural
goods that are equally shared. The power of the
politics of appropriation derives from an understanding that groups, defined by their cultural
forms, pre-exist these disputes. Organizations
that can position themselves to recapture lost
cultural forms are in a position to define local
culture and secure their own authority over it.
But it is in the dispute that group identity is
formulated and heritage is defined.

Ultimately it is not really the fact or act of
appropriation that is what is at stake here. Appropriation, from the perspective of many artists, is a
good thing in that it spreads awareness of
and promotes the popularity of certain artistic or
expressive forms, which can be good for business.
It's the recourse or control of appropriation
that matters. That credit is given or that awareness
of origins is heightened. It is the loss of the source
and consequently the disappearance of the group
as its objects float without root. Cultural amnesia
hurts the state cultural organizations that may
profit financially and symbolically from control
over unique and recognizable cultural forms.

Carnival has never been merely a collection of
roles and characters. Ultimately Carnival is only
the actions and activities of people who play with
a given framework and who may re-invent perceived traditions even as they invent novel expressive practices. Carnival provides a forum for
expression that, by necessity, needs to respond to
shifting contexts and transformations not only
within the society but also on a global scale.
The popularity of the sailor bands in the 1940s
and 1950s, the Midnight Robbers, the Dames
Lorraine and other characters was always due to
the efficacious way in which these forms engaged
with historical phenomena of immediate importance.[15] The "wine and jam" carnival of today is
actively constructed and responds to the concerns
of those who play in it. It has become middle
class, commodified and hybridized. It may be
unrecognizable to many Trinidadians who lived
through the Carnivals of the 1940s and 1950s, but
it has created a new kind of identity and community. It draws on sources from outside of Trinidad and this is a chief cause of concern for a state
preservation project that has, at least in part, the
maintenance of sovereignty as its goal. The preservationist strategy relies upon scholarly documentation and recourse to international legal
bodies to define what is properly cultural and
thereby limits or excludes significant portions of
society as they seek to construct meaningful
forms for themselves.

Notes

1 These are all names given to traditional
   Carnival characters. The initial scholarly description of these characters may be found in Crowley
   1956.

2 The only real exception being Gordon Rohlehr's
   contribution (Rohlehr 1990).

3 Again, the only exception here would be the interview
   with current Carnival bandleader Peter Minshall,

often cited for his dedication to reviving the spirit of old time mas' in his contemporary portrayals. (Schechner and Riggio 1998).

4 See Segal 1988:301–3.

5 ATSIC is responsible for a wide range of "preservationist" activities, including the repatriation of remains, protecting historical sites and preserving festivals and ceremonial activities.

6 I self-consciously use the expression "the culture" here because it is this understanding of a uniform, uncontested body of cultural content that is at issue here.

7 This is significant as the population is roughly equally divided between these two groups along with smaller numbers of Chinese, Syrians, Europeans and a category generally referred to as "mixed."

8 During the preparation of this article a subsequent visit was made to Trinidad by the WIPO and a seminar was held on the protection of folklore and traditional knowledge. (*Trinidad Guardian*, March 7, 2002:21).

9 These governing bodies are for mas' the National Carnival Bandleaders Association, for calypso, The Unified Calypsonians Organization and for pan, Pan Trinbago.

10 The chief irony of this formulation was not overlooked in the meetings WIPO had with Caribbean representatives, namely that documentation facilitates both protection and exploitation.

11 Jamaica has already implemented legislation along these lines.

12 A "band" in Carnival terminology is not a musical group, but an organization run by various entrepreneurs and designers for masqueraders. A bandleader will, each year, decide upon a theme for the band to play on Carnival Monday and Tuesday. The themes may vary widely from band to band and from year to year, but are generally meant to be something that will provide the costume designers with creative options. The band will then be subdivided into sections each one carrying out some aspect of the overall theme. Masqueraders, when choosing which bands they want to play with, will tour the masquerade camps (mas' camps) and look at the pictures of the costumes that the designers have displayed. If a masquerader likes the theme he or she will choose a section to play in. The masquerader then registers with the band and places a down payment on a costume. Just before Carnival masqueraders go to the camps and pick up their outfits that they then take home and generally modify even further.

13 *Trinidad Guardian*, February 26, 1998:1, 10.

14 In a recent essay Garth Green has demonstrated this dimension of Carnival with regard to religious controversies (Green 1999).

15 For detailed ethnographic descriptions of the Midnight Robber and Dame Lorraine characters (outside of Crowley 1956) see Riggio 1998).

References

Bakhtin, Mikhail. 1984. *Rabelais and His World*. Bloomington: Indiana University Press.

Balliger, Robin. 2002. "The Politics of Cultural Value and the Value of Cultural Politics: Intellectual Property Legislation and the Discursive Construction of Interests in Postcolonial Trinidad." Unpublished ms. Under Review in Garth Green and Philip Scher (eds.) *Critical Mas': Nationalism and Transnationalism in the Trinidad Carnival*. Indiana University Press.

Barnes, Natasha. 2000. "Body Talk: Notes on Women and Spectacle in Contemporary Trinidad Carnival." *Small Axe* Number 7.

Bettig, Ronald V. 1996. *Copyrighting Culture: The Political Economy of Intellectual Property*, Boulder: Westview Press.

Blakeney, Michael. 1999. "Intellectual Property in the Dreamtime – Protecting the Cultural Creativity of Indigenous Peoples." *Oxford Intellectual Property Research Centre Electronic Journal of Intellectual Property Rights*.

Bourne, Compton and S.M. Allgrove. n.d. "Prospects for Exports of Entertainment Services For the English Speaking Caribbean: The Case of Music." Paper prepared for The World Bank Group, Latin America and Caribbean. Online Document at www.worldbank.org.

Brown, Michael F. 1998. "Can Culture be Copyrighted?" *Current Anthropology* Vol. 39, No. 2, April, pp. 193–222.

Brush, Stephen. 1993. "Indigenous Knowledge of Biological Resources and Intellectual Property Rights." *American Anthropologist* 95: 653–86.

Brush, Stephen B. and Doreen Stabinsky (eds.) 1996. *Valuing Local Knowledge: Indigenous People and Intellectual Property Rights*. Washington DC: Island Press.

Coombe, Rosemary J. 1998. *The Cultural Life of Intellectual Properties*. Durham: Duke University Press.

Crowley, Daniel J. 1956. "The Traditional Masques of Carnival." *Caribbean Quarterly* Vol. 3/4:192–223.

Cupid, John. 1994. "Trinidad Carnival Traditional Characters." *1st Carnival King and Queen of the World Magazine* Vol. 1. pp. 16–17.

Daes, Erica-Irene. 1994. "Discrimination Against Indigenous Peoples: Protection of the Heritage of Indigenous Peoples." Report to the United Nations Commission on Human Rights Document 94-13218. TXT.

De Freitas, Patricia Ann. 1994. "Playing Mas': The Construction and Deconstruction of National Identity In the Trinidad Carnival." Unpublished PhD Dissertation, McMaster University (Canada).

Edmondson, Belinda. 1999. "Trinidad Romance: The Invention of Jamaican Carnival." In Belinda Edmondson (ed.), *Caribbean Romances: The Politics of Regional Representation*, pp. 56–75. Charlottesville: University of Virginia Press.

Franco, Pamela. 2000. "The 'Unruly Woman' in Nineteenth-Century Trinidad Carnival." *Small Axe 7*.

Franco, Pamela. 2001. "Shifting Ground: An Early History of Afro-Creole Women's Mas' in Trinidad Carnival," Unpublished PhD Dissertation, Emory University.

Franco, Pamela. n.d. "The Invention of Traditional Mas' and the Politics of Gender;" Unpublished ms. in Green and Scher, eds. *Critical Mas': Nationalism and Transnationalism in the Trinidad Carnival*. Manuscript Under Review, Indiana University Press.

Garcia Canclini, Nestor. 1995. *Hybrid Cultures: Strategies for Entering and Leaving Modernity*. Minneapolis: University of Minnesota Press, 1995.

Githaiga, Joseph W. 1998. "Intellectual Property Law and the Protection of Indigenous Folklore and Knowledge" *Murdoch University Electronic Journal of Law* Vol.5, No.2, June (online).

Green, Garth. 1999. "Blasphemy, Sacrilege and Moral Degradation in the Trinidad Carnival: The Hallelujah Controversy of 1995." In John Pulis (ed.) *Religion, Diaspora and Cultural Identity: A Reader in the Anglophone Caribbean*, pp. 189–214. Amsterdam: Gordon and Breach Publishers.

Green, Garth and Philip Scher, eds. *Critical Mas': Nationalism and Transnationalism in the Trinidad Carnival*. Manuscript Under Review, Indiana University Press, 2003.

Handler, Richard and Jocelyn Linnekin. 1984. "Tradition, Genuine or Spurious." *Journal of American Folklore* Vol. 97, No.385, pp. 273–90.

Hill, Donald R. 1993. *Calypso Calaloo: Early Carnival Music in Trinidad*. Gainsville: Universtiy Press of Florida.

Hill, Errol. 1972. *The Trinidad Carnival: Mandate for a National Theatre*, Austin: University of Texas Press.

Hill, Errol. 1985. "Traditional Figures in Carnival: Their Preservation, Development and Interpretation" *Caribbean Quarterly* Vol. 31, No. 2: 14–35.

Joseph, Francis. 1998. "Poison in Protest: Revellers Spend Two Hours on Stage." *Trinidad Guardian* February 25: 10.

Le Gall, Sharon B. 1994. "Preserving One's Narrative: Implications of Intellectual Property Protection of Folklore and the Steel Pan in Trinidad and Tobago." Unpublished Master of Laws Thesis, Osgoode Hall Law School, York University (Canada).

Liverpool, Hollis. n.d. "The Long Term Scenario: A Focus on Training, Accreditation, Education, Documentation and Marketing." Document published by the Carnival Institute of Trinidad and Tobago.

McCann, Anthony. 1998. "Traditional Music and Copyright – The Issues." In *Common Property Resource Digest* (online version), International Association for the Study of Common Property, Indiana University.

Merry, Sally Engle. 1992. "Anthropology, Law and Transnational Processes." *Annual Review of Anthropology* Vol. 21: 357–79.

Messenger, Phyllis Mauch (ed.). 1999. *The Ethics of Collecting Cultural Property*. Albuquerque: University of New Mexico Press.

Miller, Daniel (ed.). 1995. *Worlds Apart: Modernity Through the Prism of the Local*. London and New York: Routledge.

Nurse, Keith. 1999. "Globalization and Trinidad Carnival: Diaspora, Hybridity and Identity in Global Culture." *Cultural Studies* 13(4): 661–90.

Nurse, Keith. 2000. "The Caribbean Music Industry: The Case for Industrial Policy and Export Promotion." Study Prepared for Office of Cultural Affairs, Inter-American Cultural Program Organization of American States, Washington DC, June.

Pierre, Donna. 1998. "Poison Protest: Angry Revellers and Band in War of Words." *Trinidad Guardian* February 26, 1–5.

Riggio, Milla C. (Guest Ed.) 1998. "Resistance and Identity: Carnival in Trinidad and Tobago." *The Drama Review*, Fall, pp. 7–23.

Rohlehr, Gordon. 1990. *Calypso and Society in Pre-Independence Trinidad*. Port-of-Spain: Gordon Rohlehr.

Root, Deborah. 1995. *Cannibal Culture: Art, Appropriation and the Commodification of Difference*. Boulder, Westview Press.

Schechner, Richard and Milla Riggio. 1998. "Editor's Notes." *The Drama Review* Fall: 1.

Scher, Philip W. 1999. "Confounding Categories: The Global and the Local in the Process of a Caribbean Art." *Small Axe* 6: 37–56.

Scher, Philip W. In press. *A Moveable Fete: Caribbean Carnival as Transnational Cultural Process.* Gainesville: University of Florida Press

Segal, Daniel. 1988. "Nationalism, Comparatively Speaking." *Journal of Historical Sociology* Vol. 1, No.3, pp. 301–21.

Stuempfle, Stephen. 1995. *The Steelband Movement: The Forging of a National Art in Trinidad and Tobago*, Philadelphia: University of Pennsylvania Press

Turner, Victor. 1983. "Carnival in Rio: Dionysian Drama in an Industrializing Society." In Frank Manning, (ed.) *The Celebration of Society*, pp. 103–25. Bowling Green: Bowling Green University Popular Press.

Turner, Victor. 1988. *The Anthropology of Performance.* Performing Arts Journal Publications.

UNCTAD. "Report of the Expert Meeting on Systems and National Experiences for the Protection of Traditional Knowledge, Innovations and Practices." December 6, 2000.

UNESCO. "Recommendation on the Safeguarding of Traditional Culture and Folklore" Adopted by the General Conference, Paris, November 15, 1989.

UNESCO. "Draft Treaty for the Protection of Expressions of Folklore Against Illicit Exploitation and Other Prejudicial Actions" http://www.unesco.org/webworld/com/compendium/4401/html. n.d.

van Koningsbruggen, Peter. 1997. *Trinidad Carnival.* Warwick University Caribbean Studies: Macmillan, 1997.

Wilk, Richard. 1995. "Learning to be Local in Belize: Global Sytems of Common Difference," in D. Miller (ed.) *Worlds Apart: Modernity Through the Prism of the Local*, pp. 110–33. London and New York: Routledge.

WIPO-UNESCO. "Regional Consultation on the Protection of Expressions of Folklore for Latin America and the Caribbean." Quito, 1999.

World Intellectual Property Organization, "The Protection of Expressions of Folklore: Attempts to Protect Expressions of Folklore by Means of Copyright." Paper Prepared by the International Bureau of WIPO, n.d.

World Intellectual Property Organization. "Report on Fact-finding Missions on Intellectual Property and Traditional Knowledge." July 2000.

World Intellectual Property Organization. "Information Note on Traditional Knowledge," Prepared by the International Bureau of WIPO for the WIPO International Forum on "Intellectual Property and Traditional Knowledge: Our Identity, Our Future." January 21 & 22, 2002.

Yelvington, Kevin. 1993. *Trinidad Ethnicity*. Warwick University Caribbean Studies, Macmillan Caribbean, 1993.

Ziff, Bruce and Pratima Rao (eds.). 1997. *Borrowed Power. Essays on Cultural Appropriation*, New Brunswick: Rutgers University Press.

Part IV

Caribbean Cosmologies

Introduction

In bringing together peoples from across the globe, the Caribbean experience has yielded some of the richest and most varied of human spiritual and supernatural practices. Much of the scholarship on Caribbean religion has focused on that complex of creole religions that includes Santeria, Vodoun, Orisha and other forms that combine elements of West and Central African practices and Amerindian beliefs with various forms of Christianity, spiritism, and mysticism. This is understandable given the long contact between African and European religions in the region and their wide dissemination both in the Caribbean and abroad through migration. Yet much is left out if we do not pay attention to the other myriad forms of Caribbean Christianity that exist and to the role of Amerindian beliefs, Judaism, Islam and Hinduism. In compiling this section, it was important to examine forms of New World African religions such as Vodou, but also of Caribbean-African practices that reshaped Protestantism and incorporated pan-African messages such as Rastafari and Asian-Caribbean forms of worship such as Hinduism. Some major religions that could not be immediately represented in this collection, such as Santeria, Quimbois and Espiritismo are, I hope, adequately referenced in the Suggested Readings list.

Suggested Readings

Austin-Broos, Diane, 1997 Jamaica Genesis: Religion and the Politics of Moral Orders. Chicago: University of Chicago Press.

Brandon, George, 1997 Santeria from Africa to the New World: The Dead Sell Memories. Bloomington: Indiana University Press.

Brown, David, 2003 Santeria Enthroned: Art, Ritual, and Innovation in an Afro-Cuban Religion. Chicago: University of Chicago Press.

Brown, Karen McCarthy, 2001 Mama Lola: A Vodou Priestess in Brooklyn. Berkeley: University of California Press.

Cosentino, Donald J., ed., 1995 Sacred Arts of Haitian Vodou. Los Angeles: UCLA Fowler Museum of Cultural History.

Fernández Olmos, Margarite, and Lizabeth Paravisini-Gebert, 2003 Creole Religions of the Caribbean: An Introduction from Vodou and Santería to Obeah and Espiritismo. New York: New York University Press.

Gordon, Shirley, 1998 Our Cause for His Glory: Christianization and Emancipation in Jamaica. Kingston: University of the West Indies Press.

Henry, Frances, 2003 Reclaiming African Religions in Trinidad: The Socio-Political Legitimation of the Orisha and Spiritual Baptist Faiths. Kingston: University of the West Indies Press.

Houk, James, 1995 Spirit, Blood and Drums: The Orisha Religion in Trinidad. Philadelphia: Temple University Press.

Khan, Aisha, 2004 Callaloo Nation: Metaphors of Race and Religious Identity among South Asians in Trinidad. Durham, NC: Duke University Press.

Métraux, Alfred, 1974 Voodoo. Hugo Charteris, trans. London: Sphere Books.

Murphy, Joseph, 1993 Santeria: African Spirits in America. Boston: Beacon Press.

Palmié, Stephan, 2002 Wizards and Scientists: Explorations in Afro-Cuban Modernity and Tradition. Durham, NC: Duke University Press.

Taylor, Patrick, ed., 2001 Nation Dance: Religion, Identity and Cultural Difference in the Caribbean. Bloomington: Indiana University Press.

Turner, Mary, 1982 Slaves and Missionaries: The Disintegration of Jamaican Slave Society, 1787–1834. Urbana: University of Illinois Press.

11

The Faces of the Cosmic Gods

Leslie G. Desmangles

As ritual objects and persons baptized in the service of the lwas harbor spirits and thus become the portals to divine perception, so too the entire cosmos is filled with the dynamic power of the lwas to become a conduit through which these lwas can show their "faces" and be apprehended. Like many other traditional religions of the world, Vodou teaches that the universe is peopled by thousands of invisible spirits who are inherent in all persons and things, and who direct the physical operation of the universe. Hence, the repetitive patterns of change in substances in the universe – the rise and decay of things, the rotation of days and of astral bodies, the cycle of seasons, and the succession of human generations – are all parts of a grand cosmic scheme which are perceived as the manifest faces or personae of the lwas. The lwas are therefore identified not only with the substances in which they are infused, but also with the manifest changes in these substances.

But the identity of the lwas with physical substances should not lead us to conclude that Vodou is animistic. Initially coined by British anthropologist E.B. Tylor ([1871] 1970), this term was used to classify traditional thought and refers to the belief that a spirit or *anima* is an "invisible double," a shadowy "vapor" that resides in a substance, manifests itself through that substance, and is indistinguishable from the very thing that harbors it (Bergounioux and Goetz 1958, 84). In these terms, Vodou might seem to be an animistic religion, and indeed many writers have defined it as such (Salgado 1963; Métraux 1958; Price-Mars 1928). Upon closer examination, however, it becomes clear that Vodou is far from animistic, for although Vodouisants believe that the lwas reside in all matter in the cosmos, substances serve merely as vessels or conduits through which the lwas can show their faces, or manifest themselves. The relationship of a lwa to an object that harbors it is analogous to the relationship of a spirit to the body of a possessed devotee, or the relationship of the reclaimed gwo-bon-anj to the jar that lodges it. The changes in personality and deportment of a possessed Vodouisant, or the changes in physical appearance of a jar (such as its discoloration because of its age), are attributed to the spirits that are believed to reside within these substances. But these spirits are said to transcend the substances that shelter them, for they exercise their autonomy by leaving these substances and entering others as they travel from place to place either at their own will, or when they are commanded to do so by oungans or sorcerers.

In short, Vodouisants perceive the faces of the lwas when these manifest themselves in matter or in the possessed body of a devotee. They address the substances initiated in the service of the lwas by their divine names, because the lwas within them provide palpable demonstrations of abstract principles. But they perceive two modes of reality in the world by making a succinct distinction between the lwas themselves, and the substances that harbor them.

Moreover, if Vodouisants can identify the lwas with the principles that govern the universe, it is because these lwas manifest themselves not only in the material world but also in the lives of the devotees as well. Because Vodou imparts to its devotees a set of moral convictions upon which the life of the community depends, it does not ask that they understand its teachings abstractly. Vodou is a religion that does not lend itself easily to high-flown theological exercises. Instead, it makes use of every possible visible technique to involve the devotees in its rituals. Vodouisants come to know the lwas by dancing, drumming, and singing, and by reenacting or mimicking the envisaged personalities of the lwas. In Robert Marrett's sense, Vodou, like many other traditional religions, is a religion that is "danced out" rather than conceived intellectually – that is, it is imitative rather than meditative (Marrett 1920). It does not separate the mind from the body, but claims the entire person. The devotees become acquainted personally with the moral and metaphysical principles of their religion by embodying the lwas in spirit possession, by being transformed by them in mind and body, and by appropriating their envisaged personalities.

Hence, Vodou's teachings about the lwas are based upon the premises that they manifest themselves in nature, and that devotees gain knowledge of them through ritual observances in the community. It is upon these premises that the pantheons of lwas will be discussed in this chapter. The order in which the lwas are to be described reveals not only the devotees' worldview, but also the manner in which the lwas are thought to participate in the devotees' daily round of life. The description of the mythological details in the personae of the lwas reveals the subtle emphases and nuances by which each

lwa, each universal principle, is distinguished from all the others.

The description of the Vodou nanchons is here divided into two parts. This chapter deals with the lwas who manifest themselves most often in nature, and [. . .] will attempt to elucidate three main principles: first, the relationship between the African gods and the lwas; second, the nature of the transfiguration of these lwas in terms of Roman Catholicism in Haiti (to determine if the relationship between these two religions is indeed symbiotic); and third, the nature of the creole elements associated with them that are phenomena indigenous to the island. Before proceeding, however, we need to note that the existence of lwas closely related to public life does not mean that offerings, sacrifices, and other public rites are not tendered to the cosmic lwas. The reader is reminded that the present classification of the lwas as cosmic versus public is merely for the purpose of facilitating the discussion of the faces of the lwas and their relationship to Catholic saints.

The Nanchons: The Classifications of the Lwas

When Vodouisants speak of the lwas, they group them in families, pantheons, or nations, called *nanchons*. Each of these pantheons has its own characteristic ethos, which demands of its devotees corresponding attitudes. There are generally held to be seventeen nanchons of lwas, but most Haitians know only a few of these by name. They include the Wangol, Rada, Petro, Ginen, Kongo, Nago, and Ibo. Of these, the Wangol and Nago (or Anago) are the least known in Haiti; they have generally been absorbed into the Rada nanchon. The Kongo and Ibo nanchons, on the other hand, are well known, and many of their lwas have been absorbed into the Petro. The lwas of the Ginen (from Guinea) nanchon have also been absorbed into the Rada, and are the central objects of ancestral reverence of the ounfo. Although most Vodouisants recognize the Wangol nanchon (which originated in Angola), in my field research I found that no one, including oungans and mambos, could cite their names.

The Rada, Petro, and Kongo (and in some provinces, Ibo) nanchons are by far the best known in present-day Haiti. *Rada* derives from *Arada*, the name of a prominent kingdom in Dahomey during Haiti's colonial period. Similarly, the Kongo lwas originated in the Bakongo region of West Africa, which provided thousands of slaves to Haiti during the colonial period. In Vodou these words no longer designate geographical locations; rather, they characterize "categories" of lwas who are known in Haiti particularly for their cosmic functions as sustainers of the universe. *Petro* reportedly derives from a mythological character, Dom Pedro, a leader of the maroon rebellion during the latter half of the eighteenth century.

Many of the Rada lwas have Petro, Ibo, and Kongo counterparts. As if their images were reflected in a mirror, the personalities of these Rada lwas become inverted in the Petro pantheon or nanchon. In designating the Petro lwas, Vodouisants use the Rada name for each lwa and add epithets, such as *Flangbo* (Afire), *Je-Rouge* (Red-Eye), or *Zarenyen* (Spider), to designate their Petro or Kongo affiliations. For instance, Gede in his Rada persona does not usually inflict illness upon a devotee, but in his Petro persona as Gede-Zarenyen who, as the name indicates, crawls and stings like a spider, he does. Likewise, Rada's Ezili, the beneficent lwa of love, becomes Ezili Je-Rouge in her Petro affiliation, a dangerous and offensive spirit who can cause harm to recalcitrant devotees.

From early in Haitian history, the impression has persisted among scholars that the main distinction between the Rada and Petro nanchons is that between good and evil. Nothing could be more erroneous than this attempt to fit the Vodou nanchons into such rigid theological and ethical categories. It is true that in the past, the Petro lwas were most often connected with malevolent magic, while the Rada lwas were connected with benevolence (Métraux 1958, 76–8). Consequently, the Petro lwas have earned the reputation of being destructive, aggressive, and violent, whereas their Rada counterparts are said to be the gentle guardian powers of the universe. But these distinctions are not absolute. The Petro lwas can still protect a person from danger. Similarly, while the Rada lwas are usually beneficent, they can also inflict diseases on devotees who fail to fulfill their religious obligations toward them. For instance, Rada's Legba, the beneficent lwa who directs the course of human destiny, can be, in his Petro persona Kafou Legba, not only the maleficent trickster-lwa who causes accidents to alter that destiny, but also the malicious agent whose power the sorcerers propitiate in sorcery. Yet in spite of his maleficence, Kafou Legba can also protect a devotee from sorcery. The protective charms that a devotee wears to guard against misfortune are initiated in Kafou Legba's service.

Hence, the characteristic differences between the various Vodou nanchons' representations of the personalities and functions of the lwas cannot be understood exclusively in moral terms. This statement does not imply, however, that Vodouisants are morally obtuse, or that they are incapable of differentiating between good and evil. On the contrary, they have a clearly established set of ethical standards which they feel correspond to a natural cosmological order. From the point of view of empirical science, Vodouisants would say that the entire cosmos, including all of the principles inherent in its mechanical, biological, and stellar functions, can be reduced to one higher Principle, Bondye, who is the ensurer of universal order and the source of all human actions. The highest wisdom consists not only in recognizing the wholeness of the universal order as contained in Bondye, but also in affirming that same wholeness in the human community. All of life belongs to Bondye. He summons it into being and preserves it.

The strengthening and the preservation of life are Bondye's gifts to the lwas and to humankind. The divine will is a vital principle of life which expresses itself through a hierarchy of forces existing in the universe. But Vodouisants differentiate among these forces by distinguishing between "higher" and "lower" ones, all of which descend from Bondye to the lwas, to humans, to animals, and finally to physical objects in the world. World order is maintained by Bondye who controls the interaction between these forces, but each of these forces occupies a position in the order of the world and each derives from the same source.

Vodouisants' concepts of good and evil correspond to their idea of the forces that operate within the universe. They distinguish between good as a higher force and evil as a lower one, and correlate both with the natural order of forces in the world. A good act is of a higher order because it increases Bondye's power in the world, while a bad act is of a lower order because it decreases that power. Hence, every act, every detail of human behavior that militates against Bondye's vital force or against the increase of his power in the maintenance of order in the universe, is bad. For instance, Vodouisants consider murder wrong because, by a person's death, Bondye's divine influence is decreased in the human community. Sorcery is not wrong, because it increases the power of Bondye, as the sorcerers "tap" it from one of the lwas. The willful eradication of life is thought to be a sacrilege since it is not only a departure from Bondye's will for orderliness in the world, but an actual destruction of that order as Bondye established it.

The idea of Bondye as the ultimate source of power can also be seen in Vodouisants' concepts of the personalities and functions of the lwas as they present themselves in the Rada and the Petro nanchons. As already noted, the lwas have dual personalities and functions, each being the inverse of the other. In spite of the notable differences in these personalities and functions, Vodouisants do not understand them to represent two distinct divine entities, the one symbolizing beneficence and creativity and the other maleficence and destruction. Rather, they believe that both personalities and functions are attributes of the same being. This corresponds to Mircea Eliade's notion of *coincidentia oppositorum* (Eliade 1959, 174–8). On the one hand, a lwa expresses the diametric opposition of two divine personae sprung from the same Principle; and on the other, it is the nature of these personae, in the bodies of possessed devotees, to present themselves by turns, or even sometimes simultaneously, as beneficent or terrible, as creative and destructive. Although a lwa's personae appear to oppose one another, they are nevertheless reconciled (or rather transcended) by Bondye's vital force, which not only permeates the universe but fosters the forces of good and evil.

[. . .] the Petro lwas represent a *tertium quid*, New World creations whose personalities bear

the marks of neither Africa nor Europe. This can be seen particularly in the *bizango* secret society, which exists in Haiti today and whose origins probably date back to the colonial period. The bizango is a Petro secret society of sorcerers whose art includes among others the phenomenon of zombification amply described by Wade Davis (1988) and others (Craan 1988; L. Douyon 1980). As we have seen, not only does the emergence of the Petro nanchon reflect the slaves' rage against the cruelty of their masters, but the distinctions between the personae and functions of its lwas in each corresponding nanchon also reflect the theological diversity of Vodou, both during the colonial period and today. Hence, although the Petro nanchon is an extension of the Rada, it clearly reflects the socioeconomic conditions in Haiti, both past and present.

In short, the word *nanchon* in Vodou does not primarily designate the historical origin of the lwas, nor does it indicate an exclusive distinction between beneficent and maleficent forces in the universe. Rather, it presents the ethos of the lwas as well as the characteristic attitudes with which the devotees approach them. In both their Rada and Petro characterizations, or at least in the way in which these characterizations are manifested through the lwas' possessed devotees in religious ceremonies, the lwas appear as beneficent and maleficent, and possessed devotees act out these personae as the community envisages them in their local mythology. In the bodies of their devotees, the lwas are often decorative and whimsical; their notable accoutrements, which are kept in the ounfos as part of the ritual paraphernalia, and which they wear or use when their devotees are spirit-possessed during ceremonies, lend concrete physical form to their mythological personalities. Through their devotees' mannerisms, their carriage, and their dress, the lwas manifest their personalities as these correspond to the nanchons with which they are identified. By such manifestations, the community is able to recognize not only which lwa has come to "visit" it in the peristil, but also which nanchon is represented. In a sense the living depiction of the lwas in the bodies of their devotees replaces the literary and artistic vehicles upon which mythologies of other cultures often rely for the

peristil – vodou temple in centre of ounfo
ounfo – worship centre

fecundity = fertility

portrayal of their deities; one comes to know the lwas only by observing them, or by "becoming" them.

Vodouisants admit that there are more than one thousand lwas, who manifest themselves in all phenomena. Some are known to humans, but most are not. The Vodouisants can learn, however, to differentiate the personalities of many of them, and thus come to know intimately the powers that control the various events of their lives. By learning the variety of the lwas, they discover the nature of Bondye, the sacred life-force who controls the universe and who manifests himself through the multitude of the lwas. By his characterizations, each lwa reveals the varying cosmic principles inherent in the universe. Some express life and fecundity, while others are related to death and sterility; some do good, while others are maleficent. But whatever their characterizations, each reveals a different facet of that ultimate Principle. Each is, in musical terms, a variation on a theme, depicting a different cosmic Principle. Each embodies what Vodouisants deem most important to life: a life-force, which ensures fertility in the animal and vegetable kingdoms, and which establishes a power as represented in the visible community of men and women; a dynamic Principle whose beneficent and maleficent powers can be tapped and channeled through magic or sorcery. In short, the lwas are different aspects of one cosmic Principle, whose faces manifest different personae of Bondye, and whose outward appearances vary according to the context in which it operates in physical substances and in devotees' lives.

Vodou Cosmology

Beginning with the one universal Principle, the world of the lwas is rich, vast, and largely unexplored. By and large, Vodouisants say that the permanent residence of the lwas is in Dahomey in Africa, which is a mythological island below the sea, or more specifically in Ginen's mythological city of Vilokan. The events that occur there are no living person's business, though everyone has conjectures about them. It is said that few living persons have been allowed to enter Vilokan, those

privileged few having been taken there accidentally by the lwas.

Although few Vodouisants have ever visited Vilokan, most believe in its existence because they have established contact with it through the medium of the oungan in the ounfo. The oungan makes this contact at the outset of a religious ceremony by invoking Legba, the keeper of the gates to Vilokan. In Haiti, as in Benin or Nigeria, the gods are said not to speak the same language as the devotees who serve them. Legba is then the divine medium through whom human requests can be channeled to the respective lwas invoked. He is the interlocutor, the interpreter, the principle of crossing and communication with the divine world. Legba is the Hermes of the Vodou Olympus, the polyglot who translates the supplications of the devotees to the respective lwas for whom they are intended.

Legba is the one who opens the gates that separate the profane world of the living from the sacred world of the lwas. Therefore at the beginning of each religious ceremony the devotees sing to him:

> Atibo Legba, open the gates for me
> Papa Legba, open the gates for me
> Open the gates that I might enter
> When I will return (from Vilokan), I will salute the lwas.
> Vodou Legba, open the gates for me
> When I will return, I will thank the lwas.
>   Ayibobo![1]

This invocation to Legba is an important part of the Vodou ceremony. As the community dances and sings it, the oungan solemnly traces Legba's symbolic, geometric figure (vèvè), an act which is said to open the gates to Vilokan to permit passage of the devotees' supplication to the divine world. The focal image of this vèvè is Legba's symbol, the cross. In its form this cross resembles the Christian cross, but its significance is entirely African.

The symbol of the cross is central to Vodou ceremonies. Indeed, Vodouisants revere it wherever they encounter it, not only when it is traced on the floor of the peristil, but in their daily lives as well. For instance, in what might be called a

oungan - male priest - a leade- of rituals & ceremonies
manbo - a woman in the same position

territorial rite of passage, Vodouisants who pass a sacred edifice (a Catholic church, a school, or a hospital) may cross themselves reverently; to them, the Christian cross that dominates the building symbolizes Legba, the medium through which contact can be established with the world of the lwas.

Because Vodouisants usually appear to revere the Catholic cross and because the cross image has such a symbolic significance in Vodou meetings, many scholars who have written about the religion have argued that Vodou crosses are borrowings from Roman Catholicism. However, while it is true that Catholic crosses in Haiti may well have been invested with Vodou meaning, the cross symbol in Vodou did not originate in Catholicism but in African mythology. In the Fon traditional mythology in Benin, for example, the universe, as described by Paul Mercier (1968, 219–21), is conceived as a sphere transected by two mutually perpendicular and intersecting planes which, perceived in a cross-section of the sphere, represent the arms of a cross; these crossed planes provide the framework and supporting axes of the sphere. In the myths, this cross resulted from the movements of Mawu Lisa, the Godhead, to the four cardinal points of the universe when she created the world.[2] The Fon creation myth compares the universe to two halves of a gourd that are welded to each other and whose edges match perfectly;[3] the plane along which the two halves are joined constitutes the plane of the horizon. Fon mythology also conceives of two different crosses in relation to the plane of the horizon: first, it conceives of the four cardinal points of an earth that stretches flat along the plane of the horizon; second, the vertical plane intersecting the mid-point of the horizontal plane forms a cross with the horizontal plane, and the ends of these planes which penetrate the gourd represent the four cardinal points of the universe (Mercier 1968, 220–1).

Fon traditional mythology also conceives of the gourd that constitutes the cosmic sphere as surrounded by a larger gourd welded in the same manner as the small one. Beyond the larger gourd is the abode of the gods. Since the small gourd is mobile, it is said that the "little calabash floats in the larger one" (Mercier 1968, 220). The small gourd contains the visible world with its four elements: earth, water, fire, and air. In traditional societies of both Benin and Haiti, the earth is conceived to be a flat disk within the smaller cosmic sphere, surrounded by and floating on water. This is why Fon and Vodou traditional beliefs teach that one finds water when digging deeply into the earth (Mercier 1968, 220–1).

According to the Fon, when Mawu arranged the universe from preexisting materials, she did so in four days, the traditional Fon week. She traveled throughout the universe, stopping at the four "quarters of space," which correspond to the four cardinal points of the cosmos. At each halt, she gathered materials with which she formed the halves of the gourd, solidifying the dirt from which the earth is composed and determining the location of the waters.[4] The path of Mawu's primordial movements formed a cross: from west to east, and then from north to south.

The Africanness of this symbol is made clear by the fact that the cross is significant not only in the Fon traditional worldview but in those of other parts of Africa as well. Germaine Dieterlen (1951, 2–33) noted that the figure of the cross is an important symbol in the Bambara traditional worldview. Bambara cosmology is founded upon two cosmological principles: the eternal vibrations of matter, and the movement of the universe as a whole. According to the myth, the original germ of the world came out of emptiness or nothingness (glã or fu), which is enveloped by a sheath (Zuesse 1979, 153–4). Glã is also the profound silence that lies at the core of cosmic space. The first act of creation occurred when glã emitted a primal sound, which not only produced its twin (or an echo), but set in motion a series of vibrations or oscillations of "energy principles" that moved up, down, and sideways to trace the lines of a cross. From this primordial pair flowed all organic and inorganic substances in the cosmos – substances which Faro, the Godhead, later arranged at the four corners of space (Zuesse 1979, 154). The vibrations still exist in the universe today, and are responsible for the recurring dynamic flux of all world phenomena: the emergence of things, their existential changes, and their eventual destruction.[5]

Hence, the Bambara base their worldview on three active principles: a profound silence, which is an unmanifested yet most sacred primordial energy-force; the phenomenon of twinness (or the principle of efficient cause in matter and of biological reproduction in the deities and humans) deriving from that primordial energy-force; and the symbol of the cross (connecting the four cardinal points of the universe), which establishes cosmic order. The cross is the metaphysical axis around which the universe is constructed. On the one hand, it holds the entire universe in equilibrium; on the other, it provides the path for the infinite extension of the universe by the continual progression of matter. Dieterlen adds that the symbol of the cross appears in many sacred ritual objects and on many of the cooking utensils (1951, 2–3). It is also drawn on the ground at religious ceremonies and serves to frame a game of a quasi-ritualistic nature called *sumangolo*, a game to which Bambara of "all ages and both sexes abandon themselves" in order to contribute to what Dieterlen refers to as the ever-increasing "*marche du monde*" (1951, 2, nn. 1–5).[6]

An examination of the cross symbol in Vodou will make it clear that both its ritual and its theological significance derive from African mythology and not from Roman Catholicism. Like the Fon, Vodouisants see in it a cosmographic image that symbolizes their worldview. It is used in religious ceremonies that establish contact between the profane and sacred worlds. The cross represents the fact of communication between the two worlds, and the nature of the difference between their modes of reality. In the first of these symbolisms, the horizontal line of the cross represents the profane world of the living, and the vertical line the medium of communication with the sacred abyss (Deren 1972, 35). In the second symbolism, the vertical line represents the other world itself, its verticality indicating that the reality there is the inverse of the reality in the profane world of the living. This latter symbolism becomes clear when one realizes that in the Vodou worldview, the metaphysical world of the lwas is not vague and mystical, but a cosmic mirror which, like the personae of the lwas, reflects the images of the profane world of the living and in so doing inverts them. The lwas

are often referred to as mirror images reflecting the deportment and personalities of the living (Deren 1972). For example, when the oungans or mambos address or call upon the lwas, they do so in terms that describe them as reflectors of humans: Loco-Miwa (Loco in the Mirror), or Agasou-Do-Miwa (Agasou in the Back of the Mirror).

Moreover, during Vodou ceremonies the mirrored image of the world of the living is symbolized by a number of ritual observances. When the oungan greets his assistant (laplas), the two face each other while holding hands, bow to each other (reflecting the inverse motion of the other), and then perform a number of turns – first clockwise, then counterclockwise – to represent the sights of the profane world of the living as reflected in the sacred, cosmic mirror of the lwas. The double handshake, with both the right and left hands superimposed, not only traces the configuration of the cross (or the four cardinal points of the universe), but symbolizes the profane world and its mirrored inversion. Further, as Maya Deren notes (1972, 34), a mother who customarily carries her baby on her right arm will hold it on her left arm when she presents it to the lwas in the ounfo. And the ritual dance in the peristil revolves in a counterclockwise motion around a central pole (*potomitan*), which serves as an axis mundi.

Not only is the physical world inverted in the cosmic mirror of the sacred world, but so too is time. The oungan who is about to begin a ceremony often enters the peristil by emerging through the door of the holy of holies (bagi) backwards; this reverse motion symbolizes the retrogression through time to primordial times when the world was being created. The opening of the Vodou ceremony represents the sudden halt of profane time. The entire ceremony in which a large number of lwas "mount" their devotees is the archetypal reconstruction of the cosmos *ab origine*, and as the deities appear in succession, the devotees participate in the symbolic re-creation of the world. At the start of the ceremony, cosmogony is reactualized; the devotee's possession is the re-creation of the Vodou nanchons; the world of the living is refashioned, and the individual, as well as the community, is born anew (Eliade 1959, 41). The repetition of the archetype is the temporary suspension of profane time.

The principle of inversion and retrogression is fundamental to Vodou theology as well as to its rituals. Hence, in Vodou the relationship between the cosmic mirror and the profane reality that it represents takes the cosmographic form of the cross. In the cross, Vodouisants see not only the earth's surface as comprehended by the four cardinal points of the universe, but also the intersection of the two worlds, the profane world as symbolized by the horizontal line, and Vilokan as represented by the vertical line. The foot of this vertical line "plunges into the waters of the abyss" to the cosmic mirror where the lwas reside; there, in this sacred subtelluric city, is Africa (or Vilokan), the mythical home of Vodouisants, the place of the lwas' origin, and Ginen, the abode of the living-dead (Deren 1972, 36). The point at which the two lines intersect is the pivotal "zero-point" in the crossing of the two worlds. It is a point of contact at which profane existence, including time, stops, and sacred beings from Vilokan invade the peristil through the body of their possessed devotees.

The cross symbol, as Deren observes, is therefore one of the most important ritualistic symbols in Vodou, appearing wherever communication or traffic between the two worlds occurs (1972, 35). The following examples will give some idea of its pervasiveness in Haiti.

Perhaps the most prominent example is the structure of the peristil itself. It is a microcosmic representation of the universe. The four poles sustaining the structure symbolize mythologically the four cardinal points of the universe, covered by an overarching roof that represents the cosmic vault above the earth. Like the horizontal lines of the cross, the floor of the peristil symbolizes the profane world, while the vertical pole (potomitan) in the center of the peristil represents the axis mundi, the avenue of communication between the two worlds. Although the downward reach of the potomitan appears to be limited by the peristil's floor, mythologically its foot is conceived to plunge into Vilokan, the cosmic mirror. The point at which the potomitan enters the peristil's floor symbolizes the zero-point. During

the ceremonies, the potomitan becomes charged with or "polluted" by the power of the lwas. Hence, before tracing the geometrical symbols of the lwas (the vèvès), the oungan or mambo may touch the pole, a ritual act that empowers him or her to summon the lwas into the peristil. Thereafter, like the potomitan, the oungan's (or mambo's) body becomes in itself the source of power, a repetition of the microcosmic symbol, a moving embodiment of the vertical axis around which the universe revolves.

The cross structure of the peristil is repeated in the drawing of the vèvès, which are central to the rituals,[7] and the disposition of the vèvès on the peristil's floor also reflects the concept of inverted symmetry. Since each lwa has his or her own vèvè, the area where it is drawn is consecrated to him or her. In drawing each vèvè, the oungan or mambo often traces the cross (or *kwasiyen*) first; cornmeal is held between the thumb and forefinger of the right hand, and is sifted onto the floor in the configuration appropriate to each lwa. The complex representation of the deity's personality appears to hang on the two intersecting lines of the cross, and the opposing personae of each lwa are often drawn opposite each other, as if mirroring each other, on either side of the horizontal or vertical line of the cross. Once finished, they appear to the worshipers as both static and dynamic. As the principal posts of a building support the beams, so the lines of the cross provide a structure on which these images, like the cosmos, hang in equilibrium. Once drawn, notes Deren, the cross is like a revolving door; it seems to spin as if to throw off these images to the outer limits of the earth's surface (1972, 36). Both of these analogies are appropriate, for Vodouisants see the horizontal line of the vèvès as representing the secular world, while the vertical line reaches the cosmic realm of the lwas, and plunges into Vilokan.

Like the myths that they represent, vèvès can be elaborate and complex symbols, or they can be simple lines that cross each other. But their meanings are profound, for at the center of these diagrams is the zero-point of contact, where the horizontal and vertical lines intersect each other; it is the location at which all human dialogue, all the supplications of devotees that accompany the tracing of the vèvès cease to travel horizontally as they are forced downwards to Vilokan (Deren 1972). Spirit possession accompanied by glossolalia is common among devotees during the tracing of the vèvès. Possession represents a nonmaterial achievement – a profound willingness on the part of a lwa to intervene in the profane activities of humankind. That is why devotees wish to have it conferred upon them often. The possessed devotee, like the oungan, becomes the ambulant axis mundi, the point of contact between the sacred and profane worlds, and is polluted by the power of the lwa. A possessed devotee becomes a medium whose feet are planted in the sacred mirror and whose body is the vertical line whereby the revitalizing forces of the universe flow to the community.

From this examination of the use of the cross symbol in Vodou, several conclusions can be drawn. First, as among the Bambara, the tracing of the vèvès at Vodou ceremonies can be interpreted as the symbolic re-creation of the universe. In this sense, by the intricate tracery of the vèvès, and by the intervention of the lwas, Vodouisants relive the cosmological archetype not only in their retrogression through time, as represented by the movements of the oungan and his assistant as they enter the peristil, but by being possessed as well; in possession, they participate in the re-creation of the world as their bodies, now ambulant potomitans, support the world in a microcosmic way. Hence, "creation" for Vodouisants, as for the Bambara, is not a static event but a dynamic process, an ever-recurring *marche du monde*. Second, the Vodouisants' worldview corresponds to that of the Fon. In a macrocosmic dimension, Vodouisants conceive of space in the universe as limited by four cardinal points; these points are connected by intersecting lines that take the form of a cross, a metaphysical axis supporting the entire universe. In a microcosmic dimension, the peristil is the symbol of the universe. The space within it is limited by the four posts that support the structure, and the metaphysical lines that join these posts cross the floor of the peristil to form a horizontal cross which is also limited by the area of the peristil. Moreover, the vertical potomitan, around which the devotees dance in a counterclockwise direction,

intersects the floor of the structure, which mythologically supports the entire structure of the universe. As the cosmic reflection of the profane world, Vilokan is conceived by Vodouisants to be structured much like the peristil, for the potomitan that traverses the floor of the peristil also traverses the sacred world of the lwas. As already noted, during the ceremonies the vèvès and the bodies of possessed devotees become a further microcosmic reduction of the potomitan.

Hence, the cross in Vodou cannot be seen as representing a syncretistic relationship between Roman Catholicism and Vodou; rather, it is the direct product of African mythology on Haitian soil. It may be true that the African symbol of the cross among the slaves would have disappeared (as did many aspects of African religion) if it had not been reinforced by the parallel symbol in Roman Catholicism on the island during the colonial period. Yet in response to the early missionaries' catechizing efforts, the slaves learned to interpret the Catholic cross in the light of their own African traditions; if the Vodou interpretation of the cross during the colonial period was similar to that found in Vodou today, it may be conjectured that it was this interpretation that provided the slaves, as well as Vodouisants today, with the necessary means by which they could adapt themselves to a foreign religious system. Moreover, it may also be conjectured that the presence of the cross in Vodou may act to disguise actual religious practices, among Haitians today as among the slaves, under an appearance of conventional piety.

The Cosmic Lwas

Legba: Keeper of the Gates
According to Vodou mythology, one of Bondye's first creations when he fashioned the world was the sun. Without its existence, the lwas, human beings, and all the multiplicity of things could not exist. All derive from this primordial light. Among the Fon, this light, which is the fire of life, is identified with the creative power of Legba (Herskovits 1963, 2:220–30), a characterization that explains why in Haiti fires are often lit for Legba during Vodou ceremonies. Moreover, in the ritual invocations addressed to him, one finds

such words as *cléronde*, meaning circle of brightness, and *kataroulo*, meaning the four wheels of the sun's chariot as they roll on their daily path across the sky (Deren 1972, 299). In Vodou, the sun with which Legba is identified is a regenerative life-force whose rays cause the vegetation to grow and ensure the maturation and sustenance of human life.

In Vodou, as in Fon traditional beliefs, Legba is the patron of the universe, the link between the Godhead and the universe, the umbilical cord that connects the universe to its origin. Bondye fashioned the universe; Legba has nurtured it, has fostered its growth, and has sustained it. Legba is also said to be androgynous; hence, his vèvè contains the symbol of his sexual completeness, and he is invoked in matters related to sex.[8] Both the Fon and Vodouisants (as well as the Yoruba in Nigeria) know him chiefly as the cosmic phallus, and the imagery for him also expresses his androgynous nature: the potomitan of the peristil symbolizes his phallus, and the open space around it in the entire ounfò is his womb (Laguerre 1980b, 45).

Both as phallus and as umbilical cord, Legba is the guarantor of the continuity of human generations. Vodou drawings on peristil walls show him as an old man smoking a pipe; a small sack in which he carries morsels of food dangles by his side from a strap that passes over his shoulder. He totters slowly, leaning on a cane known as *baton Legba* (Legba's cane). This cane represents his phallus, the source of human life, the symbol of man's virility, and the virtual link between human generations. As cosmological symbol, Legba's cane also corresponds to the potomitan in the peristil, the "odd pole," which is the source of his power – the vertical shaft that establishes contact between the sacred and profane worlds. Like the potomitan, his power reaches the depth of Vilokan and rises to the upper regions of the universe, a cosmographic image that symbolizes his virtual access to both sides of the cosmic mirror. In short, Legba's symbol is the cross; he is a mediating principle in Vodou between the sacred world (as represented by the vertical potomitan in the peristil) and the secular (the horizontal intersecting line as symbolized by the floor of the peristil), between the center of the universe

(again represented by the potomitan) and the outer edges of the cosmos (represented by the four poles that uphold the structure at the four corners), between humankind and the lwas, and between one human generation and another. Likewise, his androgyny makes him the mediating principle between the sexes, for he is identified with the entire ounfò, a space symbolizing a sacred cosmic womb "impregnated" by its central potomitan, from which emerge the regenerative divine forces that invigorate the community of the living.

Because Legba's symbol is the potomitan, he is conceived as the keeper of the gates to Vilokan. He is also known as the lwa of the crossroads, or the *lwa Gran Chemin* (Master of the Great Way to Vilokan) (Courlander 1960, 36). As noted in the previous section of this chapter, he is believed to hold the keys to the portals of the sacred world. He is often compared to a policeman who controls traffic at a busy intersection in a large city: just as the policeman directs the orderly passage of automobiles, Legba controls the order in which the lwas appear in the possessed bodies of his devotees when they summon him to the peristil.

Vodouisants say that Legba has two personae, each corresponding to one of the aspects of his total personality. Rada's Legba is the sun, the regenerative force, the lwa of the crossroads, the mediating principle between opposites. His reflection, known as Mèt Kafou Legba (Master Legba of Intersections), is his inverted image in the Petro nanchon. Legba commands the traffic of the Rada nanchon through the potomitan, while Kafou Legba directs that of the Petro nanchon. Legba is the source and sustainer of life, whereas Kafou is a destroyer of life; his symbol is the moon (Deren 1972, 101). The persona in which Legba manifests himself varies according to the circumstances: as a Rada lwa, he is the guardian of destiny, the one who holds the keys to that destiny and makes certain that a person's life follows the preordained plan sealed by Bondye at creation; as a Petro lwa, he is the trickster who arranges unexpected accidents to cause human lives to deviate from the Almighty's plan.

In his function as the guardian of universal and individual destiny, Legba is of Yoruba origin and is known to the Fon as "Fa." The name of Fa is not known to the Haitians, but his persona is familiar to them. He holds the keys to the secrets of life, and assists Bondye in sealing the destiny of the world. As phallus, he shapes one's destiny at conception, and as umbilical cord, he sustains that destiny by maintaining one's relationship with Bondye and with the lwas. Vodouisants also imagine him to be the celestial arc, the path traveled by the sun during the day. As such, he has many lives, each corresponding to a different part of the day. In the early morning, he is as frail as a new-born child; at noon he is as fertile as a young man in the prime of life; and in the late afternoon he is a venerable and poor ancient, whose humility is like that of the revered sages of India. In this latter characterization, he is one whose age has given him a wisdom attained by no other creature, including the lwas (Deren 1972, 98).

As one who has lived through all the phases of human life, Legba knows the past and the future of the world. In Haitian folklore he is often depicted as carrying a sack that contains the world's destiny, which he dispenses at the four corners of the universe as he traverses the sky each day. He is the witness or the advocate of the destiny of humankind and the lot of the lwas: he is conceived not only as one who has access to both sides of the cosmic mirror, but also as one who has knowledge of the future as well. Because he holds such positions Vodouisants seek his advice in moments of crisis by consulting a diviner. In divination, offerings are made to him in an effort to appeal to his benevolence, and devotees "sound the cosmic mirror" to reveal what the future will bring to them. Like the Fon and the Yoruba, Haitians believe that the place that a devotee occupies in the world is established at birth. Legba determines that destiny by making a series of pronouncements, most of which may be revealed through a diviner, promising prosperity, wealth, and security to his poor devotees. He guides them through the successes and misfortunes of life.

From this idea of destiny, one might conclude that Haitians believe in an absolute determinism that enslaves each person; but like the Yoruba and Fon, they do not believe that fate binds a person

inescapably. Humans have some freedom of choice, for when Legba assumes his Petro persona as Mèt Kafou Legba, he is a trickster who invents stratagems that upset the ordinary course of that destiny. Vodouisants dread this persona because he holds the power of life and death over them. They picture Kafou as a malicious mischief-maker quite capable of causing confusion, subtle enough to complicate simple situations, and cunning enough to stimulate malice among humans.

Vodouisants believe that if there were no gates to the Petro nanchon, the worlds of both lwas and humans would be more just and less full of malice. Legba would then be free to execute the destiny of the world as Bondye and his lwas planned it. Since Kafou is an inversion of Legba, so too is his effect upon the human community's destiny an inversion of that protected by Legba. For if Legba functions to support life, Kafou attempts to undermine it. If Legba is the lwa of the four cardinal points of the universe, Kafou is the "lwa of the points in between" (Deren 1972, 19). If Legba is life as symbolized by the light of the sun which radiates during the day, Kafou is death as symbolized by the moon, the "rising sun of the night," whose mysterious nature perplexes every Vodouisant (Deren 1972, 101).

The lwas of the day are of the Rada nanchon. They are just and bring misfortune only if they are angered by the negligence of their devotees in regard to rituals, sacrifices, and offerings. At times these lwas are forced to strike hard at their devotees, but then they withdraw. Such punishments are just, because they have the purpose of disciplining recalcitrant devotees. Kafou, who releases his demons during the night, knows no mercy. The sufferings that he inflicts upon devotees do not stem from human negligence, but from the malevolent nature of Kafou and his demons. If Vodouisants believe that Kafou can inflict disease or even death on them despite their supplications to Legba, it is because they feel that ill-chance is sometimes an inescapable part of human life. As the Haitian proverb notes, "When the day of suffering arrives, even curd milk can break your head."

Because Kafou is identified with the night, Vodouisants say that he is instrumental in the

Legba = St. Peter

nocturnal machinations of *bòkòs* (sorcerers).[9] They avoid contact with the *mapou* (silk-cotton tree)[10] at night, the reputed sacred rendezvous in which Kafou and his demons meet to plan their blood-curdling activities. In his Petro characterization as Legba Pie Case (Legba with the Broken Leg) Kafou commands demonic legions that are believed to live in families, the most famous of which are the *bakas*, envisaged as small, red-eyed, fleshless mythological creatures with black-and-red skin stretched over their bones. Under the direction of bòkòs who summon them, Kafou changes his bakas into animals or *lougawous*, believed to be messengers of bad fortune. They roam throughout the countryside during the night to "eat people" (Métraux 1958, 89) – that is, to injure or kill them.

If All Saints' Day is reserved to commemorate Legba, it is because Legba and Kafou Legba are referred to in Christian terms. Because Legba is the keeper of the keys, many Vodouisants have identified him with Saint Peter.[11] This identification derives from lithographs of Saint Peter, popular among Catholics and Vodouisants in Haiti, which depict him holding the keys of the church – an iconographic image that derives from his official position as the keeper of the keys to the kingdom of heaven (Matthew 16:10–20). In Vodou, this image has been construed to be that of Legba who holds the keys to human destiny. The same lithographs also depict Saint Peter with a rooster, an image that derives from the New Testament's account of Peter's denial of Jesus. Vodouisants believe that the rooster is not only a symbol of Legba, but also his faithful companion; this perhaps explains why they always tender a rooster as an offering to him.

Although these symbols may suggest a syncretism of Vodou and Catholicism the connection is merely superficial, for Vodouisants have construed the symbols of the lithographs in African terms, as their interpretation of the details clearly shows. First, unlike Haitian Catholicism, which sees Peter as a purely benevolent saint, Vodou, as already noted, assigns two functions to Legba, corresponding to his two personae, and one of these is malevolent. Second, although the symbol of the keys in the lithographs is the principal point of contact between the saint and the lwa,

Vodouisants interpret them in African terms. Nowhere else in Vodou do the keys appear – not in drawings on the walls of the ounfos baptized in his service, in the vèvè that symbolizes him, or in the ceremonies performed in his honor. Rather, Haitians, like the Fon, identify him with the symbol of the cross. Nor is the rooster a Christian borrowing, for Melville Herskovits notes that the rooster is associated with Legba in Fon religious traditions. Two or three times a year the Fon, like Vodouisants, sacrifice several roosters (or chickens) to Legba. These ceremonies involve the pouring of the blood of the animal or the placing of cooked chicken as food for Legba (*manje lwa*) at crossroads in the countryside – religious practices similarly observed in Haiti.

Thus, symbiosis can be seen in the use of Catholic lithographs, some of whose details are interpreted in the light of African religion. Furthermore, symbiosis by ecology can also be seen in the calendrical connection between All Saints' Day and the function of Legba as the master of traffic of the lwas. Among the Fon, Herskovits notes that special religious ceremonies to Fa and Legba are observed at the beginning of each traditional new year. The first day of the year falls sometime during the harvest period. Since the slaves in Saint-Domingue were forced to adopt the Roman calendar,[12] they made the logical association between All Saints' Day and Legba by virtue of his function as master of the gates to Vilokan. All Saints' Day (November 1) falls during the period of harvest in Haiti, for, like Benin, Haiti has two rainy seasons: the first begins in March and ends in late June; the second begins about the middle of August and ends by late October or early November. Haitians, like the Fon, plant their crops shortly before the rainy season and harvest them after that season ends; the months of July and October, and the early part of November, are therefore periods of harvest. Hence, it is logical to assume that the slaves made a connection between All Saints' Day and the Fon ceremonies to Fa or Legba.

In short, symbiosis can be seen from two points of view. First, the Catholic symbols associated with Saint Peter gave Vodouisants a basis to establish the connection between Legba and the saint. Such a connection meant that the Catholic symbols in the Christian calendar were adopted to the African feast day in honor of Legba at the beginning of the traditional year. Here too, Vodouisants have fitted the Catholic holy day into the African harvest ceremonies held for Legba.

Gede: Master of Ginen

Just as Legba initiates time, so Gede ends time, for he is the master of Ginen who rules over death. Just as Legba, the lord of the sun, plunges into the sea at sunset to await his rekindling at sunrise, so too the gwo-bon-anj of the dead must remain lifeless and await its reclamation from Gede's abyss. In a sense, Gede is Legba's opponent, for whereas Legba as the sun is omnipresent during the day, Gede is lord of the night and is symbolized by the moon. Whatever Legba constructs, Gede tears down; whatever Legba sets in motion, Gede arrests; whatever Legba conceives, Gede aborts; and whatever Legba sustains, Gede destroys, for he is the lord of death, the master of destruction of things.

Although these two divine forces appear to have opposite functions, and indeed are inversions of each other, they nevertheless are similar in many ways, for both participate in the creative forces at opposite ends of the spectrum of life. Both control traffic between the profane and sacred worlds, Legba at Vilokan's gate and Gede at the portals of Ginen. Just as Legba facilitates the lwa's rebirth in the body of a possessed devotee, so too Gede ensures the reclaimed gwo-bon-anj's rebirth in the jar (govi) that serves as its vessel. To Vodouisants, Ginen is analogous to Vilokan, for both represent temporary cosmic birthplaces and cosmic graveyards from which spirits emerge and to which they return.

In a sense, therefore, Legba and Gede are divine relatives governing two distinct worlds, each of which is, for Maya Deren, the tomb and the womb of the world.[13] Gede, the master of Ginen, is lord not merely of death but of life as well. This is why Haitians often identify him with his regenerative rather than with his destructive powers. Even in his official capacity as lord of death, Vodouisants use such appellations for him as the "Giver of Life" and the "Rising Sun." These similarities explain why both lwas are

represented by the symbol of the cross (Deren 1972, 102).

Because Gede is identified with life, he is also seen, like Legba, as a phallic deity. Indeed, he symbolizes the inevitable sexual element in humankind. Pictures of him drawn on peristil walls show a man with enlarged nostrils indicating breathing, a symbol of life, but with petrified arms and feet. His large thoracic cavity is depicted as that of a skeleton, a symbol of death. In contrast, his erect phallus is large, to symbolize life; for Vodouisants say that when he walks, the movements of his body (gouyad) recall the sexual act (Laguerre 1980b, 95).

Vodouisants reserve these graphic motifs of life and death not only for their artistic expressions of Gede, but for objects and buildings initiated in his name. In the sacred chamber dedicated to his service stands Petro's Baron la Koa, represented by a black wooden cross similar to those erected on tombstones and cenotaphs at cemeteries. The tools of the gravedigger, such as pickaxes and shovels, also decorate the peristil's walls. Piles of stones, dried leaves, and skulls lie on the floor of the ounfò's sacred chamber. Amidst the macabre decor of what could be a dark and damp cosmic graveyard is the symbol of life, for dominating this grotesque arrangement is a large wooden phallus, a combination symbolizing the unity of life and death.

In the body of a possessed devotee, Gede speaks with a nasal resonance – the sound that, Vodouisants say, would be produced by a corpse if it were allowed to speak. Usually this sound incites nervous laughter on the part of those attending the ceremonies, because it reminds them of their eventual lot. The lwa is particularly noted for his rich repertoire of stories, narrated in a nasal tone and in a vocabulary that, under other circumstances, any Haitian would consider obscene. Gede always tries to provoke his devotees with his ribaldry. His stories and his songs describe the secret love affairs of the members of the community, omitting none of the lewd details. If members of the community consider sex sinful, or appear uncomfortable and embarrassed by his wantonness, he enjoys the opportunity to taunt them, displaying before them the most unrestrained and immoral mannerisms. Adept in his voluptuous art, Gede is neither ashamed of his reputation nor bothered by those who are publicly contemptuous of his sensuousness; he knows that they cannot evade their eventual confrontation with him (Deren 1972, 103).

Although Gede's devotees see him as a witty clown (Métraux 1958, 100), he nevertheless symbolizes their destiny. With a keen memory, he remembers their past lives, shrewdly watches them in their present communal life, and makes of their existential dilemmas objects of mockery and laughter. But his jocularity can never mask his omniscient and unlimited power over his devotees' destiny – a power which he does not have to manifest in the body of his devotees because they need no reminder of such a universal fact as death. Perhaps this explains why his demeanor often takes the form of mockery and defiance. When he comes to possess his devotees, he adopts the role of a young and cheerful clown, as Petro's Entretoute, or that of a frail beggar, burdened by illness, old age, and poverty. These paradoxical manifestations are reminders of the somber moment of death as an inevitable and inescapable reality from which, ironically, mirth becomes the only temporary avenue of escape.

While Gede enjoys his role as a clown, his devotees consider him wise. As lord of life, he is instrumental in giving advice to them regarding which crops they should plant, or which woman or man they should marry, or which children will be more promising. His wisdom is discernible even in his lighter moods; he is most generous in carefully advising those who seriously ask for his assistance.

Gede is probably the most complex character in Haitian folklore, for he reveals more than thirty personae,[14] each of which is associated with a different function. As Petro's Baron Sanmdi, whose fearless wife is Manman Brijit, the guardian of the past, he is the preserver of the community's religious heritage, and the protector of the history of the human race. As Baron Cimetiè, he is the "guardian of old bones" and sits at the gates of graveyards as represented by his black cross; this symbol appears at the entrance of every Vodou burial ground, to remind visitors that they are about to enter a territory where Ginen and the profane world are said to intersect each other. A

graveyard is thus like the potomitan in the ounfò, the zero-point of contact between the sacred and profane worlds. He is depicted in the Vodouisants' imagination as wearing a frock coat and striped trousers, formal apparel once worn by government officials at funerals. Amusingly enough, he has no shoes, smokes an old pipe, and wears a threadbare coat and a frayed black straw hat (Métraux 1958, 101), the stereotypical accoutrements of the Haitian undertaker. At times these accoutrements are completed by smoked glasses, which are necessary, Vodouisants say, to protect his eyes from the bright tropical sunlight, for he spends much of his time in Ginen's darkness. All the Gedes also cover their faces with thick coats of white powder, their nostrils and ears blocked with white cotton to simulate the dead. Appareled thusly, Baron holds in his hand a pickax (or hoe) and a shovel. Those who address special prayers to him may also address him as Kongo's Gede Nibo – that is, the one who lives in the shadow of the black cross. Devotees "feed" him often by bringing calabashes of food, which they place at the base of the cross. In exchange for their gifts, he counsels them on domestic matters that impinge upon the life of the community.

Baron's power, like Legba's, can be channeled through the bòkò's malevolent machinations. He can set in motion invisible forces that can harm his devotees. Whether as Baron Sanmdi, Cimetiè, Capitèn Gede, or any other characterization, his malevolent power is said to range from assisting the bòkò in animating zombies to releasing his bakas to harm those whom the sorcerer curses.

Since death consumes the world, Gede is also known for his gluttony. When his plate is set before him at a ceremony, he eats rapaciously, stuffing his mouth with both hands. In the body of a possessed devotee, he does not hesitate to snatch morsels of food from other devotees' plates, and then rushes to a corner of the peristil to eat the food privately, or runs outside to bury it. He is said to return at night, several days later, to eat it after it has decomposed (Métraux 1958, 102). In the personae of Toapel, Fatra, or Pete[15] he appears even more malevolent, as his hunger turns him not only against devotees but against other lwas as well. Angry at his devotees' occasional neglect, he invades their bodies unexpectedly, even at ceremonies not performed in his honor, to participate as an uninvited guest at sacrifices and to eat at ritual meals offered in honor of other lwas. His effrontery is perhaps most evident in the ceremonies for his younger brother, Kouzen Zaka (or Azaka).

In some ways the Vodou characterizations of Zaka resemble those of Gede, but for the most part he is differentiated from Gede by characteristics that are strictly his own. These perhaps reflect the way in which Haitian mythology conceives of him as well as the position he occupies in Haitian society. Pictures of Zaka painted on the walls of peristils (and ritual clothes worn by those possessed by him) show him dressed as Haitian peasants once did: he wears a straw hat, a blue denim shirt, trousers with one leg rolled to his knee, and a machete attached to a strap placed about his waist. With his straw sack, hung on one side of his body by a strap over his shoulder, he is believed to roam the countryside to inspect the tilled fields. Although Zaka's cosmic domain may not be as eccentric and glamorous as that of his brother, he is nevertheless the farmer's hero, for he is lord of agriculture. In this function, reminiscent of the early period of the country's history shortly after independence, he becomes an inspector of agriculture – a role that often gives him a pompous posture of authoritarianism.

Zaka is characterized as a crude and ignorant lwa. As younger brothers often do, he slavishly attempts to emulate Gede's mannerisms and character but consistently fails in his efforts. Like Gede, Zaka is said to have a ravenous appetite, but unlike Gede, Zaka's speech is neither eloquent nor his gestures clever enough to incite laughter. Gede speaks defiantly with bold vulgarity, whereas Zaka is inarticulate, his speech being the mere bleating of a goat. Gede is most often boisterous whereas Zaka is passive and quiet. In short, this unsophisticated and gauche "peasant Pan" (Deren 1972, 110) is the sort of character whom Gede would ridicule. Moreover, Zaka is docile, gentle, and kind. The Haitian peasant sees in Zaka's affection and admiration for his brother a welcome change from the fears and anxieties that Gede, as Baron, often generates in him. For although Gede produces laughter by clowning,

his presence creates a sinister atmosphere which no laughter can obscure.

Little is known about Gede's origin. Because there are no exact accounts of him in Fon mythology, it is difficult to establish a connection between Benin and Haiti, but speculations can be made on historical as well as ritualistic bases. It seems that Gede may have originated from the exploits of the Ghédévi clan in ancient Dahomey whose mythological ancestor and founder bore the name "Ghédé." In the latter part of the eighteenth century, Abomey in Dahomey became a very wealthy and powerful kingdom, having profited from the sale of slaves to the Portuguese and the French. According to Fon oral tradition,[16] Andanzan, king of Abomey, was an aged monarch whose only ambition was to enrich the state treasury by whatever means possible. He warred incessantly with neighboring peoples and plundered many of their villages, carrying away whatever wealth they possessed; he captured men, women, and children whom he kept in slave camps for a time and later sold to European slave traders. It seems that Andanzan's mother (whose name is not mentioned in the story) became displeased with her son's behavior and attempted to replace him with his younger brother Ghezo.

In order to deprive Ghezo of the counsel of his mother in the usurpation of his throne, Andanzan enslaved her as well as sixty-three of her retainers, members of the Ghédévi clan who had sided with her. Andanzan later sold them to the Portuguese and French slave traders. They were transported to Brazil and to Haiti, where they found many Dahomeans. When the descendants of Ghédé arrived in "Ame'ika," they founded the "cult of the Dahomean city." When Ghezo took his rightful place as king of Abomey, he dispatched a Portuguese friend, Da Sousa, to the New World to find his mother. After an extensive search, Da Sousa found her in Brazil, and later returned her and six other Dahomeans to Abomey. There, she is said to have ruled by the monarch's side for eighteen years until his death in 1840.

If this story is true, it would account for the connection between Dahomey and the New World, and would explain the presence of Gede in the Vodou pantheons in Haiti and in Candomblé in Brazil.[17] It would also explain why he would have been an object of ancestral reverence. As the head of a clan, and similar to the founding ancestors of other clans in Abomey, Ghédé would have been regarded as one of the focal points of social and political organizations; an altar would have been erected in his name, and clan priests who bore his name would devote their lives to him. Moreover, Ghédé would have a significant influence on the behavior of his descendants. They would have sought his counsel in matters related to marriage, and to breaches of faith between his descendants and the members of other clans. He would have been the giver of children by participating in Dã, the life-giving element of fecundity that provides continuity in perpetuating the clan, allowing the passage of ancestral souls from the underworld to be instilled in the refashioned bodies of newborns within the Ghédévi clan.

The connection between the Haitian Gede and Dahomean Ghédé can also be seen in the similarity between the Vodou rituals performed in Gede's honor and those performed by the Fon in honor of their ancestors. First, both in Dahomey (or Benin) and in Haiti, these ceremonies involve the sacrifice of chickens and goats. Second, the sacrificing of animals includes collecting their blood into calabashes, and pouring it onto the altar, or Baron Sanmdi's black cross. Third, the ceremonies in both countries take place around a tomblike structure behind which is a table serving as a shrine to the ancestors. Fourth, both in Haiti and in Benin the participants kiss the ground before they present offerings of cooked and uncooked food. Fifth, the Fon rituals, like those in Haiti, are not only an act of reverence, but are also often used for therapeutic purposes, to cure a devotee of a disease.

Because the Haitian Gede is associated with the welfare of his descendants, Vodouisants have identified him with Saint Gérard. According to Catholic hagiology, Saint Gérard was born to a wealthy family in Venice in the eleventh century. He renounced his family's wealth for the monastic life and spent much of his time healing the sick, whom he is said to have treated with uncommon tenderness. His reputation as a healer

has survived in Haiti. Lithographs of the saint (which circulate widely throughout the country) depict him as dressed in a black robe, holding a bishop's crosier in his right hand. Vodouisants recognize that lithograph to be Gede not only because of the saint's reputation as a healer but because of the color of his robe: black has traditionally been the symbolic color of the saint, as well as that of Gede. Among all the lithographs of the saints in Haiti, Saint Gérard is the only one dressed in black.

Since Gede is Zaka's brother, Vodouisants say that Saint Gérard is the brother of Saint John the Baptist, with whom Zaka is identified. It is difficult to establish Zaka's origin in Vodou mythology and folklore; most scholars provide few details about him. It is plausible that the name "Zaka," or "Azaka," is a relic of Haiti's prehistory. A brief etymological description of *zaka* shows that it probably derives from the Taino Indian word *zada*, meaning corn, or from the related *azada* or *azadon*, Taino words referring to the agricultural activities of hoeing and digging. In the northern part of Haiti, Zaka is also known as "Mazaka," a derivation from another Taino word for corn, *maza*, from which comes the English word *maize*. If this is right, Zaka, Azaka, or Mazaka in Vodou has an agrarian significance dating back to Haiti's pre-Columbian Amerindian culture (Deren 1972, 280). The inclusion of the word in Vodou mythology may have been the result of the maroons' contact with Indian culture in the interior of the island during the colonial period.

Despite these linguistic connections to the Taino, the Vodou characterizations of Zaka and the Vodou rituals related to him correspond to those for the Fon deity of agriculture, Yalóde. According to Herskovits, the rituals to Yalóde in Benin vary according to the types of crops being harvested and also according to the time of the year. As already noted, in Benin as well as in Haiti there is a well-recognized agricultural calendar based on the variations in seasonal rainfall during the year. In both countries the peasants plant, among other vegetables, corn, yams, carrots, beets, and plantains. Zaka, like Yalóde, is particularly identified with yams rather than corn. The yam harvest occurs twice during the year: during

February and March, and during July and August. These are the periods of religious ceremonies in honor of Zaka and Yalóde. In both Benin and Haiti, these ceremonies involve offerings of numerous yams and of at least one chicken and one goat. In both countries, the meat from the sacrificial animals as well as the vegetable offerings are cooked and eaten at the site of the ceremony.

If Zaka is identified with John the Baptist it is not because of the saint's life or ministry, but because of his depiction in the lithograph that is said to represent him. In reality, the lithograph that Vodouisants identify as John the Baptist is that of Saint Isidore, the patron saint of farmers and food-growers in Catholic hagiology – but Vodouisants are unaware of Saint Isidore's name, and even less aware of his persona and the symbols associated with it in Catholic iconology. In the lithograph representing Saint John (or Saint Isidore), he is depicted as a poor man wearing a blue robe, carrying a large sack hanging from a strap that passes over his shoulder and crosses his chest and back. Vodouisants identify Saint John with Zaka because his clothing and his sack resemble those of many Haitian peasants when they work in their fields. His blue robe is interpreted as the blue denim shirt and trousers that Haitian peasants have traditionally worn; likewise, Zaka's sack becomes the sack in which peasants put their personal belongings and the vegetables that they harvest as they till their fields.

By piecing together these details concerning Zaka and Gede, several conclusions can be drawn. First, unlike Zaka, Gede is entirely Fon (Herskovits 1972, 247).[18] His persona and function derive from an ancient Dahomean clan, and the Vodou rituals performed in his honor may well have originated in ceremonies performed for the royal ancestor of the Ghédévi clan in Dahomey. Second, the identification of Saint Gérard with Gede is based upon Christian hagiology and the traditional role of ancestral figures in Dahomey. As Roger Bastide suggested in the case of Brazil, the early missionaries to Brazil, as in Haiti, may have recounted stories about Saint Gérard's life to the slaves; these accounts were then interpreted in terms of African tradition

(1978). Since both Gede and Saint Gérard concerned themselves with healing the sick, it seems reasonable that Vodouisants would have made the logical connection between the African persona of Gede and the saint. Moreover, the saint's symbolic color and that of Gede were the same, so that Vodouisants would have identified them with each other.

Vodouisants' penchant for identifying a lwa with a Catholic saint on the basis of his accoutrements is made particularly clear in the case of Zaka. The Vodouisants' identification of Zaka with Saint John the Baptist rests entirely upon the similarity of the saint's accoutrements, as depicted in the lithograph that they mistakenly think represents him, to those of Haitian peasants.

Hence symbiosis can be seen in two ways. First, in the contact situation between Catholicism and African religion on the island, the African mythological personae were revived in the personae of both Gede and Zaka. Although Zaka's name is a creole phenomenon that probably derived from the contact between the Indians and the maroons during Haiti's colonial period, both the function and the persona of Zaka are essentially Fon. Second, symbiosis in the identification of these lwas with the saints is not based upon Catholic symbolism, but upon the accoutrements of the saints in popular lithographs. Moreover, these depictions have been transfigured in African terms. Third, the rituals performed in honor of these lwas recall those of Africa rather than the Catholic tradition.

Damballah: The Gentle Snake of the Primal Seas

In Fon mythology (Mercier 1968, 220–1) the story is told that at the beginning of the world Mawu Lisa traveled to the four corners of the universe in order to arrange it. She was carried in the mouth of her benevolent snake-servant Dã Aida Hwedo. Wherever Mawu directed him to take her, mountains appeared, composed of Dã's excrement.[19]

When Mawu had completed her task, she noticed that the earth would not remain buoyant upon the primordial waters, for the mountains rendered it too heavy. Like a ship weighed down by a heavy cargo, the earth was slowly sinking into the primordial waters below it. Mawu asked Dã to coil himself below the earth and form "carrying pads" to hold the earth in place. To support the earth, Dã also constructed four pillars of iron, one at each of the cardinal points of the universe, and implanted them into the cosmic waters below. The tops of these pillars were elongated to support the sky, while holding the flat and thick earth buoyant and stationary in the middle. Dã is said to have then twisted himself around these pillars in order to reinforce them and to hold them in their original position.

The Fon agree that Dã is not stationary. It is said that he also revolves around the earth by extending himself under it and across the vault of the sky, providing the circular trajectory for the sun during both day and night. Because of Dã's revolution around the earth, he is identified with eternal motion in the universe. This motion is characterized by the passage of all physical phenomena from birth to decay. According to the Fon, whatever assumes form is subject to destruction, and each world phenomenon is a link in the chain of progression of existent things. Hence, the passage from formation to destruction is seen as part of an inherent, eternal cosmic motion. This motion stems from Dã's divine energy-force, a divine essence in all world phenomena which produces the physical displacement of objects in space and in time and which manifests itself in the incessant motion of the waves of the ocean, the waters of springs and rivers in which Dã is said to reside in the form of a snake. Dã animates the wind, ensures the alternation of day and night, and impels the cyclical motion of the astral bodies. In short, Dã is a living quality expressed in all dynamic motion in the cosmos, in all things that are flexible, sinuous, and moist, in all things that fold and unfold, coil and recoil.

In humans, this energy-force is the giver of children. It is identified not only with the eternal motion of human bodies but also with motion as seen in the cycle of life and death and in the passing of human generations. The Fon, like the Haitians, give much consideration to the importance of children in the ancestral line of continuity. Children must be born not only so that the physical line can continue, but also so that the parents may be kept in a state of immortality by their children's remembrances.

Many of these characterizations of Dã have been retained in Vodou mythology and folklore in the personae of Damballah. Although few of the Fon tales about Dã have survived among Haitians, their mythological details have persisted. Like the Fon, Vodouisants say that Damballah is an aged, noble father who assisted Bondye when he created the universe. Indeed, it is said that Damballah is so ancient that in a sense, he is the father of the universe (Herskovits 1963, 2:250). As in Fon mythology, Damballah is the snake lwa, the one who twines himself around the four pillars that support the universe, and analogously around the four poles in the peristil. In some ounfòs, as in temples in Whydah in contemporary Benin, he is symbolized by a snake that lives either in an enclosed area of the temple, or in a pool of water specially constructed for him.

In the body of his devotees, Damballah crawls on the ground and speaks with an incoherent hissing. One can never communicate precisely with him, notes Maya Deren, for in his cosmic grandeur and venerable wisdom he refuses to be bothered with the petty precision of human speech (1972, 115). Yet, in spite of his aloofness, Damballah comforts Vodouisants by his willingness to possess them. As if unaffected by the events of human history, the cold, static snake-lwa's presence in the peristil brings to the devotees the assurance of a stable world whose future is secure. By each of his manifestations in the body of a devotee, Damballah promises that motion will continue to be the essence of life: time will flow, and with it physical objects will form and deteriorate, and children will be born and die, their bodies returning to the navel of the earth to await their reshaping by Bondye and his lwas.

As in the Fon solar myth, Vodouisants identify Damballah with the daily path of the sun as it travels over and under the earth, as the following song sung after sunset in Vodou ceremonies would seem to indicate:

> Oh the one in the mirror
> Damballah, you are the venerable one.

Don't you see him leaving
Oh the one in the mirror
Damballah, you are the venerable one.
Don't you see him leaving.

And at dawn, as a ceremony that has lasted throughout the night reaches its close, the community will sing:

Snake, Snake oh!
Damballah Wèdo, Papa,
Oh, Damballah Wèdo
I am calling you snake oh!
The snake cannot wake up
Damballah, Papa, you are a snake oh!
Ayibobo!

To this song Damballah answers through the body of a possessed devotee, as he unwinds himself to prepare the sun's path across the sky:

When they need me, they call me: "Papa."
The day that they don't need me, they say that
    I am a snake, oh!
Damballah has a bad disposition, oh!
Papa, they greet everyone else,
Why don't they greet me?
Papa, they greet everyone else,
Why don't they greet me?
Papa, has a bad disposition
Let me navigate!
Ayibobo!

Damballah's "bad disposition" in the song refers to the devotees' rude awakening of their lwas as they summon him to rise from his deep nocturnal sleep in the waters of the abyss to visit the peristil. The mention of navigation conjures up the image that Damballah must swim in the primordial waters under the earth before he can pass across the sky to establish the sun's trajectory at sunrise.

Vodouisants believe that when Damballah is satisfied by his devotees' devotion to him he manifests himself, as in Fon mythology, in the form of a multicolored snake, which can be seen by all the lwas and their devotees in the form of a rainbow on the horizon. One half of the arc is Damballah, and the other half is his female consort Ayida Wèdo.[20] Such manifestations reflect

Damballah's sexual completeness (Métraux 1958, 92). Since they are members of the Rada nanchon, both Damballah and Ayida are conceived to be benevolent. The oungan announces Damballah and his consort with the words,

Calling Wèdo!
Who is this lwa?
They tell me it is you, "Dan e!"

As this song is intoned, the drums sound the rhythm of the *yanvalou*, an electrifying dance that thrusts the possessed devotees' bodies into serpentine motions from shoulder to ankle. The devotees' voices surge into a powerful unison that reflects personal fulfillment, devotion, and excitement.

As one who participates in the motion of the universe, Damballah is associated with other members of the sky pantheon: Badè or Badeci, the wind; and Sogbo[21] or Agasou Tonè, the thunder. In Vodou mythology and folklore Agasou and Sogbo are inseparable companions. They share their divine functions, as the following song indicates:

Badè is blowing, blowing
He blows, Badè
Agasou roars, roars
He makes the roaring thunder.
Nadè [the wind] came from Ginen
He blows, he roars.

As Rada lwas, Badè and Sogbo are benign natural forces. Badè appears as the gentle rainfall that disperses the scorching heat of the tropical sun; while Sogbo, the thunder, heralds Badè's coming: he mounts his chariot and drives across the sky, throwing lightning bolts in the clouds. Conversely, in their Petro manifestations, Badè's gentle wind becomes a hurricane that damages crops, while Sogbo becomes a thunderstorm so violent that it shakes the earth. These latter characterizations are evident in cases of spirit possession in ceremonies in which Badè and Sogbo "mount" their devotees simultaneously. Such possessions are often violent and potentially destructive to the devotee who harbors their forces. In their brutality, it is said that Badè and Sogbo can cause death to persons who harbor them. Those sturdy enough to be occupied by them produce sounds that resemble the whistling of the wind and the roaring thunder.

Because of the notable violence that Badè and Sogbo manifest in their devotees, possession by them occurs infrequently. Indeed, in some parts of the country they have been forgotten. According to Deren, Badè and Sogbo may well be vestigial remains of another period of Haitian history. In the regions of Haiti where they are known, they may be identified with the lakou's lwa rasin. As already noted, the disintegration of the lakou in Haiti in recent years may have reduced them to mere vestiges. Yet precisely because of their vestigial nature, they embody the historical development of the lakou. Ceremonies that invoke them resemble a kind of retrogression in the lakou's history, a return to certain past events around the figure of deities who no longer are central to religious practices. As Deren notes, to revere them is to "stretch one's hand" into history and to "gather up all history into a solid contemporary ground beneath one's feet" (1972, 116).

Since by his very nature as encircler of the universe Damballah is a positive force, his contrasting equivalents in the Petro nanchon are not believed to be malevolent. However, he also has several counterparts in another frame of reference, magic. In this context, he becomes Simbi, who shares functions and characteristics not only with Damballah but with the other major deities of the Rada and Kongo nanchons. It would be logical for Simbi to be part of the Kongo pantheon rather than the Rada, for his original does not derive from Benin but from Kongo, where he is identified with pools of water (Courlander 1960, 327).

As one who is said to straddle both nanchons, Simbi epitomizes the principle of religion. He is a lwa of the crossroads, between the Kongo and Rada nanchons. In a sense, he and Legba are divine relatives, not only because he provides a path for the sun, but also because he permits communication with the lwas of the Kongo nanchon. Indeed, his vèvè shows all the symbols of Legba surrounded on both sides by two intersecting snakes. Vodouisants also say that in his Kongo persona as Simbi-yan-dé-zo

(Simbi-in-the-twin-waters), he straddles the waters of Ginen and the waters about the inner cosmic gourd of the world that separates humans from the lwas (Deren 1972, 117). In his function as a Rada lwa, Simbi is the master of springs and of ponds. Pools of water are often created in a ounfò's courtyard as a symbolic representation of his abode. Like Dã among the Fon, he is the vital force that ensures the eternal motion in the waters of the rivers. In Vodou art, he is often depicted as a powerful snake who inhabits the rivers, one who shows his strength by uprooting trees and rocks and carrying them downstream during tropical storms. In his function as a Kongo lwa, his body encircles its prey and chokes it to death. Because of these manifestations of power. Simbi is the patron lwa of magicians. In his Rada persona, he is most often summoned to assist the oungan in benevolent magic or the bòkò in his sorcery. This role is a natural one, since in his pivotal position as lord of all crossroads his power radiates to all four corners of the universe.

In both characterizations, Vodouisants believe that Simbi is a lazy lwa. He is reluctant to enter the ounfò; during meetings he is believed to coil himself outside the peristil, and, like a small child in the company of adults, he is bashful in exhibiting his knowledge. In this characterization, Simbi opposes Damballah, for while Damballah is a creative force out of which surges the energy-force that accounts for eternal motion in the universe, Simbi counteracts Damballah's creative momentum by always struggling to instill within the cosmos a lingering, static quality.

Because Damballah and Simbi are associated with snakes, Vodouisants identify them with Saint Patrick or with Moses; the first because of the well-known story about Saint Patrick driving the snakes out of Ireland, and the second because of Moses' miracle performed before the Egyptian Pharaoh when he threw down his staff on the ground and turned it into a serpent. In both cases, the personalities of Damballah and Simbi are identified with the same Catholic lithograph, which depicts Saint Patrick standing near the seashore. Wearing the liturgical accoutrements of a bishop of the church and holding a crosier in his left hand, Saint Patrick is surrounded by snakes at his feet, which he casts into the sea.

Vodouisants interpret this action to mean that Damballah and Simbi possess magical power over the snakes, power that permits them to master them.

In analyzing the depiction of Damballah in the lithograph, two observations can be made regarding symbiosis. The first deals with the interpretation of the lithograph itself, and the second with the personification of Damballah. First, the stories by the early missionaries related to the life of Saint Patrick or Moses have not been retained in Haiti. When Vodouisants are presented with the lithograph representing the saint, they identify him immediately with Damballah or Simbi. Like the Fon, they see in Damballah the manifestations of a dynamic life-force in the universe. Second, by analyzing Vodouisants' concepts of Damballah's personality, one sees that the similarities between Saint Patrick and Damballah are only apparent; for although lithographs of Saint Patrick hang in every ounfò, Vodouisants never refer to these as Saint Patrick but as Damballah. Thus, in the case of Damballah, symbiosis consists in the adoption of a lithograph, symbolic of the saint's life as depicted in Catholic hagiology, to depict a Vodou lwa who remains essentially Dahomean in character.

Notes

1 An exclamation often heard in Vodou songs which "seals" the supplications of the devotees. In a sense, it may be compared to the Judaic and Christian Amen.

2 As the Godhead, Mawu Lisa is said to be sexually complete; Mawu is the female, and Lisa the male. The Fon usually refer to the Godhead by her female designation.

3 The reference to welding here relates to one of the Fon's most sacred activities: iron smelting, an art form that is also important in Haiti.

4 Mawu therefore does not create the world *ex nihilo*, but is essentially the arranger of the universe.

5 These concepts of the emergence and maintenance of the cosmos are not unique to the Bambara, but are shared by a number of cultures around the world. In Africa, the Dogon (of Mali) traditional story of creation is that the world derives from the vibration of a primordial seed inside an egg from which all of creation flowed (Griaule and Dieterlen 1955). Similarly, the Vaisheshika school of philosophy in early Hinduism taught the eternal motion of small "factors" which coalesce continually to create the emergence of things in the world (Hiriyanna 1973, pp. 225–66). Among the Bambara, silence is the sacred principle that lies at the core of the universe and symbolizes harmony; noise (*yo*), which fills the world, derives from harmony but militates against it, disrupting that sacred order. This is why elders teach the young the profound spiritual value of silence in order to restore that order (Zuesse 1979, p. 154).

6 Translated as "the inherent forward movement of the universe." This game involves the tracing of a cross with millet (*Penincillaria spicata*).

7 Scholars disagree about the origin of the vèvès. Métraux states that they originated in Dahomey, but gives no explanation of their specific transmission (1958, p. 148). Maximilien writes that they date back to pre-Columbian Aztec culture, but likewise provides no explanation as to how these Aztec symbols come to be found in Haiti (1945, pp. 41–59). Thompson notes that the term vèvè derives from the archaic Dahomean Fon term for the palm oil used in drawing geometric symbols on the ground; their cruciform cosmograms derive from Congo and neighboring regions of West Africa (1983, p.188). While it may be correct to assume that in their use of the cross, the vèvès are essentially African, my view is that there is a strong likelihood that the configurations drawn to represent the lwas derive from Arawakan-Taino cultures, originating on the northern coast of South America. It is possible that the Tainos migrated from the northern coast of South America to the Lesser Antilles, the Greater Antilles, and Meso-America (Rouse 1964, pp. 140–44). This hypothesis is supported by evidence of similar drawings among the Bororo of Brazil. If it is correct, it would support the thesis of symbiosis – that is, the juxtaposition of religious traditions in the spatial arrangement of symbols from two different continents. It would also confirm the thesis that vèvès are creole phenomena, that the combinations of various symbols (as well as the meanings ascribed to them) are New World inventions. It is possible that these symbolic images were adopted by the maroons who, in the colonial period, came into contact with Amerindian Arawak republics in the interior of the island.

8 Like Mawu Lisa among the Fon, Bondye is thought
   to be sexually complete. In parts of Haiti, he is
   invoked as "Mother" (Bondye Manman moin).
9 *Bòkò* derives from the Fon word for sorcerer, *bocono*.
10 *Ceiba pentendra*, belonging to the same family as the
   baobab tree in West Africa.
11 In parts of Haiti, Legba is also identified with Saint
   Anthony.
12 Bastide also notes the adaptation of the traditional
   African calendar to the Roman one in the case of
   Brazilian Candomblé (see Bastide 1978, p. 198).
13 See Chapter 3.
14 Deren lists at least ten of these (1972, p. 304), and
   most of them are mentioned in works by other
   scholars (Herskovits 1972; Courlander 1960;
   Maximilien 1945).
15 Literally translated as "three shovels full" (of
   excrement, presumably), "filth," or "fart."
16 This story is recorded by Herskovits and a number
   of others (Herskovits 1963, 1:64; Paul 1962,
   pp. 278–79). Hazoumé also records another version
   of the story: Da Sousa visited Brazil, "the Antilles,
   possibly Haiti and Havana," and did not find
   Ghezo's mother (Hazoumé 1957, pp. 27–32).

17 Guédévis is a minor spirit in some sects of Bahian
   Candomblé in Brazil. It was brought to Bahia, suggests Bastide, by the Ketu priests captured by the
   Dahomean soldiers and sold into slavery (Bastide
   1978, 197).
18 Herskovits identifies Gede with the Ghédéonsu
   (about whom he does not comment), powerful
   ancestral spirits in ancient Dahomey (1972, p. 247).
19 It is interesting that "Dahomey" should derive
   from "Dã," meaning "the womb of Dã." Dahomey
   is thus the child of Dã. By logical extension, it
   is comparable to *glã* among the Bambara. As
   motion, Dã is the eternal resurrection of things.
   The future of Dahomey as a nation is assured by
   the remolding of bodies by Mawu and the gods
   (Paul 1962, p. 271).
20 The complete name for Damballah is Dã Ayida
   Wèdo. "Wèdo" is reminiscent of Whydah in
   Dahomey, the ancient city, the seat of the kingdom
   of Whydah, the lwa's place of origin.
21 Sogbo was believed to be the head of the sky pantheon in ancient Dahomean mythology (Mercier
   1968, p. 220).

References

Bastide, R. (1978) *African Religions in Brazil*. Balti-
   more, MD.: Johns Hopkins University Press.
Bergounioux, F., and J. Goetz (1958) *Les religions des
   préhistoriques et des primitifs*. Paris: Arthème Fayard.
Courlander, H. (1960) *The Drum and the Hoe*. Berkeley:
   University of California Press.
Craan, A. (1988) "Toxicologic Aspects of Voodoo in
   Haiti." *Biomedical and Environmental Sciences* 1 (1):
   372–81.
Davis, W. (1988) *Passage of Darkness: The Ethnobiology
   of the Haitian Zombie*. Chapel Hill: University of
   North Carolina Press.
Deren, M. (1972) *The Divine Horsemen: The Voodoo
   Gods of Haiti*. New York: Delta Publishing Co.
Dieterlen, G. (1951) *Essai sur la religion Bambara*. Paris:
   Presses Universitaires de France.
Douyon, L. (1980) "Les zombis dans le contexte vodou
   haïtien." *Haïti Santé* 2 (1): 19–23.
Eliade, M. (1959) *Cosmos and History: The Myth of
   the Eternal Return*. New York: Harper Torch-
   books.
Herskovits, M. (1963) *Dahomey: An Ancient West
   African Kingdom*. 2 vols. New York: J.J. Augustin.

Herskovits, M. (1972) *Life in a Haitian Valley*. New
   York: Doubleday.
Laguerre, M. (1980) *Voodoo Heritage*. Beverly Hills:
   Sage Library of Social Research.
Leclerc's Letter to Bonaparte. Paris: Archives du Minis-
   tère de la Guerre, 1802.
Marrett, R. (1920) *Psychology of Folklore*. London:
   Methuen and Co.
Mercier, P. (1968) "The Fon of Dahomey." In *African
   Worlds: Studies in Cosmological Ideas and Social Val-
   ues of African Peoples*, edited by Daryll Forde,
   pp. 210–34. New York: Oxford University Press.
Métraux, A. (1958) *Le Vaudou haïtien*. Paris: Galli-
   mard.
Price-Mars, J. (1928) *Ainsi parla l'oncle*. Port-au-
   Prince: Imprimerie de Compiègne.
Salgado, J.-M. (1963) *Le culte africain du Vodou et les
   baptisés en Haïti*. Rome: Université Pontificale de
   Propagande Fide.
Tylor, E. B. ([1871] 1970) *Religion in Primitive Society*.
   2 vols. Gloucester, MA.: P. Smith.
Zuesse, E. M. (1979) *Ritual Cosmos*. Columbus: Ohio
   State University Press.

12

Selection from *Rastafari and Other African-Caribbean Worldviews*

Barry Chevannes

Rastafari

The year, 1930; the month, November. In the remote kingdom of Ethiopia, then also known as Abyssinia, kings, princes and heads of state from all over the Western world assemble to witness the elevation of Prince Tafari Makonnen as the new Emperor of Ethiopia, Haile Selassie I. 'Haile Selassie' means 'power of the Trinity'.

The event was for Africans, both on the continent and in the Americas, a significant event. Not only is Ethiopia one of the earliest countries to have adopted Christianity, but a part of the Ethiopian nobility, including the Makonnens, had at least since the middle ages claimed descent from King Solomon of Judah and the Queen of Sheba. Self-consciously, therefore, the new Emperor in appropriating as his title 'King of Kings', 'Lord of Lords', 'Conquering Lion of the Tribe of Judah', was reaffirming the ancient roots of Ethiopian civilization and its independent place in Judaeo-Christian traditions.

In Jamaica the coronation occasioned the rise of a new religion, the Rastafari – from *Ras*, the Ethiopian for 'prince' and *Tafari*. Haile Selassie's appellations were thought to have biblical references. The 'Conquering Lion of Judah' was imagery used by the prophet Isaiah, to refer to the

messiah, as also was the description 'King of Kings' and 'Lord of Lords' by the apocalyptic visionary in the Book of Revelation.

That some Jamaicans could regard this man as the promised messiah, as Jesus Christ in fact, is insufficiently explained by the biblical references. It required other pre-determining factors. Among the most important of these was the impact of the work and ideas of Marcus Garvey in the form of a heightened Black, pan-African consciousness.

Garvey's strategy for achieving the economic advancement and liberation of Africans, 'at home and abroad', was the building up of a powerful and united Africa. To achieve this he looked to the skills and professions of New World Africans. This was the essence of his 'Back-to-Africa' scheme. Blocked by the colonial powers, the scheme failed, but not before Garvey had succeeded in galvanizing millions of Black people in the United States, the Caribbean, Central America and Africa into his Universal Negro Improvement Association (UNIA), and in influencing millions more with his concepts of Black pride, entrepreneurship, and identity based on race. His newspaper, *The Negro World*, which enjoyed a very wide readership, served not only as the main vehicle for his ideas, but also as a means of educating Blacks about their African past and thus of correcting racial prejudices and stereotypes of inferiority, some of which had been internalized. *The Negro World* was banned in most colonies, on pain of death in French West Africa. In the context of a world quickened, as far as Blacks were concerned, with White racism, Garveyism was a liberating philosophy. It denied the innateness of White supremacy and its converse, Black inferiority, fashioned a sense of national identity out of being Black, and gave to its adherents a perspective through which to view the economic and social development of Blacks.

The Afrocentricity of Garveyism would of itself have made his followers in Jamaica turn their attention to the momentous event in Ethiopia. But, regarding Garvey as a prophet, they claimed that he had indeed prophesied about it when he had told the people to 'look to Africa for the crowning of a king to know that your redemption is nigh'. Looking to Africa, looking also to the Bible, a few followers of Garvey concluded that Ras Tafari must be the messiah come back to redeem his people. The titles he bore, the homage paid by the White world through the heads and representatives of state, the antiquity of Ethiopia and its mention in both Old and New Testaments of the Bible, the Solomonic claim – like so many rivulets building up into a mighty river, all swept them away with the powerful conviction that Ras Tafari was none other than Jesus Christ. And he was Black. Now did the Song of Solomon (1:5-6) make sense:

> I *am* Black, but comely, O ye daughters of Jerusalem, as the tents of Kedar, as the curtains of Solomon.
> Look not upon me, because I *am* Black, because the sun hath looked upon me.

If Solomon was Black, so was the Christ. Both were descendants of David. Redemption of the African race was therefore at hand.

Three men are credited with being the first to begin preaching that Ras Tafari, or Haile Selassie, was God, having arrived at this conclusion independently of one another: Leonard Howell, Archibald Dunkley and Joseph Hibbert. These three, plus Robert Hinds, whose first days in the new faith were spent as an associate of Howell, were the main architects of the Rastafari movement for the first twenty years. Stretching Garvey's Back-to-Africa programme, they all saw redemption as 'Repatriation', the return of all Africans to Africa.

Phases of growth

Since its founding the Rastafari movement has gone through three distinct phases of growth. The first phase lasted through the 1930s and most of the 1940s. Theologically, the main impetus was given to propagating the idea of a Black God among a people whose image of God was of a bearded White father in the sky and of a White man on a cross. Pictures of the Black Christ, circulated at street meetings, acted as a powerful instrument of conversion. The idea of a Black God had been a part of the Garvey movement, but to the Rastafari, God was more. He was not only Black, but physically living among men. They even went further, to argue that if being Black was a divine attribute, then the African race, by being Black, shared in divinity.

Early in the movement's development, a most significant practice developed among the Rastafari, namely the wearing of facial hair by adult males, which they sacralized by claiming biblical precepts as well as emulation of the Godhead, Tafari, who was pictured with a full beard. These beliefs and practices had one common underlying motif: they were anti-establishment. Not surprisingly, the early Rastafari encountered considerable hostility, and not every male member wore a beard.

Socially, the message found fertile ground among the urban masses. This was a period which saw an intensification of internal migration, as the most destitute stratum of the peasantry flocked to the city of Kingston. Not only were the avenues of external migration to Cuba and the United States closed off but also many returning migrants preferred to settle in Kingston. Those returning from Cuba were especially receptive to the message of the Rastafari, because of their firsthand experience of racism there and the vitality of the Cuban UNIA branches. Cuba boasted the largest number of UNIA branches outside of the United States. The early preachers, thus, found a most ready audience among the uprooted peasantry (Chevannes 1989a). Early Rastafari made great headway among this section of the urban population, which provided recruits right up to the time when George Eaton Simpson conducted the first study of the brethren, in 1953. Simpson (1955) remained the only source for other writers, such as Lanternari (1963), until the Report by Smith, Augier and Nettleford (1960) which came as a result of developments in the next phase of growth.

The second phase began among second-generation converts who entered the movement in the 1940s but who were in revolt against practices they thought were compromising. The innovations and practices they instituted were to become the hallmarks of the new image of the Rastafari: dreadlocks, ganja-smoking, Rasta talk (sometimes called 'I-talk' because of the pivotal concept of *I*, the personal pronoun). Haile Selassie, who to the earlier generation was simply the King, was now praised as *Jah* or *Jah-Jah*. They intensified their practical opposition to the colonial state, using such forms as repatriation activities, illicit street marches, disruption of the court and defiance of the police. [. . .] Here it is important to trace, however briefly, the millenarian activities which the Rastas carried out during the 1950s.

Against the background of migration to the United Kingdom, Repatriation marches and other forms of agitation started. In 1958 one young leader, Prince Emmanuel Edwards, issued a successful call for an all Rasta convention. For two weeks Rastafari from all over Jamaica converged on Back-o-Wall, a notorious slum adjacent to Kingston's largest market, which hosted many a migrant fresh from the country. At the end of two weeks they marched to the central square of the city, planted a flag and symbolically 'captured' the city. It was alleged that many had sold off their belongings in the confident expectation that at the end of the convention they would be transported to Africa.

The Prince Emmanuel convention had no serious impact on either the Rastafari or the society, except that Prince lost credibility among the Rasses (or the brethren, as Rastas often style themselves) and retreated with his group into a sect known as Bobos. The millenarian activity which did have an impact, however, was led by a visionary named Claudius Henry. A returned migrant from the United States, Henry quickly established himself as the leader of a Rastafari church, with a branch in Kingston and one in the sugar belt of the parish of Clarendòn.

In 1958 Henry took a bold step. He proclaimed 5 October as 'Decision Day' when all of Israel's scattered flock would return to Africa, and towards this distributed for the price of one shilling a blue card, on which he declared that possession of the card rather than a passport was all that was needed. Hundreds of Rastafari brethren flocked to Kingston in anticipation of repatriation. There was much suffering when this prophecy also failed, but Henry managed to keep his following intact. A year and a half later, quite suddenly, news broke that a police raid on Reverend Henry's headquarters in Kingston had uncovered an arms cache and copies of a letter written by Henry and several others addressed to the new leader of neighbouring Cuba, Fidel Castro, inviting him to take over Jamaica before their departure for Africa, which the writers claimed was imminent. Henry, his wife and several other leading members were charged with treason. Before the case could be heard, however, news of yet another serious development swept the country. Two British soldiers were killed in an ambush by guerillas led by Henry's son, Ronald. Aware of untoward activities in and around the church, the police had infiltrated the group, only to discover a guerilla training camp in the Red Hills overlooking the city. The army was called in when the police contact disappeared. His body was later discovered buried near the parade ground of the camp.

These developments were to have a profound effect on Jamaica's Eurocentric middle class and on the Rastafari. Both were thrown together in a headlong confrontation long in the making. The middle class, shocked as much by the concatenation of events as by its own sense of guilt, was forced, after first reacting with expressions of hostility towards the Rastas, whom it saw as representing the very antithesis of all it aspired to, to think seriously about its own African heritage. The Rastafari, for their part, caught as they were by the aggressive posture they had cultivated over the past decade, had to act quickly to inform the public of their essentially peaceful intentions. This they were successful in doing, by appealing to the University College of the West Indies, then a college of London University, for a study of the movement. The first recommendation of the resulting study (Smith et al. 1961), namely, that Government sponsor a fact-finding mission to Africa to investigate the possibilities for migration of Jamaican nationals there, was quickly accepted and implemented. An unofficial nine-man mission was constituted, including one Dreadlock, and dispatched to Ghana, Nigeria, Ethiopia and several other countries. On its return the majority and minority (Rastafari) reports were both published in the press.

The whole Claudius Henry affair, the *University Report*, the Mission and its reports, were together the subject of intense public debate for months. They marked a new stage in the development both of the Rastafari itself and of Jamaican society; both were set on a course of forced mutual accommodation and change, which later gained momentum from the visit in 1966 of His Imperial Majesty Haile Selassie I, and the Black Power Movement started by University lecturer, Walter Rodney, in 1968 (Nettleford 1970). Through these events the Rastafari were able to effect an exorcism of the racial and colour prejudices that had possessed the middle classes from colonial times (Chevannes 1990), with the result that middle-class men and women, mulatto and Black, could feel free enough to form their own Rastafari group known as the Twelve Tribes of Israel (van Dijk 1988).

During the second phase, one other development of far-reaching import was the absorption into the movement of the urban youth, who brought with them many of their social characteristics (Chevannes 1981). This, for example, was how the Rastafari came to be associated with the development of reggae music. The youth of the 1960s, like Bob Marley, Peter Tosh, Bunny Wailer, Bob Andy, Clancy Eccles, Dennis Brown and members of such groups as the Abyssinians, forged their careers as popular artists using reggae to express Rastafari ideas, yearnings and critique (Davis 1983).

The popularity of reggae artistes was itself a measure of the popularity of the Rastafari among the masses throughout the 1970s and the main avenue of its spread abroad. The 1972 general election was contested around the use of a Rastafari symbol, a rod the Emperor had presented as a gift to one of the leaders of the two contesting parties, Michael Manley. Manley not only won, but the vote of the Rastafari-influenced youth proved decisive (Stone 1974). The 1970s also saw the growth of Rastafari throughout the other islands of the Caribbean, due in part to the influence of reggae artistes, in part to the movement throughout the region of Caribbean nationals, including students of the regional University of the West Indies. In Dominica, Grenada, Trinidad they played significant roles in radical left-wing politics (Campbell 1980). Rastafari influence in Trinidad was apparent also among the Earth People. The Rastafari movement also spread to the United Kingdom, Canada, the United States, several European countries, Africa, Australia and New Zealand. Its development in these parts of the world has not yet been the subject of serious study, with the exception of the UK, where second-generation Blacks found in Rastafari a ready vehicle of expression of their own search for identity (Cashmore 1983). Here too, both British society and Rastafari have had to find mutual accommodation, and with it change.

The third, and still current, phase of Rastafari development in Jamaica dates from the 1980s and is characterized by far-reaching changes, the result of an onset of routinization. First, the pervasiveness of Rastafari ideology among the urban youth has waned. Up to the end of the 1970s ghetto youth provided the main recruitment ground for Rastafari. The surest sign of this was the fact that most promising young reggae artistes would begin sprouting dreadlocks as soon as they began to hit the popularity charts. Now, the most successful popular musicians, the DJ artistes, manifest no Rastafari influence, neither in their lyrics nor in their hair culture. Instead, North American hair styles and bawdy lyrics predominate. Most of the young Rastas one now sees at Rastafari gatherings are the children of older Dreads.

Another noticeable development is the increasing vocality of women in the movement. One peculiarity of the Rastas is their ideological and ritual subordination of women. Women are considered essentially incapable of receiving the fullness of divine knowledge directly and must acquire this through their male spouses, their 'king-man'. They do not play any function in rituals (though their presence is not forbidden), must cover their locks at all times and must show deference to males. Menstruating women may not cook, and in one group are secluded from social contact. As a sign of change, Rastafari women have become quite vocal against these beliefs and practices, and some have defied such conventions as covering their dreadlocks, or wearing only ankle-length dress in public.

Finally, a secularization process has been underway since the 1980s, whereby identifying symbols of the Rastafari are being shorn of their religious and ethical significance and diffused to the non-Rastafari population. The most easily observable is the Rasta tricolour, the red, gold and green, which the Rasta movement adopted from the Ethiopian flag but which in part coincided with the UNIA emblem. The black in Garvey's UNIA flag stood for the African peoples, the red for their blood and the green for the vérdant wealth of the continent. By substituting the gold for the black the Rastafari forged a closer sense of identity with Ethiopia while retaining the Garveyite connection. Every Rasta tam is woven and every Rasta banner, poster, rod or other artifact painted, in red, gold and green colours. Now these colours are worn by all and sundry, without reference to any ideological commitment. The dreadlocks, also, have suffered a similar fate. While it is true that dreadlocks have been used as a symbol of defiance and rebellion in many parts of the world, it is also a fact that they have become part of 'hair couture'. A short visit to a hair stylist and one may emerge with dreadlocks either styled or woven in. Thus, especially in the tourist zones of the country, one cannot always be sure that the proud display of dreadlocks one frequently sees belongs to the genuine Rastafari believer, and not to the male prostitute locally known as the 'Rent-a-Dread'.

Notwithstanding these recent developments, the Rastafari movement in Jamaica retains great moral authority, due to its pioneering stance on issues of racial identity and colour prejudice in Jamaica and due also to its role in the development of Jamaican culture.

Organization

Rastafari is by and large an acephalous movement. Except for two highly organized groups, most brethren do not belong to a formal organization. They do, however, consider themselves members of the 'House'. The concept of House seemed to have originated in the second phase of the movement's development when, as a result of the reform activities of the emerging Dreadlocks, the movement split into two orders or Houses: the House of Dreadlocks and the House of Combsomes, that is, those who comb their hair. Since the 1960s Combsomes have all but disappeared, leaving only the House of Dreadlocks. Thus, the main distinguishing mark of members of the House today is their dreadlocks. Any Dreadlocks Rastafari, therefore, is entitled to participate in the formal rituals and deliberations of the House. An assembly of 'Elders', in truth Rastafari who show initiative, meets regularly to plan the activities of the House, such as the celebration of the Emperor's coronation, or its affairs, such as a delegation abroad.

The two organized groups are the Bobos and the Twelve Tribes of Israel. The Bobos, led by Prince Emmanuel Edwards, are the only Rastafari group living a truly communal life, on the outskirts of the city of Kingston. Distinguished from other Rastafari by their robe and turban attire and by their production and hawking of brooms, the Bobos place all their daily earnings in one central fund, from which all their material needs are met. Meals, for example, are prepared in, and shared out from, the single kitchen in the commune. The Twelve Tribes is, as indicated earlier, mainly a middle-class organization, headed by Prophet Gad. Members, organized into the twelve biblical tribes of Israel, pay dues.

Rituals

For the majority of Rastafari members rituals are of two kinds: reasonings and the 'binghi', both sometimes referred to as a 'grounding' or a 'grou-nation', from which has come the verb 'to grounds', meaning to get along well. The reasoning is an informal gathering at which a small group of brethren share in the smoking of the holy weed, ganja, and in a lofty discussion. As the brethren sit around in a circle, the host cuts up the *ganja*, mixing into it a small quantity of tobacco from a cigarette. The matter is stuffed into the chillum of a water pipe (called a 'huka' by the East Indians), from whom the whole *ganja* complex was borrowed (Rubin and Comitas 1975), but called a chalice or cup by the Rastafari, who compare this ritual to the sacred communion of the Christians. He whose honour it is to light the pipe, or chalice, pauses and recites a short prayer before, while all participants bare their heads. Once lit, the chalice is moved counter-clockwise around the circle, until all have 'supped'. Reasoning ends, not formally, but when the participants one by one don their tams or caps and depart.

The 'nyabinghi', or 'binghi' for short, is a dance held on special occasions throughout the year, to mark the coronation of His Imperial Majesty (2 November); His Majesty's ceremonial birthday (6 January); His Majesty's visit to Jamaica (25 April), His Majesty's personal birthday (23 July), Emancipation from Slavery (1 August) and Marcus Garvey's birthday (17 August). The word itself is thought to be of colonial African origin, originally referring to a secret order vowed to bring 'death to White oppressors'. During the Dreadlocks era, Rastafari would on occasion 'dance nyabinghi' to bring 'death to Black and White oppressors'. Today these dances are purely ceremonial celebrations, lasting for several days, depending on the resources of the House.

Rotated from parish to parish, the binghi brings together scores, even hundreds, of Dreadlocks from all over Jamaica. They camp in tents and makeshift lodgings on land owned by the Dreadlocks member playing host. Formal dancing takes place at night in a tabernacle especially set up for the occasion, and to a bank of Rasta drums. These are of three kinds: the bass, struck on the first of four beats and muffled on the third; the *funde*, which plays a steady one-two beat; and the repeater or *akete* (*kete* for short), which plays the improvised syncopations. The Rastas

sing and dance to their distinctive beat long into the morning. In the daytime they rest and 'reason'.

The relative dearth of religious ritual among the Rastafari, compared to Revival, is balanced by ritualization in private life. The Rastafari observe a number of personal ritual taboos and practices. The most significant of these govern food, nature and the environment, and Africa. Among foods, pork and crustaceans are universally avoided, but many Rastafari refrain from all meat and fish products. Salt is also taboo. Food cooked without salt is referred to as *ital*, that is, natural. Rastafari rejects, as much as possible, all artificial things and celebrates the use of the natural: manure instead of artificial fertilizers and sprays; herbs and barks instead of pharmaceuticals. Rastafari life is centred on Africa. Every Rasta home is adorned with photographs of Haile Selassie, sometimes referred to as 'King Alpha', his wife, known as 'Queen Omega', maps of Africa and posters with African themes and the Ethiopian colours. Every Rasta man possesses an array of decorative buttons with replicas of Emperor Haile Selassie or some other African leader, which he proudly wears in public.

[...]

The Rastafari movement has been described variously as escapist, nativist, millenarian, visionary, revitalist – all terms that reflect the impulse in our discipline towards scientific generalization. However, in only a very few cases of the many works written on the Rastas in Jamaica is the use of the particular terminology based on original field research, as opposed to secondary sources, and on the considered attempt therefrom to classify.

One notable example is that of Klaus de Albuquerque (1977), who makes the strongest case, of which I am aware, that the Rastafari is a millenarian movement. His approach is first to construct a theoretical model of millenarian movements and to test it using the Rastafari movement. To establish the relationship between any millenarian movement and the wider society, he says, one has to examine the 'prerequisites' and the 'conditions' which give rise to it. In practical terms this requires an understanding of four distinct factors. The first is the form: whether the millenarian movement is a religious or a secular one. According to de Albuquerque, what determines the form is the level of development of the society. In industrialized societies the political structure is sharply differentiated from the religious; in pre-industrial and 'modernizing' societies this is not so. As a result, millenarian movements occur mainly in the latter and are generally religious. They are not unknown in the former, but there, he says, they depend on the *locus* of the origin of oppression.

Thus, a second factor is the type of society. Industrialized societies are characterized by political structures that have developed the 'capacity to absorb and deflect protest', or to mobilize and so defuse revolutionary threats. Pre-industrial societies are lacking in this capacity.

A third factor is whether the religious belief system of the society is given to strong or weak eschatological expectations. If these are weak, the millenarian movement will likely take a secular, non-revolutionary and passive form; but if strong, the movement is more likely to be religious, revolutionary and active.

Finally, there is the aetiological origin itself. Here, de Albuquerque argues, the factors may be exogenous or endogenous. In an industrialized society endogenous factors condition the movement to be passive and escapist, appealing to bourgeois elements, whereas in pre-industrialized societies exogenous factors of origin lead to revolutionary millenarian movements, with appeals to the 'external proletariat' – external, that is, in the sense of being marginal to the system. Endogenous factors may also have the same effect, if the political structures are at the same time well developed, even if the society as a whole is not.

With a model constructed of these elements, de Albuquerque situates Jamaican society within the ranks of the pre-industrialized, or modernizing, societies, but one which also has a well-developed political structure. After examining the Rastafari, he concludes:

> Given the existence of oppression ... and the above specifying conditions, we would expect the Rastafari movement to assume a revolutionary character and appeal to the external proletariat (landless peasants and urban unemployed). The case study of the movement bears this out, with the exception that the movement had initially, and continues to have, very little impact on the Jamaican peasantry, landless or otherwise. (de Albuquerque 1977:358–9)

Apart from the fact that the theory tends to rule out the possibility of revolutionary millenarian movements in industrialized societies, the main difficulty it presents is not even so much the one acknowledged by the author in the above passage, namely that after nearly fifty years of existence the movement still lacked appeal to the external proletariat (for, it is possible to bring forward evidence to show that it is precisely this sector to which the movement has appealed), but the definition of the Rastafari as a revolutionary movement. De Albuquerque, unfortunately, does not define his use of the word 'revolutionary', so one is not absolutely sure of what he means. In the context of the discussion that would make no sense, since any movement that is radically different from the mainstream could qualify as revolutionary. However, it seems to me, given the context of the discussion, in which he defines politics as participation in some goal seeking, and in which he accords a high place in the paradigm to an activity–passivity dichotomy, that he is using the concept revolutionary in much the same way Professor Hobsbawm used it in relation to the 'primitive rebels' of Sicily: people who, in reaction to existing social and other conditions, actively take measures in pursuit of a radical transformation. If this is so, one would have to concede that the Rastafari movement is revolutionary, not just because it consistently preaches a doctrine about a new order, in which every Black man will have his own 'vine and fig tree', thus reversing the order of Black people at the bottom of society, but because it has in the past (1934, 1956 and, the most notable of all, 1959) taken measures to bring about repatriation to Africa. If one reads de Albuquerque correctly, one cannot be revolutionary and passive at the same time.

But is the Rastafari a revolutionary movement? Is that what it is all about? In what follows I wish to advance a different way of looking at the religion, one which departs from a purely social structure type of perspective and tries to see it rather in the context of cultural continuity. Specifically, I raise two issues without trying at this time to resolve them: the relationship of Rastafari to Revivalism, and the structure of the movement itself.

The Revival Past

As I have already explained in the preceding chapter, Revival grew out of Myal. One of the features of African religion, according to Alleyne (1988:59), is its receptivity to external influences. As an African-derived religion, therefore, Myal was easily able to adopt Christianity, as well as to be adopted by Christianity, as soon as the Black Baptists from the United States (George Lisle, Moses Baker and others) began preaching to the slaves late in the century. Sometimes this religion appeared under its proper name Myal, but it was content to thrive under the name Native Baptist, a development Robotham (1988:35) calls critical, because it constructed 'the synthesis for consciousness in which traditional ethnicities were dissolved' and 'established a new ethical code for the people not only in the religious but also in the *cultural* sense'.

Revival Zion is indeed a religion, and underlying its expression is a coherent worldview, which I refer to as Revivalism, or simply Revival. Briefly summarized, this worldview has three central features, which I shall briefly discuss.

God, spirits and the dead

The Jamaicans, like their African forebears, believe in a Supreme Being, a Creator, called God, or Maasa Gad, or the Father. Though He knows and sees all, God is, nevertheless, distant from human affairs. The acts of the elements are His, such as earthquake, lightning, thunder, storm and floods, and swearing by God or by the elements, particularly lightning, is regarded as a grave and solemn act, for which reason it is seldom done.

As God is distant, so are the Spirits near: in and around, and even within. In recognition of this, children used to be taught when eating always to leave a small portion by the edge of their plates, and (rum) drinkers, even today, will pour a libation before drinking. Of all spirits, Jesus is the greatest. His role in dying to save all humanity has imbued him with special powers. Jesus is the object of supplication and prayer, and is often called, Father Jesus or Pupa Jesus. The most central shrine or seal in the tabernacle is devoted to him, but he never possesses anyone as Jesus. His Spirit, though, or the Dove or Messenger, may possess devotees.

Lesser spirits include angels and archangels such as Michael, Gabriel and Raphael; prophets such as Isaiah, Jeremiah and John the Baptist; and apostles. The spirit world also includes the very powerful fallen angels, Satan being the highest among them. They too can be supplicated, especially for material favours, but they are dangerous.

Spirits of the dead, *duppies*, complete the Jamaican pantheon. The elaborate death rituals are characterized by great mourning and displays of grief among near relatives, a compulsive need to show respect for the deceased and solidarity with the bereaved, and by elaborate precautions to prevent the duppy from returning across the threshold separating the worlds of the living and the dead. Duppies are thought to roam abroad at nights, frightening and terrorizing the living. They may also be used by *obeahmen* to harm people. The most feared are East Indian, Chinese and baby duppies. To relatives, however, duppies may assume protective roles, communicating with them in sleep. Such communications from the spirit world are called visions, to distinguish them from ordinary dreams.

A function of the spirits is the possession of the living. Spirits are not feared on account of this, and spirit possession is considered not only a normal part of religious worship but an honour. It is the way some people are chosen for a higher life.

Man, nature and magic

Nature represents a zone which interfaces the material and spirit worlds, thus establishing a continuum of universal existence. Nature is material, but it is also spiritual. The same croton which makes a beautiful hedge also symbolizes the Prophet Jeremiah, and adorns graves because it is thought to keep duppies within the graves. Herbs, such as mint and sage, trees, such as the majestic cottonwood, rivers and certain species of animals, such as frogs and large moths, all have both sacred and profane identities. One never kills large moths, or bats as they are called; they are believed to represent the ancestors.

But if nature is one threshold across which the spirit world crosses into the world of the living, it is also a zone whereby one can acquire the power of the spirits and control both worlds. Here, even inanimate things may be used: a pinch of salt and a swig of rum, for example, are all the guarantees grave-diggers need. And a saucer of salt may always be found on the sacred table during mourning rituals. Red fabric, pencils and scissors are used to ward off evil spirits.

With the right knowledge, therefore, one can control even the spirit world. The *obeahman* is invested with this knowledge, which he uses mainly for harm, but which anyone may use to personal advantage: charms and amulets for protection; oils and powders to achieve certain goals.[1]

But perhaps the benefit of nature is its healing properties. A general belief is that there is no illness for which nature provides no remedy. The healing process may take place at not one but several levels, from the straightforward application until relief comes to treatment which combines nature with magic and ritual. The religious healer practises in a 'balm yard'. A good practitioner is able not only to heal but to divine and read the future.

Hence, the general attitude toward nature is one of respect and harmony. The individual is regarded as a sinful creature, but also as a vital part of nature and subject to its laws. As in the case of the children of Israel of old, enslavement and oppression are consequences of sin, a condition which will be remedied only in the next world, following a life of righteousness in this. Black skin colour is a sign of debasement. Not only are there common expressions which assume this – for example, blaming race for the failure of Blacks as an ethnic group to advance – but there are also folk-tales which tell, not without humour, how Blacks came to be black. They all tell of some aberration or weakness of character.[2] When the great Revival preacher and healer, Alexander Bedward, told ethnographer Martha Beckwith that in heaven his hand will become as lily white

as her own, he was expressing commonly held views about black skin colour, sin and oppression (Beckwith 1929:169–70). Holding such views, however, did not prevent him from calling for the overthrow of White rule (Chevannes 1971).

Humanity as a whole is sinful, but in the Revival worldview woman represents a particularly serious danger to man, even as she also represents a particularly delightful pleasure. The Adam and Eve myth tells the tale of what lies in store for man if woman is allowed to control him. Woman is therefore not to be trusted, even when she is loved. Eve and Delilah are prototypes of the female. Man is vulnerable during woman's menstrual flow, and to avoid all possibilities of contamination female underwear is strictly segregated from the laundry. Indeed, only a woman herself may wash her own underwear. Menstruating and pregnant women are also thought to have a malignant effect on certain crops.

At the same time, women are a source of male delight and comfort. Feelings about sex are not as guilt-ridden as would appear from the attitudes preached by the Christian and the Evangelical churches, though the situation could be changing, given the dramatic growth of the latter. Women are believed to be always satisfied in sexual intercourse. But it is in their role as mothers that women elicit the greatest respect from men. A woman's pride in motherhood is strong. The bond between mother and son is the strongest of all domestic relationships, and the greatest insult possible to any man is to berate his mother. Motherhood is so highly valued that the title *Mada* is given to women who gain the wide respect of their communities, and those who become Revival leaders.

Ethical and social values

The worldview fashioned by Myal in its interaction with Christianity holds to a sense of moral and cultural equality for all Blacks, as Robotham (1988) points out. It has also imbued the people with a strong sense of community. For instance, it values individualism and respects achieved status, but only if communal values are also upheld. People who achieve but by their actions and attitudes reject their community are sanctioned. 'The higher monkey climb, the more him expose'.

The world, God, spirits, nature, and humanity are all governed by order and interdependence. It is really one world. Nowhere is this more deeply manifested than in the concept of 'helping out', whereby voluntary and spontaneous acts of responsibility and sharing are undertaken, often on behalf of strangers, out of a sense of mutual interdependence and reciprocity. The good one does today will redound to one tomorrow; the good that is done one today is the result of the good one did yesterday. The concept is akin to the Christian teaching about storing up treasures in heaven, except that the reward is expected in this life rather than the next.

For this reason, the belief in retribution and fate is equally strong. The evil which one does will be repaid sooner or later. 'What is fiyu kyaan be anfiyu' (one cannot escape one's fate).

This summary of the worldview of the Jamaicans is neither exhaustive nor intended to imply that these beliefs are shared fully by everyone. I do argue, though, that they are generalized throughout the population, which is why the Revival religion could be found anywhere in the island without ever having had a centrally organized structure of the type possessed by most churches. The closest it came to this was under the great prophet Alexander Bedward, and even then not all Revival groups entered into formal affiliation with him; those that did seemed in any case to have been allowed to retain their autonomy. This process of a generalized worldview giving rise to non-centralized religious expression is replicated in identical fashion in the rise of the Rastafari.

Rastafari Beliefs

The most important belief of the Rastafari is that Haile Selassie, the late Emperor of Ethiopia, is God. This alone was enough for the general public to identify them by (Ras, the Ethiopian for Prince, and Tafari, the Emperor's personal name), although they originally called themselves the 'King of Kings people'. But underlying the belief in the Emperor's divinity is the conclusion that Black people were destined to return to their native Africa, after centuries of injustice at the

hands of the Whites. Repatriation, as the return to Africa is known, thus became the first important departure from Revival, and remained until recently a source of inspiration for the faithful as a whole and for Rastafari artistes in particular.

> Babylon is a wicked one
> Babylon is a wicked one
> Babylon is a wicked one
> O, Jah Rastafari O, Selah!
>
> Our forefathers were taken away
> Our forefathers were taken away
> Our forefathers were taken away
> O, Jah Rastafari O, Selah!
>
> Open up da gate mek I repatriate
> Open up da gate mek I repatriate
> Open up da gate mek I repatriate
> O, Jah Rastafari O, Selah!

The motif in this plaintive song, which may be heard at Rastafari celebrations, is quite common among Blacks with a Christian tradition, namely, their likeness to the ancient children of Israel who were rescued from captivity by the intervention of God. Here, the image is used not as metaphor, but as reality itself. We are the true Israelites; what is written in the Bible is only a foreshadowing of real events now unfolding. The Babylon of old is none other than the White colonial and neo-colonial world. These themes are not confined to ceremonies, but may be found in popular songs as well. *By the rivers of Babylon* is perhaps one of the best known Rastafari songs, made internationally popular by the European group, Boney M.

In Jamaica one of the most popular songs of all times evokes images of the promised land:

> There is a land, far, far away,
> Where there's no night, there's only day.
> Look into the Book of Life and you will see
> That there's a land, far, far away.
>
> The King of Kings and the Lord of Lords
> Sits upon his throne and he rules us all.
> Look into the Book of Life and you will see
> That there's a land, far, far away.

Originally sung by the Abyssinians in the 1960s, by 1980 there were over seventy different versions. The far-away land was Ethiopia, where the 'King of Kings', Haile Selassie, ruled. Its title is *Sata Amas Agauna*, the Amharic for 'Give Thanks and Praises'. *Babylon Burning*, with musical motifs of the round *London Burning*, sung by the Wailers, *I Want to go Back Home*, by Alton Ellis, *Seven Miles of Black Star Liners* by Burning Spear and numerous others express the same theme of exile and repatriation.

By contrast, one is hard put to find a single Revival song which expresses the wish to return to Africa. There is the following:

I want to go home to that land,
I want to go home to that land,
I want to go home to that land where I am from;
For there is joy in my soul,
Peace and happiness in my mind –
I want to go home to that land where I am from.

The 'land where I am from' could be interpreted as Africa, but the feelings of present joy, peace and happiness are not congruent with yearnings of return. Rather, the song expresses the readiness of the faithful, the saved, to go 'home' to heaven. This is particularly clear in another very popular Revival song, which was adopted with a change of words by the Rastafari.

Fly away home to Zion, fly away home:
One bright morning when my life is over,
I will fly away home.

The Rastafari change of the word 'life' to 'work' reflects the main difference between the two religions: salvation in the here and now of this life as against postponement into the next. 'Zion' is no longer the heaven in the skies but Ethiopia, or Africa, where God is.

A second major tenet of the Rastafari, which also marks an important divergence from Revival, is the conclusion that God is Black. It derives from the racial characteristic of Haile Selassie himself, and gives to Black people a sense of being one with, of sharing in an attribute of God. Black man is thereby elevated in status.

Two things follow. First is the rejection of the hegemonic system of values whereby 'if you are White, that's right; if you are Black, you stay back'. Second, the alienation between God and Man need no longer exist, because there is a profound way in which God shares a part of his being with those who were once poor. Man, that is Black Man, is also divine. Rastafari resist speaking of becoming converted. One does not become converted, one begins to *manifest* Rastafari, thereby implying the evolution or unfolding of something already within.

Where does this leave White people? Rastafari, instead of going the way of the Black Nationalists of the United States with a mythology that makes Whiteness an attribute of the Devil, allow the possibility of salvation for Whites, based on inward acknowledgement and rejection of the evil of White society.

Second, the elevation of Man to the status of shared identity with God is at the same time an elevation over the world of Spirits. Rastafari do not recognize the existence of, let alone communicate with, those beings which are so central to Revival. They have no need of them. If there are no spirits but only God and Man, and if Man is also part God, then God himself no longer is the distant 'Big Maasa', without a real role in the affairs of Man, but a loving Father. When Rastafari speak of 'the Father', they do so with great reverence and with an awareness of His central place in their lives. To some extent the identity with the Father gives coherence to the strong patriarchal orientation for which the movement is noted. This alteration in how the spirit world is conceived marks a radical departure from the African tradition, so far as the retention of a particular form is concerned. But, as we shall see later, there is strong retention of belief in the immanence of God.

The two tenets of Rastafari discussed above are the most fundamental, and they characterize the main divergence from Revival. They were made possible by a most important development in the history of Blacks in the Western hemisphere, the rise of Marcus Garvey as a great visionary and teacher. Although his Back-to-Africa scheme failed,[3] his shipping line and other economic enterprises foundered and his years of involvement in Jamaican politics came to naught, Garvey positively and permanently laid the foundation for a transformation in the thinking of Blacks through his tireless teachings on their past achievements and future possibilities and through the respect he won by the magnitude and daring of his schemes. He identified 'race' as the defining characteristic of a Black nationality, thereby giving a sense of common identity to millions in the new and old worlds, and a new sense of power. The early Rastafari, leaders and followers alike, all considered themselves Garveyites. To them he was John the Baptist, leading them to the one to come who would be greater than himself.

So great was Garvey's impact on popular consciousness, that the Bedwardites paired him with Bedward in the roles of Moses and Aaron, respectively. But other people also influenced by Garvey had other ideas: if Garvey was Moses (his middle name was Mosiah), the land of Jamaica must be Egypt and there must be a real promised land, not a metaphorical one.

Rastafari, then, started off as a radical departure from all that had gone before it. The image was shaped as much by the two central doctrines as by the adoption of certain symbols, notably the beard and, by the 1950s, the use of ganja and the dreadlocks, and by millenarian and non-millenarian activities to effect Repatriation.

However, despite the centrality of and insistence on this belief in Repatriation, Rastafari is essentially not a Repatriation movement. Orlando Patterson (1964) made a similar point years ago, supporting it with socio-psychological arguments backed by Peter Worsley and other scholars. In my view, the issue is how one interprets the past sixty years of the movement.

For one, repatriation initiatives have not been many in the six decades. In 1934 Leonard Howell, one of the founders of Rastafari, was believed to have preached that repatriation would take place on August 1. Following the failure of that prophecy, the main focus of attention fell on the theological concepts of God, and it was not until the mid- to late-1940s that we begin hearing about Back-to-Africa marches. These were sponsored by Garveyites like Z. Munroe Scarlett, but joined by the Rastas. Rasta-organized marches began with the appearance of the Dreadlocks, but were not explicitly Repatriation marches. In 1958 Prince Emmanuel Edwards

called an all-Rasta convention and some Rastafari reportedly sold out their belongings and gathered in expectancy of the ships to take them 'home'. In 1959, Claudius Henry distributed blue cards to be used in lieu of passports for a 'miraculous repatriation' to take place on 25 October, and in the following year his church was associated with attempts to force its way back to Africa.[4] These last episodes (one by Prince Emmanuel and two by Claudius Henry) were related to the mass migration to Britain at the time and therefore cannot be seen in isolation. Moreover, Henry's initiatives were not supported by most of the young Dreadlocks. They viewed him with suspicion, because he wore neither dreadlocks nor beard. Subsequent to the Henry affair, Repatriation activities were confined to the occasional individual such as the Rastafarian who tried to board an outgoing plane, and attempts by some leaders to pressure the Jamaican government and the United Nations. The Repatriation picture then roughly looks like this: the first twenty years, one episode at the beginning; the next ten years three episodes within a three-year time span; thereafter none.

Furthermore, Repatriation is a theological, not a political, concept. There are three aspects to it. First, Repatriation is a divine not a human act. It is different from migration, Rastafari insist. Many Rastafari even dissociated themselves from activities like the 1961 Mission, holding that while governments could bring about migration, only Jah could bring about Repatriation. This explains why other opportunities are not taken. In gratitude for their generous support of Ethiopia in the anti-fascist war, Emperor Haile Selassie made available through the Ethiopian World Federation several hundred acres of land for Blacks who wish to settle there. It is instructive that very few have seen Sheshamane and even fewer have stayed for good, including members of the Twelve Tribes of Israel, which adopts the position that since God helps those who help themselves, there is nothing wrong in trying to get its members one by one to Ethiopia. Second, Repatriation means the return of Africans not to any country of Africa, nor even to West Africa, but specifically to Ethiopia. When Rastafari sing and speak of Zion, Ethiopia is meant. Zion is where

God dwells. Third, Repatriation also includes the concept of justice, by which Europeans would give up the lands they have seized from the Amerindians and return to Europe. As a theological concept Repatriation serves as a critique of White racism against Africans and other 'coloured races' and a call for a new order of justice in the world. It functions for the Rastafari in the same way that the Second Coming of Christ functions for the Christian without Christianity as a whole being called a millenarian movement – a theological and practical criticism of evil in this world to be followed by justice in the next.

Finally, none of the Repatriation initiatives referred to above at any time had the full support of Rastafarians, for the movement is highly fragmented and unorganized, a characteristic which works against united action. This point being of some relevance to the present discussion, I think some explanation is needed.

Leadership and Organization

Rastafari is an acephalous movement. There are groups, quasi-groups and individuals, who while sharing the core beliefs, nevertheless remain separate and independent. Consequently, the fortune of the movement as a whole is not tied to the fate of any particular leader or group, and it has been able not merely to survive the ups and downs of its relations with the society over the years, but also to influence it.

Leonard Howell is generally thought to have been the very first to reach the conclusion that Haile Selassie was God. But Joseph Hibbert claimed to have done the same independently. Whether or not the initial Rastafarians influenced one another, the point is that from the very inception there were several men all preaching the same thing but doing so *independently* of one another. There was one exception: Robert Hinds first began preaching with Howell but soon went his separate way. Thus Howell, Hinds, Hibbert, Archibald Dunkley, Brother Napier, Brother Powell and a few others were preaching Rastafari on the highways and byways of the city and countryside, and organizing the converted into churches which they gave the name 'King of Kings', all at the same time,

and without reference to any one as leader, even *primus inter pares*.

A second feature was, thus, its resistance to centralized organization. Except among three very specific sects – the influential Twelve Tribes of Israel, the Bobo led by Prince Emmanuel Edwards and the remnants of Claudius Henry's church – the Rastafarian refuses to surrender his freedom and autonomy by joining any organization, Rastafari or not. A common explanation of the brethren is, 'wa jain kyan brok!' (what is joined together can be broken). But in truth it is their ethical value of complete freedom from the force of unnatural rules which informs this resistance. If one acts, it should be out of inner conviction, rather than out of the need for outward conformity. 'Man free' is another common expression, which means 'Do as you feel justified to do'. There have been repeated attempts in the past to forge a united body, to no avail. The Ethiopian International Unification Committee led by Attorney Michael Lorne is only the most recent of a series which has included the Rasta Movement Association and other initiatives.

Third, this value of freedom from outward constraint finds expression for the majority of Rastafari in the quasi-organization they refer to as the 'House', that is the House of Nyabinghi. The House is run by an 'Assembly of Elders', theoretically numbering 72, but in reality far fewer. Dr Homiak (1985:490–1) summarizes Eldership as combining cunning and resourcefulness with initiative and trust, but avoiding selfishness, arbitrariness or conceit. One does not become an Elder by appointment or election. The Elders oversee the affairs of the House, such as planning liturgical events, settling disputes, or appointing delegations as the need arises. But beyond the Assembly of Elders, there is no membership, as such. All are free to come or stay away, to participate or remain silent, to contribute or withhold financial dues. Yet one retains one's qualification as a member of the House simply by being a Rastafari. The openness of this sort of structure permits a great measure of democracy, in which all are equal, regardless of age, ability or function. But at the same time it makes a united, organized structure difficult if not impossible.

These characteristics of the Rastafari have a remarkable similarity to Revival, whose origin is traced to the incorporation by Myal of Christianity. The first Baptist to convert slaves, George Lisle, was himself a Black slave who was brought to Jamaica by his Loyalist master fleeing the American Revolution. But the more slaves Lisle converted, the less control he had, as converts went on their own, preaching their own understanding of Christianity, which in effect was Myal. Thomas Gibb, George Lewis and Moses Baker were three such preachers. They had no central organization, no mutual cooperation. Their movement reproduced itself in a cellular way.

Yet, it was clear by what the missionaries referred to as 'Myal outbreaks', beginning not long after the turn of the century and appearing as late as 1860, that there was a fairly uniform system of beliefs widely distributed across the length and breadth of the island. This allowed Revivalists everywhere to distinguish between two broad trends (or 'houses' in fact), the 'sixty' and the 'sixty-one'. The former worship only the sky-bound spirits, Jesus, the prophets, etc.; the latter worship these as well as the earth-bound spirits. Anywhere they go across the island, Revivalists are able to identify 'sixty' and 'sixty-one' and to associate with the one or the other.

No attempt was ever made to organize Revival into a united body, though scores of groups throughout the island were affiliated to Bedward.

I do not intend to stretch the comparison by saying that Revivalism, like Rasta, was impervious to organization, but the similarities in their spontaneous and acephalous nature are indeed striking.

There are similarities of a different kind, which in the context of the discussion deserve mention. I refer to the many examples where it is evident that certain crucial aspects of the Revival world outlook are very much alive in Rastafari. I distinguish two kinds: first, direct traces, where the forms are the same; and second, indirect traces, where Revival traditions provide the basis for what appear to be new Rastafari traditions. Direct traces are far more numerous than generally recognized, and may be summarized as follows:

Ritual structure

Revival meetings, as pointed out before, are basically divided into two parts: an initial period of drumming, singing, dancing and spirit possession, followed by the specific rituals which define the purpose of the meeting. Thus, the healing ritual, testimony service, and table all begin more or less the same way. The Rastafari meetings retain this element: an initial period of considerable duration in which the drumming-singing-dancing triad reigns, but without spirit possession. At the time of my fieldwork in 1975 this initial period gave way, just as in Revival, to a different element, namely Bible reading and preaching. At one ceremony I attended in Westmoreland, the Table from which the Elder spoke hosted a glass of water – another Revival trace.[5]

Ritual instruments

It is very interesting that in Professor Simpson's description of the anniversary celebration by one group of Haile Selassie's coronation in 1953 the musical instruments included rhumba boxes, saxophones, guitars, violin, banjo, tambourines and rattles (Simpson 1955:143). All this changed within ten years, as uniformly throughout the movement, a bank of drums had replaced all other instruments and a rhythm, called nyabinghi, peculiar only to the Rastafari. The drums are of three types: a huge bass, larger than Revival's but struck the same way with the padded end of a stick; the funde, which establishes the rhythm; and the repeater, which pronounces the variations. The latter two are played with the hands and fingers. These drums are central to all Rastafari gatherings. Bilby and Leib (1986:23) trace the origins of this music to a complex interpenetration of Buru, Kumina and Revival styles of drumming in West Kingston, and thus establish the accuracy of 'Rastafari insistence on the "African roots" of Nyabing[h]i' (Bilby and Leib 1986:27). Most of the ceremonial songs of the Rastafari with adjustments in certain key words, as observed above, are legacies of Revival.

Magic

To 'dance nyabinghi' against an identified oppressor was, Rastafari believed, to invoke in a sure and compelling way the power of God to destroy him. According to one informant, fire was made to consume an effigy of the person. Although the practice may have ceased, I have heard Rastafari threaten to dance nyabinghi for public personalities they considered oppressive to Rastafari. The dreadlocks are also believed to have magical properties, not to be used to harm the owner, but to be able to wreak destruction on Babylon. Such beliefs in magic are not surprising, since, according to Robert Hill (1983:38) 'popular belief in the power of the occult played a formative role in the early stages of Rastafari consciousness'.

Divination

Rastafari believe in the power of the Bible to expose evil. In one incident concerning the loss of money belonging to the House, the Holy Book was used to distinguish the guilty from the innocent.

Herbal lore

Rastafari place heavy stress on nature as a gift of the Father 'for the healing of the nation'. This attitude applies not only to ganja but to all of nature. Thus, with almost the force of doctrine, they reject artificial things pertaining to life, preferring the natural: herbal medicinal cures, herbal teas, natural spices and flavouring such as pepper and coconut milk.[6]

Visions

The same worldview which Rastafari share with other Jamaicans distinguishes dreams from visions. Dreams are the images and fantasies which appear in sleep. Visions are dreams of particular significance, usually rich in symbolic meaning, and regarded as encoded messages from the world of the spirits. Although not believing in spirits other than the Father, the Rastafari nevertheless believe in His communication through visions.

Indirect traces may be found in many new traditions which seem uniquely Rastafari but which in fact owe much to the earlier world outlook. I now present some of the more obvious.

Word power

The creation of a new mode of speech by the Rastafari has been noted by linguists (Pollard

1985; Alleyne 1988). Underlying it is a belief in the magical power of the word. Alleyne, while being too uncertain 'about the earlier stages of language development in Jamaica to be able to reconstruct a continuous process through the seventeenth, eighteenth and nineteenth centuries', does not doubt that Rastafari ideas about language are 'an expression of African culture' (Alleyne 1988:150). What he obviously implies is that more research is needed to establish the link, more research in fact on the worldview I have been calling Revival and its belief in the magical power of the word. To begin with, ethnographers have noted the predilection of the Jamaican peasant for the spoken word (Beckwith 1929), a tendency not adequately explained by the absence of a tradition of literacy, since even literate people have the feeling that to address one in person is more effective than in writing. And a predilection, one might add, not just for the spoken word but for 'big words', as if their use transforms the speaker's ability to be more effective. These traditions persist. Contemporary Jamaican culture, observes Brathwaite (1986), is essentially oral.

Names were viewed as somewhat like extensions of one's person, and therefore as the possible object of imitative magic. Hence, at night, one never answered to one's name being called, unless it was uttered three times, the number three thought to be outside the range of duppies. Similarly, one should not call out another's name in public. One attracts the other's attention either by a clapping of hands or the hissing of teeth. This custom considered it bad etiquette to do otherwise, but it was also believed that it exposed one to possible evil being conspired by strangers. The tradition still persists of giving children, especially girls, 'pet names', that is names by which they were known by family and community, and official or 'real names', sometimes known not even to the owner until read in adulthood on a birth certificate.

Nowhere is the power of the word more manifest today in non-Rastafari contexts than among the Pentecostal sects, where spirit possession takes place through the power of the preacher's words. But even in other conventional denominations the measure of satisfaction with the worship is directly a function not of the singing or the ritual but of the sermon. If good, it is described as 'sweet'.

These examples indicate that Rastafari predilection for the spoken word did not originate with them. I see no difference between the Dreadlock's preference for 'performing' over writing his complaint or petition and the peasant's. His attribution of power to the word, so beautifully expressed as 'Word, Sounds and Power!', is but a refinement of a tradition.

Contamination of death

I noted the elaborate rituals which traditionally follow death, and the fear of contamination of the world of the living by the spirits of the dead which inspires them. Rastafari carries this fear of contamination to its extreme. The brethren do not believe the true Rasta will die. I am not now in a position to say whether this belief was institutionalized from the 1930s, though it is not unlikely. None of my 'ancient' Rastafari ever mentioned death or burial. At any rate, up to the very recent past the belief that Rastafari cannot die was very strong. A change became noticeable in the 1980s, following first the report of the death of His Imperial Majesty in 1974 and that of Bob Marley in 1981. Today, some brethren admit that man is put on earth only for a time, not to live for ever. This, however, is not the majority view.

As a result of not believing he will die, the Rastafari will have nothing to do with death: he attends no funerals, takes no part in their arrangement, no matter how close the deceased, does not mourn or even discuss the event. Thus, in an ironic way, his ideological distancing has the same source as the ritualized distancing of the traditional believer: belief in the contaminating power of death.

Woman as a source of evil

Much is made of the Rastafari belief in male supremacy (Kitzinger 1971; Nettleford 1970; Rowe 1980; Yawney 1983), buttressed by beliefs in woman's natural inferiority and power to contaminate. Rastafari believe that a woman is of such wayward nature that only through her male spouse, her 'king-man', may she attain the enlightenment of Jah. Relationships are therefore marked by female submissiveness and obedience to the male, and ritual avoidance and even confinement during the menstrual flow. While this strong patriarchal tradition is indeed a direct contrast to traditional household patterns in Jamaica, its ideological root within the traditional worldview is often missed.

Man as God

I have already drawn attention to the rejection of the spirit world by the Rastafari and its replacement with a belief in the nearness of God and oneness of being between Him and Man. Yet it may be argued that the new doctrine is but an elevation of the most essential feature of the Revival beliefs about the relationship between the human and spiritual world, namely the fusion of identity which is possible in the form of ritual possession. Just as Revival possession is the means by which the spirit performs, so is Rastafari identity with God the means whereby God's works are manifest. Father Owens, to date the only presenter of a comprehensive view of Rasta theology, explains:

> Simple man is not completely divine, in the Rastafarian view, because he is still partly under the sway of Satan, the embodiment of all that is in opposition to God in man. Just as the God of the Rastas is not allowed to be an other-worldly, intangible being estranged from the ways of man, so also Satan is conceived by the brethren as being immediately present to the working of history: 'Satan is the people who live upon earth who manifest themself in Satan way. In other words, Satan is the man who trying to keep you down. Yes, that is the devil!' (Owens 1976:132)

Thus, to do good means to allow the God in you to perform his work, just as to do evil means allowing Satan to perform his. But, as Owens (1976:130) carefully notes, the brethren do not allow their identity with God to gloss over 'the real distance that they know exists between man in his present state and man in his divine state to which he is summoned'.

General Implications

The view of the Rastafari I have so far presented is one which, when silhouetted against the historical backdrop of the worldview of which Revival was the religious expression, appears as a new departure but also as a continuity. The question now is: what does it all mean? This is what I think it means.

(1) Rastafari must be included when considering Africa-derived religion in Jamaica and the Caribbean. It is more authentic an expression of that tradition than generally thought. Alleyne is hard put to find anything of African continuity in Rastafari beliefs and behaviour. 'Rastafarianism', he surmises, 'is probably an excellent example of a cultural form being generated virtually *ab initio* out of the social circumstances' (Alleyne 1988:103). But evidently conscious of the implications of such a statement,[7] he later on observes that the religion, by integrating language, music and religion at a higher level than before, merely continues an African and African-Jamaican tradition (Alleyne 1988:149). It is in this latter context that he regrets the paucity of knowledge that might have allowed linguistic, and obviously other, links to be proved.

(2) Owing so much to the Revival past, yet being so remarkably different, Rastafari may be regarded as its fulfillment. For it is clear, particularly after Marcus Garvey, that the Revival worldview was inadequate in pan-African terms, since it had no really viable answer to the problem posed by White racism. After Garvey, a return to a worldview that accommodated black skin as an ontological deficiency to be rectified only by transmogrification was out of the question.

(3) Thus, Rasta is itself essentially a worldview movement, 'a system of beliefs and a state of consciousness', as Post (1978:165) correctly put it. This accounts for its acephalous and somewhat spontaneous nature, very much in the same vein as Myal and Revival. Its greatest impact lies here, and it would be quite wrong to judge it by the failure of its prophecies of repatriation.

(4) While Rastafari has manifested millennial tendencies, which give the movement a

political character, it is much more fruitful to conceive of it as a cultural movement. What has accounted for its growth is not the dream of the millennium but the appropriation of a new and more coherent reality. There is the real revolution. As I have already said, Rastafari search for the millennium occurred four times. Yet it is a fact that its periods of greatest growth occurred *after* them: in the decade of the 1930s and first half decade of the 1940s, when the focus was on spreading the message that Selassie was God; and in the 1960s and 1970s, with the rise of the Dreadlocks and their symbolic announcement of a new and separate identity.

This is not to deny the impulse to action inherent in the appropriation of any new ideas about the cosmos, which is obviously present in the Rastafari movement. It was present, too, in Myal and Revival, which did as much in the struggle against slavery and colonialism as Vodun did in Haiti, yet no scholar, as far as I know, would regard any of them as essentially activist in the broad political sense. It is one thing to recognize these impulses, it is another to make them the essence.

No other scholar has treated the subject matter in quite the same way or has been able to document the living continuity within the Rastafari of Jamaica of a unifying worldview honed out of a variegated tribal melange. The thrust of the Nettleford essays (1970), for example, was on the issue of a Black identity. He perceived, notwithstanding the millennial dream of the movement, that the centre stage was Jamaica itself and its Black majority. But Katrin Norris (1962) had sounded a similar note almost a decade before, when she observed that the Rastafari were facing the issue of a Black identity, which the Black middle classes were avoiding. Among more recent scholars Ernest Cashmore and Laennec Hurbon adopt a similar position. Cashmore (1983) bluntly dismisses the Rastafari's potential as a revolutionary force but argues that in fact previous scholars underestimated its importance in creating a culture. Hurbon (1986:164) sees the movement as building a new identity for Jamaica and all the

Caribbean islands, but he too lapses into seeing it as a sort of nativist 'revival of the basic core of the slave and nineteenth-century cultures', again, I think, because of the failure of scholarship to uncover its living continuity with the past. And precisely this constitutes the insight of Mervyn Alleyne, whose central thesis it is that the culture of West Africa lives on in the Jamaican worldview. For example, he says:

> The reluctance of Jamaican peasants to accept modern scientific agricultural techniques, including the use of chemical fertilisers and other agents that artificially quicken growth must be seen within the philosophical framework of this oneness with nature. The Rastafarians, whose complex eating taboos reflect a belief that body, mind, and nature form an integrated whole, have developed and enriched this philosophical tradition. (Alleyne 1988:157)

It is easy to miss this because 'worldview ... cannot be observed directly like artifacts' (Alleyne 1988:157), and in the study of religion, where it could have been gleaned, the focus has been on ritual and organization to the neglect of the 'underlying philosophies'.

Alleyne's observations are well founded. Nevertheless, the approach taken in this chapter to the Rastafari phenomenon raises a number of issues which need airing. Is the existence of a worldview enough of an explanation for the lack of centralized leadership in religious movements? After all, ideas do not spread *sua sponte*. They

need human agents. And is it not often the case that what makes some people leaders is their quicker grasp of ideas and better ability to communicate them more lucidly? What, therefore, is the place of charismatic leadership in religions of this sort? Among the Rastafari all four of the most mentioned early leaders, Howell, Hinds, Hibbert and Dunkley, were invested with heroic, if not divine, abilities. De Albuquerque tells of one Rastafari who would come every morning and reverently kiss the locks of Mortimo Planno. Henry up to the time of his death was thought to be part of the triune deity, as is Prince Emmanuel presently. The lack of central leadership should not allow us to gloss over the presence and role of leaders.

Inasmuch as changes in worldviews imply changes in the conception of Man and Man's place in the world, are Africa-derived religions in the Caribbean any different from religious movements generally described as messianic, nativist and millenarian? Burridge, for example, reduces all religions to concern 'with the discovery, identification, moral relevance and ordering of different kinds of power whether these manifest themselves as thunder, or lightning, atomic fission, untrammelled desire, arrogance, impulse, apparitions, visions, or persuasive words' (Burridge 1969:5). The logic of his argument would lead us to answer no, for although each situation may be specific, what he calls the 'logic of social relations' may allow a generalized explanation. This needs to be examined.

Notes

1   According to Elkins (1986:215) oils and powders are early twentieth century additions from the influence of DeLaurence, which 'significantly influenced the development of the new type of obeah in Jamaica' known as 'Science'. DeLaurence was a publisher of books about magic and necromancy.

2   Daryl Dance (1985:5–8) collected no fewer than six, as late as the 1970s. In one, God had not made anyone Black, only straight-haired people. As a set of them laughed at monkey because his tail was on fire, he thrashed his tail around in the air. 'The fire burned the hair [and made them] black'. Similar stories may be found in the

United States. They are taken with only half-serious intent. At the same time, like all jokes which are based on real people, they have a serious side.

3   It was also grossly misunderstood. Garvey did not campaign for all Blacks to return to Africa, but for Blacks to resettle, develop and unify the continent. With united Africa a major power in the world, Blacks could command the respect denied them by Whites. Were he leading an exodus, the Black Star Shipping Line, linking Africa, North America and the Caribbean and Central America in a triangular trade, would have made no sense.

4 Significantly, some time after he returned from serving a ten-year prison sentence, Henry told his congregation that the Emperor had told him on a visit to Africa that there was no need for Black people to leave Jamaica, because Africa was already in Jamaica (Chevannes 1976).

5 That experience was very formative. It first alerted me to the existence among the Rastafari of links of continuity with the historically earlier Revival religion. The insight gained was to become my central thesis. See my *Social and Ideological Origins of the Rastafari Movement in Jamaica*, from which most of the examples of direct and indirect traces of Revivalism discussed in this chapter are drawn.

6 Even the taboo against salt may derive from this prejudice against artificial things, since as a commodity bought in shops, salt is not 'natural'. Another possibility is the re-emergence of a retention from slavery. I am grateful to Roland Littlewood for bringing this to my attention. Alleyne (1988:104) also mentions that avoidance of salt recurs among the Maroons of Jamaica and among Kumina cultists.

7 The burden of proof must be to show how it is possible for people to be bereft of culture. Even in rejecting the past they would have to do so in culturally meaningful ways, such as through language and other symbols.

References

de Albuquerque, Klaus (1977) *Millenarian Movements and the Politics of Liberation: The Rastafarians of Jamaica*. PhD dissertation, Virginia Polytechnic Institute and State University.

Alleyne, Mervyn (1988) *Roots of Jamaican Culture*. London: Pluto Press.

Beckwith, Martha (1929) *Black Roadways: A Study of Jamaican Folk Life*. Chapel Hill, NC: University of North Carolina.

Bilby, Kenneth, and Elliott Leib (1986) 'Kumina, the Howellite Church and the Emergence of Rastafarian Traditional Music in Jamaica', *Jamaica Journal*, 19 (3): 22–8.

Brathwaite, Kamau (1986) *Roots*. Havana: Casa de las Americas.

Burridge, Kenelm (1969) *New Heaven and New Earth: A Study of Millenarian Activities*. New York: Schocken.

Campbell, Horace (1980) 'Rastafari: Culture of Resistance', *Race & Class*, 22(1): 1–22.

Cashmore, E. (1983) *Rastaman*. London: George Allen & Unwin. 2nd edn (1st edn, 1979).

Chevannes, Barry (1971) 'Revival and Black Struggle', *Savacou*, 5: 27–37.

Chevannes, Barry (1976) 'The Repairer of the Breach: Reverend Claudius Henry and Jamaican Society', in Frances Henry (ed.), *Ethnicity in the Americas*. The Hague: Mouton.

Chevannes, Barry (1981) 'Rastafari and the Urban Youth', in Carl Stone and Aggrey Brown (eds), *Perspective on Jamaica in the Seventies*. Kingston: Jamaica Publishing House.

Chevannes, Barry (1989a) *The Social and Ideological Origins of the Rastafari Movement in Jamaica*. PhD dissertation, Columbia University, New York.

Chevannes, Barry (1990) 'Healing the Nation: Rastafari Exorcism of Racism in Jamaica', *Caribbean Quarterly*, 36(3&4).

Dance, Darryl C. (1985) *Folklore From Contemporary Jamaicans*. Knoxville: University of Tennessee.

Davis, Stephen (1983) *Reggae Bloodlines: In Search of the Music and Culture of Jamaica*. New York: Anchor.

van Dijk, Frank Jan (1988) 'The Twelve Tribes of Israel: Rasta and the Middle Class', *New West Indian Guide*, 62(1&2).

Hill, Robert (1983) 'Leonard Howell and Millenarian Visions in Early Rastafari', *Jamaica Journal*, 16(1).

Homiak, John P. (1985) *The 'Ancients of Days' Seated Black: Eldership, Oral Tradition and Ritual in Rastafari Culture*. PhD dissertation, Brandeis University, Waltham, MA.

Hurbon, Laennec (1986) 'New Religious Movements in the Caribbean', pp. 146–76 in J.A. Beckford (ed.), *New Religious Movements and Rapid Social Change*. London: Sage.

Kitzinger, Shiela (1971) 'The Rastafarian Brethren of Jamaica', in Michael Horowitz (ed.), *Peoples and Cultures of the Caribbean*. New York: Natural History Press.

Lanternari, Vittorio (1963) *Religions of the Oppressed: A Study of Modern Messianic Cults*. New York: Alfred Knopf, and London: MacGibbon and Kee.

Nettleford, Rex (1970) *Mirror, Mirror: Identity Race and Protest in Jamaica*. Kingston: Collins-Sangster.

Norris, Katrin (1962) *Jamaica: The Search for an Identity*. Institute of Race Relations. Oxford: Oxford University Press.

Owens, Joseph (1976) *Dread: The Rastafarians of Jamaica*. London, Kingston and Port of Spain: Heinemann.

Post, K.W.J. (1978) *Arise ye Starvlings: The Jamaica Labour Rebellion of 1938 and its Aftermath*. The Hague, Boston and London: Martinus Nijhoff.

Robotham, Don (1988) 'The Development of a Black Ethnicity in Jamaica', pp. 23–38, in Lewis Rupert and Patrick Bryan (eds), *Garvey: His Work and Impact*. Mona, Jamaica: ISER and Extra-Mural Dept., University of West Indies.

Rowe, Maureen (1980) 'The Women in Rastafari', *Caribbean Quarterly*, 26(4): 13–21.

Rubin, Vera and Comitas, Lambros (1975) *Ganja in Jamaica*. Paris and The Hague: Mouton.

Simpson, George Eaton (1955) 'Political Cultism in West Kingston, Jamaica', *Social and Economic Studies*, 4(2): 133–49.

Smith, M.G., Roy Augier, and Rex Nettleford (1961) *Report on the Rastafari Movement in Kingston, Jamaica*. Kingston: Institute of Social and Economic Research, University of the West Indies, Mona.

Stone, Carl (1974) *Electoral Behaviour and Public Opinion in Jamaica*. Kingston: Institute of Social and Economic Research, University of the West Indies.

Yawney, Carole D. (1983) 'To Grow a Daughter: Cultural Liberation and the Dynamics of Oppression in Jamaica', in A. Miller and G. Finn (eds), *Feminism in Canada*. Montreal: Black Rose Books.

13

'Official' and 'Popular' Hinduism in the Caribbean

Historical and Contemporary Trends in Surinam, Trinidad and Guyana

Steven Vertovec

The religious traditions of Hindus in the Caribbean are the products of over one hundred and forty years of inadvertent permutation, deliberate alteration or innovation, and structurally necessary modification. Caribbean Hindu traditions are also currently in process of transformation, and will doubtless continue to undergo changes for a host of reasons or purposes. This should come as no surprise since, to paraphrase Burghart,[1] reformulating Hindu beliefs and practices in light of shifting contexts is as old as Hinduism itself. In fact mutability is one of the hallmark characteristics of many concepts, rites, social forms and other phenomena generally subsumed under the rubric of 'Hinduism'. In India, the range of such phenomena is so large, varied, and variable that many scholars have criticized the use of any single notion or category 'Hinduism'.[2] However, in the Caribbean, historical courses of change have been such that a generally unitary Hindu religion has indeed arisen. Still, though a standardized and institutionalized orthodoxy has come to dominate the religious life of Hindus in each of the major communities in the Caribbean, more variegated beliefs and practices nonetheless occur on local levels.

These developments are perhaps described best in terms of 'official' and 'popular' forms of Hinduism.

Hinduism, Descriptive Categories and the Diaspora

Since the 1950s, anthropologists and others have found heuristic value in the notions of 'Little Tradition' and 'Great Tradition' for addressing the diversity within and relation between local and India-wide Hindu religious phenomena.[3] 'Little Tradition' has generally referred to highly parochial non-Brahmanic (usually low-caste) and non-Sanskritic beliefs and practices; these tend to invoke minor or potentially malevolent deities and supernaturals, often toward pragmatic ends. The 'Great Tradition' of Hinduism, on the other hand, has been said to include mainly the beliefs and practices found in Sanskrit texts and maintained by Brahmans across the entire subcontinent; these invoke the highest or most widely known pantheon of deities, and also promote transcendent or philosophical ideals.

Much of the literature describes dialectic relations between these two categories (sometimes doing so in terms of 'classical *vs* folk' or 'textual *vs* practical' religion).[4] Many scholars have come to agree that these kinds of categories can often obscure the continuity of types or 'levels' of religious phenomena by reifying an artificial polarity. Instead, perhaps, such terms should represent Weberian ideal types placed on the ends of a kind of descriptive continuum:[5] depending on what is being undertaken, the activities of Hindus in India could then be represented at one point or another on the continuum. In such a model, for example, Hindu belief and practice might be described as being towards the 'Little Tradition' or pragmatic end when a person employs a low-caste specialist to invoke a blood-demanding deity during an exorcism, and towards the 'Great Tradition' or transcendent end when the same person makes a pilgrimage to a major Vaishnavite site; subsequently, other concepts and activities (elements of domestic worship; acts or obeisance to holy men; participation in certain oblatory rites, and so on) may be placed in-between according to their means and ends as conceived by the worshipper. The most important thing to recognize is that such categories or models are merely abstractions pertaining to phenomena which are inextricably linked in believers' minds and in their social relations.[6]

With reference to the Hindus who now reside in a wide variety of contexts outside India, the categories of 'Little' and 'Great' Tradition are of even more limited value. For a host of reasons and in different ways, the range of religious phenomena so long associated with the Hindu 'Little Tradition' has been narrowed or displaced altogether among migrants and their descendants. Throughout the Hindu diaspora, there has occurred a general course of change which has 'led from village and caste beliefs and practices to wider, more universalistic definitions of Hinduism that cut across local and caste differences'.[7]

Anthropologists have described this trend in similar ways: regarding Hinduism in East Africa, one notes the occurrence of a 'complete fusion of "big" and "little" tradition elements';[8] regarding South Africa, it is suggested that migrants' beliefs and practices have evolved into a 'regional Hinduism' in their own right;[9] regarding Trinidad, Hindu phenomena characteristic of different analytical 'levels' and drawn from various regions of India have been described as historically 'homogenized' in the new context and, regarding Surinam, we read that 'Rituals and ceremonies peculiar to specific castes disappeared, as well as the division between a brahmanical religion of the higher castes and a folk religion of the lower castes.'[10] Especially due to the relatively small size and socially isolated status of their communities, a single corpus of belief and practice has usually come to be pervasive among Hindus in each post-colonial context outside India.[11] Thus to continue to describe the variety of Hindu beliefs and practices among overseas Hindus in terms of 'Little' and 'Great' Traditions – even by way of an ideal-type continuum – would be for the most part an irrelevant exercise.

Instead, it is suggested here that the notions 'official' and 'popular' religion may be more useful in describing strands or 'levels' of Hinduism in places like the Caribbean. 'Official' religion can be taken to mean a set of tenets, rites, proscriptions and prescriptions which are promulgated through some institutionalized framework: this usually entails a formal network of priests (often hierarchically structured) and/or a lay organization which determines orthodoxy and orthopraxy, arranges and administers a variety of socioreligious activities, usually controls some sort of communication network (such as publications or pronouncements dispensed through subordinate bodies – especially temples), and is often directly involved in religious education through schools and other programmes. 'Popular' religion can be understood basically as beliefs and practices undertaken or maintained by lay believers: these include orthodox practices undertaken outside 'official' auspices (especially domestic worship, but also including local festivals which celebrate mainstream deities or saints), so-called superstitious (magic–religious) and/or charismatic phenomena (such as healing rites, spirit-possession and exorcism, pursuits of miraculous ends, or steps taken to ward off evil forces), and 'cult' phenomena (collective religious activity directed toward some specific but usually unorthodox focus, such as an extraordinary person, sacred place or item, or supernatural being propitiated by a relative minority).

'Official' and 'popular' features are found in every world religion today, although in Hinduism (in India or abroad) they have a rather unique newness. Largely because it is without a founding prophet, central sacred text, geographical focal point or institutionalized priesthood, the sizeable cluster of traditions which has come to be deemed 'Hinduism' has, until relatively recently in its long history, been without an 'official' dimension. The resultant heterogeneity of belief and practice is Hinduism's leading characteristic, and has been cause for the anthropologists' conundrum of 'Great/Little Tradition'.

However, especially since the British imposition on India and the subsequent 'Hindu renaissance' of the early nineteenth century, there has been an increasing rationalization and institutionalization of Hindu beliefs and practices.[12] Consequently, a variety of organizations have arisen in India to provide Hinduism with new 'syndicated', 'corporate', or other 'official' forms. These range, for example, from the Brahmo Samaj and Arya Samaj (both of which advocate largely doctrinal and social reforms) through the Sanatana Dharma Raksini Sabha and Bharata Dharma Mahamandala (which arose, it might be said, as counter-reformist bodies seeking to standardize 'Great Tradition' tenets) to the Hindu Mahasabha and Shiv Sena (which have advocated conservative Hindu political activism). Still, their impact on Hindu religious traditions across India has been variable and sporadic (especially regarding village-level phenomena), and their membership or activity has been undercut by caste and class considerations. Outside of India in places like the Caribbean, on the other hand, such organizations have come to play a dominant role.

In order to trace adequately the development of 'official' Hinduism in the Caribbean, it is first necessary to examine migrants' religious backgrounds and early social conditions in the colonies. This chapter concentrates on the largest Hindu communities, those in Surinam, Trinidad and Guyana, where estimates suggest that Hindus respectively comprised 25 per cent, 25 per cent and 34 per cent of each country's total population of around 491,000 in Surinam, 1,062,000 in Trinidad and Tobago and 884,000 in Guyana during the mid-1980s.[13]

The Hinduism that Came

Throughout the period which witnessed the large-scale migration of Indians into the Caribbean under schemes of indentured labour, a total of 238,909 Indians arrived between 1838 and 1917 into what was then British Guiana, 143,939 into Trinidad during 1845–1917, and 34,304 into Surinam between 1873 and 1916; subsequent to the return of a number of migrants (32 per cent, 22 per cent and 34 per cent respectively) following the expiration of their five-year terms of indenture, this amounted to net immigration figures of 153,362 in British Guiana, 110,645 in Trinidad, and 22,745 in Surinam.[14] Hindus formed the overwhelming majority of these transplanted populations (around 85 per cent in each case).

Most migrants came as individuals, recruited piecemeal from vast areas of north-east and south-west India. Depending on their original region, district and village, migrants would have experienced substantial differences in culture (including language and dialect, dress, cuisine, caste composition and structure, architecture and village layout) and economy (including agricultural production and labour relations, taxation and patron-age, land distribution, local and distant markets). Their religious backgrounds, too, were highly idiosyncratic, reflecting parochial traditions of worship, pilgrimage, and festival observance as well as incorporating locally recognised sacred landscapes, varying influences of Islam or particular Hindu sects, dominating roles of castes with particular religious patterns.

The first major, geographically derived differences in socio-religious heritage can be inferred between migrant groups from North India (passing through the port of Calcutta) and South India (passing through Madras). Table 13.1 provides figures for these migrations during relevant years of operation.[15]

Thus in the early years of indentured immigration, there was a sizeable South Indian presence in the two main receiving colonies. Drawn from a number of Tamil districts (including

Table 13.1 *Migration from Calcutta and Madras to British Guiana (1845–62) and Trinidad (1845–60)*

	Madras	Calcutta	Total
British Guiana	11 459	37 270	48 729
	23.5%	76.5%	100%
Trinidad	4 992	17 624	22 616
	22.0%	78.0%	100%

Source: J. Geoghegan (1873) *Note on Emigration from India*, Calcutta: Government Printery; Government of Madras, Public Department, 1899–1916, pp. 79, 80

Trichinopoly, Ramnad, Tanjore and Salem) and Telegu districts (as far apart as Nellore, Ganjam and Vizagapatam), the South Indian Hindu migrants would tend to exhibit general religious characteristics of Shaivism (involving ascetic practices and non-Brahmanic rites directed towards Shiva), and to a lesser extent, Shaktism (involving ecstatic behaviour associated with cosmic power and healing derived from various goddesses). Regional variations in belief and practice were doubtless present among the South Indians, as they were among the far more numerous North Indian migrants. Table 13.2 provides data on the areas of origin for the latter migrants who passed through the port of Calcutta.[16]

Of the main North Indian areas of origin, Bengal, Bihar and Orissa have long been dominated by Shaktism (though Vaishnavism, or devotion to Vishnu and his incarnations, has had some influence particularly from the Chaitanya sect in Bengal), while eastern and western Uttar Pradesh (in what used to be called the Northwest Provinces or United Provinces of Agra and Oudh) and the Punjab are mainly Vaishnavite. Regardless of the regional religious patterns, however, each area is dotted with important, age-old centres of pilgrimage devoted to particular deities, which hold great sway over the religious orientation of surrounding vicinities. These include Shaivite, Vaishnavite and Shakti or Goddess sites (listed respectively for each) in West Bengal (Bishnupur, Kenduli, and Amta), Bihar (Sonpur, Gaya), eastern UP (Varamasi Ayodhya), western UP (Garmukhtesar, Soron, Deoband) and Orissa (Bhubaneswar, Puri Jaipur). In addition to propitiating the 'higher' Sanskritic gods, other

Table 13.2 *Areas of origin (by per cent) and total numbers of Indian migrants to Surinam,[1] Trinidad, British Guiana, 1874–1917*

	Surinam	Trinidad	British Guiana
Orissa	0.1	0.1	0.1
West Bengal[2]	0.9	0.9	1.0
Central Bengal	0.4	0.4	0.4
East Bengal	0.1	0.1	0.1
Bihar[3]	14.3	13.5	14.6
NW/United Provinces[4]	48.6	50.7	52.0
Oudh	28.1	24.4	24.6
Central Provinces	0.5	1.4	0.6
Central India	1.6	2.5	1.3
Ajmere	–	0.1	–
Punjab	1.6	1.9	1.5
Native States[5]	1.5	2.4	1.2
Nepal & Native States[6]	0.6	0.4	0.6
Bombay, Madras, etc.	0.9	0.7	1.4
TOTAL	99.2	99.5	99.4
Total number of migrants, 1874–1917	30 555	94 135	140 085

Source: Annual Reports, Protector of Emigrants, Calcutta
[1] No migration to Surinam recorded in 1874–5, 1875–6, 1885, 1887, 1897, 1900, 1903, 1910, 1911, 1915 or 1917.
[2] Includes Central Bengal after 1906.
[3] Includes Orissa after 1912.
[4] Called 'Northwest Provinces' (today's Uttar Pradesh) until 1902: thereafter called 'United Provinces of Agra and Oudh', though Oudh continued to be tabulated separately.
[5] Between 1897 and 1917.
[6] Migration from Nepal only recorded between 1874 and 1885; thereafter 'Nepal and Native States' recorded together between 1886 and 1896. Recruitment in Nepal discontinued after that final year.

deities are regionally popular as well, such as Gaininath, Naika, and Dharha in Bihar[17] and Bhumiya, Sitala, Joginya and Panch Pir in Uttar Pradesh.[18]

Though the bulk of Hindu migrants were drawn from three provinces, they came from a great number of districts within each, among them Cawnpore, Ghazipur, Basti and Azimgarh in the 'Northwest Provinces', Shahabad, Patna, Durbhiga and Gaya in Bihar, and Lucknow,

Fyzabad and Gonda in Oudh. Each district – and further, each village – recognized an array of supernatural beings and had various traditions associated with them. Such beings would locally include a protective village deity (*gramadevata*, often called a *dih*), saints or martyrs, ghosts, demons, witches as well as sacred or malevolent trees, river banks, wells, stones and animals.

A widely heterogeneous caste composition among Hindu immigrants also had religious consequences, since certain beliefs and practices were specific to these as well. Further, not only did certain castes have special deities and rites, but these varied from locale to locale. Thus one contemporary observer wrote that

> the manners and customs of the various castes vary from one end of the Province [UP] to the other ... A custom or mode of worship prevailing among a caste in Saharanpur or Ballia may or may not extend as far as Aligarh on the one side or Allahabad on the other.[19]

For instance, among some of the castes which came in large numbers from Uttar Pradesh to the Caribbean, Ahirs (cowherders) traditionally worshipped Bittiya and Vinchyabasini Devi in many places, but also Birnath in Mirsipur district and Bangaru Bai in south Bhandara: Kurmis (cultivators) generally worshipped Thakurji, but also Surdhir in Goruckpur and Babi Fir in Basti; and among Chamars (leatherworkers), a host of deities were worshipped from place to place, including Jagiswar, Nagarsen, Kuanwala, Sairi Devi and Parmeshwari. Finally, each lineage or clan within a caste had rites and other practices centring on a deity special to themselves (*kuldevata*).

Therefore, in sum, the Hinduism which came to the Caribbean was comprised of a profusion of religious traditions determined by the heterogeneity of the Hindu migrants themselves. Out of such a profusion, however, common forms were forged.

Early Hinduism in the Caribbean

Patterns of Hindu worship during the early years of Indian presence in the Caribbean seem to have been diffuse, by all available accounts. Goat

sacrifice – reflecting presumably non-Brahmanic activity – was observed in Trinidad in 1849 and in 1855, when a goat 'wearing garlands of red flowers and surrounded by pans of washed rice and bottles of molasses and rum ... was beheaded to the sound of drums ...'.[20] In 1865, a Christian missionary in Trinidad visited

> a place where the Hindus sacrifice. There was a pole with a small flag flying, a small altar of mud, and near it two stakes ... a sort of yoke into which the neck of the goat to be sacrificed is placed and its head severed at one blow. The blood is burned on the altar and the body made a feast of.[21]

The same missionary explained that at this time, Hindu rites were bound to occur anywhere, since 'They had no temples. Gatherings for worship were conducted at any selected spot by their Brahmans or priests': moreover, 'each priest had his own disciples'.[22]

Uncoordinated and perhaps random rites and practices at that time would be quite expectable, given the basic fact that early migrants on colonial estates were so linguistically disunited due to their diverse areas of origin. Bengali, Hindi, Maithili, Magahi, Punjabi, Telugu, Tamil, tribal languages and others were spoken by the immigrants, as were dialects such as Kanauji, Avadhi, Bhojpuri, Brajbhasa and Tondai Nadu. A missionary in British Guiana pointed out,

> nearly all these languages spoken in India are in free and constant use among them in the Colony, and only a very small portion among our immigrants can understand more than one language.[23]

He explained that

> The proprietors or managers of sugar estates purposely choose men speaking three or four separate and distinct languages not understood by each other, in order to prevent combination in cases of disturbances among them ...

'When these people meet in Trinidad,' one contemporary Englishman wrote, 'it strikes one as somewhat strange that they may have to point to water and rice, and ask each other what they call it in their language.'[24] Gradually through the years, a common, creolized Indian tongue or 'plantation Hindustani'[25] developed in each Caribbean context (based largely on Bhojpuri and Avadhi, and blended with non-Indian languages especially in the case of Sarnami in Surinam).[26] Until that time, however, collective religious activity was doubtless hindered by lack of effective communication among the transplanted Hindus.

Religious activities among the indentured Indians were quite tolerated – even facilitated – by plantation managers, as long as these activities did not conflict with economic production.[27] Yet, given the breadth of religious traditions which characterized the migrants' backgrounds, consensus on devotional focus and procedure was probably hard to achieve at first. In British Guiana, for instance, Bronkhurst suggested that Vaishnavites and Shaivites were 'strenuously contending for the supremacy of the chief object of their worship, and the consequent inferiority of the other'.[28] (It is perhaps more plausible that Bronkhurst actually discerned some division between North Indians, mainly comprising followers of the former broad orientation, and South Indians, generally equated with the latter, because among North Indians alone such contention between Vaishnavites and Shaivites would be less likely since they have co-evolved for centuries in that part of the subcontinent.) There has been no major distinction between Vaishnavites and Shaivites in Surinam,[29] basically because the colony never received shipments of South Indians.

Some Hindus may have tried to continue propitiating traditions directed toward regional, village, caste or kin group gods, but the basic fact that they were an amalgam of Indians, thrust together on plantations far from India, militated against any such successful continuity. The absence of shrines, legend-filled landscapes, and co-believers would spell the rapid relinquishment of parochial traditions – psychologically distressing though this may have been to many migrants. Certain sects or orders were more successful in maintaining their ways, however, since these were roughly institutionalized prior to migration.

Towards the end of the nineteenth century. Comins[30] described the presence of Ramanandis, Kabir panthis, Aghor panthis, and Swaminarayanis in Trinidad, the traditions of which have remained in one form or another up to the present day.

Eventually, more durable, collective modes of Hindu worship were established in the colonies, evident particularly in the creation of temples. In many estates and nascent villages, small shrines (in the form of raised platforms with clay images) persisted through the nineteenth century. Yet very gradually, more elaborate structures were constructed, often with the help and encouragement of the estate management (who, Moore suggests,[31] saw this as a way to keep the Indian workers socio-culturally isolated and therefore more easily manipulated). Underhill[32] pointed to one of the earliest temples in Trinidad, while the novelist Charles Kingsley provided the first detailed description of such structures observed in 1871:

> Their mark is, generally, a long bamboo with a pennon atop, outside a low dark hut, with a broad flat veranda, or rather shed, outside the door. Under the latter, opposite each door ... is a stone or small stump, on which offerings are made of red dust and flowers. From it the worshippers can see the images within.
>
> ... Sometimes these have been carved in the island. Sometimes the poor folk have taken the trouble to bring them all the way from India on board ship. Hung beside them on the walls are little pictures, often very well executed in the miniature-like Hindoo style by native artists in the island. Large brass pots, which have some sacred meaning, stand about, and with them a curious trident-shaped stand, about four feet high, on the horns of which garlands of flowers are hung as offerings. The visitor is told that the male figures are Mahadeva, and the female Kali. ...[33]

Bronkhurst likewise gave us a good account of Hindu temples in Guiana:

> A Hindu temple is not constructed like a Christian sanctuary. ... It is not intended to accommodate a crowd of worshippers within its walls. Its worshippers stand outside in an area

opposite the door which is the only entrance belonging to the building. The priest, the representative of the people, is the only person who enters the temple through that door in order to perform the duties of his office in the presence of the idol, which stands at the lower end of the door, and so placed that the worshippers from outside might have a full view of, and fall down before it. There is no window to a Hindu temple to let in light or admit air. The room, including the small space which is called the residence of the idol (*Swami stalam*), before which burns a small oil lamp, and the space sufficiently spacious for the temple utensils, the offerings, and the officiating priest to stir or move about, is always dark and awe-inspiring. ... These hut-temples are considered so sacred by the coolies, on account of the visible presence of the deity – the idol – they worship, that no unclean person can enter any of them without the preparatory ablutions being performed. ... (Italics in original.)

These small *shivalas* and *kitis* (or *kutiyas*), also described in Trinidad by Froude,[34] appear to have closely resembled those normally found in villages of Bihar and Uttar Pradesh. In Guiana, only two small temples were observed by a Royal Commission in the 1860s; by the onset of the 1890s, at least 33 Hindu temples were to be found, funded through individual donation or group subscription. By the early twentieth century, such structures were commonplace in most estates and Indian villages.[35]

The celebration of Hindu festivals, too, grew in number and importance by the early part of this century. Lengthy and elaborate plays (Ram Lila, Krishna) depicting stories of the gods were performed in estates and villages in the nineteenth century, and Diwali and Phagwa (Holi) were the most popular annual events celebrated by Hindus in the colonies by the turn of the century. And whereas Comins, based on a visit of a mere ten days, believed there were few Indian festivals celebrated in Surinam, Emmer suggests that no less than 32 Hindu festivals were annually recognized on Surinamese colonial estates.

Some of the earliest Hindu activities became notorious, however, which led to their suppression. One was a practice in which a devotee would impale various points of his flesh with hooks and subsequently swing by them from a pole. Oddie notes that during the nineteenth century, this was widespread in both Bengal (where it was known as *chrak puja*, a penitential rite directed to Shiva) and in South India (called *soodaloo* or *chedul*, a self-sacrificial rite to a goddess).[36] This proved too 'barbaric' for white colonists, and hook-swinging was banned in British Guiana in 1853.[37] Another extraordinary Hindu activity was fire-walking, a *shakti*-oriented practice which – though carried out in Bihar and the tribal states as well as in South India – became wholly associated with the immigrant 'Madrassis'.[38] In Trinidad, Collens reported that 'it is not observed by Hindus of Northern India, but, on the contrary, is repudiated by them'.[39] Though publicly suppressed, fire-walking continued in 'Madrassi' circles in both Trinidad and British Guiana until at least the mid-twentieth century. Animal sacrifice was abhorred by colonists as well, and was looked down upon by Brahmans and other Hindus, too; however, this still continues in the Caribbean as part of non-orthodox observances.

Apart from occasional celebrations or temple-based activity, it was the ordinary, daily practices which formed what could be considered the core of Hindu religiosity in the early years of Caribbean settlement. Sacred plants, vessels and implements used in worship, and images of deities were brought from India,[40] Hindu scriptures were imported and sold, and wandering Brahmans and sadhus gathered Hindus, told tales and expounded beliefs. All these elements contributed to the construction of a religiously affirmative environment. The domestic sphere was perhaps of greatest importance, since it was where the most common beliefs and modes of worship were perpetuated by the migrants and taught to their offspring. Household shrines, personal prayers and small acts performed by various family members constitute the essential ingredients of Hinduism in any of its forms or traditions, and these were carried out in the colonies among plantation barracks and homes in the early villages. Invoking images of village life in North India itself, Kingsley provided a print of a Hindu performing morning oblation outside of a thatched house in Trinidad, while Bronkhurst observed that in British Guiana,

> Before a Coolie eats, he places a small quantity of the prepared food before the idol or god of the house to propitiate his favour. ... Rising at dawn, the Hindu goes to the trench, or takes the water into his own yard, and there, with religious care, he cleanses his teeth, performs his sacred ablutions, imprints the emblems of his faith upon his forehead, arm, and breast, visits the idol of the house, or faces the rising sun, before which he falls down ... (The Colony of British Guiana and Its Labouring Population, 1883; pp. 257–8)

However normal such basic religious practices became in the nineteenth-century Caribbean, though, the fact remained that Hinduism was a minority religion – considered 'heathen' and even demonic by members of the ruling community – within highly pluralistic societies. This situation had the effect of stimulating self-consciousness about religious beliefs and practices, which subsequently entailed perhaps deeper reflections on choice in religious belief and practice, more attempts to justify ideas and activities, and more sharpened skills at defending religious tenets than would have been the case in villages of India. Exacerbating these circumstances were missionary activities directed primarily at Hindus, especially by Methodists and Anglicans in British Guiana, Moravians in Surinam, and Presbyterians in Trinidad.[41] While these missions were not without considerable success (some 10 per cent of Indians in British Guiana and Trinidad were Christian by 1911),[42] many Brahman pundits became quite adept at verbal combat with Christians, and through such channels, Hinduism came to be portrayed more and more as a unitary religion on social and doctrinal par with any other in the colonies. In time, formal Hindu organizations were established with the expressed goal of standardizing and promulgating such an opinion.

The Growth of 'Official' Hinduism in the Caribbean

Probably the most significant socio-religious change that occurred among Hindus in the Caribbean, and one which was a prerequisite for the rise of an institutionalized and all-embracing Hindu orthodoxy, was the attenuation of the caste system. Space does not permit a full treatment of the whys and wherefores of this process as it occurred in the Caribbean.[43] In the Caribbean, specific caste *identities* were often retained through the years (particularly in terms of *varna*, and to a much more limited extent, of *jat*, and only effectively called into play in the arrangement of marriages or sometimes with regard to claims of public status). Yet caste could never be transplanted as a *system* (as it was in India, simultaneously being a hierarchy and social relationships, a network of economic interdependence, an order of reciprocal ritual duties, and a conceptual continuum of ontological states according to notions of purity and pollution). This inability for reconstruction occurred because the caste system is a highly localized phenomenon in villages of India; it had no chance of being maintained through historical conditions in which individual members of diverse caste groups (many unheard of from one region to another) were plucked out of local hierarchies throughout North and South India and placed together in contexts where their proximity and commensality, economic activities, and social relationships were managed by non-Indians on estates and, after indenture, altered by wholly alien socio-economic circumstances. For most practical purposes, this resulted in a new kind of egalitarianism among Hindus in the Caribbean.

Yet Brahmans retained a special religious role, albeit different from that in India. 'As pandits', van der Burg and van der Veer point out, 'they monopolized the sacred knowledge of rituals and Sanskrit texts, so that ritual knowledge replaced purity as the legitimation of the Brahaman's status.'[44] In the new context of the Caribbean. Brahmans gained clients for their ritual services by offering to all – regardless of caste background – the beliefs and practices previously within their own exclusive preserve (that is, the features characterized by some as being of the 'Great Tradition' of Hinduism). The 'Brahmanization' of Hinduism thus occurred in the Caribbean, whereby throughout each Hindu community, a core of Brahmanic ritual directed towards Sanskritic gods came into ascendency.

These Brahman-dominated practices, which became the routine features of Hinduism in all three Caribbean territories, included the performance of formal *puja* (involving Sanskrit formulae governing sixteen offerings, or *shodasopachara*, made to various deities – though Hanuman *puja* was by far the most popular in all three contexts under consideration), *samskaras* (rites of passage marking key life-stages), *kathas* (routinized recitals of sacred lore, particularly a text devoted to Satyanarayan), weddings (though only the climatic formal rites were overseen by Brahmans), funerals (involving a host of ceremonies over a period of at least ten days), a *bhagwats* or *yagnas* (remarkable socio-religious activities centred on the reading of a sacred text – usually the Shrimad Bhagavata Purana – spanning seven, nine, or fourteen days and involving a variety of rites, massive communal meals [indicative of caste's demise], and much social interaction among possibly hundreds of participants). These have continued through to the present, often in vibrant and uniquely modified forms.

Organizational development of this 'Brahmanized' Hinduism was marginal for some time before undergoing a rapid acceleration. In Trinidad, for instance, a Sanatan Dharma Association was said to have existed since 1881,[45] though it is not known for having accomplished much in terms of influence or activity. By the 1920s, other small, Brahman-led groups were in existence (such as the Prabartakh Sabha of Debe and the San Fernando Hindu Sabha), but their endeavours were modest and essentially of local scope. Also, during the early decades of the century, a loose kind of pundits' *parishad* or council was said to have existed between Brahman priests in Trinidad, Surinam and British Guiana, such that their communication – though more through an informal network than through official channels – did much to standardize practices within the region. Such communication, including trips to perform rites, was most frequent between pundits in British Guiana and Surinam, owing to their common border. (It was even common for individuals from one country to have a Brahman 'godfather' [*guru*] in the other.)

In all three contexts, the undoubtable catalyst for the national organization of a unitary, standardized Brahmanic Hinduism was the introduction of the Arya Samaj into the Caribbean. The Arya Samaj, a reformist movement calling for a Vedic purification of Hindu belief and practice, was established in the Punjab by Swami Dayanand Saraswati in 1875. This radical movement had tremendous impact across North India, where it forced many Hindus to reflect on and articulate what it was they themselves believed. The result was a conservative backlash, part of which involved the creation of formal bodies to promote a formulated, 'official' orthodoxy deemed 'Sanatan Dharma' ('the eternal duty or order' – though 'dharma', here, came to mean something more like 'religion' in its Western sense). The Arya Samaj sent well-trained missionaries from India to Hindu communities throughout the diaspora, where they had identical effects.

A succession of Arya Samaji missionaries undertook prolonged visits to three Caribbean colonies. The first arrived in British Guiana in 1910, travelling that same year to Trinidad. Surinam received its first representative from the Samaj in 1912. Visits turned into sustained presence by the 1930s, highlighted by the charismatic personalities of Mehta Jaimani and Ayodhya Prasad. The Arya Samajis caused much consternation within Hindu communities through their staunch and knowledgeable advocacy of fundamental reforms in doctrine (especially by way of promoting their exclusive, Vedic-centred monotheism and rejection of idols) and in social structure (including efforts to upgrade the status of women and to criticize the Brahmans' self-ascribed authority). In each country, great debates were waged between Arya Samaji and 'Sanatanist' camps, some even ending in violent clashes.[46]

Just as in India, the forces of Brahmanism came together in each Caribbean country to create a sustained front against the Arya Samaj and to quell the air of doubt which the reformists had sent rippling through the Hindu population. This involved moves to tighten and structure their own ranks through organizational effort. In 1927, a Pundits' Council was formed in British

Guiana to act as the sole authority concerning matters of doctrine and ritual, along with the Sanatan Dharma Sabha, created to act as a national representative body for Hindus in British Guiana. In Surinam, the Sanatan Dharma (sic) was founded in 1929 to fulfil a similar role. In Trinidad, the dormant Sanatan Dharma Association was revitalized and incorporated in 1932, the same year a rival Brahmanic body was formed, the Sanatan Dharma Board of Control. And in 1934, the Sanatan Dharma Maha Sabha was established as the most prominent Hindu organization in British Guiana. (Meanwhile, the Arya Samajis had followed suit by instituting formal bodies, too: the Arya Dewaker in Surinam in 1930 and the Arya Samaj Association – later called the Arya Pritinidhi Sabha – in Trinidad in 1934.) Most of these Caribbean Hindu organizations forged links with kindred associations in India, thereby declaring further justification for the 'official' forms of Hinduism which they propagated. The unitary and Brahmanic thrust of these is exemplified by Trinidad's Sanatan Dharma Board of Control, which stated:

The registration of this society is regarded by the Hindu community as being an important step in the direction of the unification of Hindu interests ... and it is laid down as a definite policy that the Board of Control shall always be predominantly composed of orthodox, practicing pundits.[47]

These 'Sanatanist' organizations consolidated much support, especially from rural Hindus who preferred conservative modes of worship. They thereby far eclipsed the Arya Samaj, whose supporters tended to be well-educated, middle-class Hindus. In each country, the 'Sanatanist' groups achieved other important gains during the 1930s and 1940s when – after years of difficult campaigning – they succeeded in obtaining, from the respective colonial governments, legal recognition of Hindu marriages and permission to perform cremations. But perhaps the most effective organizational developments were those of Trinidad's Sanatan Dharma Maha Sabha, the body created in 1952 by Bhadase Sagan Maraj after he united the country's two

previously rival Sanatanist organizations. In addition to obtaining the affiliation of dozens of temple congregations throughout the island (coordinated by the Maha Sabha's Pundits' parishad). Maraj oversaw the construction of no less than thirty-one Hindu schools between 1952 and 1956.

With such schools, temples, publications, collective celebrations, and the participation of almost every Brahman pundit, these highly centralized Hindu bodies culminated the long processes of standardizing and routinizing Hindu belief and practice in Trinidad, Surinam and British Guiana. In each context, the national organizations dominated Hinduism in ways akin to those which Smith described regarding the Sanatan Dharma Maha Sabha in British Guiana during the 1950s and early 1960s:

This form of Hinduism [promulgated by the Maha Sabha] has gradually replaced all the lower-caste cults and special practices which used to exist among the immigrants, and it claims the affiliation of practically all the temples in the country. With its sister organisation, the British Guiana Pundits' Council, it may be said to control orthodox Hinduism (or the nearest Guianese equivalent to it), in British Guiana, and has come to constitute a 'church' in the technical sense.[48]

The 'official' Hindu bodies became so predominant, in fact, that they became major political forces. The Brahman leaders of Sanatan Dharm in Surinam established their own, short-lived Surinamese Hindoe Partij in the late 1940s; they later merged with other Indian parties to form the Verenigde Hindostaanse Partij, but continued to play a central part in this party's endeavours.[49] In Trinidad, under the strongarm tactics of Bhadase Maraj, the leadership and support of the People's Democratic Party (later becoming the Democratic Labour Party) was virtually indistinguishable from that of the Maha Sabha.[50] And in British Guiana, though the Indian-backed party was Cheddi Jagan's explicitly Marxist People's Progressive Party, it, too, was comprised of many Maha Sabha leaders.[51] Thus Hinduism had not only been 'Brahmanized' and 'officially' standardized, it had now become 'politicized'. This was particularly the case in the years immediately preceding each nation's independence (Trinidad 1962, Guyana 1966, Surinam 1975), when there were fears of political repression under Creole-backed parties – fears which have been subsequently justified.

Though the central 'Sanatanist' bodies have continued to hold much financial and organizational power, their popularity with average Hindus has greatly dwindled. This is especially so in Trinidad and Guyana. Many Hindus cite the Maha Sabhas' lack of assistance toward affiliated schools and temples, along with the arrogance of associated pundits, as reasons for this. But perhaps most damage was done in Guyana in the late 1960s and early 1970s, when the ruling, Creole-backed People's National Congress successfully gained sway over the Maha Sabha leadership, an intolerable occurrence in the eyes of average Hindus. Similarly, Trinidad's Maha Sabha suffered a crisis in leadership following the death of Maraj in 1971; much of the Hindu community grew dismayed with the Maha Sabha due to the ensuing political infighting and allegations of misconduct and corruption – made worse by its eventual leader's public support for the Creole-backed government of the People's National Movement.

Instead, new, alternative Hindu organizations have been created. While still advocating the same type of essentially Brahmanic, Sanskritic Hinduism, these have become more popular by demonstrating more grassroots activity and, importantly, more attention to the interests of young people, than the centralized organizations. These include the Nav Yuvak Sabha in Surinam, the Gandhi Youth Organisation in Guyana, the Hindu Seva Sangh in Trinidad, [and] a number of other groups operating locally through mutually supportive networks.

Today a great deal of Hindu socio-religious activity in Surinam, Trinidad and Guyana takes place under the formal direction of the national bodies and the alternative groups. Yet much occurs outside of these auspices as well. The current range of all types of practice can be described with reference to their degree of institutionalization (that is, very basically, the extent to which activities are arranged and managed by set individuals

performing specific roles) – in other words, from most 'official' to most 'popular' modes of religion.

Contemporary Caribbean Hinduism

The following list provides a classification of the most common contemporary Hindu practices in Surinam, Trinidad and Guyana. The sequence of listed items is according to the degree of ordered, collective activity (or, again, extent of institutionalization) undertaken in each type of practice.

A. Official forms

This rubric concerns those activities directly undertaken by the central, national organization (Maha Sabha) in each country. These include: weekly rites and *Kathas* held at temples; large-scale celebrations of annual holy days (particularly Divali, Phagua, Ramnaumi, Shivratri, and Krishna Janashtami – though affiliated temples also celebrate, on local levels, Navratri, Ganesh jyanti, Katik nahan, and Vasant panchmi): publications (including prayer books) and radio programmes; religious curricula in affiliated schools; contests (for Hindi language skills, debating, *chautal* singing [particular to Phagua season] and other arts); and, importantly, the pundits' *parishad* whereby doctrine and procedure is monitored.

B. Alternative official forms

Concerning most of the same activities listed above, these are only undertaken by organizations other than the Maha Sabhas, including practices in non-Maha Sabha-affiliated temples. Small-scale committees or groups (*goles* and *mandals*) also exist in villages for the specific purpose of holding *yagnas* and Ramayan *satsangs* (local meetings in which Tulsidas' epic is recited). Such alternative bodies have also creatively established practices aimed at Hindu youth, such as summer camps, marches, fund-raising bazaars, sports clubs and theatre groups.

A wholly different set of 'alternative official' Hindu phenomena is that centred on Kali worship (generally known as Kali Mai Puja), which has been gaining support in Guyana from a wide segment of the Hindu community (and among some Creoles) for many years.[52] More recently it has been reinstituted in Trinidad.[53] The tradition has developed from Shakti-oriented practices observed among the so-called 'Madrassis' in Guyana since the middle of the nineteenth century. These routinely involved animal sacrifice, possession (altered states of consciousness), and the worship of deities characteristic of South Indian Hinduism (such as Katheri, Munishwaran, Madraviran and Mariamma – the latter often identified with Kali). Such non-Brahmanic practices have long been castigated by pundits and others advocating a Sanskritic, 'Sanatanist' Hindu religion in the colonies. In Surinam, the tradition never really existed since the colony lacked South Indian practitioners: in Trinidad, it remained only in isolated pockets where 'Madrassis' had settled in number, but in [British] Guiana, Kali Mai Puja became an active religious tradition (particularly in Demerara, which is home to a large proportion of South Indian descendants). Its mode of worship became increasingly standardized in the 1920s and 1930s under the direction of Kistima Naidoo, apparently waned in attendance during the 1940s and 1950s and has undergone a prominent renewal under James Naidoo since the 1960s. There are now estimated to be some one-hundred Kali 'churches' (*koeloos*) throughout Guyana, exhibiting numerous variations from the core set of rites long associated with the tradition. There are presently formal bodies representing this form of Hinduism, such as the Guyana Maha Kali Religious Organization.

There are also other formally organized Hindu traditions, regarded as 'non-Sanatanist', which are present in the Caribbean, including those of Kabir Panthis, Sieunarinis (Swaminarayanis), Arya Samajis, devotees of Satya Sai Baba, 'Hare Krishnas' (members of the International Society for Krishna Consciousness) and followers of various Hindu-derived yoga and meditation groups. These are quite small in membership, and moreover, their members quite often participate in 'Sanatanist' activities with little dissidence.

C. Collective forms

These are religious activities self-organized by groups of people (especially networks of extended kin and/or co-villagers). They include annual festivals marking important periods of the Hindu calendar, such as celebrations for Divali (plays, Lakshmi Puja, and the building of elaborate lighting displays) and Phagua (*chautal* singing, the construction and burning of a *Holika* bonfire, and traditional forms of playing with red dye), the staging of Ram Lila or Krishna Lila plays, and the cooperative management of *yagnas* and *satsangs* sponsored by individuals. Weddings and funerals are usually fairly large events organized *ad hoc* by groups of family and friends who systematically undertake a considerable number of chores in order to perform successfully the elaborate complex of accompanying rites. Also considered under this heading are the last vestiges of caste-specific rites: namely, sacrifices of hogs to the goddess Parmeshwari, still performed privately only by a few Chamar families.

D. Domestic forms

Religious activities conducted in the home by members of Hindu families include: *pujas* (sponsored annually or for special occasions – such as birthdays or anniversaries – in which a pundit is hired to perform the necessary Sanskritic rites; this is ideally undertaken over a weekend period, with Fridays reserved for Hanuman Puja, Saturday for Satyanarayan *Katha*, and Sunday for Suruj Narayan Puja); *samskaras* (naturally held at the appropriate times of children's lives – though presently, perhaps only three to five of the prescribed 16 rites are actually performed for most Caribbean Hindus); daily rites (usually performed by children or grandparents, involving prayers and the lighting of incense and lamps at an indoor shrine and/or outside in a little sanctum at the base of the house's *jhandi*,[54] or coloured flags erected on occasion of *pujas*); and infrequent pilgrimages (to rivers or the sea [representative of the Ganges in all three countries] or to special sites such as in Trinidad, where one small temple has an allegedly growing stone [regarded as a Shiva *linga*] and a Catholic church has a reportedly miraculous statue of the Virgin Mary [regarded by many Hindus as a manifestation of the one great Goddess]).

E. Individual forms

It is harder to list religious phenomena in this category, since they are by definition idiosyncratic. These features generally involve a person's *ishtdevata*, or form of god chosen for personal worship (such as Hanuman, Krishna, Durga or Shiva), and individual mode of worship (such as paying devotion to special images or symbols, reciting certain prayers at particular times, fasting on specific days of the week or periods of the year, making votive offerings and fulfilling promises to the god in given manners, and so on). Also of an essentially individual nature is the *mantra* (Sanskrit sound or prayer) imparted to a person by their Brahman 'godfather' on occasion of *gurumukh*, the 'christening' *samskara*.

F. 'Amorphous' or peripheral forms

Because a considerable set of beliefs and practices fall far outside the 'official' forms of Hinduism, as these have come to be constructed in the Caribbean contexts, they have often been maintained in a rather clandestine and unformulated, often quite vague, manner by a decreasing minority. These are usually directed toward therapeutic or protective ends, and include: beliefs and precautions regarding the evil eye (*najar* or *malja*), *jharay* and *phukay* (the use of specific *mantras* and motions to cure various afflictions), *tabij* (talismans) and *totka* (specific acts to undo the work of malevolent forces or omens), *ojha* (black magic, often blended with Creole forms, called *obeah*), exorcism of ill-meaning spirits, and offerings to minor deities (especially Dih, originally a guardian village godling, and 'the seven sisters' – which, though few can actually name them, are conceived to be manifestations of the Goddess).

Conclusion: Ongoing Trends and Debates

The transformation of Hinduism in Surinam, Trinidad and Guyana is by no means complete. The long process of 'Brahmanization' and standardization, which culminated in domination by centralized organizations, has begun to unravel. A kind of fragmentation has begun – yet not one which necessarily divides Hindus, but rather, one

in which Hindus are again recognizing the viability of a diversity of devotional orientations and modes of worship. Thus a more 'ecumenical', rather than unitary, type of Hinduism may be developing.

The beliefs and practices of 'Sanatan Dharma' are still by far the most pervasive – particularly among older Hindus, but also among a considerable number of youths. Yet especially among the well-educated young people in each of these countries, interest is building in more philosophical and less sacerdotal forms of Hinduism (such as the teachings of Vivekananda and Aurobindo); this trend is fostered by some of the 'alternative' Hindu associations. Whatever the variety of approach taken by various groups and individuals, however, they are all being justified under the banner of *bhakti* (devotion to God) – even Kali Mai Puja, in which *bhakti* has been equated with *shakti* (such that the manifestation of divine energy is a sign of true devotion).

But the trend toward acceptable heterogeneity is not proving smooth, and several issues are presently being debated. These include: the questions as to whether only Brahmans can serve as priests, the place of Hindi and Sanskrit in Hinduism, which is a key part of the general quandary of Caribbean Hindus' relation to India, the role of women in Hinduism, and the problem of whether certain practices should be deemed 'low' and therefore undesirable.

Very much in contradiction to the statements of pessimistic observers during the 1960s, who predicted the religion's final demise in the Caribbean, Hinduism is thriving in Surinam, Trinidad and Guyana. The beliefs and practices which were drawn from throughout the subcontinent, merged and modified in new contexts, formulated and formally managed by purpose-made authoritative bodies, are now being maintained in a variety of ways, on a number of 'levels', in cities and villages of each nation.

Notes

1 Burghart, Richard, 'The perpetuation of Hinduism in an alien cultural milieu', in *Hinduism in Great Britain*, Richard Burghart (ed.) (London, 1987), pp. 224–51.
2 Frykenberg, T. 'The emergence of modern "Hinduism" as a concept and as an institution', in *Hinduism Reconsidered*, H. Kulke and G. D. Sontheimer (eds) (Delhi, 1989).
3 Marriott, McKim, 'Little communities in an indigenous civilization', in *Village India*, McKim Marriott (ed.) (Chicago; 1955), pp. 171–223.

4   Leach, Edmund (ed.), *Dialectic in Practical Religion* (Cambridge, 1968).

5   Weightman, Simon. *Hinduism in the Village Setting* (Milton Keynes, 1978).

6   Pocock, David, *Mind, Body and Wealth* (Oxford, 1978), p. xiv.

7   Jayawardena, Chandra, 'Migration and social change: a survey of Indian communities overseas', *Geographical Review* 58, pp. 426–49.

8   Bharati, Agehananda, 'A social survey', in *Portrait of a Minority: Asians in East Africa*, Dharam P. Ghai and Yash P. Ghai (eds) (Nairobi, 1970), pp. 15–67.

9   Kuper, Hilda, 'An interpretation of Hindu marriage in Durban', *African Studies* 16, pp. 221–85.

10 Van der Burg, Corstian and Peter van der Veer, 'Pundits, power and profit: religious organization and the construction of identity among the Surinamese Hindus', *Ethnic and Racial Studies* Vol. 9, no. 4, pp. 514–28.

11 This is not the case among postwar Indian migrants to Western countries like Britain and the United States: instead, these migrants have often retained many sectarian, caste-based or regionally specific Hindu traditions. Reasons for this include: migration and settlement in large group numbers (as opposed to indentured migrants' transplantation as individuals), allowing for the continued use of regional language (whereas these had been blended or attenuated in places like the Caribbean) and for the greater maintenance of caste identities (which have largely disappeared among the post-indenture descendants); also, [later] migrants have been able to retain social and economic links with India.

12 Bellah, Robert, 'Epilogue: religion [were] progress in modern Asia', in *Religion and Progress in Modern Asia*, Robert N. Bellah (ed.) (New York, 1965), pp. 168–229.

13 Population figures of Surinam [were] especially difficult to estimate due to mass emigration to the Netherlands (perhaps 80,000 or more, largely Indians) over [a period of] fifteen or more years. Similarly, Indians have been leaving Guyana increasingly since the 1960s, and a predominantly Indian exodus seems to [have] been underway in Trinidad. All of these flights stemmed from worsening economic and political circumstances.

14 Lawrence, K. O., *Immigration into the West Indies in the 19th Century* (St Lawrence, Barbados, 1971), p. 57.

15 During these years, migration from Madras was sporadic due to restriction imposed following high mortality rates at sea and abroad. The scheme for indentured migration from Madras to the Caribbean was terminated completely in 1862, long before the commencement of Indian migration to Surinam (however, over 3,000 South Indians were again shipped to Trinidad during 1905, 1910 and 1911, and a further 376 to British Guiana in 1913 and 1914; Govt of Madras, *Annual Reports 1899–1916*). Reasons for this termination included: strong competition from Mauritius in recruiting workers, lack of both a suitable depot and an active recruitment service in Madras, and colonial planters' dissatisfaction with the working and other habits of the so-called 'Madrassis' (generally attributed to the contemporary notion that these migrants were originally city dwellers, as opposed to the rurally derived 'Calcuttans'; though this may have been true in some cases, some now suggest that many of the South Indian migrants were originally coastal fishermen, an occupation which many indeed took up in Guiana following their indentureship).

16 The reader should bear in mind that these figures are cumulative, and that migration from the various districts varied importantly over the years. For instance, migration from Bihar to all colonies was high in the 1880s, but dropped substantially by the turn of the century; conversely, migration from the Native States (and therefore, of tribals or *janglis*) and from Central India rose considerably after the turn of the century, especially to Trinidad. Variation over the years is attributable to many factors, such as local droughts and famines, recruitment strategies or government restrictions. Variation between colonies is due to the fact that different numbers were requisitioned by planters in each territory, and that British Guiana (Demerara), Trinidad and Surinam had separate recruiting agencies and depots based in Calcutta.

17 Grierson, G., *Bihar Peasant Life* (London, 1885), pp. 403–7.

18 Planalp, Jack M., *Religious Life and Values in a North Indian Village*, PhD Diss., Cornell University, 1956, pp. 159–61.

19 Crooke, William, *The Tribes and Castes of the North-Western Provinces and Oudh*. 4 vols (Calcutta, 1986), Vol. I, p. vi.

20 Wood, Donald, *Trinidad in Transition* (London, 1968), p. 150.

21 Morton, S., *John Morton of Trinidad* (Toronto, 1916), p. 23.

22 Ibid., p. 52.

23 Bronkhurst. H. V. P., *The Colony of British Guiana and Its Labouring Population* (London, 1883), p. 226.

24 Gamble, W. H., *Trinidad: Historical and Descriptive* (London, 1866), p. 34.

25 Tinker, Hugh, *A New System of Slavery* (London, 1974), p. 208.

26 Durbin, Mridula Adenwala, 'Formal changes in Trinidad Hindi as a result of language adaptation', *American Anthropologist* 75, 1978, pp. 1290–1304.

27 Ramnarine, Tyran, *The Growth of the East Indian Community in British Guiana*, 1880–1920. PhD Diss., University of Sussex, 1977, p. 199.

28 Bronkhurst, H. V. P., *Among the Hindus and Creoles of British Guiana* (London, 1888), p. 17.

29 Arya, U., *Ritual Songs and Folksongs of the Hindus of Surinam* (Leiden, 1968), p. 35.

30 Comins, D. W., *Note on Emigration from India to Trinidad* (Calcutta, 1893).

31 Moore, Robert James, *East Indians and Negroes in British Guiana, 1833–1880*. PhD Diss., University of Sussex, 1970, pp. 369–70.

32 Underhill, Edward Bean, *The West Indies: Their Social and Religious Condition* (London, 1862), p. 52.

33 Kingsley, Charles, *At Last, a Christmas in the West Indies* (London, 1905), p. 300.

34 Froude, James A., *The English in the West Indies* (London, 1888), pp. 75–6.

35 MacNeill. J. and C. Lal, *Report on the Condition of Indian Immigrants in the Four British Colonies: Trinidad, British Guiana or Demerara, Jamaica and Fiji and in the Dutch Colony of Surinam or Dutch Guiana* (Simla: Government Central Press, 1914), p. 73.

36 Oddie, G. A., 'Regional and other variations in popular religion in India: Hook-swinging in Bengal and Madras in the nineteenth century', *South Asia* 10, 1987, pp. 1–10.

37 Mangru, B., *Benevolent Neutrality* (London, 1987), pp. 170–1.

38 O'Malley L. S. S., *Popular Hinduism* (Cambridge, 1935), p. 160.

39 Collens, J. H., *A Guide to Trinidad* (London, 1888), p. 235.

40 Poynting, Jeremy, *Literature and Cultural Pluralism: The East Indian in the Caribbean*. PhD Diss., University of Leeds, 1985, p. 327.

41 Samaroo Brinsley, 'Missionary methods and local responses: The Canadian Presbyterians and the East Indians in the Caribbean', in *East Indians in the Caribbean*, B. Brereton and W. Dookeran (eds). (London, 1982), pp. 93–115.

42 Singaravelou, *Les Indiens de la Caraïbe*, 3 vols. (Paris, 1987), Vol. 3, p. 69.

43 Clarke, Colin, 'Caste among Hindus in a town in Trinidad: San Fernando', in *Caste in Overseas Indian Communities*, Barton M. Schwartz (ed.), (San Francisco, 1967), pp. 165–99.

44 Van der Burg and van der Veer, 'Pundits, power and profit', p. 517.

45 Kirpalani, Murli et al., *Indian Centenary Review* (Port of Spain, 1945), p. 61.

46 Speckman, Johan D., *Marriage and Kinship among Indians in Surinam* (Assen, 1965), p. 48.

47 Forbes, Richard H., *Arya Samaj in Trinidad: An Historical Study of Hindu Organisation Process in Acculturative Conditions*, PhD Diss., University of Miami, 1984, p. 60.

48 Smith, Raymond T., *British Guiana* (London, 1962), pp. 123–4.

49 Dew, Edward, *The Difficult Flowering of Surinam* (The Hague, 1978).

50 Ryan, Selwyn, *Race and Nationalism in Trinidad and Tobago* (University of the West Indies: Institute for Social and Economic Research, 1972).

51 Vasil, Raj K., *Politics in Bi-Racial Societies* (New Delhi, 1984).

52 Phillips, Leslie H. C., 'Kali-Mai puja', *Timehri* 11, 1960, pp. 136–46.

53 Vertovec, Steven, *Hinduism and Social Change in Village Trinidad*, DPhil thesis. University of Oxford, 1987, pp. 325–7.

54 The use of *jhandi* demonstrates one important source of difference between Hindu practices in the three countries: whereas only red (for Hanuman) and, less frequently, white (for Satyanarayan) flags tend to be erected following 'Sanatanist' *pujas* in Surinam and Guyana, a range of coloured flags are displayed by 'Sanatanist' Hindus in Trinidad (including pink for Lakshmi, dark blue for Shiva, yellow for Durga, orange for Ganesha, and more).

Part V

Globalization, Migration, and Diaspora in the Caribbean

Introduction

The Caribbean region was formed by the kinds of processes we might now call globalization. It is a region not merely marked by migration, diaspora and the movement of global economic forces, but truly created by them. Unlike the gradual historical evolution that has shaped other regions of the world over millennia, we can point to the diary entry of a single man to mark the beginning of what we now know as the Caribbean. Christopher Columbus in a journal entry of Thursday October 11, 1492 wrote: "At two o'clock in the morning the land was discovered, at two leagues' distance; they took in sail and remained under the square-sail lying to till day, which was Friday, when they found themselves near a small island, one of the Lucayos, called in the Indian language Guanahani." This marks the beginning not only of sustained contact between Europe and the Caribbean, but of a process of conquest, settlement, economic development, resource exploitation, traffic in human beings, war and ultimately emancipation, independence and nation building. And these events transformed the region on a massive scale, eradicating nearly an entire civilization of indigenous people and engendering the forced migration of poor Europeans, Asian indentured laborers and millions of African slaves. Economic exploitation and migration (both internal and external) still mark the region deeply, yet here also there have always sounded the miraculous chords of survival, independence, and perseverance. This part documents some examples of the impact of global economic and cultural change on the lives of contemporary Caribbean people.

Suggested Readings

On globalization:

Dávila, Arlene M., 1997 Sponsored Identities: Cultural Politics in Puerto Rico. Philadelphia: Temple University Press.

Deere, Carmen Diana, et al., 1990 In the Shadows of the Sun: Caribbean Development Alternatives and U.S. Policy. Boulder, CO: Westview.

Kempadoo, Kamala, 1999 Sun, Sex, and Gold: Tourism and Sex Work in the Caribbean. Lanham, MD: Rowman & Littlefield.

Klak, Thomas, ed., 1998 Globalization and Neoliberalism: The Caribbean Context. Lanham, MD: Rowman & Littlefield.

Martínez-Vergne, Teresita, and Franklin W. Knight, eds., 2005 Contemporary Caribbean Cultures and Societies in a Global Context. Chapel Hill: University of North Carolina Press.

Maurer, Bill, 2000 Recharting the Caribbean: Land, Law, and Citizenship in the British Virgin Islands. Ann Arbor: University of Michigan Press.

Watson, Hilbourne A., ed., 1994 The Caribbean in the Global Political Economy. Boulder, CO: Lynne Rienner.

On migration and diaspora:

Chamberlain, Mary, ed., 1998 Caribbean Migration: Globalised Identities. London: Routledge.

Foner, Nancy, ed., 2001 Islands in the City: West Indian Migration to New York. Berkeley: University of California Press.

Gmelch, George, 1992 Double Passage: The Lives of Caribbean Migrants Abroad and Back Home. Ann Arbor: University of Michigan Press.

Olwig, Karen Fog, 2007 Caribbean Journeys: An Ethnography of Migration and Home in Three Family Networks. Durham, NC: Duke University Press.

Potter, Robert B., Dennis Conway, and Joan Phillips, 2005 The Experience of Return Migration: Caribbean Perspectives. Aldershot: Ashgate.

14

Globalization and the Development of a Caribbean Migration Culture

Elizabeth Thomas-Hope

From the outset, Caribbean colonies were part of the wider global political economy. This globalization was based first on mercantilism, the trans-Atlantic slave trade and the plantation. Later, new forms of investment were developed within the framework of various types of European and North American colonial and neo-colonial relationships. The movement of people was an integral part of these global systems and migration became an important means of adaptation to the societal changes which were induced locally.

The first profound changes were those produced by the social and economic upheavals which followed the emancipation of slaves. These had far-reaching implications for the ex-slaves in terms of their quest for an identity based upon personhood, for the freedom to move and, related to this, their incorporation into the new globalized labour markets. Migration became so important a part of the processes of adaptation to new and evolving circumstances that, ultimately, the significance of the trans-national linkages at the level of political economies was matched by that of trans-national linkages at the levels of families, households and individuals. Such globalized lives and livelihoods influenced all aspects of material culture, goals and frames of reference which characterize the identity of the contemporary Caribbean.

Emancipation, Freedom and Migration

The former slaves from the British colonies began to emigrate immediately after Emancipation (1834) and the abolition of the apprenticeship regulations (1834–8), and from the French islands after 1848. The ex-slaves, the first emigrants, inhabited lands in which they had no traditional ties or emotional attachment, quite the reverse. Ancestral attachment lay elsewhere and the disruptive and destructive system of slavery left the black population deeply alienated not only from their immediate past, but also from their present environments and, even more seriously, from themselves. Furthermore, the plantation created a single set of national criteria for social status and political power and these criteria were based on European norms. Therefore, by definition, status and power were outside the scope of the population of African descent. On grounds of race, culture, material possessions, occupation and employment, the overwhelming majority of the population in the Caribbean colonies occupied only a marginalized position.

The lack of freedom inherent in slavery meant not only an alienation of self and of identity but also a lack of those symbols with which freedom was associated. These included material posses-sions, especially ownership of land, and access to power. It also included freedom of movement. The migration from plantation to interior hill lands and the establishment of free villages pro-vided a degree of independence, but only a poor economic base. Nor was there any potential for gaining the symbols of status or power which would be accepted nationally.

The pursuit of independence from the planta-tion and from the entire societal system on which it was based led to the movement of workers not only away from the plantations but, in many cases, away from the islands altogether to return later having gained some measure of economic advantage (Thomas-Hope 1995). This made the former slaves highly responsive to new and chan-ging opportunities associated with the inter-national division of labour. The identities of the emerging societies were shaped within the con-text of movement, absenteeism and return.

Many of the Caribbean territories, for example the Netherlands Antilles, never truly constituted plantation colonies. In others, the impact of the plantation was less all-embracing of the entire economic, political and social structure because of its later development in the twentieth century under United States' dominance. Therefore, the plantation alone could not provide an adequate explanation for the evolving process of migration. But what it did explain was the early occurrence and the particular characteristics of migration in the sugar colonies. Later on and in the non-sugar colonies (too), migration was influenced by the local social and economic structures which were, in all cases, fundamentally conditioned by the nature of metropolitan political economies and the associated implications for individual Caribbean territories.

Transformations in Class Structure and Migration

The first voluntary migrations from Caribbean colonies in the nineteenth century occurred at a time of major social ferment and economic uncertainty. The adjustment to the new societal freedoms demanded major adaptations on the part of all groups in a situation where the pre-occupation of the plantocracy was the preserva-tion of their access to labour supplies, and that of the former slaves the consolidation and putting into practical effect the theoretical achievement of freedom.

With the breakdown in the formal institutions of slavery and the emergence of a new social order, social divisions and social relations, previ-ously determined by law, were then maintained by the accepted criteria of status and power – namely, race and economic wealth. The social distinctions of the plantation in the earlier period became the symbols of class in subsequent years.

The divisions between masters and other white colonists, freemen of colour and slaves evolved within the new economic order to produce coun-terparts in class terms. Internally differentiated by occupation and economic wealth, the three groups, distinct from each other principally on the basis of colour and political power, formed an upper, middle and lower class. Evidence of change in this pattern was minimal until the 1930s, though periodic challenges to the status quo (as in the Morant Bay rebellion in Jamaica in 1865 and the Federation Riots in Barbados in the 1870s) demonstrated that the society was by no means static. Nevertheless, the system was main-tained around the prevailing economic structures still fundamentally based on the plantation.

The major post-war economic changes in the Caribbean were decreased dependence on agri-cultural monoculture and increased industrial ac-tivity. In those few Caribbean countries where resources permitted, industrialization included the development of extractive industries, but in most states it has been based on some measure of tourism and manufacturing. The first stages of industrialization, and in many Caribbean territor-ies the only stage, has been manufacturing for import substitution or the formation of enclaves oriented towards the parent companies overseas. Elsewhere, the diversification of the economy has given the opportunity to former land-owning families, as well as others already prospering from commerce, to invest in and/or manage the new enterprises. As a consequence, the national capitalist class has increased in size as foreign, absentee control declined. Migration was one of the few means open to the masses to improve their material circumstances and thereby also enhance their social status.

The narrowly based, three-tiered class structure which characterized the period before the Second World War became more complex. It reflected the more varied and intricate pattern of economic relations based on a transformed and greatly reduced reliance on agriculture, alongside the expanded set of capitalist and semi-capitalist relations of the increasingly urbanized structures. A heterogeneous urban working class emerged from the former rural lower classes and urban lower service sectors; the expansion of educational opportunities facilitated the upward mobility of the children of the black lower class to fill a range of professional and urban white-collar workers, both in the private sector and in the growing civil service, as well as technical jobs in the industrial sector.

For all this class mobility and the broadening of the parameters of racial and cultural status with which class was associated, it was not accompanied by a corresponding increase in relative income levels of the upwardly mobile. The necessary economic base for sustaining such expectations simply did not exist. The reduction in the hierarchy of deference and the associated pattern of patronage and support shown towards those of lower status was not accompanied by incomes adequate to support the new aspirations for independence. Minimum wages rose beyond the reach of lower middle-class employers and thus the level of service employment declined. Social relations became less closely aligned to the former racial and cultural distinctions and much more to the capitalist commodity relations (Gordon 1987:3).

These changes were partly due to the economic transformations and the increase in capitalist activity in the islands and thus the increasing opportunities for wage labour in the non-manual and non-agricultural sectors. At the same time, the channel for obtaining such opportunities was mostly through the expanded educational facilities which came with the period of post-war capitalist expansion. By the early decades of the twentieth century, education was beginning to

play a greater role in class mobility, compensating for and, at the same time, starting the process of breaking down the rigid association of class and colour. Education became a critical factor in the acquisition of professional occupations and thus middle-class status. In addition to this was the special value accorded a foreign education, a direct legacy of the ascendant role of metropolitan frames of reference in the region.

There were limited opportunities for secondary education and vocational training, chiefly in the teaching profession, for children of the black working class. In this regard, though with difficulty, hard work and dedication, migration was beginning to play a role in providing the capital from which to start the accumulation of sufficient finance directly or indirectly to assist in the education of children. This was the means whereby the inter-generational upward mobility of an increasing number of black, working-class people was achieved by the end of the Second World War. This tendency increased in the following decades. Even where formal qualifications were not acquired, work experience or in-service skill training were important to the migrant's success and perceived migration achievement. Furthermore, it has been usual for migrants to appreciate a wide variety of migration experiences as contributing to their general educational improvement. Cultural symbols such as standard grammatical speech, public behaviour deemed 'socially respectable' and evidence that the horizons of the mind have been extended beyond the confines of insular parochialism are all highly valued. Migration takes on a special significance in this context.

The paradoxical association since the 1950s in most Caribbean countries of increased opportunities for social mobility on the one hand, and widening income disparities on the other, has reinforced the earlier role and significance of migration. As the middle class expanded, so expectations of bourgeois notions of status and living standards, based on North American norms, increased. At the same time, there was no commensurate distribution of capital to sustain these expectations. Transient flows to North America or Caribbean off-shore locations of American dollar influence, as well as longer-term circulation to North America, has ensued.

Likewise, the new urbanized working class in both formal and informal economic sectors have expectations of material acquisitiveness which cannot be readily met locally by most people. The former greater level of contentedness under conditions of rural self-sufficiency have been overtaken by much more widespread urban poverty and, at the same time, increased exposure to American television culture. Visits abroad for even very brief periods of time are perceived by the working class to provide the certain means of achieving ambitions of improved living standards.

Post-war changes in economic structures, social relations and educational opportunities were accompanied by increased not decreased migration. Where the level of industrialization was greatest, as in Puerto Rico, Jamaica and the Dominican Republic in the 1950s and 1960s, the increased available capital together with the changing pattern of class relations fuelled the migration process. For urban populations, the employment opportunities generated by the new capital intensive industries fell far short of the demand and the expectations for obtaining work. At the same time, for the agricultural smallholder, land was more valuable as a commodity for sale to the industrial and tourist enterprises than for agricultural production. This crisis in the internal development of most Caribbean territories led to worsening urban problems and to the further decline in agriculture. Migration rates increased as opportunities within the new economic order failed to meet rising expectations. Meanwhile, the growing disparities of wealth in the societies which accompanied the localization of resources heightened the potential for migration.

Capital in the hands of some was a facilitating factor in migration, while the widening gap in income, as well as in the ability of the economy to meet the new demands for urban employment, contributed to sustaining the high potential for migration for the majority. Yet again, as in the early post-Emancipation period, migration was fundamentally a means of adjusting to the changing economic and associated social stresses within society as well as providing a response to its opportunities.

Even where resources came under state control, as in Guyana in the 1960s, or state shares in the economy were extended, as in Jamaica in the 1970s, emigration did not slacken but increased. The fact that the state itself was seen to be taking over the role of entrepreneur alienated the upper strata of the society, accustomed as it was to such a role being played by either foreign corporations or local families. While manifestations of this alienation were translated into racial terms, particularly in the case of Guyana, the altered class relations and political tensions were basic to the migrations. Nationalization or localization of assets have been among the major transforming agents in the post-war era.

A second factor which occurred simultaneously in most Caribbean countries was the increased priority given to the education of the masses. Changing economic and ownership patterns with the demise of agriculture and the rise of industrialization, coupled with the expansion of secondary education, had profound influences upon the class structure and the subsequent new pattern of class relations in Caribbean societies. Despite all the new opportunities in the Caribbean and the more attainable symbols of status and power, migration was still an integral part of the society. It remained deeply embedded in social institutions and, above all, became incorporated into the new channels of social mobility.

Migration and Personal Advancement

In a situation where opportunities in the home country were perceived to be minimal or nonexistent, the migrant and high potential migrant in the Caribbean was conditioned to expect upward mobility as an outcome of migration. Migration facilitated an extension of work opportunities beyond the limitations of the local or national economic environment. Thus the role of migration in this context was closely linked to the role it played in the achievement of one or more of the objectives of work. For the majority of migrants and those who desired to migrate, it was believed that their activity or intended activity abroad would produce the additional capital which would raise their standard of living in terms of material comforts, as well as provide the assets on which independence, security and status were based. Land and a house were the principal items in this category and migration to work abroad is known to make possible the accumulation of capital for purchasing them.

Status was enhanced partly through material assets acquired and also through the fact of having lived and worked abroad. The nature of the actual work undertaken overseas was not always readily disclosed, since it was invariably of an equally low or even lower status than the work available locally. Nevertheless, there was a general view that the work done in a foreign country was automatically of higher value by the very fact of its location, whatever the work actually entailed. Furthermore, in that work commanded higher financial returns elsewhere, its value, and thus its status, was also enhanced. This was a factor of prime importance in the migration process, for what it indicated was that location, more than type of work, determined its status.

This explains why work in a neighbouring Caribbean island has been regarded as being more desirable, even though the job was essentially of the same status. Likewise, in the metropolitan centres of North America or Europe the status of the same occupation in the Caribbean is multiplied several-fold. For example, there was seen to be no comparison between agricultural work in St Vincent and the same work done on contract by Vincentians in Barbados; and definitely no comparison in the choice between Barbados and the United States or Canada whether or not the work was the same.

The international historical framework within which Caribbean societies were established and the mechanisms whereby they were structured and class relations emerged combined to produce the underlying political economy conducive to population transfers on the one hand and a *raison d'être* of those populations for moving on the other. This combination of factors has been consistently manifest in the role that Caribbean people have played in response to European and North American demands for labour in the expansion of capital both within the Caribbean region and outside the region, in the metropolises themselves.

Globalization of Labour and Migration

Emancipation had created surplus populations, though not in numerical terms, since labour for the plantations always continued to be very much in demand, necessitating in many colonies the importation of other indentured workers. But surplus labour existed to the extent that the ex-slaves withdrew their labour from the plantations. As Caribbean societies became increasingly part of the metropolitan trans-national labour force, so each generation became socialized in a way of life and livelihood conditioned by migration. To these were added the non-labour migrants: landlords were traditionally absentee and Western Europe was always regarded as a normal extension of the Caribbean for the upper and professional classes. However, the great majority of migrants comprised workers; thus the location of different types of investment in the region was especially important in determining the direction of movement. At the same time, national legislation articulated the demands and the restraints of those same metropolitan societies concerning the immigration of Caribbean people, thus controlling the timing and volume of the migrations.

Three major periods may be identified in terms of the directions of migrant flow: the period from the mid-nineteenth century to the Second World War, the post-war years until the early 1960s and the period from the mid-1960s to the present. In the mid-nineteenth century, movements were predominantly to plantations of the sugar-producing islands, especially with the expansion of sugar into the former Spanish colonies, first Puerto Rico and then the Dominican Republic and Cuba by the early twentieth century (Thomas-Hope 1978 and 1986). At the end of the nineteenth century, industrial operations employed even larger numbers of migrants within the region. The cutting of the Panama Canal and railway construction in Central America, later oil drilling and refining in Venezuela and the Netherlands Antilles of Curaçao and Aruba were among the first of West European and North American industrial operations employing migrant labour in the region.

The later expansion of North American activities was associated with military bases, aluminium plants, tourism, banking, insurance and other 'off-shore' industries. Like the earlier operations, these have employed large numbers of seasonal or more permanent migrants coming in from neighbouring islands. Indeed, the labour force of some islands, like the Bahamas and the Virgin Islands, is comprised of a high proportion of migrants, renewed on an almost continual basis (Marshall 1979, 1984). Where industry was non-labour intensive or was located in territories where populations were very large, then no migration flows occurred – as in the case of Jamaican or Guyanese bauxite, Trinidadian oil, Puerto Rican manufacturing. Likewise, no additional labour was required where development initiatives were endogenous, as in the range of import substitution industries in most Caribbean states.

The mobility of labour within the Caribbean and circum-Caribbean countries continued while the movements outside the region were occurring from the early twentieth century and with increased momentum from the mid-twentieth century. West European and North American requirements for labour and manpower for the armed forces both in the First and Second World Wars led to the recruitment of workers from the Caribbean colonies (Colonial Office Report, cited in Senior and Manley 1955: 5; Proudfoot 1950:23).

The post-war reconstruction in Western Europe also required labour, much of which was obtained from the Caribbean colonies. From the mid-1950s the hitherto small numbers of 'colonial subjects' going to their respective 'mother country' increased to flows of massive proportions. Large numbers of skilled, semi-skilled and unskilled workers were employed chiefly in industry, transport and hospital services.

Legislation in the United Kingdom in 1962 and 1965 brought that country's Caribbean migrant inflow to a virtual end. This merely resulted in a shift in the movement away from Britain and towards Canada and the United States. There, changing labour demands had led to alterations in their immigration legislation in precisely the same years – 1962 and 1965 respectively. These changes favoured Caribbean migrants, especially those falling within the professional and skilled labour categories.

The movements to France have continued to the present time because of the special departmental status which the Antilles maintain

(Domenach and Picouet 1992). In the case of the Netherlands, policies were geared towards integrating the Caribbean migrants into Dutch society rather than restricting entry (Amersfoort 1982). In the course of time, the numbers of new arrivals dwindled without legislative intervention. As in the movement of the Netherlands Antilleans to Holland, the net migration of Puerto Ricans to the United States declined as the circulation of migrants established a balance between outward and return flows.

The migration fields have changed over time, largely determined by the changing demands for labour by West European or North American capital developments either within or outside the Caribbean region itself. The Second World War brought about a shift in the focus of migrations from a predominantly regional movement to one dominated by flows to Western Europe. In the 1960s, immigration legislation induced further changes in the direction of Caribbean migrations and the pattern became dominated by movements to the USA and Canada. Intra-regional mobility continued virtually throughout the entire period.

Transnational Lives of Caribbean Peoples

The complexity of Caribbean migration is due not only to the varying types of migration which occur, but also to the wide range of movements incorporated into the overall process. Return or counter-flows have always been an integral part of Caribbean migration. As the migrations themselves have differed in purpose so, not surprisingly, have the migrants varied in regard to their intention to return and the extent to which these intentions were subsequently realized.

The volumes of counter-flow have been consistently underestimated, chiefly due to the difficulty of recording them for official statistics. Nevertheless, empirical studies have shown that not only have they been highly prevalent throughout the history of Caribbean migration but also, in various ways, they have been an integral part of the migration process. (Philpott 1973; Thomas-Hope 1985; Basch et al. 1987; Gmelch 1987). Indeed, the linkages maintained by the migrants between their households at source and destination are not only significant in perpetuating migration, but are deeply rooted in the culture. Migrants, even *in absentia*, are part of the ceremonial and sometimes the decision-making of the household in the Caribbean.

Trans-national linkages are also essential for the economic support of the migrants' households in the Caribbean. The sending of remittances involves the movement of money as well as a wide range of goods sometimes transmitted by the migrants themselves or at other times by intermediaries, usually members of the immediate family or wider kinship network (Frucht 1968; Dirks 1972; Philpott 1973; Hill 1977; Brana-Shute and Brana-Shute 1982; Pessar 1982; Richardson 1983; Georges 1990). The migrants themselves return with varying degrees of regularity, for differing periods of time and, whether or not they ever return permanently, the transnational connections are maintained by their migration orientation or the return mentality (Rubenstein 1983; Thomas-Hope 1985 and 1992). Even during a protracted absence from the home country most Caribbean migrants remain, in various ways, part of their Caribbean household and thus part of a family, household and personal transnational network. In this way, Caribbean households remain structurally linked to their absent members through the support system established. In return, migrants can, if necessary, or should they so wish, retain their places in the household with the option to return and obtain the benefits of that household and its inheritance for an indefinite period, sometimes the rest of their lives.

During the process of trans-national interaction, whatever the specific time-span in any particular case, the displacement of the migrant is only partial, though the degree and nature of displacement varies throughout the migration cycle and from one migrant to another. The displacement of the work place invariably occurs in the case of transient movements without the displacement of any other aspect of the migrant's activity. A major home base is maintained simultaneously with a secondary base, and either the one or the other may be located in the Caribbean.

The pattern of displacement is dynamic and changes as the migrant's activities alter and either he or she increases the emphasis on the home country or reduces the commitments there allowing an increase in the commitments at the destination. The balance between the two alters throughout the migration cycle and though the precise nature of the transition is not clear and varies with innumerable factors in the process, it maintains the source and destination places in a network of transnational interaction. This is a very important and hitherto little recognized aspect of the process which is significant for the perpetuation of the process through the continuing, though ever-altering nature of feedback (Thomas-Hope 1988). Depending on the purpose and duration of the absence abroad, the displacement of the individual's work activities, domestic, social and leisure activities may occur to varying extent in either the country of migration source or destination. The interaction between place of origin and destination thus remains linked in a dynamic set of relationships changing both throughout the individual's migration cycle and extended beyond, to have implications for the future pattern of migration in the household.

Overall, the greatest impact of migration upon the household or wider family is in its ability to extend the parameters of opportunity beyond national limitations. The transnational dimension of the household and the family has permitted society to preserve its viability despite continued, sometimes large-scale, migration and possibly even because of it. Thus, households, families and individual lives are fundamentally transnational in character, giving rise to a Caribbean identity which is intrinsically global.

Conclusion

The term 'migrant' includes a wide variety of persons, and 'migration' a wide range of spatial behaviour. Nor is the system static. Within the life-cycle of a household a number of migration types may occur involving one or more members of that household. It is difficult to ascertain the nature of the pattern of change from one type of mobility to another, but a transition in migration types certainly does occur and the influence is

undoubtedly carried on to subsequent generations. Thus to refer to migration as though it
were a single type of phenomenon, and to regard
a migrant as a stereotype of the worker in search of
a job, is to so oversimplify the situation as to
conceptualize the process as constituting merely
the displacement of people and ignore the institutional framework and the culture surrounding it.

The pattern of international relations with its
inherent inequalities had been set from the establishment of Caribbean societies. All developments
subsequently have simply reiterated the underlying objective in the minds of all classes alike to
aspire to the international lifestyles of which
Caribbean society is continually reminded in a
number of different ways.

The continuities in the pattern and process of
Caribbean migration, despite dramatic changes
in both international and national contexts, reflect the deeply rooted significance of migration
to the society. The value of migration to the
expansion of capital is in the labour it has provided metropolitan interests; the value of migration to Caribbean peoples themselves is in the
adjustments which it has facilitated in the face
of constitutional, economic and social change.
So successful were these strategies of adjustment that they became institutionalized to
form an important part of Caribbean lives and
livelihoods. The fact that so many are perceived
to do so well from migration continues to
endorse its value.

Freedom of movement took on special meaning to Caribbean peoples and the migration
tradition never permitted island social and economic systems to totally determine the parameters of opportunity. In a number of ways, the
island opportunities were extended to incorporate
a wider world conditioned by historical circumstances, with its legacies of colonialism and slavery, the later distribution of capital and the
pattern of labour markets.

It was in this context that the various sectors of
the society ultimately became emigrant: the white
colonists when their economic power base was
undermined; the Creole whites and coloureds
and also Asian and Middle Eastern minorities,
when economic wealth and social status were
perceived to be threatened. For the majority in
most Caribbean countries – black or mulatto – the
situation was different. Emigration was never a
response to the threat of losing wealth or status,
but rather the means of achieving it. Because of
this, the process was seen by the majority not as
permanent escape but of temporary withdrawal,
with the intention of returning later to an improved material and social situation back home.
Thus not only the initial immigrations but also
the subsequent emigrations were to have a major
impact upon the formation of society, and the
structure of society in turn stimulated a complex
pattern of emigration. It is not surprising, therefore, that an entire culture should have emerged
in which migration was an integral part.

References

Amersfoort, J.M.M. van (1982) *Immigration and the Formation of Minority Groups: The Dutch Experience, 1945–1975*, London: Cambridge University Press.

Basch, L., Wiltshire-Brodber, R., Wiltshire, W. and Toney, J. (1987) 'Caribbean regional and inter-national migration: transnational dimensions', un-published paper.

Brana-Shute, G. and Brana-Shute, R. (1982) 'The mag-nitude and impact of remittances in the Eastern Carib-bean: a research note', in W.F. Stinner, K. de Albuquerque and R.S. Bryce-Laporte (eds) *Return Migration and Remittances: Developing a Caribbean Per-spective*, Washington DC: Research Institute on Immi-gration and Ethnic Studies, Smithsonian Institution.

Dirks, R. (1972) 'Network groups and adaptation in an Afro-Caribbean community', *Man* 7: 565–85.

Domenach, H. and Picouet, M. (1992) *La Dimension Migratoire des Antilles*, Paris: Economica.

Frucht, R. (1968) 'Emigration, remittances and social change: aspects of the social field in Nevis, West Indies', *Anthropologica* 10: 193–208.

Georges, E. (1990) *The Making of a Transnational Community: Migration, Development and Cultural Change in the Dominican Republic*, New York: Columbia University Press.

Gmelch, G. (1987) 'Work, innovation, and investment: the impact of return migrants in Barbados', *Human Organization* 46, 2: 131–40.

Gordon, D. (1987) *Class, Status and Social Mobility in Jamaica*, Kingston, Jamaica: Institute of Social and Economic Research, University of the West Indies.

Griffith, D.C. (1983) 'The promise of a country: the impact of seasonal US migration on the Jamaican peasantry', unpublished PhD thesis, University of Florida.

Hill, D.R. (1977) 'The impact of migration on the metropolitan and folk society of Carriacou, Grenada', *Anthropological Papers of the American Museum of Natural History, New York* 54, 2.

Marshall, D.I. (1979) *The Haitian Problem: Illegal Migration to the Bahamas*, Kingston, Jamaica: Institute of Social and Economic Research, University of the West Indies.

Marshall, D.I. (1984) 'Vincentian contract labour migration to Barbados: the satisfaction of mutual needs?', *Social and Economic Studies* 33: 63–92.

Pessar, P. (1982) 'Kinship relations of production in the migration process: the case of the Dominican emigration to the United States', New York Research Program in Inter-American Affairs at New York University, Occasional Paper, no. 32.

Philpott, S.B. (1973) *West Indian Migration: the Montserrat Case,* London: Athlone Press.

Proudfoot, M. (1950) *Population Movements in the Caribbean*, Port of Spain, Trinidad: Caribbean Commission Central Secretariat.

Richardson, B.C. (1983) *Caribbean Migrants: Environment and Human Survival on St Kitts and Nevis*, Knoxville: University of Tennessee Press.

Rubenstein, H. (1983) 'Remittances and rural development in the English-speaking Caribbean', *Human Organization* 42(4): 295–306.

Senior, C. and Manley, D. (1955) *A Report on Jamaican Migration to Great Britain*, Kingston, Jamaica: Government Printing Office.

Thomas-Hope, E.M. (1978) 'The establishment of a migration tradition: British West Indian movements to the Hispanic Caribbean in the century after Emancipation', in Colin G. Clarke (ed.) *Caribbean Social Relations*, Liverpool: Centre for Latin American Studies Monograph Series No. 8, 66–81.

Thomas-Hope, E.M. (1985) 'Return migration and its implications for Caribbean development' in R. Pastor (ed.) *Migration and Development in the Caribbean*, Boulder, CO: Westview Press.

Thomas-Hope, E.M. (1986) 'Caribbean diaspora – the inheritance of slavery: migration from the Commonwealth Caribbean', in Colin Brock (ed.) *The Caribbean in Europe: Aspects of the West Indian Experience in Britain, France and the Netherlands*, London: Frank Cass.

Thomas-Hope, E.M. (1988) 'Caribbean skilled international migration and the transnational household', *Geoforum* 19(4): 423–32.

Thomas-Hope, E.M. (1992) *Explanation in Caribbean Migration*, London: Macmillan.

Thomas-Hope, E.M. (1995) 'Island systems and the paradox of freedom: migration in the post-Emancipation Leeward Islands', in Karen Fog Olwig (ed.) *Small Islands, Large Questions: Society, Culture and Resistance in the Post-Emancipation Caribbean*, London: Frank Cass, pp. 161–75.

15

"The Blood Remains Haitian"

Race, Nation, and Belonging in the Transmigrant Experience

Nina Glick Schiller
and Georges Eugene Fouron

"Where are you going?" The police officer asks, after stopping my car in a neighborhood near the university.

"I am going home," I say.

"Where are you coming from?" the voice in the darkness demands.

"I am coming from Stony Brook. I am a professor," I reply. Then, I show the officer my university identification that indicates that I am Professor Georges Fouron.

"Ok, Georges, be careful," comes the response. Suddenly, the police officer is all smiles and his tone of voice becomes too familiar.

"What did I do, officer?" I ask, although I know all too well that my transgression is being a black man driving through a white suburb at night.

Back comes some cockamamy excuse.

"You crossed the yellow line."

Georges sees himself as someone who has been crossing lines for a long time. In traversing borders and living his life in a transnational field that includes two nation-states, Georges experiences the lines of race and nation as they are drawn in both social orders. Haitian transmigrants live their lives within both Haitian and US understandings of blackness. These perspectives are not the same. The bitter lesson that Georges and other Haitian migrants learn as they strive to become incorporated into life in the United States reinforces their affectionate recollections of the sweetness of Haiti. In his longing for Haiti, Georges combines his daily experiences with the US racial divide and his own ongoing relationship to Haiti. In turn, Haiti reaches out and embraces him across national territorial borders as well as the divisions created by his legal status as a US citizen. This embrace contains the hopes of those left behind who have seen the Haitian diaspora as embodying a brighter future for Haiti.[1]

We have discerned three strands of Haitian long-distance nationalism. Haitian transmigrants weave one strand of their border-crossing nationalism in response to the way they experience "race" in the United States. This has a common thread, made visible in Georges's encounter above with the police officer, who is sworn to serve and protect the US public. On such occasions, persons of color, whatever their legal status, find themselves on the wrong side of the color line.[2] A second strand that makes up the warp and woof of long-distance nationalism is the complex relationship that Georges maintains to Haiti – one in which family obligation, memory, pride, and despair are intertwined. Georges's experiences in the United States shape his memories of and longing for Haiti. At the same time, he remains directly connected to Haiti through his transnational ties of family, the Haitian media – whose radio broadcasts fill his house in New York with Haitian voices, many directly from Haiti – and periodic visits that place him once again on Haitian soil.

The third and final strand of Haitian long-distance nationalism is produced by those who remain in Haiti. Throughout our trip, and the writing of our book, the fervent nationalist appeal that nineteen-year-old Marjorie made to Haitians living abroad stayed with us, compelling us to understand and explain such passion. Boldly, Marjorie had taken our tape recorder in her own hands and said: "Those who are listening to my voice, I urge them to concentrate and remember what country they left behind. It is not for you to ally with other countries. My brothers, see the one on the ground, see the one who has nothing, help him out. Those who are sick, help them as you can. All the bad ideas and bad things, remove them from our lives. Change your heart and then the country will find a solution."

Marjorie lives in a household that is connected to the United States through a flow of remittances. Yet her appeal was based on a broader sense of kinship than the boundaries of her family network. Note that Marjorie identifies those who are "left behind" as a "country" and she speaks to Haitian migrants as her "brothers." She defined all those living abroad as family members who continued to have obligations to those they "left behind."

There is much that is uniquely Haitian in Marjorie's statement about family and nation, as well as in her use of kinship metaphors to construct Haitian long-distance nationalism. It is also the case that some of the roots of Haitian long-distance nationalism spring from US soil. Moreover, the personal networks in Haiti to family members living abroad are becoming a form of intimate political connection to the United States. Many in Haiti are beginning to define migration as an expression of their nationalism. They see settlement in the United States as necessary to both their personal well-being and that of Haiti.

The United States, therefore, becomes a location that Haitians can rightfully claim as part of their birthright because of their connection to it through family, history, and political economy. In the emerging transnational realities and long-distance nationalism of Haitians, the United States is becoming the path to the future for Haiti.

In examining the experiences that have led Haitians in Haiti and the United States to develop a transnational concept of nation and make it part of their personal identity, it is important to observe that the Haitian ideology of family, blood, and nation reflects and contributes to nationalism as a set of ideas that motivates political action in countries around the world. Haitian conceptions of nation emerged as part of a more global development of nationalist ideologies that link individuals to states through notions of descent and race.[3] Haitians participated in and were influenced by this global dialogue. Today, long-distance nationalists who engage in transnational politics based in a diverse array of states all draw from a core identity narrative. In this narrative, each person inherits membership in and becomes a representative of her or his ancestral nation. Georges's story, therefore, can tell us about more than his and Haiti's particular situation. As we trace Haitian links between family and nation that extend transnationally, the tale we have to tell provides insights into the fervent attachments so many migrants claim to homelands halfway around the world.

"You Are Different"

Between 1959 and 1993, 302,458 Haitians entered the United States with permanent resident visas and 1,381,240 Haitians arrived with nonimmigrant visas. Most of those entering as nonimmigrants came with tourist visas and arrived by plane.[4] In addition, beginning in about 1971, many tens of thousands of Haitians arrived in south Florida via small wooden sailboats.[5] Until the 1990s, a great number of the migrants who came by plane as "tourists" did so for much more than a brief visit. Once in the United States, these migrants were able to find employment as factory

operatives, janitors, nannies, and domestic workers. With one of these jobs in hand, newcomers
could then obtain permanent resident visas on the
basis that workers in these occupations were in
short supply. Although this use of tourist visas
between the 1960s and 1980s differed from the
official intent, it provided for a period in which
migrants and employers could find each other
and establish whether a newcomer had the skills
to stay and prosper. Most did.

Individuals who arrived with visitors' visas
generally had a network of family members who
assisted them in purchasing a ticket and obtaining
travel documents. In the 1960s and 1970s, most
of those who followed this route came from the
middle or upper classes of Haiti, but some were
skilled urban workers. Except for the so-called
boat people, few came directly from the countryside. While many of the boat people were less
educated and came from poorer families than the
majority of other Haitian migrants, even boat
people tended to arrive with some skills and education.[6] In most cases, it took some resources to
be able to buy a place on a crowded, unseaworthy
sailboat. Increasing numbers of people from more
varied origins began to emigrate by the 1980s,
assisted by family members who had preceded
them. Most Haitians settled in south Florida
and the New York metropolitan area, but there
are also established Haitian populations in
Chicago, Philadelphia, and Stamford, Connecticut, as well as the Washington, DC, area.
New York City was the initial location of
settlement, and in 1994, 30 percent of the newly
arrived legal migrants continued to settle there.[7]

Georges is one of the many Haitians who arrived in New York with a tourist visa in the
1960s. After receiving his advanced certification
in international relations from the University of
the West Indies in Trinidad, Georges got off the
aircraft in 1970 knowing that he could not go
home, although his visa and plane ticket indicated
that he was only stopping off on the way home
to Haiti.

*I knew that in Haiti young men were being tortured,
imprisoned, and killed. Some of my friends were
disappearing. And even with university degrees,
there was no chance of employment unless you*

*were a supporter of the Duvalier dictatorship.
Meanwhile, my parents and siblings were looking
to me for support. They saw me as the lucky one,
since I was the one with the education and passport.
So I got off the plane in New York City and looked
for a job.*

Despite his ability to speak English and several
university diplomas, Georges sought a low-
paying factory job because he lacked one crucial
piece of paper: a permanent resident visa that
would have allowed him to legally remain in the
country and work.[8] Working in a succession of
small factories, Georges received his first education about race in the United States. His bosses
differentiated him from people they termed
"American Negroes" and "Spanish." "You are
different," they told him. "You are educated and
you work hard. Just stay away from the others
and you'll do fine."

But things were not so fine. Georges discovered that racism in the United States could vary
with the setting and situation. He gained some
immediate advantage when employers made distinctions between black migrants from the
Caribbean and African Americans, believing that
Caribbean migrants were superior to US blacks.[9]
But he quickly learned that when black migrants
apply for professional jobs, seek decent housing,
or walk down the street, they are suspected simply because they are black. He also discovered
that black men are particularly feared and
avoided, whether or not they are citizens of the
country. Even after Georges obtained his permanent resident visa, although he was well educated and jobs were available, he could only find
factory work.

Finally, his old friend Alex and another old
school friend who came from a well-to-do family
made Georges an offer. They set him up as the
manager of a newsstand. Georges would live off
some of the profits and send them the rest, so
they could go to medical school in Mexico. When
the friends in Mexico finished their studies, they
would come to the United States and send
Georges to graduate school. It all worked for a
while. Georges married Rolande, settled in an
apartment in Brooklyn, and their daughter Leah
was born. The hours in the newsstand were long,

but the business was good. In fact, business was too good. The mob moved in and took over the store. Georges was told to "leave the keys and don't look back."

I didn't know what I was going to do next. I didn't know what I was going to tell Rolande. I still had to send money to everyone in Haiti, and now I had a family. I took a factory job for three years and became convinced I would never be able to raise enough money to go to school. I applied for master's degree programs at the public colleges because they were less expensive than the private ones. But the public colleges would not consider my credentials from Haiti and Trinidad. They told me I would have to start college all over again. Rolande encouraged me to apply to Columbia University Teachers College. They accepted me and told me I could pay in installments. I began a master's program in education there, even though I knew that we didn't have enough money in the bank to cover the first check that I gave them. But I got a job in the college library, and Alex paid for part of one semester as he had promised when I ran the newsstand and sent him to medical school in Mexico. We managed somehow, and the next semester I was awarded a fellowship.

With US credentials in teaching, Georges was sure that he could at last be the professional educator he had struggled so hard to become. He wanted to teach poor black children, with whom he identified. But it was difficult for a black man without connections or experience to find a teaching job in the United States in the 1970s, even though there was a teacher shortage. It still is true in New York City that to turn your degree into a job in the school system, it helps to know the principal of a school. There are now Haitian school administrators who are willing to hire Haitian teachers, but in 1980, Georges had to wait until the day before school opened before anyone offered him a job. It turned out to be in a town two hours north of New York.

As soon as I got there, I knew there was something strange about them hiring me. However, it was only months later that I learned that the school district faced legal sanctions for having consistently refused to hire black faculty. That is why they called me. The town was too far for me to commute each day

from Brooklyn, but no one in the town would rent me a room. Finally, the janitor, who was the only black employee of the school district and who happened to be Haitian, took me in. But he only had a small one-bedroom apartment, and [so] I slept on his living room couch. Then a widowed Jewish Holocaust survivor who lived in the next town called me up and invited me to share her house. I moved in with her, and she insisted that I stay, even when she began to receive threatening phone calls because of my presence. The faculty sympathized with me, but they would not invite me to their homes. They explained, apologetically, that they were certain that I would be gone the next year and they had to continue to live in the community.

The next year Georges did leave. He found a teaching job in Brooklyn. After several years, he won a doctoral fellowship in education at Columbia. When he finished his advanced degree, he was able to find a faculty position at the State University of New York at Stony Brook. But that first bitter year teaching in upstate New York had served as an initiation into the experience of blackness in the United States. The lessons have continued over the years. He has had students walk into his university classroom, look right past him, and ask for the professor. Students have told him that growing up on Long Island, New York, the only other black person they have ever known was their maid.

And then there are the police. Nina, who is always late and in a hurry, often becomes impatient with Georges, who never speeds. But Georges's care in obeying every traffic regulation goes beyond his efforts to be a good citizen; he has learned that no matter how long he lives in the United States and whatever his legal status, his right to belong will always be open to question.

In all of these encounters, Georges remembers that he is a descendant of African slaves who rose up and created the new black nation of Haiti, crossing the line that defined the governance of an independent state as a whites-only privilege. He becomes a part of that black nation that continues to challenge the idea that only whites are deserving of personal and political sovereignty. In this context, his successes and the accomplishments of his family belong to Haiti and all black people. Haiti's failures similarly reflect on his self-esteem – a self in which he is a representative of his family, race, and nation.

Doing What Comes Naturally

Georges takes a chair into the small courtyard in front of his brother Alfred's home, and sits on it so that the chair leans back and rests against the wall of the house. He smiles as he looks around him, his body resting contentedly in the Haitian version of a recliner. The sky is a vivid blue, the sun is bright, and there is a lovely breeze. It is Georges's first day back to Haiti after an absence of four years. He is in a state of euphoria.

> This is home and I don't see myself spending the rest of my life in the United States. It is only here that I feel really alive. It's something in the air – the smells, the tastes, the sounds. It's something about the way things look and feel. I just finally feel right. Wow!

All his youthful memories come rushing back: the desperate days of trying to find money to leave Haiti are mixed together with the longing he has experienced ever since for the lost solidarity of close-knit friendships. He remembers the good times: hunting birds with slingshots, bathing in the river, and sitting up late and talking with friends. He also recalls the bad times: the fear that there would be no future for him in Haiti, his fear of the macoute, the scarcity of food and clothing, and the rage of his mother directed toward him because she could not provide for him. Despite these painful memories, he feels a sense of peace. Coming home as a successful professional, his sense of achievement and the differences between his past and present circumstances heighten the delights of return.

By the second day, Georges's tone has changed. He has begun to notice things. First, he sees the roads. "They are a disgrace," he tells Nina and anyone else who will listen. Even the paved ones are full of potholes so that you can't drive without zigzagging as if you were drunk. There is also the dust. It makes everything and everyone look dirty. And there is the disorder everywhere. Automobile and truck drivers respect no rules. There is garbage in the streets, too. The government doesn't repair the roads or pick up the trash. As each day goes by, Georges's discomfort with the situation in Haiti increases.

A week later, Georges goes to the airport to pick up Alex, his boyhood and best friend who comes to Haiti every summer. Georges returns muttering, "*Se pa posib. Se pa posib*" ("It's not possible. It's not possible"). After a week in Haiti, he sees the airport differently than he did in the euphoria of his arrival. He notices that the electronic sign that is supposed to flash the next flight's time of arrival continually announces that it is Thursday afternoon. He is incensed that family members are forced to stand for hours outside the terminal in the relentless sun, waiting for arriving passengers. The disorder and confusion at the airport fill him with shame. Nina is puzzled. As she records in the field notes that she writes after each day's work:

> It seems so unlike Georges to put the conditions of the pavement before the conditions of the people? Just why do these particular aspects of Haiti upset Georges so much? Why at the airport did he see the lack of order and public facilities? Why didn't he comment on the hungry women and children asking for money? Why is it that it was only after this visit to the airport that he began worrying about the impressions a white American friend who is coming for a first visit to Haiti later that summer will have about Haiti?[10]

Months later, as we sit listening to the tapes of our interviews and reading Nina's field notes, we are able to explore the complexity of Georges's feelings for the country of his birth and the United States.

> When we were in Haiti, I wanted to point to something that would make me proud. It was supposed to be a new time for Haiti, now that there was democracy and a popularly elected government. Here is a government that denounced the neglect of the country by dictators and yet they allow the same neglect. I expected a sense of renewal. And I also saw that the current leaders don't really care about Haiti. And the airport was upsetting because this is the first thing that foreigners see. I felt that foreigners use the disorder and decay as a justification for racism. They could look at everything falling in disrepair

and say: "These people need foreigners to come in and run things for them." I felt ashamed, especially at a time when a new government was in control.

It is not that the poverty didn't bother me. But couldn't the government at least get a few people together and pick up the garbage and make the streets clean? With the garbage, you have diseases and all kinds of things. And I felt that the condition of the airport and the roads made it clear that these people were not responsible leaders. And I felt it even more when we went for a trip to the Dominican Republic that summer and I saw the museums, the roads, the modernization, and the national monuments. There, you have the sense that someone is doing something in the country. Where are the museums in Haiti? Port-au-Prince was founded in 1749. Where are the historical sites? I kept thinking, we have been independent for nearly two hundred years. What do we have to show the world?

Georges's reaction to the condition of Haiti was shaped by the fact that since the Haitian revolution, European and white American leaders have devalued the culture and national independence of Haiti.[11] The white gaze that he constantly experiences in the United States reinforces his longing for Haiti and becomes part of his relationship to Haiti. When he returns to Haitian territory, the political and economic situation in Haiti becomes a source of personal shame. Nation, race, and self are tied to his experience of Haiti, whether he is on Haitian soil or in the United States.

Blood Ties

In 1804, the national identity of Haiti was forged in a successful slave rebellion that defeated the armies of Napoleon and led to Haiti becoming the first black republic. Before the Haitian Revolution, the vast majority of the population in the French colony of Saint Domingue had been enslaved Africans. The colony had also contained a vocal population of educated free mulattoes, the offspring of black slave mothers and white plantation owners. Many among the mulattoes were claimed by their wealthy fathers and educated in France. They became owners of plantations and slaves. Some of these men participated in the French Revolution and its fiery debates about

liberty and equality. They expected that Haitian mulattoes would be granted full citizenship rights in France. Black slaves in Haiti heard of the talk about the "rights of man" as well and expected an end to slavery.

By the close of the eighteenth century, political theorists seeking a way to legitimate state power over the people without reference to the divine right of kings promoted the concept of the "natural rights of man." These rights were said to be the common possession of persons who inhabited the territory controlled by the state. The state drew its authority from "the people." Inhabitants of a territory governed by such a state were said to be a "people" or "nation." As this theory was popularized, the word "nation" became transformed from earlier meanings of localized descent groups to a "fundamental political category."[12] But certain questions about "the people" remained. Were all persons living within the borders of a state to be included equally in "the people" and therefore regarded as citizens? Both the US founding fathers and the French revolutionaries struggled over whether "the people" encompassed persons of African descent.

The French revolutionary government abolished slavery, but was divided as to whether persons in their colonies, and especially those of African descent, could claim the rights of French citizenship. Some held that black people could become French citizens if they spoke the French language fluently and assimilated into French culture. But within a few years, this position was defeated, slavery was reinstituted, and even the sophisticated slave-owning mulattoes were denied French citizenship.[13]

Underlying the arguments on both sides was a conception of the nation as a community of blood.[14] Ideas of blood as a basis for citizenship were debated by Haitian and French intellectuals during the years of the French Revolution when mulattoes from Haiti claimed the rights of French citizens. There was an organized faction within the French revolutionary government that repudiated these claims. This group contended that "blacks and mulattoes, whatever they may say, are not true French" because "they are not tied by any tie to France. ... they have no blood ties from France, and they don't have patriotic feelings toward France."[15] The opposition wanted to recognize the French citizenship of Haitian mulattoes on the grounds that they had fathers of French descent so that they were indeed connected by birth to France.

In the French concept of citizenship that developed in the wake of the French Revolution, mastery of the French culture and language rather than lineage were taken to be gauges of who was sufficiently civilized to be accorded French citizenship. Nevertheless, the French discovered, as did the American revolutionaries, that one could talk about human rights yet still have slavery and colonization. To justify this seeming contradiction, US and French political theorists began to categorize all people of color as not fully civilized, and perhaps even incapable of civilization. They equated civilization, in short, with whiteness.[16]

These debates about whether or not black people were to be included in "the rights of man" helped spark the Haitian Revolution, and contributed to the conflation of concepts of family, blood, and nation that continue to be part of Haitian daily life today. In conceptualizing the newly emerging nation after the French Revolution, Haitians adopted the language of peoplehood and nation. Various declarations signed by Jean-Jacques Dessalines, the victorious general who led Haiti to independence, read "in the name of the Haitian people." In the Act of Independence of 1804, reference is also made to liberty "consecrated by the blood of the people of this island."[17] Liberty was being won through the sacrifice of the people's blood.

The Haitian state was founded on 1 January 1804. The way this moment is remembered is informative. According to Haitian historian Beaubrun Ardouin, whose 1853 accounting of the founding of the nation both reflected and became incorporated into Haitian written and oral histories, "Dessalines asked the audience and generals and the troops to swear that they would defend the freedom of the people, of the entire race of people that had up until now been vilified as slaves. As a response to that appeal made to the people, the population of Gonaïves, men and women, representing the young Haitian nation and the entire black race, pronounced also

this oath, which tied it to its future descendants from that moment into all generations as a distinct fatherland."[18]

The first Constitution of Haiti declared the Haitian people to be black, introducing the language of race into the nation's formation. In fact, in defiance of the values of the powerful cultures of Europe and their equation of civilization with whiteness, Haitians defined the "black" (nèg) to mean both a Haitian citizen and human being. No matter what your skin color, you could become a Haitian citizen if you lived in Haiti. Thus, the use of the word black for Haitian citizens did not initially equate Haitian citizenship with ancestry. The white Polish soldiers who fought on the side of the slave uprising were granted Haitian citizenship, and over the centuries, Middle Eastern Arabs and Jews, German Jewish refugees from Nazism, and various Europeans seeking their fortunes have settled in Haiti and become citizens. In so doing, they became nèg. Nonetheless, over the years, as a concept of the Haitian people developed, it became linked with a concept of a community of blood that shares, as a common ancestry, the revolutionary heroes who rose up against slavery and founded the nation.

Generally, whenever and wherever in the world new political leaders come to power through the force of arms, they face the problem of obtaining political recognition from abroad and winning acceptance from the international community. The challenge confronting the political leaders of Haiti from the beginning was of a more fundamental nature, however, and one that has engaged the poorest peasant and most urbane of the elite in a common struggle. The entire population of Haiti and its leaders found themselves marginalized because of their color.

Since its founding in 1804, Haiti has come up against various forms of exclusion or punitive treatment by the United States and the European states. By the nineteenth century, Europeans used a concept of race to distinguish between those they judged fit to rule and those they considered only capable of being ruled. Haitians – even the mulatto elite, fluent in French, dressed in the latest Parisian fashions, well read and well bred – were by these standards considered unable to govern a country. Haitian diplomats and scholars were ridiculed because they dared to assert their equality with whites. Over the years, Haitians came to understand that their claims to acceptance as human beings in the eyes of the white world were linked to the degree to which the leaders of other governments acknowledged the sovereignty of the Haitian state and accorded honor to the Haitian nation.

In struggling to win respect for their nation, Haitians found that they were ridiculed because of the religious practices of the majority of the Haitian people. The many religious beliefs of Africa and the Christianity brought from Europe had been brought together in Haiti as a new religion, which has come to be called Vodou. This syncretic religion recognizes the power of an almighty god (*Bondye* or *Gran Mèt*) as well as numerous ancestral and natural spirits (*lwa*) who are often represented by the images of Catholic saints. Beginning in 1865, the Catholic Church, which had broken its ties with Haiti after the revolution, established a formal relationship with the Haitian government and began to import European priests. These priests condemned Vodou and organized anti-Vodou campaigns. The various Protestant denominations that became increasingly important in Haiti in the twentieth century also supported campaigns against Vodou. As a result, the Haitian elite and educated people of all class backgrounds have publicly repudiated Vodou, although many privately practice it. European and US governments and intellectuals used Vodou to discredit the viability of Haiti as a black sovereign state and as a key indicator of the failure of black people to achieve civilization. Until the US occupation, though, many rural Haitians were removed from these challenges to their sense of pride and identity.

All these slights to national honor, and to the capacities and intelligence of the Haitian people, became known to the general populace when the United States invaded and occupied Haiti for nineteen years. From 1915 to 1934, the United States governed Haiti, justifying its presence in terms of the inability of Haitians to maintain order in their own country. The occupation ensured that the United States, rather than competing European powers, obtained access to Haitian bauxite and tropical products such as

rubber and sugar, all seen as essential for US industrial development. The Haitian Constitution was rewritten by the US military forces to allow foreigners to own property in Haiti. Attempts were made to build an infrastructure of roads, railroads, and sanitation facilities and services conducive to the extraction of profits for US corporations.

The occupation favored the mulattoes, putting in place light-skinned presidents and creating an army led by light-skinned officers. At the same time, the US occupiers tried to draw racial lines between themselves and all Haitians. Even the educated elites were characterized as racially different and incapable of civilization. For instance, Colonel Littleton Waller, a Marine Corps commander who became the senior US military officer in Haiti, wrote to a friend in the United States expressing his views of the Haitians among whom he worked: "Thes [sic] people are niggers in spite of the thin varnish of education and refinement. Down in their hearts they are just the same happy, idle, irresponsible people we know of."[19] As the occupation became organized, the United States racially segregated all Haitians. The Catholic Church established separate masses for white North Americans. Local hotels, which catered to whites from the United States, adopted Jim Crow regulations. White US social clubs were established that excluded all Haitians, even the president of Haiti.[20]

Haitian intellectuals responded to the racism of the US occupation by defending the intellectual capacities of all people of African descent. The US occupation ended in 1934, but the efforts of Haitian leaders and writers to defend the capacities of black people continued. They used examples of Haitian achievements in the white world as evidence. For example, Daniel Fignole, a populist political leader in the 1940s and 1950s, edited a journal *Chantier* that popularized the achievements of Haitian intellectuals such as Louis Joseph Janvier, a Haitian who had obtained distinction for his studies both of medicine and political science in Paris in the nineteenth century. Janvier's achievements were said to prove that "the brain of blacks has great elasticity, and it has the facility to acquire all sorts of knowledge without becoming exhausted."[21] Similarly, noting the death of a prominent intellectual, Dr. Justin-Chrysostome Dorsainvil, an article in *Chantier* stated, "The country, the black Race, especially our black Community, has lost in J. C. Dorsainvil one of the 'astonishing products' that you see only once every fifty years and that proves that this African Branch (section of the African race) has at its disposal an inexhaustible reservoir of intellectual and moral worth capable of flourishing in all areas of endeavor, if the natural and human obstacles are removed."[22]

Throughout the twentieth century, Haitian political leaders also have popularized a language of blood and ancestry that evokes the imagery of the nation of Haiti standing independent as a sacred patrimony of all Haitians. *Chantier* asserted, "We must remember that to break the chains of slavery our fathers had to shed their blood. In creating the Haitian Nation they dreamed, before everything else, to transmit to their children, a little corner of land where freely, they could earn their living through hard and conscientious work. Haiti is thus the inheritance of our forefathers."[23]

Duvalier took up this portrait and used it to legitimate his rule when he came to power in 1957. In taking on the name "Papa Doc," he gained patriarchal authority and legitimacy. He also transformed portions of the Catholic liturgy into a statement of obedience to be recited by all schoolchildren and at public occasions. Prayers that were well known even to the illiterate majority and incorporated into the opening rituals of Vodou services were converted into pronouncements of patriotic faith. Duvalier's version of the Lord's Prayer began: "Our Doc, who art in the Palais National for life, hallowed be Thy name, for by past, present, and future generations, Thy will be done in Port-au-Prince as it is in the provinces."[24] In this way, Duvalier surrounded his regime and its representation of the nation with an aura of the sacred. He built on the ideology of the inherent relationship between self and nation, ancestry and Haiti. His contention, "I am the flag," was widely ridiculed by foreign observers of Haitian politics. Yet, this equation of self with nation resonated with a sense of identity that he shared with both rural and urban Haitians who saw their ties to Haiti as formed from blood and

inheritance. To the Haitian poor and elite he was also saying, "you/we are the flag," the nation.

In order to legitimate his regime, Duvalier made numerous and seemingly contradictory connections between the sacred, the religious beliefs and practices of people in Haiti, and an identification with the nation. He surrounded himself with symbols of the spirits of Vodou so that as he linked himself to the nation, he was simultaneously projecting himself as an embodiment of spirit. He wore black suits and top hats, the symbols of Baron Samedi, the guardian of cemeteries who stands between life and death, controlling movement between the world of the living and that of the spirits. Many people in Haiti believed that Duvalier had these same supernatural powers. If he was the flag/nation, then there was no division between the nation and the realm of the spirits. Duvalier also rejected the white foreign church hierarchy appointed by the Vatican to serve in Haiti, and appointed in their place Haitian bishops and other church officials. In so doing, he fanned nationalist sentiments in Haiti by claiming that the Catholic Church was part of the Haitian nation.

If, in the Haiti of Georges's childhood, the conflation of self, ancestry, blood, and nation was promoted by both political and religious functionaries, these same notions were also embedded in the oral traditions and literature of Haiti. The idea of Haiti as a nation united by a common ancestry – a nation that was won through bloodshed and united by blood – was reiterated constantly in Haitian stories, songs, and writings. Haitians of all classes and colors came to define themselves as heirs to the founding ancestors of the Haitian Revolution. These founders are known to literate Haitians through school textbooks. To illiterate Haitians, they are known through oral traditions and Vodou. Several of the revolutionary heroes became *lwa* (spirits); Ezili Danto, one of the most important of the lwa, is said to have participated in the Haitian Revolution.[25]

In the Haiti of today, revolutionary ancestors and a language of blood that links family, God, and nation continue to provide a basis for community as well as a linkage between past and future. Aristide built on this legacy in his sermons, using references to national pride and religious faith to promote the agenda of the poor: "If you are a Haitian and you have Haitian blood that runs in your veins, if you are a real Haitian, stand beneath the flag of conviction and sing the national anthem. Link your faith with your commitment... like the proud Christians that you are."[26] We found echoes of this message that projects the Haitian people as a Christian family in our interviews. Twenty-seven-year-old Maurice, who had been a participant in a church-based organization, told us:

> We will see if Haiti is to make any progress. Only God will say something. There is much to be done yet. I would like to add that we would like to see that all those people who think that they are Haitian, everyone who would like to have a life, all those who have some sense of responsibility, who have love as Christians, to put their heads together to help Haiti, to help their brothers and sisters, especially those who are worse off. Those with possibility and those with goodwill. Those who do good may not find their reward on earth but life is not over when you die since we have to live again in another world, maybe we may not think it exists but it does exist because we have a creator.

To tie together the concept of family and nation, we found people in Haiti constantly using a language of blood. "Blood, that's blood that makes you a true Haitian," we heard repeatedly. "I am Haitian because my parents are Haitian. ... It is in the blood" was the way family, blood, and nation were connected by Dimase, a thirty-three-year-old man who received support from his three brothers and two sisters in New York and California. When asked to define what it meant to be Haitian, 82 percent of the people we interviewed spoke of descent. Half of the respondents began their exposition by speaking of "Haitian blood."

While the shared mythology and rituals of nationhood have been common to all classes in Haiti, linking them to a pride of nation, this mythology has not necessarily connected them to each other. Class divisions in Haiti have historically been expressed through distinctions of color and language: the dominant classes spoke French and were portrayed as mulattoes; the rural poor spoke Kreyòl and were identified as black.[27] Through most of Haiti's past, elites spoke of their pride in the Haitian nation. They also argued that Haitian culture was fundamentally French. Haitians' ability to master French culture proved to the world that black people had the capacity to participate in the highest levels of civilization. The black middle class that emerged as significant political actors after World War II generally valued French culture, too. Georges remembers that although there was no money in his house for food, his father, a poorly paid head of a vocational school in Haiti, subscribed to *Paris Match* and several other French periodicals.

Although the Haitian poor have in many ways accepted the value of French culture and whiteness, they have also created their own definitions of what it means to be Haitian, seeing Haitian culture not only as one of pride but also of proud suffering. In our interviews, we were told, "A Haitian is someone who knows poverty, suffering, and who is full of anger/resentment, and is ready for all eventualities, who embraces life the way s/he finds it." This idea of Haiti as a nation, defined not by the fact that its people share a culture and territory but by a historical experience of pain and persecution, was echoed by Vico, aged twenty-one. Vico was supported by his mother, who had emigrated to the United States and was sending money to allow her son to finish high school. As he explained, "The word Haitian means someone who is part of Haiti; finally, a Haitian is someone who has been mistreated."

The class divisions and tensions are not seen by the poor to negate the unity of the nation; their anger and illiteracy has not meant that they have been isolated from or alien to the language of national identity and unity. Rather, they have accepted the metaphor of Haitian blood as uniting the nation. They use this language to critique the ever-widening class divisions in Haiti and the use of color distinctions to justify such divides. For many of the poor, all Haitian people have the same blood, and it is black. Jeremie, who grew up in the countryside and had never been to school, had worked for years as an artisan within Haiti's tourist sector. At the age of fifty-six, with tourists no longer coming to Haiti, he had been surviving for many years on remittances. Sitting in the yard of his house, surrounded by grandchildren he was tending for family living abroad, he said: "There really is *ti wouj* [mulatto] and *ti nwa* [black]. The reason why that exists is because a lot of them do not . . . realize that if I cut myself and they also cut themselves, the blood would be the same color. But because they are looking at the skin color they are saying there is mulatto and black. But in reality we are the same nation of the same color – black, black, black – and we are the same blood." Sedye, an unemployed, impoverished musician who serves the lwa, emphasized this same theme to us. His barely habitable one-room apartment has rotted staircases and floors. While perched on a balcony that gave him a wonderful but precarious view of Port-au-Prince, he remarked: "All of the colors are from Guinea [Africa] and have value, and God created all of them. . . . When Cedras [the head of the military coup that ousted Aristide in 1991] took power, they said that all of those who are in the lower class are called black pigs [*nèg nwè kochon nwè*]. . . . The mulattoes, with the black blood in their veins, are saying these stupid things."

Changing Locations of Haiti

The language of nation as a family of persons who share a common ancestry and blood that the poor use to critique the rich, and that all classes use to unite the nation, is currently providing Haitians with a potent ideology to link emigrants and their descendants to the Haitian nation-state. When Haitians arrive in the United States, they come with a clear sense of their own national identity.[28] While they may claim a tie to a small rural hamlet, large town, or Port-au-Prince as part of their sense of self, they also firmly identify with the Haitian nation. In the late 1950s through the 1970s, however, when Haitians first began to arrive in significant numbers in New York City, they certainly did not see themselves as part of a transnational nation-state. Haitian nationalist ideology at the time portrayed those who left Haiti as having abandoned their nation.

Until the 1990s, Haitians in the United States, whether they participated in organized Haitian activities or remained distant from formal groups, tended to believe that you had to choose either to be loyal to Haiti and eventually return or "forget about Haiti" and become an American.[29] Permanent emigration was defined as an abandonment of home and family.[30] You might have multiple identities, but you could have only one political loyalty. That loyalty would ultimately determine where you physically resided. Most Haitian migrants believed that each person could have only one nation, and that to be part of that nation, you had to live within its territorial boundaries.

In this political outlook, Haitians reflected the understanding of nation-states that had become hegemonic after World War II, as well as a distinction between native and foreign that has deep historical roots in Haiti. All persons who were born on Haitian territory of Haitian parents were defined as Haitian, and all Haitians were defined as black. Blackness carried with it the sense of being human. All foreigners, whatever the color of their skin, are by definition white and therefore capable of inhuman behavior. Those Haitians who left their homeland became in a certain sense foreign; that is, they became white and could not be trusted. This division between native and foreign was reinforced and popularized by François Duvalier, when his relentless pursuit of all internal political opposition precipitated a large-scale exodus from Haiti. The Duvalier regime was able to mobilize nationalist sentiment against those who had fled. The Haitian government labeled emigrants as traitors, scum, and enemies of the nation. Organized contacts with Haitians abroad were discouraged, and Duvalier's spies were rumored to monitor Haitian migrants in New York to ascertain if they were conspiring with persons in Haiti.

Similarly, Haitian anti-Duvalier activists in the United States embraced a political rhetoric that drew a sharp line between Haitians living abroad and those in Haiti. They criticized remittances to families or hometowns and scolded any migrant organizations that contributed to projects in Haiti. These contributions, they claimed, maintained the oppressive Haitian government and thus harmed the nation. They portrayed the diaspora as political refugees in exile from repression, rather than as permanent residents.[31] These leaders feared that as Haitians became incorporated economically and socially in the United States, they would abandon the struggle against the Duvalier regime. Consequently, most Haitian migrant leaders preached a "politics of return" that called on Haitians abroad first to work for the overthrow of the Duvalier regime and then to return to rebuild Haiti. Haitians could realize their loyalty to their homeland, according to the politics of return, only by going back to Haiti. Becoming a US citizen was seen as a shameful betrayal of the Haitian homeland.

This was the political climate that greeted Georges when he arrived in New York in 1969. He, his best friends, and his close family members, who readily confided in each other about sexual trysts as well as other personal triumphs and failures, did not tell each other when they became US citizens. Nina, observing the pressures to return in the 1960s through 1980s, thought it all sounded familiar. But it was not until the two of us began systematically studying long-distance nationalism that we put together the Haitian nationalist exhortations "to return" with the Zionist appeals to American Jews "to return" to Israel. We began to realize that both the Haitian and Jewish nationalist language echoed the nationalist literature at the turn of the twentieth century. At that time, European political leaders made the same call to their compatriots settling in the United States: "Return home and rebuild your homeland."[32]

Sitting in living rooms among a circle of family and friends, men of all class backgrounds debated whether it made more sense to plan to return to or "forget about Haiti." Did they see themselves as exiles waiting for the end of the Duvalier dictatorship when they would return to rebuild Haiti, or as uprooted immigrants who had cut their ties to home? Women rarely entered into these living room debates, but they also considered the question of return as they participated in church, school, and family settings in discussions about the preservation of Haitian culture and the future of the next generation. Haiti remained the point of reference among the hundreds of Haitians we interviewed or spoke with in informal conversations in New York from the 1960s

through the 1980s. Meanwhile, of course, most Haitians were intimately engaged in the life of Haiti, monitoring news from Haiti, debating the current situation, and searching for ways to sustain their family networks. What Haitian transmigrants lacked was a political language that made visible and validated their sense of continuing to be part of Haiti.

Both the Duvalier regime and the anti-Duvalier activists began to use the word *diaspora*, which until that time had not been part of the Haitian political vocabulary. For the Duvalierists, the diaspora was those Haitians who had abandoned the nation by emigrating, and hence, were outside of and against the nation. Haitian leaders abroad labeled Haitians living outside the United States as "the diaspora" as a way of communicating that all Haitians abroad were exiles and political refugees whose goal was to return home to rebuild Haiti. Until the 1990s, however, most people in Haiti or most Haitians abroad either did not know the word or avoided using it because it was seen as being too politically charged. In our 1985 interviews with ninety-three leaders of Haitian organizations in the New York metropolitan area, only the leaders of anti-Duvalierist organizations acknowledged being familiar with the word *diaspora*.

Given the legacy of the political disconnection of emigrants from their homeland and the new realities of being categorized as black Americans, no matter what their culture or the color tone of their skin, it is not surprising that in the first decades of settlement, Haitian migrants adopted a multiplicity of alternative identities and kept a low profile. At first, many publicly identified themselves as French. Our interviews with Haitian migrant leaders in 1985 introduced to us people who, although identified as Haitians in our research, had many other identities as well. For these leaders, Christian, Haitian nationalist, Haitian American, American, Masonic, French, black, African, African American, and hometown identities could all be overlapping, noncontradictory public identities.[33]

During these first decades of settlement in the United States, Haitians did not see themselves as a distinct ethnic group or "Haitian community" in the United States. The dissemination of the concept of the Haitian community, and the different meanings imparted to this term by Haitians and non-Haitians in the United States, is a result of four decades of interaction with US-based institutions and their efforts to incorporate black migrants into the US social fabric. The first organizational identities embraced by Haitian migrants of upper- or middle-class origins in the 1960s were those of class not community. As they tried to make it in the United States, their old world beckoned, and it was not the old world of memory but that of transnational family connection to which they continued to belong. For people from the elite mulatto families or the educated middle class, there was much at stake. As they bent over a factory assembly line, parked cars, or pushed a broom, it was important to hold onto the fact that in Haiti they were people who commanded respect. To preserve their social position in Haiti, they had to maintain Haitian class divisions in the United States. This meant that persons of high status in Haiti avoided interacting in the United States with Haitians whom they saw as their social inferiors. Upper-class Haitians built elite social clubs rather than community organizations and did not speak or act in terms of a united Haitian community. They identified with Haiti, not with other Haitian migrants. Over time, many of the mulatto elite families quietly withdrew to the suburbs, where they continued to keep their distance from other Haitians.

It was only as they encountered the civic culture of New York City that Haitians began organizing as a community. The newcomers, arriving in the New York metropolitan area in increasingly large numbers in the 1960s, found no public recognition of their transnational connections and continuing identification with Haiti. They were, however, encouraged by politicians and church officials to organize as Haitians, with the connotation that they were a new US ethnic group. Before the 1960s, black migrants had not been perceived by the white mainstream as having distinctive ethnicities; they were seen simply as black. But in the wake of the civil rights and black power movements, public authorities in the 1960s began to not only recognize but actively foster black ethnic differences. Haitians were offered occasions to distinguish themselves from African Americans.[34]

To understand the meaning of this sponsorship of black ethnicity and the Haitian response, it is crucial to separate, as well as acknowledge the connections between, ethnic identity and long-distance nationalism. There is tremendous variation in the academic literature and everyday conversational practices in the English-speaking world between these two terms. Part of the confusion arises from the rapidly changing uses of the words *ethnicity* and *nation* in the course of the twentieth century. To understand the US migrant experience, we find it most useful to link both terms to the ways in which US political leaders, academics, and white mainstream institutions such as political parties and major foundations have approached the task of incorporating immigrants into the United States. These public opinion makers currently deploy both *ethnic group* and *ethnicity* as a means of acknowledging cultural difference within the fabric of US society. To the extent that they affirm the right to cultural difference, they abandon the efforts to assimilate immigrants that require newcomers to give up all other forms of identification in order to become genuine Americans. They move from a melting pot model of society in which all cultures blend into a single, unified, uniquely US culture to one of cultural pluralism or multiculturalism. Multiculturalism accords immigrants compound ethnic identities, so that Haitians become Haitian Americans.[35] While the US model of multiculturalism projects a culturally diverse society made up of multiple ethnic groups, it does not allow for long-distance nationalism. The celebration of culture within multiculturalism is one of ancestral roots, not ongoing political relationships and loyalties.

In the 1960s, the National Democratic Party created a special slot for Haitians on the All-American Council, a clustering of European ethnic groups, and encouraged the formation of the Haitian-American Citizens Society based in New York. US Catholic dioceses began to employ Haitian priests and establish special masses for Haitians. By the 1970s, the New York City Community Development Agency, an offspring of President Johnson's War On Poverty, began to fund separate Haitian community centers. Protestant organizations such as the American Baptist Convention advocated the creation of separate Haitian congregations. In the 1980s, the Ford Foundation funded the Haitian Centers Council, an umbrella group of New York community centers. The Catholic Church and Ford Foundation also supported Haitian community organizations in south Florida in the 1980s. Currently, in the various localities of Haitian settlement, Haitian priests, ministers, educators, newspaper reporters, and radio broadcasters routinely appeal to and speak in the name of the Haitian community. They portray Haitians within a US ethnic mosaic and celebrate Haitians' contributions to the "cultural diversity of America."[36]

This perception of Haitians as a new US ethnic group has been popularized in a variety of ways. The public school system has played a major role. For example, the Haitian patriotic songs that Rolande and Georges learned during their childhood in Haiti were taught to their children Leah and Jacob in their elementary school in New York City in the 1980s. During their school assemblies in Brooklyn, their teachers dressed the Haitian children in the red and blue of the Haitian flag and marched them onstage. They pledged allegiance to the Haitian flag and sang the song, "*Nous Te Voulons Chère Patrie*" ("We Love You, Dear Fatherland"), to remind them of their Haitian identity. The "Hispanic" children also sang the national anthems of their countries of origin.

More recently, school administrators in south Florida began to teach Haitian children Haitian patriotic rituals and rhetoric. Palm Beach County adopted a seventh-grade curriculum in 1998 that included the teaching of Haitian history from 1400 to 1987. Students are taught to "compare information about Haitian politics and language before and after Haiti became the first independent nation in the Caribbean."[37] The Broward County schools have started to celebrate the Battle of Vertières, a decisive 1803 contest at the end of the Haitian Revolution that has long been commemorated in Haiti. According to a Florida newspaper, local schools observed the Haitian national holiday "with patriotic songs, dance, and Haitian food" in order

to "promote recognition of the holiday among Haitian-American students and awareness of Haitian history to the public."[38]

US institutions, organizations, and political leaders – including local school systems, the Ethical Culture Society, and members of the New York City Council – also have sponsored or endorsed celebrations of Haitian Flag Day for two decades. In 1982, for instance, the United Haitian Association (UHA), which had been formed in 1978 with the support of the program director of the New York Council of Churches, organized such a celebration. US lawyers were present to provide legal advice about immigration. The Haitian founder and head of the association told his audience that his organization conducted activities "to promote the Haitian culture in the heart of the other ethnic groups living in the United States and abroad." But he went on to make an appeal on behalf of Haiti: "UHA requests your time, your participation, your enthusiasm to continue the big fight which undoubtedly will result in the liberation of the refugees and the liberation of Haiti." The evening closed with the singing of the Haitian national anthem and shouts of "Unity, Victory, Long Live Haiti." A UHA newsletter concluded its reporting of the event with a "Patriotic Appeal to the Community. ... On this commemorative day of the creation of our bicolor symbol of the sacred Union of our ancestors who forged our nation, the UHA reminds the Haitian community that the land is a continued creation, that all the Haitians should feel agitation in them, the noble feeling and the great emotions capable of feeding their patriotic flame."[39]

In 1997, 18 May was celebrated as Haitian Flag Day in New York City, as it has been for many years. The festivities began with an ecumenical service at a Catholic Church in Brooklyn that has been a center for Haitian activities since the 1960s. The same day there was a cultural fair, a theater presentation, a basketball tournament, Haitian Flag Day programs in three high schools and two colleges in Brooklyn, and a walkathon at Medgar Evers, a branch of the City University of New York that has been a center for African American and Caribbean studies. The Brooklyn Society for Ethical Culture, together with the Haitian Cultural Society, hosted an all-day event at which several Haitian intellectuals were invited to speak about the significance of Haitian Flag Day in a program titled "Haiti: The Making of a Nation."

Throughout the first decades of settlement, despite all the celebration of Haiti, there was no public acknowledgment that Haitian migrants were maintaining and reinforcing transnational familial, economic, religious, and organizational ties to Haiti. But organizations formed to represent the Haitian community as an ethnic group in the United States increasingly became engaged in activities in Haiti. Catholic parishes in New York and Miami emerged as some of the public faces of the Haitian community in the United States, advocating for Haitian refugees and providing immigrant services. At the same time, they became a catalyst for political change in Haiti. Haitian Americans United for Progress (HAUP) typified this development. Based in a Catholic Church in an area of dense middle-class Haitian settlement in Queens, New York, and led by Catholic priests and lay church leaders, HAUP received funding in 1969 from a federal antipoverty program to "empower" the Haitian community. In the following decades, the organization obtained grants for community development, assisted Haitian boat people, and provided job training and English classes. It also became a founding member of the Haitian Centers Council, an organization funded by several philanthropic groups in order to unite Haitian organizations in New York. Following what would appear to be a classic immigrant path into US politics, HAUP created ties with local political clubs along with links to state and federal elected representatives from Queens. But HAUP had another face, less visible to funders and more prominent among Haitian migrants. It served as a center for anti-Duvalier activity, hosting meetings where men and women debated the political situation in Haiti, and the "American plan" of restructuring the Haitian economy to foster export processing and agribusiness. Growing strength in local-level politics in the United States went hand in hand with an increasing political engagement in Haiti.

In the eyes of many school administrators, US politicians, and philanthropic organizations, the various community activities and celebrations of Haitian national holidays are part and parcel of US identity politics. Although the flags, songs, and dances are Haitian, they teach Haitian adults and children alike to identify with a diverse, multicultural United States. Still, Haitian transmigrants and their children may experience these "ethnic" rituals in a different light. Their growing identification with the United States may not preclude or supersede their identification with Haiti. The public celebrations and discussions of Haitian history, symbols, and politics mesh well with the transnational ties and obligations of Haitian families.[40] In response to both continuing transnational connection and the experience of publicly identifying with Haiti, although they live in the United States, Haitian transmigrants have begun to see Haitians in the United States and Haiti as living in a single social and political terrain.

Religion has played a particularly significant role in this transformation. Starting in the 1970s, Haitian Catholic priests in both Haiti and the United States, influenced by liberation theology, emerged as important leaders of the poor and began to build a transnational grassroots movement that demanded social justice. Responding to the call for prayer in indigenous languages and cultural idioms, these priests used their prestige and literacy to legitimate Kreyòl, thereby bringing the African-based culture of the rural poor into the Catholic Mass.[41] In the United States as well as Haiti, Catholic masses became occasions for discussions of the state of the Haitian nation and need for fundamental change. Haitians in both localities participated in the same political discourse, within the context of Catholic prayer. In Haiti, this developed into the *Ti Legliz* (grassroots churches), congregations of the poor that challenged both the Catholic hierarchy that remained linked to the elite and the Duvalier regime. In the United States, the same transnational religious movement influenced community organizations such as HAUP, so that it served simultaneously as a community group immersed in local ethnic politics and an extension of the movement for social change in Haiti. The Haitian Catholic Church had become fully transnational by the year 2000, regularly sponsoring activities in both the United States and Haiti. The Church continues to link saving souls and saving Haiti, although there are sharp political differences within the institution on what kind of politics saving Haiti entails.

On the surface, the Haitian Protestant churches seem to have followed a different trajectory. These churches, which range from established mainstream denominations to evangelical fundamentalists, have grown in number and significance in both Haiti and the United States in the past two decades. From their pulpits and widely disseminated radio shows, many ministers warn their congregants against political activism. They also preach that "only God can save Haiti." In these messages, religious prayer brings national as well as individual salvation. In actuality, these churches have not only promoted transnational connections but have infused into the transnational space they foster a concern for the Haitian nation.

The Haitian media, too, have played a vital role in legitimizing the concept of Haiti as a transnational nation-state. Beginning in 1986, Haitian newspapers founded by political exiles in the United States set up publishing operations in Haiti. Their coverage included the activities of the diaspora as well as political developments in Haiti, and their advertisements were for businesses and property in the United States, Canada, and Haiti. A few years later, Haitian radio programs began live broadcasts from Haiti or call-in shows where people in Haitian localities such as Montreal, New York, and south Florida could participate in the same discussion. When they turned on the radio, Haitian migrants found not simply entertainment in a familiar language. By listening to Haitian radio, they were able to identify with Haiti on a daily basis. Those living in Haiti, meanwhile, were learning to think about their national life as extending beyond the borders of their ancestral state. To legitimate this new frame of mind, Haitians formulated an ideology of long-distance nationalism.

Embracing Prodigal Sons and Daughters

Even before Haitian political leaders acknowledged Haitians living abroad as a continuing part of the Haitian body politic, impoverished people in Haiti who survived on remittances sent by family were making such claims. This became evident to us when, cognizant of the political language of the 1990s, we went back and looked at what people in Haiti had been trying to communicate to us in the 1980s, which at the time we were not able to hear.

In 1989, our research assistant in Haiti interviewed several networks of people living in the vicinity of Port-au-Prince who were supported by remittances sent from family members abroad. The thirteen people he spoke with used an ideology of blood to explain the ongoing connection between Haitians living abroad and those in Haiti. They also asserted that Haitians living abroad remained a part of Haiti, even if they became naturalized US citizens. For example, Petit-Fils, a fifty-nine-year-old painter, declared: "A person is still a Haitian [if he becomes a citizen of another country]. His blood is still Haitian blood. It is only the person's title and name that is changed. The person's skin is still Haitian, and besides that, the person was born in Haiti and even if that person doesn't consider himself Haitian the whites in the country where he's living still consider him Haitian. Therefore, I don't think a person should reject his country."

In 1990, Haitian political leaders echoed this rhetoric when Aristide, a Catholic priest who had emerged as one of the leaders of the grassroots church movement, began to campaign for president. Initially, Aristide, who had himself lived and studied abroad but had returned to Haiti, had repeated the call to the diaspora to return. As he declared in 1987 in one of his books, *In the Parish of the Poor*, "My generation is running away from Haiti, with its dark corners and by-ways. I want to call them back before they begin their fruitless travels. ... I say to them come back and make a new Haiti."[42] Yet, in 1990, while building grassroots support for his candidacy, Aristide reconsidered the politics of return in light of the part that the diaspora was playing in Haiti.

It was clear that remittances from transmigrants to family members had helped a significant sector of the Haitian population weather the most difficult periods of the Duvalier dictatorship.

Meanwhile, Catholic priests – many with substantial bases in Miami, the New York metropolitan area, and Montreal, but who were part of a growing grassroots movement in Haiti, too – had transformed the political life and consciousness of the growing numbers of Haitian transmigrants. They brought transmigrants from diverse class backgrounds into a strong, public, anti-Duvalier movement that made its voice known in the United States through frequent demonstrations and political lobbying. This US movement had become part of a Haitian transnational political struggle to rebuild Haiti. Such activities continued after the Duvalier regime ended in 1986. Individuals seeking the Haitian presidency began to campaign for the office in New York and Miami, even though Haitians living abroad could not vote. Aristide solicited the diaspora's support during his 1990 presidential campaign by asserting that Làvalas, the grassroots movement he was leading, encouraged "the participation of all citizens from all social classes. A special place will be reserved for peasants, women, all patriotic movements, and all Haitians in diaspora."[43]

Aristide, as well as many of those in his government, looked on Haitian transmigrants' financial resources and professional skills as crucial for Haiti's renewal. He spoke of the diaspora as a "bank." Haitian transmigrants could fulfill their responsibilities toward their homeland by continuing to live and work abroad while sending money back to rebuild Haiti. Their trips to Haiti should be as "Kreyòl tourists," bringing tourist dollars.[44]

The diaspora proved to be a key source of funds and personnel for political activities in Haiti. The campaign manager for Aristide's 1990 presidential bid reported that two-thirds of the three hundred thousand dollars raised for the race came from the diaspora.[45] In 1991, to provide the newly elected Aristide government with much needed funds, Haitians in Haiti and throughout the diaspora organized a "marathon of dignity" called Send Haiti Upwards (*Voye Ayiti Monte*, known by Haitians as VOAM). In less than a week, despite their dire economic conditions, overseas Haitians raised more than one million dollars for various projects in Haiti. The Family is Life (*La Fanmi Se Lavi*), a benevolent association founded by Aristide to help orphans in Port-au-Prince, received numerous contributions through minimarathons organized by various overseas Haitian communities.

Through this rhetoric, Aristide, acting as Haiti's head of state, was reclaiming all Haitian migrants and all persons of Haitian descent living abroad, no matter what their legal citizenship or place of birth, as part and parcel of the Haitian nation-state. On the day of his inauguration as president, Aristide dubbed Haitians living abroad the "Tenth Department." The territory of Haiti is divided into nine geographic divisions called departments. Aristide spoke as if they were an equivalent of France's overseas departments, although the Haitian Constitution had not been changed and Haitians abroad live within the territorial boundaries of other countries. In his first New Year's message to the Tenth Department, Aristide welcomed Haitian overseas communities anew, as Haiti's prodigal children, in the fold of the Haitian community, "under the aegis and the protection of the political power of the Haitian nation-state."[46] The diaspora was redefined. It was no longer a location of exile but an integral and vital part of Haiti.

In return for their support, Aristide pledged to the diaspora that the Haitian government would be their spokesperson and protector. Speaking at the United Nations in 1991, he deplored the negative treatment Haitian migrants had been subjected to and the lack of compassion expressed by countries that had received them. From the United Nations' podium, Aristide declared:

> **The sixth commandment of democracy: legitimate defense of the diaspora, or tenth department.** Driven out until 1991 by the blind brutality of the repressive machine or by the structures of exploitation erected in an antidemocratic system, our Haitian brothers and sisters have not always had the good fortune to find the promised land. Illegal because the brutes have not had the forethought to give their victims certificates of torture properly signed; illegal because they have had to travel as boat people without being provided with legal documents, they have nevertheless made great contributions to the economic prosperity of their patrons, preferring to do all the hardest work rather than to take charity.[47]

Aristide summarized his changed view of the diaspora in his autobiography, published in 1993. In a chapter with the revealing title "May the Peace of the Dollar Be with You," he wrote: "With Lavalas' rise to power, Haiti had grown greater, extending far beyond its 27,000 square kilometers and nine departments. Even before February 7,1991, we had created a tenth department encompassing our compatriots outside, who had multiple roles. Without them, what would become of some of the families on the island? ... Honorary ambassadors of Haiti, ties between the mother country and the rest of the world, enthusiastic supporters of renewal, the avant garde of a new definition of citizenship. ... A new citizenship was being forged, together with a new society that cooperates with its branches overseas."[48]

In response to their new welcome, many Haitian organizations that had focused their attention on the conditions faced by Haitian migrants in the United States now launched transnational activities. They began to sponsor activities to rebuild Haiti. The phrase "building Haiti" combined a collective nostalgia for an imagined past of Haitian accomplishments with a commitment to contribute not only to family but the nation. Within a very few years, the ethos of Haitian life in the United States had changed. Increasing numbers of people both in Haiti and the diaspora began to believe that emigrants could remain settled in the United States and still be patriots. With the election of Aristide in 1990, long-distance nationalism became the order of the day as both young and old contributed to Haiti by sending donations, organizing projects, or making short trips. Haitian organizations based in New York sent members to Haiti to participate in various projects, from clinics to literacy campaigns, to rebuild Haiti. The rhetoric of rebuilding was shared by those in Haiti. They embraced the project of national construction as a transnational project to restore their country.

Nevertheless, it was the political mobilization of the diaspora on behalf of Aristide, when he was exiled by a military coup after only seven months in office, that firmly implanted the concept of the Haitian people as a transnational nation among Haitians in Haiti. We found that the idea was shared in Haiti among both persons who did and did not have personal ties to the diaspora. From 1991 to 1994, the military government that overthrew Aristide carried out a reign of terror. They were responsible for massacres in poor neighborhoods, random shootings with dead bodies left in the streets to spread terror, attacks on grassroots organizations of the poor, rapes and sexual tortures of women activists, and assassinations of political leaders.[49] During these grim times, the opposition of the Haitian diaspora to the military junta and its call for the restoration of the democratically elected Aristide government provided hope to the population of Haiti. We were repeatedly told that the diaspora had "helped Haiti" by returning Aristide to office: "They are the ones who fought in Miami. They screamed for help so that Aristide could return to Haiti to rebuild the country. To build the country. To make it a smooth/silky country."

Demonstrations, statements of protest placed as paid advertisements in the *New York Times*, patient lobbying with US congresspeople, and the press of Haitian refugees seeking to enter the United States did keep the issue of Aristide's presidency alive in the United States.[50] After three years of officially condemning the Haitian military but actually providing it with various kinds of economic and military assistance, the United States changed its stance, leading a United Nations military intervention and occupation in October 1994 that restored Aristide to office.[51]

Aristide returned with a coterie of advisers and ministers who were transmigrants, adept at lobbying within the US political system, and convinced that they could help Haiti through hobnobbing with US congressional members, businesspeople, and bankers. They popularized the political inclusion of the diaspora as part of Haiti. Their presence personified Haiti as a transnational nation-state. Their political practices and transnational political networks contributed to this new conception of Haiti. The possibility and necessity for Haitian migrants to remain politically engaged in Haiti, while permanently settling in the United States, also became a central theme of Haitian transnational newspapers and radio. Broadcasters spoke not as political exiles or ethnics but as the Haitian diaspora – an influential section of the Haitian people.

Even If You Naturalize . . .

By the 1990s, poor and middle-class people in Haiti were routinely referring to blood ties to explain the long-distance nationalism of the diaspora. The fervor with which many individuals spoke about the links between those living in Haiti and those who had emigrated and lived abroad matched the intensity of the most fiery political leader.

It was this intensity that can be felt in the appeal that Marjorie made to the diaspora. Marjorie, the young woman who took our tape recorder into her hand to speak directly to her "brothers and sisters" in the diaspora, is a slender, determined nineteen-year-old whose father is a cultivator, whose mother sells meat in the market, and whose sister in the United States sends remittances to support the family she left in Aux Cayes. Readily responding to our request to define the term Haitian, Marjorie stated: "A person who is living abroad for a long time is a Haitian. Even if you are naturalized [as an American], you keep Haitian blood. The only way they can keep you from being Haitian is if they cut your meat and took all your blood."

The continuity of Haitian identity was said to hold even after persons became legally naturalized. Dimase is the thirty-three-year-old man who is supported by his five siblings in the United States. They consistently send money for the rent, clothes, and shoes. This income is supplemented by the work his wife does cooking and selling food to an engineering company. They have one child and live in a poor, though not totally impoverished, neighborhood right outside Port-au-Prince. For Dimase, nationality is a matter of descent, so that "even if you naturalize [as an American], you are still Haitian." He went on to apply this to his siblings. Of his brother who has become a US citizen, he said, "Inside of him, my brother stays Haitian. He is Haitian even if he changes his nationality."

Those who did not receive remittances could be equally as adamant. The response of an impoverished, unemployed young man designated by his friends as *Resigne* (Resigned) was typical. He is so poor that he sleeps in a tree and uses the washing facilities in the house of Yvette's

sister-in-law – a house for which Yvette pays the rent. "They don't change even if they naturalize because they have the blood. Even if they naturalize and become citizens [of another country], they have Haitian blood in them. They love Haiti."

To Resigne, the diaspora, organically a part of Haiti but with resources, "can come here and build schools. They make health centers. All these things could help. There are many children. You have five fingers, each has its own height." To express his belief that the diaspora is part of Haiti, Resigne used a folk saying that has often expressed the unity of the Haitian nation, despite the divisions of class. In this unity, each is obliged to contribute what they can, as the fingers of a hand that are unequal in size, but that all contribute to completing a task. Marc, a man in his sixties who lives in the same neighborhood and is also struggling with daily survival, echoed the affirmation of the organic link between the diaspora and Haiti, utilizing the same metaphor. "Those abroad can help ... You have your five fingers, they are not of the same height." Ninety-three percent of the people we spoke with thought that individuals born in Haiti remained all or part Haitian, wherever they lived or whatever their legal citizenship, although 7 percent of this group insisted that to claim their membership in the nation, those abroad had to contribute to Haiti.

By 1996, there was a widespread and nearly uniform knowledge of the word "diaspora" that has now become incorporated into Kreyòl to mean Haitians living abroad. The implication that those abroad were obligated to return home generally had been abandoned. Respondents differed in their judgment of the effectiveness of this assistance to Haiti. Many told us that the diaspora did help family, but had failed to help the nation as a whole. Underlying this critique was the view that it was the responsibility of the diaspora to help rebuild Haiti.

Those living in poor housing and without education envisioned the rebuilding of Haiti as a process of physical construction. For them, Haiti as a transnational nation based on the symbolic solidarity of blood ties was a visible force they could see around them. As an exhausted mother of six in Port-au-Prince told us: "Yes, the diaspora helps Haiti. They build schools, now they are talking about building houses for those who can't afford them. Those who can't send their children to school, they will give them half scholarships to send them to school, they have done many things. Even though I did not benefit from them, there are many people who do benefit from that help."

In the years since our interview, as it has been clearer that the diaspora has not provided the leadership or resources to rebuild Haiti, anger at the diaspora has grown. Many of these critics, however, are not repudiating the ties to the diaspora but admonishing the diaspora for neglecting its obligations to the nation. Depending on the context, "diaspora" can be used as a statement of solidarity or reproach, imparting into the term a pejorative undertone suggesting a person who is vain, crass, and a self-centered upstart. This negative evaluation of the diaspora speaks to some of the tensions between those who left and those who remain in Haiti, but such tensions do not amount to a severing of ties.

There also is a counternarrative to the embrace of the diaspora. The educated middle class who remained in Haiti and faced competition from those educated abroad tend to stress the differences between those abroad and in Haiti, arguing that those in the diaspora don't understand Haitian realities. The bourgeoisie, although many are transmigrants with luxurious houses in both Haiti and south Florida, have tended to see members of the diaspora as a threat to their entrenched interests. The poor and disempowered with whom we spoke were able to embrace the diaspora as part of Haiti through ties of blood and simultaneously mark the social distance created through migration. They did this by referring to visiting members of the diaspora, or those who had migrated and abandoned their family obligations, as *blan*, white. We found Georges referred to as white often.

When Nina asked Linda, aged sixteen yet having had only two years of schooling, about Georges, she said, "No, he is not Haitian. He is white." And when she talked about the role of the diaspora in Haiti, she observed that "yes, the white can help Haiti." Return migrants who come home with education, English fluency, and the look of money also reported to us they were perceived as white. Pierre-Antoine, a young man of twenty-four who had been brought by his family to the United States to finish high school in 1985, had been in the US military, and had returned to Haiti shortly before we interviewed him. He told us, "I've heard people from the masses labeling me as 'white,' which to them means 'foreigner,' or he's from the outside. Which is a connotation of the same thing.... They're probably thinking money-wise or whatever."

In discussions of the diaspora among the disempowered, blan is used as a form of social commentary about distances in education and resources, rather than nationality. Mary-Jo, who had worked in factories but currently had no work at all and five children to support, told us, "Yes, I have heard of diaspora. It is someone who is living abroad. Someone who is living in Haiti is not the same. It is not a bad thing [to be diaspora]. Like when a person comes from abroad, s/he is not the same person as you. Here ... nothing is happening. And that person was breathing a different air and therefore s/he is different from you. S/he takes on another smell. S/he breathes another air. S/he changes her or his face, her or his characteristics, but s/he is still Haitian." Here Mary-Jo was signaling some of the dissonance, distances, and life experiences that separate those in Haiti from those abroad. Whether those abroad were labeled "outsider," "foreigner," or "white," or were seen as having "a different face," these speakers were not using such distinctions to sever their connections with the diaspora. The assertion of distance can serve as an appeal for closeness, an argument within rather than an abrogation of family.

Similarly, the recent trend of Haitians living in the United States toward becoming US citizens cannot be interpreted as a rejection of Haiti. In the 1990s, migrants from many parts of the world, including Haiti, began to become US citizens at much greater rates than in the previous several decades.[52] Yvette, Rolande's cousin, worked to improve her English and became a naturalized US citizen. She returned from being awarded her citizenship papers, triumphant, and declared that she would now study even more English so that she could speak like a "real" American. Nevertheless, Yvette does not see her efforts to become incorporated into the United States as a repudiation of Haiti. Her assumption of US citizenship does not mean that she has abandoned her obligations to family in Haiti or her identification with her homeland. In part, Yvette and the myriad of other transmigrants who have become naturalized were responding to a series of punitive measures that the US Congress passed against permanent residents. These measures denied Medicaid care to elderly permanent residents and mandated that permanent residents must be deported as a result of any conviction, past or present, including traffic violations. In addition, the growth of naturalization among Haitians was an indicator that they had come to see obtaining US citizenship as an expression of their continuing commitment to Haiti. They are better able to help Haiti by taking political action as a US citizen. They are beginning to think that they may have to participate in Haiti while remaining physically in the United States.

By the millennium, the political chaos unleashed first by the coup and then US intervention, which further displaced the authority of the Haitian state, meant that it was becoming too dangerous for transmigrants to return to Haiti to settle. Even visits began to be too dangerous. In the summer of 1999, a wedding that Yvette sponsored in Haiti for a niece was attacked by robbers. The thieves cut the lights, and in the darkness, made off with all the wedding presents and the video camera being used to document the event for family in the diaspora. That winter, Rolande and a family member were robbed at gunpoint in broad daylight in the middle of a traffic jam. The robbers took Rolande's passport and her rings, the car, and all the money that Rolande had brought to pay for private hospital care for her mother, who had just experienced a stroke while visiting Haiti. They also stole Rolande and Georges's dreams of retiring in Haiti, or even their ability to visit Haiti without fearing for their lives. The loss was immeasurable. However, for Georges and many in the Haitian diaspora, despair at the violence and

disorder that plagues Haiti has yet to prompt a repudiation of their identification with and willingness to act on behalf of Haiti.

Even anger, bitter disappointment, demoralization, and denouncements of Haiti are often stated in nationalist terms, ones that fuel rather than abate the emotional pull of long-distance nationalism. A statement made on Haitian Flag Day in 1997 by Monsignor Darbouze, a Haitian priest who had been promoted to a leadership position in the Catholic Diocese of Brooklyn, expresses the complex relationship with Haiti – the intertwining of nostalgia, political critique, and ongoing identification – that compels transmigrants to adopt US citizenship as a statement of both love of and despair for Haiti:

"Long live the Haitian flag!" There used to be a time when I [used to say] these words with pride. It was the time of my youth when they celebrated May 18 [Haitian Flag Day] with pomp and circumstance. I recall the parade of primary and secondary schoolchildren in school uniform, singing and marching to the sound of music. The vibration of the marching drums still resonates in my ears. In those days Haiti was still sweet, the worth of our flag was respected. Patriotism was more than just a word that one uttered. I want to speak about the period before the macoute [the armed thugs of the Duvalier regime,] the "grands mangeurs" [the corrupt officials of the Aristide and Préval regimes], and the betrayers of the nation. ... In those days, there was a certain sense of the country and the common good. Democracy didn't exist, but there existed, nonetheless, security and order. The Constitution wasn't respected but they did not completely trammel it under foot.

Are these the words of a resentful Haitian? No! Rather these are the words of a true son of Haiti who made the choice to become an American citizen because he could no longer stand to see his dear fatherland being sullied without taking a stand. The only way for him to react was to become an American citizen. **Long live the Haitian flag!**[53]

As heirs of Africans whose enslavement was justified by Europeans on the grounds that black people were less than human, many Haitians believe that they are never subject to only individual success or failure in the eyes of the world. Father Darbouze's or Georges's accomplishments and setbacks are those of Haiti; Haiti's achievements or shortcomings are theirs. All of this feels familiar to Nina, who grew up in a family that examined both heroes and villains in the news to see if they were Jewish. Nina's parents stressed that the public successes of Jews reflected well on all Jews, while a Jewish scoundrel reinforced the anti-Semitic stereotypes that justified the Holocaust. When memories of racial, religious, or cultural persecution are transmitted across generations, one's identification with an entire nation feels like a normal and natural response. When discrimination is an ongoing daily experience, national identities are strengthened. Those who live in Haiti experience exclusion and scorn within the terrain of world public opinion. The Hollywood transformation of Haitian religious life into a realm of voodoo dolls and zombies is one source of pain. The refusal of the United States to accept most Haitians who fled from repression from Haiti's brutal governments in the 1980s and 1990s, even when refugees' bodies were scarred from torture, is a continuing denial

of Haitian human rights claims, and hence a denial of Haitians' claims to be human.[54] Much of the developing Haitian long-distance nationalism is a shared emotional state that sustains the Haitian poor as well as middle class, women as well as men, young and old – notwithstanding the differences of class, gender, and generation.

Haiti has become a transnational space that extends beyond territorial boundaries, encompassing persons of Haitian ancestry wherever they are located and whatever legal citizenship they may hold. Among those in Haiti, this reconceptualization of their nation builds on widely held ideas of blood ties and has provided a living bridge that can connect them to other lands of greater opportunity. Meanwhile, Haitian migrants living in the United States who face the racial barriers of daily life in an unwelcoming country establish links to their ancestral homeland using a concept of nationality and descent that links them to Haiti as a black nation. As the situation in Haiti becomes ever more desperate, their nostalgia for the sweet Haitian past carries them through the pain of their current situation, in which they are unable to either abandon or reclaim Haiti.

Notes

1 By 2000, many in Haiti had become disillusioned about the possibility that Haitians abroad will rebuild Haiti, and increased anger was directed at the diaspora and individuals from the diaspora returning to Haiti. Nonetheless, the diaspora continued to be seen as part of Haiti.

2 The term "color line" was used to describe the legal and informal racial barriers that divided whites and blacks in the United States until the 1960s. While water fountains, restaurants, theaters, and other public facilities are no longer segregated, black people still experience a color line in the sense that they are policed or given more intense surveillance than whites when they enter certain neighborhoods or stores. In 1999, the New Jersey highway patrol was questioned for their use of training manuals with racial profiling that led officers to search the cars of black drivers much more often than those of whites (Peterson 1999).

3 See Dikötter 1997; Herzfeld 1992; and Balibar 1991.

4 Immigration and Naturalization Service 1996.

5 Between 1971 and 1981, more than 45,000 Haitians arrived by boat (Silk 1986, 16). Most of these people were held in detention camps, despite the fact that they had fled from a brutal dictatorship. Although relatively few Haitians have ever been able to obtain official refugee status, many who fled by boat eventually gained permanent resident status through a legal amnesty program passed by Congress in 1986. Beginning in 1981, however, the United States Coast Guard began intercepting Haitian boats on the high seas, destroying the vessels and returning Haitian refugees to Haiti. Because the Duvalier dictatorship granted permission for the interceptions, these acts were deemed legal. Otherwise, such actions would have been defined as piracy. The Coast Guard's interception of people fleeing Haiti continued, even when the democratically elected government of Aristide was overthrown in 1991 and the United States refused to recognize the military government that ruled Haiti from 1991 to 1994. As political violence and general insecurity

worsened in Haiti in 1999, Haitians again began to flee Haiti in small boats.

6   See Stepick and Swartz 1982, 1986.

7   Immigration and Naturalization Service 1996, 65.

8   Until 1986, employers were not required to verify legal status. In the 1960s and 1970s, anyone who was working could obtain a social security card and pay into social security.

9   See Foner 1987, 1992.

10 Despite the increasing disorder and disarray in Haiti in the years that followed our 1996 visit, the airport waiting area was improved by 1999. Apparently those in power shared Georges's discomfort about the airport.

11 The Haitian experience of standing back and judging Haiti through the eyes of white Americans or Europeans is similar to what W. E. B. Du Bois, in writing about the African American experience, called "double consciousness, this sense of always looking at one's self through the eyes of others, of measuring one's soul by the tape of a world that looks on in amused contempt and pity" ([1903] 1989, 364). Michel-Rolph Trouillot (1987) pointed this out in "History, Power, and Ethnography in Haiti."

12 Kamenka 1976.

13 For a summary of the US founding fathers' views on race and republican government, see Takaki 1990, 3–63. For a review of the French vacillation about persons of color, citizenship, and slavery, see Madiou 1991.

14 Symbols such as blood, race, and kinship drawn from the physical world are experienced as what Mary Douglas called "natural symbols," and as such have "surreptitious force" (quoted in Herzfeld 1992, 11).

15 As quoted in Madiou 1991.

16 Henry Louis Gates Jr. (1986) in his Introduction to *"Race," Writing, and Difference* summarizes the view of Enlightenment thinkers about race and civilization. Ronald Takaki (1990) addresses the stance of US intellectuals at the time of the American Revolution. In the nineteenth century, a concept of citizenship as based on blood became popular in many states, such as Germany, that began to claim they were nations. As Walker Connor has pointed out, "Bismark's [sic] famous exhortation to the German people ... 'to think with your blood' was [an] ... attempt to activate a mass psychological vibration predicated upon an intuitive sense of consanguinity" (1994, 37).

17 Oriol 1992.

18 Ardouin [1853] 1958, 9.

19 Letter dated 26 August 1914, quoted in Schmidt 1971, 79.

20 See Schmidt 1971.

21 Déjean 1942, 3–4.

22 Ibid., 12.

23 Ibid., 12.

24 Heinl and Heinl 1978, 643.

25 See Brown 1991, 229.

26 Aristide, 1990, 90.

27 See Buchanan 1980; Dupuy 1997; and Nicholls [1979] 1996.

28 In this respect, Haitians and many contemporary migrants differ from those who came to the United States from rural Europe between 1840 and 1915 (see Connor 1990).

29 See Fouron 1985a, 1985b and Glick Schiller et al. 1987.

30 In addition, until the second half of the twentieth century, there was no Haitian tradition of permanent migration. Although some Haitians have been settling in the United States for two hundred years, most past Haitian migrants had sought, if poor, short-term work in neighboring countries, and if rich, education and cultural polish in Europe. Portugal and Greece were other countries that, until recently, defined emigrants as traitors to the nation (see Feldman-Bianco 1992; Klimt 2000; and Triandafyllidou n.d).

31 See Glick Schiller et al. [1987] 1992.

32 A typical example of these sentiments is the poem (quoted in Wyman 1993, 92) to "American Hungarians" by Emil Ábrænyi:

I know with eager zeal you'd heed,
The nation's call, and you will cross the seas
To join our brethren here, to fight, to bleed,
To die for Magyarland's sweet liberties.

33 Even the migrants who spoke Kreyòl, a distinct language with its own grammar, and knew little or no French identified themselves in the United States as French. Since only whites were recognized as having diverse cultural heritages, while all black persons were described only in racial terms, Haitians used a French rather than a Haitian identity to resist the US racial structure. We want to make it clear that Haitian attempts to avoid racial discrimination by embracing other identities than black within a US context are not a rejection of a more universal black identity or a rejection of African Americans. In general, most Haitians have tried to avoid the treatment that has been accorded to black persons in the United States

even as they have struggled for the rights of all black people. For a discussion of the multiple and changing identities of Haitian migrants between 1957 and 1987, see Glick Schiller et al. 1987; 1992 [1987].

34 See Glick [Schiller] 1975; and Glick Schiller 1977.

35 Beginning in the 1960s, influential social scientists began to designate all immigrant groups except those from England as ethnic groups. In so doing, they negated the differentiation between immigrants such as the Italians, who were seen as white after World War II, and those from outside Europe, who continued to be viewed as people of color. In subtle ways, the attribution and celebration of ethnic difference has maintained the distinction between white Anglo-Saxon Protestants (WASPs) and all others. This differentiation was heightened from the 1880s to 1945 and has still not completely disappeared, as became evident in the excitement when Al Gore chose Joseph Lieberman, a Jew, as the Democratic Party nominee for vice president in 2000. Even as such identities acknowledge the validity of diverse cultural roots, they perpetuate the notion that only those who can claim English ancestry are fully part of the US mainstream and can qualify as real Americans. At the same time, the practice of designating immigrants and their descendants from Ireland, eastern and southern Europe, as well as immigrants of color as US ethnic groups, negates the continuing significance of race in the United States. European immigrants are accorded and experience the social acceptance that accompanies whiteness that is not accorded those populations viewed as people of color, such as Haitians. An additional complication is the tendency to use the term *multicultural America* in a way that highlights racialized categories such as Hispanic, Asian, and black, contrasting these groupings with normative white America. The seminal work that popularized the concept of ethnic group for all multi-identity populations in the United States was Nathan Glazer and Daniel Moynihan's *Beyond the Melting Pot* (1970). Matthew Frye Jacobson (1998) discusses the changing ascription of whiteness in the United States. For a look at the continuing significance of race, see Bell 1993; Dyson 1997; Hill 1997; Harrison 1995, 2000; Lieberson 1980; Steinberg 1981; and Williams 1989.

36 Portes and Stepick 1993. For discussion of Haitian radio in South Florida, see Eugene 1998.

37 Solomon 1998.

38 Benjamin 1998.

39 United Haitian Association Newsletter, June 1982, 1.

40 Beginning in the 1990s, some US politicians were actually encouraging a Haitian transnational identity. For example, in a 1996 statement to the Haitian community, Howard Golden, the president of the borough of Brooklyn, described Haitian Flag Day as an event that "will focus on social and cultural issues facing Haitians at home and in the United States, with particular attention to young people" (1997, 1).

41 See Buchanan 1980; Glick [Schiller] 1975.

42 Aristide 1990, 8.

43 Aristide n.d.

44 Richman 1992a, 196.

45 Jean-Pierre 1994, 59.

46 *Radyo Moman Kreyòl* 1991. *Moman Kreyòl* is a popular Haitian radio program aired on WLIB-AM every Sunday from 10:00 A.M. to 4:00 P.M. WLIB-AM is a minority-owned and -operated business with roots in the Caribbean community in New York.

47 Aristide 1993, 195–6. It is important to note here that the English translation by Linda Maloney, which was completed during Aristide's exile in the United States, strays strikingly from the original French document. The translation's tone is less threatening and the language less militant.

48 Aristide 1993, 141–2.

49 See Americas Watch and the National Coalition for Haitian Refugees 1993; and Human Rights Watch and National Coalition for Haitian Refugees 1994a, 1994b, 1996.

50 Fifty-five thousand fleeing Haitians were intercepted by the United States Coast Guard on the high seas during the first year of the coup. Despite the fact that the US government did not recognize the Haitian government after the coup as legitimate, at least thirty-five thousand of these refugees were forcibly sent back. In 1993, as a presidential candidate, Bill Clinton stated, "I am appalled by the decision of the Bush administration to pick up fleeing Haitians on the high seas and forcibly return them to Haiti before considering their claim to political asylum. ... This policy must not stand." When Clinton became president, however, he continued the policy of "interdiction." Many of those who were returned were beaten or imprisoned by the de facto military government (see Poppen and Wright 1994, 20).

51 See Dupuy 1997.

52 The Immigration and Naturalization Service reported that in 1996, the most recent year for which it had a full tabulation of immigrant

naturalizations, 24,556 Haitian migrants became US citizens. In 1985, only 2,545 Haitians became US citizens (Immigration and Naturalization Service 1996, 141; 1999, 149). For a discussion of the increased rate of naturalization among all nationalities, see Dao 1999.

53 Darbouze 1997, 10. Bold in the original.

54 In the years 1992 and 1993, a period of intensive and well-documented repression of the Haitian grassroots movement, only 756 Haitians were granted political asylum (Immigration and Naturalization Service 1999, 86). In 1994, 3,284 applications were pending when the year began and 10,400 people applied. Of these, only 1,436 people were granted refugee status during 1994 (Immigration and Naturalization Service 1996, 79). Most individuals who fled Haiti were sent home without a chance to even formally apply for refugee status. In the same year, almost all of those who applied for refugee status from Iraq, Iran, Cuba, Laos, and Vietnam were approved.

References

Americas Watch and the National Coalition for Haitian Refugees. 1993. *Silencing a People: The Destruction of Civil Society in Haiti*. New York: Human Rights Watch.

Ardouin, Beaubrun ([1853] 1958) *Etudes sur l'histoire d'Haiti*. Edited by Dr. François Dalencour. Condés-Noireau, France: Condéenne.

Aristide, Jean-Bertrand, (nd) Pwojè Lavalas. Mimeograph, in files of Georges Fouron.

Aristide, Jean-Bertrand, (1990) *In the Parish of the Poor: Writings from Haiti*. Maryknoll, NY: Orbis Press.

Aristide, Jean-Bertrand, (1993) *An Autobiography*. Maryknoll, NY: Orbis Books.

Balibar, Etienne (1991) Racism and Nationalism. In *Race, Nation, Class: Ambiguous Identities*, edited by Etienne Balibar and Immanuel Wallerstein. London: Verso.

Bell, Derrick A. (1993) *Faces at the Bottom of the Well*. New York: Basic Books.

Benjamin, Jody (1998) Observing Haitian Holiday. *Sun Sentinel*, 19 November, 20B.

Brown, Karen McCarthy (1991) *Mama Lola: A Vodou Priestess in Brooklyn*. Berkeley: University of California Press.

Buchanan, Susan (1980) Scattered Seeds: The Meaning of the Migration of Haitians in New York City. PhD diss., New York University.

Connor, Walker (1990) When is a Nation? *Ethnic and Racial Studies* 13, (1):92–100.

Connor, Walker (1994) A Nation is a Nation, is a State, is an Ethnic Group, is a .... In *Nationalism*, edited by John Hutchinson and Anthony D. Smith. Oxford: Oxford University Press.

Dao, James (1999) Immigrant Diversity Slows Traditional Political Climb. *New York Times* (New England edn), 29 December, A1, A20.

Darbouze, Roland (1997) Vive le drapeau haïtien. *Builder's Journal*, 18 May, 3.

Déjean, Leon (1942) Notre combat. *Chantiers* 1(2) (15 July):3–4, 12.

Dikötter, Frank, ed. (1997) *The Construction of Racial Identities in China and Japan: Historical and Contemporary Perspectives*. Honolulu: University of Hawaii Press.

Du Bois, W.E.B. ([1903] 1989) *The Souls of Black Folks*. New York: Bantam Books.

Dupuy, Alex (1997) *Haiti in the New World Order: The Limits of the Democratic Revolution*. Boulder, CO: Westview Press.

Dyson, Michael Eric, (1997) *Race Rules: Navigating the Color Line*. New York: Vintage Books.

Eugene, Emmanuel (1998) Transnational Migrant Media: A Study of South Florida Haitian Radio. Master's thesis, Florida International University.

Feldman-Bianco, Bela (1992) Multiple Layers of Time and Space: The Construction of Class, Race, Ethnicity, and Nationalism among Portuguese Immigrants. In *Towards a Transnational Perspective on Migration: Race, Class, Ethnicity, and Nationalism Reconsidered*, edited by Nina Glick Schiller, Linda Basch and Cristina Blanc-Szanton. New York: New York Academy of Sciences.

Foner, Nancy (1987) The Jamaicans: Race and Ethnicity among Migrants in New York City. In *New Immigrants in New York City*, edited by Nancy Foner. New York: Columbia University Press.

Foner, Nancy (1992) West Indians in New York City and London: A Comparative Analysis. In *Caribbean Life in New York City: Sociocultural Dimensions*, edited by Constance Sutton and Elsa Chaney. Rev. edn. New York: Center for Migration Studies.

Fouron, Georges (1985a) The Black Immigrant Dilemma in the United States: The Haitian Experience. *Journal of Caribbean Studies* 3(3): 242–65.

Fouron, Georges (1985b) Patterns of Adaption of Haitian Immigrants of the 1970s in New York City. Ed.D. diss., Teachers College, Columbia University.

Gates, Henry Louis, Jr. (1986) Editor's Introduction: Writing "Race" and the Difference it Makes. In "Race," Writing, and Difference, edited by Henry Louis Gates Jr. Chicago: University of Chicago Press.

Glazer, Nathan, and Daniel Moynihan (1970) Beyond the Melting Pot. Cambridge: MIT Press.

Glick [Schiller], Nina Barnett (1975) The Formation of a Haitian Ethnic Group. PhD diss., Columbia University.

Glick Schiller, Nina (1977) Ethnic Groups are Made Not Born. In Ethnic Encounters: Identities and Contexts, edited by George L. Hicks and Philip E. Leis. North Scituate, MA: Duxbury Press.

Glick Schiller, Nina, Josh DeWind, Marie Lucie Brutus, Carrolle Charles, Georges Fouron and Louis Thomas ([1987] 1992) All in the Same Boat? Unity and Diversity among Haitian Immigrants. In Caribbean Life in New York City: Sociocultural Dimensions, edited by Constance R. Sutton and Elsa M. Chaney. Rev. edn. New York: Center for Migration Studies.

Golden, Howard (1997) Statement in Honor of Haitian Flag Day. In Builder's Journal. New York: Flag Day Committee.

Harrison, Faye (1995) The Persistent Power of "Race" in the Cultural and Political Economy of Racism. Annual Review of Athropology 24:47–74.

Harrison, Faye (2000) Facing Racism and the Moral Responsibility of Human Rights Knowledge. Annals of the New York Academy of Sciences 925:45–69.

Heinl, Robert Debs, and Nancy Gordon Heinl (1978) Written in Blood: The Story of the Haitian People, 1492–1971. Boston: Houghton Mifflin.

Herzfeld, Michael (1992) The Social Production of Indifference: Exploring the Symbolic Roots of Western Bureaucracy. Chicago: University of Chicago Press.

Hill, Mike (1997) Whiteness, a Critical Reader. New York: New York University Press.

Human Rights Watch and National Coalition for Haitian Refugees (1994a) Rape in Haiti: A Weapon of Terror. Human Rights Watch Report 6 (8).

Human Rights Watch and National Coalition for Haitian Refugees (1994b) Terror Prevails in Haiti: Human Rights Violations and Failed Democracy. Human Rights Watch Report 6 (5).

Human Rights Watch and National Coalition for Haitian Refugees (1996) Haiti, Thirst for Justice: A Decade of Impunity in Haiti. Human Rights Watch Report 8 (7).

Jacobson, Matthew Frye (1998) Whiteness of a Different Color: European Immigrants and the Alchemy of Race. Cambridge: Harvard University Press.

Jean-Pierre, Jean (1994) The Tenth Department. In The Haiti Files: Decoding the Crisis, edited by James Ridgeway, Washington, DC: Essential Books.

Kamenka, Eugene (1976) Political Nationalism – The Evolution of an Idea. In Nationalism: The Nature and Evolution of an Idea, edited by Eugene Kamenka. New York: St Martin's Press.

Klimt, Andrea, (2000) Enacting National Selves: Authenticity, Adventure, and Disaffection in the Portuguese Diaspora. Identities: Global Studies in Culture and Power 6 (4):513–50.

Lieberson, Stanley (1980) A Piece of the Pie: Blacks and White Immigrants since 1880. Berkeley: University of California Press.

Madiou, Thomas (1991) Histoire d'Haiti. 8 vols. Port-au-Prince: Editions Deschamps. Originally published in 4 vols from 1847 to 1904.

Nicholls, David ([1979] 1996) From Dessalines to Duvalier: Race, Color, and National Independence in Haiti. Cambridge, MA: Cambridge University Press.

Oriol, Michel, (1992) 185 images de la révolution à St. Domingue. Port-au-Prince: Henri Deschamps.

Peterson, Iver (1999) Whitman Says Troopers Used Racial Profiling. New York Times, 21 April, section A1.

Poppen, Cinny, and Scott Wright, eds. (1994) Beyond the Mountains, More Mountains: Haiti Faces the Future. Washington, DO: Ecumenical Program on Central America and the Carribean.

Portes, Alejandro, and Alex Stepick (1993) City on the Edge: The Transformation of Miami. Berkeley: University of California Press.

Radyo Moman Kreyòl. 1991 WLIB-AM, 5 January.

Richman, Karen (1992a) "A Lavalas at home/a Lavalas for home": Inflections of Transnationalism in the Discourse of Haitian President Aristide. In Towards a Transnational Perspective on Migration: Race, Class, Ethnicity, and Nationalism Reconsidered, edited by Nina Glick Schiller, Linda Basch, and Cristina Blanc-Szanton. New York: New York Academy of Sciences.

Schmidt, Hans (1971) The United States Occupation of Haiti, 1915–1934. New Brunswick, NJ: Rutgers University Press.

Silk, James (1986) Despite a Generous Spirit: Denying Asylum in the United States. Washington, DC: US Committee for Refugees, American Council for Nationalities Service.

Solomon, Lois (1998) History of Africa, Holocaust in Classes. Sun Sentinel, 2 August, 1B.

Steinberg, Stephen (1981) *The Ethnic Myth: Race, Ethnicity, and Class in America*. Boston: Beacon Press.

Stepick, Alex, and Dale Swartz (1982) Haitian Refugees in the US. *Minority Rights Group Report*, 52.

Stepick, Alex, and Dale Swartz (1986) Flight into Despair: A Profile of Recent Haitian Refugees in South Florida. *International Migration Review* 20 (74):329–50.

Takaki, Ronald (1990) *Iron Cages: Race and Culture in Nineteenth-century America*. New York: Oxford University Press.

Triandafyllidou, Anna, (nd) Immigration, Nationalist Discourse, and the Rhetoric of Exclusion: The Case of Greece. Manuscript, in the files of Nina Glick Schiller.

Trouiliot, Michel-Rolph (1987) History, Power, and Ethnography in Haiti. Paper presented at the 86th Annual Meeting of the American Anthropological Association, 20 November, Chicago.

United Haitian Association (1982) Patriotic Appeal to the Community. *United Haitian Association Newsletter* (June).

US Immigration and Naturalization Service (1996) *Statistical Yearbook of the Immigration and Naturalization Service, 1994*. Washington, DC: Government Printing Office.

US Immigration and Naturalization Service (1999) *Statistical Yearbook of the Immigration and Naturalization Service, 1997*. Washington, DC: Government Printing Office.

Williams, Brackette (1989) A Class Act: Anthropology and the Race to Nation across Ethnic Terrain. *Annual Reviews of Anthropology* 18:401–44.

Wyman, Mark, (1993) *Round-trip to America: The Immigrants Return to Europe, 1880–1930*. Ithaca, NY: Cornell University Press.

16

Designing Women

Corporate Discipline and Barbados's Off-shore Pink-Collar Sector

Carla Freeman

The Off-shore Office as Scene for Research

The bright yellow awning-shaded tables of Chefette are crowded with young Bajan women animated in their lunchtime conversation; their colorful and fashionable dress turns the heads of passersby. Within moments, the fast-food tables empty, and the high-heeled workers of Data Air[1] escape the midday Caribbean sun, hurrying back to the air-conditioned hum of the "open office." These women represent vast changes in labor patterns and technology in the international arena. Their lives have suddenly become intertwined with service workers in such disparate places as Ireland, the Dominican Republic, Jamaica, Mauritius, and the United States, as the information age signals the virtual collapse of national boundaries and as labor and capital become increasingly internationalized. On the data-entry floor of this off-shore information processing facility, more than 100 women sit at clustered computer stations, entering data from some 300,000 ticket stubs from one airline's 2,000 daily flights. One floor below, an equal number of women work as "approvers," entering data from medical claims sent for processing by one of the largest insurance companies in the United States.

This expanding company alone hires close to 1,000 Barbadian workers – almost all of whom are young women. Their fingers fly and the frenetic clicking of keys fills a vast and chilly room as Walkman-clad women work eight-hour shifts at video display terminals – constantly monitored for productivity and accuracy – typing to the latest dub, calypso, or easy-listening station. The muffled clatter of keys creates a sort of white noise, and the green glow of a sea of computer screens lends a sort of Orwellian aura to the tropical setting outside.

Data Air and Multitext Corporation are both foreign-owned off-shore companies, one owned by an American and the other by a British multinational. Both set up shop in Barbados in the mid-1980s, and with the exception of the English general manager of Multitext, they are managed almost entirely by Bajans. The move from the American Southwest to Barbados has saved Data Air's parent company roughly 35 percent on its data-entry costs, in addition to the profits made from its expansion into insurance claims processing for one of America's largest firms. From the Barbadian standpoint, this company provides close to a thousand jobs, and its Bajan general manager anticipates that a recent expansion will generate significant foreign exchange, desperately needed as the country now faces newly introduced IMF structural adjustment measures.

Located under the general umbrella of manufacturing, and marking the latest version of high-tech rationalization of the labor process, the expansion of this new off-shore industry represents a massive and international commodification of information – in forms ranging from academic texts to airline tickets, consumer warranty cards, pornographic novels, specialized scientific articles, and literary classics. Data in various forms are currently either flown back and forth between "core" and "periphery" for overnight transactions or sent over fiber optic telephone lines for almost immediate return. New satellite technology facilitates fast and relatively inexpensive transmission of information between "offices" all over the world. In many ways, the shift of information-based work off-shore looks much like a newer, spruced-up version of the export processing model à la Arthur Lewis and Puerto Rico's Operation Bootstrap. In addition to management-level incentives and the arrangements made between local government and foreign industry, these information-based enterprises closely model their traditional manufacturing counterparts, and what looks like clerical work (generally considered white-collar "head" work) begins more closely to resemble low-skilled, highly rationalized assembly-line work in corporate garb.

A number of recent studies have addressed the ways in which the global economy, with its vast movements of capital, labor, and changing technology, is radically reshaping people's (and particularly women's) lives (e.g., Abraham-Van der Mark 1983; Beneria and Roldan 1987; Bolles 1983; Kelly 1987; Mies 1986; Nash and Fernandez-Kelly 1983; Ong 1987; Safa 1981; Sassen 1988; Ward 1990). Within the global orderings, traditional notions of boundaries and space have suddenly given way, while capital, labor, and relations of production and consumption that used to be structured along geographic lines are conflating as borders vanish altogether.

This discussion moves between personal narratives of working women's lives and corporate doctrines and ideologies about gender and work in the context of both Barbados's economic development strategy and a burgeoning and globalized information age.

Although international movements of people, goods, culture, and ideologies are certainly not new historical phenomena in the West Indies, the current character and scale of these processes *are* arguably distinct. As these newly incorporated pink-collar workers so clearly reveal, "natives" (and this is particularly evident within the Caribbean) travel between "first" and "third" worlds in increasing numbers, and in their lives in Barbados, imported "first world" artifacts and ideologies (disseminated through the media, advertising, music, et cetera) abound. There are internationalized relations of production in which not only does the information to be "processed" zoom instantly between countries, but so, in a sense, do the processors themselves. This enormous mobility manifests itself at various levels within the labor process. In the case of Data Air, the airline tickets being processed are fitting emblems of the overall collapse of space and distance in this new information age. As part of the company incentive plan, employees are rewarded for exceptional production rates with "thank you cards" in the form of travel vouchers that can be exchanged for trips to other Caribbean islands, Canada, or the United States. In turn, such voyages reveal these women's further entrenchment in the international economy as they purchase clothes, jewelry, and household goods from abroad, both for their own consumption and for marketing back home in an active and diverse informal sector.

The critical labor process school, which followed in the tradition of Harry Braverman's *Labor and Monopoly Capitalism* (1974), argues that the radical restructuring of work currently occurring in the clerical arena is part of a generalized process whereby work is fragmented and deskilled as a necessary part of capitalism's "forward march . . . that will ultimately degrade all but the most skilled labor" (Baran and Teegarden 1987:202). In the context of office work, however, it becomes increasingly clear that these processes take on a distinct character, and that we are witnessing the forging of a very particular, newly gendered working class. A number of recent feminist analyses have gone beyond early critical labor process frameworks to look at the particular ways in which restructurings of labor and capital and technological change have had gender-specific implications. These studies, along with recent research about women's massive recruitment into the "global assembly line," can help us better situate the experiences of Barbadian off-shore office workers.

The assumption is often made that clerical jobs constitute middle-class "mental" or "non-manual" work. However, the contemporary range of new "office" contexts (with a one-to-one boss: secretary ratio at one extreme and vast data-processing pools at the other) forces us to look more closely at the organization of the labor process and to differentiate between types of office work, revising the oversimplified link between "clerical" and "middle class." Moreover, if we accept the importance of the distinction between manual and nonmanual work (versus manual and mental), then, as Braverman implies, clerical work in the form of high-volume information processing – with its low skill level, low pay, and repetitive, fragmented nature – more closely resembles factory work than traditional office work. The nature and spatial organization of clerical work has changed dramatically from its traditional boss–secretary arrangement. Alongside the development of the off-shore office has been the emergence of home-based clerical work in the United States, where women seeking autonomy, flexibility, and a better balance of work and family responsibilities perform a "double day" while simultaneously absorbing overhead costs and forgoing the benefits offered to full-time office staff. These parallel forms of information-based work make an interesting counterpoint to controversial presumptions about "available pools of labor" and their distinctly feminized makeup. Some feminist analyses of automation in the workplace argue that, although increased computerization of offices has led to a decline in some areas of boss–secretary exploitation, it simultaneously gives rise to other forms of control and oppression (Barker

and Downing 1980). Rosemary Pringle (1989) argues that the decline in status of clerical work in the 1950s and 1960s marked changes in the structure of femininity. "Rather than being 'proletarianized,' clerical workers lost some of their status as 'ladies' and were thrown into the mass category of 'girls.'" This happened, she says, through a process of "sexualization rather than through loss of control over the 'means of production'" (p. 193). In the case of clerical workers in vast word-processing pools and off-shore data-entry houses, I would argue that *both* processes are taking place together, creating a class of newly proletarianized and distinctly feminine subjects. The notion of "pink-collar" workers here implies these simultaneous feminization and proletarianization processes.

Woman as "Better Suited": Reinvention of a Familiar Myth

One development officer who specializes in the arena of off-shore information processing in Barbados put forth a familiar explanation for why women workers are preferred for this work. The preference, he said, is not a matter of deliberate selection, but due, rather, to the nature of the production process itself, as well as to the educational and cultural climate.

> Women tend to do light assembly work which involves sitting and manipulating fine objects. Some persons claim that men don't have that good coordination. ... I don't know how true that is, but ... some people claim that. I think it might more be a matter of aptitude – and aptitude is probably cultivated by your society and so on. A man is seen in movies and in real life doing things, moving and so on. A man is never seen sitting ... sitting especially on a line manipulating fine things. And he may not have had the practice, because in terms of practice, women have had practice manipulating needles and doing fine intricate things, embroidery or cake icing, or being more delicate. And also they have smaller hands, so if you're going to manipulate fine things the physical structure may have some impact. Whatever the reason is, it so happens that women tend to do data entry, garments, electronic assembly, and men tend to do heavier type work. As for the reasons, I wouldn't try to imagine.

Like many other managers and government representatives, this development office resorts both to the biological rationale that women's passive, patient, and dexterous nature makes them best suited for sedentary, monotonous, and meticulous work, and to the liberal position of choice – that women do these jobs because they have the requisite skills and because they exercise individual free will. He vacillates between the "nature" and "culture" rationales for the selection of women, but in the final analysis he implies that these patterns are natural, matter-of-fact, and not up for challenge. From management through rank-and-file data-entry clerks, many with whom I spoke echo similar "commonsense" essentialist explanations: women perform these jobs because they are simply "better suited" for the work. One of the few male employees in a non-typing job at Data Air explained, "I never really thought about one of the keying jobs. I probably think my fingers are too big for the keyboard. To me, a lady would handle that a lot more better than a gentleman ... 'cause ... the touch a lady has, it would be much more comfortable to her. And I personally am the type of guy that likes to be moving around – active – I mean lifting things and that kind of thing." More often than not, female keyers themselves stated simply that women know how to type, and that because these jobs require typing, men do not bother to apply. In Barbados, as in many other places, girls take typing in school, not boys. So, the logic behind "why women?" appears self-evident – since typing is the main requirement for data processing, only girls and women tend to apply for the jobs. A certain tautology pervades this logic and obviously ignores deeper levels of cultural ideologies surrounding gender-based occupational categories. In light of the usual argument, it is noteworthy that in the sister plant of Data Air located in the Dominican Republic, the work force (performing virtually identical jobs) is roughly half male and half female, a majority of whom hold postsecondary technical degrees.

A Data Air personnel assistant, who was conducting interviews to fill the current demand for 190 new insurance claims approvers, revealed an interesting twist not only to the question of why women are recruited, but specifically why young (and often single) mothers are recruited. She commented that the six women she had interviewed one day ranged in age from 18 to 22, and *all* had children. Although she sympathetically "wondered how they manage it all," she expressed the view that "in the long run they make the best workers. ... They have better family values and a greater sense of responsibility" than many of the others, who are "too flashy" and "in there just for their paychecks." The implication here is that because these women bear the primary responsibility for their children, they work harder and exhibit greater commitment to their jobs. Interestingly, this assumption was strongly contradicted by an American manager of Multitext who argued that, although he had heard (and frankly had counted on the fact) that Barbadian women make good workers because they bear the bulk of the responsibility for their children, he sensed that the matriarchal and extended family instead provides young people with a "guaranteed safety net," thereby obviating precisely the autonomy and sense of responsibility on which he had banked.

A recent increase in crime, the emergence of gang violence, and widespread "indiscipline" among the youth of the country have led to numerous public outcries and a general fear that the traditionally conservative and peaceful social fabric of Barbadian life is quickly being worn thin. Most notable is a lament over the demise both of The Family, the primary locus of social life and economic resourcefulness, and of Christian morality. A number of contradictory arguments and accusations are made in the local press in a scramble to explain these recent and disturbing social changes. On the one hand, working women are blamed for neglecting their maternal obligations; on the other, the diminished role played by grandmothers and other extended female kin, who once bore great responsibility for socialization, is also acknowledged. Women are widely believed to be the natural and necessary minders of children across racial and class groups. From the standpoint of young employed women, the continued formal employment of their mothers and other female relations, and a tendency to idealize marriage and the formation of nuclear families, pose serious implications for the historical precedence of family-based child care and shared domestic responsibilities offered by the traditional extended household (Powell 1986; Senior 1991).

In the context of the data-entry industry, two contradictory profiles of "ideal" workers underlie management's conceptualization of, and rationalizations for, hiring women workers. They reveal international corporate notions about women as workers, as well as long-held stereotypes about West Indian women as strong and independent matriarchs. The young single woman continues to be perceived as the quintessential off-shore worker. Family metaphors that incorporate her as a "daughter" portray her as a first-time worker, enjoying the freedom and independence that comes from earning a wage, and as a contributing but nonessential earner in her own household.[2] At the same time, "older" women with children (regardless of their household composition), whose wage-earning roles cast them as the backbone of their families, constitute an alternative stereotype. As the manager makes clear, the expectation is that "older" women will make up a particularly committed and responsible work force and thus ensure high-quality production. Indeed, these women are viewed as a distinct worker "generation" and are often referred to as the "old guard" – those who came to work for Data Air when the company opened its doors in 1983 and continue to constitute a committed work force nine years later. One member of the old guard described the distinctions between generations: they have different views regarding salaries, and the older women identify more with the growth of the company:

> Now I'm 25. When I came here I was 18. ... I was one of the youngest in my department. ... Down here, although the age difference is only about 5–7 years apart, I think it is very noticeable. When I came here I was working for BDS $187.50 (US$93.75 biweekly). That is one figure I will never forget. How many of these people do you think are going to work for that? What they are making now is considerably more than what I was making then, but they don't think it's enough. I know people that even resign from here and just went home and sat down because they didn't think that coming in here and

working for that salary made it worthwhile ... they don't really stick it out. ... I think that generation now are different ... they don't take the same hassles that we have in our day. They're less tolerant. Most of these people in here was born in the '70s and I was born in the '60s. I think if you want you could call it a generation gap ... they haven't seen this company transformed and maybe they don't feel a part of it, but we that were here saw the progress.

Contrary to the usual trend in export-processing industries around the globe, the old guard of Data Air represents a significant presence not only in numbers, but also in creating an alternative worker profile. In contrast to the more common tendency for women with children (or those who become pregnant) to be turned down or terminated from jobs, the old guard are often favored over younger "school leavers" in the Barbados-based data-entry industry.

Corporate Discipline in the Open Office

A number of elements distinguish the new information-processing enterprises from the off-shore assembly plants that preceded them, from the labor process itself to the ideologies that underlie the construction of an ideal feminine work force. Although the garment and electronic industries have also targeted young Third World women (Ong 1987), the particular methods of control and surveillance fostered by computer technology lend a new and multidimensional shape to the "corporate discipline" exercised in other off-shore factories. The video display terminal (VDT) is undoubtedly a manager's dream come true: every employee can be electronically observed without pause or error; her productivity can be measured for specific increments or longitudinally; and she need never be engaged in face-to-face contact. The computer thus becomes a tool that not only speeds specific job tasks, but that evaluates the worker as well.

Early industrialists devised numerous methods to regulate and direct bodies and bodily energies for productive labor. Foucault described these processes of industrial management as "laying the groundwork for a new kind of society, a 'disciplinary society,' one in which bodily discipline, regulation and surveillance are taken for granted" (as quoted in Zuboff 1988:319). His analysis of the panopticon as a form of control can be applied to new labor contexts, thus allowing the intensely powerful and unrelenting eye of the computer to be seen as a reinvention of an old form of control. This old form was based on the 1787 architectural plan of Jeremy Bentham, the panopticon of which Foucault writes, which was designed to contain convicts and paupers and was used ultimately in prisons, asylums, and factories. The design included a "twelve sided polygon formed in iron and sheathed in glass in order to create the effect of ... 'universal transparency'" (as quoted in Zuboff 1988: 320). As Foucault described it, "each individual, in his place, is securely confined to a cell from which he is seen from the front by the supervisor; but the side walls prevent him from coming into contact with his companions. He is seen but he does not see; he is the object of information, never a subject in communication" (Foucault 1979:200).

The phenomenon of VDT workers in the information industry is, even in its clean and "cool" appearance, a haunting reminder of Bentham's eighteenth-century panopticon. The individual nature of the work process, whereby keyers are physically divided from one another at cellular stations, is coupled with a double layer of surveillance: the deep level of computer monitoring and the surface layer of human supervision. Managers' and supervisors' glass-enclosed offices surround the data-entry floor so that they can observe the overall hum of the shift, while workers, susceptible to their gaze, focus on the VDT screens. The information industry lends itself to a level of worker control and surveillance that far exceeds other forms of manufacturing industries in capitalizing on the power of the panopticon: the computer systems at which keyers work are capable of monitoring the workers' error rates, speed, and quantity of items processed. Lapses in keying, length and frequency of breaks, and worker productivity and discipline can be thus calculated and compared in precise and systematic ways.

As much as the computer facilitates this intense level of surveillance, technology *per se* cannot, however, be held singularly responsible for job deskilling and a newly configured corporate discipline. Focusing on hardware alone ignores the processes by which the technology is mediated through a host of other social practices (language, dress, et cetera). It is these processes that deserve greater attention within critical feminist labor studies. Technological transformations carry ideological, social, and economic implications that are distinctly gendered. Similarly, deskilling and new technologies cannot completely explain the greater preference for women within this or other labor-intensive industries. Such transformations are cleverly and integrally bound up in the forms of supervision as well as in the general expectation that clerical workers conform to so-called traditional female stereotypes (e.g., that they be pleasant, loyal, courteous, well groomed, and perhaps attractive, cheerful). Although discipline and control have been central to sex-selectivity in the electronics and garment (manufacturing) industries, their role in the management of this new "clerical" enclave is even more pronounced and multifaceted – markedly in terms of dress. One corporate officer proudly proclaimed that the information-processing industry offers a work environment on a par with that of other offices and distinctly separate from manufacturing. "Women are expected to dress professionally here," he said. "This is not a production mentality like jeans and tee shirts." And, in fact, with a number of manufacturing industries located next to these data-entry facilities, many of the women themselves stated quite unequivocally that "you can tell by the way (a woman) looks" whether she is going to work at one of the garment factories or in data entry. Although they note little difference in the pay between the two, they clearly think that working in data entry was a step above the garment factories. Vividly illustrating this point was the expression of disbelief and even indignation on the part of several data processors when they learned of a fellow worker who quit her job as a keyer to work at a piece rate in a neighboring cigar factory. Discussing the pros and cons of her job and the general atmosphere of this information enclave, buzzing with the sound of computer keys and "plenty of gossip," one young woman emphasized the importance of dress and appearance in maintaining the professional character of the workplace, as well as the ambivalence on the part of some of the workers about the true nature of the industry:

> They had to talk to one or two people in there already about the way that they dress, but I never had to be spoken to like that. You should dress in a place like that not like if you're going to a party or a disco or going to town ... [you should] dress as if you are working at an office ... 'cause some people don't really look at it as being an office. ... But if they were working in an office they would dress a certain way, so I think that if you think that way about working at an office, think that way about working at Multi-text and dress to suit the occasion.

The corporate officer's emphasis on women's "professional" presentation as bound up in a particular worker "mentality" implies that the way one looks both reflects and shapes one's work ethic and productive capacity. The importance of this notion is expressed and absorbed in numerous ways. Such subtle additional job requirements as codes of dress and behavior, although obvious to the onlooker as setting workers apart from other industries, become invisible as forms of labor. In the arena of the "open office," dress and fashion become not only powerful metaphors of corporate discipline, but also a form of individual expression and pleasure. A few quotes from Data Air's employee-produced newsletter give a sense of the grave importance attributed to dressing and appearance and the complex way in which messages about dress are bound up in corporate ideals as well as in broader cultural values:

> What you wear is really who you are and how you feel about yourself.

> Clothing sends a message, a statement to others about you.

> Clothing can whisper stability and high moral standards, or it can shout rebellion and discontent. It can serve as a form of identification.

Supervisors are concerned about the way you dress; for them it is more than an issue of personal taste. They want you to send the right message, one that projects you as a balanced, responsible person.

Ladies, before you select what to wear, you must decide whether the clothing is suitable for work. Materials that are so revealing should be reserved for the bedroom. Stop and think about the impression you are giving to onlookers; and it matters not whether you are on the night or day shift. You are dressing for work!

Deodorants! What you wear with what you wear! People won't notice how neatly and appropriately dressed you are if they're gasping for fresh air when you're in the same room!

Despite the fact that this service job is performed behind the scenes, in large, open production floors geographically remote and forever removed from face-to-face contact with its customers, off-shore data-entry operators are expected to present themselves as though they are indeed serving a client in a professional office place, face-to-face.

The enticing appeal of the clean, cool look of the "open office," the dress codes, and the slick-carpeted and air-conditioned work environment (much of which is demanded by the computer technology itself) go a long way in persuading the workers of the "professional" nature of their jobs. The contradictions between their factory wages and fancy titles, such as "material controller," "instructor specialist," and "assistant trainer," help heighten the ambiguities. Although women generally denied that their work experience in the data-processing industry had changed their images of themselves in any identifiable way, their clearly defined notions about how one should dress and behave at work – with a "professional" demeanor and appearance – stand in contrast with their descriptions of their previous work experiences and, to some extent, their class base. This "professional" identity is perceived as contradictory in their own minds and in the reality of the jobs they perform. For example, when comparing their present jobs in data entry to those in other industries (in terms of status, monetary reward, job mobility, and so forth), some women said that they could be making more money working as domestic or agricultural workers, and that their wages are comparable to those in a garment or electronics factory. Many of these women have actually had these jobs, but state that in the final analysis they would rather be in data entry because of the job setting and the "cool" look of the place. The manager-owner of one of the smaller, local data-entry operations explained the phenomenon as follows:

> When you see a group of the young ladies, like the ones from Data Air, you can see that they're much better dressed than the ones from the assembly plant. That's my observation. They're probably not getting paid much better but their work environment is a cleaner one, a purer one, and they in fact live out that environment. ... The Data Air office is very plush, so the young ladies working in there perceive that they are working in an office and they dress like it and they live like it. It's a very interesting phenomenon – it only got started when the data entry business got started – this new breed of office-type workers. They equate themselves with ... clerical staff in an office and they carry themselves in that way.

Although, to greater or lesser degrees, women acknowledge exploitative production quotas, labor practices, and what one called the "we say and you do attitude," their pride associated with working in a "professional enterprise" (whether real or imagined) helps to quell some of these frustrations and, in the face of rising unemployment and economic uncertainty, assists in maintaining very low attrition rates (2 percent). For example, although excessive discipline is one of the most often mentioned complaints about the job (along with pay and favoritism), it is also, in a peculiar way, cited as a contributing factor to the workplace professionalism so eagerly sought and identified with the "office" environment. One woman put the contradiction well, as she described, on the one hand, the company's obsessive concern for time and order – a half-hour lunch, constant monitoring, and "rules and regulations on everything under the sun" – and complained, on the other hand, that many of the

"new girls don't understand the importance of a serious professional approach" to their jobs. They talk when they should be working and dress as though they're going out dancing or shopping in town, wearing "short short skirts and off-the-shoulder tops or rolled-up pant legs and flat shoes." Peer pressure in dress and demeanor both contradicts and plays into the hands of the corporate prescriptions: groups of workers may at one moment voice complaints to management about bathroom conditions or excessive overtime, and at the next moment tease and harass a fellow worker for her "inappropriate" clothes or her "unmannerly" work habits.

One young data worker and home needleworker, who bemoans the fact that she has to get up at 5:30 every morning and work overtime without fail each day, expressed no regret over leaving a more flexible (and profitable) arrangement where she worked part-time at the university law library and part-time as a seamstress at home. This by no means implies, as Lim claims (1985), that employment within these foreign, off-shore high-tech companies liberates women from the constraints of a patriarchal tradition, or that it promotes greater economic autonomy among them. Rather, like multinationals in other parts of the world (Ong 1987), these high-tech enterprises have shrewdly tapped into a strong Barbadian concern with appearance and have turned this set of cultural values to the advantage of international capital by encouraging workers to identify with a well-defined corporate image. Corporate ideologies about femininity and work, and disciplinary measures that subtly enforce them, contribute to pink-collar workers' pride as "professional" workers. In other words, dress as a manifestation of corporate discipline becomes interwoven with the pervasive and conservative Barbadian ethic that places great emphasis on grooming and deportment.

A number of social critics have debated the fashion question – whether fashionable dress is a form of female oppression or self-expression and adult play. "Is it part of empty consumerism, or is it a site of struggle symbolized in dress codes? Does it muffle the self, or create it?" (Wilson 1990:231). I would argue that dress becomes an arena in which local (class-based) and international corporate values are simultaneously contested and consented to. As Wilson convincingly states, the puritanical position that construes consumer culture as an opiate, "duping the masses into a state of false consciousness," fails to do justice to the complexities involved in women's decision-making and the psychological pleasures derived from fashion and dress. Women's experimentation with clothes reveals an aesthetic inventiveness that can be interpreted either as conformity to international corporate consumer culture or as enhancing their exploration of alternative subjectivities. Women of all ranks refer to their enjoyment and expenditure in clothes, as well as to the "pressure to dress hard" and the rampant gossip and teasing to which they are subject when their hairstyles and clothes fail to conform. One woman, who began as a supervisor for Data Air when the company opened and has since been promoted to shift manager, expressed her contradictory sense of the dress question in the following way:

> Our policy is governed by a dress code. ... We are not a factory. We call ourselves an "open office" and if you were working in an office, you wouldn't go in a jean skirt or jean pants or short skirts. You would dress as if you were an executive. That's what we expect our persons to do. Now when we realize that our people are not dressing the way we think they should, we speak with them; we have even gone as far as to ask persons to go back home and change because their attire was not properly suited for the work atmosphere. And we instill that in our people, so by practice and counseling, we have reached the stage where people recognize us for the way we look. They usually say we work for a lot of money [she laughs]. It's not that, but you're governed by a particular code you have to adhere to – *you are being watched*. And not only that but, because there are so many young persons, they usually talk about you if you don't look good. They say "how could you come in here looking like that?" and they want to keep the image up, and certainly as a manager, I wouldn't like to think that my people are coming in here and looking better than me [laughs again]. So you want to dress a certain way to be in line with them, because they do speak about you.

Even as a manager, she describes a sense of surveillance. In her position she is watched not only from above, but also from below, as she fears the scrutiny and criticism from younger fashion-conscious women on the production floor. [Later], and independently, work groups within these vast data-processing facilities have designed and commissioned needleworkers to make them uniforms – brightly colored skirt suits and dresses with distinctive scarves and pocket handkerchiefs to match. Although in some workplaces one might read the imposition of a uniform as a means of suppressing individuality and personal choice, in this case, women derive a sense of pride and shared identification from the uniform that they have fashioned themselves. For them, the uniform is a symbol of professional status comparable to airline workers and bank tellers, and presents an economical way of adhering to the style protocol.

Naming through titles, and image-making in general, can become an element of corporate control. Along with more conscious and direct measures (work quotas, overtime demands, incentive policies, time restrictions, et cetera), forms of image making are often so subtly bound up in a sort of internationalized mainstream feminine stereotype that it becomes hard to differentiate between corporate discipline – with its concomitant imposition of particular gender ideologies, culturally specific notions of women's work and femininity – and women's own changing, and perhaps contradictory, subjectivities. Whereas the Malaysian factory women in Aihwa Ong's work (1987) are reputed in their local contexts to be "loose" and "modern" for having adopted western-style clothes, the Barbadian women are often reputed to look well-off, and even showy, their dress obscuring the reality of their low-skilled, low-paid, tedious work. Following Ong, we might ask how, if at all, the "traditional" or stereotypic notion of the West Indian woman as matriarch, with varying but marked degrees of independence (Barrow 1986), and other ideologies are incorporated into women's new roles as workers at these new industries. Or, conversely, how is the ideology of western individualism and feminine docility reinscribed in the Caribbean context as a way of constructing its "ideal" female

work force? These apparently contradictory notions become simultaneously intertwined in the
corporate arena of the off-shore office.

In the tradition of Esther Boserup (1970),
Linda Lim (1985) asserts that as women become
incorporated into multinational factories as wage
workers, as part of a community of other women
and through exposure to the bright lights and
modernity of urban free-trade zones, they gain
independence. Wittingly or not, she echoes the
promotional materials of many multinational corporations and business optimists selling their
hardware or off-shore enterprises to Third
World governments. Although these factors,
may, in fact, represent an element of the incorporation experience (and one that the women
themselves often note), it is important also to
recognize that the use of such rationales by foreign companies, local governments, and even
popular cultural texts may entail clever ideological manipulation on the part of corporate
capital that masks much of the reality of the
work performed. The relative prestige associated
with being one of "the Data Air family," however, along with the promise of independence
(amorphous as it may be) and the fact that jobs
are increasingly hard to come by in the context of
newly implemented structural adjustment measures, seems to effectively convince many of the
young women that they are fortunate to be where
they are. One should look further, perhaps.

Many of the women testified that their motivations for working in the industry clearly
extended beyond basic economic necessity.
Some remarked on the importance of "getting
out" and being among friends in addition to earning a wage and contributing to a household economy. Others alluded to the pride they feel in
holding down a regular job, getting dressed up,
and being "a working woman." Significantly,
these other aspects of the work experience tend
to be downplayed in the development literature
about women's incorporation into these industries, whereas they are highlighted by development officers and industry managers. One might
conclude, therefore, that this discourse is part of a
deception or a ploy to distract the workers from
the reality of their meager wages and the limits of
their jobs. I would argue, however, that this con-

clusion precludes a more subtle analysis of the
women's working experience and the contradictions between their "real" and "perceived"
motivations and responses. In a similar vein,
Sharon Stichter described textile workers in
Egypt and Morocco who justified their employment purely in economic terms, as religious and
social mores would otherwise dictate against their
working for wages (1990:55–6). In Barbados, and
in the Caribbean in general, women's engagement
in wage work has a long and extensive history,
and female independence is considered high relative to other parts of the developing world (Barrow 1986). There is little need, therefore, for
women to justify their desire for employment in
the data-entry industry. Not one woman of the 85
women I interviewed indicated that her job created disdain or turbulence within her family.
Most reported, instead, that their families were
pleased about their work both because of the
contribution it would make to the household
economy and, more generally, because of the
sense of responsibility associated with a full-
time job and the prestige still surrounding any
work involving a computer. No one described
being either pressured to take a job in data entry
or prohibited from doing so by a father or husband, as has been noted by others in Mexico,
Malaysia, and so on (Beneria and Roldan 1987;
Ong 1987).

This is not to say that many data processors do
not express grave frustrations and see their jobs as
"boring," "dead-end," and "stressful." Rather,
the women's messages are complex and often
contradictory. Some say that sitting in front of a
computer for eight hours every day is "easy" or
"cool" compared to other jobs that "have you on
your feet all day" (e.g., shop assistant or garment
assembly worker). Others, however, describe
being "chained" to the machine. They express
enormous frustration and annoyance at being
treated like "school girls" with rules and regulations, and time constraints they must obey. They
resent being surrounded by so many other
"girls," where "every day is the same," and,
perhaps worst of all, "with nowhere to go from
there." At both Data Air and Multitext Corporation, incidents of computer-based theft or sabotage reveal ingenuity on the part of the workers as

well as an unexpected sort of mastery over a fragmented and apparently sealed system. In each case, individual keyers figured out ways of "tricking the computer" by copying disks or hitting particular keys in such a way as to achieve exceptional speed and accuracy reports and effectively double their paychecks in the process. When the scandals were uncovered, management at both companies was forced to "tighten security" either by reorganizing the distribution of work to ensure greater control or, in the more extreme case, by making an enormous capital investment in an entirely new computer system. As in many other industries, and even under the exceedingly close supervision and control of the computer, workers have discovered high-tech loopholes that, if even for a short time and in the form of theft, enable them to gain an element of control over their labor.

Woman's Body: Site/Sight of Corporate Discipline and Style

I have alluded to a sort of "corporate style" that underlies the relations of production in the off-shore information-processing industry, and that plays a significant role in the constitution of the Barbadian off-shore data processor in ways that set her apart from other enclave workers (e.g., garment and electronics workers). Elements of ergonomic design that turn a factory shell into an "open office," along with an identifiable fashion statement on the part of employees from management down to rank-and-file production workers, become bound up in the overall labor process through a notion of corporate "style." Corporate image makers deploy this style through a variety of means, the most obvious being an official dress code that prescribes a "smart, professional" look. Corporate style molds discipline as well as ideologies. The image reinforces several contradictory messages and subjectivities for the workers themselves. When asked to account for the reputation of Data Air workers as exceptionally well dressed, some (including supervisors and managers) noted the pressure they feel to keep up with the fashion of the young workers on the floor. Many said that Bajan women simply love to dress. Therefore, even though they acknow-

ledge the company's strict dress code, they may locate the distinguishing mark of the "Data Air girls" in themselves – their own cultural practices and sets of values. It is thus difficult to determine if and where the lines should be drawn between corporate control, worker consent and complicity in presenting themselves as the company prescribes, and broader cultural mores regarding dress and fashion.

The "well-dressed" reputation of the Bajan processors is accompanied by the assumption – expressed by a wide array of people outside the industry who witnessed the parade of young women workers en route to or from work – that they must be making good salaries to be able to afford such extensive and expensive-looking wardrobes. Thus, the notion of "professional style" is a powerful expression of a particular corporate ideology and discipline that runs through the labor process as well. Not only does it create a work force that looks distinct from other manufacturing industries, but it also helps shape the women's notions of themselves and the jobs they do. They dress "professionally" because there is a stated dress code and because peer pressure runs deep. Simultaneously, their dress persuades them that they work in a professional place and do a professional job. Along with the other aspects of decor and ergonomic design – the framed floral prints in the offices, the muted colors of the walls and carpeting, the high-tech look of the computer work stations with their swivel chairs and divided desk spaces, the soft lighting and air conditioning – the women's presentation of themselves as professional workers set this off-shore industry strikingly apart from others whose labor processes are remarkably similar. If, on the one hand, dress becomes a form of discipline by which the company can insist upon a certain look, which presumably translates into a certain work ethic, on the other hand, many women willingly consent to this demand, claiming it as part of their own cultural identity and individual expression.

In a recent article, Bolles and D'Amico-Samuels remark that, "like all people, folk in the Caribbean are often caught between conflicting notions of what they want, and are also responding to economic conditions beyond their immediate control" (1989:175). In the context of what appear to be contradictory impulses, responses, and subjectivities on the part of the Barbadian data processors, this reminder is well taken. Women are being employed in low-skilled, low-paid jobs, which, despite the comfort of their air-conditioned environments and the status and appearance of being well-off as signified by their dress, entail monotonous and frequently stress-inducing work that presents little in the way of transferable skills or opportunity for advancement. Some of these women acknowledge these constraints in clear and direct terms, expressing a strong desire to find better jobs or go back to school. Others, however, seem essentially content with their data-processing jobs. Whether because of the "friendly atmosphere" and "nice working conditions," or because of the simple fact that, with or without prior work experience, jobs in Barbados are hard to find, many women clearly like their jobs and express great loyalty toward their employers. Several women repeated lines resonating from Data Air's corporate "mission": "We're like one big family," "We're all in it together," and "We [the company] will continue to grow as long as we keep our production high and do good quality work." Despite the fact that they work for a foreign company and have witnessed (and/or personally experienced) the sudden flight of similar off-shore companies (notably INTEL, an electronics assembly plant that closed its doors in 1985, but also garment factories that have shut down), most seem to have a surprising degree of faith in the company's commitment to them and to Barbados. Most women assumed that because people will always fly on airplanes and always get sick (therefore using tickets and submitting insurance claims forms), Data Air should always be in business, and as long as they work hard and do their jobs to the company's satisfaction, they assured themselves there should be no reason to worry. Again, as Bolles and D'Amico-Samuels put it, "work, no matter how dead-end, has meaning in terms of how a woman attempts to meet her familial responsibilities, and is also an essential part of her self-image and her conception of womanhood" (1989:175).

The fact that women consent to corporate guidelines does not necessarily imply that they are simply and effectively duped by some sort of monolithic corporate construction of a feminine worker; rather, it emphasizes the complex and contradictory nature of their positions as workers and women. As revealed in the development officer's quotation above, the focus on women's "inherent" sense of responsibility, manual dexterity, patience, and so on, conceals very real measures of control within the workplace and reinforces, at the same time, a sexual division of labor that consistently places women in low-skilled, low-paid, dead-end jobs (Fernandez-Kelly 1989:27).

Advances in computer technology itself are well underway, and it is only a matter of time (and a brief one at that) before the shape of data-entry jobs and the locus of information-based work are again radically altered. High-volume, low-skilled data-entry work will continue to exist as enclave industries off-shore, only until electronic scanning devices (or Optical Character Readers) are improved for accuracy and produced at lower costs. Barbadian workers are already in a wage bracket that increasingly prohibits them from competing for this low-end work with their lower-waged neighbors in Jamaica, the Dominican Republic, St Lucia, Dominica, and St Vincent. Although its English-speaking work force and proximity to the United States made Barbados attractive to companies years ago, strikingly high accuracy rates and comparatively low wages in Asia and Central and South America, as well as rapidly expanding satellite facilities, are making these drawing cards less enticing. As automated technologies replace the need for a vast data-entry arena off shore, it seems clear that some companies will again shift operations closer to their North American or European home offices. Increasing numbers of companies are thus poised to move into more "up-market," off-shore computer-based arenas (e.g., software design, computer graphics, data-based research, animated video production services, computer-aided design (CAD)), such that developing countries are again forced to scramble to come to terms with the labor and technological demands that will enable them to vie for these potentially lucrative contracts. Although it is yet unclear how Barbados will respond to these impending changes, it seems clear that these shifts promise higher-skilled jobs for more-educated people and pose important questions in light of the gender-based incorporation patterns of those industries that preceded them. As the work becomes increasingly skilled, will the work force become less and less a female domain? Will we witness a reversal of the feminization of information processing as it ceases to entail only the rudimentary entering of data and moves into higher level, truly "white-collar" work? Predictions of this sort were made in Singapore's "second stage" of export-oriented manufacturing, which similarly emphasized higher-skilled, higher-value-added industries. Barbados might very well be following close behind in its scramble for high-tech development.

Notes

1   The names of companies and individuals have been changed.
2   This profile is consistent with off-shore workers in numerous industries around the world, and similar tactics of patronage and the factory as "family" metaphor are cited by others as well (Ong 1987).

References

Abraham-Van der Mark, Eve E.
  1983   The Impact of Industrialization on Women: A Caribbean Case. In *Women, Men and the International Division of Labor*. June Nash and Maria Patricia Fernandez-Kelly, eds. Albany: SUNY Press.
Baran, Barbara, and Suzanne Teegarden
  1987   Women's Labor in the Office of the Future: A Case Study of the Insurance Industry. In *Women, Households and the Economy*. Lourdes Beneria and Catherine R. Stimpson, eds. New Brunswick, NJ: Rutgers University Press.
Barker, Jane, and Hazel Downing
  1980   Word Processing and the Transformation of the Patriarchal Relations of Control in the Office. *Capital and Class* 10: 64–99.
Barrow, Christine
  1986   Autonomy, Equality and Women in Barbados. Paper presented at the 11th Annual Caribbean Studies Association Meeting, Caracas, Venezuela.
Beneria, Lourdes, and Martha Roldan
  1987   *The Crossroads of Gender: Industrial Homework, Subcontracting and Household Dynamics in Mexico City*. Chicago: University of Chicago Press.
Bolles, A. Lynn
  1983   Kitchens Hit By Priorities: Employed Working-Class Jamaican Women Confront the IMF. In *Women, Men and the International Division of Labor*. June Nash and Maria Patricia Fernandez-Kelly, eds. Albany: SUNY Press.
Bolles, A. Lynn, and Deborah D'Amico-Samuels
  1989   Anthropological Scholarship on Gender in the English-Speaking Caribbean. In *Gender and Anthropology: Critical Reviews and Research and Training*. Sandra Morgen, ed. Washington, DC: American Anthropological Association.
Boserup, Esther
  1970   *Women's Role in Economic Development*. New York: St. Martin's Press.
Braverman, Harry
  1974   *Labour and Monopoly Capital: The Degradation of Work in the Twentieth Century*. New York: Month Review Press.
Fernandez-Kelly, Maria Patricia
  1989   Broadening of Purview: Gender and International Economic Development. Paper presented at the International Conference on Women and Development, State University of New York, Albany.
Foucault, Michel
  1979   *Discipline and Punish: The Birth of the Prison*. New York: Vintage Books.
Kelly, Deidre
  1987   *Hard Work, Hard Choices: A Survey of Women in St Lucia's Export-Oriented Electronics Factories*. Institute of Social and Economic Research, Occasional Paper No. 20. Cave Hill, Barbados: University of the West Indies.
Lim, Linda
  1985   *Women Workers in the Multinational Enterprises in Developing Countries*. Geneva: Intenational Labor Organization.
Mies, Maria
  1986   *Patriarchy and Accumulation on a World Scale: Women in the International Division of Labour*. London: Zed Books.
Nash, June, and Maria Patricia Fernandez-Kelly, eds.
  1983   *Women, Men and the International Division of Labor*. Albany: SUNY Press.

Ong, Aihwa
    1987   *Spirits of Resistance and Capitalist Discipline: Factory Women in Malaysia*. Albany: SUNY Press.
Powell, Dorian
    1986   Caribbean Women and their Response to Familial Experiences. *Social and Economic Studies* (35)2: 83–130.
Pringle, Rosemary
    1989   *Secretaries Talk: Sexuality, Power and Work*. New York: Verso.
Safa, Helen I.
    1981   Runaway Shops and Female Employment: The Search for Cheap Labor. *Signs 6*: 418–23.
Sassen, Saskia
    1988   *The Mobility of Labor and Capital: A Study in International Investment and Labor Flow*. Cambridge: Cambridge University Press.
Senior, Olive
    1991   *Working Miracles: Women's Lives in the English-Speaking Caribbean*. Cave Hill, Barbados: Institute for Social and Economic Research, University of the West Indies.
Stichter, Sharon
    1990   Women, Employment and the Family. In *Women, Employment, and the Family in the International Division of Labor*. Philadelphia: Temple University Press.
Ward, Kathryn, ed.
    1990   *Women Workers and Global Restructuring*. Ithaca, NY: ILR Press.
Wilson, Elizabeth
    1990   The Postmodern Chameleon. *New Left Review* 180 (March/April): 187–90.
Zuboff, Shoshana
    1988   *In the Age of the Smart Machine: The Future of Work and Power*. New York: Basic Books.

Index